LITERARY THEMES
for Students

LITERARY THEMES
for Students

Examining Diverse Literature to Understand and Compare Universal Themes

RACE AND PREJUDICE
VOLUME 2

Anne Marie Hacht, Editor

Foreword by Margaret Brantley

THOMSON

GALE

Detroit • New York • San Francisco • New Haven, Conn. • Waterville, Maine • London

Literary Themes for Students: Race and Prejudice

Project Editor
Anne Marie Hacht

Editorial
Sara Constantakis, Ira Mark Milne

Rights Acquisition and Management
Lisa Kincade, Ronald Montgomery,
and Jessica Sitt

Manufacturing
Rita Wimberley

Imaging
Leitha Eheridge-Sims, Lezlie Light,
and Mike Logusz

Product Design
Pamela A. E. Galbreath

Vendor Administration
Civie Green

Product Manager
Meggin Condino

LIBRARY OF CONGRESS CATALOGING-IN-PUBLICATION DATA

Literary themes for students – race and prejudice : examining diverse literature to understand and compare universal themes / Anne Marie Hacht, project editor.
   p. cm. – (Literary themes for students)
   Includes bibliographical references and index.
   ISBN-13: 978-1-4144-0275-9 (set)
   ISBN-10: 1-4144-0275-9 (set)
   ISBN-13: 978-1-4144-0284-0 (vol. 2)
   ISBN-10: 1-4144-0284-8 (vol. 2)
   [etc.]
   1. Race in literature. 2. Prejudices in literature. I. Hacht, Anne Marie. II. Series.
PN56.R16L58 2006
809'.933355 – dc22
                            2006017454

ISBN-13:
978-1-4144-0275-9 (set)
978-1-4144-0274-1 (vol. 1)
978-1-4144-0284-0 (vol. 2)

ISBN-10:
1-4144-0275-9 (set)
1-4144-0274-0 (vol. 1)
1-4144-0284-8 (vol. 2)

This title is also available as an e-book.
ISBN-13: 978-1-4144-1887-2 (set)
ISBN-10: 1-4144-1887-6 (set)
Contact your Thomson Gale sales representative for ordering information.

Printed in the United States of America
10 9 8 7 6 5 4 3 2

Table of Contents

Foreword

SPEAKING UP: THE LITERATURE OF RACE AND PREJUDICE

Each volume of *Literary Themes for Students* brings together dozens of renowned works of literature that share a specific theme. The theme for this set of *Literary Themes for Students* is race and prejudice.

Examples of fear, ignorance, and misunderstanding dominate written human history until just a few hundred years ago. Written declarations of human rights date to the sixth century B.C. and Persia's Cyrus Cylinder. More than two millennia later, literature that gives voice to the voiceless began to flourish. With the Industrial Revolution came a boom in publishing, which was accompanied by a rise in literacy. The eighteenth century was also the Age of Enlightenment, which spawned the American and French Revolutions. At that time, people with inferior positions in society—namely women and slaves—began to tell their stories and make the case for equal rights.

The literature of race and prejudice serves a twofold purpose: to advance freedom and to protect it. Concentration camp survivor Martin Niemöller, vividly captures the power of testimony with this statement, which is engraved on the New England Holocaust Memorial:

They came first for the Communists,

and I didn't speak up because I wasn't a Communist.

Then they came for the Jews,
and I didn't speak up because I wasn't a Jew.
Then they came for the trade unionists,
and I didn't speak up because I wasn't a trade unionist.
Then they came for the Catholics,
and I didn't speak up because I was a Protestant.
Then they came for me,
and by that time no one was left to speak up.

*(New England Holocaust Memorial,
www.nehm.com/contents/niemoller.html
(April 30, 2006).)*

Some of the selections in *Literary Themes for Students: Race and Prejudice* represent the capacity of literature to change history. Abraham Lincoln famously called Harriet Beecher Stowe "the little lady who started the big war" after her novel *Uncle Tom's Cabin* brought the horrors of slavery to life in the American imagination and rallied support to the cause of abolition. A century later, Martin Luther King Jr.'s celebrated speech "I Have a Dream" became the icon of the Civil Rights movement in the United States. Both masterpieces are as potent today as when they were written.

Literature can also change the way history is understood. For instance, Dee Brown's *Bury My Heart at Wounded Knee* explodes the myth of civilization's victory over savagery in the settlement of the American West, describing episode after episode of ethnic cleansing. Anne Frank's *Diary of a Young Girl* (1947) gave a shocking look inside the Holocaust and helped a still-reeling world comprehend the terror of the war and the basic humanity of its victims. Both these books, along with many others that inform the modern view of the past, are included in this exploration of race and prejudice.

Literary Themes for Students: Race and Prejudice represents many perspectives on the struggle for equal rights. Mary Wollstonecraft acts as a passionate, reasoned advocate in her essay "A Vindication of the Rights of Woman" (1792). Mark Twain's protagonist in *Adventures of Huckleberry Finn* (1884) observes, records, and reacts to the injustice of slavery, even as he accepts it as a given. The nameless protagonist of Ralph Ellison's "King of the Bingo Game" (1944) is a victim of societal racism, while the narrator of Ernest Gaines's *Autobiography of Miss Jane Pittman* (1971) is a survivor. Selections that are studied include memoirs, polemics, novels, dramas, poetry, and histories—all bearing important contributions to the theme.

The works included in *Literary Themes for Students* represent a wide range of circumstances in which individuals experience prejudice. The discussion goes well beyond race, religion, and gender into ethnicity, social status, mental and physical health, and personal beliefs and behaviors. Among the titles presented are *Nisei Daughter*, which recalls the internment of Japanese Americans and *Angels in America*, which dramatizes the early years of the AIDS epidemic. Several essays examine dominant and recurring subthemes in the literature of prejudice. Each entry further explores the component themes particular to that specific work, such as education, sexuality, and violence.

Literary Themes for Students cannot take the place of experiencing firsthand the books it presents. This overview of the topics, historical contexts, and critical interpretations presented in these entries can guide readers who want to discover more. It gives learners a platform from which to launch their own exploration of race, prejudice, history, and literature. It celebrates how far human rights have come in a relatively short time and underscores how much further there is yet to go. It pays tribute to those who have spoken up, because they speak for all humanity.

Margaret Brantley
Brantley is a literature critic and a
literary reference editor.

Introduction

The purpose of *Literary Themes for Students* is to provide readers with an overview of literary works that explore a specific theme. The volumes analyze poetry, plays, short stories, novels, and works of nonfiction that address the theme in some capacity, and the reader discovers how that theme has been treated in literature at different times in history and across diverse cultures. *Literary Themes for Students: Race and Prejudice* (LTSRP) includes "classic" human rights literature often used in the classroom curriculum, as well as more contemporary accounts of race and prejudice and works by minority, international, and female writers.

These volumes begin with three overview essays that introduce the theme of race and prejudice in literature, dividing it by geography and culture into American literature, British literature, and world literature. There are also nine sub-essays, which break these themes down further into subthemes that correspond to recurring ideas in the literature of race and prejudice. Sub-essays examine particular titles that exemplify the subthemes and show how that subtheme has developed over time.

Each work is discussed in a separate entry. These entries include: an introduction to the work and the work's author; a plot summary, to help readers understand the action and story of the work; an analysis of themes that relate to the subjects of race and prejudice, to provide readers with a multifaceted look at the complexity of human rights literature; and a section on important historical and cultural events that shaped the author and the work, as well as events in the real world (from the time of the author or another time in history) that affect the plot or characters in the work.

Additionally, readers are presented with a critical overview discussing how the work was initially received by critics and how the work is presently viewed. Accompanying the critical overview is an excerpt from a previously published critical essay discussing the work's relation to the theme of race and prejudice. For further analysis and enjoyment, an extended list of media adaptations is also included, as well as a list of poems, short stories, novels, plays, and works of nonfiction that further address the theme of race and prejudice, and thus students are encouraged to continue their study of this theme.

The titles of each volume of *LTSRP* were selected by surveying numerous sources on teaching literature and analyzing course curricula for a number of school districts. Our advisory board provided input, as did educators in various areas.

HOW EACH ENTRY IS ORGANIZED

Each chapter focuses on the ways in which an entry relates to the theme of race and prejudice. Each entry heading includes the author's name, the title of the work being discussed, and the year it was published. The following sections are included in the discussion of each entry:

Introduction: a brief overview of the work being discussed. It provides information about the work's first appearance, any controversies surrounding its publication, its literary reputation, and general details about the work's connection to the theme of race and prejudice.

Plot Summary: a description of the events that occur in the work. For poems, some additional insight into the context and interpretation of the poem—and discussion of symbols and elements—is provided. The plot summary is broken down by subheadings, usually organized by chapter, section, or stanza.

Themes: a discussion of how the work approaches the issues of race and prejudice through various themes. Each theme is addressed under a separate subheading. Several of the major recurring themes are discussed at more length in individual sub-essays.

Historical and Cultural Context: a discussion of the historical and cultural events that appear in the work or that affected the writer while the work was being written. This can include large-scale events such as wars, social movements, and political decisions, as well as smaller-scale events such as cultural trends and literary movements. If the work is set during a different time period from that in which the author wrote it, historical and cultural events from both periods are included.

Critical Overview: a discussion of the work's general critical reputation, including how it was initially received by reviewers, critics, and the general public. Any controversy surrounding the work is treated in this section. For older works, this section also includes information on the ways that views of the work have changed over time.

Criticism: a previously published critical essay discussing how the work addresses the issues of race and/or prejudice. When no appropriate criticism could be found, commissioned essays were written to deal specifically with the work.

Sources: an alphabetical list of sources used in compiling the entry, including bibliographic information.

In addition, each entry includes the following sidebars, set apart from the rest of the text:

Author Biography Sidebar: a brief biography of the author, including how he or she was affected by or led to write about race and prejudice.

Media Adaptations: a list of film, television, and/or stage adaptations, audio versions, and other forms of media related to the work. Source information is included.

OTHER FEATURES

LTSRP includes "Speaking Up: The Literature of Race and Prejudice," by Mo Brantley, a writer and editor of language arts reference books. This is a foreword about how the literature of race and prejudice can help contemporary readers appreciate how far human rights have come in a relatively short time and how far there is yet to go.

Each entry may have several illustrations, including photos of the author, depictions of key elements of the plot, stills from film adaptations, and/or historical photos of the people, places, or events discussed in the entry.

Nine sub-essays discuss various subthemes of race and prejudice literature: ethnicity; gender; religion; sexual orientation; social class and caste; disability, illness, and social stigma; ethnic cleansing, genocide, and exile; slavery; and segregation. Each sub-essay addresses approximately ten works that deal directly with the subtheme, and discusses how treatment of that theme has changed over time.

A Media Adaptation list compiles nearly seventy films, plays, television series, and other media that deal with the subjects of race and prejudice. The adaptations are organized by subtheme for easy access.

The *What Do I Read Next?* section provides over ninety plays, short stories, poems, novels, and nonfiction works on the subject of race and prejudice. These works are also organized by subtheme.

An overview essay about prejudice in British literature analyzes how the depiction of prejudice and the quest for equality have changed since Shakespeare's time. Poems, plays, short stories, novels, and nonfiction works that exemplify Britain's attitude toward race and prejudice are examined and provide students with an overview of British literature about human differences since the country's days as a colonial superpower.

An overview essay on the themes of race and prejudice in American literature analyzes how the history of the nation is tied to its "melting pot" identity and the ways in which its literature reflects America's attitude toward race and its relationship with peace. Discussion of key poems, plays, short stories, novels, and nonfiction works reflect the evolving place of race and prejudice in the literature and culture of the United States.

An overview essay on the themes of race and prejudice in world literature analyzes how such issues have been viewed in differing cultures and time periods around the world. Discovery, interaction, fear, and the quest for understanding have left their imprint on world literature throughout history, and this essay provides students with a brief survey of how that literature reflects the values and attitudes of the cultures that produced it.

CITING

When writing papers, students who quote directly from any volume of *Literary Themes for Students: Race and Prejudice* may use the following general formats. These examples are based on MLA style. Teachers may request that students adhere to a different style, so the following examples should be adapted as needed.

When citing text from *LTSRP* that is not attributed to a particular author (i.e., from the Themes or Historical Context sections), the following format should be used in the bibliography section:

> *"The Awakening." Literary Themes for Students: Race and Prejudice.* Ed. TK. Vol. TK. Detroit: Thomson Gale, 2006. TK–TK.

When quoting a journal or newspaper essay that is reprinted in a volume of *LTfS*, the following format may be used:

> Khan, Shahnaz, "Reconfiguring the Native Informant: Positionality in the Global Age," in *Signs: Journal of Women and Culture and Society*, Vol. 30, No. 4, 2005, pp. 2022–2023; excerpted and reprinted in *Literary Themes for Students: Race and Prejudice*, Vol. TK, ed. TK (Detroit: Thomson Gale, 2006), pp. TK–TK.

When quoting material reprinted from a book that appears in a volume of *LTSRP*, the following form may be used:

> Sinsheimer, Hermann, *Shylock: The History of a Character*, Benjamin Blom, 1963, p. 17; excerpted and reprinted in *Literary Themes for Students: Race and Prejudice*, Vol. TK, ed. TK (Detroit: Thomson Gale, 2006), pp. TK–TK.

WE WELCOME YOUR SUGGESTIONS

The editorial staff of *LTSRP* welcomes your comments, ideas, and suggestions. Readers who wish to suggest themes and works for future volumes, or who have any other suggestions, are cordially invited to contact the editor. You may do so via email at ForStudentsEditors@thomson.com or via mail at:

Editor, *Literary Themes for Students*
Thomson Gale
27500 Drake Road
Farmington Hills, MI 48331-3535

Acknowledgments

The editors wish to thank the copyright holders of the excerpted criticism included in this volume and the permissions managers of many book and magazine publishing companies for assisting us in securing reproduction rights. We are also grateful to the staffs of the Detroit Public Library, the Library of Congress, the University of Detroit Mercy Library, Wayne State University Purdy/Kresge Library Complex, and the University of Michigan Libraries for making their resources available to us. Following is a list of the copyright holders who have granted us permission to reproduce material in this volume of *Literary Themes for Students: Race and Prejudice (LTSRP)*. Every effort has been made to trace copyright, but if omissions have been made, please let us know.

COPYRIGHTED MATERIALS IN *LITNM*, VOLUME 2, WERE REPRO DUCED FROM THE FOLLOWING PERIODICALS:

African American Review, v. 29, spring, 1995 for "Race and Domesticity in 'The Color Purple'" by Linda Selzer. Reproduced by permission of the author./ v. 35, spring, 2001 for "Invented by Horror: The Gothic and African American Literary Ideology in 'Native Son'" by James Smethurst. © 2001 James Smethurst. Both reproduced by permission of the respective authors.—*The American Enterprise,* v. 14, September 3, 2003. Copyright 2003 American Enterprise Institute for Public Policy Research. Reproduced with permission of *The American Enterprise*, a national magazine of Politics, Business, and Culture (TAEmag.com).—*The American Indian Quarterly,* v. 21, summer, 1998. Copyright © 1998 by the University of Nebraska Press. All rights reserved. Reproduced by permission of the University of Nebraska Press.—*Black American Literature Forum,* v. 24, summer, 1990 for "Singing the Black Mother: Maya Angelou and Autobiographical Continuity" by Mary Jane Lupton. Reproduced by permission of the author.—*College Literature,* v. 19, October-February, 1992. Copyright © 1992 by West Chester University. Reproduced by permission.—*Criticism,* v. 28, summer, 1976. Copyright © 1976 Wayne State University Press. Reproduced with permission of the Wayne State University Press.—*Critique: Studies in Contemporary Fiction,* v. 33, winter, 1992. Copyright © 1992 by Helen Dwight Reid Educational Foundation. Reproduced with permission of the Helen Dwight Reid Educational Foundation, published by Heldref Publications, 1319 18th Street, NW, Washington, DC 20036-1802.—*ELH,* v. 70, summer, 2003. Copyright © 2003 The Johns Hopkins University Press. Reproduced by permission.—*Explicator,* v. 58, summer, 2000; v. 60, summer, 2002. Copyright © 2000, 2002 by Helen Dwight Reid Educational Foundation. Both reproduced with permission of the Helen Dwight Reid Educational Foundation, published by Heldref Publications, 1319 18th

Street, NW, Washington, DC 20036-1802.—
Frontiers: A Journal of Women's Studies, v. 26, June 5, 2005. Copyright © 2005 by the Frontiers Editorial Collective. All rights reserved. Reproduced by permission of the University of Nebraska Press.—*Journal of American & Comparative Cultures,* v. 24, spring, 2001. Copyright © 2001 Basil Blackwell Ltd. www.blackwell-synergy.com. Reproduced by permission of Blackwell Publishers.—*Journal of American Culture,* v. 22, winter, 1999. Copyright © 1999 Basil Blackwell Ltd. www.blackwell-synergy.com. Reproduced by permission of Blackwell Publishers.—*Journal of the West,* v. 39, January, 2000. Copyright © 2000 by Journal of the West, Inc. Reproduced by permission.—*Judaism: A Quarterly Journal of Jewish Life and Thought,* v. 48, winter, 1999. Copyright 1999 American Jewish Congress. Reproduced by permission.—*Melus,* v. 19, winter, 1994; v. 22, summer, 1997. Copyright *MELUS: The Society for the Study of Multi-Ethnic Literature of the United States,* 1994, 1997. Both reproduced by permission.—*The Midwest Quarterly,* v. 43, spring, 2002. Copyright © 2002 by *The Midwest Quarterly,* Pittsburgh State University. Reproduced by permission.—*Modern Drama,* spring, 1999. Copyright © 1999 by the University of Toronto, Graduate Centre for Study of Drama. Reproduced by permission.—*New Statesman & Society,* v. 6, February 12, 1993. Copyright © 1993 New Statesman, Ltd. Reproduced by permission.—*Partisan Review,* v. 70, winter, 2003 for "Anne Frank: The Redemptive Myth" by Judith Goldstein. Reproduced by permission of the author.—*Perspectives on Political Science,* v. 31, fall, 2002. Copyright © 2002 by Helen Dwight Reid Educational Foundation. Reproduced with permission of the Helen Dwight Reid Educational Foundation, published by Heldref Publications, 1319 18th Street, NW, Washington, DC 20036-1802.—*South Atlantic Review,* January, 1993. Copyright © 1993 by the South Atlantic Modern Language Association. Reproduced by permission.—*Southern Cultures,* v. 6, summer, 2000. Reproduced by permission.—*Studies in American Fiction,* v. 24, spring, 1996. Copyright © 1996 Northeastern University. Reproduced by permission.—*Texas Studies in Literature and Language,* v. 36, 1994 for "Freedom, Uncertainty, and Diversity: 'A Passage to India' as a Critique of Imperialist Law" by Kieran Dolin. Copyright © 1994 by the University of Texas Press.

Reproduced by permission of the publisher and the author.—*U.S. News and World Report* v. 115, August 30, 1993. Copyright 1993 U.S. News and World Report, L.P. Reprinted with permission.—*USA Today,* December 12, 2001 for "Like the Taliban, Some U.S. Parents Fear Free Minds" by Mark Mathabane. © 2001 by Mark Mathabane. Reproduced by permission of the author.—*Western Folklore,* v. 51, 1992. © 1992 by the California Folklore Society. Reproduced by permission.—*The World and I Online,* v. 13, June, 1998. Copyright 1998 News World Communications, Inc. Reproduced by permission.

COPYRIGHTED MATERIALS IN LITERARY THEMES FOR STUDENTS: RACE AND PREJUDICE, WERE REPRODUCED FROM THE FOLLOWING BOOKS:

Achebe, Chinua. From *Hopes and Impediments: Selected Essays.* Copyright © 1988 by Chinua Achebe. Used by permission of Doubleday, a division of Random House, Inc., and in Canada and the UK by Emma Sweeney Agency on behalf of the author.—Bosmajian, Hamida. From *Children's Literature.* Yale University Press, 1996. Copyright © 1996 by Hollins College. All rights reserved. Reproduced by permission.—Cassedy, Patrice. From *Understanding 'Flowers for Algernon.'* Lucent Books, 2001. Copyright 2001 by Lucent Books, Inc. Reproduced by permission of Thomson Gale.—Kruger, Steven F.. From "Identity and Conversion in 'Angels in America'," in *Approaching the Millennium: Essays on 'Angels in America'.* Edited by Deborah R. Geis and Steven F. Kruger. The University of Michigan Press, 1997. Copyright © 1997 by the University of Michigan. All rights reserved. Reproduced by permission.—Powers, Jessica, "'Kaffir Boy': An Analysis," *www.Suite101.com,* October 17, 2001. Reproduced by permission of the author.—Tompkins, Jane. From *Sensational Designs: The Cultural Work of American Fiction 1790-1860.* Oxford University Press, 1985. Copyright © 1985 by Oxford University Press, Inc. Used by permission of Oxford University Press, Inc.—Yamamoto, Traise. From *Masking Selves, Making Subjects: Japanese American Women, Identity, and the Body.* University of California Press, 1999. Copyright © 1999 by The Regents of the University of California. Reproduced by permission of the publisher and the author.

National Advisory Board

Contributors

Sylvia M. DeSantis: DeSantis holds a master's degree in English and is an instructional designer and instructor for the Pennsylvania State University libraries. "Disabilities, Illness, and Social Stigma" essay.

Carrie Evans: Evans is a writer and editor with a bachelor's degree in journalism and a master's degree in social work from The University of Texas at Austin. Major work on *The House on Mango Street* and *Roll of Thunder, Hear My Cry.*

Koryn Fisher: Fisher holds a master's degree in English education and is a freelance writer and editor. Major Work on "King of the Bingo Game" and "Sexual Orientation" essay.

William F. Gillard: Gillard holds a master's degree in English and teaches at Fairleigh Dickinson University. Major work on *Ceremony*

Joyce E. Haines: Haines holds a Ph.D. in educational policy and administration, and teaches at the University of Kansas Division of Continuing Education, Kansas City Kansas Community College, and online courses for Community College of Southern Nevada. Major Work on *Farewell to Manzanar.*

Jonathan Lampley: Lampley is a doctoral candidate in English at Middle Tennessee State University and is a freelance writer. "Gender" essay.

David Layton: Layton holds a Ph.D. in English literature and teaches at Santa Monica College, University of Phoenix, and American Intercontinental University. Major Work on *Kaffir Boy.*

Cambria Lovelady: Lovelady holds an M.A. in creative writing from the University of Memphis and is a writer and editor for educational materials. Major work on *A Room of One's Own, Angels in America, The Awakening,* "Everything that Rises Must Converge," "I Have a Dream," and "Slavery" essay.

Natasha Marin: Marin is a freelance writer and poet. Major work on *A Raisin in the Sun, Blacks, The Color Purple,* and "What You Pawn, I Will Redeem." Critical essay on "What You Pawn, I Will Redeem."

W. Todd Martin: Martin holds a Ph.D. in English and teaches at Huntington College. "Ethnicity" essay.

Kate McCafferty: McCafferty holds a Ph.D. in American literature and teaches ESL abroad. Major Work on *Native Son* and *Vindication of the Rights of Woman.*

David L. McLean: McLean holds a master's degree in English and is a freelance writer. Major Work on *The Merchant of Venice* and *A Passage to India.*

Ray Mescallado: Mescallado holds a master's degree in English and is a freelance writer. Major Work on "A Good Day."

Annette Petrusso: Petrusso is a freelance writer and editor with a B.A. in history from the University of Michigan and an M.A. in screenwriting from The University of Texas at Austin. Major work on *The Autobiography of Miss Jane Pittman* and *Flowers for Algernon*.

Tom Pearson: Pearson is a freelance writer and editor. Major work on *The Autobiography of Malcolm X*.

Laura Baker Shearer: Shearer holds a Ph.D. in American literature and works as an English professor and freelance writer. Major work on *The Souls of Black Folk* and *Uncle Tom's Cabin*.

Paula R. Stiles: Stiles holds a Ph.D. in medieval history and works as an English tutor. "Ethnic Cleansing, Genocide, and Exile" essay.

Melanie Ulrich: Ulrich holds a Ph.D. in English literature from The University of Texas at Austin and is a freelance writer. Major work on *To Kill a Mockingbird*.

Frederic Will: Will holds a Ph.D. in comparative literature and teaches at Mellen University. Major essays on Race and Prejudice in World Literature, Race and Prejudice in British Literature, and Race and Prejudice in American Literature.

Greg Wilson: Wilson is a freelance literature and popular culture writer. Major work on *Bury My Heart at Wounded Knee, Anne Frank: The Diary of a Young Girl, Heart of Darkness, The Adventures of Huckleberry Finn, I Know Why the Caged Bird Sings, Nisei Daughter,* and "The Negro Speaks of Rivers." Critical essays on "The Negro Speaks of Rivers" and *Nisei Daughter.* "Religion," "Class and Caste," and "Segregation" essays.

Literary Chronology

1564: William Shakespeare was born on or about April 23 in Stratford-upon-Avon, Warwickshire, England.

1596: William Shakespeare's *The Merchant of Venice* is published.

1616: Shakespeare died on April 23 in Stratford-upon-Avon, Warwickshire, England.

1759: Mary Wollstonecraft was born on April 27 in Hoxton, England.

1792: Mary Wollstonecraft's *A Vindication of the Rights of Woman* is published.

1797: Wollstonecraft died on September 10 of complications from childbirth.

1811: Harriet Beecher was born on June 14 in Litchfield, Connecticut.

1835: Mark Twain was born Samuel Langhorne Clemens in 1835 in Missouri.

1850: Katherine O'Flaherty Chopin was born on February 8 in St. Louis, Missouri.

1852: Harriet Beecher Stowe's *Uncle Tom's Cabin* is published.

1857: Joseph Conrad was born Jozef Teodor Konrad Korzeniowski on December 3 in Berdiczew, Podolia, Russia (now Ukraine).

1868: William Edward Burghardt Du Bois was born on February 23 in Great Barrington, Massachusetts.

1879: Edward Morgan Forster was born on January 1 in London, England.

1882: Adeline Virginia Stephen was born January 25 in London, England.

1884: Mark Twain's *The Adventures of Huckleberry Finn* is published.

1896: Stowe died on July 1 in Hartford, Connecticut.

1899: Kate Chopin's *The Awakening* is published.

1902: James Mercer Langston Hughes was born on February 1 in Joplin, Missouri.

1902: Joseph Conrad's *Heart of Darkness* is published.

1903: Alan Paton was born on January 11 in Pietermaritzburg, Natal, South Africa.

1903: W. E. B. Du Bois's *The Souls of Black Folk* is published.

1904: Chopin died on August 20 of a brain hemorrhage in St. Louis, Missouri.

1908: Dorris (Dee) Alexander Brown was born on February 28 near Alberta, Louisiana.

1908: Richard Wright was born on September 4 in Roxic, Mississippi.

1910: Twain died of heart disease on April 21 in Redding, Connecticut.

1914: Ralph Waldo Ellison was born on March 1 in Oklahoma City.

1917: Gwendolyn Brooks was born June 7 in Topeka, Kansas.

1919: Primo Michele Levi was born on July 31 in Turin, Italy.

1919: Monica Sone was born Kazuko Monica Itoi in Seattle, Washington.

1921: Langston Hughes's "The Negro Speaks of Rivers" is published.

1921: Alex Haley was born on August 11 in Ithaca, New York.

1924: E. M. Forster's *A Passage to India* is published.

1924: Conrad died on August 3 of a heart attack in Bishopsbourne, Kent, England.

1925: Mary Flannery O'Connor was born March 25 in Savannah, Georgia.

1925: Malcolm Little was born on May 19, 1925, in Omaha, Nebraska.

1926: Nelle Harper Lee was born on April 28 in Monroeville, Alabama.

1927: Daniel Keyes was born August 9 in Brooklyn, New York.

1929: Martin Luther King Jr. was born on January 15 in Atlanta, Georgia.

1929: Virginia Woolf's *A Room of One's Own* is published.

1929: Anne Frank was born on June 12 in Frankfurt, Germany.

1930: Lorraine Hansberry was born on May 19 in Chicago, Illinois.

1933: Ernest James Gaines was born in 1933 on a plantation in Louisiana.

1934: Jeanne Wakatsuki Houston was born on September 26 in California.

1940: Richard Wright's *Native Son* is published.

1941: Woolf committed suicide by drowning on March 28 in Lewes, Sussex, England.

1943: Mildred Delois Taylor was born on September 13 in Jackson, Mississippi.

1944: Ralph Ellison's "King of the Bingo Game" is published.

1944: Alice Walker was born February 9 in Eatonton, Georgia.

1945: Frank died in March at the Bergen-Belsen concentration camp.

1947: Primo Levi's "A Good Day" is published.

1947: Anne Frank's *The Diary of a Young Girl* is published.

1948: Leslie Marmon Silko was born on March 5 in Albuquerque, New Mexico.

1948: Alan Paton's *Cry, the Beloved Country* is published.

1953: Monica Sone's *Nisei Daughter* is published.

1954: Sandra Cisneros was born December 20 in Chicago, Illinois.

1959: Lorraine Hansberry's *A Raisin in the Sun* is published.

1960: Wright died on November 28 of a heart attack in Paris, France.

1960: Harper Lee's *To Kill a Mockingbird* is published.

1961: Flannery O'Connor's "Everything that Rises Must Converge" is published.

1963: Martin Luther King Jr.'s "I Have a Dream" is published.

1963: Du Bois died on August 27 in Accra, Ghana.

1964: O'Connor died on August 3 of lupus in Milledgeville, Georgia.

1965: Hansberry died of lung cancer on January 12 in New York, New York.

1965: Malcolm X was assassinated on February 21 in New York, New York.

1965: Malcolm X's *The Autobiography of Malcolm X* is published.

1966: Daniel Keyes's *Flowers for Algernon* is published.

1967: Hughes died on August 22 of a cerebral hemorrhage in St. Louis, Missouri.

1968: King was assassinated on April 4 in Memphis, Tennessee.

1970: Forster died on June 7 in Coventry, England.

1970: Dee Brown's *Bury My Heart at Wounded Knee: An Indian History of the American West* is published.

1971: Ernest J. Gaines's *The Autobiography of Miss Jane Pittman* is published.

1973: Jeanne Wakatsuki Houston's *Farewell to Manzanar: A True Story of Japanese American Experience during and after the World War II Internment* is published.

1976: Mildred D. Taylor's *Roll of Thunder, Hear My Cry* is published.

1977: Leslie Marmon Silko's *Ceremony* is published.

1982: Alice Walker's *The Color Purple* is published.

1984: Sandra Cisneros's *The House on Mango Street* is published.

1987: Levi died of an alleged suicide on April 11.

1987: Gwendolyn Brooks's *Blacks* is published.

1988: Alan Paton died of throat cancer on April 12 in Botha's Hill, Natal, South Africa.

1992: Alex Haley died of cardiac arrest on February 10 in Seattle, Washington.

1994: Ellison died on April 16 of cancer in New York, New York.

2000: Gwendolyn Brooks died on December 3 of cancer in Chicago, Illinois.

2002: Brown died on December 12 in Little Rock, Arkansas.

I Know Why the Caged Bird Sings

MAYA ANGELOU

1969

Maya Angelou's memoir *I Know Why the Caged Bird Sings* was her first published full-length literary work. The book takes its title from a poem by Paul Laurence Dunbar titled "Sympathy," in which he expresses his feelings of imprisonment due to racial prejudice. Similarly, Angelou's detailed memoir recounts her early years and the hardships she faced as a young black girl in America. However, the book also documents many of her childhood joys, learning experiences, and accomplishments, as well as hardships that transcend race.

In the book, the author—known to her family as Marguerite—chronicles a period of her young life filled with displacement and a complete absence of any sense of belonging. She and her brother Bailey are shuffled back and forth among family members after their parents divorce, living most of their early years with their grandmother in Arkansas. From there, they are shipped off to St. Louis, then back to Arkansas, and finally they move out to California with their mother. The only real source of stability for the two siblings, separated by just a year in age, is each other.

I Know Why the Caged Bird Sings has attracted controversy in recent years for its chilling depiction of Marguerite's rape at the hands of one of her mother's boyfriends, Mr. Freeman. In "Learning to Live: When the Bird Breaks

from the Cage," critic Opal Moore notes that the book has also received criticism for

> its exploration of the ugly spectre of racism in America, its recounting of the circumstances of Angelou's own out-of-wedlock teen pregnancy, and its humorous poking at the foibles of the institutional church.

However, as Moore points out, "Self empowerment, faith, struggle as quest, survival, intellectual curiosity, complexity of choice—these ideas are the underpinning of Maya Angelou's story." The book touches on serious issues in a serious way, which some feel is inappropriate for younger readers. In fact, the American Library Association lists *I Know Why the Caged Bird Sings* as one of the most frequently challenged books in American libraries, which reflects the number of attempts that have been made to pull a book from library circulation due to "offensive" content.

Still, the book continues to receive steady attention and praise and is frequently listed as part of the curriculum in classes dealing with race, literature, and women's issues. Angelou has written several more volumes of autobiography, including *Gather Together in My Name*, which focuses on the author's late teen years and early adulthood; *Singin' and Swingin' and Gettin' Merry Like Christmas*, which documents her subsequent short-lived marriage and stage career; *The Heart of a Woman*, which covers Angelou's burgeoning interest in civil rights and writing; and *All God's Children Need Traveling Shoes*, which chronicles her experiences living in Ghana in the 1960s. However, neither these books nor her extensive work as a poet and screenwriter have come close to the success Angelou achieved with her very first memoir.

PLOT SUMMARY

Chapters 1–3

I Know Why the Caged Bird Sings begins when the author, known by her given name Marguerite Johnson, is only three years old. She and her four-year-old brother Bailey are sent by train from their former home in Long Beach, California, to live with their paternal grandmother in Stamps, Arkansas. Marguerite and Bailey's parents have decided to divorce, and neither is prepared to take on the full responsibility of raising the two children. Though she does not recall many details of the trip, she

> " RITIE, DON'T WORRY 'CAUSE YOU AIN'T PRETTY. PLENTY PRETTY WOMEN I SEEN DIGGING DITCHES OR WORSE. YOU SMART. I SWEAR TO GOD, I RATHER YOU HAVE A GOOD MIND THAN A CUTE BEHIND."

does note that black passengers are segregated on part of the journey through the South; she also mentions that many black passengers, feeling bad for the unaccompanied children, offer them food and sympathy.

Marguerite's grandmother—whom the children soon come to call "Momma"—owns and operates a general store in Stamps. In the twenty-five years since it was built, the store has come to be "the lay center of activities in town." The store caters especially to the black workers who toil in the cotton fields; even as a child, Marguerite can sense the harsh truth of Southern economics as it applies to the cotton pickers:

> No matter how much they had picked, it wasn't enough. Their wages wouldn't even get them out of debt to my grandmother, not to mention the staggering bill that waited on them at the white commissary downtown.

In Chapters 2 and 3, Marguerite describes her responsibilities at the store and her Uncle Willie, who lives with the children and Momma in Stamps. Willie is physically disabled, a condition Momma attributes to a careless babysitter having repeatedly dropped him. Willie is a proud, well-dressed man who does not hide his disability from others. Marguerite recalls the only occasion she ever saw him try to stand fully erect, when an unfamiliar couple from Little Rock visited the store. She can only guess that Willie "must have tired of being crippled, as prisoners tire of penitentiary bars and the guilty tire of blame." One day, the former sheriff stops by the store to let Momma know that the Klan will be out that night, looking to avenge the actions of a black man who reportedly "messed with a white lady" that day. The family hides Willie in the vegetable bin, covered in potatoes and onions, until morning.

BIOGRAPHY

MAYA ANGELOU

Maya Angelou was born Marguerite Ann Johnson in St. Louis, Missouri, in 1928. Soon after her birth, her family relocated to California. When she was three years old, her parents divorced and she and her brother, Bailey, were sent to live with their paternal grandmother in Stamps, Arkansas. Her experiences from age three to age sixteen are documented in her bestselling memoir, *I Know Why the Caged Bird Sings*.

After having a son soon after finishing high school, Angelou spent several years at different jobs, including dancing and acting. In 1959, at the request of Dr. Martin Luther King Jr., she was appointed the Northern Coordinator of the Southern Christian Leadership Conference. She eventually turned her attention to writing and achieved success as both a journalist and a poet. Her first full-length literary work was *I Know Why the Caged Bird Sings*, which was nominated for a National Book Award; she has since written several more autobiographical books covering different periods of her unique life, as well as numerous essays, poetry collections, and children's books. Angelou has also written for television, film, and stage.

In 1992, Angelou was designated as a poet laureate by newly elected President of the United States Bill Clinton. She composed and recited an original poem for his inauguration titled "On the Pulse of Morning." As of 2006, Angelou continues to write and appears regularly in films and on television.

Chapters 4–6

Throughout her youth, Marguerite looks to her older brother Bailey for support, friendship, and protection. She describes him as "the greatest person in my world." Whenever anyone makes a remark to hurt or insult Marguerite, Bailey is always there to seek revenge in his own way.

Because Bailey is "the pride of the Henderson/ Johnson family," he is rarely punished.

Twice each year, the Johnson children are sent to the white part of Stamps to buy fresh liver. As the author notes, "In Stamps the segregation was so complete that most Black children didn't really, absolutely know what whites looked like." Although Marguerite knows they are real—she has seen their clothing, carried by their servants when the servants stopped by the store—she still has a difficult time picturing them as people.

A subset of the enigmatic "whitefolks" is what the author calls the "powhitetrash," the poorest of the whites who often visit Momma's store. The children show no respect, climbing on counters and getting into anything within reach. Even worse in Marguerite's eyes, they do not address Momma with the respect she deserves. Despite this, Momma responds to the impudent children with patience and dignity. Though Marguerite does not fully understand her actions, she sees Momma's strength and knows that somehow, "Momma had won."

In their petty, childish way, Marguerite and Bailey grow to hate Reverend Howard Thomas, the presiding elder over their church's district. Every three months when he comes to visit the parish, the reverend stays overnight at their house; when he does, Reverend Thomas always gets to eat the best parts of the chicken at Sunday dinner. The children get their satisfaction one Sunday when another member of the congregation, Sister Monroe, is so overcome by his sermon that she runs to the pulpit and literally knocks the preacher's dentures out of his mouth.

Chapters 7–9

Although the Johnson family is one of the few black families in Stamps who does not receive government welfare, Momma allows her customers to exchange their government-issued provisions—like powdered milk and powdered eggs—for goods from her store. This means that the Johnson children end up eating the government provisions regularly, much to Marguerite's dismay. This is just one example of Momma's life philosophy: "Waste not, want not."

One Christmas, the children receive gifts from their parents in California. Both Marguerite and Bailey, who barely remember their real parents or California, react badly; it had been easier for them to believe that their parents might be dead than to face the reality that their parents just did not want them around.

The following year, their father, Bailey Senior, comes to Stamps. The children are dazzled by his sophisticated clothes and speech, but when he tells them he is taking them to live in St. Louis with their mother, Marguerite does not want to go. In St. Louis, the children meet their mother as if for the first time. Marguerite notes, "I knew immediately why she had sent me away. She was too beautiful to have children." Their father leaves them in St. Louis with their mother and returns to California.

Chapters 10–12
In St. Louis, the children live at first with their grandparents. Though the big city is a far cry from Stamps, they adapt well and find that their rural schooling has been far superior to that of their urban classmates. Both children are moved up a grade level and still manage to excel beyond the levels of the other students. The children also find that their mother's side of the family, the Baxters, are a close-knit and fiercely loyal group.

The children eventually move in with Mother and her boyfriend, Mr. Freeman. Marguerite, stricken with nightmares, begins sleeping in the same bed as Mother and Mr. Freeman. One morning, after Mother has left, Mr. Freeman molests Marguerite and tells her that if she tells anyone, he will have to kill her brother Bailey. Marguerite does not understand what has happened, but she knows she cannot tell.

Later, when Marguerite and Mr. Freeman are home alone, he rapes her. The author describes the pain as "a breaking and entering when even the senses are torn apart." Marguerite falls ill afterward and is bedridden until the next day. While Mother and Bailey change her sheets, they discover the blood-soaked panties Marguerite has hidden under her mattress.

Chapters 13–15
In the hospital, Bailey convinces Marguerite to tell him who raped her. Mr. Freeman is arrested and, as the author notes, "spared the awful wrath of my pistol-whipping uncles." Marguerite testifies against Mr. Freeman at his trial, and he is sentenced to one year and one day—a sentence he never serves. Soon after, a policeman stops by to inform the family that Mr. Freeman has been found dead.

Marguerite, upon hearing that Mr. Freeman has died, stops talking to everyone except Bailey. She fears that her words are responsible for Mr. Freeman's death and does not want to risk harming others. Though the family accepts her unusual behavior after such a traumatic experience, the children are sent back to Stamps to live with Momma.

Marguerite remains mute for a year. Her life changes thanks to a woman named Mrs. Bertha Flowers, whom she considers "the aristocrat of Black Stamps." Mrs. Flowers invites Marguerite to her house and treats her with the respect of an adult, serving her fresh-baked cookies and reading to her from *A Tale of Two Cities*; in return, Mrs. Flowers asks Marguerite to recite passages from her books aloud. This marks the beginning of the end of Marguerite's self-imposed isolation.

Chapters 16–18
At ten years old, Marguerite is sent to work part-time at the home of a white woman named Viola Cullinan. This, she explains, was her "finishing school"—the place where she learns all the skills a woman should possess, like setting a table with silverware and cooking meals. Under the tutelage of Miss Glory, Mrs. Cullinan's black cook, Marguerite endures the tedious tasks she is assigned. When Mrs. Cullinan begins calling her "Mary" instead of Marguerite for her own convenience, she decides to quit. Knowing Momma would not allow this, though, she devises a plan to get fired. After getting Mrs. Cullinan's attention, Marguerite drops the woman's favorite dishes—family heirlooms—right in front of her, shattering them. The plan works, and she never has to return.

One Saturday, Bailey goes to the movies and fails to return before evening. Momma is worried but tries not to show it; she knows the dangers that await a black boy in the South at night. As the author notes: "The Black woman in the South who raises sons, grandsons and nephews had her heart-strings tied to a hanging noose. Any break from routine may herald for them unbearable news." Bailey finally returns after dark and receives a severe whipping for his actions. Soon after, Bailey tells Marguerite why he came home so late: he was watching a movie, over and over, that starred a woman named Kay Francis who looks just like their mother. Two months later, when another Kay Francis movie comes to town, Bailey and

Marguerite both go to see it and are comforted by the fact that they can see their "mother" on movie screens since they cannot see her in person.

Chapter 18 describes an annual church revival for the local black parish in Stamps. The author notes the emphasis on suffering through the toils of this life—including racism, segregation, and other inequities of black life in the South—in order to secure a place in heaven.

Chapters 19–21

In Chapter 19, the entire black community gathers at Momma's store radio to listen to black heavyweight champion Joe Louis take on a white challenger. For the listeners, it is much more than just a boxing match. The author describes a moment when Louis is on the ropes, and defeat seems imminent:

> My race groaned. It was our people falling. It was another lynching, yet another Black man hanging on a tree. One more woman ambushed and raped. A Black boy whipped and maimed. It was hounds on the trail of a man running through slimy swamps. It was a white woman slapping her maid for being forgetful.

But Louis comes back, pounding away at his opponent until he goes down for the count. The crowd in the store celebrates with candy and soda. Those who live far away make arrangements to stay in town; as the author puts it, "It wouldn't do for a Black man and his family to be caught on a lonely country road on a night when Joe Louis had proved that we were the strongest people in the world."

Shortly before Valentine's Day, Marguerite receives a letter from a boy she scarcely knows named Tommy Valdon who wants Marguerite to be his valentine. Wary of males since her experience with Mr. Freeman, she tears up the letter; Tommy sends her a thoughtful valentine letter anyway, and Marguerite regrets rejecting him so hastily.

Just before he turns eleven, Marguerite's brother Bailey has a more serious love affair with a girl named Joyce, four years his senior. As their relationship grows in intensity, Bailey steals more and more goods from Momma's store to give to Joyce. Suddenly, she disappears one day. Marguerite later finds out that Joyce ran off to marry a railroad porter she met one day when he stopped at Momma's store.

Chapters 22–24

One windy night, the Johnsons are visited by a widower neighbor named George Taylor. Momma and Willie welcome the man into their home, and he recounts a tale that terrifies Marguerite. Lying in bed the night before, Mr. Taylor opened his eyes to see an apparition of a baby angel. The angel, according to Mr. Taylor, had his dead wife's voice; it told him that it wanted children. Sensing the man's loneliness, Momma and Willie let him stay the night. Momma tells Mr. Taylor he should take in a child to help him with his farm.

In Chapter 23, Marguerite's eighth-grade graduation ceremony is nearly spoiled when a white politician named Donleavy delivers the commencement address. Donleavy proudly promises that the school will soon receive equipment and resources to take advantage of the male students' athletic skills; in contrast, the local white school will receive a new art instructor and the latest scientific equipment for their lab. This enrages Marguerite, who suddenly sees the futility of her education: "We were maids and farmers, handymen and washer-women, and anything higher that we aspired to was farcical and presumptuous." Afterward, however, class valedictorian Henry Reed restores their spirit and pride by leading the class in a rendition of the "Negro national anthem."

In Chapter 24, Marguerite's fondness for candy has resulted in two deep cavities that cannot be dealt with using traditional home remedies. Momma takes her to the only dentist in town, Dentist Lincoln. Though he has a policy against treating blacks, Momma had lent him money in the past, and she feels that he owes her a favor. Dentist Lincoln refuses, saying that he would "rather stick my hand in a dog's mouth than in a nigger's." Momma tells Marguerite to wait for her outside, then demands that Dentist Lincoln pay her interest for money she once lent him; she then uses this money to take Marguerite on a bus to the nearest black dentist, in Texarkana.

Chapters 25–27

After an incident in which Bailey sees the dead body of a black man who has been fished out of a pond, Momma tells the children that she will be taking them out to live in Oakland, California with their mother, Vivian. Not long after moving in with several other members of the Baxter clan—relocated from St. Louis to

Oakland—Vivian marries a man Marguerite comes to know as Daddy Clidell, and the four move to San Francisco as a newly formed family.

As America enters World War II, San Francisco is cleared of all Japanese citizens, and they are largely replaced by Southern blacks looking for economic opportunities on the West Coast. None of the blacks Marguerite knows have ever seen the Japanese people whose former homes and businesses they have adopted as their own. Marguerite feels a connection to the city and, for the first time in her life, feels as if she is in a place where she belongs.

Chapters 28–30

Marguerite does well in high school, and at fourteen she is given a scholarship to an adult college called the California Labor School where she takes evening classes in drama and dance. Over time, she grows to admire her stepfather, Daddy Clidell; he is successful without being arrogant and seems honorable despite the many con men he calls friends.

Marguerite's real father, Daddy Bailey, invites her to visit him in Los Angeles for the summer. When she arrives, she discovers that her father's life does not match the glamorous vision she had created in her mind: he lives "in a trailer park on the outskirts of a town that was itself the outskirts of town," and his girlfriend Dolores is a small, uptight woman not much older than Marguerite herself.

One day, Daddy Bailey takes Marguerite to Mexico to buy supplies for the Mexican food he loves to make. Marguerite soon realizes that the purpose of the trip is not just to buy food, which can be obtained just as easily near their home; Bailey takes her all the way to a bar near Ensenada, where he is recognized and welcomed as a regular. Marguerite gets a glimpse of her father's secret life, which includes a Mexican girlfriend surely unknown to Dolores.

Daddy Bailey disappears for a while and is eventually brought out to his car in a drunken stupor. Marguerite, facing the possibility of spending the night in Mexico, attempts to drive the car back to California with her father passed out in the backseat. She manages quite well until she crashes into another car at a checkpoint near the border. Daddy Bailey wakes up and is able to smooth things over with the owner of the other car; suddenly clearheaded and not the least bit angry, he drives them the rest of the way home.

Chapters 31–33

After the two return from Mexico, Daddy Bailey and Dolores—who has been patiently awaiting his return—get into an argument over Marguerite. After her father has stormed out of the house, Marguerite realizes that he has treated Dolores cruelly. Marguerite tries to comfort Dolores, but she responds with insults. When Dolores calls Marguerite's mother a whore, Marguerite slaps her and the two begin brawling. In the ensuing chaos, Dolores stabs Marguerite in the side. Daddy Bailey returns soon after; he takes Marguerite to a nurse friend who treats her wound and then deposits her at the trailer of another friend where she can stay the night safe from Dolores.

Marguerite decides to run away and ends up in a junkyard where other runaways—made up of blacks, whites, and Hispanics, all with equal regard for each other—also live. She stays there for a month, collecting bottles for redemption money and entering a local dance contest each week just to try and collect the prize money. She eventually calls her mother Vivian, who arranges for the airfare back home. The sense of community and tolerance that she learned with the runaways remains with her long after she leaves.

During Marguerite's absence, her brother Bailey has started hanging out with unsavory friends and arguing with Vivian. After defying a curfew she has set, Bailey is thrown out of the house. Though he does not return home, he and Vivian make up, and she arranges for him to work on the Southern Pacific railroad as a dining-car waiter.

Chapters 34–36

Left without her brother, Marguerite decides that she wants to get a job. She chooses streetcar conductor as her desired profession, but is disappointed when her mother tells her that black people are not allowed to work the streetcars. Undaunted, Marguerite begins a campaign to become the first black streetcar operator in San Francisco. Her tenacity ultimately pays off, and she gets her wish.

When high school resumes, she realizes that she and her fellow students are "on paths moving diametrically away from each other." She begins to cut classes, believing that school has little else to teach her. Her mother is understanding, but insists that Marguerite let her know if she wants to stay home.

After reading a book called *The Well of Loneliness*, Marguerite becomes concerned that she might be a lesbian. Even though she is not entirely clear on what the term *lesbian* means, she feels that she must find a boyfriend to "clarify [her] position to the world." She seeks out a handsome boy she knows and asks if he would like to have sex with her. Although the encounter leaves her less than fulfilled, she discovers three weeks later that she is pregnant.

This realization leaves her "suffocating in the nightmare." Still, she manages to hide her pregnancy from her family for eight months and throws herself back into her studies. She receives her diploma and then summons up the courage to tell her family about the coming baby. Her family treats her with more understanding than she expects. Soon after, she gives birth to a boy. At first she is terrified to hold him, afraid she does not know what to do; her mother reassures her, telling her, "See, you don't have to worry about doing the right thing. If you're for the right thing, then you do it without thinking."

THEMES

Segregation

In *I Know Why the Caged Bird Sings*, Marguerite experiences firsthand the segregation prevalent in the American South during her childhood. She first notes segregation on the train trip from California to Arkansas when she is three years old; for Marguerite and her brother, however, the experience is positive. Once the two children are surrounded by other black people, sympathy and camaraderie show themselves, and the children are treated to food from strangers' lunch boxes.

In Stamps, the author notes that "the segregation was so complete that most Black children didn't really, absolutely know what whites looked like." This leads Marguerite to view whites as something entirely different from her and the people she knows:

> People were those who lived on my side of town. I didn't like them all, or, in fact, any of them very much, but they were people. These others, the strange pale creatures that lived in their alien unlife, weren't considered folks. They were whitefolks.

When Marguerite suffers from two painful dental cavities, Momma takes her to a white dentist in Stamps for treatment. Even though Momma has previously loaned the dentist money, the dentist states firmly that it is his policy not to treat blacks. Momma's only option is to take Marguerite on a bus to Texarkana, where the nearest black dentist practices.

In another way, Marguerite's frequent relocation throughout her youth results in a sort of self-segregation. She rarely becomes close with other people, and constantly views herself as an outsider or visitor wherever she lives. When Marguerite runs away from her father's home in Los Angeles, she stays in a junkyard along with other runaways; some are black, some are white, and some are Hispanic. It is here that Marguerite first develops a sense of community and tolerance outside the primarily black areas in which she has been raised. After the experience she notes, "I was never again to sense myself so solidly outside the pale of the human race."

Inequality

In the book, Marguerite sees massive inequalities between the resources and opportunities available to blacks as compared to whites. At her eighth-grade graduation, a white politician reminds her of those inequalities when he talks about the improvements their Negro school will receive—all of which relate to athletics. The white school, by contrast, will receive new scientific equipment and a new art instructor. As Marguerite sums it up:

> The white kids were going to have a chance to become Galileos and Madame Curies and Edisons and Gauguins, and our boys (the girls weren't even in on it) would try to be Jesse Owenses and Joe Louises.

Even in San Francisco, a far cry from the segregated South, Marguerite encounters a conspicuous inequality in the opportunities available to blacks. When she tells her mother that she would like to work as a streetcar conductor, her mother says simply: "They don't accept colored people on the streetcars." Marguerite spends weeks displaying her determination to the railway company that runs the streetcars, and eventually gets hired; however, this does not change the fact that she must exhibit great strength and tenacity just to obtain the same job application that any white person would be handed for the asking.

Racial Violence

Although very little racially motivated violence occurs in *I Know Why the Caged Bird Sings*, the threat of violence hangs over the black population of Stamps like a veil. Early in the book, a former sheriff stops by Momma's store to tell her that the Ku Klux Klan, a group he refers to simply as "the boys," will be out that night looking for black men. Momma and the children hide Uncle Willie in the vegetable bin for his safety.

A similar fear strikes again when Bailey is late returning from the movies one evening. Nightfall brings with it the possibility of terrible things for a black man in the South, including lynchings. As Marguerite states, "The night suddenly became enemy territory, and I knew that if my brother was lost in this land he was forever lost."

Later, a crowd gathers at Momma's store to listen to a radio broadcast of Joe Louis's heavyweight boxing match. Those who live far away from the store make arrangements to stay overnight in Stamps; on a night when a black man has just proven his title "Heavyweight Champion of the World" by defeating a white contender, it is considered unwise for black people to be traveling on isolated roads where bitter white men might be out looking for trouble.

The children find themselves headed for California after Bailey tells of seeing a dead black man pulled out of a pond. The man is never identified and the cause of his death is not stated, but the white men Bailey sees dealing with the body clearly find the dead man amusing. Bailey recognizes that the white men hate the black men and are capable of doing them harm. After the incident, Momma immediately begins planning to send the children to their mother, who now lives in the less-threatening environment of northern California.

Class and Race

Although class is often associated with race in *I Know Why the Caged Bird Sings*, the author includes numerous examples where the two diverge. Daddy Clidell, Marguerite's stepfather in the end, is a black man who has become quite a financial success even though he lives in relative modesty when compared to the lavish excess Marguerite sees in the lifestyles of white people.

By contrast, there are some whites in the book who inhabit an economic realm below Momma and many other blacks. As Marguerite says, "My grandmother had more money than all the powhitetrash. We owned land and houses." In fact, some of these destitute white people live on land owned by Momma. Still, even though the "powhitetrash" are much worse off than Momma economically, they act superior to all black people. On one occasion, a group of poor white children mock her and try their best to evoke some sort of negative emotion from her, but Momma refuses to dignify their antics with any sort of response. She has been raised to believe that it is unsafe to speak to white people at all, but when necessary, she always speaks with politeness and deference—regardless of the white person's class.

HISTORICAL OVERVIEW

Segregation in the American South

The era of segregation began in the South when the era of Reconstruction, or rebuilding after the Civil War, ended in 1877. When federal troops withdrew from the South, individual states passed laws that allowed whites to refuse accommodations or facilities (such as restrooms and drinking fountains) to blacks at their discretion. Although the Supreme Court upheld these laws on the premise that blacks were entitled to "separate but equal" facilities, this was rarely the case. More often than not, facilities reserved for blacks were not functional or not maintained with the same diligence as those reserved for whites.

In *I Know Why the Caged Bird Sings*, Marguerite describes the segregated black school in the town of Stamps, Arkansas: "Unlike the white high school, Lafayette County Training School distinguished itself by having neither lawn, nor hedges, nor tennis court, nor climbing ivy." It was not until 1954, when the Supreme Court ruled in *Brown v. Board of Education of Topeka, Kansas* that segregated schools were inherently not equal, that official state-sanctioned segregation in the South began to come to an end. Still, some states like Arkansas—where Marguerite had lived with Momma years earlier—resisted the court ruling. In 1957, Arkansas Governor Orval Faubus deployed Arkansas National Guard to prevent nine black students from attending a formerly whites-only high school in Little Rock.

The Great Depression and Southern Blacks

In *I Know Why the Caged Bird Sings*, Marguerite spends her youth in Stamps, Arkansas, during the Great Depression. However, she notes, "The country had been in the throes of the Great Depression for two years before the Negroes in Stamps knew it." Since blacks in the South often had little to begin with, they had little to lose, and therefore were not immediately affected. However, as labor-intensive industries such as cotton farming felt the financial squeeze of the Depression, the black field workers suffered even lower wages than normal.

Blacks, who were already foundering in an economic system designed to promote and sustain debt, fell even further behind. In *I Know Why the Caged Bird Sings*, Momma manages to keep her store running primarily by accepting trade instead of money from her impoverished customers. Fortunately, these poorest of the poor were also among the first to benefit from President Franklin Roosevelt's social welfare programs in the 1930s, which provided food to those who could not afford to feed themselves.

World War II and the Great Migration

With the advent of World War II, the economy of the United States received just the jolt it needed to shake off the last stages of the Great Depression. The war caused such a drain on American labor resources that many blacks found themselves able to secure jobs that would have otherwise proved unattainable. Although this was true throughout the country, it held especially true for the West Coast, where tens of thousands of Japanese American citizens and Japanese immigrants were removed from the labor force and sent to internment camps. In *I Know Why the Caged Bird Sings*, Marguerite notes of San Francisco: "The Japanese area became San Francisco's Harlem in a matter of months."

This demand for wartime labor drew many blacks from their longtime homes in the South into factories in the Northeast and along the West Coast. This was one of the key factors in what has come to be called the Great Migration, the dispersion of African Americans from the South to other parts of the United States. The continued economic growth of the country after World War II, as well as more progressive attitudes about civil rights in other parts of the country, resulted in a steady flow of blacks out of the South for many years.

CRITICAL OVERVIEW

When *I Know Why the Caged Bird Sings* was first published in 1969, critical response was warmly positive. Robert A. Gross, reviewing the book for *Newsweek*, notes that the author "regularly throws out rich, dazzling images which delight and surprise with their simplicity." He also says of the book that "one has to read it to appreciate its sensitivity and life." Christopher Lehmann-Haupt, in a review for the *New York Times*, calls the book "a carefully wrought, simultaneously touching and comic memoir." Like Gross, Lehmann-Haupt specifically points out the author's skill with words: "The beauty is not in the story, but in the telling."*I Know Why the Caged Bird Sings* spent the initial months after its publication on the New York Times Bestseller List, and was a finalist for the 1970 National Book Award.

E. M. Guiney, in a review for *Library Journal*, notes that the story itself "is horrifying and painful to read"; however, the reviewer also notes the author's writing "ranges from beautifully lyrical prose to earthy metaphor, and her descriptions have power and sensitivity." Despite the sometimes unpleasant subject matter, the reviewer considers it "one of the best autobiographies of its kind."

However, many feel that the book's graphic depictions of both rape and consensual sex, as well as its frank discussion of the maturing female body, are inappropriate for younger readers. *I Know Why the Caged Bird Sings* is listed as number three on the American Library Association's list of 100 Most Frequently Challenged Books of 1990–2000; a "challenge" consists of a formal complaint to the ALA that a book be removed from library circulation due to offensive content. Maya Angelou is herself listed by the ALA as one of the Top Ten Challenged Authors of 1990–2004.

Despite these challenges, *I Know Why the Caged Bird Sings* remains a popular title in high-school and college curricula. The book's open discussion of race and gender issues has opened the door for similar discussions in classrooms across the country.

MEDIA ADAPTATIONS

An abridged audio recording of *I Know Why the Caged Bird Sings* was released on audio cassette by Random House Audio in 1986 and rereleased on compact disc in 1996. It is read by the author, and both formats are currently widely available. This abridged audio recording is also available as an audio download through audible.com.

I Know Why the Caged Bird Sings was adapted into a television movie in 1979. The film stars Diahann Carroll as Vivian and Esther Rolle as Momma. The film was directed by Fielder Cook, from a screenplay cowritten by Angelou. This adaptation was released on VHS by Live/Artisan, but is not currently available.

The Book-It Repertory Theatre in Seattle staged an adaptation of the book in 2003 scripted by Myra Platt. This adaptation is not currently available.

CRITICISM

Mary Jane Lupton

In the following excerpt, Lupton discusses unifying stylistic and thematic elements in Angelou's autobiographies.

> Now my problem I have is I love life, I love living life and I love the art of living, so I try to live my life as a poetic adventure, everything I do from the way I keep my house, cook, make my husband happy, or welcome my friends, raise my son; everything is part of a large canvas I am creating, I am living beneath.

This energetic statement from [an] interview with Maya Angelou [in *Black Scholar*, January–February, 1977] merely hints at the variety of roles and experiences which sweep through what is presently her five-volume autobiographical series: *I Know Why the Caged Bird Sings* (1970), *Gather Together in My Name* (1974), *Singin' and Swingin' and Gettin' Merry Like Christmas* (1976), *The Heart of a Woman* (1981), and *All*

God's Children Need Traveling Shoes (1986). It is fitting that Angelou, so adept at metaphor, should compare her "poetic adventure" to the act of painting: "[E]verything is part of a large canvas I am creating, I am living beneath." Like an unfinished painting, the autobiographical series is an ongoing creation, in a form that rejects the finality of a restricting frame. Its continuity is achieved through characters who enter the picture, leave, and reappear, and through certain interlaced themes—self-acceptance, race, men, work, separation, sexuality, motherhood. All the while Angelou lives "beneath," recording the minutest of details in a constantly shifting environment and giving attention to the "mundane, though essential, ordinary moments of life" [Sondra O'Neale in *Black Women Writers (1950–1980): A Critical Evaluation*, 1984].

I Know Why the Caged Bird Sings is the first and most highly praised volume in the series. It begins with the humiliations of childhood and ends with the birth of a child. At its publication, critics, not anticipating a series, readily appreciated the clearly developed narrative form. In 1973, for example, Sidonie Smith discussed the "sense of an ending" in *Caged Bird* as it relates to Angelou's acceptance of Black womanhood [in "The Song of a Caged Bird: Maya Angelou's Quest after Self-Acceptance," *Southern Humanities Review*, Vol. 7, 1973]: "With the birth of her child Maya is herself born into a mature engagement with the forces of life." But with the introduction in 1974 of Angelou's second autobiographical volume, *Gather Together in My Name*, the tight structure appeared to crumble; childhood experiences were replaced by episodes which a number of critics consider disjointed or bizarre. Selwyn Cudjoe, for instance, noted the shift from the "intense solidity and moral center" in *Caged Bird* to the "conditions of *alienation* and *fragmentation* "in *Gather Together*, conditions which affect its organization and its quality, making it "conspicuously weak." Lynn Z. Bloom [in *Dictionary of Literary Biography*, Vol. 38] found the sequel "less satisfactory" because the narrator "abandons or jeopardizes the maturity, honesty, and intuitive good judgment toward which she had been moving in *Caged Bird*." Crucial to Bloom's judgment is her concept of movement *toward*, which insinuates the achievement of an ending.

The narrator, as authentic recorder of the life, indeed changes during the second volume, as does the book's structure; the later volumes abandon the tighter form of *Caged Bird* for an episodic series of adventures whose so-called "fragments" are reflections of the kind of chaos found in actual living. In altering the narrative structure, Angelou shifts the emphasis from herself as an isolated consciousness to herself as a Black woman participating in diverse experiences among a diverse class of peoples. As the world of experience widens, so does the canvas.

What distinguishes, then, Angelou's autobiographical method from more conventional autobiographical forms is her very denial of closure. The reader of autobiography expects a beginning, a middle, and an end—as occurs in *Caged Bird*. She or he also expects a central experience, as we indeed are given in the extraordinary rape sequence of *Caged Bird*. But Angelou, by continuing her narrative, denies the form and its history, creating from each ending a new beginning, relocating the center to some luminous place in a volume yet to be. Stretching the autobiographical canvas, she moves forward: from being a child; to being a mother; to leaving the child; to having the child, in the fifth volume, achieve his independence. Nor would I be so unwise as to call the fifth volume the end. For Maya Angelou, now a grandmother, has already published a moving, first-person account in *Woman's Day* of the four years of anguish surrounding the maternal kidnapping of her grandson Colin.

Throughout the more episodic volumes, the theme of motherhood remains a unifying element, with Momma Henderson being Angelou's link with the Black folk tradition—as George Kent, Elizabeth Schultz, and other critics have mentioned. Since traditional solidity of development is absent, one must sometimes search through three or four books to trace Vivian Baxter's changing lovers, Maya Angelou's ambivalence towards motherhood, or her son Guy's various reactions to his non-traditional upbringing. Nonetheless, the volumes are intricately related through a number of essential elements: the ambivalent autobiographical voice, the flexibility of structure to echo the life process, the intertextual commentary on character and theme, and the use of certain recurring patterns to establish both continuity and continuation. I have isolated the mother-child pattern as a way

of approaching the complexity of Angelou's methods. One could as well select other kinds of interconnected themes: the absent and/or substitute father, the use of food as a psychosexual symbol, the dramatic/symbolic use of images of staring or gazing, and other motifs which establish continuity within and among the volumes.

Stephen Butterfield says of *Caged Bird* [in his *Black Autobiography in America*, 1974]: "Continuity is achieved by the contact of mother and child, the sense of life begetting life that happens automatically in spite of all confusion—perhaps also because of it." The consistent yet changing connection for Maya Angelou through the four subsequent narratives is that same contact of mother and child—with herself and her son Guy; with herself and her own mother, Vivian Baxter; with herself and her paternal grandmother; and, finally, with the child-mother in herself.

Moreover, in extending the traditional one-volume form, Angelou has metaphorically mothered another book. The "sense of life begetting life" at the end of *Caged Bird* can no longer signal the conclusion of the narrative. The autobiographical moment has been reopened and expanded; Guy's birth can now be seen symbolically as the birth of another text. In a 1975 interview with Carol Benson [in the January issue of *Writer's Digest*], Angelou uses such a birthing metaphor in describing the writing of *Gather Together*": If you have a child, it takes nine months. It took me three-and-a-half years to write *Gather Together*, so I couldn't just drop it." This statement makes emphatic what in the autobiographies are much more elusive comparisons between creative work and motherhood; after a three-and-a-half-year pregnancy she gives birth to *Gather Together*, indicating that she must have planned the conception of the second volume shortly after the 1970 delivery of *Caged Bird*.

Each of the five volumes explores, both literally and metaphorically, the significance of motherhood. I will examine this theme from two specific perspectives: first, Angelou's relationship to her mother and to mother substitutes, especially to Momma Henderson; second, Angelou's relationship to her son as she struggles to define her own role as mother/artist. Throughout the volumes Angelou moves backwards and forwards, from connection to conflict. This dialectic of Black mother-daughterhood, introduced in the childhood narrative, enlarges and contracts during the series, finding its fullest expression in *Singin' and Swingin' and Gettin' Merry Like Christmas.*

In flux, in defiance of chronological time, the mother-child configuration forms the basic pattern against which other relationships are measured and around which episodes and volumes begin or end. Motherhood also provides the series with a literary unity, as Angelou shifts positions—from mother to granddaughter to child—in a non-ending text that, through its repetitions of maternal motifs, provides an ironic comment on her own sense of identity. For Angelou, despite her insistence on mother love, is trapped in the conflicts between working and mothering, independence and nurturing— conflicts that echo her ambivalence towards her mother, Vivian Baxter, and her apparent sanctification of Grandmother Henderson, the major adult figure in *Caged Bird.*

Annie Henderson is a solid, God-fearing, economically independent woman whose general store in Stamps, Arkansas, is the "lay center of activities in town," much as Annie is the moral center of the family. According to Mildred A. Hill-Lubin [in *Ngambika: Studies of Women in African Literature,* 1986], the grandmother, both in Africa and in America, "has been a significant force in the stability and the continuity of the Black family and the community." Hill-Lubin selects Annie Henderson as her primary example of the strong grandmother in African American literature—the traditional preserver of the family, the source of folk wisdom, and the instiller of values within the Black community. Throughout *Caged Bird* Maya has ambivalent feelings for this awesome woman, whose values of self-determination and personal dignity gradually chip away at Maya's dreadful sense of being "shit color." As a self-made woman, Annie Henderson has the economic power to lend money to whites; as a practical Black woman, however, she is convinced that whites cannot be directly confronted: "If she had been asked and had chosen to answer the question of whether she was cowardly or not, she would have said that she was a realist." To survive in a racist society, Momma Henderson has had to develop a realistic strategy of submission that Maya finds unacceptable. Maya, in her need to re-image her grandmother, creates a metaphor

that places Momma's power above any apparent submissiveness: Momma "did an excellent job of sagging from her waist down, but from the waist up she seemed to be pulling for the top of the oak tree across the road."

There are numerous episodes, both in *Caged Bird* and *Gather Together,* which involve the conflict between Maya and her grandmother over how to deal with racism. When taunted by three "powhitetrash" girls, Momma quietly sings a hymn; Maya, enraged, would like to have a rifle. Or, when humiliated by a white dentist who'd rather put his "hand in a dog's mouth than in a nigger's," Annie is passive; Maya subsequently invents a fantasy in which Momma runs the dentist out of town. In the italicized dream text, Maya endows her grandmother with superhuman powers; Momma magically changes the dentist's nurse into a bag of chicken seed. In reality the grandmother has been defeated and humiliated, her only reward a mere ten dollars in interest for a loan she had made to the dentist. In Maya's fantasy Momma's *"eyes were blazing like live coals and her arms had doubled themselves in length"*; in actuality she "looked tired."

This richly textured passage is rendered from the perspective of an imaginative child who recreates her grandmother—but in a language that ironically transforms Annie Henderson from a Southern Black storekeeper into an eloquent heroine from a romantic novel: *"Her tongue had thinned and the words rolled off well enunciated."* Instead of the silent "nigra" of the actual experience, Momma Henderson is now the articulate defender of her granddaughter against the stuttering dentist. Momma Henderson orders the *"contemptuous scoundrel"* to leave Stamps *"now and herewith."* The narrator eventually lets Momma speak normally, then comments: *"She could afford to slip into the vernacular because she had such eloquent command of English."*

This fantasy is the narrator's way of dealing with her ambivalence towards Momma Henderson—a woman who throughout *Caged Bird* represents to Maya both strength and weakness, both generosity and punishment, both affection and the denial of affection. Here her defender is *"ten feet tall with eight-foot arms"* quite capable, to recall the former tree image, of reaching the top of an oak from across the road. Momma's physical transformation in the dream text also recalls an earlier description: "I saw only her power and strength. She was taller than any woman in my personal world, and her hands were so large they could span my head from ear to ear." In the dentist fantasy, Maya eliminates all of Momma Henderson's "negative" traits—submissiveness, severity, religiosity, sternness, down-home speech. It would seem that Maya is so shattered by her grandmother's reaction to Dentist Lincoln, so destroyed by her illusions of Annie Henderson's power in relationship to white people, that she compensates by reversing the true situation and having the salivating dentist be the target of Momma's wrath. Significantly, this transformation occurs immediately before Momma Henderson tells Maya and Bailey that they are going to California. Its position in the text gives it the impression of finality. Any negative attitudes become submerged, only to surface later, in *Gather Together*, as aspects of Angelou's own ambiguity towards race, power, and identity.

Source: Mary Jane Lupton, "Singing the Black Mother: Maya Angelou and Autobiographical Continuity," in *Black American Literature Forum*, Vol. 24, No. 2, Summer 1990, pp. 257–76.

SOURCES

Angelou, Maya, *I Know Why the Caged Bird Sings*, Bantam Books, 1993, originally published in 1970.

Berson, Misha, "Angelou Adaptation is a Rough Gem that Needs Polishing," in *Seattle Times*, January 28, 2003, p. E3.

Gross, Robert A., Review of *I Know Why the Caged Bird Sings*, in *Newsweek*, March 2, 1970, pp. 89–90.

Guiney, E. M., Review of *I Know Why the Caged Bird Sings*, in *Library Journal*, March 15, 1970, Vol. 95, p. 1018, quoted in *Book Review Digest: Sixty-Sixth Annual Cumulation*, The H. W. Wilson Company, 1971, p. 34.

Lehmann-Haupt, Christopher, "Books of the Times," in the *New York Times*, February 25, 1970, p. 45.

Moore, Opal, "Learning to Live: When the Bird Breaks from the Cage," in *Censored Books: Critical Viewpoints*, Nicholas J. Karolides, Lee Burress, and John M. Kean, eds., 1993, pp. 306–16, as reproduced in *EXPLORING Novels*, Online Edition, Gale, 2003, Student Resource Center, Thomson Gale, galenet.galegroup.com/servlet/SRC (March 23, 2006).

"The 100 Most Frequently Challenged Books of 1990–2000," on the American Library Association website, www.ala.org/ala/oif/bannedbooksweek/bbwlinks/100mostfrequently.htm (March 23, 2006).

Kaffir Boy: The True Story of a Black Youth's Coming of Age in Apartheid South Africa

MARK MATHABANE

1986

In *Kaffir Boy: The True Story of a Black Youth's Coming of Age in Apartheid South Africa*, Mark Mathabane presents the remarkable story of his childhood and his rise to prominence as a journalist, lecturer, and humanitarian. Mathabane grew up in the terrifying shantytowns of Alexandra, outside of Johannesburg, South Africa. In these urban slums, he witnessed and survived the most repressive period of apartheid, the South African government's system of legalized racism. On a page of explanation before the narrative begins, Mathabane tells the reader, "In South Africa [the word *Kaffir*] is used disparagingly by most whites to refer to blacks. It is the equivalent of the term *nigger*. I was called a 'Kaffir' many times."

Kaffir Boy tells the story of his life under apartheid, as well as how he escaped South Africa to attend an American university, leaving his family behind. Mathabane's unwavering honesty is the book's main strength. One section, "The Road to Alexandra," offers a particularly relentless depiction of brutality and squalor. From the first page, Mathabane shows his readers the devastating personal costs of institutionalized racism: destroyed families, demolished personal pride, psychological pain, and ceaseless physical suffering. Mathabane does not lecture the reader; instead, the details of his story show what happens when racist brutality is made law. Mathabane does not shrink from relating his own failures, which include hanging out in

gangs, battling with his father, and feeling hatred for all white people. Mathabane dwells on his own attitudes in the second half of the book, demonstrating how he overcomes his hatred for whites and learns to judge people as individuals.

When *Kaffir Boy* was published in 1986, apartheid was still an official government policy in South Africa. Most educated people and governments in the rest of the world knew about apartheid in a vague sense, but few knew the full extent of the South African government's stance. Mathabane's autobiography thus became an important historical document. Mathabane describes significant events in the history of apartheid that were poorly covered by the Western press, such as the Sharpeville Massacre and the Soweto riots. *Kaffir Boy* is an important political work, as well. As Mathabane explains in the preface, his goal in writing the book was to help abolish apartheid. Now that apartheid has ended, the book still serves to demonstrate the horrifying consequences of institutionalized injustice and inequity. Like Frederick Douglass's autobiography, *Narrative of the Life of Frederick Douglass, An American Slave*, and Richard Wright's *Black Boy*, *Kaffir Boy* makes real for readers events that are often lost in the abstraction of law and social policy.

Mathabane's autobiography became an international bestseller and was translated into several languages. He won a Christopher Award for his book, an honor presented to writers and others whose work reveals something about the human condition. Since its publication, *Kaffir Boy* has become a familiar part of high school and college curricula. Mathabane continues to write about South Africa, as well as his more recent experiences. *Kaffir Boy in America: An Encounter with Apartheid* (1990) is a sequel to *Kaffir Boy*, in which Mathabane describes his life after coming to America and his struggles with American society. His other books include *Love in Black and White* (1992), co-written by Mathabane's white American wife, Gail, about their experiences as an interracial couple; *African Women* (1994), a non-fiction account of his mother, grandmother, and great-grandmother's experiences; *Ubuntu* (1999), a fictional thriller set in South Africa; and *Miriam's Song* (2000), the story of Mark's younger sister Miriam's coming of age amid the violence of apartheid resistance.

"MY CONCEPTION OF THE WORLD, OF LIFE, WAS WHOLLY IN RACIAL TERMS; AND THAT CONCEPTION WAS NOT MINE ALONE. IT WAS ECHOED BY ALL BLACK PEOPLE I HAD COME ACROSS. THERE WERE TWO WORLDS AS FAR AS WE WERE CONCERNED, SEPARATED ABSOLUTELY IN EVERY SENSE. BUT SOMEHOW, IN MY KNOWING ABOUT THESE TWO WORLDS, IT HAD NEVER OCCURRED TO ME THAT THOUGH THE TWO WERE AS DIFFERENT AS NIGHT AND DAY, AS SEPARATE AS EAST AND WEST, THEY HAD EVERYTHING TO DO WITH EACH OTHER; THAT ONE COULD NOT BE WITHOUT THE OTHER, AND THAT THEIR DEPENDENCY WAS THAT OF MASTER AND SLAVE."

PLOT SUMMARY

Part I: The Road to Alexandra
Chapters 1–20

Mark Mathabane, born Johannes Mathabane, begins by describing Alexandra, one of the many black shantytowns (sometimes called townships) created under apartheid. Alexandra is where Mathabane grew up and where most of the book's events take place. He writes that apartheid laws allow "more than 90 percent of white South Africans go through a lifetime without seeing firsthand the inhuman conditions under which blacks have to survive." He defines his purpose as showing the white man "with words a world he would otherwise not see because of a sign and a conscience racked with guilt."

Chapter 2 plunges the reader into these conditions, as they occur in Alexandra. One night in 1965, the black Alexandra police, known as Peri-Urban, raid the township. They arrest as many residents as they can, for reasons ranging from not having a pass (an internal passport) to participating in a gang. Johannes's mother must flee because her pass does not have correct documentation; she leaves the children alone in their

BIOGRAPHY

MARK MATHABANE

Mark Mathabane was born Johannes Mathabane in 1960, the first of seven children, to a Tsonga mother and a Venda father. He grew up in the black ghetto shantytown of Alexandra, outside of Johannesburg, South Africa, under the oppressive government system known as apartheid. When Mathabane was seven years old, his mother and grandmother collected enough money to send him to a local school. At the age of fourteen, he learned to play tennis, eventually becoming good enough to gain the attention of star American tennis player Stan Smith, who arranged for Mathabane to receive a scholarship to an American university. In 1983, he graduated *cum laude* from Dowling University, where he was the first black editor of the college newspaper. He then went on to study journalism at Columbia University. At the same time, he began publishing essays about South Africa and apartheid. In 1986, he published his first autobiography, *Kaffir Boy*, which won widespread recognition in the United States and Great Britain.

As of 2006, he continues to write and lecture about racism and South Africa. Additionally, he has established a scholarship fund to provide books and uniforms for school children of the Bovet Primary School in Alexandra, where he and his siblings studied.

---

house. Johannes and his sister Florah watch the chaos through a window until their baby brother George gashes his head in a fall. In another raid, Johannes sees black policemen humiliate his father. Though common in Alexandra, these raids strengthen Johannes's deep fear of and hatred toward black police officers and whites in general.

Johannes's father, Jackson, belongs to the Venda tribe, and the family speaks a language called Venda. As Johannes grows up, he begins to question and resent many aspects of his life, including his father's respect for tribal rules. Johannes talks during a meal, setting off the first of many father-son conflicts over tribal ways. His father is short-tempered and abusive, habits that only intensify in later years. On the other hand, Johannes's mother is a considerate and strong-willed woman.

Late in 1966, Johannes's father is arrested and imprisoned because his passbook is not in order. Without his support for almost a year, the family struggles to feed themselves. Johannes's sister Maria is born during this time, making the food scarcity even worse. His mother spends much of her time looking for work or begging for money and food. Johannes's maternal grandmother contributes some money, but it is not enough and runs out quickly. At one point, the Mathabanes and other black families rummage through a garbage dump, searching for food and household items discarded by whites. Johannes's mother discovers a dead black baby in a box left at the dump.

Jackson returns from prison a bitter man, prone to drinking and gambling. He manages to get his old job back, but he squanders his money and the family still goes hungry. Johannes spends his time with gangs of young boys to avoid troubles at home. He sees his first film with the gangs; it terrifies him because no one tells him that the images do not depict someone else's real life: "To me the illusions and fantasy of the movies were the stark reality of a world I was forbidden to enter."

In 1967, Johannes has his first encounter with Christianity. His father hates Christianity; for him it is a white belief system used to oppress black men. Johannes's mother, however, is curious about Christianity, having noticed that Christian black families tend to fare better than those that cling to tribal ways. His father takes the family to an evangelical service to show them that Christianity is foolish. At the service, the sermon mirrors the white Christian view of South Africa: black people are especially cursed as the "sons of Ham" and so must work harder to redeem themselves. Several of the black men in the audience, including Johannes's father, denounce the minister and leave. The scene establishes a persistent conflict between Johannes's parents. His father insists on devotion to the tribal religion and continuously denounces

Christianity, while his mother secretly, and later openly, accepts Christianity as a way to improve her family's circumstances.

Later that year, Johannes has one of the most frightening experiences of his life. Wandering the streets as he often does, he comes across a group of boys waiting in front of a barracks. The boys promise him all the food he can eat. When Johannes and the other boys enter the compound, black men greet them and offer food. Johannes notices beds in the back of the room and begins to feel uncomfortable. He refuses to eat and watches as the others strip and line up near the bed. Johannes panics when he realizes the men intend to have sex with the boys and runs away. The boys call Johannes a fool for not participating, but Johannes realizes that in "the black world, one could only survive if one played the fool, and bided his time." He vows to keep his experience a secret but later discovers that such occurrences are common. Mathabane writes that most of the boys involved later end up dead or in prison.

Johannes's trip to the Venda tribal reserve with his father is a defining moment in his intellectual development. Johannes's father has lost his job; worrying that witches have cursed him, he seeks help from a tribal witch doctor. The reserve is "mountainous, rugged and bone-dry," and the people there lead empty, impoverished lives. Johannes is particularly struck by the fact that there are nearly no men there; they must go to the cities to work in mines. He decides he would rather die than live on the reserve.

Part I ends when Johannes's mother tries to obtain the documents he needs to attend school. This turns out to be a long and humiliating process, one that begins at four in the morning when she walks the younger children to their grandmother's house. She then takes Johannes to the appropriate office, where they stand in line for over twelve hours. Her first attempt fails because her brother, Piet, gets arrested; she has to use the money she had planned to use for Johannes to secure Piet's release. On her second attempt, the white officer who issues the paperwork decides to take the afternoon off. Her third attempt is thwarted when bureaucrats demand Johannes's birth certificate. A black officer refuses to issue the birth certificate, but a white nurse intervenes. After his mother gets the necessary papers, she tells Johannes that not all white people are bad, but he does not believe her.

Part II: Passport to Knowledge
Chapters 21–34

Johannes's mother and grandmother collect enough money to send him to school, but Johannes refuses to go because he has heard horror stories about it from other boys. His mother and grandmother have to tie him up and take him to see the principal, who makes it clear that Johannes will be physically punished if he does not go to school. Johannes remains opposed until his drunken father kicks the family out of the house, furious about his children going to school. He believes tribal education is the only kind that matters—school is just another white man's trick. Johannes's mother explains to Johannes that she is sending him to school because she does not "want [him] growing up to be like [his] father," which shatters Johannes's resistance.

Still, the reality of school is a harsh one. Children crowd into an outside square to listen to long speeches from the principal and the teachers; they are then taken to overcrowded classrooms. Johannes's teacher is an inexperienced young woman who cannot control her pupils. Frustrated, she goes into a violent frenzy, whipping the children indiscriminately and making Johannes increasingly skeptical about school. He is unable to afford books or a uniform, and his teachers whip him frequently. Nevertheless, he manages to finish the first year at the top of his class. Johannes's success softens his father's prejudice against formal education.

The following school year, Johannes's teachers beat him again for not having proper school supplies. He confronts his mother about his desire to drop out, but she urges him to continue. As soon as she finds a job, she says, she is going to spend her first paycheck on schoolbooks for him. She is six months pregnant, but his mother takes a job cleaning for a large Indian family. Her income helps with Johannes's school expenses, even though his father now often refuses to give her money for groceries. Johannes continues to excel in school, but he still cannot grasp the value of education. He has no experience with educated black role models, so he has never seen the tangible benefits of education.

Two American events make their way to black South Africa. The first is Muhammad Ali's championship fight, in which he knocks out a white man and thus becomes a hero to underprivileged blacks. "Ali fever" sweeps the men and boys in Alexandra. Many of the boys misunderstand what *knockout* means, and Johannes dreams of someday becoming a boxer so that he can beat white men to death and do even worse to black policemen who victimize other blacks. One evening, Johannes and a group of neighborhood boys go to a boxing club, where the owner puts Johannes into the ring with an experienced fighter and has Johannes "play" Ali. Johannes gets beaten senseless and shuns boxing afterward. The other notable American event is the assassination of Martin Luther King Jr., known only as "King" to the black South Africans. This event introduces Johannes to the concept of equal rights.

One evening after ditching school, Johannes witnesses a murder. A group of *tsotsis*, teenage gang members, hunt a man down and kill him for his meager possessions. Though Johannes has seen dead black people before, he is profoundly affected by witnessing this incident. He cannot understand why people kill each other, and he can make even less sense of a black person killing another black person. He longs to escape to some place of "love and compassion" but has no idea where such a place would be. He broods over these thoughts for days. A few months later, his despair remains so great that he considers suicide. His mother eventually convinces him that his siblings need him and that she would not want to live without him.

Johannes's grandmother gets a gardening job with the Smiths, a white family. The Smiths are English, not Afrikaner (white South Africans descended from Dutch immigrants). They are vaguely opposed to apartheid and supply Johannes's grandmother with comic books and clothes for Johannes. Johannes begins to learn English from the comic books. This connection to the Smiths will affect Johannes's life significantly.

Johannes's father decides to run a beer club, known as a *stockvel*, to earn money. He promises to give up gambling and stop spending money on alcohol; he even hands over an entire week's wages as proof of his good intentions. From these *stockvel* parties, Johannes learns to keep accounts, a job that falls to him because of his knowledge of math. When illiterate customers see that Johannes is trustworthy, they begin to bring their letters to him. They cannot read or respond to the letters their far-away family

members send, but in their letters Johannes learns about the terrible hardships many people on the black reserves face. In many of them, Johannes sees the "death of the mind and soul," which he believes is worse than physical death.

Johannes gets his first real glimpse of the white world when he accompanies his grandmother to work at the Smiths. He is startled to find that a large house and many cars can belong to just one family in the white world. Mrs. Smith is pleasant, but she is patronizing to Johannes. The Smiths' son, Clyde, is one year older than Johannes and goes to a Boer school. ("Boer" is another term for Afrikaner; it refers specifically to Afrikaners who were farmers.) Clyde learns the ways and attitudes of apartheid at school, though his mother tries to dissuade him from those views. He treats Johannes as an idiot, while showing off his books and toys. Clyde claims to have learned that black people are incapable of civilization because they have smaller brains than whites. His remark infuriates Johannes, who resolves to prove that he can be the intellectual superior of any white man. Mrs. Smith gives Johannes a copy of *Treasure Island*, which he uses to begin studying English in earnest.

Johannes realizes the pointlessness of gang life when he is coerced into participating in a gang battle in which a boy loses his eye. He renounces the gangs, preferring constant studying.

At home, Johannes continues to fight with his father. When his father has no money for bus fare because he has gambled it away, Johannes refuses to give him some. Johannes sees their struggle as a conflict between worldviews. His father is unable to see any hope in the future and lives for past days of tribal glories. Johannes, however, looks for ways to escape the terror of shantytown existence and make his life better: "The thick veil of tribalism which so covered his eyes and mind and heart was absolutely of no use to me." Part II ends when Mrs. Smith gives Johannes a tennis racket. Johannes practices tennis on the Alexandra sand court, watched by a "coloured" man—"his official designation as one of over two million people of mixed race who … were neither black nor white." The man's name is Scaramouche; known as one of the best tennis players in the area, he becomes Johannes's coach.

Part III: Passport to Freedom
Chapters 35–53

Scaramouche gives Johannes tennis books and magazines. Johannes learns about famous black and colored tennis players, including Arthur Ashe, Althea Gibson, and Evonne Goolagong. Johannes's father, however, considers tennis a "sissy sport" and tries to shame Johannes out of playing it.

Johannes dislikes and distrusts his father's tribal beliefs; he feels similarly about his mother's Christianity, though he never argues with her about it openly. He does, however, argue with a pair of evangelists. Johannes calls them liars for making people forget reality and dwell on a fantasy life in Heaven; he says they are cheats for taking money away from poor people. He says they have betrayed their own people by shaping their lives according to a book of white stories.

Johannes has a major altercation with his father when he appears with two men to take Johannes to "mountain school." This is a Venda manhood ritual, involving circumcision. Brandishing a knife, Johannes refuses to go and threatens to kill anyone who tries to make him. After this incident, he goes to live with his grandmother for two weeks. When he returns, he and his father hardly speak.

Johannes's academic success pays off when he wins a scholarship that pays for three years of secondary school. His loathing for the tribal traditions leads him to choose Alexandra Secondary School rather than the boarding school on the Tsonga reserve. This proves a fateful decision, because the Alexandra school has a tennis team. Johannes begins devoting most of his spare time to tennis. He takes up yoga, reads tennis instruction magazines and books, and vows to postpone sex. His regimen pays off; he wins often, becomes captain of the team, and enters several black tennis tournaments. In 1973, he meets a tennis player named Tom who plans to quit his job at a tennis club run by liberal whites. Johannes immediately suggests that he replace Tom. When he meets the German who runs the club, Johannes "for some reason" gives his name as "Mark." He is known as Mark from that day on.

The South African government allows black American tennis star Arthur Ashe to play a tournament in South Africa late in 1973. Ashe is a hero to politically conscious South Africans because of his public denouncements of apartheid. Whenever he can, Mark goes to watch Ashe play: "[He] had never seen a black man walk that proudly among whites." Ashe's wins are major news in black South Africa. Because of Ashe's success, Mark begins to believe that the only chance he has to excel is to leave South Africa and live in America. Before leaving South Africa, Ashe helps establish the Black Tennis Foundation to train aspiring black athletes.

Mark continues winning tennis tournaments and excelling in school. At the tennis club, he is able to develop the "unheard of" habit of talking to whites as equals. He feels that this is his "true self" and finds it increasingly difficult to pretend inferiority around whites. At a black tennis tournament in Pretoria, Mark realizes that working at the white tennis club has given him tremendous advantages. If he had stuck to black training facilities, Mathabane believes he would not have had any chance at escaping poverty.

Mark begins to have eye problems after the tournament, eventually losing most of his sight. He gets no attention at overcrowded clinics and hospitals, so he agrees to follow his mother's advice and see a witch doctor. The witch doctor says that devils are pursuing Mark, reaching him through his work reading and writing letters for strangers. She tells him that to get better, he must be a "son of Africa." He follows the witch doctor's prescriptions, and he stops reading and writing letters for illiterate people. He eventually sees a specialist, who gives him eye drops. The problem goes away, but Mark is never certain which prescription provided the cure. His ambivalence indicates his divided cultural identity.

During his third year at secondary school, Mark has a conversation with his principal, who worries that Mark reads too many "white" books. Mark reveals that "white" books have shown him that he can never have real freedom in South Africa. The principal tells Mark that the older generation of black South Africans misunderstood the political situation, believing too strongly that they could reason with white society. He tells Mark to cultivate his rebellious spirit but to be careful because he risks turning blacks against him, too.

In June of 1976, the South African government decrees that blacks must be educated in

Afrikaans, not English. Many black students view Afrikaans as the language of the oppressor and refuse to speak it. On June 16, ten thousand students march down the streets of Soweto Township in protest, only to run into a police barricade. Police officers fire on the unarmed protesters, killing several children. This incident sparks intense anger in the black community, and Mark decides to join a protest with his fellow students. The police respond with overwhelming force, killing more protesters. Rioting and looting break out; whites flee the country, fearing a black revolution. After the police kill a girl who lives near Mark, he fears that there will never be a peaceful resolution to apartheid.

Police officers begin raiding students' schools and homes, arresting hundreds. Mark decides that home and school are not safe and begins to spend most of his time at the tennis club. There he meets Helmut, a German opposed to apartheid. They play tennis in whites-only facilities, openly flouting the law. From Helmut, Mark learns about Germany's Nazi past and the Holocaust. Helmut takes foolish risks, such as dropping Mark off at home. Many in Alexandra suspect that Mark is an informant. Some gang members attack Mark, and he is lucky to escape them.

Mark meets and befriends Andre Zietsman, a rising young white South African tennis star. He tells Mark about blacks and whites living and working together in America. Andre describes the shock he felt when no American called him *bass* (Afrikaans for "boss" or "master"); blacks and whites played on the same sports teams, ate in the same restaurants, mixed freely at social gatherings, and slept in the same dormitories. These descriptions make Mark even more eager to experience life in America.

Mark makes two important decisions about his future during his final year of secondary school. He turns down a job with the company sponsoring his scholarship. Though the job would make him middle class, Mark wants freedom more than money. Mark also decides to play in his first professional tournament. He loses his first match and ends up banned from the black tennis league. With time to spare, Mark watches a famous American doubles team practice. One of the team members, the legendary Stan Smith, asks Mark to practice with him. Afterward, over lunch with Smith and his wife, Mark tells them about his life and

his desire for a scholarship to an American university. He becomes friends with the Smiths, and they provide funds that allow Mark to enter some tournaments. He does not play well in the tournaments, so he conducts some clinics in the Cape Town shanty areas.

Things seem to get worse for Mark. The government officially allows some blacks to join white tennis clubs, but Mark finds it an empty policy with the usual racist barriers still in place. Mark encounters similar racism in his academic life. The white-run exams administration deliberately downgrades many students' final exam results, including Mark's, making it impossible for them to be admitted to a South African university. Mark begins doing well in some South African tennis tournaments though, and joins South Africa's best junior tennis squad as its first black player. Mark eventually finds a job at a bank, where he makes more money than his parents ever did.

When Mark accepts a full scholarship to Limestone College in South Carolina, he becomes "the first black boy to ever leave South Africa on a tennis scholarship." He initially has trouble getting a passport, but liberal whites come to his aid once again, providing the money and influence necessary to get the required paperwork. After a tearful farewell with his family, including his father, he wonders, "Why does apartheid do this to us? . . . Why had it created within my father's heart a granite wall?" However, he notes that the wall shatters in the face of this monumental departure. He leaves feeling that he has a duty to his race and his country to succeed personally and work toward the betterment of black life in South Africa.

THEMES

Identity

Mathabane's attempt to relate to different cultural identities is a recurring theme in *Kaffir Boy*. He is ambivalent about the various group identities that are open to him: tribal, Christian, South African, and black. He eventually accepts his racial heritage as his defining "culture" because it allows him to come to terms with the harshness of apartheid, but he never relinquishes his individuality. Mathabane argues that he had to reject some of these identities, especially his mother's Christianity and his father's tribal heritage. Nonetheless, by the end of the book Mathabane recognizes that people cannot escape their culture or upbringing: "[D]eep within me I knew that I could never really leave South Africa or Alexandra. I was Alexandra, I was South Africa." Mathabane thus acknowledges that his parents' attitudes and values shape his own. Even though they do not define him, they are a part of South Africa that he takes with him to America.

Oppression

As Mathabane matures, he learns that both religion and culture can become tools of oppression. He sees how apartheid distorts tribal customs and traditional black identities, using them to dominate and dismiss black South Africans. Superstition plays a significant role in tribal traditions, and blacks who live on the reserves suffer under the "double yoke of apartheid and tribalism." Mathabane sees a similar problem when township men, like his father, bow to superstitious beliefs. He shares his mother's view that township blacks who cling to tribalism usually fare worse than those who become more modern.

Mathabane never accepts Christianity as an alternative to tribalism, pointing out that it, too, has worked to keep black people oppressed. South Africa's white government calls itself Christian while arguing that God gives whites the authority to rule over blacks. Black churches are not much better, claiming that blacks suffer a special burden of sin and thus must work especially hard for divine rewards—mainly by giving money to the churches. At one point, Johannes angrily denounces a pair of evangelists, calling them traitors. He and a friend burn pamphlets that the evangelists leave behind, an act that symbolizes their general disdain for the Christian message.

Eventually, Mathabane acknowledges that his mother benefited from her faith. However, he could never join her; he cannot accept that God favors whites while allowing injustices against black Africans to continue unabated. He rejects Christianity for the same basic reason he rejects tribal beliefs—he knows that neither system can provide the answers he needs about white power and black oppression.

The Power of Education

Kaffir Boy contends that education is the best route to a better life. Mathabane's story establishes a relationship between knowledge and opportunity, and shows how possessing knowledge means having power. Learning English, in particular, is the "crucial key" that grants access to the white world. It seems to Mathabane that white people gain power over black people by reading books. He also repeatedly sees how illiteracy keeps blacks impoverished and comes to understand that literacy is essential to the struggle for black liberation. Mathabane finds that reading changes his views, allowing him to see both freedom and slavery for what they are. Moreover, books teach him about America and show that apartheid is not the only possible social system.

The relationship between education, opportunity, and political power becomes even clearer to Mathabane during the Soweto riots. These riots start with the government's ruling that black South Africans must be educated in Afrikaans instead of English, a decision that angers many black students. As Mathabane watches a public library burn, a friend explains that it was set on fire to destroy evidence of white oppression and Bantu Education (the segregated schooling that black South Africans received). Mathabane agrees that Bantu Education hurts black people, but he is still angry: "Why burn the only things that taught one to believe in the future, to fight for one's right to live in freedom and dignity?" He understands that schools and libraries offer what little hope there is for blacks and risks his life to rescue some books from the burning library. Later, he tells a group of white men that rioters burn libraries and schools because black protesters cannot burn their real targets, the homes and institutions of white people.

Mathabane thinks about quitting school several times, and the Soweto riots raise this question again. During the riots, he decides that the best way to help destroy apartheid is to flee to another country and join a rebel force. Before he can act on this idea, a man with relatives among the Zimbabwean freedom fighters tells him that the gun is one of many tools for achieving freedom. He tells Mathabane that this struggle is not just a matter of force. Victory over apartheid will require thinkers and writers as well, people who can show the rest of the world what is happening. Eventually, Mathabane makes his contribution to the struggle by writing *Kaffir Boy*.

Throughout the book, Mathabane emphasizes that his academic success made special opportunities available to him. His education improves his potential earning power, allows him to negotiate the bureaucratic system more effectively, and connects him to people who can help further his ambitions. Though Mathabane questions the value of his education while he is in the midst of it, the existence of his book underscores its influence on his life.

HISTORICAL OVERVIEW

Apartheid

Apartheid was a policy of social and political segregation that typified South Africa for much of its history.

The Union of South Africa was formed in 1910. Two British colonies, the Cape Colony and Natal Colony, combined with the South African Republic and Orange Free State (two states defeated in the Second Boer War). These states were thereafter known as the Cape Province, Natal, Transvaal and the Orange Free State, respectively. The Union's constitution contained provisions establishing that blacks were legally inferior to whites.

In 1948, the all-white Nationalist Party gained control of the South African government and immediately instituted the policy of apartheid as the official law of South Africa. Most of the apartheid laws created during the 1950s became known as "petty apartheid." Under these laws, every citizen was classified by race; classification boards were established to decide difficult cases. These laws created many obstacles and hardships for non-white citizens. Mixed-race marriages were illegal, as was interracial sex. The Group Areas Act of 1950 aimed to separate various racial groups geographically. Blacks needed special permission to visit white areas, and they could not live there. In 1953, the Separate Amenities Act required separate public facilities for blacks, whites, and "coloureds" (a group that included non-European and non-African nationals, such as Indians and mixed-race South Africans). These "separate amenities" included hospitals, schools, and beaches. Blacks and "coloureds" had to carry a pass, or internal passport, to travel in and out of their designated reserves and townships. A person without a pass could be arrested on the spot. These identity papers had to be constantly updated, as well.

The government claimed that apartheid policies were simply sensible procedures for separating groups that could never get along. In reality, apartheid was the use of force to create total economic and political inequality along racial lines. After the anti-pass protests of 1960, the white South African government stepped up its apartheid policy, announcing "Grand Apartheid." Prime Minister Hendrik Verwoerd led the movement to create reservations for black tribes, calling them independent nations. Blacks thus became recognized as foreigners and were treated as such, though they outnumbered whites seven to one. Passes, labor permits, and Bantu Education policies often separated families, and many were kept in total poverty.

Other nations expressed their disapproval of apartheid with economic and political sanctions against South Africa. By the 1980s, international pressure began to affect the South African economy and influence domestic attitudes toward apartheid. Black protests against apartheid became bolder and more frequent as pro-African parties realized that South Africa was under international scrutiny. The government gradually repealed many of the petty apartheid laws. By 1993, all of the apartheid laws were repealed, and President F. W. de Klerk called for a new constitution and a more democratically representative government. The African National Congress (ANC) took power in the 1994 elections, and Nelson Mandela, a black man who spent three decades in jail for opposing apartheid, was elected president.

The Sharpeville Massacre

On March 21, 1960, the Pan-Africanist Party (PAC) arranged a peaceful demonstration in Sharpeville, a shantytown, to protest laws requiring blacks to carry passes to travel in white areas of South Africa. White authorities responded by killing sixty-nine unarmed protesters and wounding more than one hundred eighty. Protests elsewhere were similarly suppressed, but less violently. The government declared a state of emergency; detention without trial was legalized and pro-African political parties were banned. South Africa was condemned by many of the world's governments for its handling of the Sharpeville protest.

The Soweto Riots

In 1974, the South African government issued the Afrikaans Medium Decree. This law required that all black students learn Afrikaans and that all tribal schools be taught largely in Afrikaans, rather than English. The law angered black South Africans, for a variety of reasons. Afrikaans, originally derived from Dutch, was commonly spoken by South African whites—most blacks could not speak or write Afrikaans. Furthermore, most blacks viewed Afrikaans as the language of their oppressors; they preferred to learn their tribal languages and English. On June 16, 1976, thousands of black schoolchildren gathered to protest the new law in Soweto, a shantytown outside of Johannesburg. The students threw stones and white South African police responded, using real bullets—not plastic bullets, as expected—to disperse the crowd. By the time the protests were brought under control, more than five hundred blacks had been killed, most of them children. Widespread shock and fury among blacks led to uprisings in other townships. Thousands of young men and women fled to neighboring African nations, joining anti-apartheid movements among the exiled there. Media coverage of the violence was strictly limited, and most foreign journalists were denied access. Nevertheless, information and photographs escaped, sparking international sanctions and public condemnation of South Africa.

CRITICAL OVERVIEW

When *Kaffir Boy* was published, it was hailed as an important contribution to global understanding of apartheid. It peaked at number three on the *New York Times* Paperback Best Sellers List in the fall of 1987. *Publishers Weekly*, reviewing the book in February 1986, called it a "powerful account" that makes the reader "feel intensely the horrors of apartheid." In a review of Mathabane's follow-up memoir, *Kaffir Boy in America: An Encounter with Apartheid*, *Publishers Weekly* refers to the original as "one of the best books ever written about apartheid." In "After Apartheid, a New Struggle," the *Chicago Sun-Times* calls Mathabane's autobiography "searing," noting that his frank treatment of apartheid's horrors make it "almost painful reading."

Kaffir Boy won a Christopher Award for its service to humanity and was placed on the American Library Association's list of

MEDIA ADAPTATIONS

An abridged version of *Kaffir Boy*, read by Howard Rollins, is available on cassette from New Millennium Books Audio.

Mark Mathabane maintains a website at www.mathabane.com with links to reviews, articles, photos, and excerpts from many of his books.

Outstanding Books for the College Bound. Positive reviews and Mathabane's appearance on an episode of the *Oprah Winfrey Show* led to *Kaffir Boy* appearing on many high school reading lists, as well. From time to time, however, there is controversy about whether *Kaffir Boy* is appropriate for young adult readers. Most of the controversy surrounds a small part of the book: the passage involving boys who prostitute themselves for food. Some parents and teachers see this passage as pornographic or as promoting homosexuality. Neither characterization is accurate, but this passage has sometimes resulted in the book being removed from curricula or being placed on restricted access in school libraries.

Mathabane objects to this reaction. In an article entitled "Like the Taliban, Some U.S. Parents Fear Free Minds," in *USA Today*, Mathabane admits that some parts of his autobiography are violent and unpleasant, but "books are not written with readers' comfort in mind. I wrote *Kaffir Boy* to show the world the inhumanity of apartheid and the consequences of dehumanizing others, and to educate people about racial hate." In his article "If You Assign My Book, Don't Censor It," published in the *Washington Post*, Mathabane argues against the practice of partial censoring, in which teachers cover or mark out parts of the book that they find objectionable. He asks that *Kaffir Boy* either be taught as it was written to students of an appropriate age, or not taught at all. According to the "Attempts to Ban *Kaffir Boy*" page of Mathabane's website, Mathabane released an "international edition" of the book that omits the contentious scene to make his book more accessible to middle-school students. *Kaffir Boy* remains controversial. *Kaffir Boy* is ranked thirty-first on the American Library Association's list of the 100 Most Frequently Challenged Books of 1990–2000. South Africa initially banned the book, though that ban lasted only a couple of months.

CRITICISM

Jessica Powers

In the following essay Powers argues that although Mathabane sought to completely separate himself from South Africa, he has been unable to leave it behind and it has become his life's work.

The recurring question of *Kaffir Boy*—the autobiography of Mark Mathabane, a young black who grew up in Alexandra, a ghetto of South Africa—is one of identity: "What race, religion, country, and class do I/ should I belong to?" To survive the reality of apartheid, to affirm his racial heritage and individual identity as an autonomous human being, Mathabane argues he had to reject his parents' religious and tribal heritage and leave South Africa.

Yet despite the fact that he strips away many of the most obvious elements of South African life, at the end of the book Mathabane claims he can never escape his culture or his country. "Deep within me," he states, "I knew that I could never really leave South Africa or Alexandra. I was Alexandra, I was South Africa." The question of whether this is true becomes more acute throughout the book as it becomes clearer how separate Mathabane keeps himself from other black South Africans. Yet he resents any inference that he rejected African culture and allowed white culture to shape or define him. Rather, Mathabane firmly believes that every decision he makes—and the elements of black and white culture that he accepts or rejects—are self-determined exercises of autonomy.

One of the first observations Mathabane made as a young child was how apartheid had twisted tribalism and used it as a form of oppression against Africans. At seven years old, he realized that his father's life was "controlled" by superstition. Even at that young age, Mathabane's individual consciousness was highly developed, and he deliberately rejected the superstition of his parents, claiming his

right to do so because "my life was my own to do with as I pleased." When he recognized his father's slavery to the "double yoke of apartheid and tribalism," he realized that African "superstition" and tribal culture were not for him. His scorn for his father lay in the fact that his father clung to values which had "outlived" their "usefulness," values which discriminated against him while he attempted to function within the white man's world.

Equally, Mathabane rejected Christianity, claiming it was misused by all sides. The government used it to claim that God had given whites the divine right to rule over blacks; the black churches misused it by demanding money from Africans who were already destitute; and black churches further misused it by resigning themselves to the idea that this was their "lot" in life, God's will for black men and women.

Although Mathabane came to accept his mother's faith, and recognized the legitimacy in her relationship with the Christian God, he stated that he could never share in her faith because he could never believe in a God who favored whites and stood by, "oblivious" to Africans' pain. His rejection of Christianity, like his rejection of tribalism and African superstition, was based on an understanding that he could not give up his "free will" in order to submit to these cultural and religious institutions.

What Mathabane did accept, though it took some trial and error, was his mother's understanding that education would lead him to a better life. Learning English, he decided, was the "crucial key" to unlocking the doors of the white world. The books that white people read led to the "power" they had over black people. Mathabane eventually decided that literacy was a necessary element in the liberation struggle. How can the illiterate function, he wondered, in a world ruled by sign? Books had taught him about places where he could be "free to think and feel the way I want, instead of the way apartheid wants."

Mathabane's understanding became even more acute in the middle of the Soweto riots, which were sparked by anger over the government's ruling that African education be taught in Afrikaans instead of English. As he watched a library burn down, he asked for an explanation from one of his friends, who stated that they were burning the library down to destroy all traces of white oppression and Bantu Education. Mathabane's angry internal response was the question: "Why burn the only thing that taught one to believe in the future, to fight for one's right to live in freedom and dignity?"

Though Mathabane left South Africa, it is clear he took it with him. It has become his life's work. During the middle of the Soweto riots, despite his love of learning, he had wondered if he should quit school and become a guerilla fighter. An African who had relatives among the freedom fighters in Zimbabwe told him not to sacrifice everything for the gun. "There's room for people with your brains in the struggle," he said. "Your kind fight a different fight … Writers are also needed to tell the rest of the world what the struggle is all about." *Kaffir Boy* fulfills this prophetic calling.

Source: Jessica Powers, "*Kaffir Boy*: An Analysis," in *Suite101.com*, October 17, 2001, pp. 1–2.

Mark Mathabane

In the following essay, Mathabane explains his stance on Kaffir Boy*'s place in the classroom, arguing for the book's use for appropriate grades and ages rather than an all-out ban.*

The Taliban of Afghanistan was notorious for its disdain of independent minds. Its demise gives me hope in the war against America's version of the Taliban: bands of parents who anoint themselves as thought and morality police.

They are found in communities across America, demanding that our high school classrooms and libraries be purged of books whose contents they disagree with. An American Library Association list of their top targets includes the *Harry Potter* series, *I Know Why the Caged Bird Sings*, *The Catcher in the Rye*, *To Kill a Mockingbird*, *The Color Purple* and *Huckleberry Finn*.

My own memoir of my South African childhood, *Kaffir Boy*, is on the list. The mullahs of public schools in North Carolina, Texas, California, Nevada, New York, Virginia, and more than a dozen other states have tried to either restrict the book's use or ban it from the curriculum and the school library.

The main charges are that the book uses "offensive language" and "promotes homosexuality." This stems from my graphic description of one of the most harrowing experiences in my life. When I was 7, hunger drove me to tag along with a ring of boys going to a nearby men's hostel, where, unbeknownst to me, they planned to prostitute themselves for food. I hadn't eaten a square meal

in days, but I declined the food the men were offering in exchange for sexual favors and bolted from the hostel when the boys began undressing.

A reason I included the scene is that resisting peer pressure is one of the toughest things for young people to do. Yet they make such tough choices daily, particularly if they live where abuse, poverty, violence and death are commonplace and innocence dies young.

Stories teach children

That lesson seems lost on censors who want *Kaffir Boy* banned from high schools. Yet hardly any students among the tens of thousands who've read the book, which is required reading in many high schools, complain about the scene. Instead, students tell me in impassioned letters and e-mails that the book teaches them to never give up in the face of adversity, to never waste food, to value books and libraries, to regard education as a powerful weapon of hope, to always strive to do the right thing and to never take freedom for granted.

When I came to America in 1978 to attend college, I was stunned—and exhilarated—to discover that students here could read any book without fear of being harassed, jailed or killed. I remember how my peers died during the 1976 Soweto student rebellion for only dreaming of such freedom. To me, the First Amendment is the jewel in the crown of American democracy.

A proper response

As a parent of three school-age children, I understand some parents' concern about what their children are assigned to read. But should my child bring home a book whose contents I find objectionable, the proper thing to do would be to request that my child be assigned a different book.

But that's not what critics of *Kaffir Boy* and other books are doing. They want to rob all of a school's students of the right to decide. Worse, they insist on imposing their own taste and morality on others. But books are not written with readers' comfort in mind. I wrote *Kaffir Boy* to show the world the inhumanity of apartheid and the consequences of dehumanizing others, and to educate people about racial hatred.

It boggles my mind why, given the complex nature of life, any parents would want to deny their children the opportunity to grapple with its exigencies, especially in light of how complicated our world has become since Sept. 11. American students need to learn more rather than less about different cultures and different ways of life.

To those brave teachers out there who are being subpoenaed to defend *Kaffir Boy* and other books they've chosen to broaden the minds of their students and deepen their sensibilities, I say fight such narrow-mindedness, continue to expose your students to the realities of life and continue to challenge them to value the sanctity of their minds. Do not allow them to be invaded by America's Taliban, whose goal is to extinguish the precious lamp of independent thinking, which is the hallmark of the truly free.

Source: Mark Mathabane, "Like the Taliban, Some U.S. Parents Fear Free Minds," in *USA Today*, December 12, 2001, pp. 1–2.

SOURCES

"The 100 Most Frequently Challenged Books of 1990–2000," *American Library Association*, www.ala.org (December 13, 2005).

"After Apartheid, a New Struggle," in the *Chicago Sun-Times*, July 2, 1989, p. 14.

"Attempts to Ban *Kaffir Boy*," *Mathabane Books & Lectures: Knowledge is Power*, www.mathabane.com (August 26, 2005).

Mathabane, Mark, "If You Assign My Book, Don't Censor It," *Mathabane Books & Lectures: Knowledge is Power*, www.mathabane.com (December 13, 2005), originally published in the *Washington Post*, November 28, 1999, p. B1.

———, *Kaffir Boy: The True Story of a Black Youth's Coming of Age in Apartheid South Africa*, Free Press, 1986.

———, "Like the Taliban, Some U.S. Parents Fear Free Minds," *USA Today*, www.usatoday.com (December 18, 2001).

Review of *Kaffir Boy: The True Story of a Black Youth's Coming of Age in Apartheid South Africa*, *Publishers Weekly*, reviews.publishersweekly.com (December 13, 2005), originally published in *Publishers Weekly*, February 28, 1986.

Review of *Kaffir Boy in America: An Encounter with Apartheid*, *Publishers Weekly*, reviews.publishersweekly.com (December 13, 2005), originally published in *Publishers Weekly*, April 28, 1989.

"King of the Bingo Game"

First published in the literary journal *Tomorrow* in November 1944, Ralph Ellison's short story "King of the Bingo Game" explores black men's alienation in white society. In the story, the main character struggles with the reality of his existence. The protagonist feels hopeless: he lives in an unfamiliar city in an unfamiliar part of the country and is further isolated by the threat of his wife's death from a sickness they cannot afford to treat. He is poor, hungry, and afraid of what his future holds. His vulnerable position in society speaks to the plight of blacks living in America at the time the story was written, particularly to those who have come north with hopes of realizing their dreams.

Throughout "King of the Bingo Game," Ellison creates an atmosphere that is at once harshly realistic and dreamily surreal, mirroring the character's state of mind as he alternates between hopelessness and hope. The protagonist goes unnamed throughout the story, allowing him to serve as a generic representation of the black experience. His experience is not just that of an individual: he could be any black man in the 1940s. A nameless protagonist also allows Ellison to address issues of identity and naming, a prominent theme in much of his work. This nameless figure is the product of an oppressive society that robs blacks of identity, dignity, and the opportunity to make something of themselves.

Fate is an equally significant theme, as the protagonist attempts to control his destiny despite

RALPH ELLISON

1944

BIOGRAPHY

RALPH ELLISON

Ralph Waldo Ellison was born March 1, 1914, in Oklahoma City. His father named him after the famous intellectual and essayist Ralph Waldo Emerson. Following in the footsteps of his namesake, Ellison became a thinker and a writer, best known for his novel *Invisible Man*. Although *Invisible Man* was Ellison's only novel, his many short stories and critical essays helped him earn a place as one of twentieth-century America's most influential and accomplished authors. Many of his stories and essays concentrate on the themes of human equality and the need for racial pride.

Ellison began his career studying music at the Tuskegee Institute in 1933, on a scholarship. He moved to New York City in 1936, hoping to earn money for his senior year of college. There, he met Richard Wright, author of *Native Son*, who encouraged Ellison to write. Having found some success publishing articles and reviews, as well as some intellectual community in New York, he decided not to return to Tuskegee. He joined the Merchant Marines during World War II, and in 1946 he married Fanny McConnell. *Invisible Man* won the National Book Award in 1953. Ellison died of cancer in 1994.

In "King of the Bingo Game," Ellison integrates his knowledge of politics and history with the tradition of African American folklore. His ability to bring a realistic world view together with a fantastical one in a unified theme distinguished his work and helped him earn a position as one of the most influential African American writers. Ellison wrote "King of the Bingo Game" eight years before he published *Invisible Man* (1952), the novel that made him famous. Many people see "King of the Bingo Game" as a natural precursor to *Invisible Man* because the story and the novel share many themes. However, even though "King of the Bingo Game" presents readers with themes characteristic of Ellison's later writing, he intended for the short story to stand on its own as a complete work.

"King of the Bingo Game" can be found in the collection *Flying Home and Other Stories*, published in 1996 by Vintage Books. The collection includes thirteen stories written by Ellison between 1937 and 1954.

PLOT SUMMARY

"King of the Bingo Game" begins with the unnamed protagonist sitting in a movie theater, watching a movie he has already seen. He is waiting for the movie to end, so that the bingo game that takes place in the theater can begin. The woman in front of him is eating peanuts and the two men beside him are drinking wine; as he waits, the smell of food and drink cause his stomach to gurgle and growl. He is hungry, and he reminisces about living in the South where people were friendlier and he would feel comfortable asking the woman or the men to share with him.

The protagonist's memories of the South remind him of his current predicament. He has no money and is unable to find a job because he does not have a birth certificate. To make matters worse, his wife, Laura, is sick and needs to see a doctor, which they cannot afford. The protagonist momentarily questions his own sanity before his attention is drawn back to the movie. It is one of his favorite scenes, in which the hero finds a trap door that leads him to the girl who is tied to a bed. The men sitting next to him find this scene interesting, and they discuss the possibility of the hero leaving the girl tied up. The protagonist tries to involve himself in the scene, but he cannot stop thinking of Laura.

recognizing that life is little more than a game of chance. In this sense, "King of the Bingo Game" can be seen as a black man's struggle to accept that his fate is out of his hands and that the American dream is, at least for him, an unattainable myth. When the protagonist holds the button to the bingo wheel in his hand with the potential to win money that could save his wife, he begins to feel power for the first time in his life. However, this unfamiliar experience causes him to forget who he is, unable to remember even his name. His determination to control the wheel—his destiny—becomes overwhelming, and he loses everything.

> LET THEM YELL. ALL THE NEGROES DOWN THERE WERE JUST ASHAMED BECAUSE HE WAS BLACK LIKE THEM. HE SMILED INWARDLY, KNOWING HOW IT WAS. MOST OF THE TIME HE WAS ASHAMED OF WHAT NEGROES DID HIMSELF. WELL, LET THEM BE ASHAMED FOR SOMETHING THIS TIME. LIKE HIM.''

Tired of the film and impatient for the bingo game to begin, the protagonist looks around the theater. He is drawn to the white beam emanating from the projection room. Considering the beam, the protagonist is intrigued by its whiteness and its ability to land squarely on the screen. He takes this as evidence that everything is prearranged and imagines what would happen if things did not go as planned. For instance, he wonders how the men in the projection room would react if the movie suddenly changed and instead of untying the girl, the hero began undressing himself and the girl.

The men beside him take another swig from their bottle, and he cannot help but notice the gurgle. Closing his eyes in an attempt to escape, the protagonist begins to drift off to the dreamy music accompanying the final scenes of the movie. He hears a train whistle in the distance, and he recalls a time that he walked along a railroad trestle as a boy down South. A train is coming, and he runs as fast as he can, getting off the trestle to the ground just in time. But in his dream, the train leaves the track and begins barreling after him. It follows him down the road, and he runs screaming while white onlookers laugh.

The protagonist is awakened from his nightmare by the men next to him. The men tell him he is ruining the movie with his hollering and offer him a drink to calm his nerves. The protagonist is glad they woke him and accepts a drink from the bottle, which turns out to be whiskey, not wine. As the drink warms him, he again feels the pangs of hunger. He has not eaten all day; his hunger, combined with the whiskey, makes him feel lightheaded. He finds a seat farther from the smell of the peanuts.

The protagonist chooses a new seat in the dark; as he sits down, the lights come on in the theater. The screen disappears behind a curtain, and a man with a microphone and a uniformed attendant emerge on the stage. This is the moment the protagonist has been waiting for: the beginning of the bingo game. He feels in his pocket for his bingo cards and touches his five of them. He knows that having five cards is against the rules, but he hopes having that many cards will improve his chances of winning. Examining his cards, the protagonist thinks about Laura again. Though he does not think he is likely to win, he decides that he must have faith for Laura's sake.

The lights fade, and the man with the microphone begins to spin the bingo wheel and call out numbers. Each time a number is called, the protagonist scrambles to find the numbers on his five cards. He has to move fast, and he becomes nervous because he is having difficulty following along. For a moment he contemplates choosing one card and throwing the others out, but he remembers the cost of Laura's doctors and how important it is for him to win. He tries to focus on the bingo game and concentrate on finding the numbers on his cards. With his attention back on the game, the protagonist realizes that he has bingo on his third card. He stands up and yells, "Bingo! Bingo!" As he stumbles onto the stage, he is blinded by the bright light. The light has a strange affect on him and he feels as though he is under a spell.

Once on stage, the man with the microphone begins to check the numbers on the card against those that were called. The protagonist is trembling, and he feels faint. Fearing that he has made a mistake, he backs away from the man with the microphone. He hears the man call the numbers over the microphone, and he remains frozen with tension, listening. When he sees the man with the microphone smile at the audience, he begins to relax, realizing that he does indeed have bingo. The man with the microphone announces to the audience that the man on stage is one of the "chosen people," and the audience responds with laughter and applause. He then instructs the protagonist to move to the front of the stage. The protagonist does so, moving slowly forward into the bright light. The man with the microphone then explains the rules for the bingo jackpot, telling the protagonist and the audience that to win the jackpot of thirty-six

Ralph Ellison AP Images

dollars and ninety cents, the bingo wheel "must stop between the double zero."

Having attended other bingo games, the protagonist knows the ritual. Nonetheless, he is extremely tense, feeling that his whole life depends on how he spins the bingo wheel. The wheel will determine not only his future, but his past as well. He feels as though the wheel has always been there, playing a part in his parents' lives as well as his own, even when he was unaware of it. Unable to shake this strange sensation, the protagonist momentarily considers leaving the stage before he makes a fool of himself; he is stopped by the smiling man with the microphone. The man talks to him and the protagonist smiles in return, unable to speak. Even though the protagonist feels that he is on the brink of embarrassment, he has no choice but to stay where he is and let fate take its course.

Meanwhile, the man with the microphone asks the protagonist where he is from. He says he is from Rocky Mont, North Carolina, and the

man with a microphone makes a joke about him having come down off the mountain to join the United States. The protagonist feels that the man is making fun of him, but he remembers his purpose when the control for the bingo wheel is placed in his hand.

Standing in front of the wheel in the white projection beam, the protagonist feels as though he is alone. He recalls his plan to give the wheel a short twirl, hoping it will land on double zero. Less nervous now and extremely hopeful, the protagonist believes that he is finally going to be repaid for all the suffering in his life. He presses the button for the wheel and the lights begin to whirl, but he quickly realizes that he is powerless to release the button. The wheel increases in speed, and the protagonist feels drawn into its power.

With the button in his hand, the protagonist confronts his ability to control his own destiny. He can hear the man speaking into the microphone, advising him about what to do, but he continues squeezing the button until his fist hurts. For a moment he is tormented with a sense of doubt, wondering how he can tell when to stop the wheel. But soon his doubt is replaced with hope as he realizes that as long as keeps pressing the button he is in control of the jackpot, and by extension, his fate.

Suddenly, he realizes that the audience is yelling at him. Most of the audience is criticizing him, yelling for him to let someone else have a chance. The protagonist ignores them and turns his back to the crowd. He is set in his purpose and refuses to let go of the button. As he watches the numbers on the wheel spin by, the protagonist feels exalted and declares aloud, "This is God!"

The crowd continues yelling, disregarding the protagonist's revelation. He thinks they are fools to ignore him. As he listens to them shout, he feels a hand on his shoulder. It is the man with the microphone who tells the protagonist he has taken too long. The protagonist violently brushes the hand away and insists that he knows what he is doing. Then the protagonist reconsiders his actions and smiles at the man, hoping he has not hurt the man's feelings. He calls the man over toward him and questions him about the rules of the game. The protagonist concludes that since anyone can play the game and anyone who gets the lucky number can win, then he is doing nothing wrong. He assures the man with the microphone that he is not going to hurt anyone, and he tells the man to move aside and to watch him show the whole world how to win the jackpot. The protagonist flashes the man with the microphone another smile to show him that he does not hold his whiteness or his impatience against him. He continues pressing the button, ignoring the noise from the audience; he believes they are only upset because they are black, too, and are ashamed of him. The protagonist can sympathize with them because he is often ashamed of what other blacks do, but he decides it is their turn to be ashamed of him. He feels that he is in control at last; because of this, he finally allows himself to believe that Laura will be all right.

Unexpectedly, the lights flicker and the protagonist stumbles backward in surprise. He realizes that the wheel controls him as much as he controls it. He believes that he must hold the button forever, or else he will be left hopeless and Laura will die. Deciding that his only hope is to do whatever the wheel demands, he continues to push the button, deriving a certain sense of power from the action.

In defiance of the crowd's continued screams, the protagonist continues to spin the wheel. He is the one running the show, and he is enjoying his power. Yet he is also beginning to lose his sense of self, and he realizes with a start that he has forgotten his own name. Although the name was given to his grandfather by white slave owners, he still feels the need to recall it. Thinking that perhaps the people in the crowd know his name, he asks "Who am I?" They just tell him to hurry up and bingo.

For a moment the protagonist feels sad that he has lost himself, but he quickly decides that he does not need his old name. He is reborn in playing the bingo game and as long as he presses the button he knows that he is "the King of Bingo." Even if no one understands his purpose—including Laura—he is determined to continue pressing the button. Overcome by emotions, he begins to scream aloud, yelling for Laura to live: "Live, Laura, baby. I got holt of it now sugar. LIVE! . . . I got nobody but YOU!" His scream is so intense that he feels as if his head is going to burst and indeed he sees small droplets of blood landing on his shoe. He realizes that his nose is bleeding and wonders what is happening. He becomes paranoid, wondering if the audience has somehow entered him and is trying to steal his prize. Totally out of control, the protagonist vomits, and to escape his own confusion he retreats to his thoughts of Laura. He imagines himself running, with Laura in his arms and a subway train in hot pursuit. People are yelling for him to come out of the subway tunnel, but he knows the only way out is to stop and get smashed by the train, or to jump onto the other track and risk the electrified third rail.

The audience begins singing and clapping. The protagonist realizes they think he is crazy, which makes him angry. As he stands listening to the crowd, he notices that they are watching something on the stage behind him. It is two men in uniform and they begin to approach the protagonist. He scrambles, looking for something to fight the men with, but he has nothing but the button for the bingo wheel. His only escape is to run around the stage, trying to avoid the uniformed men without letting go of the button to the wheel.

Someone calls for the stage curtain to be lowered, and the protagonist fears that if it is, the light from the projection room will be cut off. Before he can voice his concern, he finds himself in the grips of the guards. The guards wrestle him to the ground and try to pry the button from his hand. The protagonist clings desperately to the button, "for it [is] his life," but eventually the guards are able to remove it from his hand.

The protagonist watches the wheel as it slowly spins to a stop, and he is not surprised to see that it has landed at double zero. He points out the winning number to the guards whose reactions make him think he will be given his prize after all. He does not notice their patronizing tone, or that the curtain is descending swiftly towards him. It crashes down, as one of the uniformed men delivers a devastating blow to the protagonist's skull. As his consciousness fades, he realizes with finality that his luck has run out.

THEMES

Racism

Race plays a vital role in Ellison's "King of the Bingo Game." Whites' power and social dominance appear throughout the story, highlighting the power denied to blacks and the degree to which whiteness is valued over blackness. The black protagonist's internal monologue and his interactions with other characters reflect the extent to which blacks were marginalized in 1930s America.

The black protagonist of Ellison's story dreams of finding success, even if it only means winning a thirty-six-dollar bingo jackpot. Yet his ambition is largely a dream that he has little hope of realizing. As Hal Blythe and Charlie Sweet suggest in their article "Ellison's 'King of the Bingo Game,'" "By contrasting the main character's major fantasy with his real-life situation, Ellison makes more poignant the gap between white and black America in the 1930s." Indeed, it would seem that the protagonist is caught in a losing situation; he "got no birth certificate to get a job" and his wife Laura is about to die because he "got no money for a doctor." This situation is directly related to the fact that he is a black man, and further emphasizes his marginalization.

Throughout "King of the Bingo Game," symbols of white control appear in the protagonist's monologue. For example, he is preoccupied with

the "white beam" of light emanating from the projection room (and controlling the movie and the bingo game), leading to his declaration that "Everything [is] fixed." As Troy Urquhart notes in "Ellison's 'King of the Bingo Game,'" the story "establishes the bingo hall as firmly controlled by the white male, ... despite the protagonist's insistence that 'anybody can win.'" Though the protagonist feels power while he is clutching the button that controls the bingo wheel, he is constantly under the heat and glare of the white light from the projection room.

Racism also affects the way other characters respond to the protagonist. During the narrative, whites condescend to the protagonist. He is called "boy" on three occasions, and he is frequently described as a "fool," even as a "jerk." Moreover, the protagonist is subjected to the audience's laughter. Significantly, it is not only whites, but also blacks who look down on him. The protagonist notes that "All the Negroes ... there were ... ashamed because he was black like them." Here Ellison shows black men judging each other in much the same that white society judges them, further emphasizing the protagonist's alienation.

Destiny and Powerlessness

The theme of fate and destiny is closely connected to the inequality that runs throughout "King of the Bingo Game." The black man's lack of control over his own destiny is vitally important to the story. The protagonist's foolhardy attempt to regain some power over his fate through the bingo wheel underscores the desperation with which the black man approaches life in a world controlled by whites.

In a broad sense, the protagonist's fantasies throughout the story help to express his feelings of hopelessness in a society that denies him any real power. His nightmare about being chased by a train represents his inability to control his own destiny, and "all the white people laughing" signifies whites' refusal to do anything other than ensure his desperate condition. When the dream is updated later in the story to show the protagonist carrying Laura in a subway tunnel, a crowd tells him to jump onto the electrified third rail of an adjacent track. Either choice—staying on the track or jumping—means death. It is only once the protagonist wins the chance to spin the wheel that he is afforded any power over his destiny. In "Ellison's 'King of the Bingo

Game,'" Urquhart points out that "As the bingo wheel spins, the feeling of total power that accompanies becoming the master of his own destiny overcomes [the protagonist]." Indeed, the protagonist describes himself as "drunk" with the power he feels. Ironically, it may be this ability finally to influence his destiny that brings about his downfall. Having never had such power, the protagonist does not know how to respond to it. He grips the button, afraid to let go, because the decisive action of releasing the button includes the risk of losing influence over the jackpot. Even though the protagonist's inaction leads to disaster, Urquhart suggests that he still gains something important, because he achieves, "if only for a moment, the power held by the white patriarchy in American society."

In "King of the Bingo Game," Ellison explores the power structure of American society in the 1930s and how it denied blacks meaningful control over their own destinies. According to Pearl I. Saunders in "Symbolism in Ralph Ellison's 'King of the Bingo Game,'" the protagonist of the story ultimately "realizes that his destiny has always been guided by hatred; hatred of self and of his race, caused by the repressiveness of a white controlled and white dominated society." The protagonist struggles against this maddening, senseless situation, leading to the story's tragic conclusion.

Identity and Naming

Identity is another important key to understanding Ellison's "King of the Bingo Game." The protagonist of the story is nameless throughout the narrative, emphasizing the anonymity of the black man in a white society. This theme is common in much of Ellison's writing; it is vital for grasping the situation of the black man as presented in "King of the Bingo Game." As Pearl I. Saunders asserts in "Symbolism in Ralph Ellison's 'King of the Bingo Game,'" Ellison's "unnamed protagonist represents the namelessness, the invisibility, or lack of identity experienced by the black American." The protagonist feels invisible to those around him; he sits alone in the darkness of the theater, in stark contrast to the camaraderie shared by others attending the film. He feels alienated and lonely, far from the friendliness he remembers from his past in the South. On stage holding the button, he temporarily feels alone, as if he is the only one in the theater. The crux of his problem seems to be his inability to define himself and find a place in which he belongs.

At one point in the narrative, the protagonist realizes "he [has] forgotten his own name." This incident underscores the protagonist's lack of individual identity, but even more importantly, it allows him to escape from a confining identity imposed on upon him by the white world. Forgetting the name that "had been given him by the white man who had owned his grandfather," allows the protagonist to feel free—he describes himself as "reborn." Furthermore, by renaming himself "the-man-who-pressed-the-button-who-held-the-prize-who-was-the-King-of-Bingo," the protagonist exerts control over his own identity. The power acquired from this renaming is only temporary, but it allows the reader to see how issues surrounding identity contribute to the inequalities blacks face.

HISTORICAL OVERVIEW

Pre–Civil Rights America

When "King of the Bingo Game" was published, the movement for African American civil rights was just beginning take shape. In 1896, the Supreme Court upheld the constitutionality of "separate but equal" public facilities for blacks and whites, setting the stage for generations of legal segregation and racism. The National Association for the Advancement of Colored People (NAACP) was established in 1909, and the white supremacist group the Ku Klux Klan re-emerged in 1915. Segregation, institutionalized through what were known as Jim Crow laws, was the standard for most aspects of American life in the South. There were more than 1,200 lynchings (mob murders of blacks by whites) in the American South between 1900 and 1918. Racially motivated violence was not confined to the South; lingering, deadly race riots erupted in St. Louis, Chicago, Detroit, and Harlem over the next quarter-century. Even without Jim Crow laws in the North, blacks often lived as second-class citizens. The Supreme Court made several decisions in support of equal rights in the late 1930s, but momentum would not shift firmly in favor of equality until after World War II. The atmosphere of discrimination that surrounded Ellison as he wrote is evident in his work.

In particular, in "King of the Bingo Game," Ellison considered the hopelessness that engulfed many blacks after they moved north seeking better opportunities than those available in the Jim Crow South. Believing that the North was a place of possibility and freedom, they were often crushed to discover that they still faced extensive discrimination there. Ellison's protagonist remembers the South fondly, as if life was actually better there. He claims that "Folks down South stuck together.... But up here [in the North] it was different." Life for African Americans was different in the two regions, but difficult in both. Without the forced segregation of the South, black communities were often less concentrated. The North was also highly industrialized and urban, a radical change from the largely agrarian South.

Ellison himself struggled to find his place in a society that was often hostile to him, which shaped his life and his writing. By depicting this experience and giving voice to its nameless participants, he helped in the struggle for civil rights.

The Great Depression and the Federal Writers' Project

The stock market crash of 1929 triggered a massive, worldwide economic collapse that lasted a decade, until the start of World War II. Americans confronted a situation for which they were completely unprepared; the post–World War I prosperity that characterized the 1920s was quickly replaced with poverty and unemployment on a devastating scale. Lasting throughout the 1930s, the economic slump of the Great Depression profoundly affected the landscape of the American workforce and the mindset of those who endured the crisis.

By 1932, the unemployment rate in America had risen to twenty-five percent. With joblessness so high, no one was immune to the consequences of the Depression. African Americans, many of whom were already living in poverty, were hit particularly hard. Unemployment among African Americans was twice as high as the national average. Blacks who had jobs were often forced to give them up to whites. As a black man living is this economic environment, Ellison was clearly influenced by the desperation around him. This is particularly evident in "King of the Bingo Game," in which the protagonist is jobless, broke, hungry, and—most significantly—

hopeless. This attitude characterized many of the African Americans fighting to survive in a depressed economy that did not have room for them.

Aside from becoming a theme in Ellison's work, the economic conditions of the Depression directly shaped his writing career. The Works Progress Administration (WPA) was a federal government program under President Roosevelt's New Deal. It helped create work for Americans during the Depression, and it included a provision for unemployed writers: the Federal Writers' Project (FWP). Under the FWP, unemployed writers were given a variety of paid work. Many got their start in this program, including Ellison, who was a literary intern for the Federal Writers' Project. The Depression thus played a profound role in Ellison's development as a writer, providing inspiration for his later work and giving him an early forum in which to write.

Harlem Renaissance

African Americans were shut out of most parts of white society during the early- to mid-twentieth century. Racism and other obstacles often stood in the way of black writers, dancers, artists, and thinkers. However, there was one place in America where African American social thought and culture flourished: Harlem, a neighborhood in New York City. African Americans seeking to express and enjoy themselves flocked to this Manhattan neighborhood, which quickly became a center of black culture. Black artists could create art here, but perhaps more importantly, they also found a receptive audience largely made up of people who shared their life experiences as black people in America. They were united by this experience—not politics or religion, and not artistic style.

This period of creativity and originality is known as the Harlem Renaissance, which extended from the end of World War I to the late 1930s. Talented young blacks in Harlem—including Zora Neale Hurston, Eubie Blake, W. E. B. DuBois, Josephine Baker, Marcus Garvey, and Paul Robeson—launched pioneering efforts in writing, music, theater, painting, dance, and other cultural media. Known at the time as the "New Negro Movement," the Harlem Renaissance created a place in society where the black perspective mattered; not only was it welcome, it was nurtured. Places like the Apollo Theater, the Savoy Ballroom, the

Lafayette Theater, and the WPA Negro Theater Company all provided a meaningful forum for blacks to explore their racial consciousness. Moreover, the Harlem Renaissance marked the first time that black culture crossed racial lines; these talented people created works that were absorbed into mainstream culture, affecting whites and blacks alike.

Ellison moved to Harlem in 1936, and he developed as a writer here. Exposed to the proliferation of black thought and creativity, as well as to the most prominent black literary figures of the time, Ellison began to write about blacks in American society. It was in Harlem that Ellison became friends with Richard Wright (author of *Native Son*), who influenced Ellison's approach to racial issues in his writing. Wright himself was outspoken about the evils of racism. Following Wright's lead, Ellison explored the conflicts that the black man faced in a society that did not see him as a viable and equal contributor.

CRITICAL OVERVIEW

Ellison's short story "King of the Bingo Game" was not widely reviewed when it was first published in 1944. To understand the importance of Ellison's work, it is worthwhile to consider how his novel *Invisible Man* (1952) was received by critics. His previous short stories and critical essays had not attracted much attention, but the publication of his first and only novel changed that. With *Invisible Man*, Ellison earned a reputation as a literary giant.

An unsigned article from Barron's Booknotes, "Ralph Ellison: The Author and His Times," notes that "reviews of the novel [*Invisible Man*] were ecstatic." Reviewers admired the depth to which Ellison explored the black experience, and stressed the literary merit of the novel. In "Man Underground," author Saul Bellow calls *Invisible Man* "a superb book." Other critics expressed similar judgments. Rather than viewing the novel only in terms of its author's race, they heralded *Invisible Man* as an outstanding American novel. Wright Morris, in "A Tale from Underground," declares that Ellison's novel "is a resolutely honest, tormented, profoundly American book." Ellison's *Invisible Man* was so widely prized for its literary worth that in 1953 it won the prestigious National Book Award for

fiction—the first of these awards ever bestowed on a black writer.

Even though many critics and scholars consider Ellison an important voice in black literature, his work often faced criticism from African Americans during the 1960s and early 1970s. The author of "Ralph Ellison: The Author and His Times" writes that many blacks "did not think that Ellison spoke for them because he was too much of an 'Uncle Tom,' a black who served the white man's interests." At a time when outspoken and radical black leaders like Malcolm X took center stage, some resented Ellison's approach to racial issues. They believed that Ellison defined blackness in white terms, and they begrudged him for doing so. In "A Critical Look at Ellison's Fiction & at Social & Literary Criticism by and About the Author" (1970), Ernest Kaiser says:

> *Invisible Man* is not rated highly as a meaningful novel dealing with the Black experience. There is a sense of anger with Ellison that he has sold out, that he has not dealt with things as they are, that he says little to Black people today.... There is in *Invisible Man* a sense of accommodation and willingness to try and change the prevalent white views. . . . [T]his is out-of-date with the current mood of young Black people in general.

Despite these negative reactions, Ellison's reputation as a vital and important writer of the twentieth century has prevailed. The posthumous publication of *Flying Home and Other Stories* rekindled interest in Ellison's work and its broader significance. This collection includes "King of the Bingo Game" and is the only published collection of Ellison's stories; it drew special attention because it included six stories not published during Ellison's lifetime. As the book's editor John F. Callahan explains in the introduction, no one knew that those stories existed until they were discovered in a box under Ellison's dining room table.

Writing in the *New York Times Book Review*, Gary Giddens calls the collection "a slim but shining installment." Elizabeth Judd, reviewing the collection for Salon.com, acknowledges that the stories are "sometimes slight," but "gracefully written and insightful." A review in *Melus* says the book is "at times, equally surreal and poignantly raw." Some writers consider the collection in light of previous responses to Ellison's work. In the *African American Review*, Robert J. Butler addresses "those who have

MEDIA ADAPTATIONS

"King of the Bingo Game" was adapted into a short feature film by Elise Robertson, starring Coleman Domingo. The short drama originally aired on PBS's American Storytellers series in 1999 and was later released as a video recording by PBS Home Video in 2001.

---

unfairly charged Ellison ... of lacking sufficient anger and militance," saying the six new stories in particular "smolder with anger and repulsion." Most important, Butler says, "what these thirteen stories emphatically demonstrate is that Ellison's *Invisible Man* did not spring ... out of nowhere, but [was] the product of a long period of artistic and philosophical growth."

CRITICISM

Troy Urquhart

In the following excerpt, Urquhart explores Ellison's "King of the Bingo Game," examining the relationship between black and white and further considering the power of naming in that relationship.

In her essay "Playing in the Dark," Toni Morrison asserts that in a "wholly racialized society" "there is no escape from racially inflected language." In a postcolonial view of American society, this assertion suggests both that the dichotomous relationship between the colonizer and the colonized is inescapable and that this relationship is reinforced or even constructed by language. The act of naming, then, enforces ideological hierarchies, including what Armitjit Singh and Peter Schmidt term "the socially constructed binary of black/white" in American culture. While John F. Callahan, editor of a collection of Ralph Ellison's short stories, describes Ellison's "King of the Bingo Game" as the tale of a "migrant" who "draws bingo and the right to take a turn at the wheel of fortune and the jackpot," Ellison's text seems to comment on the position of post-Reconstruction African Americans as defined by something more than chance. The question at the center of "King of the Bingo Game" is, perhaps, 'Who am I?" for the narrative never names its protagonist, relying almost to the point of absurdity on the use of the third-person pronoun *he*. When Ellison's story is viewed in terms of Morrison's assertion about the power of language, it reveals a pattern of naming that reinforces the hierarchy which values "whiteness" over "blackness" and suggests that the relationship between white and black remains a relationship between colonizer and colonized.

The text establishes the bingo hall as firmly controlled by the white male, and despite the protagonist's insistence that "anybody can win," the language in the bingo hall reinforces the racial hierarchy. The hall, a place where "everything was fixed" (209), is dominated by a "white beam" and is filled with an audience that repeatedly addresses the protagonist in condescending terms: "boy," "fool," and "jerk." The only character to name the protagonist in a positive manner is the old man who calls him "buddy," and their sharing of "not wine, but whiskey" suggests a religious communion and indicates that they are equals in the social hierarchy. Further, the replacement of "wine" with "whiskey" implies an attempt to subvert traditional white power structures to meet black purposes. When the protagonist calls " 'Bingo !' ", someone from the audience yells, "Let that fool up there" ; moments later, the protagonist fears that he will "make a fool of [himself]" and feels that the man on stage is "making a fool of him." This rapid internalization of the name "fool" suggests the "double-consciousness" that W. E. B. Du Bois describes as a "sense of looking at one's self through the eyes of others, of measuring one's soul by the tape of a world that looks on in amused contempt and pity." The protagonist cannot—or at least does not—respond to the "jive talk" and jokes of the man on stage; he simply "nod[s] vacantly" and "grin[s]", allowing his own identity, his own powers of assertion and articulation, to reflect the projection made by the dominant white male.

However, at the moment of crisis, when the protagonist asks, " 'Who am I?' ", he seems to overcome this internalization of social labels. An unnamed member of the audience yells, "Hurry up and bingo, you jerk!", but the protagonist refuses this label and insists that "he was reborn," echoing the religious image of the whiskey communion and suggesting that he has overcome white subjugation by subverting its power. The protagonist's receipt of power from the dominant white male ("The button rested snugly in his palm where the man had placed it" and his use of the rules that white society has constructed to justify his remaining on stage reinforce his internalization of American ideology: to win, he must receive the means to power from the dominant white male, and he must follow the rules established by white society. At the same time, the necessity of rebirth before taking a name of power implies that he sees his former, pre-bingo self in the pejorative terms used by the audience.

The protagonist's renaming of himself expresses the elation that he feels as he attempts to grasp power, yet it also implies the emptiness of that power. He casts off his old, "white" name and declares that he is "The-man-who-pressed-the-button-who-held-the-prize-who-was-the- King-of-Bingo " ; and, significantly, the story takes its title from this act of naming. While this title suggests that he does hold "a certain power" by defining himself as a "King," it deflates that power by indicating that it is over something trivial: a bingo game. Further, this self-aggrandizement quickly breaks down as the protagonist again internalizes the social messages: "He felt that the whole audience had somehow entered him … and he was unable to throw them out." Even as he holds the button, as he grasps power, and as the uniformed enforcers of the white patriarchy threaten him with physical harm, the protagonist "couldn't afford to break the cord." This image of an umbilical cord that cannot be cut suggests the "twoness" of the African American psyche described by Du Bois and reinforces his inability to define himself except in terms given to him by the dominant white male.

The protagonist's intoxication with power brings about his demise, but he recognizes, if only for a moment, the power held by the white patriarchy in American society. As the bingo wheel spins, the feeling of total power that accompanies becoming the master of his own destiny overcomes him: "This is God! This is the really truly God! He said it aloud, 'This is God!'" His equation of control with "God"

echoes the images of communion and rebirth and suggests that complete power lies not in control of others, but in control of the self and in hope, however slight, for success. For the protagonist, "God" is freedom from economic desperation and freedom from the nameless condition imposed upon him by the racial hierarchy of American ideology. And, perhaps more than these, "God" is the freedom to hold onto desperate hope and to name himself "the *King* -of-Bingo."

Source: Troy Urquhart, "Ellison's '*King of the Bingo Game*,'" in *Explicator*, Vol. 60, No. 4, Summer 2002, pp. 217–19.

Hal Blythe and Charlie Sweet

In the following essay, Blythe and Sweet analyze how Ellison's use of juxtaposition in the "King of the Bingo Game" is indicative of the racist theme of the story. In addition, they describe the black protagonist's recurring cinematic fantasy in the story as it relates to race.

Critics have long recognized symbolism as one of Ralph Ellison's favorite devices. However, a lesser-known technique, juxtaposition, illuminates the racism theme so prominent in his classic short story "King of the Bingo Game." By contrasting the main character's major fantasy with his real-life situation, Ellison makes more poignant the gap between white and black America in the 1930s.

Ellison opens the story by describing his black protagonist's recurring cinematic fantasy. For the fourth time his character is in a theater watching the same stereotypic action-adventure movie. In it the hero, enshrouded by darkness within a room, probes with "the beam of a flashlight" to locate a trapdoor, then the heroine, who is tied to a bed. Freeing her, he escapes with his beloved, presumably to live happily ever after. In short, the protagonist's fantasy is one of control wherein a man by himself defeats overwhelming odds to save the woman he loves.

Ellison then juxtaposes this "reel-life" escape and escapism to the protagonist's desperate real-life situation by establishing some obvious parallels. The man's purpose in coming to this dark theater is to win a game of chance and use the prize money to buy needed medicine for his ailing woman, Laura, who is home in bed. Ellison emphasizes that his protagonist is a stranger in a strange land: He is unemployed because he has no birth certificate, and he is a displaced Southerner in a Northern city. Ellison has given him no name. Before he can obtain his goal, the man must again watch the movie that comes from the projector and flashes in a "white beam" onto a white screen. He particularly observes how the beam always lands on the screen because "they had it all fixed. Everything was fixed." Indeed, in this strange land "they"— not he—control even more than the protagonist realizes. On this particular night, the protagonist assumes the role of hero when he wins at bingo and has the opportunity to play the wheel of fortune.

From this point Ellison stresses the dramatic divergence of the protagonist's path from that of the cinematic hero. In real life the odds are too overwhelming for a single man—especially a black man in white society—to overcome. As the man stumbles down the aisle, he is caught in a "light so bright and sharp" that it almost blinds him. Ellison uses the light to signal a role reversal. Just as in the movie the girl-victim was illuminated by the flashlight, so too the protagonist is lit, moving him from would-be hero to victim. Ellison emphasizes this transition by immediately having the protagonist feel "he had moved into the spell of some mysterious power." As the white announcer grabs his winning bingo card and checks it out with the "cold light" flashing from his finger, the protagonist has yet to realize the change—that like the film on the white screen, he is "fixed" by his role in a white-run society.

The protagonist's ignorance continues while he watches the spin of the wheel. He still believes that as long as he holds the button he is in control, yet he is tethered to the wheel by the electrical cord, unable to escape the white policemen who have been called to remove him from the stage so that the game can continue. His moment of triumph, in which he seemingly finds a "trap-door" to escape the hold of white dominance with the godlike act of changing "the name that had been given him by the white man who had owned his grandfather," is short-lived. Despite landing on the prize-winning double zero, the protagonist, who has diverged from the fixed role dictated to him by those running the game, is denied his win, beaten, and dragged from the scene. At the end there is no trapdoor (he lies on the stage floor unable to disappear beneath it), and there is no money to rescue Laura. (Ellison's

choice of the name Laura firmly places the protagonist within the heroic tradition because Laura is the archetypal name for the beloved in many works from the Renaissance where the wheel of fortune and its fickleness were so prominent.) Given a chance to control destiny, to replicate the fantasy's heroism, the protagonist fails. Through this telling juxtaposition of the "reel" and real, Ellison establishes that the cinematic fantasy of controlling one's destiny cannot become reality for a black man, for in 1930s America it is just that—a fantasy.

Source: Hal Blythe and Charlie Sweet, "Ellison's '*King of the Bingo Game*,'" in *Explicator*, Vol. 58, No. 4, Summer 2000, pp. 218–20.

SOURCES

Becker, Becky, Review of *Flying Home and Other Stories*, in *Melus*, Vol. 24, No. 2, Summer 1999, pp.179–81.

Bellow, Saul, "Man Underground: Review of Ralph Ellison's *Invisible Man*," in *Commentary*, June 1952, pp. 608–10.

Blythe, Hal, and Charlie Sweet, "Ellison's 'King of the Bingo Game,'" in *Explicator*, Vol. 58, Issue 4, Summer 2002, pp. 218–21.

Butler, Robert J., Review of *Flying Home and Other Stories*, in *African American Review*, Vol. 32, No. 1, Spring 1998, pp.164–67.

Ellison, Ralph, "King of the Bingo Game," in *Flying Home and Other Stories*, Vintage International, 1996, pp. 123–36.

Giddens, Gary, "A Review of *Flying Home and Other Stories*," in *New York Times Book Review*, January 19, 1997, p. 13.

Judd, Elizabeth, Review of *Flying Home and Other Stories*, *Salon Magazine*, www.salon.com/sneaks/sneak peeks961216.html (December 16, 1996).

Kaiser, Ernest, "A Critical Look at Ellison's Fiction & at Social & Literary Criticism By and About the Author," in *Black World*, December 1970.

Morris, Wright, "A Tale from Underground," in *New York Times*, April 13, 1952.

"Ralph Ellison: The Author and His Times," *Barron's Booknotes*, www.pinkmonkey.com/booknotes/barrons/ invismn1.asp, (1985).

Saunders, Pearl I., "Symbolism in Ralph Ellison's 'King of the Bingo Game,'" in *CLA Journal*, Vol. 20, No. 1, September 1976, pp. 35–39.

Urquhart, Troy, "Ellison's 'King of the Bingo Game,'" in *Explicator*, Vol. 69, Issue 4, Summer 2002, pp. 217–20.

The Merchant of Venice

WILLIAM SHAKESPEARE

1596

The Merchant of Venice, by Elizabethan playwright William Shakespeare, ranks among the most popular and frequently performed of the Bard's thirty-seven plays. Because of its presentation of a single character—Shylock, a Jewish moneylender—it is also his most controversial. In Shylock, Shakespeare created one of the most memorable, timeless characters in theatrical history, a dramatic figure so important that he has become a milestone role in the careers of mature actors. By pitting Shylock against a play full of Christians, Shakespeare also created a remarkable dramatic vehicle for exploring issues of race, religion, and prejudice.

The play likely dates from 1596 or 1597 and is one of what critics call Shakespeare's "great" or "middle" comedies, which he wrote during a fruitful period from roughly 1596 to 1601, a group of plays including works such as *A Midsummer Night's Dream*, *As You Like It*, and *Twelfth Night*. As was common in Shakespeare's day, the play was not an original plot but was based on two older tales. Specifically, an Italian work called *Il Pecorone* provided Shakespeare with his plot involving Antonio, Bassanio, Portia, and Shylock, while a number of stories, including the famous *Decameron* by Italian writer Boccaccio, provided the story related to selecting caskets to win a lady's hand in marriage. Shakespeare, of course, altered these older stories and added his own unique elements to the play.

The figure of a Jew was not entirely unknown to the Elizabethan audience, though Jews on stage were relatively rare. Jews had been expelled from England in the thirteenth century (and later from other European countries) and were only allowed to return a few decades after Shakespeare's death. Thus, the contemporary audience would have had little or no contact with either the Jewish faith or Jewish people, as no known Jews had lived legally in England for centuries. Jews were convenient outsiders, who in the past had been accused of a variety of wild rituals involving their faith and blamed, among other things, for causing the deadly Black Plague in Europe. In 1588, Shakespeare's contemporary, Christopher Marlowe, wrote his successful play *The Jew of Malta*, which employed the stereotype of a Jew as a monstrous, amoral moneylender. Then in 1594, a Portuguese doctor living in London, one Roderigo Lopez, was accused of trying to poison Queen Elizabeth. While being tortured on the rack, he admitted to being Jewish and keeping it a secret. This admission and his subsequent execution were a great sensation and may have prompted Shakespeare to create his Shylock to capitalize on the scandal. The incident also gave rise to an immediate revival of Marlowe's play.

The "merchant" of the title is Antonio, a Christian whose great antagonist is Shylock. It is the character of Shylock that has dominated the play historically. Shakespeare titled the play after Antonio, yet created such a forceful character in Shylock that he, too, seems to compete for a position in the title. Probably as a result of audience reaction to early productions, the play was quickly subtitled, so when it was registered for printing in the year 1598, it was listed under the lengthy title of *The Comical History of the Merchant of Venice, or Otherwise Called the Jew of Venice.*

Shylock is not the only great role in the play, however. In Portia, Shakespeare creates the first of his great female heroines, in whose footsteps later followed the likes of Rosalind of *As You Like It* and Viola of *Twelfth Night*. Through Portia, as with future heroines, Shakespeare explores the position of women in Elizabethan society, both their perceived powerlessness in a male-controlled world and their actual power to act when given the opportunity. Thus at its core, *The Merchant of Venice* is a play about prejudice, though not everyone agrees about the interpretation of the play, with the ambiguity mostly regarding Shylock.

> " HE HATH DISGRACED ME, AND HINDERED ME HALF A MILLION; LAUGHED AT MY LOSSES, MOCKED AT MY GAINS, SCORNED MY NATION, THWARTED MY BARGAINS, COOLED MY FRIENDS, HEATED MINE ENEMIES, AND WHAT'S HIS REASON?—I AM A JEW. HATH NOT A JEW EYES? HATH NOT A JEW HANDS, ORGANS, DIMENSIONS, SENSES, AFFECTIONS, PASSIONS; FED WITH THE SAME FOOD, HURT WITH THE SAME WEAPONS, SUBJECT TO THE SAME DISEASES, HEALED BY THE SAME MEANS, WARMED AND COOLED BY THE SAME WINTER AND SUMMER AS A CHRISTIAN IS? IF YOU PRICK US DO WE NOT BLEED? IF YOU TICKLE US DO WE NOT LAUGH? IF YOU POISON US DO WE NOT DIE? AND IF YOU WRONG US SHALL WE NOT REVENGE?"

The great question about *The Merchant of Venice* is whether it is an anti-Semitic play or is a play about anti-Semitism. The answer, provided by over four hundred years of production, presentation, and critical debate, seems to be an ambiguous "yes"—it is both. The play and its questions about religious prejudice transcend Elizabethan England. The way it is interpreted offers a glimpse into the collective psyche of each era in which it is produced. In the anti-Semitic worlds of eighteenth-century England or Nazi Germany in the 1930s and 1940s, it was a play for deriding Jews and presenting them as monsters. In gentler times, it has been a play that reveals the pain and conflict caused by intolerance and shows how such prejudice can plant the seeds of hate. This ambiguity is a part of the play's greatness and is why it remains among the most frequently performed and most heatedly debated of Shakespeare's plays.

PLOT SUMMARY

Act 1, Scene 1

Antonio, the merchant of Venice in the play's title, is melancholy but cannot explain why.

Salerio tells him it is because his ships are at sea and he is worried about his investments. Solanio agrees. Antonio denies this reasoning, pointing out the diversity of his investments and saying that he feels secure in his business deals. Bassanio, Lorenzo, and Graziano enter and Salerio and Solanio depart. Graziano also comments on Antonio's serious demeanor before leaving with Lorenzo. Bassanio mentions the debts he owes to Antonio and others, and Antonio offers to help him. Antonio then asks Bassanio about a lady whom Bassanio is supposed to have met; Bassanio then tells him about Portia, but says that he needs money to travel to Belmont to compete with her other suitors. Antonio tells Bassanio that all of his cash is tied up in trade, but that his good reputation should allow him to borrow money to help his friend.

Act 1, Scene 2

The scene shifts to Belmont, home of Portia. She enters with Nerissa, her waiting woman. Portia is melancholy because she has no choice in marriage as a result of her late father's decree. He created a riddle involving caskets of gold, silver, and lead and declared that any man who could solve the riddle will make a worthy husband for Portia. Nerissa assures her that it will work out in the end. They comically review the various suitors who have already come, with Portia criticizing all their faults. Nerissa tells Portia that the suitors have decided to leave upon hearing the conditions of the lottery. One condition is that if a suitor fails, he must promise never to get married. Nerissa asks if Portia remembers Bassanio and says that he above all deserves her. A servant arrives saying four suitors are leaving and another, from Morocco, has just arrived.

Act 1, Scene 3

Bassanio is arranging a loan of three thousand ducats with Shylock, a Jewish moneylender, saying that Antonio will guarantee the loan. Antonio arrives, and in an aside, Shylock remarks how much he hates Antonio and that his policy of lending out money for free brings down the interest rates on loans: "How like a fawning publican he looks. / I hate him for he is a Christian." He also mentions how Antonio hates Jews and rails against Shylock and his lending practices, to which Shylock thinks, "Cursèd be my tribe / If I forgive him." Antonio and Shylock negotiate the contract, and Antonio mentions

BIOGRAPHY

WILLIAM SHAKESPEARE

William Shakespeare was born on or about April 23, 1564, in Stratford-upon-Avon in Warwickshire, England. The exact birth date is uncertain, but his baptism, likely performed within days of his birth, was recorded on April 26, 1564. His father, John Shakespeare, was a successful merchant, and his mother, Mary, was the daughter of local gentry. In 1582, at the age of eighteen, Shakespeare married twenty-six-year-old Anne Hathaway. They had their first child six months later.

Little is known of Shakespeare's life from the time of his marriage until he appeared in London around 1590. He quickly became well known as an actor and playwright for the Lord Chamberlain's Men theatrical company, producing his first history plays and his earliest comedies. *The Merchant of Venice* dates from the mid-1590s, and is one of the works critics frequently call Shakespeare's "great" or "middle" comedies. Among the other comedies written at this time were *A Midsummer Night's Dream, As You Like It, Twelfth Night,* and *Much Ado About Nothing.*

In the early 1600s, Shakespeare wrote his great tragedies, including *Hamlet, Othello, King Lear,* and *Macbeth.* He completed his last work around 1613 and likely retired to Stratford, where died on April 23, 1616, at the age of fifty-two.

that he never loans money at interest. Shylock offers an Old Testament story in his defense, but Antonio retorts, "The devil can cite Scripture for his purpose." He then asks if the deal is settled. Shylock, growing angry, points out how Antonio insults him in public and wonders about the hypocrisy of criticizing him on one hand and asking him for money on the other. Antonio replies that he will likely insult Shylock

William Shakespeare The Library of Congress

again, and that he should lend the money to an enemy so that the penalty may be more enjoyable. Shylock says that he would like to be friends with Antonio and will lend the money free, but Antonio clearly does not want his friendship. Shylock then says that instead of charging interest, he will secure the loan with "an equal pound / Of your fair flesh to be cut off and taken / In what part of your body pleaseth me," should Antonio fail to pay. Despite Bassanio's protests, Antonio agrees to this term.

Act 2, Scene 1

The Prince of Morocco arrives at Belmont. He begins by telling Portia to "Mislike me not for my complexion," and explains why the color of his skin should not matter to her. Portia tells him that she has no choice in her selection of a husband but that if she did, the prince is as good as any she has yet seen. The prince is ready to choose, though he acknowledges that the lottery is a random choice and that a lesser man than he may win. Portia invites him to dine before he risks the lottery.

Act 2, Scene 2

Lancelot the clown is debating out loud whether or not he should run away from Shylock, his

master. His conscience tells him not to, even though his master is "a kind of devil." Ultimately, he decides to leave. Enter Gobbo, Lancelot's father. He is blind and does not recognize his son. Gobbo asks Lancelot how to get to Shylock's house and Lancelot pretends to be a stranger. He asks about Gobbo's son Lancelot, then tells Gobbo that his son is dead. Gobbo is horrified, saying that Lancelot "was the very staff of my age, my very prop." Lancelot, feeling bad about the trick he has played, then humbly reveals himself to his father. He learns that Gobbo has come with a gift for Shylock, but Lancelot complains about how Shylock treats him, complaining "My master's a very Jew," and that "I am famished in his service." He wants to work for Bassanio instead, and says "If I serve not him, I will run as far as God has any ground." He asks Gobbo to give his gift to Bassanio instead. Bassanio arrives and Lancelot asks him to take him into service. Bassanio agrees, saying that Shylock has already agreed to such an arrangement. Lancelot and Gobbo depart as Graziano arrives to tell Bassanio that he wants to travel with him to Belmont. Bassanio says that he can go, but he must "take pain / To allay with some cold drops of modesty / Thy skipping spirit, lest through thy wild behavior / I be misconstrued in the place I go to."

Act 2, Scene 3–Scene 5

Shylock's daughter, Jessica, tells Lancelot that she is sorry he is leaving. "Our house is hell, and thou, a merry devil, / Didst rob it of some taste of tediousness," she says. She gives Lancelot a letter to deliver secretly to Lorenzo. Lancelot departs and Jessica admits that she is ashamed to be her father's child and that if Lorenzo is willing, she will convert to Christianity and marry him.

Lorenzo tells Graziano, Salerio, and Solanio that they will all sneak away from supper and meet later in disguise. Lancelot arrives and gives Lorenzo the letter. Lorenzo reads it and then asks Lancelot to tell Jessica that "I will not fail her." Lancelot, Salerio, and Solanio depart. Lorenzo then tells Graziano that Jessica has given him instructions for stealing her away from her father's house that very night.

Shylock tells Lancelot that he will soon see the difference between working for him and working for Bassanio. He then tells Jessica that he is going to supper at Bassanio's and gives her the keys so that she can lock up the house. He tells her to watch the house carefully, as he has had a bad dream and feels something is amiss. Lancelot privately tells Jessica to keep an eye out for Lorenzo, then leaves. Shylock then sends Jessica to her room and Jessica thinks aloud how Shylock is about to lose a daughter: "if my fortune be not crossed, / I have a father, you a daughter lost."

Act 2, Scene 6

A parade of people wearing masks enter, including Graziano, Salerio, and torchbearers. They stop beneath Jessica's window and wait for Lorenzo to arrive. Once he does, he calls to the upper window of the house. Jessica appears and throws down a purse full of money. She tells Lorenzo that she is disguised as a boy. Jessica steals more from her father's house and then appears below. Lorenzo, Salerio, and Jessica leave while Graziano lingers behind. Antonio enters and says that he has been looking for Graziano because Bassanio sails for Belmont tonight and is waiting for Graziano to board.

Act 2, Scene 7–Scene 9

The Prince of Morocco is ready to try the riddle of the caskets. Portia explains that the correct casket contains her picture. Morocco selects the gold casket, but inside only finds a scroll explaining his failure. He reads it aloud and then quickly departs, remarking, "I have too grieved a heart / To take a tedious leave. Thus losers part."

Back in Venice, Salerio tells Solanio that Bassanio and Graziano have left, but he does not think Lorenzo went with them. Solanio tells Salerio how Shylock, upon discovering his daughter gone, called for the Duke to search Bassanio's ship. Salerio adds that it was already under sail and that Lorenzo and Jessica were seen leaving in a gondola. Solanio then tells how Shylock cried for his lost money and his lost daughter, alternating over which loss pains him more: "My daughter! O, my ducats! O, my daughter! / Fled with a Christian! O, my Christian ducats!" Salerio reports that he has heard of a Venetian ship sinking off the French coast; he hopes that it was not Antonio's.

Back at Belmont, the Prince of Aragon has come to try the lottery. He chooses the silver casket, but it is not the right one. As he leaves, a messenger arrives reporting that a young Venetian is on his way. Nerissa says she hopes it is Bassanio.

Act 3, Scene 1

Salerio tells Solanio of gossip circulating that one of Antonio's ships has sunk; Solanio confirms the rumor. Shylock arrives and accuses them of knowing of Jessica's flight and doing nothing to prevent it. They admit it, and Shylock says she will be damned for it. They ask Shylock if he has heard of Antonio's losses and he confirms them. Salerio asks Shylock if he will really take his pound of flesh and Shylock answers yes, because Antonio "hath disgraced me ... laughed at my losses, mocked at my gains, scorned my nation." Shylock then gives an impassioned speech, asking, "If you prick [Jews] do we not bleed? If you tickle us do we not laugh?" The loss of his daughter has embittered him, and he has decided to seek revenge via the bond. Tubal, a fellow Jew, enters. He has been searching for Jessica in Genoa but has not found her. He reports rumors of her spending the money freely in Genoa and mentions that Antonio has lost a ship and that his creditors are searching for him. Shylock is ecstatic at the news. He sends Tubal off to find an officer of the law.

Act 3, Scene 2

Again at Belmont, Portia asks Bassanio to wait for the lottery because she would like to have his company for a while so she can teach him how to choose correctly. Bassanio wants to choose immediately. Portia asks for music and while Bassanio prepares to choose, one of her servants sings. Interestingly, the first three lines of the short first song all rhyme with the word "lead." Bassanio then selects the lead casket, which is the correct one. Portia offers herself to him and gives him a ring, saying, "Which when you part from, lose, or give away, / Let it presage the ruin of your love." He says if he ever parts from the ring, he will be dead. Graziano then steps in and asks if he can marry Nerissa. Lorenzo, Jessica, Salerio, and a messenger arrive. Salerio gives Bassanio a letter from Antonio and reports that Shylock is bent on revenge: he no longer wants the money to be returned; he wants to literally cut off a pound of Antonio's flesh. Portia tells Bassanio to go to Venice and pay the debt while she and Nerissa wait.

Act 3, Scene 3–Scene 5

Shylock enters with Solanio, Antonio, and the city jailer. Shylock is ranting at Antonio, saying, "Thou called'st me dog before thou hadst a cause, / But since I am a dog, beware my fangs." He refuses to hear Antonio's pleas for mercy. Antonio admits that the Duke cannot deny the contract and that to do so would make a mockery of the law and business for which Venice is so famous.

At Belmont, Portia entrusts the duties of running her house to Lorenzo while she and Nerissa are away. She says they will wait for Bassanio's return at a nearby monastery, but after Lorenzo and Jessica leave, she gives her servant Balthasar a letter. She tells him to take it to her cousin, Doctor Bellario, in Padua, and then to meet her at the ferry for Venice. Portia tells Nerissa of her plans for the two women to secretly travel to Venice dressed as young men.

Lancelot tells Jessica, "truly I think you are damned" because she is Jewish, and that her only hope "is but a kind of bastard hope"; literally, that she is not her father's child. She says she will be saved because her husband has made her a Christian. Lorenzo enters and Jessica explains Lancelot's jesting. Lorenzo counters by telling Lancelot that "the Moor is with child by you," referring to one of Portia's ladies-in-waiting.

Act 4, Scene 1–Scene 2

The climactic trial scene begins with the entrance of the Duke of Venice, Antonio, Bassanio, Graziano, and Salerio. The Duke tells Antonio, "I am sorry for thee. Thou art come to answer / A stony adversary, an inhuman wretch / Uncapable of pity, void and empty / From any dram of mercy." Antonio says that he is willing to take his punishment "with a quietness of spirit." Shylock arrives and insists that he will have the "forfeit of my bond" as he has "a lodged hate and a certain loathing" for Antonio. Bassanio offers Shylock six thousand ducats, twice the original debt, and is refused. Shylock then throws their anger back in their faces, pointing out that they themselves are slave owners, that they buy and sell human beings like animals and would never allow him to interfere with them.

The Duke says that a learned lawyer named Bellario is due to arrive, but Nerissa, dressed as a male legal clerk, comes in with a letter. Shylock begins to sharpen his knife, a brazen act that angers Bassanio. The Duke announces that Bellario has sent a letter commending a young lawyer named Balthasar, who will soon arrive. Portia comes, dressed as Balthasar. She introduces herself to Shylock and to Antonio, then offers a speech about mercy, beginning "The quality of mercy is not strained." She argues that mercy does not just save the life of the offender but honors the power that grants the mercy, too; thus, it is "twice blest" and "is enthroned in the hearts of kings." She asks if Antonio has the money and Bassanio says yes and begs for mercy on Antonio, but Portia says that the bond is forfeit and Shylock is entitled to his pound of flesh.

Portia bids Shylock to be merciful and take the money, but he says no. She tells him to prepare his knife and he does so, praising the judge for his wisdom. Portia finally issues the final judgment: "A pound of that same merchant's flesh is thine. / The court awards it, and the law doth give it." However, she adds, there is nothing in the bond about blood, so that if Shylock sheds even one drop of blood, all of his lands and property are forfeit to the state. Shylock, recognizing the truth of the statement, quickly retreats. He decides he will take the money instead, but Portia denies him, saying he can only have his penalty and if he cuts off any more or less than an exact pound, he dies.

Shylock again asks for his money and is again refused. Portia then mentions another law. Since Shylock has, in effect, threatened to kill a citizen of Venice, the threatened man has the right to half of Shylock's estate while the other half is forfeit to the state. The state also has the right to sentence Shylock to death. The Duke quickly claims Shylock's property and asks Antonio what he should do with him. Antonio, ostensibly showing mercy, asks that Shylock be left with half of his estate but asks for the other half to use for himself, saying that upon Shylock's death, he will leave it to Lorenzo and Jessica. He then asks that Shylock be forced to become a Christian and that upon his death, the remaining part of his estate will also go to Lorenzo and Jessica. The Duke agrees and Shylock, defeated, says, "I am content" and leaves.

Once Shylock leaves, the Duke asks Portia to dinner but she says she is leaving immediately for Padua. The Duke departs and Bassanio offers Portia the three thousand ducats, but she refuses the money. Bassanio then asks her to take some token and Portia asks Antonio for his gloves. Testing her new husband, she asks Bassanio for the ring that she gave him.

Embarrassed, he refuses it with an apology, saying that his wife gave it to him. Portia, feigning offense, leaves with Nerissa. But Antonio, appalled by Bassanio's refusal, implores him to give up the ring. Bassanio gives Graziano the ring and tells him to find the departed lawyer and to give it to him.

Graziano catches up with Portia and Nerissa and hands over the ring. Portia asks Graziano to show Nerissa the way to Shylock's house so that Nerissa can deliver the deed of gift for him to sign. Nerissa decides she will try to get Graziano's ring, too.

Act 5, Scene 1

Act 5 takes the play back to Belmont and to the realm of romantic comedy after the seriousness of the trial scene. On a moonlit night, Lorenzo and Jessica exchange romantic speeches that may suggest early signs of marital strife. Portia returns with Nerissa and Bassanio. Graziano and Antonio soon follow. Bassanio introduces Antonio, whom Portia pretends to meet for the first time. As they talk, Nerissa and Graziano speak together privately until Graziano admits that he gave Nerissa's ring away to Balthasar's clerk. Portia criticizes Graziano for parting with the ring too easily, suggesting his love is not true. Graziano says that Bassanio gave his ring to the judge and Portia feigns anger. Bassanio defends himself, but Portia refuses to accept his reasoning. She eventually gives Antonio the ring and tells him to give it to Bassanio, claiming that the young lawyer "lay with me." Nerissa also claims that the clerk "did lie with me" and both Bassanio and Graziano are shocked, believing their wives have been unfaithful. Portia quickly tells of their hidden identities, however. She also tells Antonio that three of his ships have indeed survived and that he is again well-off. Nerissa gives Lorenzo the deed to Shylock's property and Lorenzo, amazed, says, "Fair ladies, you drop manna in the way / Of starved people." The play seemingly ends happily for all except Shylock.

THEMES

Religion and Race

Religious prejudice dominates *The Merchant of Venice*. Though the play is a romantic comedy and the character of Shylock appears in only five

of the play's twenty scenes, there is no doubt that the conflict between Christian and Jew is the greatest source of both interest in and controversy about the play. The conflict lies in the clash of religions, in Christian Europe's fear or dislike of Jews based on their beliefs. It lies in culture: the perceived strangeness of the Jews in dress, appearance, and business practices. And it lies in the hypocrisy of Christians as they marginalize Jews, but turn to them as moneylenders and traders when needed.

Shylock makes it clear from his first meeting with Antonio that he despises him, citing two reasons: "I hate him for he is a Christian; / But more, for that in low simplicity / He lends out money gratis, and brings down / The rate of usance here with us in Venice." The antagonism is immediately established and it is based partly on religion, though Shylock makes it clear that money issues are more prominent. Given the different views of moneylending between Christians and Jews, however, even the economic conflict has cultural and religious overtones. The antagonism is not one-way, however. Shylock also makes it clear that he frequently suffers abuse at the hand of the openly anti-Semitic Antonio: "He hates our sacred nation, and he rails, / Even there where merchants most do congregate / On me, my bargains, and my well-won thrift."

Shylock is by no means a particularly sympathetic figure. He is harsh, curt, and prejudiced himself. He can be vengeful when angered. According to his daughter Jessica, theirs is a difficult home. She does not run away with Lorenzo just for love, but because her home is a "hell" to her. Modern film and theater directors point out that they often have to cut lines in order to make Shylock more palatable to modern audiences, as some of his utterances are as nasty as those thrown at him. Given his position as a barely tolerated outsider, his insistence on not quietly putting up with insults makes him stronger and more sympathetic than a meek character might be.

The Christians in the play are problematic, too. They are arguably worse, given the gap between their rhetoric about generosity and Christian mercy and their acts. Shylock is the constant target of their derision. He is referred to as a "devil." He is berated in the streets and laughed at for the painful loss of his daughter, who besides eloping has stolen a large sum of money from him. To the Christians in the play,

A drawing by Charles A. Buchel of Shylock from Act II of The Merchant of Venice *Public Domain*

Shylock is a stereotype, a monstrous Jewish moneylender not worthy of sympathy. Shylock points out Antonio's hypocrisy reminding him, "You call me misbeliever, cut-throat, dog, / And spit upon my Jewish gabardine" but then asks him for a loan. Antonio, whom the Venetians constantly refer to as a good Christian, replies unapologetically: "I am as like to call thee so again, / To spit on thee again, to spurn thee too."

This debatable Christian mercy is another core theme in the play, for the Christians are certain of their own merciful behavior when they decide not to put Shylock to death. They are convinced of their Christian mercy when they steal half of his estate and leave him the other half. They are confident in their mercy when they force Shylock to convert to Christianity. Portia, in disguise as the lawyer Balthasar, offers Shylock multiple chances to show such Christian mercy and to spare Antonio. His failure to act like a Christian damns him.

Gender

Though questions about Shylock dominate *The Merchant of Venice,* race and religion are by no

means the only area in which prejudice is examined in the play. The few women that are in the play, like women generally in Shakespeare's age, are themselves bound by restrictions. Though they are not outsiders to the extent of Shylock, they are nonetheless placed in a position of inferiority and powerlessness that must be resolved if they are to find happiness. There are only three women characters in *The Merchant of Venice*: Portia; her waiting-woman, Nerissa; and Jessica, Shylock's daughter. By the play's end, all three are married, though two of them have had to overcome substantial obstacles to marry according to their choice.

Portia begins the play in an oddly powerless situation that leaves her melancholy. She is attractive, wealthy, and intelligent yet she, even more so than most women in Shakespeare age, has absolutely no say in who shall be her husband. She is bound by the absurd edict of her dead father: her husband will be the man who solves a riddle involving three caskets, and any man that tries and fails must promise to leave immediately and forswear marriage for the rest of his life. The stakes are therefore high, and many suitors are unwilling to take the chance and depart without trying. Portia is thankful for their departure, however, as she seems to have already set her heart on Bassanio.

Jessica is similarly powerless. While Portia is bound to marry any man who takes the risk and solves the riddle, Jessica is bound to marry within her religion. In order to marry Lorenzo, a Christian and the man of her choice, she not only has to elope from her father's house but has to convert to Christianity. It is a heavy price to pay for the freedom to choose, but she is willing; early on she tells the clown Lancelot "[o]ur house is hell," letting it be known how miserable she is living with her father.

Both female characters are transformed, however, by donning the clothing of men and moving through the world as men. Freedom comes with the clothing. Jessica requires the clothing of a boy to escape her father's house and run off with Lorenzo. Later, both Portia and Nerissa disguise themselves as men in order to follow their husbands to Venice, where Portia, dressed as a male lawyer, suddenly dominates the action of the play. As Carol Hansen writes in her book *Woman as Individual in English Renaissance Drama: A Defiance of the Masculine Code*:

> While garbed as a learned Doctor of Laws from Rome, a disguise which allows [Portia] to test both the fidelity of her new husband, Bassanio, and to distinguish between the efficacy of the Old and New Testaments' definitions of justice, she determines the fate of both Shylock and Antonio.

Besides determining fates, the disguise allows two other things to happen. It allows both Nerissa and Portia to gain the upper hand in their marriages by tricking their new husbands into giving up the rings they had promised to wear forever. The other effect is, according again to Hansen, that "Shakespeare appears to be suggesting an extraordinary resolution: that after disguised entrance into the male world, the disguise once lifted, she may emerge as the man's equal or friend." As the play ends and the ruse of the disguise is revealed, the men appear to give in to their wives and accept them as equal partners. Their prejudices are lifted by the fact that their women have shown themselves capable of being more powerful than they are themselves.

Sexuality

In recent years, the issue of sexuality in *The Merchant of Venice* has come increasingly under critical scrutiny, specifically in relation to the friendships among the Venetian men in the play and the potentially homophobic overtones they create. The great English poet W. H. Auden, for instance, pointed out that the play makes a great deal more sense if Antonio is not just Bassanio's patron but his lover, too, or at the very least is deeply in love with Bassanio. If this scenario is taken as a given, an interesting rivalry arises, not between Antonio and Shylock, but between Portia and Antonio over Bassanio's affections. As critic Alan Sinfield writes in his essay "How to Read *The Merchant of Venice* Without Being Heterosexist":

> The seriousness of the love between Antonio and Bassanio is manifest, above all, in Portia's determination to contest it. Simply, she is at a disadvantage because of her father's casket device, and wants to ensure that her husband really is committed to her.

With this reading, Portia must "defeat" Antonio and, in effect, "convert" her new husband Bassanio to socially sanctioned heterosexual relations. Sinfield and others have made the strong case that Portia systematically slights Antonio, and that even saving him from Shylock's knife is a form of triumph as it prevents Antonio making the ultimate sacrifice of his life for Bassanio.

HISTORICAL OVERVIEW

The Power of Venice

To audiences in Shakespeare's England, Venice was something of a magical place. There was a "myth of Venice" that drew travelers to the city, which was known widely for its wealth, its tolerance, its political power, its liberty, and even its licentiousness. Even though Venice the city-state was well past its peak in the 1590s, the city's reputation remained strong throughout Europe.

The city had been an independent entity, a so-called city-state, since the late seventh century. Its service during the eleventh and twelfth centuries as a gathering point for the Crusades, in which European soldiers sought to "free" the Holy Land (Jerusalem and its surroundings) from its Islamic "occupiers," helped the city develop into a major political and commercial power. By the thirteenth century, it was the strongest commercial and military power in Mediterranean Europe. Venetian Marco Polo had traveled the Silk Road to China, increasing interest in trade with the East. The city had thousands of merchant ships carrying goods around the Mediterranean and beyond. Thus, Shakespeare's Antonio, with his ships trading in faraway lands, is an accurate reflection of the Venetian merchant class during the height of the city's powers.

The Republic of Venice was also known for a relatively high level of religious tolerance. Jews had been officially expelled from a number of countries, including England, in previous centuries and had been persecuted in others, but the city of Venice had allowed them to settle, albeit with some restrictions. In 1516, the first genuine Jewish ghetto in Europe formed in the city. It could have been home to Shakespeare's Shylock.

Jews in Europe

After the eighth century, Jews had been welcomed in parts of Europe, largely because they were assumed to be good at business, useful for the local economies, and no threat to the standing powers since they neither owned nor worked the land. They were never fully accepted by these communities, but neither were they persecuted. Then the Crusades started in the eleventh century, and though they were rooted in conflicts between Christians and Muslims, the wars deeply affected European Jews.

The gathering armies of the Crusaders attacked Jews in northern Europe, killing many and wiping out whole communities. Life for Jews in northern Europe became even more difficult after the Crusades. Jews became more isolated from their surroundings. They were forced to wear badges and to live in poverty. Wild rumors spread about their religious practices and they were blamed for outbreaks of the bubonic plague. They were expelled from England in 1290, from France in the fourteenth century, and later from Germany and Spain. Upon expulsion, most Jews moved east, to Poland. Others moved south, settling in Venice in what is considered the first Jewish ghetto.

By the time Shakespeare wrote *The Merchant of Venice*, Jews had been banned from England for three hundred years. It is likely that few people watching a production of the play had ever come in contact with a Jew, as they were practically unknown to Elizabethan audiences. Jews were seen largely a rumor, a collection of prejudices and myths, figments of the wild imagination. Shakespeare's contemporary, Christopher Marlowe, had written *The Jew of Malta* in 1588, portraying the Jewish moneylender Barabas as a one-dimensional monster. Then in 1594, a Portuguese physician named Roderigo Lopez was accused of trying to poison Queen Elizabeth and while under torture, he admitted that he was secretly a Jew. His trail and execution were a sensation and led to an immediate revival of Marlowe's play.

Usury

At the core of the plot in *The Merchant of Venice* is the question of moneylending at interest, a practice once termed as "usury." The original sense of usury meant charging a fee for the use of money. It is the same thing that is commonly called "interest" today, though a variety of other fees for monetary transactions could also be classified as usury in its original sense. Interest is commonly accepted today and the term "usury" has now narrowed to mean the charging of excessive interest on borrowed money.

This acceptance of charging interest, of "usury" in its original form, is relatively new, however. The practice of usury is an ancient moral, religious, and economic question. It was denounced by thinkers such as Greek philosopher Aristotle and Christian philosopher St. Thomas Aquinas. In the sixteenth century, despite the relatively new culture of exploration and ever-expanding trade, it was still a hot topic of debate. Christians were implored not to lend money at interest. As critic Jay Halio writes of the England at the time in *Understanding* The Merchant of Venice*: A Student Casebook to Issues, Sources and Historical Documents,* "a compromise bill was passed in 1571 called the Act against Usury, which stated that usury was morally wrong but nevertheless permitted lending at interest at a rate not to exceed 10 percent."

Jewish law allowed Jews like Shylock to lend money at interest to non-Jews, though it forbade the charging of interest to a fellow Jew. This practice of charging Gentiles interest helped create the stereotype of the Jewish moneylender, in part fostering the anti-Semitism that was common in Europe at the time. Christianity also forbade the lending of money at interest, thus the Jew as moneylender was in many ways a creation of the system that later persecuted them for lending money. Shylock makes it clear that one thing he dislikes about Antonio is that he lends money for free, thus taking business away from Shylock and pushing down the rate of interest he can charge borrowers. In doing so, Antonio is following his Christian conscience. But Shylock is following his Jewish edicts. This clash of cultures regarding usury establishes the great conflict in the play.

CRITICAL OVERVIEW

None of Shakespeare's other plays have generated the critical controversy that surrounds *The Merchant of Venice*, and nearly all of that debate has been centered on the character of Shylock. The central question has simply been this: is *The Merchant of Venice* a play about anti-Semitism, or is it an anti-Semitic play? That is, does Shakespeare attempt to honestly reflect and even criticize the anti-Semitism common to his time, or is he pandering to it and agreeing with it in his portrayal of Shylock?

Initially, there was no need for such a debate. Anti-Semitism was not only a commonplace across Europe in Shakespeare's time, but it was an accepted norm. Jews were disliked, banned, feared, hated, and persecuted. They had been expelled from England three hundred years before and only allowed to legally return some thirty years after Shakespeare's death. Thus, there was no debate about this aspect of the play. To Elizabethan audiences, Shylock would have been an evil, money-grubbing, vengeful—and perfectly normal—Jew. He would have been portrayed in comic and monstrous form and the play would have been seen as providing a happy end for him by forcing him to convert to Christianity. He was saved from himself and his creed by Christian mercy.

The famous nineteenth-century actor Edmund Kean is usually credited with changing the way Shylock was performed. In 1814, he portrayed Shylock as younger, more vigorous, and more sympathetic than had previously been done. The point is illustrated by English critic William Hazlitt, in his "Characters of Shakespeare's Plays" (1817):

> When we first went to see Mr. Kean in Shylock, we expected to see, what we had been used to see, a decrepit old man, bent with age and ugly

with mental deformity, grinning with deadly malice, with the venom of his heart congealed in the expression of his countenance....We were disappointed, because we had taken our idea from other actors, not from the play.

Kean's Romantic reading of the play, in which Shylock became as much victim as victimizer, caught on and dominated interpretations of the play through the early twentieth century.

The rise of Nazi Germany and the Holocaust in the 1930s and 1940s obviously affected the way *The Merchant of Venice* was perceived. The play was popular in Nazi Germany as anti-Jewish propaganda. Shylock, interpreted sympathetically for well over a hundred years, returned to his original form as a monster. Writer Harriet Hawkins, quoted by Harold Bloom in his book *Shylock* (1991), reports, "In the earlier Nazi years, *Merchant* was put on quite often; there were about fifty German productions between 1933 and 1939, according to the known statistics." In contrast, German Jewish critic Herman Sinsheimer, who was forced to flee Nazi Germany in the late 1930s, asserted in his book *Shylock: The History of a Character* (1963), that "Shakespeare created the greatest Jewish character since the Bible."

As might be expected, criticism has also reflected the changing times. While the character of Shylock still dominates the scholarship about the play, recent critics have approached *The Merchant of Venice* from, for instance, a feminist or homosexual perspective. The poet W. H. Auden argued that the play made much more sense if one could see Antonio as deeply in love with Bassanio.

The debate over Shylock continues, however. Well-known American critic Harold Bloom, a great admirer of Shakespeare, places the play firmly on the side of anti-Semitism. Bloom contends that the ease with which Shylock accepts his forced conversion is wildly inconsistent with his otherwise formidable, tenacious character and therefore a sign of the play's inherent anti-Semitism. Bloom writes in his book *Shylock* that "[i]n this one play alone, Shakespeare was very much of his age, and not for all time." Bloom feels the play reflects the rampant, accepted anti-Semitism of Elizabethan England, and attempts to justify Shylock's forced conversion are willful misreadings of the play. Recent adaptations both on stage and on film still argue against Bloom, with portrayals of Shylock as ultimately sympathetic despite his faults.

MEDIA ADAPTATIONS

The Merchant of Venice has been frequently adapted to film from the very beginning of the commercial film industry. An early example is a silent version from 1914, which has the distinction of being the first feature film directed by a woman, Lois Weber. Weber also played the role of Portia in the film. It is currently unavailable.

A famous 1974 British television version of the film, directed by John Sichel, stars the great Laurence Olivier as Shylock and Joan Plowright as Portia. The film, adapted from a 1970 British National Theatre production, gives the play a Victorian setting. It is currently unavailable.

An unusual adaptation to film is *The Maori Merchant of Venice,* (2002) directed by Don C. Selwyn. The play was translated into Maori, the native language of New Zealand, and is the first feature-length film to be made in the language. The English subtitles, translated back from Maori, appear in modern English from rather than as Shakespeare's original text. Both a DVD and video of the film are available at homepages. ihug.co.nz/~hetaonga/merchant/Product_Store/ product_store.html, the film's producers' website.

The 2004 screen adaptation features an all-star cast, including Al Pacino as Shylock, Jeremy Irons as Antonio, and Joseph Fiennes as Bassanio. Set in the sixteenth century, the film is directed by Michael Radford. It is available on DVD from Sony Pictures.

In 1999, Canadian Pierre Lasry made an hour-long documentary called *Shylock*. The film discusses the history of the character and includes footage from a variety of Shylocks who have appeared on film or stage, plus interviews with the actors who played him, theater directors, and theologians. The film is available from the National Film Board of Canada.

The play is also available in numerous audio productions. One version, available from the Pearl label, is narrated and acted by great American actor and director Orson Welles. Welles also filmed the play for television in 1969 but two of its three audio reels were stolen and never recovered, leaving the completed project unreleased.

CRITICISM

James O'Rourke

In the following excerpt, O'Rourke argues that both standard interpretations of The Merchant of Venice, *that Shakespeare either shamefully endorses or presciently critiques traditional anti-Semitism, are too simplistic when the play is considered in its historical context and from the perspective of sexual politics.*

Recent historically inflected criticism on *The Merchant of Venice* has generally accepted the premise that William Shakespeare wrote an anti-Semitic work structured on "the central dramatic conflict of Jew and Gentile, or more precisely, of Jewish fiscalism and Gentile mercantilism." Those who find the play frankly insulting to modern sensibilities have reason to be suspicious of the various, sometimes contradictory, ways in which the anti-Semitism expressed in the play has been excused or even reversed in critical commentary. The argument that *The Merchant* might have been intended as a satire on the sanctimonious avarice of the Christian characters and of their hypocrisy in projecting their own worst traits onto the scapegoated figure of the Jew has prompted an emphatic rejoinder from Alan Sinfield, who argues that there is less difference than there seems between those who idealize the play's Christian characters and those who see the play as a critique of the flaws of those characters. Sinfield contends that "even a 'sympathetic' presentation, with Shylock as victim" ends up saying that "the Christians are as bad as the Jews-who function, therefore, as an index of badness." Both an idealized reading of the play, which portrays the Venetians as exemplars of a civil generosity that reflects theological values, and the darker reading, Sinfield argues, accept "an underlying us-and-them pattern" in the play.

While historicist readings have gathered their persuasive force by placing *The Merchant* within broad historical currents, I will argue here that a close reading of the play within the micro-politics of its immediate historical moment suggests that *The Merchant* is in fact an antiracist response to the hanging of Rodrigo Lopez in 1594. The stability of the Jewish/Christian opposition in the play, which seems to be anchored by the repeated use of the word "Christian" to refer to the Venetian characters, is unsettled by the repeated juxtaposition of inconsistencies, contradictions, and hypocrisies in the Tudor stereotyping of Jews and Italians; and the very frequency with which the Venetians are called "Christians" indicates the stress borne by the word as it tries to persuade a Tudor audience to see Italian Catholics standing for the same values as English Protestants. The words "Christian" and "Christians" appear twenty-seven times in *The Merchant*, which constitutes over a third of all of their appearances in Shakespeare's works, and is over three times the count for any other individual play. This insistent repetition functions like the double crossdressing that occurs later in the play; the slippage of the signifier exposes the unstable relation between the sign and the referent. Just as double crossdressing forces a recognition of the artificiality of representing women with male actors, the repeated references to Italian Catholics as "Christians" call attention to the ambiguity of this designation for a Tudor audience.

In arguing that Shakespeare deliberately constructs a critical distance on the phenomenon of anti-Semitism, I am departing from a presumption of realist theater, the premise that the play must solicit some sort of identification from the audience, either with the Venetians as exemplary Christians or with Shylock as a victim. I will argue here that *The Merchant* deliberately frustrates any possibility of identification with its characters as it cites, rather than iterates, the stereotypical Jewish/Christian opposition. Its critical force then emerges from the production of a denaturalized perspective that makes it possible, in Bertoldt Brecht's terms, to "alienate the familiar" and make an audience "distrust what they are used to."

The Tudor audience was certainly "used to" anti-Semitism, and that prejudice is initially aroused both by Shylock's self-caricaturing statement that he will avoid the smell of pork and by his first aside to the audience, where his willingness to charge interest seems to mark an essential moral difference between Jew and Christian. But the identification of the Tudor audience with the Venetian Catholic Antonio could only be equivocal at best, especially when financial matters were involved. Not only were there no Jewish moneylenders in London in 1594, but the hated foreign usurers in London in the 1590s were mostly Italians, known popularly as "Lombards," and there was a long history of English resentment of Lombard merchants. A royal edict of 1559 that tightened the currency regulations on "merchant strangers" warned that "[t]he Italians above all other to be taken heed of, for they ... lick the fat even from our beards." From the time of the expulsion of the Jews from England in 1290, Italians served as the primary source of foreign capital, and from the fourteenth through the sixteenth centuries Italian moneylenders were subject to a series of parliamentary petitions calling for their expulsion and to xenophobic riots by the London working class. When *The Merchant* opens with three Italians discussing their concerns over their "merchandise," it presents a familiar tableau of acquisitive Lombard merchants. It was not axiomatic to an Elizabethan theater audience that Italian merchants were more economically virtuous than Jews; Robert Wilson had a good deal of success in the 1580s and 1590s with *The Three Ladies of London* (revived in 1588 and reprinted in 1592), a play that pitted a morally upright Jewish merchant against a thoroughly unscrupulous Venetian.

The proximity of Italians and Jews in the Tudor imaginary is shown in a handbill from an anti-alien riot in Southwark in 1593 that complained, "Your Machiavellian merchant spoils the state, / Your usury doth leave us all for dead / ... And like the Jews you eat us up like bread." The metaphoric equivalence of the "Machiavellian merchant" and "the Jews" might suggest that Elizabethan xenophobia did not make much of a distinction between Italian merchants and Jews were it not for the fact that the handbill appeared in the year before Lopez's trial, when there was no "Jewish question" in London. The simile of the Machiavellian merchant and the Jews describes a structural relation between the Italians widely present in London and the archetypal figure of the Jew in the Tudor imaginary, a structure that is reflected in the first confrontation between Shylock and Antonio. When Shylock easily gets the better of Antonio at every turn in their battle of wits, he gives the crowd an opportunity to see the alien usurers in their midst being beaten, at what was supposed to be their own game, by a figure who is seen as their prototype. The scene solicits a series of contradictory responses as it plays one prejudice against the other; anti-Italian xenophobia is partly disabled by the use of the word "Christian," which encourages the audience to sympathize with Antonio, but the certainty of the moral superiority of the Christian/Catholic over the Jew is eroded in the course of the scene by Shylock's scathing account of his customary treatment by Antonio, which suggests that Shylock's hatred for Antonio does not originate in his nature as a Jew but is the result of having been continually harassed by Antonio while conducting a business that is legal by the laws of both Venice and London.

Antonio's status as an exemplary Christian is further clouded by his offer to Bassanio that "my person ... lie[s] all unlocked to your occasions" (1.1.138–39). The suggestiveness of Antonio's metaphor is reinforced by English stereotypes of the sexual behavior of Italians. As Edward Coke asserted, "Bugeria is an Italian word," and according to his parliamentary history, the fourteenth-century appeal for the expulsion of "Lombard merchants" charged not only usurious business practices but also the accusation that the Lombards had "brought into the realm the shamefull sin of sodomy, that is not to be named." This accusation appears in a similar context and in a similarly euphemistic form in Thomas Wilson's *Discourse Upon Usury* in 1572, where Wilson charges Italians with a propensity "to sin horribly in suche sorte as is not to be named." This stereotype allows the Tudor audience to complete the innuendo of Solanio's teasing challenge to Antonio, "Why then you are in love" (1.1.46), when they see Antonio's response to the arrival of Bassanio, and it enables them to understand what is not quite named when Solanio says of Antonio's tears at Bassanio's

departure, "I think he only loves the world for him" (2.8.50). As Bruce Smith puts it, "In order not to say something one has to have a precise sense of what that thing is." One can avoid naming "[w]hat is not to be named" out of more or less sympathy; something can remain unspoken either because it is too horrible to be named or too inconsequential to be mentioned.

As the work of James Shapiro and Alan Bray has shown, both the presence of Jews and the practice of sodomy were open secrets in Tudor England. What was forbidden by law was routinely overlooked in day to day affairs, unless a Jew or a "sodomite" ran afoul of the law, in which case his sexuality or his Jewishness quickly became a marker of his probable guilt. Another way of describing this phenomenon would be to say that in Tudor times both homophobia and anti-Semitism were ordinarily latent presences; it took some special circumstances to make them active forces. The hanging of Lopez in 1594 was one of these circumstances, which involved the exposure of one open secret and the maintenance of another. When Lopez, a convert, protested his innocence on the scaffold and claimed that he "loved the Queen as he loved Jesus Christ," the crowd responded with derisive laughter, and the proof of his guilt was easily adduced: " 'He is a Jew,' they shouted." Even as the Elizabethan mob easily articulated the common understanding of Lopez's true religious allegiance, they overlooked a second open secret maintained by his prosecutors. Lopez's chief antagonists consisted of the homosocial network of the Earl of Essex's men, and the task of chronicling the Lopez trial for the Essex faction was undertaken by Francis Bacon, whose openly secret homosexuality was well protected by the Essex clique. At the time of the Lopez trial, Essex was attempting to secure Bacon's appointment as Attorney General, at the same time that he was pursuing a vendetta against Lopez over the resistance of William Cecil and of Elizabeth herself. But Bacon's homosexuality, and particularly his association with Antonio Ferez, were probably among the reasons for Elizabeth's resistance to his appointment.

Perez, a Spanish emigre who had been investigated by the Inquisition for sodomy in 1592 and who was particularly disliked by Elizabeth, was one of two "Antonios" in the Essex circle at the time of the Lopez prosecution, and Francis Bacon was intimately involved in the circulation of political, financial and personal favors with both of them. The other "Antonio" was Anthony Bacon, Francis's brother, who had been charged with sodomy in France in 1586, and who was by 1594 deeply in debt for money he had borrowed and passed on to Francis. When Francis Bacon lost the Attorney General's position to Coke and was widely supported by many of Essex's enemies for the Solicitorship as a compensatory gesture to Essex, Coke, who was to become a forceful polemicist against "the shamefull sin of sodomy, that is not to be named," continued to argue strongly (and successfully) to Elizabeth against Bacon's advancement. Bacon's description of Lopez in his True Report of the Detestable Treason Intended by Doctor Lopez, that he was "of nation a Portugese, and suspected to be in sect secretly a Jew, (though here he conformed himself to the rites of the Christian religion)," shadows Bacon's own maintenance of his openly secret sex life.

The outcomes allotted to Shylock and Antonio at the conclusion of *The Merchant* reflect the fates of Lopez and Bacon in 1594: the Jew's life is destroyed, and the semi-covert homosexual is excluded from the center of the social structure. The downfalls of both characters are produced by the figure of Christian feminine authority, Portia, whose success, as Jonathan Goldberg has argued, "unleashes energies that are racist and homophobic." Both Antonio and Shylock function as scapegoats to the play's comic resolution, and the asymmetrical parallel between them takes its form from the Book of Leviticus, where two goats are chosen, one to be sacrificed, the other to be sent to wander in the wilderness. Portia's question, "Which is the merchant here? and which the Jew?" (4.1.170), recreates the moment in Leviticus when the two goats are poised to discover which is to get the worse news. Through this double scapegoat structure, *The Merchant* outlines the structural similarity of the positions occupied by homosexuals and Jews in Tudor England.

Source: James O'Rourke, "Racism and Homophobia in *The Merchant of Venice*," in *ELH*, Vol. 70, No. 2, Summer 2003, pp. 375–80.

SOURCES

Bloom, Harold, Introduction, in *Shylock*, edited by Harold Bloom, Chelsea House, 1991, p. 7.

Halio, Jay L., *Understanding* The Merchant of Venice: *A Student Casebook to Issues, Sources and Historical Documents*, Greenwood Press, 2000, p. xvi.

Hansen, Carol, *Woman as Individual in English Renaissance Drama: A Defiance of the Masculine Code*, Peter Lang, 1993, pp. 165–66.

Hazlitt, William, "Characters of Shakespeare's Plays," in *Shylock*, edited by Harold Bloom, Chelsea House, 1991, p. 12.

Shakespeare, William, *The Merchant of Venice*, in Vol. 2 of *The Complete Oxford Shakespeare: Comedies*, edited by Stanley Wells and Gary Taylor, Oxford University Press, 1987, originally performed in 1596.

Sinfield, Alan, "How to Read *The Merchant of Venice* Without Being Heterosexist," in Vol. 2 of *The Alternative Shakespeare*, edited by Terence Hawkes, Routledge, 1996, p. 126.

Sinsheimer, Hermann, *Shylock: The History of a Character*, Benjamin Blom, 1963, p. 17.

Native Son

RICHARD WRIGHT

1940

Richard Wright's *Native Son*, the first bestselling novel by an African American man, broke new literary ground—although, like all groundbreaking events, it involved upheaval. First published in March 1940, this story of a young ghetto man's erupting fury sold a quarter of a million copies in its first month. Bigger Thomas's extreme violence and his aggressive reaction to a society that has him cornered were intended to alert America to the mounting rage of disenfranchised blacks. In "How Bigger was Born," Wright describes his desire to warn people that there would be dues to pay for "the moral ... horror of Negro life in the United States." In its message and subject matter, *Native Son* undeniably foreshadowed the civil rights and black liberation struggles to come.

Much of the criticism that still swirls around Wright's confrontational novel concerns its genre: *Native Son* is a hybrid of styles. Based on lived experience as well as imagination, the author combines aspects of melodrama and gothic horror with urban realism. The novel draws on diverse influences, including Dostoyevsky's *Crime and Punishment*; the novels of Americans Henry James, Sinclair Lewis, and Theodore Dreiser; the social analysis of H. L. Mencken; the economic theory of Karl Marx; and Frederick Douglass's slave narrative. Wright also emphasized the effect of cinema on his novel. There are moments that reflect anti-slavery texts, as well as expressionist scenes in which realism is set aside

> TO BIGGER AND HIS KIND WHITE PEOPLE WERE NOT REALLY PEOPLE; THEY WERE A SORT OF GREAT NATURAL FORCE, LIKE A STORMY SKY LOOMING OVERHEAD, OR LIKE A DEEP SWIRLING RIVER STRETCHING SUDDENLY AT ONE'S FEET IN THE DARK. AS LONG AS HE AND HIS BLACK FOLKS DID NOT GO BEYOND CERTAIN LIMITS, THERE WAS NO NEED TO FEAR THAT WHITE FORCE."

to bring forth Bigger's disturbing vision. These components meld to produce a new dynamic—a novel that smashes the stereotype of the passively enduring African American. For the first time, a black man's pen allowed white America to see itself as a potential target of retaliation.

Native Son was Wright's second book. The reviews of the first, *Uncle Tom's Children*, were so warm and sympathetic that in "How Bigger was Born," the author reveals that he resolved to write another book "so hard and deep" that its audience would have to face reality "without the consolation of tears." Depending on the reader, Bigger may inspire shock, apprehension, understanding, or fear, but never easy sympathy.

Native Son was the first book by an African American writer recommended by the Book-of-the-Month Club, but the organization requested significant changes to the original manuscript. The 1940 version reflects their demands; in particular, Wright changed the scene in which Bigger and Jack go the movies before their planned robbery. This edited version is what was originally published, so it is known as the "original version." In 1991, Harper Perennial published Wright's manuscript without these changes, in a version known as the "restored text." This entry follows the restored version of *Native Son*.

Although Wright's later work never achieved the acclaim of *Native Son* and his autobiography *Black Boy* (1945), he continued to publish both fiction and non-fiction until his death, and more of his writing was published posthumously. Even though generations have passed since its

publication, *Native Son* is no artifact. The ideas and attitudes it expresses are still relevant to American race relations; issues like ghettos, gangs, police bigotry, and the shame, fear, and anger of the marginalized still await resolution all over the world.

PLOT SUMMARY

Book I: Fear

Book I begins with the sound of an alarm clock in the Thomases' one-room apartment in the Chicago ghetto. The two sons, twenty-year-old Bigger and adolescent Buddy, sleep together in one bed. Vera, their sister, and Mama are separated from them by only a narrow space. Tempers are always short in this squalid place, yet they cannot afford a larger apartment unless Bigger takes a job he does not want, as a chauffeur for a rich white man. Jobs are scarce as America pulls out of the Great Depression, especially for blacks. Bigger's situation is more difficult than most, because he has a reform school record and little education. His family survives on welfare, which will be terminated unless Bigger takes the job.

Before the Thomases are even dressed they have to face the day's first challenge. An enormous black rat runs into the room from a hole in the wall. The sons shout and scramble to kill it while the women scream and try to avoid it. This despised creature, its body "puls[ing] with fear" and the life-or-death rage that fuels its struggle, is Bigger's symbolic double or *doppelganger*. He kills the rat, taunting his sister with its corpse. The women berate his manhood and destructive mentality, prophesying that he will come to harm. Little do they know that behind his curtain of tough reserve, Bigger feels shame, hopelessness, and despair at the way they live. The omniscient narrator (one that can see into the thoughts and motives of all characters), says of Bigger, "He knew that the moment he allowed what his life meant to enter fully into his consciousness, he would either kill himself or someone else."

Bigger leaves his family's kitchenette and meets up with his gang. He and his friends Gus, G. H., and Jack discuss a plan to rob Blum's Delicatessen. They have pulled off smaller robberies in the past, targeting African Americans because the police do not bother prosecuting crimes against blacks. This robbery would be

BIOGRAPHY

RICHARD WRIGHT

Richard Wright was born in 1908 in rural Mississippi. His poverty-stricken family moved to Memphis with high hopes, but his father soon abandoned them. The Wright children lived for a time in an orphanage while their mother worked odd jobs. When she suffered a major stroke, they returned to Jackson, Mississippi, to live with their maternal grandmother.

Although Wright was valedictorian of his ninth-grade class, he left high school to earn a living. He moved to Chicago in 1927, where he worked as a postal clerk until the Great Depression forced cutbacks in the mail service. He reacted to the socio-economic woes of the era by developing an interest in the Communist Party, which he joined in 1934. He moved to New York in 1937 and became the Harlem editor of the *Daily Worker*. After receiving a Guggenheim Fellowship, he completed *Uncle Tom's Children* in 1938.

Two years later, Harper and Row released the first African American protest novel, *Native Son*.

Wright left the Communist Party in 1942. The next year he wrote *Black Boy*, his early autobiography, as well as a variety of fiction and non-fiction works, including plays and poetry. He moved to Paris in 1947 with his wife and daughter, where the mixed-race family found more acceptance. There, he wrote novels that explored social problems from an existentialist perspective, abandoning the determinism found in *Native Son*. Determinism is the belief that people's acts and mental states are caused by preceding events or laws; individual choice has little effect on a person's life. Existentialism, on the other hand, maintains that each individual makes choices, and thus is responsible for his or her actions, even without knowing right from wrong. Wright died on November 28, 1960.

---

different, though, because Blum is white. Although Bigger is desperate to find some money, he is afraid to commit a crime against a white man. He convinces his partners to let him bring his gun, and they agree to get together to rob the shop later that afternoon.

Jack and Bigger go to see a movie to distract themselves while they wait. Before the movie begins, they make a game of masturbating in the theater. A newsreel shows a beautiful young woman playing on the beach in Florida. When Jack says he would like to be there, Bigger tells him if he went somewhere like that, he would be "hanging from a tree like a bunch of bananas." Bigger recognizes girl in newsreel as Mary Dalton, the daughter of his future employer. Jack tells Bigger that "them rich white women'll go to bed with anybody.... They even have their chauffeurs." The newsreel mentions Mary's Communist friend, and Jack and Bigger discuss their idea of Communism. Bigger considers the exotic possibilities of his new job, thinking that if everything he has heard about white people is true, he will get to "see a lot of things from the inside; he'd get the dope, the low-down."

The feature film *Trader Horn* depicts "primitive" Africans dancing. Bigger has a hard time focusing on this film, although the Africans seem "secure from fear and hysteria" in their homeland. Bigger is lost in thoughts of white society and privilege. He rethinks his upcoming job interview in terms of what he has just seen in the newsreel. He enjoys fantasizing about wealthy Mary Dalton, wondering if she might be the kind of girl to give him money, or at least make him her confidant.

Although Bigger does not want to rob Blum's store because it might hurt his chances at his new job, it is too late to back down. He rushes home to get his gun and preserve his tough-guy image. Jack, Bigger, and G. H. meet at the hall earlier than agreed. When Gus shows up late, a tense and anxious Bigger beats him up, then draws his knife and makes Gus lick the blade. When the proprietor kicks them out, Bigger slashes the pool table with his knife. This quells his fear: after taking violent action, Bigger feels equal to those around him—at least for a time. He insists it is too late for the robbery, even though he realizes they still have plenty of

Richard Wright Archive Photos, Inc. / Getty Images

time. He goes home until it is time for his job interview.

Later, he heads to the Daltons' and feels self conscious just walking in the rich, white neighborhood. The Daltons are slumlords who think of themselves as philanthropists. While he is speaking to Mr. Dalton, Mrs. Dalton appears, followed by her large, white housecat; she does not acknowledge him. Her pallid skin, snow white hair, and faded eyes make her seem "like a ghost." Mr. Dalton tells him that she is blind and that "she has a very deep interest in colored people." Mary Dalton, the girl from the newsreel, comes in during the interview and baffles Bigger by asking him questions about unions and capitalism. He worries that she will ruin his chances to get the job. Bigger limits his remarks primarily to "Yessuh" and "Nawsuh," while trying to hide his confusion and fear. Mr. Dalton decides to hire him because, as he explains, he supports the NAACP (National Association for the Advancement of Colored People).

Peggy, the Daltons' maid, shows Bigger how to feed the furnace in the cellar—one of his reponsibilities—and then shows him the room where he will sleep. He lies on the soft bed in

the large room he will have to himself and thinks about how good things could be there. His only concern is that Mary will get him into trouble, with her political talk and overly familiar manner. When he gets thirsty, he goes to the kitchen where he finds Mrs. Dalton and her cat. Mrs. Dalton wants to know about his hopes to better himself through education, but Bigger has no such plans.

Bigger thinks he is supposed to drive Mary to the university that evening; he is surprised when it turns out that she wants to meet a friend. Bigger wonders to himself if her friend is a Communist, and is wary. They pick up Mary's boyfriend, Jan, whom Bigger recognizes as her "communist friend" from the newsreel. He makes Bigger uncomfortable by shaking his hand and insisting that Bigger not call him "sir," and deciding that he will drive. Bigger feels that Jan and Mary are far too chummy with him. They say he is their equal and they want to be friends, but Bigger feels threatened and confused. He wishes they would leave him alone and let him follow the accepted rules about how blacks and whites should interact. He wonders if they are making fun of him. They ask Bigger to recommend a restaurant on the South Side, then insist that Bigger eat and drink with them. He does not know how to behave when he sees friends inside. Jan buys them a fifth of rum, which helps Bigger relax. He is finally able to look them in the eye as he answers their questions about his background. Mary mentions that she is traveling to Detroit in the morning and tells Bigger to take her trunk to the station before she leaves.

After they leave the restaurant, Bigger drives Jan and Mary around the park while the three continue to drink in the car. He notices the pair's amorous activities in the back seat and becomes aroused himself. After dropping Jan off, Mary joins Bigger in the front seat and they continue drinking as they drive back to the Dalton place. Bigger has to help Mary into the house because she is too drunk to stand. He worries that he will lose his job if he is caught and is angry at Mary for creating the situation. He carries her into her room, and as she clings to him, he becomes aroused by the smell of her hair and feel of her body. He kisses her, and the inebriated girl moves toward him. He lays her on her bed and is kissing her when the door opens, revealing "silent, ghostlike," blind Mrs. Dalton. She calls to her daughter, who mumbles in response. Bigger is terrified of being found in the girl's room. Mrs. Dalton calls to Mary several more times, and Bigger covers Mary's mouth with her pillow to keep her silent. The drunken girl struggles hard, and he pushes until she stops. He eases off the bed and into a corner, watching while the mother approaches her daughter, smells alcohol, assumes Mary has passed out, and kneels to pray before she leaves the room.

Bigger panics when he discovers that Mary is dead. He starts planning a story that will direct suspicion toward Jan while he decides what to do with the body. He stuffs her body inside her trunk and carries it downstairs. He hopes her parents will assume she has gone to Detroit. Down in the cellar, Bigger decides to burn the body in the furnace. He shoves her in feet first, and winds up having to cut her head off to make the body fit. He notices Mrs. Dalton's cat watching him and considers killing it, but does not. After dumping more coal on the fire, Bigger tidies the cellar, turns on the exhaust fan to blow out the smell, and leaves the house. He steals Mary's purse from the car outside and finds it full of cash. He returns home and quickly falls asleep.

Book II: Flight

Though he is even more tense than usual, Bigger tries to act normal with his family on Sunday morning. He answers their questions about his new job, but he is quick to anger. Reflecting on the events of the night before, he thinks of a few ways to improve the cover-up and starts to feel less worried about committing the crime. As he leaves for work, Buddy runs after him to ask if anything is wrong and to give him the wad of money he had dropped—the money from Mary's purse. He gives Buddy some money and swears him to secrecy. He runs into his three friends at the corner drugstore. His mood lifts when he buys each of them a pack of cigarettes and a beer, and giving each one a dollar as well. He tells them he got the job and that he likes it "swell."

He leaves his friends and heads to the Daltons' on the streetcar. He thinks more about Mary's death and decides that she deserved it because of "the fear and shame she had made him feel." He is excited and empowered by his newfound philosophy, a commitment to "act like other people thought you ought to

act, yet do what you wanted." He wishes that black people could find a strong leader, one who could inspire them to act together and "end fear and shame."

At the Daltons' house, Bigger continues his cover-up. He burns a bloody scrap of paper he had overlooked the night before and leaves out some Communist pamphlets Jan had given him. He mentions to Peggy that Mary had a gentleman friend over the night before. Then he waits in the car as if he expects Mary to emerge. When she does not come down, Peggy suggests that she might have already gone to the station and that Bigger should take her trunk to the train. When he returns to the house, he listens as Mrs. Dalton and Peggy share details about the previous night and that morning, and realize that Mary's absence is strange. Mrs. Dalton asks Bigger about the last time he saw Mary, and he again mentions that Mary had a gentleman friend with her. She gives Bigger the day off, and he decides to visit his girlfriend Bessie to relax and forget. The idea that he should have planned the murder and been able to get more money from it nags him. When Bessie mentions a famous kidnapping case, he decides to ask for Bessie's help arranging a ransom scam to get money from Mary's family.

They go out for a drink and Bigger outlines his plan, but Bessie wonders why Bigger is not worried that Mary will turn up. He tells her Mary eloped with a Communist, but Bessie probes, asking "you ain't done nothing to that girl, is you?" Bigger denies that he has hurt Mary and insists no one will suspect a black man of being smart enough to mastermind a kidnapping. He leaves Bessie with the money and returns to the Daltons', feeling that at last "he had his destiny in his grasp."

Back at the mansion, Mr. Dalton has hired a private detective. This man, Britten, suspects Bigger because he is black. Bigger acts intimidated, subservient, and befuddled. He sees their fear for Mary and is pleased to have made these white people feel afraid and insecure, just as he has always felt with them. As Bigger reveals the tale of an inebriated Mary and her Communist boyfriend slumming on the South Side, Britten shifts his suspicions to Jan, who is brought to the house to be questioned. Accused of being the last person to see Mary, at first Jan says he did not see her, then starts supporting Bigger's story that he came home with Mary. But soon he tells the truth, that he took the streetcar, leaving Bigger to drive Mary home. He wonders why Bigger is lying, but Bigger will not change his story, and Britten and the distraught Mr. Dalton believe him. Jan waits outside for Bigger, and when he tries to talk to him, Bigger, in a frenzy, draws his gun. Jan assumes that the powerful people have manipulated Bigger and offers to help him, but Bigger shouts at him and runs away.

Bigger buys an envelope, paper and a pencil to write the ransom note, still debating about whether to send it. He is more interested in "cower[ing] Jan and Britten into awe, into fear of him" than in getting away with the crime. He suddenly realizes that Mr. Dalton owns the company from which Bigger and his family rent their small, rat-infested room—the millionaire philanthropist is responsible for the squalid living conditions that poor blacks face all over his neighborhood. He decides: "Yes; he would send the kidnap note. He would jar them out of their senses."

Bigger goes back to Bessie's because they will have to act fast to get the ransom. He writes a note demanding ten thousand dollars and signs it "Red." Bessie no longer wants to be part of the scheme and asks him directly whether he killed Mary. He denies it at first, but then admits it. He tries to coerce Bessie into going along with the plan, saying that she is already an accomplice because she received the money he stole. Then he flatly threatens to kill her, too, if she betrays him now. He walks Bessie through what he wants her to do the following night to collect the ransom.

Bigger returns to the Daltons' house and slips the ransom note under the front door. After Mr. Dalton reads that his daughter has been kidnapped by "Red," Britten has Jan picked up by the police. He also interrogates Bigger down in the cellar. Bigger worries that Mary's bones will block the ash pan in the furnace, so he keeps pouring more coal on the fire. Reporters show up, and Mr. Dalton tells them about the note. Jan turns out to have a solid alibi and can prove he did not come home with Mary. Bigger is ordered to shake down the ashes in the cooling furnace, but when he adds more coal, leery of sifting the pan in front of the reporters, the room fills with smoke. A journalist grabs the shovel from the corner; he rakes and scrapes the ashes, revealing bone shards and an earring. In the excitement, Bigger escapes unnoticed.

Bigger rushes over to Bessie's to stop her from going to pick up the ransom. He tells her everything about how he killed Mary and burned her body. Bessie thinks he will be accused of raping her, as well. Bessie is upset about being involved with this crime, but Bigger forces her to hide with him in a deserted building. He rapes her there, and because she knows too much to be left behind, he kills her. He throws her body down an air shaft to hide it, afterward realizing that his getaway money was in the pocket of her dress. With seven cents left, he flees to another building at dawn. He reads newspaper reports about the police systematically searching the black neighborhood for him; racial tensions have flared because of the manhunt. He also reads that the police suspect a sex crime; they still suspect Jan was involved, because "the plan of the murder and kidnapping was too elaborate to be the work of a Negro mind." Bigger is proud to have fooled the whites all by himself.

He wanders through the night looking for a place to hide. He buys a loaf of bread and breaks into a vacant apartment. He hears two men discussing whether the black community should hide the murderer or turn him in. He eats his bread and sleeps. When he goes out for the next day's newspaper and a new place to hide, he learns that the white force hunting the "Negro rapist and killer" is closing in on his block. Bigger tries to escape over the frozen ghetto rooftops, but he is cornered and the police drench him with a fire hose. Freezing and exhausted, he is dragged down four flights of stairs to the sea of white faces waiting below.

Book III: Fate

In jail, Bigger initially refuses to speak or accept food and water, and he faints at the inquest. He reads about himself in the newspaper, which likens him to an uncivilized beast, a "missing link in the human species." A local police captain says that death is the only solution for a problem like Bigger, while a southern newspaper editor wires to add, "We have found that the injection of an element of constant fear has aided us greatly in handling the problem [of Negro restlessness]." His mother's minister appears, then Jan, who forgives him and introduces a communist lawyer, Max, who will defend him for free. Bigger's mother, his siblings, his friends, the Daltons, and the prosecutor Buckley all come with their own beliefs and agendas. Buckley is the last to leave after interrogating Bigger, trying to trick him into admitting to murders of white women that he did not commit. Bigger confesses to killing Mary and Bessie.

Testimony before the grand jury highlights Mr. Dalton's institutionalized racism; it also raises doubts about Jan's motives for associating with black people and presents Bessie's corpse as evidence that Bigger is a monster. He is indicted for Mary's rape and murder. As he leaves the building for jail, the mob outside screams for his death. Police officers take him to the Dalton mansion and up to Mary's room, where they try to make him act out the rape and murder. Bigger refuses. He sees a Ku Klux Klan cross burning on a roof across the street. He feels that Jesus' love and the hope of salvation have been lost to him. At the jail, he throws away the cross that a minister had given him to comfort him.

Max interviews Bigger before preparing his defense. Max's questions focus mostly on the young man's feelings, and Bigger finds himself opening up and trying to express himself in ways that are new to him. His feelings reflect the fear and hopelessness of his life as an African American. He feels sorry for Max because people will hate him for trying to help a black killer. Max says, "The fear of hate keeps many whites from trying to help you and your kind." The conversation with Max inspires Bigger: he wants to be involved with the world, and to live, now, so he will have time to understand what his life means.

Bigger pleads guilty to the crime but Max tries to save his life in the sentencing phase of the trial by offering evidence of mitigating circumstances. Both the prosecution and defense present their ideas about oppressed blacks and white defenders of the status quo. Max argues that Bigger is a victim of lifelong oppression, so society should accept responsibility for its role in making him a murderer. Despite Max's heroic effort to save him, Bigger is sentenced to death. Max tries to get a pardon from the governor, but fails. He says goodbye to Bigger and encourages him to believe in himself. Bigger says he knows that he killed for something and feels good about that—until he killed, he never felt alive. He is trying to console Max but understands that his explanation is terrifying him. In the end, he can only assure Max that he is all right. Max leaves him to his fate without looking at him again.

THEMES

Ethnicity and Social Stigma

Freed slaves and their descendants encountered racism of an astounding depth and breadth in the late 1800s and early 1900s. African Americans were said to be sub-human, or at the very least different and less developed than whites. Many ethnic minorities endured similar prejudice, but African Americans were said to be particularly "savage" and "primitive" in their instincts. In *Native Son*, Buckley, the prosecuting attorney, describes Bigger as a "mad black dog," "a subhuman killer," and an "infernal monster." He labels the young man "a piece of human scum" and "a maddened ape." Buckley argues that any white American male should relish the "opportunity to crush with his heel the woolly head of this black lizard." Racist whites used this sort of defective reasoning to justify discrimination in both public and private interactions with African Americans. Wright said that he was strongly influenced by media coverage of the Robert Nixon murder case. In 1938, Nixon, a black Chicago man, murdered a white woman with a brick during the course of a robbery. The Chicago papers described him as a brute and an animal, going on to point out that a rabid wild animal is usually exterminated.

In *Native Son*, Wright portrays the way African Americans were affected by accepting and internalizing this negative characterization. When Bigger complains to his friends about how society limits blacks, Gus says, "Aw, nigger, quit thinking about it. You'll go nuts." They accept that their skin color automatically disqualifies them from flying airplanes or living in nice houses. Still, Bigger hopes for something more. Later, when he works as Mary's chauffeur, it might seem that some of Bigger's wishes are going to come true: as he drives Mary and Jan around the city in a luxury car, they insist he is their equal and express admiration for ghetto people, whom they romanticize. But instead of feeling warmed by their overtures, Bigger feels suspicious and angry:

> He was very conscious of his black skin. . . . Did not white people despise a black skin?. . . he was something he hated, the badge of shame which he knew was attached to a black skin.

When the barriers of race and prejudice are pushed away from Bigger, a violent explosion ensues. Wright states in "How Bigger was Born" that Bigger "is a product of a dislocated society," and that his response is a protest against a dehumanized life, which has driven him over the edge.

Gender and Sexuality

The gender expectations imposed on black ghetto men is one of the burdens that Bigger shoulders every day. As the oldest male in his family, Bigger is expected to help his family out of poverty without breaking the law. After a rat wakes the family, Bigger's mother declares, "We wouldn't have to live in this garbage dump if you had any manhood in you." Later she cries, "Bigger, honest, you the most no-countest man I ever seen in all my life!" Bigger, barely past his teens, replies, "You done told me that a thousand times." In the ghetto, a "real" man must save his family from financial disaster, even though he is at the bottom of the employment ladder. He must also command respect from his peers on the street. He laughs off broken dreams and social obstacles; "real" men are not allowed to be scared, so he carries weapons, which he uses to maintain dominance. These expectations weigh heavily on twenty-year-old Bigger.

Social pressure also shapes Bigger's sexuality. He is expected to have a girlfriend and be sexually active, even if the relationship is not sincere or lasting. Bessie lets him have sex with her because he brings her money, or things that money can buy, like the oblivion of alcohol. This trade-off is the best thing he experiences with her, because men are not encouraged to feel tenderness or express affection—sex is the only venue for closeness with a woman. In addition to the physical pleasure it provides, sex helps diminish the tensions of walking the world as a black man: something "laid a quiet finger of peace upon the restless tossing of his spirit" after sex. Even after Bigger knows he will murder Bessie, he forces her into one final sexual act, trying to relieve his overpowering sense of hunger and tension.

Racist whites stereotype African American males as hypersexual and uncontrollably attracted to white females, and rape plays an important role in the white mob hysteria that develops in Wright's novel. The newspapers convict Bigger of raping and murdering Mary Dalton long before he is tried. Described as a "Negro sex-slayer," they suggest he killed her in "a brain-numbing sex passion." A Southern newspaper editor advises that in the future, Northerners should follow Southerners' example and keep "Negroes firmly in their places and ... make them know if they so much as touch a white woman, good or bad, they cannot live." Bigger is condemned to death, punished for Mary's murder, but just as much for a rape that exists only in the public's racist imagination. Wright's story also shows how racism affects views of female sexuality. Bigger rapes Bessie, but this rape does not merit punishment; on the other hand, the mere *suspicion* that he might have raped Mary inspires lynch mobs and a cross burning, because she was white. The myth of white women's purity supports white men's violent, racist acts, while black women's suffering is dismissed.

HISTORICAL OVERVIEW

Post–Civil War America

The Civil War ended in 1865; in March of that year, all of the remaining slaves in the United States were freed. The Confederate states were readmitted to the Union only after accepting the Fourteenth and Fifteenth Amendments to the U.S. Constitution. The Fourteenth Amendment guaranteed African Americans the same rights as whites, and the Fifteenth Amendment granted them the right to vote. Black voters outnumbered whites in many parts of the South, and whites were frightened they would lose political control of those areas. For a time, the U.S. Army occupied the defeated South during Reconstruction to ensure that blacks could vote. When Reconstruction ended and federal troops withdrew, however, African Americans and their rights were at the mercy of local governments, which were often virulently racist.

Freed slaves faced poverty and a terrifying general hostility, leading many to feel that slavery was better than freedom. Belinda Hurmence's book *Before Freedom: 48 Oral Histories of Former North and South Carolina Slaves* includes testimony from Patsy Mitchener, who was a nineteen-year-old slave in 1865. She describes slavery and freedom as poisonous snakes. "The snake called slavery," Mitchener said, "lay with his head pointed south, and the snake called freedom lay with his head pointed north. Both bit the nigger and they was both bad." Hurmence explains that the post-war South was concerned with its own grievous war wounds, not with the survival of ex-slaves. Though the North was opposed to slavery and somewhat less racist, it struggled "to cope with four million needy new citizens clamoring for jobs, education, some land of their own." In both the North and the South, Hurmence writes, whites responded with "righteous indignation: the slaves had been set free; why weren't they properly appreciative? ... If they wouldn't put their past behind them, they ought at least, for history's sake, to keep quiet about it."

Southern Response to Black Emancipation

Every state had to respect the federal Constitution, which guaranteed equal voting rights to all men. But in 1890, after Reconstruction had ended, Mississippi held a convention to rewrite its state laws, with the goal of excluding black citizens through voter restrictions. A poll tax was levied: a black man who wanted to vote was required to pay a special tax for two years before he could register. If he found money to pay this tax, he next faced a literacy test. This test excluded the sixty percent of black men who were illiterate because, as slaves, they had not been permitted to read or write. The white county voting clerk required literate blacks to read and interpret a difficult passage from the state constitution. Usually they failed, but if they passed, the famous "grandfather clause" restricted voter eligibility to those whose grandfathers could vote before the Civil War. Data released by the Constitutional Rights Foundation shows that racist policies like these caused the percentage of black voters in Mississippi to drop to less than six percent in 1892, down from over ninety percent during Reconstruction.

Other Southern states saw how Mississippi's racist policies affected blacks and quickly enacted their own laws, called Black Codes. Jim Crow laws were another popular strategy for oppressing blacks, stemming from the Supreme Court's "separate but equal" decision in *Plessy v. Ferguson* (1896). These laws denied African Americans access to white housing, schools, hospitals, restaurants, and even drinking fountains and toilets.

The Northern Response to Emancipation

The South was primarily a failed agrarian economy by the end of the Civil War, while the North had been successfully industrialized. Fleeing white violence and dreaming of prosperity, millions of African Americans fled north to the great ports, steel mills, and slaughterhouses. The North also received waves of immigrants from Western Europe, Mexico, and Asia. However, the urban, industrialized North was not free of racism and offered its own kinds of prejudice and oppression.

Prejudice forced blacks into slums, where they struggled to survive. Slum landlords exploited segregated housing policies, providing non-whites with substandard shelter at exorbitant rents. These ghettoes were frequently attacked by inner-city gangs (often Irish or Jewish), waging street battles that furthered the aims of white politicians and mobsters. The Chicago race riots of 1919 were touched off by a gang attack. On July 30, over two hundred members of the Ragen's Colts gang attacked nine houses along the west border of the ghetto with bricks, stones, and guns, driving black residents out. Thirty-eight African Americans were killed, over five hundred were injured, and a thousand were left homeless—but not one of the gang members was prosecuted. In large Northern cities, there were also "voting gangs," white gangs that tried to scare African Americans away from the polls. In the first half of the twentieth century, the North was scarcely more hospitable to black Americans than the South.

The Communist Party and the Black Community

The Communist Party of the United States of America (CPUSA) made a policy of defending the black working class in the early and mid-1900s. It rallied against Jim Crow laws, integrating its own social events and expelling members for "white chauvinism." The CPUSA organized black miners, steel and smelter workers, and the huge force of Chicago meatpackers. It also sought to help blacks unionize for equal pay, which led to "hate strikes" and race riots by white workers. The party worked to help blacks gain admission to industries that had excluded them, such as transport, and to integrate professional sports like baseball. Emerging communities of urban African Americans responded with hope and trust, and many illustrious blacks became involved with the CPUSA, including Ralph Ellison, Langston Hughes, Paul Robeson, and Richard Wright.

The Communist Party, and later the National Association for the Advancement of Colored People (NAACP), directed public attention to the false rape charges that were frequently pressed against black men. The claim that a black man had raped a white woman often resulted in white mob executions called lynchings. (According to R. L. Zangrando's "About Lynching," the 3,330 recorded lynchings of blacks in post–Civil War America is only the tip of the iceberg.) The "Scottsboro Boys" case is one famous example of this rape hysteria. In March 1931, nine black teenagers were accused of raping two white women in Alabama. A group of white men and black youths had fought while they were riding as hoboes on a freight train, and the white men had been forced from the train. When the train stopped in Paint Rock, Alabama, the black teenagers were arrested. Two white women found hiding on the train claimed the boys had raped them. Within ten days, local white jurors convicted all nine and sentenced all but one of them to die.

The International Labor Defense (a communist legal organization) and the NAACP worked to defend the innocent Scottsboro boys and prevented their executions. During the six years of trials surrounding the Scottsboro case, a rift developed between the CPUSA and the NAACP. Many African Americans began to separate from the party, defining their problems as matters of race and prejudice, not class.

CRITICAL OVERVIEW

Native Son was published in 1940 by Harper and Brothers. Before publishing the book, Harper and Brothers sent bound copies of the manuscript's proof pages to the Book-of-the-Month Club, which was interested in the novel as an upcoming selection. In "Notes on the Text" in the Harper Perennial edition of the novel, Arnold Rampersad records that Wright's editor told him that the Book Club's was particularly concerned about the masturbation scene in the movie theater, writing, "I think you will ... understand why the Book Club finds it objectionable. They are not a particularly squeamish crowd, but that scene, after all, is a bit on the raw side." Wright agreed to alter the section, omitting the masturbation scene and substituting a fictional movie (*The Gay Woman*) for what had been a newsreel about Mary Dalton. This altered version, known as the "original text," was published in March 1940 and the Book Club chose it as one of its selections that year.

The first piece of criticism on *Native Son* came from Wright himself, in an essay entitled "How Bigger Was Born." This essay was originally published separately, but is included in many later editions of the book. In it, Wright explains that a proper portrayal of Bigger Thomas's disturbed awareness required him to avoid the inner workings of his other characters: "[F]rom the start to the finish, it was Bigger's story, Bigger's fear, Bigger's flight, and Bigger's fate that I tried to depict." Wright is most interested in what he calls Bigger's "character-destiny"; as the archetypal black youth of the ghetto, Bigger's "social, political, and personal [experiences]" are the foundation and reality of Wright's story.

Native Son was published in a climate of racial tension stoked by the Great Depression. Many whites (especially those in Southern states) took the novel as evidence that black people hated whites and were awaiting their chance to be violent. The novel also fueled the racist delusions of extremist organizations such as the Ku Klux Klan. Nonetheless, the book was an instant success. It sold a quarter of a million copies in its first month. The 1930s produced the most vicious racism the country had seen since the Civil War; in "How Bigger Was Born," Wright challenges black and white readers to become aware of "Bigger's relationship with white America, both North and South, ... a relationship whose effects are carried by every Negro, like scars, somewhere in his body and mind."

A flood of critical interest made *Native Son* the first bestseller by an American black man. Charles Poore reviewed it in the *New York Times* on the day it was published, calling the book "enormously stirring." Poore agreed with critic Henry Seidel Canby's judgment that *Native Son* was the best novel that had been written by a black American. Great writers of the day—including Zora Neale Hurston, Sinclair Lewis, and James Farrell—weighed in on it, as did groups like the Communist Party and the NAACP. More than twenty years after Wright's book was published, critic Irving Howe's "Black Boys and Native Sons" validates the initial response to the work:

> The day *Native Son* appeared, American culture was changed forever. No matter how much qualifying the book might later need, it made impossible a repetition of the old lies.... Richard Wright's novel brought into the open,

as no one ever had before, the hatred, fear, and
violence that have crippled and may yet destroy
our culture.

Many passionate critical debates center on
Native Son. One recurring argument focuses on
the women in Wright's novel. Bessie, Mama,
Mrs. Dalton, and Mary Dalton are not especially admirable characters; among their faults
are passivity, impotence, "blindness," thrill-
seeking, and shallowness. Some critics believe
that Wright was guilty of misogyny (the hatred
of women). Others argue that these figures accurately portray the narrow lives and cultural
norms available to women, both white and
black, in male-dominated, 1930s America.

In 1949, author James Baldwin started a
discussion that continues today. Baldwin suggests that Bigger is isolated from the black community. African American scholar Cornel West
agrees in his essay "Philosophy and the Afro-
American Experience": "Wright tried to create
an Afro-American self-image that rests solely on
personal revolt," rather than an identity that
"presupposes a community, a set of common
values and goals, at which a marginal man like
Wright can only sneer." Scholar Aime J. Ellis
rejects this interpretation in his recent essay
"Where is Bigger's Humanity? Black Male
Community in Richard Wright's Native Son":

> However unsavory Bigger's male world might
> have appeared ... [his] deeply emotional con-
> versations with his homeboys constitute a site
> of black male community that allows them to
> purge the psychic pain of urban blight as well as
> to create an intimate space for sharing their
> dreams, aspirations, and joys.

The principal debate, still hotly contested, is
illustrated in a longstanding critical duel
between eminent black author Ralph Ellison
and Irving Howe, Jewish American critic and
founder of the journal *Dissent*. Howe and
Ellison clashed in four essays published in that
journal. In "Black Boys and Native Sons," Howe
insists that Wright created Bigger Thomas to
illustrate the prototypical African American
"experience of a man with a black skin....
How could a Negro put pen to paper, how
could he so much as think or breathe, without
some impulsion to protest?" Ellison argues that
protest fiction robbed blacks of both diversity
and potential, by locking them into roles built
around rage and violence. Baldwin and Ellison
defend the perspective of the black intellectual,

MEDIA ADAPTATIONS

In collaboration with Paul Green, Richard
Wright wrote a version of *Native Son* for the
stage, entitled *Native Son (The Biography of a
Young American): A Play in Ten Scenes*. It was
performed in 1941 at the St. James Theatre
in New York City. The script is published by
Harper.

The first film version of *Native Son* was
written by Richard Wright and starred Wright
as Bigger Thomas. Released by Classic Films in
1951, the film was directed by Pierre Chenal. It is
currently unavailable.

The most recent film version of *Native Son*
appeared in 1986. Released by Cinecom Pictures
and American Playhouse (PBS), it was directed
by Jerrold Freedman and starred Vincent Love,
Oprah Winfrey, Matt Dillon, and Carroll Baker.
Critics were disappointed in this film because
it omitted elements crucial to the book's plot
(such as Bessie's murder) and became a more
mundane tale of a boy-gone-wrong, rather than
the story of a boy tormented by complex race
relationships.

James Earl Jones reads *Native Son* on an
abridged audiocassette edition released by Caedmon in June 1998. Jones's rendition is praised,
though the work has been significantly cut to fit
a one-cassette format.

rather than that of Bigger Thomas, whose intellect was undeveloped and largely untapped.

In the twenty-first century, notable scholars
such as Henry Louis Gates Jr., Houston Baker
Jr., and Harold Bloom have offered further
insight into *Native Son*. Regardless of critical
opinions, Wright seems to have achieved his
goal of informing the world that poor, black
males are not passive, patient, or pardoning.
The Modern Library recently named *Native
Son* as one of the one hundred most important
books of the twentieth century.

CRITICISM

James Smethurst

In the following excerpt, Smethurst traces a strong thread of gothic horror throughout Native Son *and African American experience in general. However, he points out that this novel, after following the main features of a gothic tale, moves beyond endless terror to become "anti-gothic," the forerunner of a new kind of African American literature.*

Native Son intimates that the Daltons of the world will continue to encounter the Biggers. And neither will be able to understand the other because the rules which guide their world are hidden in a web of gothic figuration. In fact, that both the Biggers and the Daltons perceive each of their worlds as largely disjunct from that of the other is actually another form of mystification which will hinder them from objectively apprehending the nature of their social order.

The fundamental reason that none of the characters that we see in the first two sections of the novel understands the underlying rules of society is that they are caught up in various narratives the function of which is to perpetuate the power relations of American society and, again, to mystify the true nature of those relations. Some of these narratives are basically ghosts of a past era of American society. These narratives are not simply accounts of the past which make sense of the present and offer a guide to conduct—this is implicitly or explicitly true of all the narratives in the text—but are holdovers from the past. This category of ghosts would include both Mrs. Thomas's stoic and accommodationist Christianity, which has its ultimate origin in the slave South, as well as the older Daltons' paternalistic narrative of philanthropy. Both of these older narratives no longer have the desired impact on a new generation of uprooted and marginalized young people represented by Bigger and his gang: They have no desire to defer desire until the next world or go to night school in order to become better educated servants. Of course, the Daltons have an interest in not demystifying these narratives despite the death of their daughter.

Wright sees virtually all black literature before *Native Son* as essentially part of these mirroring narratives of stoic deference and paternalism. It is also interesting, though disturbing, to see how Wright, like Claude McKay

in the novels *Home to Harlem* (1928) and *Banjo* (1929), assigns gender to these narratives so that the conservatism of the black folk culture and its accommodation to white paternalism are seen as feminine, as opposed to an implicit masculine narrative of rebellion and liberation. Even in the case of the equally uprooted and marginalized Bessie, her response to her confinement in the face of extravagant mass culture narratives of desire is basically passive, whereas Bigger's is active. It is also notable that Bigger's greatest sense of validation comes from acts of extreme misogyny which are not fully repudiated by the novel.

Bigger and his gang are alienated from the folk culture that his mother represents, from the black politicians of the South Side who hold their positions through accommodation with the white power structure, and from the white power structure itself, whether in its more blatantly corrupt and hostile form, as represented by State's Attorney Buckley, or in the more apparently benign and unconscious form represented by the Daltons. Bigger and his peers are caught in narratives of mass culture and the hungers and fears inculcated by those narratives which glamorize the lifestyles of the rich and famous while demonizing the poor, particularly African Americans, and the politically radical, especially the Communists. For example, the first of the two movies that Bigger and Jack see, *The Gay Woman*, titillates with the possibility of a chaotic modern world of unlimited gratification, represented as threatening in the figure of a Communist assassin, which ultimately is repelled with a return to a mythic past of "family values." The second movie, *Trader Horn*, is an equally eroticized narrative of a mythic Africa in which Africans, and by extension African Americans, are shown to be "savage" and therefore terrifying as well as "natural" and therefore desirable. In both cases, what is seen is ultimately a justification of the present social order through narratives of the past which are literally projections of the present. The problem for society is that the desire that these mass culture products incite to attract consumers is not so easily sated or repressed.

Practically all Bigger's knowledge of the world, particularly outside the ghetto, and of how to conduct oneself in that world whether as a lover or as the writer of a ransom note, comes from mass culture—tabloids, news-reels, movies, detective stories, and so on. Like Emma Bovary, and in a less tragic manner Catherine Morland in Jane Austen's *Northanger Abbey*, Bigger is the victim of these mass culture narratives. As models of how to act, they cannot help but lead him to disaster.

And as models of normative desire, desire that he can never satisfy, they are equally disastrous. Of course, African Americans are not the only ones caught in such narratives. The posse of the 8,000 racist white police and the racist mob screaming for Bigger's blood outside the courthouse in the third section are clearly inflamed by a narrative of black bestiality retailed by the popular press. Ironically, this mob is comprised largely of people who might be categorized as white Biggers, other uprooted and marginalized people whom—along with marginalized blacks such as Bigger—Wright sees as the potential basis for a mass fascist movement in America.

One could argue that what makes Bigger's existence truly gothic is the wild terror and the extravagant desire that are produced when these narratives of mass culture act on an individual for whom the normative markers of identity—markers of class, race, gender, sexuality—have broken down and who is confined within the rigid and narrow limits of the ghetto. It is this intersection of fear, desire, and confinement that produces the doubling, the projection, the transference, the transgressive sexuality—which includes rape—both real and imagined, followed by murder, real and imagined miscegenation, symbolic homosexual coupling and the possibility of incest, the anxiety about who one is and how one should act, the apprehension and misapprehension of possible meanings, and the sense of an inescapable past which is also the future so common to the gothic genre.

Perhaps the most telling moment of *Native Son* is the book's opening. First, an alarm clock goes off. The clock ostensibly is a reminder of linear time. But in fact the alarm clock is a symbolical of cyclical time marking the beginning of a day, a journey that will be almost exactly like yesterday and tomorrow. Immediately after the bell goes off, we are introduced to themes of confinement and transgressive sexuality. Then a black rat appears, both terrified and terrifying. In the first moment of doubling in the text, Bigger kills his rat double, who attacks Bigger in a fit of terror, hunger, and defiance. Bigger goes on to terrify his sister with the dead rat, enjoying her

fear. Bigger's mother prophesies a tragic end for him. End of story. But not really. There will be more rats. The slum buildings of the ghetto produce an endless stream of hungry and fearful rats.

Native Son, then, would seem to be a gothic text in which history is destined to repeat itself as both tragedy and farce. In fact, if the book ended with Bigger's capture and the signing of the confession the State's Attorney gives him, then it would be a sort of gothic. Why is it an antigothic? Bigger, primarily through his interaction with the Communist lawyer Boris Max and the particular Marxist-Leninist ideology that Max embodies, attains a genuine self-consciousness or at least recognizes his ability to attain some sort of true self-consciousness, even if his execution will cut the process short. Of course, it is important to note that it is not merely Max's ideas that begin to move Bigger in a new direction away from the gothic, but also Max's willingness to act on those ideas:

> Bigger was not at that moment really bothered about whether Max's speech had saved his life or not. He was hugging the proud thought that Max had made the speech for him, to save his life. It was not the meaning of the speech that gave him pride, but the mere act of it. That in itself was something.

This willingness to act on his stated ideals, as well as to expound them directly and clearly, are at least as important in distinguishing Max from the other white speakers who either disassociate their acts from their ideals (as in the case of the slumlord Mr. Dalton) or conceal the real significance of their acts with appeals to allegedly commonly held ideals (as does the corrupt State's Attorney Buckley, who invokes God and civilization in his opening statement at Bigger's trial).

Bigger begins to understand the motivations for his actions and the social laws which have shaped his actions, or at least he sees that such an understanding may be possible. The way Wright represents the process is not as a simple linear progression—and how far the process has moved by the end is ambiguous. Rather it is a process that moves in fits and starts. Neither is it a process by which the Communist Party gives Bigger the truth: The white Communists Boris Max and Jan Erlone learn at least as much from Bigger as Bigger learns from them. In fact, Bigger's vision of himself at the end may well be clearer than Max's own self-knowledge. Ultimately, Bigger rejects the various narratives which have shaped his life and his self-perception and takes responsibility for his actions. He no longer feels terror, even about his impending execution. In essence, he takes control of his own narrative, basing it on himself rather than trying to conform himself to the various narratives of mass culture.

The gothic then is crucial to Wright's project because it is the perfect literary analogue to what Wright sees as the ideology and psychology guiding the relations between black and white Americans under what he viewed as late capitalism. The highly developed gothic rhetoric of extreme social anxiety or terror on the part of the individual subject with respect to social identity as well as the repression of that anxiety by the subject with the concomitant return of the repressed as the uncanny allowed Wright graphically to represent the pathology of American racism. Yet as in the Communist critique of Freudianism which gothic literature prefigured and influenced, it is in part rejected because of its focus on individual terror rather broader social forces—a limitation that remains even when the gothic is used to figure social conflict and anxieties. Also, because of the relation of black literature to the gothic genre, the representation of the gothic and its limitations can also be seen as a critique of black expressive culture, particularly literature, and a statement of the need for a new type of African American literature of which *Native Son* was to be the forerunner.

Source: James Smethurst, "Invented by Horror: The Gothic and African American Literary Ideology in *Native Son*," in *African American Review*, Vol. 35, No. 1, Spring 2001, pp. 29–40.

SOURCES

Constitutional Rights Foundation, www.crf-usa.org/brown 50th/race_voting.html (November 21, 2005).

Ellis, Aime J., "Where is Bigger's Humanity? Black Male Community in Richard Wright's *Native Son*," in *ANQ: A Quarterly Journal of Short Articles, Notes, and Reviews,* Vol. 15, No.3, Summer 2002, pp.23–24.

Howe, Irving, "Black Boys and Native Sons," in *Dissent,* Vol. 10, No. 4, Autumn 1963, pp. 353–54.

Hurmence, Belinda, ed., *Before Freedom: 48 Oral Histories of Former North and South Carolina Slaves,* Mentor Books, 1990, pp. viii–ix, 64–69.

Poore, Charles, "Books of the Times," in *New York Times,* March 1, 1940, p. 25.

Rampersad, Arnold, "Notes on the Texts," in *Native Son,* Harper Perennial, 2001, pp. 574–75.

West, Cornel, "Philosophy and the Afro-American Experience," in *Philosophical Forum,* Vol. 9, Winter/Spring, 1977–1978, pp. 117–48.

Wright, Richard, *Native Son,* Harper Perennial, 2001, originally published in 1940.

———, "How Bigger Was Born," in *Native Son,* Harper Perennial, 2001, pp. vii–xxxiv.

Zangrando, R. L., "About Lynching," *Modern American Poetry: An Online Journal and Multimedia Companion to Anthology of Modern American Poetry,* Department of English of the University of Illinois at Urbana-Champaign, www.liu.edu/cwis/cwp/library/african/2000/lynching.html (2002).

"The Negro Speaks of Rivers"

LANGSTON HUGHES

1921

"The Negro Speaks of Rivers" is a short, evocative poem written by Langston Hughes when he was only seventeen. Despite Hughes's relative lack of real-world experience, the work embodies a wisdom and cultural awareness far beyond the poet's years. The poem's narrator evokes images that span thousands of years and thousands of miles, relating the experiences of all black people throughout history to himself in his present day.

Hughes wrote the poem while traveling by train across the Mississippi River on a trip to Mexico. Biographer Arnold Rampersad, in his book *The Life of Langston Hughes*, tells the story:

> The beauty of the hour and the setting—the great muddy river glinting in the sun, the banked and tinted summer clouds, the rush of the train toward the dark, all touched an adolescent sensibility tender after the gloomy day. The sense of beauty and death, of hope and despair, fused in his imagination. A phrase came to him, then a sentence. Drawing an envelope from his pocket, he began to scribble.

The poem was published in *The Crisis,* the official publication of the National Association for the Advancement of Colored People (NAACP), in June of 1921; it was Hughes's first professionally published work. From this short debut poem, however, readers could already see that Hughes had the potential to become an influential voice in American

literature. When Jessie Fauset, literary editor of *The Crisis,* first read the poem, she showed it to W. E. B. Du Bois—cofounder of the NAACP—and asked, "What colored person is there, do you suppose, in the United States who writes like that and is yet unknown to us?"

"The Negro Speaks of Rivers" offers a sweeping portrayal of the vast black experience in just over one hundred words. The poem focuses on four rivers—the Euphrates, the Congo, the Nile, and the Mississippi—and nods to each river's role in the narrator's cultural history. Despite the narrator's repeated use of the pronoun "I," the reader quickly realizes that the narrator is not an actual individual person and indeed could not be since the events described in the poem take place over such a wide span of human history. The narrator is the embodiment of all black people and shares in the experiences of all who have come before him. The poem carries a message of unity and connectedness among Africans and their descendants—a message not frequently heard at the time.

Hughes continued his successful career as a poet even as he attended college at Columbia University pursing a degree in engineering. He eventually left Columbia, completing his education at Lincoln University while continuing to write. His first published book, a collection of poetry called *The Weary Blues* (1926), marked the first book publication of"The Negro Speaks of Rivers." The poem appeared again in Hughes's *The Dream Keeper and Other Poems,* a collection aimed at young readers and first published in 1932.

Despite Hughes's youth and comparative lack of practice as a poet when it was written, "The Negro Speaks of Rivers" remains one of his most anthologized poems. It has also inspired composers, two of whom have set the poem's words to music as a song. The poem's positive message extends beyond the time in which it was written and invites modern readers to share in a celebration of cultural awareness just as relevant today as it was in 1920. As Jean Wagner writes in *Black Poets of the United States:*

> "The Negro Speaks of Rivers" heralded the existence of a mystic union of Negroes in every country and every age. It pushed their history back to the creation of the world, and credited them with possessing a wisdom no less profound than that of the greatest rivers of civilization that humanity had ever known.

I'VE KNOWN RIVERS:

ANCIENT, DUSKY RIVERS.

MY SOUL HAS GROWN DEEP LIKE THE RIVERS."

PLOT SUMMARY

"The Negro Speaks of Rivers" is written from the first-person perspective, or the viewpoint of the main character of the poem. The protagonist and narrator is described only by the term "Negro" in the title. The entire work consists of a mere thirteen lines of free verse. Although it does not employ a set rhyme scheme or stanza pattern, the poem does feature parallel structure within several lines as well as two simple phrases that act as a refrain, or a repeated section similar to a chorus in a song. The poem begins with a simple declaration—"I've known rivers"—that implies the narrator's experience and wisdom.

The narrator elaborates on this depth of knowledge in the next lines, noting that he has known rivers "older than the flow of human blood in human veins." This comparison ties humanity to the oldest parts of nature and suggests that the flow human life force is much like the flow of a river. The narrator then notes that his "soul has grown deep like the rivers." Again the narrator compares a human attribute—the soul—to a river. This image, however, contrasts with the description of a moving river. At its deepest points, the flow of a river seems to almost cease; as it becomes shallower, the water flows more quickly. The narrator, then, is comparing his soul to the deceptive stillness of a deep river.

In the next lines, the narrator lists several personal experiences involving rivers. All begin with the pronoun "I." First, he says that he has cleansed himself in the Euphrates River. This river, which begins in Turkey and flows through Syria and Iraq, is mentioned in the Bible as one of four rivers flowing out from the Garden of Eden. The river also forms the western border of a region known as Mesopotamia, where many of the earliest recorded civilizations flourished. For this reason, the area near the Euphrates is

BIOGRAPHY

LANGSTON HUGHES

James Mercer Langston Hughes was born in Joplin, Missouri, in 1902, and spent much of his youth in Kansas and Illinois. Though he wrote poetry from an early age—"The Negro Speaks of Rivers" was published while still in his teens—he attended Columbia University to study engineering. He was successful in school, but dropped out and spent several years in Europe.

Hughes returned to the United States in 1924, continuing his career as a poet and a novelist. His first full-length book, a collection of poetry titled *The Weary Blues,* was published in 1926. He quickly became one of the artists most associated with the Harlem Renaissance, a period of great productivity among African American writers of the 1920s and 1930s, and his works often focus on capturing the black experience in urban America. However, many of Hughes's works reach beyond race: they depict the economically downtrodden of all races and cultures, and spotlight the ever-growing chasm between the rich and poor in the United States.

Hughes received a great deal of recognition during his lifetime; his first novel, *Not Without Laughter* (1930), received the William E. Harmon Gold Medal for literature, and Hughes received a Guggenheim Fellowship in 1935. In 1960, Hughes received the Spingarn Medal from the National Association for the Advancement of Colored People and was inducted into the National Institute of Arts and Letters the following year. Hughes died in 1967 due to complications from prostate cancer. In 1973, the City College of New York instituted the Langston Hughes Medal, an annual literary award given to a work by an African American writer who follows in the tradition of Hughes.

---

often called the "Cradle of Civilization." The act of bathing also recalls the rite of baptism, which in some denominations of Christianity is meant to cleanse the recipient of sin. Thus, in more ways than one, this line provides images of purification for the narrator.

The narrator tells that he was in the Euphrates "when dawns were young." This implies a time in the distant past, and this in turn reflects the region's status as the birthplace of humankind. It is also the reader's first clue that the narrator might not be describing personal, individual experiences—despite the use of the pronoun "I"—since the event apparently happened several thousand years ago.

The narrator next mentions that he once built a hut along the Congo River, which is in central Africa. The gentle sound of the river serves as his lullaby and helps him to sleep. Again, the narrator is evidently describing an event from the distant past, though perhaps more recent than the experience in the Euphrates. The Congo River has long served as one of the most important geographic features of central Africa, providing a steady year-round flow of water throughout the region. For this reason, many tribes have settled on its banks over the millennia.

In the next line, the narrator claims not only to have seen Egypt's Nile, but to have "raised the pyramids above it." This phrase seems to refer to the Great Pyramids and is the first event the reader can place into the context of recorded history. The Great Pyramids of Egypt, according to historians, were mostly built between 2600 and 1600 B.C.. The narrator implies that he played an active part in constructing the pyramids; in the early twentieth century when the poem was written, it was widely accepted that slaves were responsible for the construction of the pyramids. Egyptian slaves were often traded up the Nile River, so it is conceivable that many of these slaves originally came from more southern regions of Africa. The narrator, therefore, seems to be describing an early and notable example of African enslavement. In recent years, however, evidence uncovered by archeologists suggests that the builders of the pyramids were treated more as craftspeople than as slaves.

It is also possible that narrator is referring to the Nubian Pyramids, also found along the banks of the Nile River in an area once called Nubia, currently known as Sudan. Like the Egyptian pyramids, these structures were built to honor the highest members of Nubian society. If the narrator is referring to these pyramids, the line is more likely an expression of cultural pride than of weathering the adversity of enslavement. However, it seems likely that the narrator's rather casual reference to "the pyramids" is meant to refer to those pyramids most familiar to the audience—in other words, the Great Pyramids of Egypt.

With his claim that he helped build the pyramids, it becomes increasingly clear that the narrator is speaking not just for himself as a person, but for an entire race. Since the only fact the reader knows about the narrator is that he is black, this suggests that the narrator is describing the history of the black experience against the backdrop of different rivers.

In the next line, the narrator speaks of the Mississippi River. He describes the sound it makes as "singing," and notes in particular a time when Abraham Lincoln traveled down to New Orleans, where the Mississippi River empties into the Gulf of Mexico. This echoes a popular legend about Lincoln from his young adulthood. It is established that in his early twenties, Lincoln was hired to transport goods down the Mississippi River in 1831; he traveled by river from his home in Illinois to New Orleans. Some believe that once in New Orleans, Lincoln witnessed a slave auction. Such auctions were commonplace in a southern port city such as New Orleans. According to legend, seeing this slave auction strengthened Lincoln's resolve to end slavery in the United States. The "singing" of the Mississippi can be interpreted as a celebration of coming end to slavery in America.

The narrator also describes how he has seen the river's "muddy bosom turn all golden in the sunset." The Mississippi River is frequently referred to as "The Muddy Mississippi" due to the amount of silt carried in its water. The technique Hughes uses when referring to the river's "bosom" is called personification—the attribution of human characteristics to nonhuman things. By referring to the river's "bosom," the narrator clearly intends to draw parallels between the river and a person. A person's bosom is often considered the source of human emotion, and the bosom also calls to mind a motherly embrace. To say that the river's bosom was muddy calls to mind the darkness it had represented for African Americans in the past. He then notes that the river becomes "all

Langston Hughes Library of Congress

golden in the sunset," as if in the afterglow of Lincoln's visit, the Mississippi has come to offer warmer, brighter possibilities.

The final lines of the poem echo the first lines. Again, the narrator issues the simple statement, "I've known rivers"; and again, the narrator describes those rivers as ancient. However, the narrator here also describes the rivers as "dusky." The word "dusky" can be interpreted as "dim" or "hazy," but is most often used to mean "dark in color." This definition reinforces the relationship the narrator has established between the rivers and black people.

The narrator concludes with another line repeated from the opening of the poem: "My soul has grown deep like the rivers." In addition to stillness, this line also suggests the depth of cultural history signified by the rivers. Rivers are used to connect the past with the present; in this way, the experiences of blacks throughout history are connected to the narrator. Just as a river is a single body that can span eons, the narrator's soul, having grown deep, represents the cumulative history of his people in a single body.

A litograph by Currier and Ives showing a steamboat race Bettmann/Corbis

THEMES

Cultural Awareness

In "The Negro Speaks of Rivers," the narrator—never referred to by name, and therefore known only as "The Negro"—stands as a representative for all black people throughout history. By offering snapshots from several different periods of time, the narrator is expressing a personal awareness of and connection to his roots. Appreciation of this connection appears to be what allows the narrator's soul to grow deep.

The poem suggests that by remaining in touch with the heritage of one's ancestors, a person can achieve a certain degree of inner peace and wisdom. In the case of the narrator, the heritage is a centuries-long narrative of struggle in which the tide may finally be turning. The poem mentions Abraham Lincoln's trip to New Orleans, which according to legend, was when Lincoln resolved to end slavery. This reading is reinforced by the uplifting image of the muddy Mississippi River looking "golden in the sunset."

The flow of a river might also be compared to the flow of Africans from their native homelands to other parts of the world, such as Egypt and the United States. Though this large-scale flow of people was in many cases forced—a by-product of the African slave trade—the narrator of the poem helps the reader follow this "river of culture" back to its source, establishing an ancestral connection in particular for black Americans. Slaves and their descendants were often forced to abandon their traditions, or denied the tools and community needed to keep those traditions alive. Hughes's poem represents a deliberate attempt to reestablish those roots in the mind of the reader.

Slavery

"The Negro Speaks of Rivers" refers to slavery only indirectly, though the theme plays in important part in the poem. The narrator asserts that he "raised the pyramids" near the Nile. It was once commonly believed that slaves performed the work of building the Great Pyramids of Egypt. Although historical evidence now supports a different explanation for the building of the pyramids—that the workers were skilled craftspeople, and were respected in Egyptian society—the author and his readers in the 1920s would clearly have understood this line as a reference to slavery in ancient Egypt. Even modern scholars recognize this connection: in his 1987 essay "From the Bottom Up: Three Radicals of the Thirties," Adrian Oktenberg notes, "Raising the pyramids above the Nile was the act of slaves."

The poem also evokes slavery in its mention of Abraham Lincoln traveling to New Orleans. Lincoln may have decided to dedicate himself to the abolition of slavery in the United States after witnessing a slave auction in New Orleans. Although this legend might be obscure to a modern reader, it is likely that the story was well-known to the author's readers in 1921, less than sixty years after Lincoln issued the Emancipation Proclamation.

Though "The Negro Speaks of Rivers" never refers to slavery explicitly, the poem nevertheless narrates black people's struggle against oppression. The narrator first recounts the experiences of free people, bathing and sleeping without fear. Then he implies the toil of building the pyramids, clearly meant to bring images of enslavement to mind. Finally, he portrays the twilight of slavery in America as embodied by Abraham Lincoln. In the end, the narrator has achieved a certain resolve; while the struggle against oppression may not be over, his knowledge of his own cultural history has given him the strength and steadfastness of a great river.

HISTORICAL OVERVIEW

The Euphrates and Ancient Civilization

The Euphrates River winds from modern-day Turkey to Iraq and empties into the Persian Gulf. It marks the western border of a large floodplain known as Mesopotamia. The Tigris River, which merges with the Euphrates in southern Iraq, forms the eastern boundary of Mesopotamia. The region of Mesopotamia is often called the "Cradle of Civilization" because it was home to several of the earliest organized human societies, such as the Sumerians. The Euphrates is mentioned in the ancient writings of many religions, including Christianity, Judaism, and Islam. In the Bible, the Euphrates is one of the four rivers flowing out from the Garden of Eden. Its associations with both paradise and early civilization secure its regard as one of the most important rivers in human history.

The Pyramids of Egypt

Most of the pyramids of Egypt were created between 2600 B.C. and 1600 B.C.. These massive monuments, at least eighty of which still remain in some form, were primarily built along the west bank of the Nile River and served as tombs for Egyptian leaders, known as pharaohs. The earliest and most durable pyramids were constructed entirely from limestone, while later pyramids were made primarily from granite or mud bricks. Each pyramid was then covered with a polished outer casing of limestone, though most have lost this layer over the centuries.

For over two thousand years, many people believed that the pyramids had been constructed by slaves forced into labor by the mighty pharaohs. However, modern archeological findings cast doubt on this belief. Excavations at Deir el-Medina, home to hundreds of workers who built tombs for the pharaohs between 1600 B.C. and 1000 B.C., indicate that workers were granted significant wealth and status in recognition of their talents. According to Rosalie David, author of *Pyramid Builders of Ancient Egypt: A Modern Investigation of Pharaoh's Workforce*, "There is never any indication that they were slaves ... and ... there is no indication that there was any strict regulation of their domestic lives or religious practices."

The Mississippi River and the American Slave Trade

The Mississippi River is the longest river in the United States. In the early 1800s, before the advent of rail travel, the Mississippi River was the primary means of transporting goods to and from newly settled frontier areas such as Illinois and Missouri. Cities located along the river include Minneapolis, St. Louis, and Memphis, as it makes its way south to the Gulf of Mexico. The Mississippi River was essential in providing a way of transporting slaves to the many cotton plantations along its banks. Because of this, New Orleans—often considered the "port city" of the Mississippi River, even though the mouth of the Mississippi is actually located many miles south—became a booming market in the slave trade.

During the early and mid-1800s, slavery became a big business in the South. Territories farther north along the Mississippi, such as Illinois and Iowa, became established "free states"—they did not allow the practice of slavery. So in addition to facilitating the slave trade among southern states, the Mississippi River was also instrumental in providing a route northward for escaped slaves to reach freedom prior to the Civil War.

The Harlem Renaissance

Langston Hughes was a teenager when "The Negro Speaks of Rivers" was first published in 1921; at the same time, art and culture were blossoming in black urban communities throughout the United States, most notably in the Harlem neighborhood of New York City. This period of artistic achievement, lasting roughly from 1920 until 1940, is known as the Harlem Renaissance.

The neighborhood of Harlem, originally settled by the Dutch and named after an important city in the Netherlands, was home to many different cultural and ethnic groups over the centuries. In the early 1900s, a large number of educated, middle-class black families relocated to Harlem. In addition, with the advent of World War I, thousands of black laborers from the South moved to New York City and other urban centers to work in factories that supported the war effort.

As more blacks achieved middle-class status, they began forming organizations dedicated to addressing the concerns and needs of black Americans in general. In 1909, the National Association for the Advancement of Colored People (NAACP) was created in an effort to achieve racial equality. Many black Americans, for the first time feeling the freedom to choose their own career paths, sought self-expression through the arts. Jazz and blues music, brought to New York by black southern musicians, became wildly popular in both white and black communities. Harlem became a haven for those seeking to become part of a thriving creative community.

Like countless others, Langston Hughes himself was drawn to New York by this newly flourishing arts environment. As biographer Arnold Rampersad quotes Hughes himself in *The Life of Langston Hughes*, "I had come to New York to attend Columbia,...but *really* why I had come was to see Harlem." Over the next several years Hughes became a fixture on the Harlem literary scene, along with other influential writers like James Weldon Johnson and Zora Neale Hurston.

During the Great Depression, Harlem and its arts-heavy economy were hit especially hard. Many of the most influential figures of the Harlem Renaissance moved away during the 1930s, and mainstream America turned its interest to social welfare and world politics. However, the seeds planted in Harlem during the 1920s and 1930s brought a greater awareness of African American culture in the population at large, and a determination among African Americans to demand greater racial equality in the United States.

CRITICAL OVERVIEW

"The Negro Speaks of Rivers" was first published in book form as part of the poetry collection *Weary Blues* in 1926. Though the book's initial print run was small, it received positive reviews from several respected publications. An unnamed reviewer for the *New York Times* remarks, "We sincerely hope that Langston Hughes will receive the wide reading he deserves." Du Bose Heyward, a reviewer for the *New York Herald Tribune,* calls the book "[a]lways intensely subjective, passionate, keenly sensitive to beauty and possessed of an unfaltering musical sense."

However, some reviewers felt that Hughes had clearly not yet reached his potential. A reviewer for the *Independent* notes, "Time may give more depth and beauty to his work, which is crude in texture and lacking in distinction." In the *London Times Literary Supplement,* an unnamed reviewer dismisses the weight of Hughes's works with these words: "Civilization merely excites his senses, and he becomes the poet, flamboyant or sentimental, of the cabaret."

"The Negro Speaks of Rivers" also appeared in *The Dream Keeper and Other Poems,* published in 1932 as a poetry collection intended for young readers. A reviewer for the *Boston Transcript* calls the poems in this collection "simple, human, vivid, tingling with sincerity." In a review for the *New York Times,* A. T. Eaton applauds the author, stating, "It is not hard to understand the appeal of Langston Hughes to young people sensitive to poetry." In the *Saturday Review of Literature,* W. R. Benét offers the poet both compliment and criticism in the same sentence: "Langston Hughes is not a first-rate poet, even among those of his own race, but he is distinctly

MEDIA ADAPTATIONS

A spoken performance of "The Negro Speaks of Rivers," read by the author himself, is included on the audiocassette *Langston Hughes Reads*. It was released by Caedmon in 2000.

In 1932, composer Howard Swanson wrote a song incorporating the words of the poem as lyrics. A version of this song, performed by David Korevaar and Odekhiren Amaize, is found on *The Negro Speaks of Rivers: Art Songs by African American Composers,* released on compact disc by MSR Classics in 2000.

Another song built around Hughes's lyrics, also known by the same title as the poem, was written in 1942 by Margaret Bonds. A performance of the song by Darryl Taylor and Maria Corley is included on the compact disc *Dreamer: A Portrait of Langston Hughes,* released by Naxos in 2002.

---

an appealing one, a melodist who touches with sensitiveness the stops of his black flute."

Hughes's popularity has only grown with time. Today, Hughes remains one of the most anthologized American poets. In 2001, the Academy of American Poets placed a poll on their website allowing visitors to vote for the American poet they most wanted to see on a postage stamp. Hughes won by a landslide, and the United States Postal Service issued a Langston Hughes postage stamp in 2002, further celebrating his reputation as one of America's most popular poets.

CRITICISM

Greg Wilson

Wilson is a popular-culture writer. In the following excerpt, he discusses Langston Hughes's "The Negro Speaks of Rivers" and casts a critical eye

> AS A CELEBRATION OF RACIAL CULTURE AND HISTORY, AS IT IS OFTEN CREDITED, THE POEM HAS PROBLEMS—SOME SPECIFIC TO THE LANGUAGE AND IMAGERY HUGHES EMPLOYS, AND SOME ENDEMIC TO ANY LITERATURE THAT PURPORTS TO CELEBRATE A CERTAIN RACE."

---

on its modern relevance as "a celebration of racial culture and history."

Langston Hughes wrote "The Negro Speaks of Rivers" when he was only seventeen. As a poem, it succeeds brilliantly in conveying mood and tone while offering glimpses of human existence in times past. As a celebration of racial culture and history, as it is often credited, the poem has problems—some specific to the language and imagery Hughes employs, and some endemic to any literature that purports to celebrate a certain race.

Since the purpose of the poem seems to be to evoke feelings of cultural connectedness and racial pride, the "historical snapshots" chosen by Hughes should be historically relevant. Unfortunately, if one assumes that Hughes means to convey a sweeping portrait of the "black experience"—as most literary scholars seem to accept—then the poem becomes problematic at nearly every stage of its central stanza.

First, Hughes—through the narrator "the Negro"—mentions bathing in the Euphrates River. Certainly Hughes knew the actual location of the Euphrates: in modern geopolitical terms, the river begins in Turkey, flows through Syria and Iraq, and empties into the Persian Gulf. Inhabitants of this middle eastern region are Middle Easterners, not Africans, as the narrator implies. Most readers overlook this detail, though George Hutchinson, in *The Harlem Renaissance in Black and White*, addresses the issue directly:

> Readers rarely notice that if the soul of the Negro in this poem goes back to the Euphrates, it goes back to a pre-"racial" dawn and a geography far from Africa that is identified with neither blackness nor whiteness—a geography

at the time of Hughes's writing considered the cradle of all the world's civilizations and possibly the location of the Garden of Eden. Thus, even in this poem about the depth of the Negro's soul Hughes avoids racial essentialism while nonetheless stressing the existential, racialized conditions of black and modern identity.

Another problematic line is the narrator's discussion of the pyramids built along the Nile River. Hughes clearly means to suggest that black slaves were used to construct the pyramids. The notion that slave labor built the pyramids is an old one, probably originating with the Greeks, that was still accepted when Hughes was a young man. However, in the last fifty years, archeologists have uncovered evidence to suggest that the builders of the pyramids were not merely slaves, but were regarded by ancient Egyptians as talented craftspeople. Although Hughes could not have foreseen the revised understanding of ancient history that would come later in his life, a modern reader's modern understanding of this historical detail weakens the poet's imagery.

Finally, we come to the last historical snapshot of the poem's central stanza: that of Abraham Lincoln traveling to New Orleans. This references the legend that Lincoln, during a trip down the river to New Orleans as a young man, witnessed a slave auction and was so horrified that he decided to work to end slavery if he possibly could. While it is well established that Lincoln did travel on a flatboat to New Orleans as a young man, the rest of the tale occupies the same shaky historical ground as other presidential legends, like George Washington's infamous chopping down of a cherry tree. As Benjamin Quarles points out in *Lincoln and the Negro,* the "story will not stand up, as it was told by a man who did not accompany Lincoln on either of his trips [to New Orleans]."

A reader could assume that Hughes intends to address not just the "black experience" but the "human experience"; readers of all races find the poem moving and resonant. However, the other deliberate choices made by Hughes in the poem belie this notion. First, the title quite pointedly mentions that the narrator is "Negro." Additionally, three of the four historical snapshots relate to Africa and/or slavery, and are clearly particularly relevant to the author and his narrator.

It could be that Hughes did not mean to reference real historical events so much as suggest a symbolic racial history. Even in this case, though, we run into the problems inherent in any literary work that espouses any type of "racial pride." The concept of racial pride fails in two ways; first, because "race" has no truly quantifiable meaning without delving into absurdity, and second, because "group pride" is often just prejudice in disguise.

Race is a distinction based solely on the idea of exclusion. The concept of race is used to identify outsiders so they can be effectively marginalized by the distinguishing population. To accept any racial designation—and worse, to do it with pride—is to accept and legitimize the false premise that race is in any way a real thing.

If different people have different colors of skin, one might ask, how can race not be a real thing? No one considers redheads a different race, though their features are distinctive. By the same token, Jews are considered by many to comprise a different racial group, though there are no reliable physical characteristics to distinguish them from non-Jews. Is race based on pedigree, then, instead of appearance? What if a person has an Anglo parent and an African parent? It should come as no surprise that, historically, children of such mixed parentage have almost always been lumped in this group as a member of the more maligned "race." In particular, American history is rife with absurd terms and laws meant to either prevent the mixing of races, or to stigmatize children of such unions for many generations. (Thus, "whites" invented terms like "octoroon" to describe a person who was one-eighth "black," and seven-eighths "white"—but still, according to prevailing prejudice, legally "black.")

In fact, Langston Hughes himself was the product of a mixing of "races." According to Arnold Rampersad, one of the poet's great-grandfathers was "a white Virginia planter." Rampersad also quotes one of Hughes's schoolteachers, describing her former student: "he was a bad combination—part Indian, part Nigra, and part white." Hughes's skin tone was lighter than that of many "blacks"; in fact, on the very same trip to Mexico during which he wrote "The Negro Speaks of Rivers," several people assumed that Hughes was Mexican. He did not correct them. Indeed, Hughes welcomed the notion that a certain camaraderie existed between all people with comparatively dark skin, as Rampersad quotes from Hughes's journal: "I am among my own people, for ... Mexico is a brown man's country."

Hughes—despite having a mixed heritage himself—buys into the premise that race is quantifiable. He even offers a sweeping generalization of Jewish people in his journal from his trip to Mexico, noting that "Jews are warm hearted people and seldom prejudiced." This is in reference to one of the very same people Hughes chose not to tell he was actually African American and not Latino.

Pride—in its most positive sense—is something earned through accomplishment, by the actions of an individual or group. Whether someone is "proud to be a Daughter of the American Revolution," "proud to be black," or "proud to be white," these are not achievements in and of themselves, but accidents of parentage and genetics. Would it not be silly for someone to say he or she is "proud to be tall" or "proud to have green eyes"? What did such an individual do to achieve these qualities? Not a thing. In a more common usage, pride can mean the absence of shame. For a person to say she is "proud to be the grandchild of immigrants" or "proud to be Native American" may mean that she is not ashamed of her heritage. Just as the uncontrollable traits of one's ancestors are shaky ground on which to base one's sense of worth, neither should they be secrets to be hidden or denied.

This is not to suggest that people should not be comfortable with their own heritage and appreciate the histories of different cultures and societies. The more one studies human history, the less likely one is to judge oneself or another on something as arbitrary as a racial designation. This is also not to suggest that living as a part of an oppressed population does not require effort worthy of pride; however, oppressed groups should be wary of subscribing to the very notions that enable their oppression.

It is important to point out, further, that Hughes had not even reached the age of majority when he wrote the poem and visited Mexico, and he lived in an environment where prejudice was dangerous and real—even if the oppressors sometimes had difficulty figuring out who should be oppressed. One can hardly fault him for not exhibiting a way of thinking that was not widely popularized until four decades later.

However, those who continue to overemphasize the poem's importance as a call for racial awareness only serve to perpetuate divisiveness between groups of people, as well as steal attention from the poem's other merits.

None of the aforementioned criticisms take away from this simple fact: a seventeen-year-old boy, looked down upon as a Negro by the society in which he lived, was inspired to write an eloquent meditation on humanity's connection to its ancestry. In a mere 103 words, the teenaged Hughes conjures feelings of dignity, nobility, and optimism in his readers. The poem rings true even if it is not true, and with its expertly crafted use of imagery and tone, foreshadows the greatness that its author would achieve: Hughes became one of the finest and best-loved American poets of the twentieth century. "The Negro Speaks of Rivers" is as beautiful as it is important, and whether the poet meant to speak for all humankind, all humankind can see itself in the brief but moving meditation on an individual's relationship to the multitudes of human history.

SOURCES

Benét, W. R., Review of *The Dream Keeper and Other Poems,* in the *Saturday Review of Literature,* November 12, 1932, Vol. 9, p. 241, as quoted in *The Book Review Digest,* Twenty-Eighth Annual Cumulation, edited by Marion A. Knight, Mertice M. James and Dorothy Brown, The H. W. Wilson Company, 1933, p. 466.

David, Rosalie, *Pyramid Builders of Ancient Egypt: A Modern Investigation of Pharaoh's Workforce,* Routledge, 1997, p. 76.

Eaton, A. T., "Review of *The Dream Keeper and Other Poems,*" in *New York Times,* July 17, 1932, sec. V, p. 13.

Heyward, Du Bose, Review of *Weary Blues,* in *New York Herald Tribune,* August 1, 1926, Books, p. 4, as quoted in *The Book Review Digest,* Twenty-Second Annual Cumulation, edited by Marion A. Knight and Mertice M. James, The H. W. Wilson Company, 1927, p. 350.

Hughes, Langston, "The Negro Speaks of Rivers," in *The Dream Keeper and Other Poems,* 1932, reprint, Alfred A. Knopf, 1994, p. 62.

Humes, James C., *The Wit and Wisdom of Abraham Lincoln,* Gramercy, 1999, p. 55.

Hutchinson, George, *The Harlem Renaissance in Black and White,* Belknap Press, 1997, as quoted on Modern American Poetry: An Online Journal and Multimedia Companion to *Anthology of Modern American Poetry,* www.english.uiuc.edu/MAPS/poets/g_l/hughes/rivers.htm (April 12, 2006).

Oktenberg, Adrian, "From the Bottom Up: Three Radicals of the Thirties," in *A Gift of Tongues: Critical Challenges in Contemporary American Poetry,* edited by Marie Harris and Kathleen Aguero, University of Georgia Press, 1987, pp. 83–111.

Quarles, Benjamin, *Lincoln and the Negro,* Da Capo Press, 1991, p. 18.

Rampersad, Arnold, *The Life of Langston Hughes,* Vol. 1, Oxford University Press, 2d ed., 2002, pp. 4, 18, 40, 51.

Review of *Weary Blues,* in *New York Times,* March 21, 1926, p. 6, as quoted in *The Book Review Digest,* Twenty-Second Annual Cumulation, edited by Marion A. Knight and Mertice M. James, The H. W. Wilson Company, 1927, p. 350.

Review of *Weary Blues,* in the *Independent,* April 3, 1926, Vol. 116, p. 404, as quoted in *The Book Review Digest,* Twenty-Second Annual Cumulation, edited by Marion A. Knight and Mertice M. James, The H. W. Wilson Company, 1927, p. 350.

Review of *Weary Blues,* in the *Times (London) Literary Supplement,* July 29, 1926, p. 515, as quoted in *The Book Review Digest,* Twenty-Second Annual Cumulation, edited by Marion A. Knight and Mertice M. James, The H. W. Wilson Company, 1927, p. 350.

Review of *The Dream Keeper and Other Poems,* in the *Boston Transcript,* July 30, 1932, p. 2, as quoted in *The Book Review Digest,* Twenty-Eighth Annual Cumulation, edited by Marion A. Knight, Mertice M. James and Dorothy Brown, The H. W. Wilson Company, 1933, p. 466.

Wagner, Jean, *Black Poets of the United States: From Paul Laurence Dunbar to Langston Hughes,* University of Illinois Press, 1973, p. 394.

Younge, Gary, "Review: Live and Letters: Renaissance Man of the South: Gary Younge Remembers Langston Hughes, America's Most Popular Poet, Whose Centenary is Celebrated in London Next Week (Guardian Saturday Pages) (Letter to the Editor)," *Guardian,* October 26, 2002, p. 34, in *InfoTrac Custom Newspapers* (April 5, 2006).

Nisei Daughter

MONICA SONE

1953

Monica Sone's *Nisei Daughter* is a memoir about growing up as a Japanese American in the United States prior to and during World War II. The author, born on American soil to Japanese immigrant parents, is a *Nisei*, or second-generation Japanese American. Her parents, as first-generation Japanese immigrants to America, are considered *Issei*. Being born in the United States meant that a Nisei was an American citizen, but strict immigration laws prevented any Issei from becoming citizens until long after World War II.

Nisei found themselves torn between their Japanese ancestry and their thoroughly American lifestyles. They often had to serve as cultural or linguistic interpreters for their Issei parents, many of whom had not fully mastered the English language or American customs. Nisei were often criticized by Japanese nationals for abandoning their roots, yet they were unable to fully assimilate into the American mainstream thanks to widespread fear and prejudice toward the Japanese during the first half of the twentieth century.

As World War II approached, both genera-tions of Japanese Americans faced especially harsh persecution along the West Coast, where most had established roots. Sone recounts her experiences as a young Nisei in Seattle in the years leading up to and shortly after the Japanese attack on Pearl Harbor in 1941. She chronicles the virtual loss of her rights as an American citizen and her family's

WE HAD HEARD THE CLAMORING OF SUPERPATRIOTS WHO INSISTED LOUDLY, 'THROW THE WHOLE KABOODLE OUT. A JAP'S A JAP, NO MATTER HOW YOU SLICE HIM. YOU CAN'T MAKE AN AMERICAN OUT OF LITTLE JAP JUNIOR JUST BY HANDING HIM AN AMERICAN BIRTH CERTIFICATE.' BUT WE HAD DISMISSED THESE REMARKS AS JUST HOT BLASTS OF AIR FROM AN OVERHEATED PATRIOT. WE WERE QUITE SURE THAT OUR RIGHTS AS AMERICAN CITIZENS WOULD NOT BE VIOLATED, AND WE WOULD NOT BE MARCHED OUT OF OUR HOMES ON THE SAME BASIS AS ENEMY ALIENS."

BIOGRAPHY

MONICA SONE

Monica Sone was born Kazuko Monica Itoi in Seattle in 1919. Like many Nisei, her name was a bridge between her Japanese past and her American future: *Kazuko* is Japanese for "peace," while Monica is the name of St. Augustine's mother. She spent her childhood helping her parents run the Carrollton Hotel on Seattle's Skid Row. In 1942, she and her entire family were forced into a Japanese internment camp in Puyallup, Washington. The family was eventually relocated, along with hundreds of others, to Camp Minidoka in Idaho, where many Japanese Americans remained until 1946.

Sone was released from internment in 1943 to work in Chicago as a dental assistant. She eventually returned to college (which she had begun before internment) in Indiana, studying clinical psychology. She married another Nisei, Geary Sone, and the two eventually settled in Canton, Ohio. As of 2006, *Nisei Daughter* remains the only book Sone has written.

forced relocation to an internment camp in Idaho. Nevertheless, *Nisei Daughter* is hardly a bitter or accusatory book. Instead, it focuses on one family's strength in the face of adversity, and their willingness to sacrifice for the benefit of the country they love.

Although readers often focus on the book's depiction of Japanese relocation and internment during World War II, Sone was also one of the first authors to offer a detailed view of day-to-day life as a Japanese American in the 1920s and 1930s. It is through these mundane interactions that Sone illustrates the process of assimilation, wherein members of a minority group adopt the behaviors and attitudes of the majority population among which they live. In *Nisei Daughter*, the issue of assimilation becomes especially complex. While most Nisei make great efforts to assimilate, a significant segment of the American population seems to resist, and even thwart, these efforts.

While *Nisei Daughter* was not particularly successful when it was originally published in 1953, renewed interest in the matter of Japanese internment resulted in a 1979 reprint edition through the University of Washington Press. This edition has spawned the book's widespread popularity, and it is often assigned as required

reading in many classes dealing with multicultural issues in America.

PLOT SUMMARY

Chapter I: A Shocking Fact of Life

Sone—referred to throughout the book by her first name, Kazuko—begins *Nisei Daughter* with the moment, at the age of six, that she first realizes she has Japanese ancestry. Before that, she notes that she lived "in amoebic bliss, not knowing whether I was plant or animal," in her family's low-rent hotel on Seattle's Skid Row. She and her older brother Henry are indifferent to the revelation until they learn that their parents have enrolled them in Japanese school, which they must attend every day after grammar school. Kazuko and Henry protest, but they know it will do no good.

The author then tells how her parents came to the United States. Her father, a law student from Tochigi-ken politely referred to as Mr. Itoi, sails to America in 1904 with dreams of continuing his law studies in Ann Arbor, Michigan. He arrives in Seattle and takes a string of odd jobs to save money for his journey to Michigan; eventually, he gives up his dream of Ann Arbor and becomes a business owner in Seattle. Soon after, the author's mother, Benko, arrives in America with her family. Mr. Itoi is impressed by Benko and her sisters; through a go-between, he first asks for the hand of Benko's sister Yasuko. When he learns that Yasuko is spoken for, he asks about Benko. With some persuasion, Benko agrees to marry Mr. Itoi.

The two work together to run a dry-cleaning business until their first child, Henry Seichi, is born. At that time, Mr. Itoi sells the business and buys the Carrollton Hotel, a "flea-ridden" place along the economically decaying Skid Row. The couple improves the hotel as much as they can but still relies on a working-class clientele of "sea-hardened mariners, shipyard workers, airplane workers, fruit pickers and factory workers." A year after buying the hotel, the couple's second child, Kazuko Monica, is born. Brother Kenji William and sister Sumiko follow later.

Kazuko has fond memories of growing up in the Carrollton, where her family sets aside several of the rooms for use as their own living quarters. Skid Row is her childhood playground, with its union office, Salvation Army, and forbidden burlesque house. Upon entering grammar school, a whole new world opens up to Kazuko: a world of people her own age of many different races. Still, she has trouble reconciling her Japanese ancestry with her thoroughly American attitudes.

Chapter II: The Stubborn Twig

Kazuko and Henry attend their first day of *Nihon Gakko*, or Japanese school. Upon being introduced to Mr. Ohashi, the principal, Kazuko and Henry are immediately reprimanded for not bowing properly. Despite her resistance, Kazuko soon starts to enjoy her Japanese schooling. Her experience there is quite unlike her days at grammar school, and she even notices that her personality and behavior differ dramatically between the two. While at Japanese school, Kazuko learns to read and write in Japanese and also learns the finer points of Japanese manners and etiquette.

Kazuko and her fellow Japanese students all dislike a boy named Genji Yamada. He is a star pupil, primarily because his parents sent him to Japan when he was young to become immersed in Japanese culture. Now, back in the United States, he is "a stranger among us with stiff mannerisms and an arrogant attitude." His posture is always perfect, and his Japanese writing is beautiful. He is Mr. Ohashi's pride.

There are several workers at the Carrollton Hotel that the Itois consider a part of their family. Sam, "a tall, rugged, blue-eyed retired mariner with a photographic mind," runs a dormitory owned by the Itois next to the hotel. Joe, "a portly, cheerful man with a tiny black mustache," works as a night watchman at the hotel and becomes Mr. Itoi's good friend. Peter, "a soft-spoken, gentle old Bohemian," eventually takes charge of a second dormitory for the family. Montana, "over six feet tall with a tightly curled, black beard growing rampant down over his faded flannel shirt," works as a bouncer at the hotel. One night, when a disgruntled guest calls Mr. Itoi a "Jap," Montana literally picks the man up and tosses him down the exit stairs.

Unfortunately, even Montana cannot protect the family from corrupt policemen. One night, as the family eats dinner, two police officers visit and accuse Mr. Itoi of selling bootleg alcohol. They offer to forget about the accusation if Mr. Itoi pays them fifty dollars. He refuses, and they take him to jail. At the trial, the alleged witness in the case incorrectly identifies another man as Mr. Itoi, and all charges are dismissed.

Chapter III: An Unpredictable Japanese Lady

After attending a children's talent show, Kazuko decides she wants to become a dancer. Her father refuses, believing all American dancers to be lewd and skimpily dressed. Still, Kazuko volunteers to create a dance routine for a Christmas program at grammar school; she secures her father's approval by portraying a fully dressed clown. Even though the performance is well received, Kazuko realizes that dance is not for her.

Kazuko's mother is more accepting of American ways than her father but still has her own struggles. Her main hurdle is the language.

Once, while speaking to Kazuko's teacher, she accidentally says that she is Kazuko's "big sister" and refers to a dress she made for Kazuko as "lousy" instead of "loud." Another time, while attending a Mickey Mouse Club meeting, Mrs. Itoi is mistaken for the wife of the Japanese consul without even realizing it; she is whisked away and treated like a dignitary while Kazuko and her younger sister Sumiko fear their mother has gotten lost.

Chapter IV: The Japanese Touch

Although Kazuko and her family celebrate most of the same holidays as white Americans, there is the special holiday for Japanese called *Tenchosetsu,* or the Japanese Emperor's birthday. For this celebration, Japanese gather together to ceremoniously view a picture of the emperor; it is the only time an image of the emperor can be shown. Kazuko and the other Japanese American children she knows endure the ceremony because their parents demand it, even though the children, having been born in the United States, are all American citizens.

Another more enjoyable event for Kazuko is the annual picnic sponsored by the Nihon Gakko. For this occasion, the entire Japanese American community shows up at Jefferson Park to celebrate with food, games, and traditional folk songs. Mothers cook huge meals and share their food with other families, like a potluck; the children participate in the sort of games and contests common at other American picnics, like a three-legged race and a baseball tournament.

The New Year's holiday for the Itoi family is a mix of Japanese and American traditions. On New Year's Eve, Kazuko's mother makes everyone take a bath so that they can "greet the new year clean and refreshed in body and spirit." They gather together to play a Japanese card game until midnight, when they turn on the radio and sing along to "Auld Lang Syne." They forego the traditional New Year's Day breakfast of *ozoni,* a thick chicken stew, but must still attend a formal Japanese get-together that tests the children's ability to remain polite.

Chapter V: We Meet Real Japanese

In the spring, the Itoi family takes a ship to visit Mr. Itoi's family in Japan. The children are all excited except for the youngest son, Kenji, who is afraid of the deadly earthquakes that happen

there. The children, dressed in American clothing, feel like outsiders; the local Japanese children make it worse by shouting "American-jin!" and throwing rocks at the house where they stay. One morning, Kazuko and Henry are ambushed by several local boys and start to fight. Kazuko feels a special need to defend the name of America: "The land where we were born was being put to a test." A maid puts a stop to the fight, but Henry has won respect from the Japanese boys, who later invite him to join them fishing.

Shortly before they plan to leave Japan, Kenji and Henry both become ill with dysentery, an intestinal disorder that often proves fatal. Henry survives, but young Kenji does not. Once Henry has sufficiently recovered, the family returns to the United States.

Chapter VI: We Are Outcasts

Back in America, Sumiko develops a worsening asthma condition. Mr. and Mrs. Itoi decide to rent a summer house near the beach, hoping that it will improve Sumiko's health. Kazuko and her mother drive to Alki Beach to search for a rental property. They find the perfect house, but when they talk to the owner, they are told that the place has just been rented to someone else. As they continue to search, they hear the same story: either the rent is much too high or the house is suddenly unavailable. Finally, one woman is honest enough to tell them the truth: "I'm sorry, but we don't want Japs around here."

The family settles for a small apartment near Lake Washington looked after by a Scandinavian couple named the Olsens. They are quite sympathetic to Japanese Americans and have many as tenants. Still, anti-Japanese sentiment runs high in the western United States. As the Japanese national army is a quickly developing military power in Asia, Japanese Americans are openly denied service in stores and other businesses, while newspapers carry grotesque cartoons stereotyping Japanese people. Many Nisei, like Kazuko, have an especially hard time accepting such treatment since they are full citizens of the United States. They endure it because they do not want to leave their beloved homeland and because they believe it will soon pass.

Chapter VII: Paradise Sighted

On her last day of grammar school, Kazuko receives a picture from a boy named Haruo. He is handsome and seems to be interested in Kazuko, but her parents strictly forbid her from dating. At the same time, one of Henry's friends, Kazuo, becomes a regular visitor to the Itoi home. Kazuo is American, but he spent much of his time growing up in Japan; he often boasts about how Japan's military could defeat America's military. Annoyed at his arrogance, Kazuko tells Kazuo she hates him and hopes never to see him again. He leaves and does not return. Henry is upset and tells Kazuko that the main reason Kazuo kept visiting was to see her. Years later, she sees Kazuo again. He is more subdued, having learned that Nisei girls do not respond to the arrogant posturing he learned in Japan. Kazuko exchanges letters with Haruo for two years, but she sees him only at the annual Japanese school picnic. Finally, they are at last set to be in the same class at Nihon Gakko. Haruo takes a seat next to her, and everything seems perfect. Then, when they rise to bow to their instructor, they both realize that Kazuko stands a full head taller than Haruo. From that point on, the relationship is doomed.

Eventually, Kazuko graduates from high school and excitedly prepares for college. Her father, sensing the mounting tensions between Japan and the United States, suggests that she attend business school first, "so you can step into a job and be independent, just in case." Kazuko does not want to attend business school, but she feels she must abide by her parents' request. She decides to complete the two years of business school in a single year so she can get to college sooner. She finishes business school ahead of schedule, but then suffers a devastating bout of tuberculosis. She is hospitalized for nine months while she recovers from the dangerous disease. When she is released, she sees that her family has bought a lovely new house on Beacon Hill. She also finds that her brother Henry is engaged to his girlfriend, Minnie.

Chapter VIII: Pearl Harbor Echoes in Seattle

On December 7, 1941, as Kazuko, Henry, and Sumiko rehearse for a church choir Christmas program, they learn that the Japanese have bombed the U.S. Navy base at Pearl Harbor, Hawaii. Shocked and frightened, the family gathers at home and listens to the radio for additional news. Mr. Itoi dismisses the reports as American propaganda until he hears the same information on a Japanese shortwave radio broadcast.

Japanese men in the United States and Hawaii are promptly rounded up for questioning. The government freezes the bank assets of Japanese nationals like Mr. and Mrs. Itoi; Mrs. Itoi prepares a suitcase for her husband, dreading the day FBI agents will knock on their door and lead him away. The family destroys many of the Japanese artifacts in their house, fearful that they will be mistaken for loyalist spies. In February 1942, President Franklin Roosevelt signs Executive Order 9066, which allows the War Department to remove people of Japanese ancestry from any area they deemed necessary. The Itoi family, like all other Japanese American families along the West Coast, is ordered to dispose of its property, homes, and businesses, and to report to a relocation center. Mr. Itoi searches for someone to care for his business in his absence so he will not lose it.

Chapter IX: Life in Camp Harmony

As evacuation day approaches, Mr. Itoi arranges for someone to manage his hotel. On April 21, they receive the official word: all people of Japanese ancestry in Seattle will be relocated to a temporary camp in Puyallup, Washington, by May 1. Each person is allowed to bring one seabag and two suitcases; they pack only the essentials, like winter clothes, sheets, blankets, and eating utensils. Mrs. Itoi also sneaks a gallon of soy sauce, figuring it will be hard to come by. The Itoi family is officially registered as Family Number 10710, and they are transported by bus to the Washington state fairgrounds in Puyallup. They pass long rows of what look like chicken houses. Someone on the bus notes, "They sure go in for poultry in a big way here." Then they realize that these are not chicken houses—these are their new homes, known collectively as "Camp Harmony."

The five members of the Itoi family share a single room about eighteen by twenty feet. It is bare except for a small wood-burning stove, and individual army cots that are distributed later. The walls do not extend all the way to the ceiling, leaving large gaps for sound to travel throughout the barracks. It rains the first night, and they discover that the roof leaks badly; they also discover that Camp Harmony is built on muddy ground. This spawns a trend of wearing *getas*, or traditional wooden platform shoes, to keep out of the sticky mud.

Joe, the night watchman at the Itois' hotel, visits them at Puyallup. He brings fresh grapefruit, nuts, and candy bars for the family to enjoy. Looking at the wire fences that imprison them in the camp, Joe says, "I don't like it, to see you in here. I don't understand it. I know you all my life. You're my friend."

Kazuko works as a stenographer at the camp's administration office, and Henry, who had been a medical student before the evacuation, gets a job at the camp hospital. This allows him to be closer to his fiancée Minnie, who also works at the hospital. Just as the family settles into camp life, they are told the entire population of the camp will be relocated to Idaho.

Chapter X: Henry's Wedding and a Most Curious Tea Party

The residents of Camp Harmony arrive at their new Idaho home, Camp Minidoka, during the oppressive heat of August. The accommodations are much the same: one room for the whole family to share, only slightly larger than their previous dwelling. Kazuko, Sumiko, Henry, and Minnie all take jobs at the camp hospital, and Mr. Itoi takes a job as one of the camp's internal policemen. The minister who had served the family back in Washington, Reverend Thompson, moves to Idaho to remain with his congregation. The weather turns bitterly cold as winter sets in, and one member of the camp dies from exposure.

Representatives of the War Department visit the camp looking for soldier recruits among the eligible men. The camp members first react with justifiable hostility; however, a sincere military officer explains that he sees this as an opportunity for Japanese Americans to show the rest of America how much they love their country. Henry volunteers and the families decide that he and Minnie will get married before he is shipped out. The families secure passes to leave the camp for the wedding, which is held at Reverend Thompson's apartment. After the wedding, they return to camp for a large reception. The American-style party is confusing to the many Issei attendees and appears to be a complete failure, but the guests finally relax just as it is scheduled to end.

Chapter XI: Eastward, Nisei

After nearly a year of internment, some Nisei are allowed to leave camp for jobs further east. With the help of a friend, Kazuko is invited to live with a pastor in Chicago and work as a dental assistant there. Her host family, the Richardsons, provide her with a warm and loving home. She writes to Sumiko, Minnie, and Henry—who had been rejected for military service due to his poor eyesight—and urges them to try to find placement outside the camp. Soon after, Henry and Minnie get jobs in a hospital in St. Louis, while Sumiko is accepted into the Cadet Nurse's Corps in Long Island. After being treated badly by her employer, Kazuko quits her job as a dental assistant. With the help of the Richardsons, she is able to enroll as a student at Wendell College in Indiana.

Chapter XII: Deeper into the Land

Kazuko thrives in the multicultural environment she finds at Wendell College. She pays for her tuition by working first as a waitress and later as a secretary for one of the professors. During summers, she returns to Chicago to work as a stenographer. She admits, "Father's foresight in persuading me to go to business school was paying off at last."

During her second year of college, she receives a letter from her parents asking her to return to Camp Minidoka for Christmas. She does and spends days recounting her experiences while her parents, in return, update her on happenings within the camp. As she prepares to leave, she tells her parents how they have taught her to be proud of both her Japanese heritage and her American heritage. She no longer feels like a divided person: "The Japanese and American parts of me were now blended into one."

THEMES

Segregation

Segregation, or the separation of people based on their ethnicity, race, or culture, is at the heart of *Nisei Daughter*. The internment camps created by the War Department are designed to separate Japanese Americans from their non-Japanese counterparts. The interned Japanese are forced to leave the communities they know well, and are taken to areas far removed from other human activity.

A small Japanese American girl, with her baggage, waiting for internment, 1942 National Archives and Records Administration

When a group of people is segregated from the larger society, it generally does not receive access to the same quality of amenities or services as the rest of the population. In *Nisei Daughter*, each family of internees is required to live in a single room within larger barracks, devoid of insulation or plumbing. Although the internees staff their own schools and medical facilities within the camp, they are routinely denied basic supplies like lumber and tools. For instance, when Henry's fiancée wants to purchase a dress for their upcoming wedding, she must get special permission to leave the camp and visit a nearby town. In these ways, the camps more closely resemble prisons than communities. Even in the face of such treatment, the internees continue life as well as they can manage. Early into the internment, Kazuko's father holds an especially optimistic view of the situation when he notes, "The government gave me the first vacation of my life and no one's going to interfere with it."

Prejudice

Prejudice toward Japanese Americans appears throughout *Nisei Daughter*. In chapter II, when Mr. Itoi refuses to refund a hotel guest's money after he uses a room for most of the day, the man tells Mr. Itoi that he is a lawyer and will have Mr. Itoi arrested. He assumes that a Japanese immigrant like Mr. Itoi does not know American laws; however, Mr. Itoi—once a law student in Japan—reveals that he is knowledgeable and will not be fooled.

Later, when tensions grow between Japan and the United States, white Americans routinely eye fellow citizen Kazuko with suspicion simply because of her appearance. She observes, "I felt their resentment in a hundred ways—the way a saleswoman in a large department store never saw me waiting at the counter." Before they have even met her, strangers judge her to be in league with the enemy.

After the attack on Pearl Harbor, FBI agents raid the home of another Japanese American, Mrs. Matsui. When they cannot find her husband, they assume she is hiding him because he is a spy. After scouring the place, the agents discover that Mr. Matsui had died years before. This sort of widespread prejudice even prompts Chinese Americans to begin wearing badges identifying themselves as Chinese so they will not be mistaken for Japanese.

Nationalism

Nationalism, or devotion to one's own country above all others, is an important theme throughout *Nisei Daughter*. It is a source of pride, a source of resentment, and a source of conflict.

The Itoi children, even before they are aware of their Japanese ancestry, are proud to be American. "I had always thought I was a Yankee," Kazuko notes of her childhood. After the Japanese attack on Pearl Harbor, most Japanese Americans cooperate fully with the government in spite of their persecution, believing that their sacrifice will contribute to the war effort and help the country they love achieve victory. However, after being placed in internment camps, some Japanese Americans become understandably resentful. When a War Department representative visits the Minidoka camp and asks for volunteers to fight in a Japanese combat unit, the reaction is initially negative. As one young man puts it, "First they change my army status ... because of my ancestry, run me out of town, and now they want me to volunteer for a suicide squad so I could get killed for this damn democracy." Still, many young men eager to prove their loyalty to the

United States—including Kazuko's brother Henry—volunteer for the unit.

Misguided nationalism is also undoubtedly one factor motivating the white Americans who call for the internment of Japanese along the West Coast. They believe that the presence of these immigrants from the land of the enemy poses a direct threat to national security, though the author notes that "there had not been a single case of sabotage committed by a Japanese living in Hawaii or on the Mainland during the Pearl Harbor attack or after."

Nationalism, of course, is not limited to the United States; it also leads to conflict when the Itoi family visits Japan. Native Japanese children, convinced that the Japanese Americans have forsaken their loyalty to Japan, criticize the visitors, vandalize the home where they stay, and ultimately taunt Kazuko and her brother Henry into a fight.

Assimilation

Assimilation is the process by which a minority population integrates itself into the majority population around it. This can mean adopting new habits of social interaction, changing one's diet, and learning another language. In *Nisei Daughter*, Mr. and Mrs. Itoi embrace all of these changes to some degree. They dress like typical Americans, and in their pantry, rice and soy sauce stand "next to the ivory-painted canisters of flour, sugar, tea and coffee." They use both chopsticks and traditional western tableware.

The Itoi children, having been born in America, assimilate far more quickly and fully than their parents could ever hope to do. On one New Year's Eve, for example, Mrs. Itoi considers making the traditional Japanese holiday meal of buckwheat noodles. The family rejects this idea, and they eat apple pie instead. When Mr. and Mrs. Itoi tell Henry and Kazuko that they will attend Japanese school after regular school each day, Kazuko protests; she does not want to learn about being Japanese because she sees herself as American.

Since the Nisei children have already thoroughly assimilated into American culture, they are shocked by other Americans who view them as foreigners. Though they have done everything possible to fit in, their physical features betray their ancestry to those who seek to exclude them. As S. Frank Miyamoto writes in his introduction to *Nisei Daughter,* "Thus a Nisei was American, but not truly a part of American society. A Nisei was certainly not Japanese, but Japanese influences seeped into aspects of his character and behavior." They want nothing more than to be seen as American, yet even their own government, at least during World War II, takes an active role in preventing that assimilation.

HISTORICAL OVERVIEW

Japanese Immigrants in America

In 1854, the Treaty of Kanagawa, which allowed for trade with the United States, ended Japan's two hundred years of relative seclusion from foreign trading partners. Within a few decades, many Japanese had relocated to Washington, Oregon, and California to work for railroad companies and other booming industries. This influx became even greater after the Chinese Exclusion Act in 1882, which prohibited Chinese people from entering the United States. Until then, the Chinese had played an important part in the development of many industries along the West Coast.

By 1907, paralleling events with Chinese immigrants decades earlier, West Coast landowners and businessmen called for a halt on all Japanese immigration to the United States. The American and Japanese governments settled on an informal agreement, and Japan stopped issuing passports for new laborers. However, Japanese "picture brides" were still allowed to travel to America to meet their pre-arranged husbands. In 1913, Japanese people were banned from owning land in California after white farmers feared they might be driven out of business. In 1924, all immigration from Japan was officially halted. This ban remained in place until the 1950s.

Japanese and other Asian immigrants were summarily denied the right to citizenship since they did not meet the naturalization requirement of being "free white persons." However, the children of Japanese immigrants born on American soil were automatically recognized as U.S. citizens.

In recent decades, Japanese immigration has fallen well below past levels, with other Asian nationalities appearing in much larger numbers. Although Japanese Americans can be found across the United States—primarily due to the West Coast exodus caused by internment during World War II—the largest established communities are still found in Hawaii, California, Oregon, and Washington.

World War II and the Internment of Japanese Americans

On December 7, 1941, when Japanese bombers attacked the American naval base at Pearl Harbor, Hawaii, the United States was home to over one hundred thousand Japanese Americans. The majority of these were full American citizens, born in the United States. (The rest, despite living in the United States for many years, were prohibited by law from becoming citizens.) American military leaders feared that spies operating among them—citizens or not—would cripple their efforts to wage war against Japan.

Despite the fact that his own State Department officials reported no threat from Japanese people on the West Coast, President Franklin Roosevelt was convinced to issue Executive Order 9066. This order allowed the War Department to remove anyone, of any ethnic makeup, from "exclusion zones" that were deemed to be of military significance. The War Department then declared all of California, most of Oregon and Washington, and part of Arizona as an exclusion zone and announced that anyone of Japanese ancestry within the region would be forced to relocate. Hawaii was noticeably absent from the relocation, despite the fact that one-third of its population was Japanese. Some historians claim this is because removing the Japanese from this territory would have been economically devastating to the region.

These Japanese Americans were required to rid themselves of their assets—homes, businesses, and other valuable property—before reporting to their local relocation center. In many cases, the bank assets of Japanese nationals were frozen even before relocation. Internees were frequently held in temporary barracks until more permanent camps were finished in Idaho, Utah, Colorado, California, and other states. The camps offered bare-bones barracks with no insulation or personal plumbing and no appliances or furniture beyond a single wood burning stove in each dwelling. Weather at the camps ranged from extreme heat during the summer to extreme cold during the winter. Most of the internees, having spent their entire lives in temperate West Coast regions, were ill equipped for such conditions.

The camps wsurrounded by wire fences monitored by armed guards, and contraband materials such as tools were routinely seized from internees.

By 1943, some college-age Nisei internees were allowed to leave the camps if they could provide proof of an employment offer or acceptance to a college outside the exclusion zone. Several hundred Nisei men volunteered for U.S. military service alongside Japanese volunteers from Hawaii; their unit, the 442nd Regimental Combat Team, became one of the most decorated combat units in American military history. The majority of internees were allowed to return to the West Coast in 1945. Many thousands of these, left with nothing to return to on the West Coast, started new lives in areas throughout the rest of the United States.

The legality of creating an "exclusion zone" (and the subsequent internment camps) was challenged in the 1944 Supreme Court case *Korematsu v. United States*. The court ruled in favor of the government, pointing out that extreme measures were sometimes necessary in times of war. The case was appealed in 1983, and the ruling was finally reversed. In addition, several U.S. presidents, beginning with Gerald Ford in 1976, acknowledged that the internment of Japanese American citizens during World War II was unnecessary and wrong. In 1988, President Ronald Reagan signed a bill that allowed for compensation in the amount of twenty thousand dollars for each living internee who filed a claim. In 1992, President George H. W. Bush approved additional reparation funds and issued a formal apology to all internees.

Several of the former internment camp sites, including the Minidoka camp at which the Itoi family was held, have been marked by historical monuments that aim to educate Americans about this often-overlooked event in their history.

CRITICAL OVERVIEW

At the time of its initial publication in 1953, *Nisei Daughter* was one of the only notable memoirs written from a Japanese American perspective. Critics were generally favorable in their discussion of the book. A reviewer for the *San Francisco Chronicle,* quoted on the cover of the reprint edition, enthuses "The deepest impression this unaffected, honest little story made on me was one of smiling courage." In "American Uses of Japanese American

Memory: How Internment Narratives are 'Put into Discourse,' " Brian Lain quotes Georgianne Sampson's review for the *New York Herald Tribune*, which calls the book "warmly affecting and entertaining," and notes that it seems to be "composed more with love than with protest."

Still, the book is not without its faults. A reviewer for *Newsweek* writes that "the book has an unfinished air" and suggests that "it does not do justice to the Japanese or to the Americans" (quoted in Lain). Whatever the reason, sales of the book during its first printing were modest, and the book was quickly forgotten. It was out of print for over twenty-five years before renewed interest in the Japanese American internment brought it back to the public's attention in the late 1970s. The 1979 reprint was issued by the University of Washington Press, and has remained steadily popular ever since. On the *Nisei Daughter* webpage on the University of Washington Press website, Sone is noted as writing with "charm, humor, and deep understanding." S. Frank Miyamoto, who wrote the introduction to that edition, calls *Nisei Daughter* a "lively, ingenuous, and charming book." *Kliatt Young Adult Paperback Book Guide* calls the book "ideal … for young adults," and rates it as "highly recommended" (quoted in Lain). Still, some modern readers have expressed the opinion that the book deals too gently with the issue of Japanese American relocation and internment.

CRITICISM

Greg Wilson

In the following essay, American popular culture writer Wilson examines Sone's depiction of white Americans in Nisei Daughter *and argues that their overly positive portrayal serves to weaken the impact of the internment tragedy in the mind of the reader.*

There are precious few literary accounts of the tragedy that befell Japanese Americans at the hands of their own government during World War II. Monica Sone's *Nisei Daughter* is certainly one of the best-regarded, despite the fact that only about one-fifth of the rather slim book covers the author's own experiences in internment camps in Washington and Idaho. Those looking for a hard-hitting account of this appalling, government-sanctioned imprisonment may be left unsatisfied for another reason as well: the author's depiction of white Americans—especially during wartime—is surprisingly gentle. In fact, the relative absence of animosity expressed by whites in the book may lead someone without an understanding of Japanese culture to regard it with a certain amount of suspicion.

The negative portrayals of white Americans' behavior toward those of Japanese ancestry in the book are so few, in fact, that each can be mentioned here in some detail. Almost all take place before World War II, and most are qualified by the author in some way. The first occurs when a guest at the Itoi family's hotel demands a refund for his room, even though he has stayed there most of the day. The man, who is referred to as a "grizzly bear," calls the author's father a "damn Jap," and threatens to turn him in to the police. However, the man gets his comeuppance at the hands of the hotel's bouncer, who removes him from the premises by tossing him down a long stairway.

The next incident involves two police officers looking to extort money from the author's father. They interrupt the family dinner and accuse Mr. Itoi of selling bootleg alcohol. The police call him "Shorty" and "Charlie" (likely a reference to Charlie Chan, though the term was later used for different reasons to refer to Vietnamese people during the Vietnam War), and take him to jail when he refuses to pay a fifty-dollar bribe. Still, the author makes it clear that this incident had little to do with ancestry, and was a common occurrence on Skid Row where the family lived; just before this, she describes how she and her siblings would often see police shaking down drunks—white drunks, the reader can assume—for whatever pocket money they had.

The most dramatic and sweeping negative portrayal of white Americans occurs when the family attempts to rent a summer beach house so the author's young sister, Sumiko, can get fresh air and sunshine to improve her asthma. The family does not know that the people in the area in which they are looking are not hospitable to Japanese people. They are repeatedly told that empty houses are no longer for rent, or scared off with quotes of exorbitant rates. One woman says flatly, "I'm sorry, but we don't want Japs around here." Aside from this one instance, though,

> THOSE LOOKING FOR A HARD-HITTING ACCOUNT OF THIS APPALLING, GOVERNMENT-SANCTIONED IMPRISONMENT MAY BE LEFT UNSATISFIED FOR ANOTHER REASON AS WELL: THE AUTHOR'S DEPICTION OF WHITE AMERICANS—ESPECIALLY DURING WARTIME—IS SURPRISINGLY GENTLE."

the author notes, "They all turned us down politely." Even when the white proprietors behave despicably, the author feels the need to soften the blow by complimenting their method of delivery.

In the months leading up to World War II, with relations between Japanese and whites undoubtedly tense, there are only a few brief incidents mentioned: two uses of the word "Jap," a couple of instances of service denied to the author at a store and a lodge, and the occasional cold stare from a white stranger. Even after Pearl Harbor, as government officials are arresting and holding Japanese Americans without just cause, the author relates the rather tame story of a Japanese woman whose husband had died years before: government officials show up and ransack her shop looking for the husband, but when they realize he is dead, they are apologetic. After Executive Order 9066 is issued, the author quotes some generic racist statements without attribution, but notes that the family "had dismissed these remarks as just hot blasts of air from an overheated patriot."

By contrast, the positive portrayals of white Americans are abundant throughout the book, most particularly when the author is finally able to leave the internment camp during the war. Furthermore, these are invariably lengthier and more detailed passages than the negative portrayals. All of the white men who work for the author's father at the hotel seem particularly tolerant; during the family's internment, one of them visits, bringing fresh fruits, candies, and expressions of sorrow at their confinement. The many people who help Sone gain freedom from the camp are described in loving detail. Here is a description of a man whose family boards the author after her release:

> Dr. Richardson came out of his study, beaming. He was a great oak of a man, tall and solidly built. The rugged cut of his features, his deep vibrant voice, everything about him revealed a personality of strong purpose and will.

The author even counterbalances some of her scant negative portrayals of West Coast whites with more glowing depictions of white Americans in the Midwest. The following scene, set in Chicago, serves as an effective rejoinder to the time she was ignored at a department store counter in Washington:

> Sometimes there were decided advantages to having an Oriental face, especially when shopping. When I stepped into a department store or market, a clerk would spot me instantly and rush up to wait on me, burning with curiosity. The clerks were invariably sociable and pleasant and they complimented me on my English.

Interestingly, the author reports this as a positive experience, but makes no mention of how the "compliment" on her English is based on the prejudiced—and incorrect—assumption that she is not a native speaker.

In a memoir, of course—especially one written while the characters within it are very much alive—it is not uncommon to focus more on those who have made a positive impact on one's life. It is also possible that the author subscribes to the simple philosophy, "If you don't have anything nice to say, then don't say anything at all." Then again, most who subscribe to such a philosophy have probably not spent years unjustly imprisoned.

This oddly gentle treatment of white Americans reaches a climax at the end of the book, when the author returns to the Minidoka internment camp to visit her parents for Christmas. Just before she leaves, the three discuss the situation of the Japanese in America. Her mother says, "When the war came and we were all evacuated, Papa and I were heartsick. We felt terribly bad about being your Japanese parents." To someone without an understanding of the Japanese culture, this statement may seem ridiculous. The parents are blaming *themselves* for being Japanese? Equally frustrating are the author's own thoughts about her parents as she leaves the internment camp: "I wondered when they would be able to leave their no-man's land, pass through the legal barrier and become naturalized citizens. Then I thought, in America,

many things are possible." Indeed, in America, many things are possible; unfortunately, some of those things are reprehensible, and should not be quite so easily excused lest they be forgotten.

It is worth mentioning that the most violent race-based conflict in the book does not involve white people at all; it happens when the author and her family visit their relatives in Japan. The local Japanese youths brazenly slur the visitors with cries of "America-jin! America-jin!" and throw rocks through the paper walls of the house where they stay. One morning, the author and her older brother are confronted by several of the local boys, and a fight ensues.

Why, one might ask, do white Americans get off so easily in Sone's memoir? Perhaps this can all be explained by the distinctly Japanese tendency toward extreme diplomacy that sometimes seems, to an outsider, to border on self-punishment. For example, at a potluck picnic, the author relates a plea her mother makes to another Japanese woman: "I'd like to have you try some fried chicken. I did a very poor job on it, but please take pieces to your family."

Perhaps it has something to do with the book's original 1953 publication date. This was a time of nationalist fervor, when the United States was battling a new Asian foe (the Communist Chinese, via North Korea) and Senator Joe McCarthy was riding high on his quest to ferret out "un-American" activities. Japanese Americans were undoubtedly eager to reaffirm their patriotism, especially in light of their home country's eagerness to revoke their most basic rights only a decade before. Such a desire could at least explain the insistent flag-waving found at the end of the book.

Then again, it could simply be that the author's individual encounters with white Americans were not representative of the greater, abstract national consciousness. This is a common occurrence in matters of race: those in the ethnic or racial majority often consider themselves "good people," and treat individual members of a minority as equals. At the same time, they allow terrible things to happen to the minority group as a whole, as if it were somehow beyond their control. This may be the most insidious kind of racism, because it is so hard to pin to a slab and dissect.

Sone should not be criticized for writing a memoir that has become, by virtue of its uniqueness more than its quality, required reading for those curious about the Japanese internment tragedy. However, impressionable readers might assume that her feel-good account is the full story; at the very least, instructors who include the book as part of their curricula should also demand a more critical and detailed examination of these events than this book can ever provide.

SOURCES

Lain, Brian, "American Uses of Japanese American Memory: How Internment Narratives are 'Put into Discourse,'" *University of North Texas*, www.comm. unt.edu/faculty/american_uses_of_japanese_americ.htm (January 4, 2006).

Miyamoto, S. Frank, Introduction, in *Nisei Daughter*, by Monica Sone, University of Washington Press, 1979, pp. xi, xiv, originally published by Little, Brown in 1953.

"Nisei Daughter," *University of Washington Press*, www.washington.edu/uwpress/search/books/SONNIS. html (January 6, 2006).

Sone, Monica, *Nisei Daughter*, University of Washington Press, 1979, originally published by Little, Brown in 1953.

A Passage to India

E. M. FORSTER

1924

A Passage to India is the sixth and final novel by English writer Edward Morgan (E. M.) Forster. It received almost universal acclaim when it was published in 1924. The novel depicts life in British colonial India during the early part of the twentieth century, offering a balanced look at both the English and the Indians they ruled. At the time of publication, its unflattering portrayal of the English caused many to view the book as a critique of the British government's colonial policies. Only later did critics begin to see themes in the novel that transcended the immediate politics of the time.

Forster began writing the book in 1913, the year after his first visit to India. The start of World War I delayed his work, and it was only after another visit to India in 1921 that Forster decided to finish the novel. When *A Passage to India* was published, fourteen years had passed since the publication of his previous novel, *Howards End*, and his new novel was the publishing event of the year. Expectations were high and they proved to be justified by the almost uniformly positive critical assessments of the book. *A Passage to India* is frequently cited as Forster's best work. It is praised for its intelligent and sensitive portraits of race relations and prejudice in British colonial India, as well as for its larger spiritual themes and for its beauty, economy, and polish as a work of art.

'I HAVE HAD TWENTY-FIVE YEARS' EXPERIENCE OF THIS COUNTRY'—HE PAUSED, AND 'TWENTY-FIVE YEARS' SEEMED TO FILL THE WAITING-ROOM WITH THEIR STALENESS AND UNGENEROSITY—'AND DURING THOSE TWENTY-FIVE YEARS I HAVE NEVER KNOWN ANYTHING BUT DISASTER RESULT WHEN ENGLISH PEOPLE AND INDIANS ATTEMPT TO BE INTIMATE SOCIALLY. INTERCOURSE, YES. COURTESY, BY ALL MEANS. INTIMACY—NEVER, NEVER.' "

BIOGRAPHY

E. M. FORSTER

E. M. Forster was born in London, England, on January 1, 1879. His father, an architect, died soon after, and Forster was raised by his mother and great-aunt. After attending university at King's College, Cambridge, he spent time traveling Europe with his mother. On his return to England, he began to focus seriously on writing.

By the time he visited India in 1912, he was an accomplished novelist. He began writing *A Passage to India* the following year, but World War I delayed his work on the novel. After the war and a second trip to India, he finally finished the novel, some ten years after starting it. Published in 1924, it was his sixth and final novel. Forster later returned to King's College, where he spent many years teaching and writing.

A Passage to India was a great success, in part because of the controversy it created. Some readers were offended by the novel's portrait of a racist English ruling class, though Forster himself considered the novel more spiritual than political. Some of his best-known novels include *A Room with a View* (1908), *Howards End* (1910), and *Maurice* (published posthumously in 1971).

Forster died in Coventry, England, on June 7, 1970.

Despite its political overtones, *A Passage to India* was already somewhat politically dated at the time of its publication. The situation in India had begun to change, in part because World War I had affected the British Empire and in part because of the early independence movements in India. What had not changed were the colonialist attitudes portrayed in the book. Conflicts between people of different races and religions remained relevant, as they do today. At the heart of all Forster's novels lie the relationships between human beings, the fragility—and in the case of *A Passage to India*, the impossibility—of friendship between the rulers and the ruled. For Forster, the most damning aspects of colonialism were the facts that it divided human beings, kept potential friends apart, and prevented understanding between people of different races or cultures.

With a certain amount of irony, Forster named his book after a poem by American poet Walt Whitman. Whitman's "Passage to India," written after the opening of the Suez Canal in 1869, celebrates connecting of East and West through the achievements of modern technology. It is a poem about the convergence of the human race, so long divided by geographic, racial, and cultural differences. Forster, writing half a century later, is far more skeptical about such a connection and whether it really represents advancement, though there is still a sense of longing for it in the novel. *A Passage to India* suggests that there is a long way to go before

human beings truly come together; the politics of the time, along with ethnic and religious divisions, are among the obstacles in their way.

Forster was forty-five years old when *A Passage to India* was published. He lived another forty-five years but wrote no more fiction, concentrating instead on biography, criticism, and essays. *A Passage to India* remains his most popular novel, translated into more languages than any of his other fiction.

PLOT SUMMARY

A Passage to India is divided into three sections titled "Mosque," "Caves," and "Temple." Each section roughly represents one of the groups portrayed in the novel: "Mosque" depicts the Muslims; "Caves," the English; and "Temple," the Hindus.

Part I: Mosque
Chapters 1–6

The novel opens with a broad introduction to the fictional city of Chandrapore, India, which is a rather ordinary place. Aside from the nearby Marabar Caves, there is little of interest in Chandrapore. Dr. Aziz, a young Muslim physician, arrives at the home of Hamidullah, a prominent local lawyer, and they discuss whether it is possible to be friends with an Englishman. Aziz then receives a note from Major Callendar, his supervisor at the hospital, asking him to come to Callendar's bungalow. On the way, however, his bicycle gets a flat tire and he is forced to hire a carriage. By the time he arrives, Callendar has gone. Aziz is angry at the slight and he is further incensed when two English ladies ignore his presence and take his hired carriage.

On his way home he stops at a mosque, where he is interrupted by an elderly English woman. He is rude to her at first, assuming she has not removed her shoes as required, but then regrets his rudeness when he learns of her respect for Islam. They strike up a friendship. The woman is Mrs. Moore, newly arrived from England. Her son Ronny Heaslop is the local city magistrate. Aziz complains about how he has been treated by the English, then sees Mrs. Moore off and walks happily home.

Mrs. Moore goes to the local social center for the English, or Anglo-Indians, as they are called. There, she meets her friend Adela Quested, who has traveled from England with Mrs. Moore to see Heaslop, whom she is thinking of marrying. Miss Quested remarks "I want to see the *real* India" and is soon introduced to some of the local Anglo-Indians. They generally have nothing good to say about the native Indians, but Mr. Turton, the local political leader, says he will throw a party so that Miss Quested can meet some Indians. Mrs. Moore mentions her meeting at the mosque. Heaslop is curious, assuming his mother has met an

E. M. Forster Hulton Archive / Getty Images

English doctor, and is shocked when he realizes it was a local Muslim. Miss Quested—enthralled by the notion of meeting a local—is put off by Heaslop's obvious prejudice.

Turton's party is a failure. The English stand aside gossiping about the Indians, cynically assessing their motives. Miss Quested tries to start a conversation with a group of Indian women but the attempt fails. She suddenly shudders at the thought of marrying Heaslop and living among the snobbish Anglo-Indians. The exception is Cyril Fielding, the principal of the local college, who is open and generous with the Indians. He learns that the Indian women approve of Mrs. Moore and Miss Quested, and he invites the two ladies to tea. That night Heaslop talks with his mother and they argue about colonialism. Heaslop proudly supports the harshness of British rule while Mrs. Moore argues for Christian love and charity.

Aziz decides to attend the party, but then changes his mind because it falls on the anniversary of his wife's death. By skipping the event, he disappoints his Hindu colleague, Dr. Panna Lal. Later, Aziz plays polo at Hamidullah's with an English soldier. Lal arrives and complains to Aziz about his missing the party, but Aziz refuses to show contrition. Aziz claims that he is not beholden to the English but fears he may have angered Callendar by not attending the party. When he gets home, he is pleased to find an invitation to tea from Fielding, a man he has never met.

Chapters 7–11

Aziz goes to Fielding's for tea and quickly strikes up a friendly rapport with Fielding. They are joined by Mrs. Moore, Miss Quested, and Professor Godbole, a local Hindu man. Miss Quested lets on that she has decided not to marry Heaslop, upsetting Mrs. Moore. While Fielding shows Mrs. Moore around the college, Miss Quested stays to talk with Aziz and Godbole. Aziz invites Miss Quested and Mrs. Moore to see the Marabar Caves. Heaslop comes in and is rude to both Indians. He criticizes Fielding for leaving Miss Quested with two Indians, then takes her away. Mrs. Moore, upset with Miss Quested for revealing she will not marry Heaslop, asks to go home; Miss Quested and Heaslop go to a polo match where Miss Quested tells him that they will not be married. The Nawab Bahadur, a prominent local Muslim landowner, then arrives and invites them for a drive. In the dark car, Heaslop and Miss Quested accidentally touch hands and let the contact linger, thus rekindling their affair. The car then strikes something on the road and skids into a tree. Miss Derek, an Englishwoman who works for an Indian official, takes them away in her car. The accident has brought Heaslop and Miss Quested together and they are again engaged.

Aziz, slightly ill, lies in bed thinking about Fielding, the only Englishman he likes. A group of friends arrives and they gossip about Godbole and Hindus more generally. Lal comes in to check Aziz's health and to spy on Aziz for Callendar. They begin to argue, pitting Muslims against Hindus, and Fielding enters. They then all speak frankly about why England is in India, but Aziz remains silent, embarrassed by the poverty of his room. Before he leaves, Aziz calls Fielding back into the house and shows him a picture of his late wife. Fielding is honored. As Fielding leaves, he and Aziz feel they have solidified their growing friendship.

Part II: Caves
Chapters 12–16

The second section of the book, "Caves," opens with myths of India's geographical creation followed by a description of the Marabar Caves' qualities—both ordinary and extraordinary. Nothing has come of Aziz's invitation to see the caves, and Miss Quested casually comments on her disappointment. A servant overhears her and passes along the word. Aziz, feeling he has offended, quickly arranges the outing with Fielding, Godbole, and the ladies. Heaslop agrees only on the condition that Fielding takes responsibility for the ladies' comfort. On the day of the outing, Fielding and Godbole miss the train to the caves, which surprises Aziz because "Fielding [is] an Englishman, and they never do miss trains, and Godbole [is] a Hindu, and [does] not count." The train stops near an elephant that Aziz has hired, which the group rides to the caves. Miss Quested asks Aziz about her becoming a typical Anglo-Indian, but he does not want to talk about it. In the first cave, Mrs. Moore finds the atmosphere stifling and nearly faints amid the crush of servants and local people. The dead echo, the "boum" sound that the cave produces, horrifies her, and she refuses to enter any more caves. She tells Aziz to take Miss Quested with a guide and leave the others behind. As they leave, she contemplates the echo she heard in the cave and feels immensely distressed.

Miss Quested, Aziz, and the guide climb up a ridge to a large section of caves. Miss Quested thinks about her impending marriage, her plans, and her life in India, and suddenly realizes that she does not love Heaslop. She asks Aziz if he is married, and when he says yes, asks him if he has more than one wife. Aziz, shocked and offended, disappears into a nearby cave to avoid insulting Miss Quested. When he returns, Miss Quested is gone, having apparently disappeared into a different cave. The guide does not know where she has gone, and Aziz angrily strikes him for not doing his job. A motorcar approaches below and Aziz suddenly sees Miss Quested walking toward the parked car. As he heads down, he spots Miss Quested's field glasses at a cave entrance. He notices that strap is broken and then puts them in his pocket. Below he finds Fielding, who has come by car with Miss Derek. Miss Derek's chauffeur says that Miss Derek and Miss Quested have returned to Chandrapore. Fielding thinks this is odd, but Aziz is not worried. They return to Chandrapore by train; when they arrive, Aziz is arrested and taken to prison for an unnamed charge. Fielding is taken to see Turton in the station.

Chapters 17–23

Turton is enraged. He tells Fielding that Miss Quested has accused Aziz of attacking her in a cave. Fielding refuses to believe it, claiming Aziz is innocent; Turton gets angry with him for not rallying around his English comrades. He tells Fielding about a meeting at the club that evening and Fielding says he will come. Fielding goes to see McBryde, the superintendent of police; he hears the details of the charge, but still refuses to believe it. He tells McBryde that Aziz is innocent and insists that they ask Miss Quested to clear things up before trouble starts. McBryde warns Fielding to keep quiet, informs him that Miss Quested is ill, and denies him access to Aziz. Outside, Fielding meets Hamidullah, Aziz's friend and lawyer, and decides that he will side with the Indians. Hamidullah suggests a Hindu lawyer to broaden support for the case and mentions an anti-British lawyer in Calcutta named Amritrao. Fielding fears the incident will explode into violence. Later, Fielding writes Miss Quested a letter asking her to rethink her accusation.

Ignoring their initial dislike of Miss Quested, the Anglo-Indians now rally to her cause, exaggerating and inventing dangers. At the meeting, Turton and the others want to exact revenge on all of India for the insult to Miss Quested. The news arrives that Miss Quested is feeling better, much to everyone's relief. Callendar persuades a subordinate to try baiting Fielding into a fight, but Fielding keeps a cool head despite his anger. Heaslop, who has refused to grant Aziz bail, arrives. Fielding is the only person who refuses to stand up as a show of support and respect. The others attack Fielding, who declares his belief in Aziz's innocence. He then resigns from the club and leaves. He goes to see the Indians and gets involved in their campaign on Aziz's behalf.

Miss Quested is staying at the McBrydes' while she recovers. After her scramble down from the cave, she had to have hundreds of cactus spines removed from her body. She tries to recall the incident clearly but is exhausted and confused. She hears about tensions and near riots caused by her accusations, which are to be tried before Das, an Indian assistant to Heaslop. McBryde admits that he opened and read Fielding's letter to Miss Quested and mentions that Fielding thinks she has made a mistake. Heaslop takes Miss Quested home, where she finds Mrs. Moore distant and detached, still disturbed by her experience in the cave. Mrs. Moore wants to go home to England and only becomes talkative when Miss Quested mentions the cave's echo, which Miss Quested says she hears in her head. Mrs. Moore refuses to testify at the trial. Miss Quested wonders if she has made a mistake and even tells Heaslop that Aziz is innocent, but Heaslop refuses to believe her. Mrs. Moore then also says that Aziz is innocent and Heaslop decides to send his mother home after all. Mrs. Moore leaves before the trial begins.

Chapters 24–25

The trial begins. Miss Quested, who is now staying with the Turtons, has rehearsed her testimony and is ready. There is great unrest in the town the day of the trial. The courtroom is hot and crowded, and tempers flare over Fielding's aid to the Indians. McBryde prosecutes, and plans to have Lal and Callendar testify against Aziz. McBryde's opening statement mentions Mrs. Moore, prompting Aziz's lawyer to rage about how Mrs. Moore was spirited away so that she could not testify. He criticizes English justice and the crowd outside begins to chant Mrs. Moore's name, pronouncing it "Esmiss Esmoor." Miss Quested takes the stand but when asked about the caves, she suddenly recants her original charge. The charges are dismissed, Aziz faints, the English are enraged, and the court erupts in chaos. Miss Quested encounters a crowd of celebrating Indians and the surge flings her against Fielding, who protects her, leaving Aziz behind. Fielding takes Miss Quested to his place, amazed but also angry with her. Aziz, meanwhile, is driven away with his supporters, distraught that Fielding has not followed.

Chapters 26–32

Fielding and Miss Quested talk, and she asks him if he can explain her behavior. Her echo is gone now and Fielding thinks that she suffered a nervous breakdown in the cave. They speculate over whether she had a hallucination or whether the guide may have assaulted her. Then Hamidullah comes in; he is deeply resentful of Miss Quested. Having been denounced by the English for recanting her story, Miss Quested now has no place to stay, so Fielding offers to let her stay at the college. Heaslop arrives and tells Fielding that Mrs. Moore has died on her way back to England. Fielding and Hamidullah leave for Aziz's victory banquet and Hamidullah begins talking about how much compensation Aziz should request from Miss Quested. After the banquet, Fielding tells Aziz he should drop the request for money and argues in Miss Quested's favor, telling Aziz how bravely she acted by changing her story. Aziz refuses and Fielding is disappointed with Aziz's bitterness. Aziz says he will ask Mrs. Moore for her advice, forcing Fielding to tell him that his friend has died.

Fielding rejoins the English club and develops a friendship with Miss Quested. She writes a letter apologizing to Aziz, and Fielding uses the memory of Mrs. Moore to convince Aziz not to ruin Miss Quested by demanding compensation. Heaslop breaks his engagement with Miss Quested and she leaves for England. Once she is gone, however, an Indian servant starts a rumor that Miss Quested and Fielding had become lovers while she was his guest at the college. Aziz believes the rumor and turns cool toward Fielding. Aziz tells Fielding about the rumor and Fielding tries to dismiss such talk until he realizes that Aziz believes it. He then gets angry at Aziz, who is both ashamed of his suspicions and hurt by Fielding's reaction. Fielding tells Aziz that he is going to England and Aziz is convinced that Fielding will marry Miss Quested for her money. Their friendship now strained, Fielding leaves for England.

Temple
Chapters 33–37

The final section of the novel, "Temple," serves as an epilogue—a conclusion that reveals something about the lives of the main characters after the central story has ended. Two years have passed and Aziz is now working with Godbole at Mau, in a Hindu state. He has escaped English rule to some extent and is happy. A Hindu festival is taking place and Godbole tells Aziz that Fielding, traveling on business, has arrived at the local guest house with his wife and her brother. He sends a note, but Aziz, assuming that Fielding's wife is Miss Quested, tears it up.

While on a walk with his children, Aziz meets Fielding and his young brother-in-law, Ralph, who has been stung by a bee. Fielding asks why Aziz has not answered his letters, which in fact he has never even read, and Aziz is distant and ironic. Then Aziz refers to Ralph as "Mr. Quested" and his mistake is revealed.

Ralph is not Miss Quested's brother; he is Mrs. Moore's son, Fielding's wife's brother. Aziz is mortified at his mistake but Fielding is amused. Then Aziz becomes genuinely angry, denouncing Fielding and all the English. He leaves, but finds himself happy that the exchange rekindled him memories of Mrs. Moore. He later delivers an ointment for Ralph. Seeing Fielding and his wife in a boat below the guest house, Aziz thinks the guest house empty and lets himself in. He finds and reads two of Fielding's letters, one from Heaslop and one from Miss Quested, and learns that Fielding has become a member of the ruling English establishment. Ralph appears and surprises Aziz, who treats the young man roughly at first. After Ralph tells Aziz that Mrs. Moore genuinely loved him and had written about him in her letters, Aziz invites him to see the Hindu procession from a boat. Their boat collides with Fielding's and both boats capsize in shallow water. The incident renews the friendship between Fielding and Aziz.

Fielding and Aziz go for a horseback ride, and their conversation reveals that Fielding now views colonialism more positively. Aziz has written a letter to Miss Quested, forgiving her. The two men talk politics and Aziz, now entirely anti-English, declares that he would like to throw all the English out and let India be a nation, " 'and then' he concluded, half kissing him, 'you and I shall be friends.' " Fielding protests, but they know it is not yet time for Englishmen and Indians to be true friends.

THEMES

Race

Race is among the most important and controversial issues in *A Passage to India*. Immediately after the novel's publication, Forster was accused of exaggerating the English colonists' racism, though he was also praised for describing their attitudes honestly and accurately. The typical colonists' attitudes are portrayed early in the novel, when Mrs. Callendar, amused at Miss Quested's interest in meeting the natives, says, "Why, the kindest thing one can do to a native is to let him die." She then adds that a native "can go where he likes as long as he doesn't come near me. They give me the creeps." Miss Quested, new to India, is appalled by such remarks, as were many of the novel's English readers. But

Mrs. Callendar is by no means exceptional—she is the colonial British norm. Later in the book, Mrs. Turton reminds Mrs. Moore, "You're superior to them, anyway. Don't forget that. You're superior to everyone in India except one or two of the Ranis, and they're on an equality."

Ronny Heaslop, too, offers a number of racist generalizations about the Indians, though Heaslop's attitudes reveal how the English become much more aware of race after arriving in India. His comment after Fielding's tea party is one example. Before the party, Fielding breaks his collar stud and Aziz generously gives him his own, leaving his own collar partially detached. Heaslop, unaware of this small act of friendship, makes a sweeping and unfair judgment: "Aziz was exquisitely dressed, from tie-pin to spats, but he had forgotten his back collar-stud, and there you have the Indian all over: inattention to detail; the fundamental slackness that reveals the race." The reader, knowing the truth, can laugh at Heaslop's ignorance, but the point remains: prejudice is often based on easy judgments made in ignorance. Forster also makes it clear that Heaslop has learned to make these judgments during his year in India. "You never used to judge people like this at home," his mother says to him, suggesting that he has changed for the worse over the course of the year.

Though race is an issue throughout the book, it becomes a central concern in the novel when Miss Quested accuses Aziz of attempting to assault her in the cave. A British man would have been scandalized by this accusation, but for a native it is the ultimate disgrace. The English people at the club assume not only that Aziz is guilty but that he is typical in his guilt. Only Fielding, who "had no racial feeling," publicly disagrees with their racism (though Mrs. Moore later declares Aziz's innocence privately, to her son and Miss Quested). The Anglo-Indians cannot accept Fielding's assumption that Aziz is innocent; they take it as not only an insult to Miss Quested but to the English nation and the entire race:

> [T]he Collector looked at him sternly, because he was keeping his head. He had not gone mad at the phrase "an English girl fresh from England," he had not rallied to the banner of race. He was still after facts, though the herd had decided on emotion

Fielding does indeed keep his head, and as a result is at least temporarily ostracized by his white countrymen. They accept him again only later, after the trial, which is overseen by a Hindu judge.

Religion

The British ruling classes are not the only people concerned with racial or religious differences in *A Passage to India*. The Indians display prejudices in the novel, as well. Much of their prejudice is focused on their British rulers, of course, but they also show prejudice toward one another. Religion creates a major division between the Indians: the Muslims and Hindus do not quite trust each other and they often get along only when joining forces to oppose the British. Aziz, for instance, offers a number of prejudiced comments about Hindus, including "I wish they did not remind me of cow-dung." Miss Quested's accusation rallies both Hindus and Muslims to defend Aziz's innocence, but it is clear that this is a short-term alliance between the groups.

The portrayal of these religious differences and prejudices provides balance to the novel. The English use these religious rifts to justify their presence in the country, claiming that their overriding rule prevents Hindus, Muslims, and Sikhs from fighting. The Indians themselves are aware of these divisions and use them to their advantage at times. Shortly after Aziz is arrested, his friend and lawyer Hamidullah decides to bring in a prominent anti-English Hindu lawyer from Calcutta, specifically to broaden support for the Muslim Aziz. He wants to make a political issue of the accusation.

Frustrated Brotherhood

The balanced portrayal of different cultures in Forster's novel suggests that he intended it to be more than simply a critique of British colonialism and racism. He examines relations between human beings, lingering on the differences that divide them and make them strangers. Time and again in the novel, characters feel slighted by a comment, question, or act that has been misinterpreted or that was based in cultural ignorance. At times, clear communication seems impossible. Cultural and racial differences keep characters apart, as do class and language.

A Passage to India is an attempt to analyze the spiritual journey of human beings, regardless of their religion. Forester's statement in the book that "The song of the future must transcend creed" could just as easily conclude "transcend race" or "transcend gender" or "transcend class." Ultimately, the novel leaves readers uncertain whether human beings can transcend these differences any time soon. It ends with Fielding and Aziz on their horses coming to terrain through which they must pass single file. The physical separation is symbolic of a larger, human separation. As critic Norman Page summarizes in *McMillan Modern Novelists: E. M. Forster*, "The conclusion ... is neither optimistic nor pessimistic but presents a clear-eyed, unillusioned acknowledgment of the vastness of the issues and the problems that render difficult—not impossible, but very difficult—the quest for universal brotherhood."

HISTORICAL OVERVIEW

The British Empire at its Peak

A Passage to India is set in British colonial India, which—at the time Forster wrote the novel—was the largest and most important of Britain's numerous colonies. The British Empire was at its peak when Forster visited India in 1912. In the early twentieth century, the Empire controlled roughly 20 percent of the land on earth and governed more than 400 million people. It was a truly global empire, with colonies on every inhabited continent. Britain ruled India through a civil and military administration answerable directly to the government in London. The British colonialists brought with them their own class system, which existed as a ruling hierarchy above India's own rigid social hierarchy, the caste system. The British characters in the novel, for example, are ultimately answerable to the highest local British official, Mr. Turton.

The English had been in India for three hundred years and had ruled the land extensively for over two hundred years, first through the privately owned East India Company and later directly through the British government. British rule in India was repressive and dictatorial at times. When Ronny Heaslop says, "We're not pleasant in India, and we don't intend to be pleasant. We've something more important to do," he gives voice to a widely held Anglo-Indians belief, one shared by many people in

Britain. Aziz jokes about having to please the English police, but after his trial, even though he is proven innocent, he is labeled a troublemaker and followed by colonial agents for the rest of his life.

Colonial Unrest

Despite the reach of the British Empire, social unrest was increasing in India during the time in which *A Passage to India* is set. The independence movement was led largely by Mohandas Gandhi, a leader in the Indian National Congress political party; it had begun some years before and gathered steam after World War I. Forster includes vague references to this unrest in the novel, both in Chandrapore and beyond. Through the police superintendent McBryde, Forster also mentions the first anti-colonial rebellion in India, known as the Sepoy Rebellion. It occurred in 1857 when Indian soldiers, or sepoys, rebelled against their colonial rulers. After the Sepoy Rebellion, the British government ruled India directly rather than through the East India Company, though the company's huge army was incorporated into the British colonial army. The shadow of the Sepoy Rebellion lingers over the unrest in the novel.

The growing independence movement led to bloodshed shortly before Forster finished *A Passage to India*. In response to a series of repressive new laws passed by the British government, Gandhi called for a series of nationwide strikes. On April 13, 1919, British soldiers fired into a crowd of demonstrators in Amritsar, a holy city of the Sikh religion, where the demonstrators had come primarily to attend a religious festival. Nearly four hundred Indians were killed and more than a thousand were wounded. The incident was still fresh in the public's mind when Forster published *A Passage to India* and helped increase interest in the book. The Amritsar incident was a turning point in India's drive towards independence.

Internal Unrest

The tensions in India between Indians and Anglos were compounded by tensions within the native Indian population. Forster depicts tension between Hindus and Muslims in the novel, which the British used to justify their own presence in India. Near the end of the novel, Aziz points this out to Fielding:

Old story of "We will rob every man and rape every woman from Peshawar to Calcutta," I suppose, which you get some nobody to repeat and then quote every week in the *Pioneer* in order to frighten us into retaining you!

Aziz is right, but Fielding's skepticism about Indian independence is reasonable as well. The British did help keep the peace internally, but the anti-British feeling shared by Hindus and Muslims often allowed them to agree and cooperate. When India finally did gain independence in 1947, it was divided. Despite Gandhi's attempts to keep the country united, the Muslim regions split to form their own country, Pakistan, while mainly Hindu India became an independent nation.

India's Caste System

Another source of division in India at the time (one that still persists today) was the caste system, a social class system native to India. The caste system, which is derived from Hindu culture, originally divided people into four social classes. In descending order of social importance, the classes are Brahmans (priests and scholars), Kshatriyas (warriors and rulers), Vaishyas (farmers, merchants, and traders), and Sudras (common laborers born to serve the three higher castes). Another group, Dalit, often called the Untouchables, was considered so lowly as to be completely outside the social system. They traditionally performed "unclean" work such as slaughtering animals, but they were also farmers and laborers. Over centuries, the basic castes were further divided so that today in India there are more than two thousand levels of this complex social system. In *A Passage to India*, the Hindu character Professor Godbole is a Brahman; even though the caste system originated in Hindu culture, it came to be applied more generally, encompassing even Muslim Indians like Aziz. This caste system leads to a certain irony in the novel; Aziz and Hamidullah bristle at disrespectful treatment from the British, but think nothing of slapping a servant or insulting someone from a lower caste.

Because the caste system restricts social mobility, it has been often cited as a major obstacle to the modernization of India. People almost always marry within their caste, and in the past, caste status frequently determined one's profession, as well. Ironically, British rule in India made the system more flexible, opening the door for more social mobility. The designation "untouchable" was officially abolished by the Indian Constitution in 1948, though it continues to be applied today, especially in rural areas.

CRITICAL OVERVIEW

When *A Passage to India* first appeared in June 1924, it was an immediate hit, both critically and commercially. Fourteen years had passed since Forster's previous novel, *Howards End*; the arrival of a new Forster novel was a publishing event in itself, even before the work had been assessed by critics.

The critics received the novel with almost uniform praise. Critic Philip Gardner, in his book *E. M. Forster: The Critical Heritage*, writes, "The generally accepted verdict that *A Passage to India* is Forster's best book is confirmed both by the volume and by the almost complete unanimity of the response when it was published in 1924." The book was widely reviewed not only in England and the United States, but in India as well. By and large, English and Indian critics both praised Forster's damning portrayal of the English and his unusually balanced depiction of Indians. Edward Arnold's review in the *Guardian* (London), "*A Passage to India* by E. M. Forster," describes Forster's evenhandedness as "the involuntary fairness of the man who sees," suggesting his artistic sense is so developed that he sees and hears "internally, without any obligation to fancy." The book was also commended for its literary beauty. In a review for the *New York Times* titled "Challenge and Indictment in E. M. Forster's Novel," Herbert S. Gorman says, "*A Passage to India* is one of the saddest, keenest, most beautifully written ironic novels of the time." It was far and away Forster's best-selling novel.

Initially, *A Passage to India* was interpreted as a political work. Given the status of the British Empire in 1924, there was a great immediacy to the novel's subject matter. Gardner writes, "There seems little doubt that, coming only a few years after the still hotly-debated Amritsar massacre, Forster's novel had a topical relevance and an excitement that increased its acceptability to the more general reader of the time." It also angered many British readers, especially among those who lived, had lived, or were planning to live in India. Stories of civil servants throwing the novel overboard in disgust on their way to India may or may not be true, but there is no doubt that Forster's portrayal of English arrogance and racism irritated many people. According to critic Norman Page, writing in *McMillan Modern Novelists: E. M. Forster*, Forster referred in a letter "to the possibility that it might be banned by the British government." This measure, however, was never taken.

There were other negative reactions to the novel as well, of a less political nature. Indians and English alike criticized the technical, at times almost laughable, inaccuracies of the trial scene. Forster was writing well beyond his experience and they felt that he had sacrificed truthfulness for dramatic effect, a point Forster himself later acknowledged as a fair one. Yet artistically, most readers agreed that the courtroom scene is riveting material.

The primary fault found with the novel, however, concerns the third and final section of the novel, "Temple." Most critics found it odd and strangely out of place. They felt the natural climax of the book was Miss Quested's recantation of her charges and that an epilogue set during a Hindu celebration was a mistake on Forster's part. Removed from the immediate political atmosphere of the time of publication, later critics began to see the role of this section with regard to the novel's larger concerns. They noticed that the book's three-section organization suggested a larger spiritual theme involving the three groups in the novel: the Muslims, the English, and the Hindus. Even though the "Temple" section occurs after the novel's dramatic climax, it was recognized as an important part of a larger literary strategy. In his 1962 book *The Achievement of E. M. Forster*, critic J. B. Beer alludes to Forster's larger purpose as he summarizes the problem with some early criticisms of the novel:

> But the novel ought never to have been read as an essay in *realpolitik* (meant to advance a national interest). It is at once too local and too universal. As a contribution to a "practical" solution of the Indian problem as it existed at that time its value was limited, and the last chapter acknowledges the fact.

In his work "E. M. Forster as Victorian and Modern: *Howards End* and *A Passage to India*,"

MEDIA ADAPTATIONS

Indian playwright Santha Ramu Rau adapted *A Passage to India* for the stage. It was performed by the Meadow Players and opened at the Oxford Playhouse in January 1960. Forster wrote a program note for the production. An American edition of the play was published by Harcourt, Brace in 1961.

British writer John Maynard adapted Rau's play for television, and a production of this adaptation was broadcast in Britain in 1965. It is currently unavailable.

In 1984, the noted British film director David Lean wrote and directed a full-length feature film of *A Passage to India*. The film garnered eleven Oscar nominations and won two: Best Original Score and Best Supporting Actress for Judy Davis's portrayal of Adela Quested. The film is available on DVD from Columbia-Tri Star.

The novel was again adapted for the stage in 2002, this time by playwright Martin Sherman. It is available as a book from Methuen Drama.

novelist and critic Malcolm Bradbury describes Forster's larger purpose:

> [The book] is about human and cosmic wholeness, the reconciling of man to man in a global sense, and then of man to the infinite. A book of decidedly symbolist aspirations, its world is one in which social existence is dwarfed and made a feeble invasion on the surface of a harsh, implacable, yet also spiritually demanding earth.

Further testament to the novel's enduring reputation is the fact that, although it was Forster's last novel, it was the first of his works to be translated into another language. It appeared in French in 1927, a full twenty years before any other Forster novel was translated, and has been by far his most frequently translated work.

CRITICISM

Kieran Dolin

In the following excerpt, Dolin shows how Forster criticises the inherent race-based inequalities of the legal structures of Colonial India and how British history in India influenced the punitive attitudes of the British towards any Indian accused of a crime or a simple misdeed, even when evidence argues for their innocence.

The treatment of individuals under the law, by other individuals who have been appointed officials, is one of the major motifs of the legal novel. However, it acquires peculiar force in the colonial setting because of the diminished legal status of the conquered peoples. Forster registers the "race-bound" quality of freedom in India at a number of points in the plot and in different modes. An early, comic example occurs when Aziz observes to Fielding that Indians of his class wear a collar "to pass the police." Another is the passionate, vengeful outburst of Mrs. Turton in the anteroom at the courthouse:

> You're weak, weak, weak, weak. Why, they ought to crawl from here to the caves on their hands and knees whenever an Englishwoman's in sight, they oughtn't to be spoken to, they ought to be spat at, they ought to be ground into the dust, we've been far too kind with our Bridge Parties and the rest.

The authoritarianism of this statement by the wife of the "Burra Sahib" is emphasized by its juxtaposition with the actual trial. Its irrationality and extreme punitiveness provide less a contrast with than a denial of the English claims to juridical reason, impartiality and objectivity. G. K. Das has demonstrated that this small passage not only condenses an attitude but alludes to an actual punishment imposed after the Amritsar massacre of 1919. A "crawling-order" was enforced in the Amritsar street where a female English missionary was assaulted: every Indian entering the street was required to crawl its length. Moreover, suspects were publicly flogged; and a "salaaming-order" was imposed requiring all Indians to "salaam" or respectfully salute English civil and military officers. These repressive orders arose partly from a policy of severe curtailment of Indians' rights, but that general approach was tightened by a local atmosphere of hysterical fear. The policy led to the "show of force" in which hundreds of unarmed demonstrators were killed by troops. Das argues that Forster draws from this event the assault on "a young girl fresh from England," the outbreak of panic among the English community, and the violently reactionary feelings of Mrs. Turton, Callendar, and the Collector himself. Just as important as the historical plausibility of the Aziz fiasco is the "eruption of reality" created by the pressure of these events. Mrs. Turton's violence is the violence of Anglo-India made plain, and the degradations imposed on Nureddin, Aziz, and others manifest the dehumanizing cruelty of the conquerors.

The officials themselves lack this insight. McBryde, who is reputedly the most philosophical of them, tells Fielding that "the Mutiny Records rather than the Bhagavad-Gita should be your bible in this country," but his succeeding question, "Am I being beastly?" is rhetorical and idiomatic rather than self-searching. Beastliness is projected onto Indians in the criminology of the Raj. The 1857 Mutiny revealed this quality once and for all and became enshrined as the decisive event in AngloIndian history, the figura and antitype of every subsequent act of resistance or crime. The incident in the Marabar Caves is not simply a case to be tried in the Chandrapore police court but a "case-study" in Indian perfidy, a demonstration of something already known. The narrator evokes the majority view at the club through *style indirect libre*: "The crime was even worse than they had supposed—the unspeakable limit of cynicism, untouched since 1857." The British place the case of Aziz and Adela in a narrative context that is partly historical and partly mythic. The latter dimension arises because the club members begin to five in the mutiny story, viewing themselves as besieged and playing out symbolic roles. The fretful Mrs. Blakiston, with her babe in arms and her husband away, "with her abundant figure and masses of corngold hair, ... symbolized all that is worth fighting and dying for." Mrs. Turton becomes her protector, her "Pallas Athene." Individual stories are subsumed into the communal myth. Adela, too, is received into the Turton household, "but it was her position not her character that moved them." In consequence, her own story and especially her doubts are overlooked. She sits unregarded during Mrs. Turton's tirade: "The issues Miss Quested raised were so much more important than she was herself that people inevitably forgot her."

Fielding alone resists this magnification of the Marabar incident into a myth of imperial martyrdom. He assiduously keeps "the lantern of reason" alight, and coolly analyses the processes by which the authorities convert a mystery into a conspiracy. He notes the emotional "rallying-cry" intended in characterizing Adela as "a young girl fresh from England." Despite being its butt, he refuses to react to the escalating anger in the club and combines detachment with moral discernment in recognizing that "evil was propagating" through Major Callendar's rumor bearing. At the first opportunity he asks McBryde, "What is the charge, precisely?" and receives a periphrastic reply, "that he followed her into the cave and made insulting advances." Most important, he believes that Adela's story is partly constructed by its AngloIndian audience and wishes to question her himself:

> " . . . I want someone who believes in him to ask her."
>
> "What difference does that make?"
>
> "She is among people who disbelieve in Indians."
>
> "Well, she tells her own story, doesn't she?"
>
> "Yes, but she tells it to you."

The point is lost on McBryde, but its importance is proved in the conversation between Ronny and Adela in chapter 22, when he dismisses her statement that Aziz is innocent. The gaps in Adela's story are readily filled by the community that rallies round her, while her own doubts are silenced. In effect, the narrative presented by the prosecution at the subsequent trial is a collective one. Chapter 22 foreshadows the trial in three respects: when Adela articulates her belief in Aziz's innocence, her "echo" briefly dies away; Mrs. Moore also pronounces him innocent, and Adela intuits this belief before it is actually spoken, just as the crowd's chant outside the court, "Esmiss Esmoor," fortifies her in the witness box; and finally, Ronny's reaction to his mother's statement, "She can think, and Fielding too, but there's such a thing as evidence, I suppose," ironically anticipates the *lack* of evidence in support of the charge.

Source: Kieran Dolin, "Freedom, Uncertainty, and Diversity: *A Passage to India* as a Critique of Imperialist Law," in *Texas Studies in Literature and Language*, Vol. 36, No. 3, 1994, pp. 337–39.

Hunt Hawkins

In the following excerpt, Hawkins argues that Forester's primary criticism of British imperialism is that it makes personal friendships between rulers and the ruled impossible. He traces the change in attitude of the character Fielding, who is initially sympathetic to the Indians until becoming a member of the British ruling establishment, at which point his thinking begins to conform to the common prejudices of the English.

The chief argument against imperialism in E. M. Forster's *A Passage to India* is that it prevents personal relationships. The central question of the novel is posed at the very beginning when Mahmoud Ali and Hamidullah ask each other "whether or no it is possible to be friends with an Englishman." The answer, given by Forster himself on the last page, is "No, not yet. . . . No, notthere."

Such friendship is made impossible, on a political level, by the existence of the British Raj. While having several important drawbacks, Forster's anti-imperial argument has the advantage of being concrete, clear, moving, and presumably persuasive. It is also particularly well-suited to pursuit in the novel form, which traditionally has focused on interactions among individuals.

Forster's most obvious target is the unfriendly bigotry of the English in India, or the Anglo-Indians as they were called. At times he scores them for their pure malice, as when Mrs. Callendar says, "The kindest thing one can do to a native is to let him die." More tellingly, Forster shows up their bigotry as prejudice in the literal sense of pre-judgment. The Anglo-Indians, as Forster presents them, act on emotional preconceptions rather than rational and open-minded examination of facts. They therefore fall into logical inconsistencies which the author exposes with his favorite weapon: irony. For example, at the hysterical Club meeting following Dr. Aziz's arrest for allegedly molesting Adela Quested, the subaltern defends an anonymous native with whom he had played polo the previous month: "Any native who plays polo is all right. What you've got to stamp on is these educated classes." The reader knows, as the subaltern doesn't, that the native was Aziz himself. Against the bigotry of the Anglo-Indians, Forster urged tolerance and understanding in the widest sense.

Forster does much more in his book ... than simply deride the intolerance of a few accidental individuals. He carefully shows how this intolerance results from the unequal power relationship between English and Indians, from the imperialistic relationship itself... The process is best shown in the book in the case of Ronny, who has only recently come out from England to be City Magistrate of Chandrapore.

Ronny was at first friendly towards the Indians, but he soon found that his position prevented such friendship. Shortly after his arrival he invited the lawyer Mahmoud Ali to have a smoke with him, only to learn later that clients began flocking to Ali in the belief that he had an in with the Magistrate. Ronny subsequently "dropped on him in Court as hard as I could. It's taught me a lesson, and I hope him." In this instance, it is clearly Ronny's official position rather than any prior defect of the heart which disrupts the potential friendship. And it is his position in the imperial structure which causes his later defect, his lack of true regret when he tells his mother that now "I prefer my smoke at the club amongst my own sort, I'm afraid."

Forster tells us that "every human act in the East is tainted with officialism" and that "where there is officialism every human relationship suffers." People cannot establish a friendship of equals when the Raj is based on an inequality of power.

The one possible exception to this process of corruption among Englishmen is Fielding. He is partially immune to the influence of the imperialistic power relationship because he works in education rather than government, and because, as he puts it, he "travels light"— he has no hostages to fortune. Fielding establishes a friendship with Aziz and maintains it in defiance of all the other Ango-Indians. There is some doubt, however, whether he can maintain this course and still remain in imperial India. He is obliged to quit the Club and says he will leave India altogether should Aziz be convicted. After Fielding marries Stella, thereby ceasing to travel light, and after he becomes associated with the government as a school inspector, he undergoes a marked change of attitude toward the Raj. It would surely be a mistake to continue, as several critics do, to identify Forster

with Fielding past this point. The omniscient narrator pulls back and summarizes Fielding's situation: "He had thrown in his lot with Anglo-India by marrying a countrywoman, and he was acquiring some of its limitations." Like Ronny and the other English officials, Fielding begins to be corrupted by his position. Thinking of how Godbole's school has degenerated into a granary, the new school inspector asserts that "Indians go to seed at once" away from the British. Fielding almost exactly echoes Ronny's defense of the Raj to his mother when he excuses unpleasantness in the supposedly necessary imperial presence: he had "'no further use for politeness,' he said, meaning that the British Empire really can't be abolished because it's rude." Fielding certainly did not start with a defect of the heart, but, as a result of his new position in the imperial structure, he is acquiring one.

The English, of course, aren't the only ones corrupted by imperialism. Although most of the Indians in the book have a nearly unbelievable desire to befriend Englishmen, they are ultimately turned from it by the political reality. Some succumb to self-interest. Mahmoud Ali, for example, seems to have been the first to subvert his budding friendship with Ronny by advertising their smoke to potential litigants. More often the Indians succumb to the fear, largely justified but occasionally erroneous, that they will be scorned and betrayed. The prime example is Aziz. He makes the horrible mistake of assuming that Fielding back in England has married his enemy Adela and further that Fielding had urged him not to press damages against his false accuser so Fielding himself could enjoy Adela's money. Aziz, of course, has been conditioned to expect betrayal from his experience with other Anglo-Indians, and this expectation provides an undercurrent to the friendship from the very beginning. After Fielding returns to India, and Aziz learns he really married Stella Moore, their relationship is partially retrieved, but the damage has been done. The new school inspector has shifted toward the Raj, and Aziz, now leery of all Englishmen, has become a nationalist, saying of India, "Not until she is a nation will her sons be treated with respect."

Source: Hunt Hawkins, "Forester's Critique of Imperialism in *A Passage to India*," in *South Atlantic Review*, January 1983, pp. 54–65.

SOURCES

Arnold, Edward, "*A Passage to India* by E. M. Forster," in the *Guardian* (London), June 20, 1924.

Beer, J. B., *The Achievement of E. M. Forster*, Chatto & Windus, 1962, pp. 134–35.

Bradbury, Malcolm, "E. M. Forster as Victorian and Modern: *Howards End* and *A Passage to India*," in *Possibilities: Essays on the State of the Novel*, Oxford University Press, 1973, p. 91.

Forster, E. M., *A Passage to India*, Penguin Books, 1989; originally published in 1924.

Gardner, Philip, ed., *E. M. Forster: The Critical Heritage*, Routledge, 1997, pp. 3, 6.

Gorman, Herbert S., "Challenge and Indictment in E. M. Forster's Novel," in *New York Times*, August 17, 1924, p. BR6.

Page, Norman, *McMillan Modern Novelists: E. M. Forster*, The MacMillan Press, 1987, pp. 96, 116.

A Raisin in the Sun

LORRAINE HANSBERRY

1959

Lorraine Hansberry's play *A Raisin in the Sun* opened on March 11, 1959, at the Ethel Barrymore Theatre on Broadway and ran for 530 performances. Directed by Lloyd Richards and starring Sidney Poitier in the role of Walter, it was the first play ever written by an African American woman to be produced on Broadway. Its overwhelming success led to a New York Drama Circle Award for Hansberry, who also became the youngest person to win in the 1958–1959 season. *A Raisin in the Sun* is a domestic drama set in an apartment building on the South Side of Chicago sometime between 1945 and 1959. The play's title refers to a line from the Langston Hughes poem "Harlem," also known as "A Dream Deferred": "What happens to a dream deferred? / Does it dry up / like a raisin in the sun?"

The play examines the "deferred dreams" of the Younger family, who live in a tenement building on the South Side of Chicago. Mama and her daughter-in-law Ruth both dream of a better place to live than their cramped apartment, while Walter hopes for the financial independence he believes will come if he can open a liquor store. Beneatha, the only formally educated member of the family, hopes to become a doctor. All these dreams hinge on a ten-thousand-dollar insurance check that comes to the family as a result of Big Walter Younger's death, but as is soon shown, not everyone's dream can survive. Events within the family as

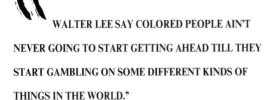

" WALTER LEE SAY COLORED PEOPLE AIN'T
NEVER GOING TO START GETTING AHEAD TILL THEY
START GAMBLING ON SOME DIFFERENT KINDS OF
THINGS IN THE WORLD."

BIOGRAPHY

LORRAINE HANSBERRY

Lorraine Hansberry was born in Chicago on May 19, 1930. She was the youngest of four children born to schoolteacher and civil rights activist Nannie Perry and her husband, prominent real-estate broker Carl Hansberry. When Hansberry was eight, the family moved into the all-white neighborhood of Woodlawn in Chicago. Despite vicious acts of vandalism and visits from angry mobs, Mr. Hansberry defended his family's right to live there—even taking the matter as far as the Supreme Court (he won in *Hansberry v. Lee*, 1940). This transition period and the experiences of racism and sexism that followed it played a significant role in Hansberry's childhood, growing up as an African American child in a white, middle-class neighborhood.

Hansberry attended the University of Wisconsin from 1948–1950 and later studied African culture and history with legendary scholar W. E. B. Du Bois at the Jefferson School for Social Sciences in New York. During that time, she also wrote for Paul Robeson's *Freedom* magazine. In 1953, Hansberry married Robert Nemiroff, a Jewish literature student, songwriter, and activist. The couple divorced in 1964.

Just six years after her initial success with *A Raisin in the Sun*, Hansberry died of lung cancer on January 12, 1965, at the age of thirty-four.

well as outside of it cause each person to make a choice that none of them could imagine making at the beginning of the play.

Set between the end of World War II in 1945 and the full momentum of the civil rights movement of the 1960s, *A Raisin in the Sun* examines racial prejudice and discrimination from several perspectives. When the Youngers buy a house in the white neighborhood of Clybourne Park, they are subjected to racist neighbors who try to keep the black family out of their neighborhood. In addition to this external racism, the Youngers also grapple with prejudice and racial identity within their own family. From Beneatha's desire to commune with her African heritage to Walter's rejection of what he calls "the world's most backward race of people," the expectations of race within the Younger family are complex and varied. Each character sees his or her responsibility to their race differently, which creates tension and disagreement until they are able to, temporarily, unite against Karl Lindner, who has come to make a racist offer to the family on move-in day.

The play was significantly cut before its first staging in 1959 to reduce its runtime. The Vintage Book edition of the play restores the cut scenes that were initially excluded. It is considered the most complete edition available. Hansberry is also the author of several other plays, including *The Drinking Gourd* (1960) and *The Sign in Sidney Brustein's Window* (1965), and an autobiography: *To Be Young, Gifted and Black: Lorraine Hansberry in Her Own Words* (1970).

A Raisin in the Sun continues to be one of the most performed and anthologized plays in the history of American theater. A revival was performed on Broadway in the summer of 2004, starring Sean "Diddy" Combs as Walter and Phylicia Rashad as Mama. The success of the revival and the four Tony Award nominations it received underscore the enduring truth present in Hansberry's play.

PLOT SUMMARY

Act 1, Scene 1
The play begins with lengthy stage directions. It is set on Chicago's South Side "sometime between World War II and the present," which at the time was 1959. The scene opens at the Youngers' house, in what "would be a

Lorraine Hansberry The Library of Congress

comfortable and well-ordered [living] room" that is beginning to show its wear. While it is apparent that at one time the objects in the room were carefully selected and cared for, it is clear now that "Weariness has, in fact, won in this room." Concern about decorum and comfort has given way to the simple act of living. Hansberry establishes this space as one that represents financial struggle, strain, and depression.

It is early on a Friday morning when Ruth Younger, a woman in her thirties with a look of "disappointment [that] has already begun to hang in her face," wakes to assist her family in getting prepared for the day's activities. She rouses her ten-year-old son Travis from the living room couch where he sleeps. He heads toward the washroom that the Youngers must share with other families in their apartment building. Next, Ruth goes to the bedroom to wake her husband, Walter Lee Younger. Walter is described as an "intense young man in his middle thirties, inclined to quick nervous movements and erratic speech habits." While Travis is bathing, Walter and Ruth chat as she prepares his breakfast. Shortly thereafter, Travis

emerges from the bathroom and his father hurries to take his place. Travis reminds his mother that he needs fifty cents to bring to school, but Ruth tells him, "I ain't got it." When Walter returns, he disagrees with Ruth's decision not to give Travis the money. He gives the boy the fifty cents he requested for school, and an additional fifty cents for "fruit . . . or [to] take a taxi-cab to school."

After Travis leaves, Ruth and Walter continue arguing about their precarious financial situation. The Younger family is expecting a life insurance check for ten thousand dollars as a result of Walter's father's death. The money is due to arrive the next day and everyone in the household is anticipating the relief it will bring. Walter works as a chauffeur for a man named Mr. Arnold, and he hopes to use some of the money to put a down payment on a liquor store. Ruth reminds Walter that the check is really his mother's to spend and encourages her husband to finish his breakfast and get to work. It is clear from their dialogue that Walter is dissatisfied with his job and is looking for a way out, but his idea to co-own a liquor store with his friends Bobo and Willy is a risky one that conflicts with Ruth's more cautious approach to survival. Walter equates his wife's hesitance to sabotage and tells her, "That is just what is wrong with the colored woman in this world . . . Don't understand about building their men up and making 'em feel like they somebody. Like they can do something."

Walter's sister Beneatha enters, "about twenty, [and] as slim and intense as her brother . . . [but] not as pretty as her sister-in-law." She and Walter engage in morning banter and the topic of conversation quickly turns to Beneatha's ambition to be a doctor. Both Walter and Ruth muse at the rarity of Beneatha's aspirations, noting there "Ain't many girls" who decide to become doctors. The sibling rivalry continues when Walter accuses Beneatha of "acting holy 'round here," because she is in school while the rest of the adult household must work grueling, thankless jobs just to make ends meet. Beneatha responds to Walter's accusation by dropping to her knees and pleading, "forgive me for ever wanting to be anything at all!" It seems that everyone has a reason to want a portion of the money to come—Walter to become an entrepreneur and Beneatha to become a doctor.

The argument comes to a halt when Walter and Beneatha's mother enters the room. Mama, "a woman in her early sixties, full-bodied and strong," wants to know what the ruckus is about. Her first act of the day is to tend to a "feeble little plant growing doggedly in a small pot on the windowsill." Ruth and Mama discuss all the possibilities that the ten-thousand-dollar check allows the family. After listening to Ruth's suggestions, Mama reminisces about her late husband, Big Walter, whose lifelong struggle to provide for his family makes her decision regarding how to spend the money that much more challenging. She tells Ruth that Big Walter once said to her, "Seem like God didn't see fit to give the black man nothing but dreams—but He did give us children to make them dreams seem worth while." This leads Beneatha to denounce the existence of the God, telling her mother that she gets "tired of Him getting credit for all the things the human race achieves through its own stubborn effort." Beneatha's outburst sends her mother reeling. She tells Ruth that her household is changing, with Walter always thinking about money and Beneatha talking about things Mama does not understand. Mama daydreams of owning a house with a garden in the back she can tend. While looking out the window, she does not notice that Ruth has fainted.

Act 1, Scene 2

The following morning, the Youngers are cleaning the house. They are interrupted by a visit from Joseph Asagai, a Nigerian student whom Beneatha has recently met on campus. Asagai, who is referred to by only his last name, senses tension in the household. When he asks Beneatha why she looks so "disturbed," she jokingly responds, "we've all got acute ghetto-itis." In truth, Ruth has just returned from the doctor, having learned that she is two months pregnant. The information is not good news, especially considering the family's already cramped living arrangements. Ruth's pregnancy reveals the dire nature of the Youngers' financial situation. Asagai has come to court Beneatha, bringing some records of Nigerian folk music as well as a traditional Nigerian woman's robe from his sister's own wardrobe. Beneatha is thrilled with the gifts and accepts the compliments Asagai gives her.

His only criticism involves Beneatha's "mutilated hair"—so called because it has been straightened and is therefore unnatural. Beneatha disagrees with Asagai's use of the word "mutilation" to describe her hair, defending her decision to straighten her hair because "it's so hard to manage when it's, well—raw." The two of them discuss how assimilation and identity relate to both African and African American cultures. Asagai attempts to convey his romantic intentions towards Beneatha, telling her, "Between a man and a woman there need be only one kind of feeling. I have that for you." The feeling is not reciprocated, and she tells him, "I'm not interested in being someone's little episode in America." As Asagai prepares to leave, Mama enters the room and exchanges pleasantries with Asagai. Having already been warned by Beneatha to avoid seeming ignorant to their guest, Mama casually mentions, "I would love to hear all about ... your country. I think it's so sad the way our American Negroes don't know nothing about Africa 'cept Tarzan and all that." Asagai bids Beneatha farewell, calling her "Alaiyo." He tells her it means "One for Whom Bread—Food—Is Not Enough."

After Asagai leaves, the mailman delivers the much-anticipated insurance check. Mama is reminded that her husband had to die in order for the family to have this money. Walter arrives shortly thereafter, excited by the prospect of his latest endeavor. The first words from his mouth are, "Did it come?" Mama informs him that she will not be using any of the money to help him open a liquor store, no matter what the arrangements are between him, Bobo, and Willy. Outraged by what he believes to be a betrayal of their relationship, Walter asks his mother, "Do you know what this money means to me? Do you know what this money can do for us?" Mama tries to console her son, but his frustration and hopelessness persist. Unsure of how to reconcile the disagreement, Mama tells Walter that Ruth is expecting another baby and considering having an abortion. Walter reacts to the news with disbelief: "You don't know Ruth, Mama, if you think she would do that."

Ruth, whose voice the stage directions indicate is "beaten," tells Walter that she would, in fact, have an abortion. Mama, who clearly does not support this option, turns to Walter. She tells him she is waiting to hear him act like his father and tell Ruth that their family is not the kind that would "destroy" a child. Walter says nothing and leaves. Mama continues, saying that he is a disgrace to his father's memory.

Act 2, Scene 1

Later that same day, Beneatha dons the traditional Nigerian robes Asagai brought for her. While she is listening to her new folk music records, Walter enters the room, drunk. Beneatha is dancing what she says is the traditional dance of welcome that Nigerian women use upon their men's return from the hunt. Beneatha and Walter engage in an impromptu performance celebrating their African heritage. Ruth watches disapprovingly, "embarrassed for the family." George Murchison arrives to take Beneatha out to the theater. Beneatha's enthusiasm for her African heritage is cut short by George's comment: "Look honey, we're going *to* the theatre—we're not going to be *in* it."

Beneatha takes off the headdress and reveals her new hairstyle—a short, natural afro. Shocked by Beneatha's decision to change her hair, Ruth asks her, "You expect this boy to go out with you with your head all nappy like that?" Beneatha responds by telling Ruth that she hates "assimilationist Negroes." Then Walter starts talking to George about business ideas and says that they should get together to talk about them. George reacts to the suggestion with indifference. Infuriated, Walter insults George, calling him a "busy little boy," too preoccupied with his own privileged college life to "be a man." George and Beneatha manage to leave before Walter's anger escalates to the boiling point. Ruth reassures her husband by telling him that "life don't have to be like this."

When Mama returns, she announces that she has placed a down payment on a house at 406 Clybourne Street in Clybourne Park, an all-white, working-class neighborhood. Ruth is thrilled at the prospect of moving, but worried about moving into an all-white neighborhood. She embraces the joy of the news and goes to see to Travis. Walter feels completely defeated and accuses his mother of shattering his dreams: "So you butchered up a dream of mine—you—who always talking 'bout your children's dreams."

Act 2, Scene 2

A few weeks later, on Friday night, Beneatha and George return to the apartment after a date. He tries to kiss her but she wants to talk.

They argue about the nature of their relationship. Mama returns as George leaves, and the women talk about Beneatha's feelings for George. Beneatha explains that she is unable to continue her relationship with him because he refuses to engage her as an equal. Beneatha appreciates her mother's understanding.

Mrs. Johnson, a gossipy neighbor, knocks on the door. Her perspective about blacks is noticeably limited, as she makes statements like, "I always thinks like Booker T. Washington said that time—'Education has spoiled many a good plow hand.'" Her antagonism is most apparent when she suggests that the family's impending move to a white neighborhood, although "wonderful," will result in headlines like "NEGROS INVADE CLYBOURNE PARK—BOMBED!" This bigoted attitude leads Beneatha to tell her mother, "if there are two things we, as a people, have got to overcome, one is the Ku Klux Klan—and the other is Mrs. Johnson."

After Mrs. Johnson's visit, the family learns that Walter has not been to work for three days. When he says that he has spent the time drinking in a jazz club, his mother feels bad for ruining his dreams. She gives Walter the sixty-five hundred dollars she has left over from the house down payment. She tells him to put aside three thousand dollars for Beneatha's schooling and spend the rest as he wants. Walter, who is shocked by his mother's unexpected support, tells Travis, "Daddy ain't going to never be drunk again." Walter and Travis discuss manhood and their own dreams for the future. The scene ends with Walter telling him, "You just name it, son . . . and I hand you the world!"

Act 2, Scene 3

It is one week later on moving day. The curtain opens on Ruth and Beneatha discussing their plans for their new home. Even Walter is agreeable, dancing with his wife as the excitement spreads. In the midst of everyone's happiness, a white man who identifies himself as Karl Lindner of the Clybourne Park Improvement Association, comes to the door. Mr. Lindner explains that as chairman of the welcoming committee, it is his job to "go around and see the new people who move into the neighborhood and sort of give them the lowdown on the way we do things out in Clybourne Park." He tells the Youngers that the community in Clybourne

Park would rather that blacks stay in their own neighborhood. To encourage this, they have pooled their money to buy the Youngers' new house back from them at a price higher than they paid for it. Mr. Lindner reminds the Youngers "of some of the incidents which have happened in various parts of the city when colored people have moved into certain areas"—a comment referring to acts of violence, the equivalent of a politely worded threat.

By mentioning that the community he represents is made up of those who are "not rich and fancy people; just hard-working, honest people," Mr. Lindner hopes that the racist agenda of his visit will be instead thought of as a means to achieve "the happiness of all concerned." Even after Walter tells Mr. Lindner to leave, the man protests, saying, "You just can't force people to change their hearts, son." As the only white character in the entire play, one might expect Mr. Lindner to be unnecessarily demonized. However, the script notes much to the contrary, indicating that Mr. Lindner is not a tyrant but, "a gentle man; thoughtful and somewhat labored in his manner."

When Mama returns, Beneatha informs her of Mr. Lindner's visit. Mama asks if he threatened the family. Beneatha tell her, "they don't do it like that any more.... He said everybody ought to learn how to sit down and hate each other with good Christian fellowship." Beneatha and Ruth speculate as to why the community has a problem with black neighbors, suggesting sarcastically that the whites are afraid they might "eat 'em" or "marry 'em." As Mama carefully prepares her little plant for the trip, the family teases her for even wanting to bring it to the new house.

Ruth, Walter, and Beneatha present a gift of gardening tools to Mama in preparation for her dream house, and Travis gives her a large gardening hat. The family tries to recapture the excitement that Mr. Lindner's visit had interrupted earlier. Bobo arrives at the door with more bad news. Willy, Bobo and Walter's friend and would-be business associate, has apparently fled with all their money. Walter reveals that instead of following Mama's directions and setting aside money for Beneatha's schooling, he gave all sixty-five hundred dollars to Willy as an investment on the liquor store. The family is shocked and silent at Walter's revelation. Mama "looks at her son without recognition,"

hitting him in the face. She speaks of her late husband, saying, "I seen him grow thin and old before he was forty ... working and working and working like somebody's old horse ... and you—you give it all away in a day." Mama looks up to the heavens, begging God to give her strength.

Act 3, Scene 1

One hour later, Asagai enters, "smiling broadly, striding ... with energy and happy expectation," unaware of what has just transpired. He has come to help with the packing and asks Beneatha what is wrong. Beneatha tells him that Walter gave away the insurance money in an investment not even Travis would have made. Beneatha explains to Asagai why she has wanted to be a doctor since she was a child and how now it is pointless because "it doesn't seem deep enough, close enough to what ails mankind!" Disillusioned by her brother's betrayal and Asagai's attempt to put it in perspective with idealism, she tells Asagai that his idealism is useless, and that he thinks he can "Cure the Great Sore of Colonialism ... with the Penicillin of Independence." Asagai attempts to restore Beneatha's optimism by inviting her to come live with him in Africa. He leaves her to contemplate his offer.

When Walter enters the room, Beneatha, disgusted, calls him "*Monsieur le petit bourgeois noir* (Mr. little middle-class black).... Symbol of a Rising Class! Entrepreneur!" Walter leaves as his sister hurls insults after him. Mama and Ruth discuss whether or not to call and cancel with the movers. Mama thinks they cannot afford the house now, but Ruth insists that the four of them can. Walter announces that the family is "going to do business" with Mr. Lindner (whom he also refers to here as "The Man," "Captain Boss," "Mistuh Charley," and "Mr. Bossman"). Walter demonstrates how he plans to "get down on [his] black knees" and beg Mr. Lindner for the money he had offered. His mother and sister are appalled at his "groveling and grinning" behavior because they feel that accepting the payoff is the same as admitting that they are not good enough. Mama agrees to let him accept Mr. Lindner's offer as long as he does so in his son's presence so the boy understands what Walter is doing and why. When Mr. Lindner returns, Walter shocks everyone by refusing his offer, telling him "we come from people who had a lot of *pride*," and that the Youngers "don't want to make no trouble for nobody or fight

Sidney Poitier and Claudia McNeil in a stage production of A Raisin in the Sun *AP Images*

no causes, and we will try to be good neighbors." Mr. Lindner leaves and the Youngers celebrate the reemergence of Walter's pride. As the family leaves the apartment to meet the movers, who have arrived downstairs, Beneatha tells Mama of Asagai's proposal. While the family goes downstairs, Mama returns to get her plant from the window.

THEMES

Internalized Racism

While scholars debate the meaning of internalized racism, critics agree that this concept is key to a complete understanding of *A Raisin in the Sun*. In "Internalized Racism: A Definition," Donna Bivens, co-director of the Boston Theological Institute, defines internalized racism as "the situation that occurs in a racist system," when members of an oppressed group maintain or participate in "the set of attitudes, behaviors, social structures and ideologies that undergird the dominating group's power." In other words, when characters such as Walter, George, and Beneatha start to believe the stereotypes about their own race, they have internalized racism.

In act 2, scene 1 of *A Raisin in the Sun*, George tells Beneatha that her African heritage "is nothing but a bunch of raggedy-assed spirituals and some grass huts." With this statement, he clearly demonstrates his own internalized racism. A member of a well-to-do black family, George distances himself from his African heritage, preferring instead to adopt the attitudes and tastes of affluent white Americans. Beneatha describes George's family as "honest-to-God-real-*live*-rich colored people, and the only people in the world who are more snobbish than rich white people are rich colored people." Emphasis on George's wealth accompanies his presence throughout the play. Presumably,

George's status as both "rich" and "colored" set him apart from other characters, who see him as a fake.

The echo of internalized racism continues to resonate when Walter, a poor chauffeur, complains to his wife, "we all tied up in a race of people that don't know how to do nothing but moan, pray, and have babies!" This statement reveals Walter's own internalization of anti-black/pro-white racism. In an article titled, "Levels of Racism: A Theoretical Framework and a Gardener's Tale," Camara Phyllis Jones insists, "It is important to note that the association between socioeconomic status and race in the United States has its origins in discrete historical events," and that "Institutional racism manifests itself both in material conditions and in access to power." In this way, one can see that regardless of their differing economic positions, both Walter and George are affected, and consequently defined, by their own internalized racism.

External Racism

Though the dynamics within the Younger household indicate various levels of internalized racism, racism from external forces also finds its way into their living room. When Mama receives the insurance check from her husband's death, she uses part of the money to put a down payment on a house with a garden, which is her dream. The family is excited to be moving into a house with more room and in a nicer neighborhood. That happiness is temporarily dashed when Karl Lindner from the Clybourne Park Improvement Association pays them a visit on the day they are set to move. He tells the family that he is there to "give them the lowdown on the way we do things out in Clybourne Park." That "way" turns out to be striving to keep the neighborhood all white. Though Lindner tells the Youngers he is here to talk to them "friendly like," his message is anything but friendly. In order to keep the black Youngers out of white Clybourne Park, the neighbors have pooled their money together to try and buy out the Youngers' house:

> I want you to believe me when I tell you that race prejudice simply doesn't enter into it. It is a matter of the people of Clybourne Park believing, rightly or wrongly, as I say, that for the happiness of all concerned that our Negro families are happier when they live in their *own* communities.

Although Lindner is careful to point out that the actions of Clybourne Park residents are not a matter of "race prejudice," that is exactly the case. The neighbors fear the prospect of blacks moving into their white neighborhood, and do everything they can to stop it. When Walter throws Lindner out of the house, Lindner tells the family that they have nothing to gain "by moving into a neighborhood where [they] just aren't wanted." Soon after, Walter learns that Willy has run off with the rest of the insurance money. He suddenly thinks the family should take Lindner up on his offer after all. But Mama refuses: "ain't nobody in my family never let nobody pay 'em no money that was a way of telling us we wasn't fit to walk the earth." When Walter meets Lindner again, he tells him that the Youngers will be moving into their new house because their father "earned it for [them] brick by brick." Selling out to the Clybourne Park neighbors might otherwise have seemed a windfall, but the option is untenable because it would make the Youngers complicit in their own oppression.

African Heritage

African heritage and culture play a significant role in *A Raisin in the Sun*. The Nigerian Asagai represents the entire continent and culture of Africa for the Younger family. When Beneatha first mentions Asagai to Mama, she reminds her not to "ask him a whole lot of ignorant questions," like "do they wear clothes and all that" because Beneatha is acutely aware that popular conceptions of Africans are often negative. Beneatha says, "All anyone seems to know about when it comes to Africa is Tarzan." Upon learning that Asagai is Nigerian, Mama mistakenly assumes, "that's the little country that was founded by slaves way back." Beneatha corrects her mother's mistake, indicating that it is Liberia, not Nigeria that was founded by slaves. Mama responds, "I don't think I never met no African before," revealing an extremely limited understanding of Africa.

With the character of Asagai, the author creates an avenue through which to educate both her characters and her audience about certain details of African culture. By doing this, she also points out the fact that many African Americans have the desire, but not the resources, to reconnect with their African ancestry. Because slavery largely prevented African Americans from preserving their various

African cultures, assimilation became the primary method of survival for black African slaves and their descendants in America. Beneatha, who has a strong interest in African heritage and appears in act 2, scene 1 dressed in tribal clothing and singing traditional songs, tells Ruth that she "hate[s] assimilationist Negroes!" She defines an assimilationist as "someone who is willing to give up his own culture and submerge himself completely in the dominant, and in this case *oppressive* culture." This assessment does not acknowledge why one might employ assimilationist tactics to survive. For example, George Murchison, who embodies this "assimilationist" viewpoint, is depicted in a negative light in the play—however, he is the play's most socio-economically successful character. George's disdain for his own African ancestry is set in stark contrast to Beneatha's embrace of it.

This dynamic plays out in act 2, scene 1, when Beneatha emerges "grandly from the doorway ... thoroughly robed in the (Nigerian) costume Asagai brought," and she and Walter enthusiastically enact what they imagine to be scenes from their African heritage. The performance includes much dancing, yelling, posturing, and references to such things as warriors, drums, flaming spears, lions, and chiefs—all of which call to mind the image of "the noble savage," a people unspoiled by civilization, which has often been romanticized in literature and film. This cultural reclamation highlights Beneatha and Walter's limited knowledge of their ancestral past. It is Asagai who represents the true Africa, and Beneatha's attempts to claim her identity by connecting with him seem absurd in the light of the overtly dramatic portrayal of African-ness that dominates this scene.

HISTORICAL OVERVIEW

Chicago and the Great Black Migration
In the wake of the Civil War and subsequent Reconstruction, hundreds of thousands of black Southerners moved north to escape the legalized oppression of Jim Crow laws and find work in industrialized cities. Chicago became a main destination for these migrants in the early twentieth century. The so-called "Great Black Migration" of the early twentieth century changed the makeup of Chicago, which until then had been largely inhabited by Irish and other European immigrants. According to *Encyclopedia of African-American Culture and History*, the black population in Chicago was 44,000 in 1910. After World War II and during the time in which *A Raisin in the Sun* is set, the black population had increased tenfold. By 1960, there were nearly 813,000 blacks residing in Chicago.

Despite their optimism about life in the North, African Americans discovered that racism and prejudice were not strictly southern problems. Discrimination and rapid population growth soon created separate black neighborhoods, including the South Side of Chicago. While many blacks flourished in the community and became entrepreneurs and business owners, those who could not find suitable work fell into poverty. The South Side, also known as the "Black Belt," became a cultural, musical, and educational capital for African Americans in the 1940s, much like New York's Harlem in the 1920s.

In the mid-1960s, Congress passed open-housing laws that helped give blacks and other minorities a greater choice of neighborhoods in which they could live. As I. F. Stone notes in an article entitled "The Rat and Res Judicata," prior to this legislation, residents of Chicago's Black Belt had been paying some of the highest rent in the city relative to income. Because they were not entitled to live wherever they pleased, there was a crunch for available housing that led to exorbitant rents. This reality is reflected in Mama's choosing a house in Clybourne Park—a white neighborhood—over a house in an African American neighborhood. As Mama explains, "Them houses they put up for colored in them areas way out all seem to cost twice as much as other houses."

Hansberry v. Lee
As a child, Hansberry's family moved to a white neighborhood in Chicago known as Woodlawn only to be faced with racist mobs. Upon learning of the race of her new neighbors, white Woodlawn resident Anna M. Lee filed suit against the seller of the house and the Hansberrys for one hundred thousand dollars, alleging that both had violated the restrictive race covenant in the neighborhood designed to keep blacks out the area. This covenant was not unique to Woodlawn; it is estimated that at the time, some eighty percent of Chicago housing was

controlled by similar covenants. Both a circuit court and the Supreme Court of Illinois upheld the covenant and found in Lee's favor. The Illinois Supreme Court even called for the Hansberrys' property to be confiscated. Hansberry's father took his family's right to live in this neighborhood all the way to the U.S. Supreme Court in *Hansberry v. Lee* (1940), which reversed the decision of the Illinois courts. It did not, however, find fault with the existence of restrictive covenants. This was nearly thirty years before the Federal Fair Housing Act outlawed such restrictions. *Hansberry v. Lee* rocked the perception that the North was any more welcoming to blacks than the South had been.

CRITICAL OVERVIEW

When Lorraine Hansberry's play *A Raisin in the Sun* opened on Broadway in 1959, no one knew it would become such a huge success. In a 1959 article for the *New York Times*, Sam Zolotow notes that all seven major New York drama critics endorsed the play; however, many critics were not as positive in their assessments. In his article "*A Raisin in the Sun* Revisited," J. Charles Washington points out that

> In the eyes of some critics ... [the play] was passé almost before it closed, because they saw it only as a protest play or social drama about a Black family's struggle to buy a house in a white neighborhood.

Washington also cites critic C. W. E. Bigsby's review of the play, quoting, "[*A Raisin in the Sun*] is an unhappy crossbreed of *social protest* and reassuring resolution." The negativity of these reactions was hardly unusual, and stemmed from a general discomfort surrounding political and racial issues at the time. Washington also refers to critic Harold Cruse's evaluation that the play is "the most cleverly written piece of glorified soap opera" that he had ever seen. From this feedback, one might be surprised that *A Raisin in the Sun* is considered a classic of American theater. However, aside from the less-than-exultant response to the play's obvious political message, many critics praised the play's universality, noting the far-reaching appeal of the individual characters, whose eloquence and dignity make them accessible to a diverse audience.

In "*A Raisin in the Sun*'s Enduring Passion," Amiri Baraka notes that at the time of its staging, the play itself was "political agitation," explaining, "It dealt with the very same issues of democratic rights and equality that were being aired in the streets." In this way, *A Raisin in the Sun* has come to represent not only the humanist ideals embodied by the Younger family, but also the far-reaching socio-political conflicts that continue to affect life in America. In "Hansberry's *A Raisin in the Sun*," David Cooper surmises that at its heart, this play is about "the human condition, human aspiration and human relationship—the persistence of dreams, of the bonds and conflicts between men and women, parents and children, old ways and new." With these timeless themes, *A Raisin in the Sun* has continued to thrive both on and off the stage.

That the play continues to be performed is a testament to its universal and lasting qualities. As Robert Nemiroff notes in his introduction to the Vintage Books edition of the play, the revivals staged on the twenty-fifth anniversary of the play were warmly received. He quotes a *New York Times* review that says, "The events of every passing year add resonance to *A Raisin in the Sun*. It is as if history is conspiring to make the play a classic." Nemiroff also quotes a *Washington Post* review that calls it "one of a handful of great American dramas." In a 1999 review of the play for *Curtain Up*, Elyse Sommer notes, "The play's surface issues may have changed but ... this compassionate human drama still works its magic on our emotions." David Chadderton's review of a London staging for *The British Theatre Guide* applauds Hansberry's ability to create "a number of characters—none of which is portrayed as wholly good or wholly bad—that represent radically different points of view convincingly." A 2004 Broadway revival of *A Raisin in the Sun*, starring Phylicia Rashad and Sean "Diddy" Combs, also met with critical praise. In a review of the revival, Anna Deavere Smith of the *New York Times* writes in "Two Visions of Love, Family and Race Across the Generations" that *A Raisin in the Sun* offers "a new and refreshing lens on our history and on the theater's potential." The production was nominated for four Tony Awards in 2004, including Best Revival of a Play.

MEDIA ADAPTATIONS

A Raisin in the Sun was adapted as a film directed by Daniel Petrie, starring Sidney Poitier, Claudia McNeil, and Ruby Dee in 1961. It is available on DVD from Sony Pictures.

A Raisin in the Sun was adapted as a Broadway musical in 1973 produced by Hansberry's ex-husband Robert Nemiroff, and starring Joe Morton, Ernestine Jackson, and Ralph Carter. The original cast recording is available from Sony.

A Raisin in the Sun was adapted as a made-for-television film in 1989 directed by Bill Duke, starring Danny Glover, Esther Rolle, and several members of the original Broadway cast. It is available on VHS from Monterey Video.

An audio version of the play is available from Caedmon on audio cassette. It is narrated by Ossie Davis.

CRITICISM

Robin Bernstein

In the following excerpt, Bernstein provides a favorable evaluation of the play, and discusses the dynamic of universalism in the critical reception of A Raisin in the Sun.

When Lorraine Hansberry's *A Raisin in the Sun* opened on Broadway in 1959, the vast majority of white critics praised the play's "universality." One reviewer wrote, "A Negro wrote this show. It is played, with one exception, by Negroes. Half the audiences here are Negroes. Even so, it isn't written for Negroes... It's a show about people, white or colored ... I see *A Raisin in the Sun* as part of the general culture of the U.S." The phrase "happens to be" appeared with remarkable frequency among reviews: the play was "about human beings, who happen to be Negroes" (or "a family that happens to be colored"); Sidney Poitier played "the angry young man who happens to be a Negro."

Other white reviewers, however, praised the play not for its universality, but for its particularity. "The play is honest," wrote Brooks Atkinson, critic for the *New York Times.* "[Hansberry] has told the inner as well as the outer truth about a Negro family in the southside of Chicago at the present time." "This Negro play," wrote another reviewer, "celebrates with slow impressiveness a triumph of racial pride."

How can a play be simultaneously specific and universal? This apparent paradox is easily resolved with the assertion that African-Americans are precisely as human—and African-American cultures just as universal or particular—as any other group. Hansberry herself pointed out the non-existence of the paradox:

> Interviewer: The question, I'm sure, is asked you many times—you must be tired of it—someone comes up to you and says: "This is not really a Negro play; why, this could be about anybody! It's a play about people!" What is your reaction? What do you say?

> Hansberry: Well[,] I hadn't noticed the contradiction because I'd always been under the impression that Negroes *are* people... One of the most sound ideas in dramatic writing is that in order to create the universal, you must pay very great attention to the specific.

Hansberry's solution to the apparent paradox did not go unnoticed or unremarked. Novelist John Oliver Killens, for example, wrote,

> Lorraine believed that ... the literary road to universality is through local identity. Many critics said of *Raisin* that it is "universal," that it isn't specifically about Blacks. "It is about people. It could be about anybody." But a play that could be about anybody would most probably be about nobody at all. Lorraine was very clear on this point [in the above-quoted interview].

Historian and editor Lerone Bennett Jr. found precisely the same solution to the apparent paradox:

> From my reading of Lorraine Hansberry, I get the feeling that she struggled all her life with the whole question of "universality." And I interpret her as having struggled against *false* definitions of "universality." ... To my way of thinking, an artist is most universal when he's

discussing the concrete issues of his own culture. It's the task of the artist to take the concrete and make it universal... She was universal in her particularity.

The paradox, then, is that a paradox was perceived at all, or that it continued to be perceived after Hansberry (and later, Killens, Bennett, and others) had publicly resolved it. Why did critics persistently categorize *Raisin* as universal *or* specifically black? Why, when critics noted the fact that the play successfully communicated both universal and particular concerns, did they remark on this fact as a paradox or contradiction? In other words, why was the appearance of a paradox created and maintained?

The claim that the play's characters are universal "people" without specific ties to African-American culture appears simply racist ("This is a well-written play; white people can relate to it; therefore it cannot be a black play"). Conversely, the assertion that the play is *not* universal but exclusively specific to African-Americans—that is, that the characters exist outside the category of "human"—seems equally racist. Upon closer examination, however, it is possible to discern both racist and anti-racist impulses in each claim.

The "particularizing" assertion can be separated into several different strands. In the most racist form, critics in this mode refused to acknowledge any difference between Hansberry's characters and stereotyped images of blacks. A few months after the play opened, Lorraine Hansberry noted "some of the prior attitudes which were brought into the theatre from the world outside. For in the minds of many, [the character of] Walter remains, despite the play, despite performance, what American racial traditions *wish* him to be: an exotic." If audiences went to the theatre to see "the simple, lovable, and glandular 'Negro,'" they would find him, regardless of what actually occurred on stage. Hansberry wrote,

> My colleagues and I were reduced to mirth and tears by that gentleman writing his review of our play in a Connecticut paper who remarked of his pleasure at seeing how "our dusky brethren" could "come up with a song and hum their troubles away." It did not disturb the writer in the least that there is no such implication in the entire three acts. He did not need it in the play; he had it in his head.

Such blatant racism is related to the more subtle "people's culture" approach Eric Lott attacked in *Love and Theft: Blackface Minstrelsy and the American Working Class*. Lott defined the "people's culture" position as one that views minstrelsy as a more-or-less accurate reflection or aspect of "authentic" Negro culture. Lott's attack on this approach's ahistoricity and inaccuracy might seem not to apply to *Raisin*, which was obviously and deliberately locatable in black culture. However, the "people's culture" stance resembled that of some of the reviewers in that both approaches sought—or demanded—access to "authentic" black culture, as evidenced in critics' repeated praising of *Raisin* as "honest drama" with "vigor as well as veracity." In other words, the "people's culture" approach and that of some of *Raisin*'s critics shared a common *impulse to access* perceived authentic black culture. And in doing so, they re-asserted whiteness as the norm.

The play's ability to appear to encapsulate "Negro experience" in the readily knowable, digestible, and non-threatening form of theatrical realism arguably satisfied this impulse and thus constituted the primary reason for the play's success among white audiences. In other words, the play's realism satisfied its white viewers in much the same way that minstrelsy satisfied its viewers by providing them with easy access to consumable perceived "Negro culture." *A Raisin in the Sun*, then, by making black experiences appear understandable to and consumable by white audiences, simultaneously made those experiences *collectable*. The bourgeois white viewer could display his or her newfound knowledge much as one might display a collection of "primitive" art; as James Clifford argues, "cultural description [can be] presented as a form of collecting."

Collecting is a performance of power. To collect is to construct, limit, contain, display, and define. As Clifford observed, collections (even nonmaterial ones such as collected experiences of theatregoing) are necessarily organized taxonomically and hierarchically; thus collectors assert power over their possessions (which serve as menonyms for cultures). The impulse for the white theatregoer to collect knowledge of "authentic" black experiences—through minstrelsy or *Raisin's* realism—is therefore an impulse to perform (and thus actualize) white power.

Collecting is closely related to conservation, another performance of power to which Clifford devoted some attention: "Collecting—at least in the West, where time is generally thought to be linear and irreversible—implies a rescue of phenomena from inevitable historical decay or loss." Clifford described the collecting of "primitive" visual art and the anthropological collecting of nonmaterial knowledge as similarly conservative projects: "both discourses assume a primitive world in need of preservation, redemption, and representation." White audiences' nonmaterial collecting of minority experiences through theatre attendance, then, could involve a similar conservative impulse. And as Clifford's colleague Donna Haraway noted, conservation is always intertwined with subjugation: "Once domination is complete, conservation is urgent."

Finally, the assertion that *A Raisin in the Sun* was specifically and exclusively black effectively erased from the play Hansberry's class analysis. Many African-American critics and scholars have noticed and commented on this aspect of the play, but almost no white commentators have. Hansberry complained,

> Some writers have been astonishingly incapable of discussing [the character of Walter's] purely *class* aspirations and have persistently confounded them with what they consider to be an exotic being's longing to "wheel and deal" in what they consider to be (and what Walter never can) "the white man's world."

The erasure of Hansberry's class analysis suggests white critics' unwillingness to engage with a black writer's intellect. In other words, white audiences who came to the theatre to see (and collect the experiences of) the "simple, lovable, and glandular 'Negro'" (and encountering, to their disappointment, non-stereotyped characters) could have preserved their mission by willfully ignoring anything that did not contribute to that project. Even the FBI, which investigated Lorraine Hansberry as a possible "danger to the Republic," labeled the play "not propagandistic." This description, regarded as flattering by the FBI, revealed an unwillingness to engage with—or even recognize—the politics of the play.

By ignoring Hansberry's politics and recognizing only the play's specificity to black culture, white critics erased Hansberry's authority to speak about anything but herself. This action positioned blacks as if in a fishbowl: they could look at each other, but not at anything beyond their immediate context. This fishbowl could sit comfortably, decoratively, on a shelf in a white household; white people could peer through the glass (which contained and controlled the exotics and simultaneously kept the white spectator safely separated from the creatures) and enjoy their collection. In other words, erasing Hansberry's authority to speak about anything but her (white-defined) culture created a "glass" barrier which separated white audiences from the play's black creators and characters and rendered the subaltern collectable—and thus produced white power.

Furthermore, this "fishbowl" dynamic created a unidirectional gaze; that is to say, it positioned blacks as the object of both blacks' and whites' gazes, and simultaneously positioned whites as the empowered, invisible inspector. This action reified blacks' lives and experiences as collectable and simultaneously precluded the possibility of blacks inverting the dynamic and collecting (and thus disempowering) whites and their experiences. The fish cannot collect the human outside the bowl.

Black audiences apparently also read the play in the context of racist stereotypes. According to James Baldwin, the play drew unprecedented numbers of African-Americans to the theatre because "never before in American theater history had so much of the truth of black people's lives been seen on stage." Overlap occurred, then, between the racist impulse to collect black experiences and the anti-racist impulse to see one's own experience reflected on stage (and to see stereotypes extirpated): both impulses hinged on the highly suspect notion of authenticity. The fact that two opposing impulses could exist in the same space contributed to the appearance of a paradox.

The play itself emphasized particularity within particularity through the character of Joseph Asagai, a Nigerian. According to Alex Haley, Hansberry achieved two goals through the character of Asagai. First, she helped to dispel the myth of the "cannibal" with a bone in his hair. Her educated African character ... was certainly the first time a large audience had seen and heard an African portrayed as carrying himself with dignity and being, moreover, a primary spokesman for sanity and progress. It must also have been the first time a mass audience had ever seen a black woman gracefully don African robes or wear an "afro" hairstyle.

Asagai, then, continued Hansberry's project of creating individual, specifically black characters who testified against stereotypes. Second, as Haley noted, *A Raisin in the Sun* was the first artistic work to popularize (on a large scale) the concept of a relationship between African-Americans and Africans. By teasing out this relationship that specifically separated African-Americans from all other Americans, Hansberry again employed the particularizing approach—but to anti-racist ends.

Source: Robin Bernstein, "Inventing a Fishbowl: White Supremacy and the Critical Reception of Lorraine Hansberry's *A Raisin in the Sun*," in *Modern Drama*, Spring 1999, pp. 1–4.

SOURCES

"African-American Population Data," in Vol. 6 of *Encyclopedia of African-American Culture and History*, 2d edition, edited by Colin Palmer, Macmillan Reference USA, 2006, p. 2567.

Baraka, Amiri, "*A Raisin in the Sun's* Enduring Passion," in *A Raisin in the Sun; The Sign in Sidney Brustein's Window*, by Lorraine Hansberry, edited by Robert Nemiroff, New American Library, 1987, pp. 9–20.

Bivens, Donna, "Internalized Racism: A Definition," *Women's Theological Center*, www.thewtc.org/ Internalized_Racism.pdf (1995).

Chadderton, David, Review of *A Raisin in the Sun*, *The British Theatre Guide*, www.britishtheatreguide.info/ reviews/raisininsun-rev.htm (January 16, 2006).

Cooper, David D., "Hansberry's *A Raisin in the Sun*," in *The Explicator*, Fall, 1993, pp. 59–61.

Hansberry, Lorraine, *A Raisin in the Sun*, Vintage, 1994, originally published in 1959.

Jones, Camara Phyllis, "Levels of Racism: A Theoretical Framework and a Gardener's Tale," in *American Journal of Public Health*, Vol. 90, No. 8, August 2000, pp. 1212–15.

Nemiroff, Robert, Introduction, in *A Raisin in the Sun*, Vintage, 1994, p. 5.

Sommer, Elyse, "A *Curtain Up* Berkshire Review: *A Raisin in the Sun*," *Curtain Up*, www.curtainup.com/ raisininthesun.html (July 22, 1999).

Smith, Ana Deavere, "Two Visions of Love, Family and Race Across the Generations," *News and Reviews About* A Raisin in the Sun *on Broadway*, www.raisinonbroadway. com/news.html (January 16, 2006), originally published in *New York Times*, May 29, 2004.

Stone, I. F., "The Rat and Res Judicata," in *Nation*, Vol. 151, No. 21, November 23, 1940, pp. 495–96.

Trotter, Joe, Jr., "U.S. Migration/Population," in Vol. 4 of *Encyclopedia of African-American Culture and History*, 2d edition, edited by Colin Palmer, Macmillan Reference USA, 2006, p. 1442.

Washington, J. Charles, "*A Raisin in the Sun* Revisited," in *Black American Literature Forum*, Vol. 22, No. 1, Spring, 1988, pp. 109–124.

Zolotow, Sam, "*A Raisin in the Sun* Basks in Praise; 7 Critics Welcome Play by Miss Hansberry," in *New York Times*, March 13, 1959, p. 25.

Roll of Thunder, Hear My Cry

MILDRED D. TAYLOR

1976

Mildred D. Taylor's novel *Roll of Thunder, Hear My Cry* examines the hardships and struggles of the Logans, a black family living in rural Mississippi during the early 1930s. It is Taylor's second account of the Logans, whom she follows in six other books, including a prequel, a sequel, and several novellas, all written for a child and/or young adult audience. Based on Taylor's father's experiences growing up, the books reflect some of the South's most troubling history, when Jim Crow laws ruled and civil rights were not yet within reach. Taylor uses her family's past as a lens through which to explore the legacy of the American South, deftly making a case for its modern relevance in the process.

Taylor grew up listening to her father's reminisces about his family's struggle to keep its land despite the Great Depression and hostility from white neighbors. She thought of the tales often before she finally succeeded in crafting one into her own short story. The breakthrough was her creation of protagonist Cassie Logan, originally eight years old, who is loosely based on Taylor's aunt. She tried telling the stories from other characters' perspectives, but none felt as natural as Cassie's. Taylor's first story, about a white man cutting and selling trees from the Logans' land without their permission, won first prize in the African American category in a competition sponsored by the Council on Interracial Books for

" SO NOW, EVEN THOUGH SEVENTY YEARS HAVE PASSED SINCE SLAVERY, MOST WHITE PEOPLE STILL THINK OF US AS THEY DID THEN—THAT WE'RE NOT AS GOOD AS THEY ARE—AND PEOPLE LIKE MR. SIMMS HOLD ON TO THAT BELIEF HARDER THAN SOME OTHER FOLKS BECAUSE THEY HAVE LITTLE ELSE TO HOLD ON TO. FOR HIM TO BELIEVE THAT HE IS BETTER THAN WE ARE MAKES HIM THINK THAT HE'S IMPORTANT, SIMPLY BECAUSE HE'S WHITE."

BIOGRAPHY

MILDRED D. TAYLOR

Mildred D. Taylor was born in Jackson, Mississippi, on September 13, 1943. Her family moved to Toledo, Ohio, soon afterward. Though her own childhood was spent in Ohio, Taylor experienced Mississippi through her father's stories and through annual summer trips to visit family; her father's stories especially left an impression. As a student, Taylor noticed that the blacks described in books often did not resemble the ones in her father's stories, and by high school she felt almost obligated to help alter the literary landscape. She excelled in English, where she was often the only black student in her college preparatory classes, but she did not begin writing fiction until years later.

She earned a bachelor's degree from the University of Toledo before joining the Peace Corps and moving to Ethiopia. When she returned, she went to graduate school to study journalism at the University of Colorado. She thought often of her father's stories and struggled to develop them into fictional narratives. After her first story, "Song of the Trees," won first prize in a contest, she found a publisher and quickly developed the story into a novella for young adults. Taylor has been devoted to writing fiction ever since.

In 2004, the University of Mississippi celebrated Mildred D. Taylor Day as part of the Oxford Conference for the Book. As of 2006, Taylor lives in Colorado.

Children, and a publishing offer soon followed. Taylor elaborated on the story, turning it into a novella called *Song of the Trees* (1975).

A year later she published *Roll of Thunder, Hear My Cry*, which was an immediate success. The American Library Association (ALA) named it a Notable Book of 1976, and the following year it won the Newbery Medal and was a finalist for a National Book Award. Taylor was writing during a blossoming of African American culture. Fresh out of the civil rights movement, black men and women were making strides toward equality, especially in areas such as music, film, and literature. Maya Angelou had recently published her famed memoir *I Know Why the Caged Bird Sings* (1969). Alex Haley received the National Book Award for his epic family drama *Roots* (1976) the same year Taylor published *Roll of Thunder, Hear My Cry*. Just a couple of years before Taylor's award-winning book, Virginia Hamilton won the Newbery Medal and the National Book Award for her young adult novel *M. C. Higgins, the Great*, which also dealt with issues of race and property. It was a time, perhaps more so than any other before or since, when the issue of race was acknowledged and discussed in the public arena, and perspectives from African Americans were welcomed with new enthusiasm.

Both the political climate and Taylor's own journey prepared her to write the Logan family chronicles. She had recently completed a master's

degree in journalism from the University of Colorado, where she helped create a black studies program. Before graduate school, as a member of the Peace Corps, she spent two years teaching English and history to children in Ethiopia—an assignment she had requested. No doubt these experiences helped shape Taylor's sense of self and provided a context in which to develop her family's stories. The result is a breadth of memorable characters and settings that are both painful and inspiring. In *Roll of Thunder, Hear My Cry* for example, the Logans repeatedly confront racism as they struggle to keep their land, but retain a strong sense of identity. Cassie especially becomes more conscious of prejudice, moving from indignation and anger to cautious resistance and grief. Her evolution speaks to the harsh reality of racism, as well as to the strength of those who endure it.

Roll of Thunder, Hear My Cry is available in a twenty-fifth anniversary edition, published in 2000 by Phyllis Fogelman books, that includes an introduction by the author.

PLOT SUMMARY

Chapter 1

The Logan children—Cassie, the narrator, and her brothers Stacey, Christopher-John, and Little Man—walk to school. It is October and their first day back after cotton-picking season began in early spring. They are dressed in Sunday clothes, a tradition Mama enforces on the first day of school. Cassie describes the Mississippi scenery on the way to school: forest on one side and a cotton field on the other. She notes the barbed-wire fence that runs "the length of the deep field, stretching eastward for over a quarter of a mile" where the family's four hundred acres ends.

Beyond the forest is Harlan Granger's plantation, where many sharecroppers live. Cassie explains the story of how the Logans came to own their land. Many years ago it had belonged to the Grangers, but during Reconstruction, the period after the Civil War when the Confederate states were being reintegrated with the Union, the Grangers had had to sell much of their land to pay taxes. Grandpa Logan bought two hundred acres, and years later when he had paid off the debt, he bought two hundred more. Now, during the Great Depression, the price of cotton has dropped and the expense of the land has become almost too much for the family to bear. Papa, the children's father, is in Louisiana working on the railroad. He tells Cassie she will never have to live on someone else's land. Mama teaches seventh grade and runs the farm while Big Ma, Papa's mother, works in the fields and tends to the house.

Mildred Taylor The Toledo Blade. Reproduced by permission

T. J. Avery and his younger brother Claude, children of black sharecroppers, meet the Logans on their way to school. T. J., known for his bullying, rebellious ways, is a friend of Stacey. He shares information about a burning into the conversation, but the others have no idea what he is talking about. T. J. tells them that "some white men took a match" to Mr. Berry and his two nephews.

Stacey suddenly urges everyone off the road and onto the clay bank at the edge of the forest. Little Man does not follow because he does not want to get his clothes dirty. He is covered in a "scarlet haze" of red-clay dirt and dust when a school bus shoots past him. White school children laugh in the windows of the bus. Along the way, a "towheaded boy" named Jeremy Simms joins the group. The Logan children are baffled at his decision to walk with them. He has been doing it for years, though they know he has been whipped for it. When they reach the crossroads, they pass white children, including Jeremy's sister Lillian Jean, who does not acknowledge the black children. The Logan children stop to gaze at the white school, which has a sports field, two buses, and a big front lawn.

Down the road, the black school is "a dismal end to an hour's journey." The teacher announces that the students will get books this year and instructs them to "take extra-good care of them." Cassie immediately notices the books are in terrible shape and opens hers to find pictures and illustrations of "girls with blond braids and boys with blue eyes." After Little Man looks inside his book, he flings it to the floor and stomps on it. Cassie realizes why Little Man is upset when she sees the chart on the inside cover of the book: this is its twelfth "issuance" to a student, its condition is "very poor," and the race of student is listed as "nigra." Cassie tries to defend Little Man by showing the teacher the chart, specifically pointing out "what they called us," but the teacher is not sympathetic. In the end, both Cassie and Little Man refuse their books and get a whipping.

Chapter 2

Papa comes home, bringing with him "the most formidable-looking being" the children have ever seen. The children are disappointed to hear that Papa can only stay one night before he has to get back to Louisiana, but he explains that he "come home special . . . [to] bring Mr. Morrison." Papa says that Mr. Morrison lost his job on the railroad and that he has offered him work as a "hired hand." Morrison tells Mama that he got fired from his job for fighting with some men, but they did not get fired because they were white. She says they are glad to have him "especially now," leaving the children wondering what she means. Later, while working in the field, they speculate that Papa brought Morrison home because of the burnings T. J. told them about.

The big news at church the next morning is that one of Mr. Berry's nephews has died. The children finally hear the story of the burning when neighbors come to visit. Mr. Berry's two nephews had stopped to get gas when drunken white men appeared, accusing one of the Berry men of flirting with a white woman. The Berry brothers left without getting gas, but the white men later caught up with them. The brothers, afraid they would run out of gas, stopped at their uncle's house. The white men dragged the brothers out of the house "and when old man Berry tried to stop it, they lit him afire with them boys." A Berry relative told the sheriff what happened, but he "called her a liar and sent her on home." Papa suddenly tells the people at

church that his family does not shop at the Wallace store. An uncomfortable silence follows. Papa tells the children to stay away from the Wallace store as well, where youngsters are going after school to buy liquor and cigarettes and get into trouble. The children promise to stay away.

Chapter 3

When the rains come, the walk to school is especially dreadful as the school bus "zoom[s] from behind" and splashes the children with "the murky waters of the road." One morning, the bus swerves close to the children. They attempt to jump the gully but it is too full of water, and they fall short and land "in the slime." The white children laugh at them and call "nigger" and "mud eater" out the windows. Stacey promises his siblings that the bus will not get them again, "least not for a long while."

At lunch time, Stacey takes some shovels and buckets from the school's tool shed and the group walks to the place where the bus forced them off the road. Stacey decides not to tell T. J. about this because he talks too much. At the gully, Stacey tells them to dig. Soon there is a large ditch from one side of the road to the other, and they use the buckets to fill it with water. That afternoon it pours rain. On their way home from school, they notice the ditch has transformed into a "twelve-foot lake." They hide in the forest and watch as the bus speeds toward their trap. They hear the white children on the bus laughing and then a "tremendous crack" as the bust gets stuck in the rut "like a lopsided billy goat on its knees." The bus driver tells the children on board they will have to walk to school for at least the next two weeks.

Chapter 4

Granger's car is leaving the driveway as they get home. Big Ma says he was pestering her about the land. Cassie follows her into the forest and they sit in a clearing. Big Ma talks of her late husband, Grandpa Logan, and how he acquired the land. When he bought his first two hundred acres from the Grangers, Mr. Jamison, "a good neighbor," also bought a portion of the Granger land. Later, when Harlan Granger became head of the Granger plantation, "he wanted to buy back every inch of land that used to belong to the Grangers." Grandpa Logan and Mr. Jamison refused to sell. When Mr. Jamison died, his son Wade had no interest in farming. Wade Jamison sold most of his land to Harlan Granger, except for two hundred acres that he sold to Grandpa Logan, a move that Harlan Granger resented.

Mama takes the children to see Mr. Berry, one of the burn victims. Mama advises the children to be themselves, but they are dumbfounded by what they see: "The face [has] no nose, and the head no hair; the skin [is] scarred, burned, and the lips [are] wizened black, like charcoal." On the way home, Mama tells them that "the Wallaces did that." They visit sharecropping families, and Mama speaks "of the bad influence of the Wallaces" and of "finding another store to patronize." Most people only nod. Mr. Turner agrees but says he has credit at the Wallace store because Mr. Montier, his plantation owner, signs for him. Mama says her family has found stores in Vicksburg that treat them well and suggests that someone might be "willing to make the trip" for others. Mr. Turner says he has no cash and does not think anyone in Vicksburg will give him credit. Mama does not relent, asking "what if someone backed your signature? Would you shop up in Vicksburg then?" Mr. Turner says he will "consider it deeply."

Chapter 5

Big Ma takes Stacey and Cassie with her to Strawberry, the nearest town, to sell goods at the market. T. J. comes along, too. At the farmer's market, Cassie immediately notices that the black families are situated far from the entrance where nobody can see them. She is irritated by this but Big Ma tells her to be quiet.

In town, Big Ma goes to see Wade Jamison, now a lawyer. She tells the children to wait in the wagon, but T. J. urges them to go ahead to the store. T. J. places his order but a white customer cuts in with a long list, and "the storekeeper, without a word of apology," begins to fill hers. He finishes her order and goes back to T. J.'s, but he is interrupted again by white customers and walks away. When Cassie sees him wrapping up a pork chop for a white girl, she walks over and reminds the storekeeper that they are waiting and that they were there before the girl. He tells her to get her "little black self back over there and wait some more." The situation escalates until he calls out, "Whose little nigger is this!" and she screams, "I ain't nobody's little nigger!" Finally, Stacey pulls Cassie out of the store.

On the way to find Big Ma, Cassie bumps into Lillian Jean. She apologizes, but Lillian Jean insists Cassie "get down in the road" and stop using the sidewalk where the "decent white folks" are. When Cassie will not move, Mr. Simms twists her arm from behind and shoves her into the road. Then he tells her to apologize to "Miz Lillian Jean this minute." Big Ma arrives and meekly defends Cassie before she also instructs Cassie to apologize. Cassie considers this day the cruelest in her life.

Chapter 6

Cassie is angry with Big Ma, but Stacey suggests there are things Cassie does not understand. At home, there is a silver car in the barn. The children worry it is Granger's, but it turns out to belong to Uncle Hammer. When Uncle Hammer asks Cassie about her first trip to Strawberry, she bursts out with the story of Lillian Jean. Uncle Hammer is angered when he hears Mr. Simms pushed her and heads toward the door. Big Ma begs him to let it go. Mama tells Stacey to go get Morrison while she tries to persuade Uncle Hammer that Cassie is all right, and he should not make any trouble. He responds with urgency: "If I'd've knocked his girl down, you know what'd've happened to me? ... Right now I'd be hanging from that oak over yonder."

Before Cassie goes to sleep, Mama talks to her about the events in Strawberry. Mama tells her that Mr. Simms thinks Lillian Jean is better than Cassie because Lillian Jean is white, that "he's one of those people who has to believe that white people are better than black people to make himself feel big."

After church the next day, Uncle Hammer takes the family for a drive in his car. At Soldiers Bridge, where only one car can pass at a time, Uncle Hammer sees the Wallace truck approaching. Instead of allowing it to pass first, he rushes onto the bridge, knowing the Wallaces will think it is Granger's car. As the car comes off the bridge, the Wallaces "touch their hats respectfully, then immediately freeze." Uncle Hammer calmly touches his hat too before speeding away. Everyone laughs but Mama, who says one day they will have to pay for it.

Chapter 7

Papa comes home for Christmas, and the family sits around and tells stories. As it gets late, Morrison shares a story about when he lived with his family in a shantytown outside of Shreveport, Louisiana. Two teenage boys came to their door one night "scairt, clean out of their heads with fright," after a white woman accused them of molesting her. As the boys had finished their story, "devilish night men swept down," killing and burning the family out of its home. Morrison's parents and sisters died that night.

After Christmas dinner, the children are surprised to find Jeremy standing at their door. He offers a burlap bag full of nuts to Mama and gives Stacey a wooden flute that he has made. Papa asks Jeremy if his daddy knows he is there, and Jeremy says that he does not. Papa suggests he go home before his daddy comes looking for him. After Jeremy leaves, Papa and Stacey talk. Papa discourages Stacey from being friends with Jeremy because "friendship between black and white don't mean that much 'cause it usually ain't on a equal basis." When Stacey defends Jeremy, Papa explains that someday blacks and whites might be able to be friends, "but right now the country ain't built that way."

The next day, Jamison brings papers for Big Ma to sign. Cassie figures out that she is signing over the land to Uncle Hammer and Papa. Before Jamison leaves, he says he has heard that people are "looking to shop in Vicksburg" and that thirty families are trying to get credit. He offers to back the credit himself. Jamison admits that he is a "Southerner, born and bred," but that that does not mean he approves of everything that goes on in the South. They discuss the possible consequences of the arrangement.

Granger stops by the Logan house a few days later. He suggests they are "stirring up something" and threatens that their "mortgage could come due anytime." Papa tells him not to plan on getting the land.

Chapter 8

Cassie sets out to ingratiate herself to Lillian Jean by walking with her to school and carrying her books. Papa talks to Cassie about the incident in Strawberry and says that "Lillian Jean probably won't be the last white person" to disrespect her. He encourages her to "think real hard on whether or not Lillian Jean's worth taking a stand about."

For the next month, Cassie carries her books in the morning, and Lillian Jean tells Cassie her secrets. After school one day, Cassie claims to

have a surprise for Lillian Jean in the forest. Cassie smashes Lillian Jean's books and taunts Lillian Jean into hitting her. When she does, Cassie tackles her, knocking them both down. Cassie beats her up, careful not to touch Lillian Jean's face and demands an apology. Lillian Jean apologizes profusely, though after she is released, threatens to tell her father. Smirking, Cassie tells Lillian Jean that if she says "one word of this to anybody … everybody [at the white school] is gonna know who you crazy 'bout and all your other business."

Granger, Kaleb Wallace, and another man show up at the school to observe Mama teaching. They discover she is teaching material not found in the books, and Granger suggests if she is so smart, she can write her own book and "forget about teaching." The next day, a student tells Stacey that T. J., who had recently failed a test, complained about Mrs. Logan at the Wallace store. The kid says T. J. also told the Wallace men that the Wallace store boycott was her idea. T. J. denies that he said anything, but the Logan children decide not to be T. J.'s friend any longer.

Chapter 9

Just before school ends, the children hear from Jeremy that T. J. is "running 'round" with Jeremy's older brothers R. W. and Melvin. Jeremy says his brothers do not treat T. J. well.

Mr. Lanier and Mr. Avery come by to withdraw their shopping lists for the upcoming trip to Vicksburg because Granger and Montier have demanded an increased share of the families' crops. On top of that, the Wallaces have threatened to send the sheriff after them unless they pay their debts at the store. Papa, Morrison, and Stacey make a trip to Vicksburg for the seven families that continue to boycott the Wallace store. They do not arrive home when the family expects them, and everyone worries. When they finally do return, Papa is injured. The back wheels came off the wagon on the way home from Vicksburg. When they stopped to fix the wagon, someone in a passing truck driving with the lights off shot Papa. At the same time, the mule reared and the wagon rolled over Papa's leg and broke it. Morrison fought the men, apparently hurting them badly. The bullet only skimmed the side of Papa's head. Stacey thinks it was the Wallaces.

Chapter 10

The children go to a neighbor's house with Morrison. On the way back, Kaleb Wallace blocks the road with his truck, gets out, and yells at Morrison. Morrison calmly asks if he is going to move his truck. Finally, "his muscles flexing tightly against his thin shirt," Morrison moves the truck himself. When they are halfway down the road, they hear Kaleb Wallace scream, "One of these nights ... I'm gonna come get you for what you done!" Shortly thereafter, Papa receives a letter from the bank demanding the mortgage be paid in full immediately. Papa, who has been unable to work since breaking his leg, calls Uncle Hammer, who says he will get the money. Uncle Hammer shows up sometime later with the money, but no longer driving the silver car.

T. J. shows up at the local revival with the Simms brothers. He loudly tells the group about his "mighty fine friends" who give him whatever he wants, "Including the pearl-handled pistol in Barnett's Mercantile." Stacey, disgusted, ignores him. The Simms brothers tell T. J. that since they went with him to the revival, he is going with them to Strawberry.

Chapter 11

This chapter begins with an epigraph patterned after a slave song. Beginning with the line, "Roll of thunder / hear my cry," because "Ole man comin' / down the line," it foreshadows the events to come. Much later on the night of the revival, Cassie finds T. J. on the porch knocking on the door of the boys' room. He tells her and Stacey that he is in trouble and shows them the "deep blue-black swelling of his stomach and chest" where R. W. and Melvin beat him. He tells them the store in Strawberry was closed, but the Simms brothers decided to break in to get the pistol. When they were caught by Mr. Barnett, R. W. hit him hard on the back of the head with an axe. Mrs. Barnett, hysterical, came into the room, mistaking R. W. and Melvin for black men because they had stockings on their heads. R. W. slapped her and she fell back, hitting her head on a stove. The brothers beat T. J. when he said he would tell people what happened.

T. J. asks Stacey to help him get home before his father finds out he is gone, and the other children insist on going with them. As the Logan children are leaving T. J.'s house after walking him home, six vehicles pull into the yard and Kaleb Wallace gets out, yelling for "that thieving, murdering nigger." The group of men, which includes R. W. and Melvin, drag the Avery family out of the house while the Logan children watch from the forest. Suddenly, one of the men holds up the pistol from the store. He tells of Mrs. Barnett's claim that three black boys robbed her store and attacked both her and her husband. The men beat T. J. when he tries to defend himself. Then Jamison arrives with the sheriff, who says, "Mr. Granger sent word by me that he ain't gonna stand for no hanging on *his* place." When the men suggest they take T. J. down the road, Jamison stands in front of T. J. Stacey tells Cassie and the others to go get Papa and Morrison.

Chapter 12

Cassie tells the adults of the events at T. J.'s house, and Papa gets his shotgun. Mama, afraid he will be killed, tells him to find a way to get Granger to stop the men. Big Ma prays and the family sits quietly. Soon, Mama smells smoke and sees fire on the land near the Granger forest. In a panic, she and Big Ma fill a tub with water and head toward the blaze. Jeremy shows up later and tells Cassie that his father, older brothers, and many of the men from town are fighting the fire. He also says their father is working on it, and they are relieved to hear Papa is okay. The cause of the fire is assumed to be lightning.

Jamison comes by later and tells them that Mr. Barnett died in the early morning. T. J. is being held by the sheriff in Strawberry. Jamison advises Papa to "stay clear of this whole thing now ... and don't give anybody cause to think about you at all," implying he assumes Papa started the fire. The children want to know what will happen to T. J., and Papa says he could "go on the chain gang." Stacey asks if T. J. might die. Papa says he has never lied to them, but he wishes he could now. Stacey, crying, runs toward the forest. Cassie goes to bed and cries also "for those things which had happened in the night and would not pass."

THEMES

Racism

Racism tinges almost every experience of the Logans and their sharecropping neighbors in *Roll of Thunder, Hear My Cry*. The children

A large lynch mob surrounds the burning body of an African American man tied to a tree trunk, Waco, Texas, 1917 Corbis

look over their shoulders while they walk to school for fear the white children's school bus will cover them with dust, or worse, run them off the road. Blacks are variously ignored and provoked by whites, but never forgotten. In turn, blacks never forget the threat that whites pose; more often than not, that threat is followed by action.

On the trip to Strawberry with the Logans, T. J., typically irreverent and unpredictable, is quiet and easygoing in the store, even when the storekeeper drops his order to help a white customer. It is Cassie, not yet attuned to the subtleties of racism, who confronts the storekeeper about the injustice. T. J. knows there is worse treatment than having his order delayed, indeed, Cassie is insulted and ordered out of the store after she complains. The black characters in the novel react to the ill treatment according to their personal experience. Uncle Hammer, used to a more progressive way of life in Chicago, is quick

to defend the family against the rural Southern whites. Cassie, with her fiery outrage, patterns herself after the adults in her family. As landowners, the Logans are better able than most to actively challenge the status quo. Papa talks explicitly about the threat of racism when he warns Stacey not to befriend Jeremy, a seemingly harmless boy; the color of Jeremy's skin alone means he might "turn on [Stacey] in a minute." In fact, it is Jeremy's older brothers R. W. and Melvin, T. J.'s new friends, who fulfill Papa's prediction.

Racism is also expressed through economics. Many sharecropping families are kept from participating in the Wallace store boycott even after Jamison agrees to back their credit at a store in Vicksburg. They are caught in a cycle of debt: their plantation owners charge them "risk" interest in exchange for backing their credit at the Wallace store, and the Wallace store charges them interest on all of their purchases made on the credit. When some share-croppers attempt the boycott anyway, the plantation owners simply demand a larger share of the crops—income the families cannot afford to lose. In this way, the black families are kept largely dependent on their plantation owners and the Wallaces, and unable to assert their freedom of choice.

Property and Empowerment

When *Roll of Thunder, Hear My Cry* begins, Cassie questions why Papa would travel as far as Louisiana for work just to pay for their land. She does not yet understand why the land is so important that her father would leave the family for months at a time to preserve it. Papa explains that there is a difference between living on one's own land and living on somebody else's, but eight-year-old Cassie only recognizes the inconveniences.

The Logans are the only black landowners in the book. They are also a brave, risk-taking family, leaders of the black community with enough influence to start a boycott of the Wallace store. The land represents both a burden and a blessing for them. It requires the family's constant attention, often threatening to bankrupt them even as it offers them stability and important leverage within both the black and white communities. From connecting them with Jamison, an educated white man who becomes an ally, to shielding them from dependence on underhanded plantation owners, the land is a tangible source of empowerment for the Logans. More importantly, it is what the land represents—possession and ownership—that provides the family with the strength and will to fight racism. With ownership comes a level of freedom. Papa chooses to burn part of his land in a ploy to get Granger's attention and distract the Wallace men from T. J. He is free to sacrifice a portion of his crop without danger of being implicated, or even suspected, for wrongdoing. This act, and in turn the land itself, ultimately saves T. J.'s life.

Denial and Acceptance

Throughout the book, Cassie struggles with the realities of racism. As an eight-year-old, she is only beginning to realize the extent to which the color of her skin defines her experiences. She encounters racial disparity again and again, beginning in chapter 1 when she discovers the chart on the inside cover of the worn-out schoolbook. Cassie cannot believe the county has listed the black schoolchildren's race as "nigra." When she desperately shows the chart to her teacher, she is confused by her teacher's casual reaction. This scene offers examples of both extreme denial and extreme acceptance. Cassie's immature understanding of race relations causes her to reject the book, while her teacher, Miss Crocker, after a lifetime of experiencing such offenses, passively accepts it. When Miss Crocker speaks with Mama about Cassie and Little Man's behavior after school, Cassie expects Mama to react with as much indignation as she did. Instead, Mama calmly begins covering the charts on all of the books in her classroom. In this way, Mama serves as Taylor's ideal, someone who accepts that racism exists but speaks openly about its harm and actively tries to undermine it. As Kelly McDowell writes of Mama in "*Roll of Thunder, Hear My Cry*: A Culturally Specific, Subversive Concept of Child Agency":

> In an almost seditious act, [Mama] exerts an agency to resist the racist practice. By doing so, she displays to her students, as well as to her own children, that agency is possible and, in fact, crucial and that there are always ways to resist domination.

At the height of Cassie's awakening is her experience in Strawberry with Lillian Jean and Mr. Simms. In the end, she is more hurt and angered by Big Ma's submissive reaction than the physical assault and the insults of Mrs. Simms. Part of the denial of racism is the denial of its power. Cassie is stunned and hurt to see her grandmother subservient to Mr. Simms. Later, Mama explains that Big Ma was protecting Cassie from further violence by Mr. Simms, and Cassie begins to glimpse the complex game of give-and-take involved in relationships with whites. Mama tells Cassie outright that she has to accept the fact that the world is not ideal, and that "white is something just like black is something." McDowell notes that she also "hints of a tactic for resistance and, thus, encourages her daughter's own subversive agency."

Cassie displays a deeper understanding of racial dynamics later when she avenges Lillian Jean's mistreatment of her in such a way that Lillian Jean is powerless to do anything about it. At the book's end, Cassie discovers that T. J. may be put to death for a crime he did not commit. She desperately asks Papa, "d-does it have to be?" but she already knows the answer.

In bed, she finally cries, mourning not just for T. J. but for the way things are—a sign she is beginning to come to terms with the reality of racism.

HISTORICAL OVERVIEW

Sharecropping

After the Civil War, slavery often gave way to a tenuous form of freedom known as sharecropping, or tenant farming. The slave system had created a co-dependency between white plantation owners and black labor. After the abolition of slavery, property owners could not maintain their land without slaves; likewise, slaves had nowhere to live and nothing to eat without the property owner. Though many former slaves migrated to the North, many stayed in the South and fell into an arrangement between white landowners and former black slaves in which former slaves farmed the land in exchange for a portion (half or less) of the crops. Landowners were especially happy with the arrangement, since the war had left their Confederate money worthless and they could not afford to pay workers. At first, newly freed slaves looking for autonomy saw sharecropping as an improvement. However, it soon became clear that sharecropping was simply another form of servitude.

To begin with, sharecroppers had to buy their own seeds, fertilizer, and equipment, as well as food to live on until harvest time. As in *Roll of Thunder, Hear My Cry*, landowners would ensure sharecroppers had credit at the general store, but then both the landowner and the store owner would charge sharecroppers interest on that credit. Before the seeds were even in the ground, sharecroppers were in debt. After selling their share of the crops (often at prices set by the landowner), sharecroppers had to put most of the money toward their increasing debt; soon they would have no choice but to rely on credit again. On top of this, the work was constant and grueling, and sharecroppers often developed permanently stooped backs from bending over to work in the fields.

Continuing into the twentieth century, sharecropping was the work of the poorest of the poor, including whites. The arrangement became even less rewarding during the Great Depression as crop prices plummeted. Not long after, sharecroppers were replaced by mechanized farm tools.

Post-Reconstruction Racial Violence

During the period of Reconstruction (1865–1877) after the Civil War, many people in the South reacted to their defeat in the war with violence toward recently freed slaves, as well as white abolitionists. But it was not until Reconstruction officially ended in 1877 that the pattern of violence almost exclusively targeted black people, often in the form of public hangings by vigilantes, or lynchings.

As soon as federal troops left the South, white supremacists began deliberately defying the laws of Reconstruction, intending to impede black citizens' progress at every turn. Jim Crow laws, which spread throughout the South beginning around 1890, served to reinforce the prevailing racist attitudes by creating "separate but equal" facilities for "colored" people. For many whites, Jim Crow laws simply became an excuse to harass and threaten black people with more violence. If blacks were seen as stepping outside of their narrowly defined place in society, they were often bullied and sometimes even murdered.

In *An American Dilemma: The Negro Problem and Modern Democracy* (1944), Gunnar Myrdal writes that lynchers were typically rural, lower-class white men who, among other things, had a fear of being displaced by blacks. Large groups, known as lynch mobs, would hunt down a victim, creating a spectacle of brutality before the climactic hanging. Sometimes victims were tortured first. Rarely were the lynchers punished, and in fact, local sheriffs and government officials commonly took part in the scene. In some cases, lynch mobs even retrieved the victim from a local jail. Blacks were terrorized for everything from impertinence to suspicion of raping a white woman. According to journalist Ida B. Wells-Barnett, who documented her findings in *The Red Record* (1895), more lynching victims were accused of murder or attempted murder—like T. J. in *Roll of Thunder, Hear My Cry*—than any other crime. Racial violence did not always come in the form of lynching. Beatings and burnings were also common methods of abuse, as was the destruction of property.

In the mid-1920s, the number of lynchings began to decrease. Many factors played a role in

this, especially the work of civil rights organization National Association for the Advancement
of Colored People (NAACP) to bring awareness
of the problem into the mainstream. Though an
anti-lynching bill was passed in the House of
Representatives in 1922, it was stifled in the
Senate. Still, the bill prompted lengthy discussions of lynching, which may have aided in redu-
cing its prevalence. Lynchings continued to
decline throughout the twentieth century,
though as Phillip Dray points out in *At the
Hands of Persons Unknown: The Lynching of
Black America* (2002), it was not until 1952 that
a year went by without a single reported
incident.

CRITICAL OVERVIEW

When *Roll of Thunder, Hear My Cry* was first
published by Dial Books in 1976, it steadily
attracted attention from critics, especially those
interested in children's and young adult fiction,
like *The Horn Book* and the American Library
Association's *Booklist*. The novel received a
starred review in *Booklist*, which, as quoted in
the Puffin paperback edition of *Roll of Thunder,
Hear My Cry*, notes the book "grows with con-
vincing detail of character and situation." *The
Horn Book*, also quoted in the Puffin paperback
edition of the book, recognizes the story's "verisimilitude" and "carefully drawn" characters.

Writing in the *New York Times* in "For
Young Readers," Jean Fritz calls the book
powerful and acknowledges that "Mildred
Taylor's truth is on a ... terrifying level."
However, Leah Deland Stenson in the *School
Library Journal* considers the book's focus on
"indignities and injustices" too heavy for readers
to "discover who the Logans are or how they've
changed by virtue of their struggles." The review
goes on to concede, though, that "readers will
undoubtedly be propelled by the forceful
momentum of mounting conflicts."

The year after it was published, *Roll of
Thunder, Hear My Cry* won the Newbery
Medal, the most prestigious children's book
award in the country. The award garnered the
book even more attention and practically guaranteed its place on school reading lists. Typically
assigned in seventh or eighth grade, the book has
regularly been challenged by both black and
white parents and school administrators, who

MEDIA ADAPTATIONS

Adapted to film shortly after it was published,
Roll of Thunder, Hear My Cry (1976) aired as a
three-part television miniseries. The movie stars
Claudia McNeil as Mama and Morgan Freeman
as Uncle Hammer and was nominated for two
Emmys. Released on VHS in 1999 from Live/
Artisan, it is currently unavailable.

An abridged audio version of *Roll of
Thunder, Hear My Cry* is available on CD from
Listening Library. It is narrated by Lynne
Thigpen.

most often find offense with its use of the word
"nigger." In 2002, it made the American Library
Association's "Ten Most Frequently Challenged
Books" list. According to Leslie Postal's "Take
Book Out of Schools in Seminole, Parents Ask,"
in 2004 a Florida family challenged the book for
its "harsh depictions of racism and its use of
racial slurs." In spite of the challenges, though,
the book is rarely banned. In a 2001 interview
with Hazel Rochman of *Booklist*, Taylor says
she understands these reactions to an extent,
but she believes children need to know their
heritage: "I think each of us needs to know
where America was in the past, where we came
from."

In 2003, Taylor won the first NSK Neustadt
Prize for Children's Literature, sponsored by
World Literature Today and the University of
Oklahoma. Reflecting on this in "Mildred D.
Taylor and the Art of Making a Difference,"
Robert Con Davis-Undiano writes that
Taylor's "work has marked a huge cultural
shift in the lives of many American families
who have suffered the indignities of poverty
and racial discrimination." Davis-Undiano suggests Taylor's significance lies in the fact that she
is "socially engaged," and chooses "to serve her
community steadfastly through the fiercest
adherence imaginable to the truth of the
African American experience."

African American children gathered around a porch Library of Congress

CRITICISM

Hamida Bosmajian

In the following excerpt, Bosmajian considers how Taylor's protagonist grows to understand the precarious relationship between law and justice.

Mildred Taylor's rich chronicle about an African American family in rural Mississippi during the years 1933–41 is narrated by the main character, Cassie Logan. The story she tells is not only about the adventures of her childhood and adolescence, not only about the deep bonds she has with her family, but also about the injustices a white, racist, and lawless society inflicts on the Logans and their neighbors. Although they are citizens in a nation that is framed by one of the most important legal documents in Western civilization, the Constitution of the United States, black Americans find themselves in Taylor's chronicle constituted in an unjust system of local laws and customs. It is not surprising, therefore, that as a child the intelligent and inquisitive Cassie is already quite aware of the binary injustice/justice. The first term of the binary is privileged in her life experience; it is the second, justice, that she yearns for.

It is a theme that is unusual in children's literature. Most often the law, especially in fairy tales, is expressed through irrational or tyrannical rules imposed upon the hero by persons in authority. The hero's trial, then, consists often of impossible hardships and tasks to fulfill these rules. The mysteries of adult law and legal systems may also befuddle the child hero who, like Alice in Wonderland, finds herself or himself in an absurd world. We may well conclude that children's literature tends to depict law in a preconscious, even dreamlike sense. Taylor's chronicle, however, shows us characters who are conscious of the value of American law as a heritage of an age of reason. Although the titles *Roll of Thunder, Hear My Cry* and *Let the Circle Be Unbroken* are prayerful imperatives that reflect the religious heritage of African Americans—the first asking for vertical divine intervention, the second for the continued connectedness on the horizontal level of human experience—the novels do not invoke or appeal to divine law, but place the responsibility for justice on laws made by humans.

As far as the values of law and justice are concerned, fictions such as the *Oresteia* or Taylor's trilogy are pedagogical in their rhetorical ethos. The Greek poet of antiquity instructs the polis through the mythic mode, where the gods are the authoritative teachers. Mildred Taylor, a writer in the psychologically and socially realistic mode, focuses on justice and law issues by recording the ordinary routines and events of human life, as with Cassie Logan, who grows from a pranksterish tomboy to an aspiring student of the law. In the Mississippi of her childhood and adolescence, custom and the unjust statutes of segregation have institutionalized racism, and those in power can vent their rage with impunity whenever they feel that "colored folk" are "forgetting their place." The victims of this willful power must constantly be vigilant and self-controlled, even if they are infuriated by the injustices inflicted upon them. To protect herself and her family, young Cassie has to learn that she cannot vent her anger. As she matures, she begins to place her hope for empowerment in the knowledge and interpretation of the law, particularly the law of the U.S. Constitution, which potentially can supersede the unjust law and custom of Mississippi.

Mildred Taylor shows us Cassie's development not only in the context of growing up in a warm and nurturing family but also in the context of the middle-class values of life, liberty, and the pursuit of property (happiness). It is the Logan's landownership, threatened though it is by the difficulty of meeting tax payments, that is essential to their dignity, their life, and the liberty they claim. Her family's self-respect is based largely on the fact that they farm their own land, even though Mrs. Logan also teaches and Mr. Logan works on the railroad. This status helps Cassie avoid becoming the child Martin Luther King describes in his "Letter from Birmingham Jail": "The depressing clouds of inferiority begin to form in her little mental sky, and we see her begin to distort her little personality by unconsciously developing a bitterness toward white people." Cassie gets angry at anyone who wants to designate her as inferior; she would agree with King's argument that "any law that uplifts the human personality is just. All segregation statutes are unjust because segregation distorts the soul and damages the personality." Her childhood experiences and observations give her ample evidence to observe that effect.

Socially and politically, Mildred Taylor's chronicle is squarely within the context of the values of constitutionally guaranteed rights, no matter how these rights are violated in temporal local statutes. Such values give her story an affirmative narrative pattern that has the reader consistently root for Cassie Logan's struggle toward right and lawful actualization of herself and her community. Nevertheless, the narrative is filled with ambivalent countermemories and subtexts, for the building of the temple of justice is indefinitely deferred in the three novels and the furies have no intentions of becoming the "kindly ones." Taylor's storytelling skill manages to include all these ambivalences yet lets her young hero continue her struggle. In examining Cassie's growth and education in awareness of justice and law, I shall limit the discussion to several key incidents.

The first example is the prank as a relatively harmless tactic of revenge against persistent abuse. *Roll of Thunder* begins with the Logan children's trek to school along the narrow road that "wound like a long red serpent dividing the high forest bank of quiet old trees on the left from the cotton field ... on the right." The school bus would come "roaring down the road spewing red dust over the children" while "laughing white faces pressed against the bus windows." On a rainy day, "the bus driver would entertain his passengers by sending us slipping along the road to the almost inaccessible forest banks … [and] we consequently found ourselves comic objects to cruel eyes that gave no thought to our misery."

Cassie's younger brother, Clayton Chester, or "Little Man," is enraged by this humiliation and eager for revenge. The children decide to dig a ditch across the road that, filled with water, traps the school bus whose passengers now get soaked in return: "Oh, how sweet was well maneuvered revenge!" exclaims the narrator in retrospect. Their prank is a playful retaliation, a momentary empowerment against daily mistreatment, but it could easily become a more serious matter, with disastrous consequences.

Revenge, argues Judge Posner, is the irresistible impulse to avenge wrongful injuries, but it is also the underpinning of the corrective justice of criminal punishment and the breakdown of law and order when legal channels have become blocked. Revenge, however, precludes the possibility of eventual cooperation. Taylor's characters feel repeatedly the upsurge of anger that could lead them to revenge, but only in *The Road to Memphis* does that anger lead to violence; usually Taylor depicts the black community as venting its anger only in a prank or an attitude. An organized attempt at community action, such as the boycott of the Strawberry store organized by the Logans and supported by Jamison, is bound to fail as whites react by terrorizing blacks. Blacks experience the constant threat of violence, for anxiety makes the oppressor permanently vigilant against the slightest signs of insubordination, signs that nearly always trigger an excessive response. Shortly after the bus prank, therefore, when "night riders" terrorize the neighborhood, the Logan children connect it with their prank and Cassie is overwhelmed by the terror she will feel often during her childhood and adolescence.

How can a young person in such an environment still learn to value the idea of law? The values of personhood and community are instilled through the deep bonding among the members of the Logan family and their ability to "talk things out." Mary Logan's personal courage against injustice and David Logan's kind and disciplined nature provide the children with strong values. Moreover, David teaches his children separateness from whites as a means of

survival. The family survives by finding strength in one another, for all attempts to reach out and change the injustices in the community fail, as the attempted boycott in *Roll of Thunder* or the thwarted labor union in *Let the Circle Be Unbroken* demonstrate. Publicly, the importance of law is projected for Cassie through Wade Jamison.

In spite of his ineffectualness, Jamison is a mentor to Cassie. It is he who gives her her favorite book, *The Law: Case Histories of a Free Society*. Not only is Cassie intrigued by the lines of argument, whose conclusions she likes to predict, but the case histories actualize the concepts of law through interpretation. Beginning with *Let the Circle Be Unbroken,* Cassie begins to be attracted to legal texts. Although the justice implicit in the texts prevails nowhere in the novels, Cassie increasingly sees in the texts the possibility for a just society.

In *Let the Circle Be Unbroken,* Cassie begins to be interested in the nature and argument of legal texts. The inciting moment occurs when the aged Mrs. Lee Annie decides to exercise her right to vote. In order to pass the literacy test, Mrs. Lee Annie needs to study her copy of the 1890 Mississippi Constitution, given to her by a judge. She wants Cassie to tutor her, but Cassie finds the print too small and the words too hard to understand, though Mrs. Lee Annie's decision interests her. As Mama tutors Mrs. Lee Annie, Cassie experiences a breakthrough in the thorny language of the text: "I suddenly found the dry words of the constitution beginning to take meaning. Mama explained that a number of the laws were quite good and in theory quite fair. The problem, however, was in the application, and if the judges and the courts really saw everyone as equal instead of as black or white, life would have been a lot pleasanter."

Although Taylor does not appeal to the "higher law" of God that motivated Martin Luther King Jr. so profoundly in his struggle for change through civil disobedience, she does accept the assumptions and enlightenment traditions that enabled King and the Civil Rights Movement to achieve major legal transformations. Without the framework of the Constitution as guarantor of the transcendent rights of individual equality, that struggle could not have led to the civil rights legislation of the 1960s. Taylor's faith can, of course, be problematized when we ask ourselves how the content and structures established by the Constitution institutionalize the privileges and differences a free and equal society seeks to avoid. The subtextual problematic of the Civil Rights Movement and of Taylor's novel, particularly in relation to Wade Jamison and Cassie, is the assumption that law is a sufficient means in the transformation of a racist society rather than a necessary first step. In the end Cassie begins to get in touch with this core problem as she senses that great historical struggles may not really eradicate the roots of prejudice. Young Cassie is on her way to becoming a rational and just individual who is aware that the temple of justice is always constructed on the Areopagus, the Hill of Ares, where the Furies are at best only tentatively persuaded to become the Eumenides, the kindly ones.

Source: Hamida Bosmajian, "Mildred Taylor's Story of Cassie Logan: A Search for Law and Justice in a Racist Society," in *Children's Literature*, Yale University Press, 1996, pp. 141–147, 151, 152, 159.

SOURCES

Davis-Undiano, Robert Con, "Mildred D. Taylor and the Art of Making a Difference," in *World Literature Today*, May-August 2004, pp. 11–13.

Dray, Phillip, *At the Hands of Persons Unknown: The Lynching of Black America*, Modern Library, 2002, p. iii.

Fritz, Jean, "For Young Readers," in *New York Times*, November 21, 1976, p. 262.

McDowell, Kelly, "*Roll of Thunder, Hear My Cry*: A Culturally Specific, Subversive Concept of Child Agency," in *Children's Literature in Education*, Vol. 33, No. 3, September 2002, pp. 213–25.

Myrdal, Gunnar, *An American Dilemma: The Negro Problem and Modern Democracy*, Transaction Publishers, 1995, originally published by Harper and Brothers, 1944.

Review of *Roll of Thunder, Hear My Cry*, by *Booklist*, excerpted in *Roll of Thunder, Hear My Cry*, by Mildred D. Taylor, Puffin Books, 1991.

Review of *Roll of Thunder, Hear My Cry*, by *The Horn Book*, excerpted in *Roll of Thunder, Hear My Cry*, by Mildred D. Taylor, Puffin Books, 1991.

Rochman, Hazel, "The Booklist Interview: Mildred Taylor," in *Booklist*, September 15, 2001, p. 221.

Stenson, Leah Deland, Review of *Roll of Thunder, Hear My Cry*, in *School Library Journal*, September 1976, p. 140.

Taylor, Mildred D., *Roll of Thunder, Hear My Cry*, Puffin Books, 1991, originally published by Dial Books, 1976.

Wells-Barnett, Ida B., *The Red Record*, IndyPublish.com, 2005, originally published in 1895.

A Room of One's Own

VIRGINIA WOOLF

1929

In *A Room of One's Own* (1929), Woolf asserts that some of the most interesting and intellectual characters in literature have been women. However, off the printed page, women have primarily played second-class roles, kept in place by men determined to dominate them. Women have long been denied access to education and have historically been denied the personal rights and leisure time that are the precondition of creative writing. Addressing her audience in 1929, she notes that authors such as Jane Austen and the Brontë sisters have made important contributions to literature, but much remains to be done. Woolf famously insists that creative works require freedom, both financial and intellectual; a woman must have independent means (at least five hundred pounds a year, a large sum at the time) and a room of her own. At the time this essay was published, Woolf's message was unprecedented and radical.

A Room of One's Own is based on two lectures that Virginia Woolf presented in 1928 at Newnham and Girton colleges, women's colleges at Cambridge University. She expanded the lectures and published them together as one long essay in 1929. In it, Woolf starts with the subject of women and fiction, but quickly expands into the wider issue of sexism and art, particularly as it affects women's creativity. She frames the essay as a description of her own thinking on the matter, and as she sets out to learn more about women and literature, she

"INDEED, IF WOMAN HAD NO EXISTENCE SAVE IN THE FICTION WRITTEN BY MEN, ONE WOULD IMAGINE HER A PERSON OF THE UTMOST IMPORTANCE; VERY VARIOUS; HEROIC AND MEAN; SPLENDID AND SORDID; INFINITELY BEAUTIFUL AND HIDEOUS IN THE EXTREME; AS GREAT AS A MAN, SOME THINK EVEN GREATER. BUT THIS IS A WOMAN IN FICTION.... SOME OF THE MOST INSPIRED WORDS, SOME OF THE MOST PROFOUND THOUGHTS IN LITERATURE FALL FROM HER LIPS; IN REAL LIFE SHE COULD HARDLY READ, COULD SCARCELY SPELL, AND WAS THE PROPERTY OF HER HUSBAND."

BIOGRAPHY

VIRGINIA WOOLF

Adeline Virginia Stephen was born January 25, 1882. Her father was an editor, critic, and biographer; Woolf had full run of his library as part of her at-home education. Her mother died in 1895, leading her to experience the first in a series of nervous breakdowns. When her father died in 1904, Woolf suffered another mental collapse. When she recovered, she and three of her siblings moved into a house in the Bloomsbury neighborhood in London. In 1912, she married Leonard Woolf, and the next year she suffered another breakdown. Her first novel, *The Voyage Out,* was published in 1915.

In 1917, the Woolfs began their own publishing imprint, Hogarth Press. They also became the center of an intellectual circle known as the Bloomsbury Group, an assemblage of creative intellectuals that included E. M. Forester, Dora Carrington, John Maynard Keynes, and Vita Sackville-West. Woolf became well known for her modernist style and non-traditional novel structure. Woolf's fiction often focused on ordinary female lives that had been overlooked in literature.

Fearing another nervous breakdown and a possible Nazi invasion of England (her husband Leonard was Jewish), Woolf filled her pockets with stones and drowned herself in the river Ouse near her home in Sussex, England, on March 28, 1941.

finds a shortage of significant female authors prior to the nineteenth century. Seeking an explanation—poverty, lack of education, social expectations that tied women to the domestic sphere—she makes another startling discovery: not only is there a paucity of female authors, there is a lack of information about women's everyday lives before the eighteenth century. The historical picture makes it seem as though women existed only in literature written by men, from a man's point of view. Woolf responds by imagining women's lives, as a way of understanding why female authors are historically such a minor presence in literature.

Woolf's literary reputation was already well established by the time *A Room of One's Own* was published. She was deeply affected by the carnage and devastation of World War I and was part of the modernist movement in literature. Modernism called for a new worldview and the use of new modes of expression in traditional genres such as novels and poetry. In her writing, Woolf used a method she called "tunneling," in which she dug into a character's inner life, dreams, and thought processes in order to present a more complete picture. She strove to uncover genuine meaning, the truth underneath the observed details of daily life. This technique is evident in her novels *Jacob's Room* (1922), *Mrs. Dalloway* (1925), and *To the Lighthouse* (1927). In *Orlando: A Biography* (1928), Woolf explored her title character even more deeply, presenting a protagonist who chooses not to grow old and moves between genders. Her thoughts on a new literary perspective and the concept of androgyny (sexual identity neither exclusively male nor female) are fully articulated in *A Room of One's Own.*

A Room of One's Own is considered a landmark feminist text and is itself a significant critical contribution to the subject of women and literature. Though some of Woolf's suggestions and methods have been questioned in the seventy years since its publication, it holds an important place in the British and feminist literary canon as an essay that empowered generations of women writers to pick up their pens.

Virginia Woolf AP Images

PLOT SUMMARY

Chapter One

Having been asked to speak on the topic of women and literature, Virginia Woolf wonders what that topic means: the type of literature women write? The type of literature women read? The type of literature written about women? She thinks a mixture of the three is the most interesting take on the topic. She quickly realizes, however, that she will never be able to come to a conclusion, as both women and fiction remain "unsolved problems." Because of the controversial nature of the topic, Woolf says, she can only give her opinions and show she arrived at them, leaving the audience to draw its own conclusions.

She begins by talking about the days preceding the lecture, during which she visits a men's college she calls Oxbridge (a hybrid of "Oxford" and "Cambridge," traditionally male, elite universities), and women's college she calls Fernham. Thinking about the topic of women and fiction, Woolf absent-mindedly begins to walk across the grassy grounds at Oxbridge. She is quickly intercepted by a security official, who tells her to get off the grass and return to the gravel path. Only students and professors of the college are permitted to walk on the grass; as a woman, Woolf can be neither. Having lost the idea she was developing before she was chased from the grass, she thinks about an essay by Charles Lamb, in which he recalls revisiting Oxbridge and discusses one of Milton's manuscripts. Curious to see it for herself, Woolf makes her way over to the library only to find the entrance is barred to her. Women are only allowed in the library if they have a letter of introduction, or are accompanied by a student or professor.

Woolf angrily leaves, following music she hears coming from a chapel nearby. She stays outside, listening and watching. Reflecting on the chapel's architecture, Woolf thinks of the money it took to build this and all the other university buildings. She thinks of all the kings, noblemen, merchants, and clergy members who have contributed to the college and continue to do so. She then goes to a luncheon, at which several courses of sumptuous food are served. She thinks about "how trivial this grudge or that grievance, how admirable friendship and the society of one's kind, as, lighting a cigarette, one sunk among the cushions in the window-seat." The lunch guests enjoy conversation and laughter, and the feast lasts late into the afternoon. Afterward, Woolf ventures down the road to Fernham, a woman's college.

The meal at Fernham contrasts sharply with her luxurious lunch at Oxbridge. The food is plain and the women drink water rather than wine. Everyone leaves the dining hall immediately after eating, no one stays to talk or smoke a cigarette. Woolf talks to a friend, a science professor at the college, about the money flowing into Oxbridge and asks why it is not the same at Fernham. The professor recounts the struggle to find benefactors for the women's college and the time and energy it took just to raise enough money to get the college started. There is simply no money left over for things like rich food or even private rooms and sofas for students.

As they consider the difficulty female students have gathering money for tuition, Woolf and the professor wonder: "What had our mothers been doing then that they had no wealth to leave us?" They realize that their mothers were busy having children and running homes, too busy to build fortunes. If mothers and grandmothers had been able to support Fernham, Woolf and the professor would not be discussing a lack of funds; instead, they would be talking about art, biology, mathematics, and other scholarly pursuits. However, they also realize that if their mothers had gone into business and made money, they would have never been born, remarking that "making a fortune and bearing thirteen children—no human being could stand it." Woolf decides it is useless to think about these women amassing financial fortunes, because it would have been impossible. Moreover, any money they made would have been the legal property of their husbands, not their own to donate to a women's college. Thus there are no amenities at Fernham; "to raise bare walls out of bare earth was the utmost they could do."

Chapter Two

The scene shifts to the British Museum in London. Woolf's visits to Oxbridge and Fernham have shown her new questions about women and fiction, and she wants to consult experts about the answers. Looking at the card catalog, she is stunned by the number of books about women written by men. She notes that it is not just biologists or doctors writing about women, but seemingly anyone and everyone, "men who have no apparent qualification save that they are not women." The sheer number of men writing on women transforms Woolf's initial question—why are women poor—into dozens of new questions. She makes a list of topics that she encounters in these books about women, such as "Small size of brain of," "Mental, moral and physical inferiority of," and "Weaker muscles of." She discovers a wellspring of contradictory opinions about women, and despairs at the difficulty of finding the truth. Woolf imagines one of the male experts on women and sketches his picture; she draws him looking angry. She imagines him writing his book about the inferiority of women angrily as well, and wonders about the source of this anger.

Having lunch at a nearby restaurant, she resumes thinking about why the expert was angry when he wrote his book, wondering why any man should be angry at women, given that men hold power over women. Perhaps the expert insists that women are inferior not because he is concerned with the truth about women, but because he wants to make sure that he remains superior. Women, Woolf argues, have long been a magnifying glass for men, making them seem bigger than they are. If women were to abandon this function, the civilized world would cease to exist. Men therefore have a motivation to keep women in a subservient position.

As Woolf pays her check at the cafe, she thinks about the money her aunt left her: five hundred pounds each year for the rest of her life. The money has liberated her from the demeaning odd jobs she used to work. It allows for freedom and security, and she is no longer bound by the bitterness that used to accompany her working life. She describes her independence and freedom, writing, "I need not hate any man; he cannot hurt me. I need not flatter any man; he has nothing to give me." Woolf considers the shifting value of women's labor. She imagines a time when women are no longer denied simple rights and freedoms, wondering how these thoughts relate to women and fiction.

Chapter Three

Woolf rejects the opinions she read in the British Museum's books, choosing instead to consult the historical facts of women's lives. Great works of fiction, she notes, do not simply materialize; they are crucially supported by the writer's livelihood, income, and health. Perhaps an examination of history can explain why, for centuries, women did not write.

Woolf notes that women were long handed off between families via arranged marriages; legally, they were the property of their fathers or husbands. She is struck by the contrast between reality and the way women are depicted in literature: characters from Antigone to Anna Karenina have been powerful, competent individuals. Off the page, they were beaten, kept illiterate, and treated as though they were insignificant. Literary women often surpass the male characters' intelligence and heroism, but living women were not allowed in public without a male escort. Woolf believes that a combined analysis of historical women and fictional women provides a better understanding than either one taken alone. Historians write only of heroes and victors, roles that women were simply not allowed to play. When women cannot read or write, they cannot record their own history; until the nineteenth century, there are few diaries, personal histories, plays, or poems by women. Woolf laments that little is known about women's lives before the eighteenth century. It is thus impossible to know with certainty why women did not write; their private lives, hopes, and expectations are unknown.

Woolf imagines the life of Shakespeare's gifted sister, Judith. Shakespeare leaves Stratford, going to London to write, act, and choose his own path in life. Judith wants the same things, but she is forced to stay home, cobbling together her own education, condemned to domestic chores. She writes in secret, hiding her work or destroying it for fear it will be found. Her father loves her, but believes that this is the best life for her. She is still quite young when her father arranges her marriage. She tries to convince him that she should remain unmarried, but he beats her and begs her not to shame the family. She runs away to London, hoping to become an actress, but stage managers ridicule her and tell her that women cannot be actors. She has a romantic relationship with an actor-manager and becomes pregnant; despairing at her situation, she commits suicide and her grave is long forgotten.

Woolf believes a life like William Shakespeare's was not a practical possibility for the women around him. Given Judith Shakespeare's aspirations, her life could not have been anything but a frustrating tragedy, because "genius like Shakespeare's is not born among labouring, uneducated, servile people." Woolf does not deny that working class people may possess extraordinary talent and genius (as evidenced by Robert Burns and Emily Brontë). Her point is that limited education, exhausting work, and domestic demands leave little energy or time to express oneself creatively. Woolf believes that any woman with Shakespeare's gift in Elizabethan England would have either killed herself or lost her mind, reasonable responses to being continually thwarted in the pursuit of one's goals. In later centuries, women who dared to write often used pseudonyms or submitted their work anonymously, for "Anonymity runs in [women's] blood."

Though Shakespeare never wrote about his inner life or his experiences as a playwright, later authors have written extensively about the challenges of the creative process. Thus, modern readers know that completing a work of fiction takes enormous strength and commitment, in the best circumstances. The task was that much more formidable for women, Woolf argues, because women could rarely, if ever, obtain the education, quiet, and privacy that most people need to express themselves creatively. This was nearly impossible for women, even in the upper classes, until the nineteenth century. Female artists and writers faced significant material challenges, but they also confronted problematic public attitudes. The world does not *need* poetry or art, and male writers have often met with an indifferent audience. Women writers faced this indifference, but received hostility, as well. She notes, "the world did not say to her as it said to them, Write if you choose; it makes no difference to me. The world said with a guffaw, Write? What's the good of your writing?" A large body of work claiming that women are intellectually inferior only supported this hostility, confirming and perpetuating men's self-serving ideas about women. Taken together, these challenges are major obstacles to female artists. In 1928, Woolf feels that female novelists have largely overcome these hurdles, but women painters and especially musicians are still struggle under the weight of prejudice. Woolf sees men's collective goal as "not so much that *she* shall be inferior as that *he* shall be superior....The history of men's opposition to women's emancipation is more interesting perhaps than the story of that emancipation itself."

Woolf reminds her audience of the great difficulty of forging ahead artistically, in the face of the prevailing view of women. It is difficult to convince oneself that the view is wrong, and it is a further challenge to persuade a prejudiced public to accept one's artistic creations. Nonetheless, true creativity requires that an author be able to write beyond her environment. Truly great literature is not burdened with details of the author's personal life and unaddressed grievances. We do not know Shakespeare's purpose in writing his plays. His work stands on its own; it is his *writing* we know, not him. Creative freedom allows artists to reach beyond themselves, but it requires social and material independence.

Chapter Four

Free and complete expression, like Shakespeare's, would not have been possible for a middle-class Elizabethan woman. On the other hand, one can imagine women of nobility or means being able to indulge their creativity. Still, these women were constrained as human beings, and emotions such as fear or anger would emerge in their work, compromising the greatness of their efforts. As an example, Woolf offers Lady Winchilsea, whose poetry focuses on women's oppression. If she could have overcome that, Woolf believes that purer poetry would have come from her pen. Woolf examines other female writers of the seventeenth and eighteenth centuries, who risked—and received—ridicule for their poetry and instead wrote in solitude for themselves.

Aphra Behn, however, is different. With her, "we turn a very important corner on the road." Behn, a middle-class widow in the eighteenth century, had to make her own living by writing. With Behn, Woolf claims, the capacities of an unconstrained female author are first evident. Behn's work signaled the dawning realization that women could write and make money, and those who followed her laid a foundation for better-known female writers like Austen and the Brontë sisters. Though one needs solitude to write, one also needs the supportive presence of those who have come before.

Woolf notes that the nineteenth century produced more female novelists than poets. Because women writers usually worked in a common family sitting room, any writing done there would be frequently interrupted. It would thus be easier to write prose than poetry, because it requires less concentration. Jane Austen's *Pride and Prejudice* was written in this sort of environment. Woolf notes that Austen writes without bitterness or fear, in an open manner much like Shakespeare. This was not the case with Charlotte Brontë, in whose writing Woolf sees signs of bitterness and rage. *Jane Eyre,* like others novels written by women at the time, is marked by the author's lack of real-world experience. Woolf argues that all novelists need such experience. A novel's quality, regardless of the author's gender, derives from its integrity, the sense that the writer is telling the truth. Social dictates about proper subject matter (which, for example, value war stories over stories of family life) can lead female writers away from integrity. Remaining true to oneself and one's experience must have been an enormous struggle, Woolf admits. Only Jane Austen and

Emily Brontë were able to do it in their time, ignoring what they were told they should write about or think.

Woolf admires the bravery of nineteenth-century women because they had no female literary tradition to consult for help or guidance. Going to male writers for advice was useless; male writers' style, methods, and genres were not suited to female writers. Therefore they took up the novel—the newest literary form—and tried to make it fit their needs.

Chapter Five

Looking at her bookshelf of modern writers, Woolf sees that women's writing changed in the twentieth century. Self-expression became an art form. Woolf examines a hypothetical contemporary author she calls Mary Carmichael. Carmichael writes about two women in a relationship, a departure from the traditional depiction of women. Until Austen, she argues, women were "almost without exception ... shown in their relation to men" and not in relation to each other. Portraying women's relationships with one another acknowledges that they have meaningful interests outside the home. Showing women eternally in the shadow of men diminishes them as literary characters and as people. If the men in Shakespeare's plays could only have played women's lovers, there would have been no Caesar, Hamlet, or Lear. Likewise, "literature is impoverished beyond our counting by the doors that have been shut upon women." If Carmichael—and the contemporary female authors she symbolizes—can maintain the momentum and direction of her writing, Woolf thinks that she will light "a torch in that vast chamber where nobody has yet been." Women outside the domestic sphere, away from men, are new creatures in literature.

For Woolf, female writers offer a different perspective than male authors, and they use their creative powers differently. Woolf praises these differences, and suggests that education should encourage these differences rather than seek to eliminate them. Women should not hide the fact that they are women writing about ostensibly female subjects, for millions of obscure lives remain to be written. "Be truthful," she says, "and the result is bound to be amazingly interesting."

Continuing her critique of Carmichael's novel, Woolf notes that Carmichael is writing like a woman who has forgotten she is a woman, which is good. Woolf worries that the scholars, experts, and men of the world are conspiring against Carmichael's writing and style, waiting in the wings for her to listen to their dissent.

Chapter Six

Looking at a busy London street, Woolf watches a man and woman get into a cab together and considers the difficulties of evaluating the sexes separately. To concentrate on one thing, other things must be held back. Woolf wonders whether there is a state of mind in which nothing is held back at all, and feels that watching the man and woman come together in the cab is just such a state. She believes that the sexes naturally want to cooperate, and that perhaps there are two sexes in the brain that must be united for complete satisfaction. When both the male and female sides of the brain are working together, they create what Samuel Taylor Coleridge called "the androgynous mind." Creative minds are truly "man-womanly" or "woman-manly"—the sexes are not separated. Unfortunately, a divided mind is much more typical; for example, the angry men writing books about female inferiority are writing strictly from a male perspective, and their works are unbalanced and less interesting as a result.

Woolf blames the prevalence of divided minds on anyone who perpetuates division of the sexes. An androgynous mind is essential, Woolf argues, because "it is fatal for any one who writes to think of their sex." Writing has neither greatness nor longevity if it is sex-conscious.

Woolf reiterates the importance of financial independence and private space for the creative writer. She closes by addressing two possible objections to her views. First, her point is not that women are better writers; she is not debating the merits of female writers versus those of male writers. Writing cannot be measured like ingredients in a cake, and as people mature intellectually, they no longer believe in choosing sides. She exhorts her audience to write whatever they want, and not to sacrifice their vision.

The second objection she foresees has to do with her claims about the need for material security and financial independence. Some might claim that a true artist can rise above any circumstances, but this is unrealistic. Woolf quotes a professor of literature, who writes that the best British poets of the past two hundred years have been well-to-do, saying, "the poor poet has not in these days, nor has had for two hundred years, a dog's chance." Woolf agrees, and says that "intellectual freedom depends on material things." Women's historical poverty means that they have had little opportunity for the intellectual freedom required to write poetry or fiction. But she does not wish to confine women to writing fiction. Fiction is enriched in the company of other books, on wide-ranging topics such as archeology, travel, and philosophy, and women have important contributions to make in many fields. Good books—of all sorts—make the world a better place.

Woolf ends her speech by encouraging her female listeners to refuse ignorance and limitation. The world offers them women's colleges, the right to own property, the right to vote, and more professions open to women than at any other time in history. Old excuses about lack of opportunity and education are no longer valid. Reminding her audience of Judith Shakespeare, William's imaginary, restricted sister, Woolf tells them that Judith "lives in you." If women continue to make progress and write about reality, then Judith Shakespeare has a chance to live. Women's historical struggles, in poverty and obscurity, have been worthwhile if they finally allow Judith to speak.

THEMES

Women and Literature

The impetus behind *A Room of One's Own* was an invitation to lecture college students on the subject of women and fiction. As Woolf considers her topic, she reaches an interesting conclusion: women in literature have little in common with actual women—a woman becomes an "odd monster" when one compares fact to fiction. Female characters such as Antigone, the Wife of Bath, Juliet, Penelope, and Cleopatra have some of the "most inspired words, some of the most profound thoughts in literature," but in reality, at the times these works were written, women could "hardly read, could scarcely spell, and [were] the property of [their] husband[s]." Because female characters are depicted only in relation to male characters, "the splendid portrait of the fictitious woman is much too simple and much too monotonous."

Women's real-world lives also suffered as a result of this limited, stifling picture of their role and capabilities. In one of the most famous sections of *A Room of One's Own,* Woolf imagines that William Shakespeare has a similarly gifted sister named Judith. While Shakespeare is free to leave Stratford, seek his fortune on the stage, and fulfill his creative goals, Judith has none of these opportunities. She cannot spend time cultivating her talents because her parents (and society) tell her to "mend the stockings or mind the stew and not moon about with books and papers." Judith's stifled creativity and subjugation lead to her suicide. Woolf believes that any woman "born with a great gift in the sixteenth century would certainly have gone crazed, shot herself, or ended her days in some lonely cottage … half witch, half wizard, feared and mocked at." Until the nineteenth century, women were rare in writing because their fundamental task was to serve their fathers or husbands, and their days were filled with domestic responsibilities.

At the end of the eighteenth century, however, a shift occurred in which women began to be able to make their own livings by writing. This momentous trend opened the doors for women to express themselves in a way that had been previously off-limits. For Woolf, this achievement is "of greater importance than the Crusades or the Wars of the Roses." These early female writers established a female literary tradition, a new foundation of support for other women who wrote later. From that tradition sprang the novels of Jane Austen and the Brontë sisters; from that time onward, women were increasingly able to represent female lives truthfully and completely. As long as women continue to develop creatively and to make their voices heard in the arts, Judith Shakespeare's suffering will not have been in vain. With a room of one's own in which to write and financial independence, women may write without restriction. She declares, "So long as you write what you wish to write, that is all that matters; and whether it matters for ages or only for hours, nobody can say."

Gender

A Room of One's Own begins with an illustration of the inequality and prejudice confronting women at the time. Woolf presents her experiences at two colleges: Oxbridge, a male college (a theoretical amalgam of eminent English universities Oxford and Cambridge), and Fernham, a college for women. At Oxbridge, she is chided for walking on the grass and barred from the library, in both cases because she is a woman. She reflects on Oxbridge's beautiful architecture and the money it must have taken to build the school. At an afternoon luncheon, she dines richly and engages in intellectual conversation. In comparison, her dinner in Fernham's cramped facilities is bland and joyless. She wonders why there are no individual rooms for students, or even couches in the lounges. Woolf discovers that it was an enormous struggle for the founders to get the college established, and they must fight for every penny. There is no money for luxuries. Wealthy men support Oxbridge, but Fernham suffers because women—the students' mothers and grandmothers—do not have the money to endow a fully equipped university.

Woolf sees inequality between the sexes in terms of a struggle for superiority. She believes men have a vested interest in keeping women uneducated and under men's financial control—as long as they do so, men remain superior. This desire, she writes, "plants him wherever one looks, not only in front of the arts, but barring the way to politics too." Woolf suggests that men need women as magnifying mirrors, objects reflecting their image in a positive light, and this might not happen if women were truly independent:

> Women have served all these centuries as looking-glasses possessing the magic and delicious power of reflecting the figure of man at twice its natural size. Without that power probably the earth would still be swamp and jungle.

Therefore, the stakes of female independence are high; men stand to lose a distorted (but precious) picture of their own importance, and women stand to gain valuable rights and freedoms. Woolf writes in 1929, when women could obtain considerably more of this independence than previous generations: they can vote, be educated, work outside the home, and most importantly for Woolf, they can write as women. Though there is "no mark on the wall to measure the precise height of women," women now have the ability not only to make a mark, but to exceed it with every effort. Woolf imagines a day when every opportunity will be open to women and "womanhood [will have] ceased to be a protected occupation."

Class and Poverty

For Woolf, social class and poverty played a major role in keeping women from writing significantly until the eighteenth century; these factors are still barriers to women's creative expression. As Woolf analyzes women and poverty, she concludes that women have historically been poor because they have never been allowed the means or opportunity to support themselves. They have spent their lives as property to fathers and husbands, tending the house and bearing children, legally unable to hold wealth or property. There was neither time for jobs outside the home, nor for creative endeavors. The same can be said for the contemporary working-class. Woolf notes that they do not have idle time to create, as their days are filled with making a living. Because of this, she posits, "genius like Shakespeare's is not born among labouring, uneducated, servile people.... It is not born today among the working classes." She goes on to quote Arthur Quiller-Couch's *The Art of Writing,* which substantiates her claim by examining the lives of England's most renowned authors over the past three centuries: with the exceptions of Robert Burns and John Keats, all had been university-educated—an avenue open to middle- and upper-class men only. Quiller-Couch regrets to admit that "the poor poet has not in these days, nor has had for two hundred years, a dog's chance."

Woolf argues that in order to create, one must be financially secure, that "intellectual freedom depends upon material things." This is why she repeatedly points to the importance of having a stable income; combined with a solitary place to write, these are the keys to creative freedom. "Five hundred pounds a year stands for the power to contemplate [and] a lock on the door means the power to think for oneself," she says. Free of constant worries about survival, one can concentrate on creating. She herself knows of the liberty that money brings, as she inherited a five hundred pound annual income from an aunt (at the time, a fair amount of money). This money, she writes, has freed her of the need to depend on men for support: "my aunt's legacy unveiled the sky to me, and substituted for the large and imposing figure of a gentleman ... a view of the open sky."

Androgyny

Though *A Room of One's Own* is often considered a foundational feminist text, Woolf is concerned with more than promoting female independence. After spending three-quarters of the essay examining the place and role of women in literature, Woolf discusses the next step in literary and human development: "the androgynous mind." An androgynous mind is neither female nor male; it combines the two in a seamless, transcendent intellect, one that has the strengths and capacities of both genders. Rather than spend time and energy dividing the sexes and thinking of the world in dichotomous terms—as either male or female—Woolf believes that gifted writers must move beyond those distinctions to achieve the incandescence that marks great literature.

She posits that much writing is compromised by being too clearly the product of one sex or the other. Women's writing fails when it is raging and suppressed; men's writing, when it is angry and condescending. Woolf agrees with Coleridge in his assertion that "a great mind is androgynous." When women write consciously as women, Woolf argues, their work is too strongly colored by rage, limitations, and self-consciousness—natural and valid responses to their oppression, but not the foundation for great literature. Men suffer from different, but equally ruinous, flaws when they write consciously as men. When the different sexes write this way, they cannot find satisfaction in one another's work. Instead, "one must be woman-manly or man-womanly," and abandon all thoughts of gender while writing. Failing to do so is a "fatal" mistake, and produces literature that cannot possibly have the lasting impact of true art.

Woolf is often referred to as a feminist. However, critic Bernard Blackstone suggests another label in his essay "Virginia Woolf" for *Scribner's Writers Series.* He believes a more appropriate title for Woolf is that of an androgynist: "she puts the emphasis every time on what a man and a woman have to give to each other, on the mystery of completion, and not on the assertion of separate superiorities."

HISTORICAL OVERVIEW

Elizabethan England

The Elizabethan Era in England is typically considered the country's golden age and is also known as the English Renaissance. During the reign of Queen Elizabeth I (1558–1603), British literature flourished, as did British exploration and colonization, while the Protestant Reformation fought against Catholic influences in Europe. It was a time of relative tolerance and economic prosperity. Playwrights—Shakespeare, Christopher Marlowe, and Ben Johnson—found success and popularity in London playhouses. The Church of England, created by Elizabeth's father, Henry VIII, continued to evolve as the country's official church. Sir Walter Raleigh colonized the east coast of America, and Sir Francis Drake circumnavigated the globe.

As Woolf points out in *A Room of One's Own,* the notable men of the era take up nearly all the space in Elizabethan history. There is little information about Elizabethan women other than the queen. What is known is that the average woman did not work outside the house and was passed as property from her father to her husband. Childbearing was dangerous and resulted in many women's deaths. Women were not permitted on stage, so female roles (such as Juliet, Helen of Troy, Lady Macbeth, and Cleopatra) were played by men. Historical sources suggest that Woolf's picture of Judith Shakespeare's life is roughly accurate.

World War I

The seeds of World War I were sown long before the actual fighting began in 1914. Political alliances and military expansion combined with fervent nationalism (the belief that one's identity is tied to a specific country or ethnicity) to create a powder keg of tension and animosity. The spark that set the war in motion was the assassination of Austro-Hungarian Archduke Franz Ferdinand; he and his wife were killed in Sarajevo on June 24, 1914, by a young Serbian nationalist. A series of invasions and declarations of war followed, with participants aligning into two main groups. The Allies—France, Russia, Britain, Serbia, and later the United States—fought the Central Powers—Germany, Austria, Turkey, and Italy—for four bloody years. At the time, it was the second deadliest conflict in recorded history. Over sixteen million soldiers and civilians were killed.

World War I introduced a new type of fighting that replaced centuries-old hand-to-hand combat and chivalric conduct. Men fought with long-range guns, submarines, chemical weapons, tanks and, for the first time in history,

aircraft. Fighting was impersonal and conducted at a distance, eliminating many of the opportunities for individual bravery and valor that were highly prized in earlier forms of warfare. Fighting ended on November 11, 1918, and the Treaty of Versailles was officially ended the war on June 28, 1919.

The devastation caused by World War I shook the world. Many felt that their old ways of thinking no longer applied in a world so horribly changed. In *A Room of One's Own,* Woolf notes the poetic hum that has disappeared from gatherings—and life—since the war. She asks, "When the guns fired in August 1914, did the faces of men and women show so plain in each other's eyes that romance was killed?" Woolf was profoundly affected by the war, and was a key member of the modernist movement that sought to find new modes of expression in its wake.

Modernism

The modernist movement began in the last decade of the nineteenth century as a reaction against strict Victorian morals and values. It did not become widespread, however, until World War I began changing people's understanding of the world. The modernist aesthetic (guiding principles) embraced the concept of "making it new," replacing outdated traditional modes of artistic expression in music, art, and literature. In the face of a mechanized sacrifice of human life for pieces of earth, pre-war conceptions of society, humanity, and the world were no longer recognizable, and a new generation of creative artists began speaking their minds. Virginia Woolf was a key figure in modern literature, and some of her suggestions in *A Room of One's Own*—most notably her support for the androgynous mind—reflect the movement's ideals. Woolf's novels *Jacob's Room, Mrs. Dalloway,* and *To the Lighthouse* are considered classic modernist texts. As Bernard Blackstone points out in his biographical essay "Virginia Woolf" for *Scribner's Writers Series,* "Woolf was, from first to last, intensely conscious of making a different thing out of the novel," just as she encourages her audience to do in *A Room of One's Own.*

Suffrage Movement in Britain

The British suffrage movement began in England in the late nineteenth century, aiming to secure women's right to vote in government elections ("suffrage" means the right to vote). Two groups supported women's suffrage in Britain: suffragists, a nonviolent collection of both men and women who sought change through legislation; and suffragettes, an exclusively female group that sometimes resorted to violence and vandalism in their attempts to effect change. Suffragettes were known for tactics such as hunger strikes, breaking store windows, lighting mailboxes on fire, and chaining themselves to fences in order to be heard. In popular history, many people specifically credit the suffragettes with achieving the women's right to vote in Britain.

During World War I (1914–1918), women were called upon to fill the roles of working men who were fighting the war. They were given greater social responsibilities in addition to their new workplace roles, and proved that they were capable of many tasks that were traditionally assigned to men. In 1918, the British Parliament passed a resolution allowing a woman to vote as long as she met at least one of the following conditions: she was over thirty, she was a homeowner or married to a homeowner, she was a renter, or she was college educated. It was not until 1928 that *all* women were able to vote on the same terms as men. In the United States, the Nineteenth Amendment (ratified in 1920) granted women the right to vote.

CRITICAL OVERVIEW

As Mary Gordon notes in her foreword to *A Room of One's Own,* Virginia Woolf forecasted the reviews to her published essays: "I shall get no criticism, except for the evasive jocular kind; ... also, I shall be attacked for a feminist; ... I am afraid it will not be taken seriously." Gordon writes that the essay was published at a time when feminist writing was not "in vogue," and many accused Woolf of "snobbery [and] aestheticism." It was published near the time of the stock market crash that lead to the Great Depression, and the rise of fascist powers in Italy and Spain. As a result, much of the world's attention was elsewhere, and the essay did not receive the same critical attention paid to her previous works. "The Literary Debate between Virginia Woolf and Arnold Bennett" records Bennett's review of *A Room*

of One's Own in a November 1929 issue of the *Evening Standard.* In it, Bennett argues that Woolf's main point about a fixed income and a solitary place to write are not fully supported in the essay, which is instead full of padding and filler:

> Virginia Woolf's thesis is not apparently important to her, since she talks about everything but the thesis. ... She is merely a victim of her extraordinary gift of fancy (not imagination). ... Whereas a woman cannot walk through a meadow in June without wandering all over the place to pick attractive blossoms, a man can. Virginia Woolf cannot resist the floral enticement.

In the latter part of the twentieth century, the essay attracted countless critics and scholars. Beth Carole Rosenberg calls the book a "classic in Anglo-feminist literary theory" in her essay "Virginia Woolf: Overview" in *Feminist Writers.* In "Virginia Woolf's Shakespeare: Why Woolf Made Room for the Stratford Lad in *A Room of One's Own,*" Andrew Werth calls the essay "a bombshell that would become the cornerstone of feminist criticism," and notes that Woolf's section on Judith Shakespeare is "a dazzling feat of imaginative writing." In the Virginia Woolf entry in *Dictionary of Literary Biography,* Alan Kennedy writes that "one can only regard with admiration and wonder the lightness of touch with which [Woolf] dissects male power and injustice." While most agree that *A Room of One's Own* is a foundational feminist text, feminists have not accepted it uncritically. In "Virginia Woolf: Overview" in *Gay & Lesbian Biography,* Renee R. Curry writes that "*A Room of One's Own* has never ceased to be a controversial text worthy of debate and long discussion." She points to well-known feminist critic Elaine Showalter, who criticized the essay for a "naive insistence on an equality gained only by running away from being a woman."

In the early 1990s, *A Room of One's Own* was adapted into a one-woman play. Critics praised the adaptation, and often commented on Woolf's original text. In a review of the adaptation in *Library Journal,* Philip Fryer marvels at the way Woolf "was able so freely to articulate and express in 1929 the state of women throughout history and literature. Her pointed critique is at once devastating and luminous." Michael Sommers's review in *Back Stage* praises Woolf's writing as "quicksilver ... and often dryly humorous." In a later issue of *Back*

MEDIA ADAPTATIONS

A Room of One's Own was adapted into a one-woman play of the same name by Patrick Garland. It has been performed off-Broadway at the Lamb's Theatre in New York City and in various cities across the country. A video version with Eileen Atkins as Virginia Woolf is available from Films for the Humanities & Sciences.

An abridged audio version of *A Room of One's Own* is available from Penguin Audio on audio cassette. It is narrated by Eileen Atkins.

Stage, Jane Hogan calls the essay a "wonderfully intelligent text."

Today, Woolf's essay remains a landmark literary achievement of the twentieth century. The Modern Library placed *A Room of One's Own* in the fourth position on its "100 Best Nonfiction" list in 1999.

CRITICISM

Arthur Scherr

In the following excerpt, Scherr argues that both Virginia Woolf and noted philosopher Friedrich Nietzsche embraced the idea of an "androgynous" mind that was bias toward neither male or female. Scherr writes that both Woolf and Nietzsche believed that only by using an androgynous mind can a person truly tap his or her creativity.

Although few writers have perceived similarities between Friedrich Nietzsche and the great English novelist, feminist writer, and literary critic, Virginia Woolf (1882–1941), her antipathy toward the male gender resembled Nietzsche's against women. A victim of childhood sexual abuse by her half-brothers (and possibly her father), she had additional cause to resent the callous, brooding male patriarchy's domination of the life and literature of her time. Her father, the famous English critic, historian, and biographer Sir Leslie Stephen

(1832–1904), epitomized many of the literary and personality traits she despised. She deplored his despotic, hardheaded, and hardhearted rule in the home and his bullying of her uncomplaining mother, which she suspected contributed to her premature death when Virginia was only thirteen. She abhorred the Victorian middle-class British male's analytic intellect as a "prick of steel," which rendered him unable to feel the profound emotions of sympathy, pity, and love of nature.

In her famous lecture, *A Room of One's Own* (1929), Woolf first fully expressed her feminism and her conviction that women could not gain intellectual autonomy and an opportunity for self-realization as novelists unless and until they achieved economic independence and privacy ("a room of one's own") apart from the men who had hitherto controlled their lives. Vaguely purporting to discuss "women and fiction," Woolf's brief classic eschewed specific topics. Inventing the trope of "Judith Shakespeare," William Shakespeare's mythical, "wonderfully gifted" sister, who is denied an education, degraded and beaten by her father, sexually exploited by the men she meets, and never encouraged to develop her literary talents, Woolf vividly depicted women's dehumanization by hegemonic patriarchal economic, social, and educational institutions. She urged women to take pride in their emotions and develop the "female sentence," a language more spontaneous and less rigidly rational than male structures. Feminist scholar Jane Marcus considers *A Room of One's Own* the "first modern text of feminist criticism, the model in both theory and practice of a specifically socialist feminist criticism."

Few scholars note that Woolf's final pages in *A Room of One's Own* expound a more inclusive theory of literary creativity. She asserts that the most innovative writers, whether male or female, possessed an "androgynous mind" (a phrase she borrowed from Samuel Taylor Coleridge). The androgynous writer alone achieved true artistic greatness, leaving behind her/his resentments and bitterness and depicting universally resonant themes that transcended differences in gender, class, race, or religion. Woolf's androgynous ideal *prima facie* struck a blow against male cultural domination. Nathaniel Brown, an expert on the concept of bisexuality during the Romantic Period, observes: "Androgyny is associated in her [Woolf's] mind with the ability to transcend the confining limitations of the patriarchal mentality."

In several of their writings, Virginia Woolf and Friedrich Nietzsche viewed the opposite gender dispassionately if not sympathetically, implying that incorporating the opposite's elements within the self would heighten individual artistic creativity. Yet students of Woolf and Nietzsche seem to have ignored the intellectual impetus for their transitory "androgynous" periods: an ultimate goal to achieve universal, "objective" standards of artistic value and creativity.

In spite of the reputation for feminism Virginia Woolf acquired after writing *A Room of One's Own* (1929), this work transcended man-hating vituperation. Analyzing the desirable characteristics for a female novelist, Woolf decried self-righteous indignation at the oppression that women had undergone in a male-dominated society and literary milieu. Positing integrity, truth, and objectivity as the primary qualifications of any good novelist, male or female, she argued that a female novelist should be unbiased. Stooping to defend herself against charges that she flouted "male" values and canons, a woman writer preoccupied with her resentments and sufferings in a man's world ruined her creativity. Woolf disapproved of her hypothetical budding novelist busily engaged in refuting male critics: "She met that criticism as her temperament dictated, with docility and diffidence, or with anger and emphasis. It does not matter which it was; she was thinking of something other than the thing [the novel] itself." Pressured to justify herself against male aspersions upon women's fitness for writing, Woolf feared, a weak-willed female novelist would abandon the search for universal, objective truths and degrade her mission by fighting on men's terms.

Woolf admired Jane Austen and Emily Brontë for writing as women wrote, with women's language, state of mind, and themes. Since men had long dominated the genres encompassed by epics and plays with their traditional, straightforward, "masculine" style of writing, Woolf argued, "The novel alone was young enough to be soft in her [woman's] hands—another reason, perhaps, why she wrote novels."

Particularly offended that male novelists had previously avoided discussing women's friendships, Woolf advised burgeoning female writers to put female camaraderie at the center of their narratives. She pointed out that men had previously examined only women's relationships with men, which she considered far less interesting and relatively superficial compared to women's more profound relationships with each other. Moreover, men's biases disqualified them to depict conversations between the sexes: "And how small a part of a woman's life is that; and how little can a man know even of that when he observed it through the black or rosy spectacles which sex puts upon his nose." Thus, Woolf reasonably pointed out, when men described conversations between themselves and women they were telling only half the story; insofar as dialogues between women were concerned, they groped totally in the dark.

Striving to evaluate male novelists' treatment of women impartially, Woolf observed that, in the nineteenth century, men began to write more objectively about women than had classical playwrights, who depicted them as either angels or monsters. Conceding that few writers of either gender could easily comprehend the other's feelings or existence, she perceived that, as late as the close of the nineteenth century, "it remains obvious, even in the writing of Proust, that a man is terribly hampered and partial in his knowledge of women, as a woman in her knowledge of men." On the other hand, she argued that the 18th-century Enlightenment's poets and novelists had gained renewed inspiration from their love affairs with women, which gave them "something that their own sex was unable to supply ... some stimulus, some renewal of creative power which is in the gift only of the opposite sex to bestow."

Exercising her imagination, Woolf pondered the consequences of men's confining women's creative powers to the indoor household's world. She speculated that this constraint explained why women's rooms were so much more decorative and interesting than men's, an appropriate comment for a book entitled *A Room of One's Own*. Thereby men's oppression of women had inadvertently created a milieu in which females could develop facets of their creativity, producing some unintended salutary consequences, Woolf pointed out. She hoped that the genders' writings would preserve their unique (albeit socially-molded) personhood. In a forthright, "male" manner, she commented: "It would be a thousand pities if women wrote like men, or lived like men, or looked like men, for if two sexes are quite inadequate, considering the vastness and variety of the world, how should we manage with one only?" Extolling human diversity, Woolf acclaimed two sexes as a good thing: perhaps three or four sexes would even better suit "humanity."

Unlike Nietzsche, who, as shown earlier, at the outset of his career believed that the idea of innate intellectual differences between the sexes was spurious and man-made, Woolf discerned intrinsic variations. At the same time, she was ambivalent, arguing that men's control of society—the limited options they had kept open for women—played a major role in conditioning women's interests, identities, and worldview in such matters as their preoccupation with household cleanliness and adornment. Her views were, so to speak, "Lamarckian" in that, at least to a degree, she believed in women's "inheritance" of "acquired characteristics," i.e., social attributes and concerns which Western man had ascribed to them practically throughout history. Although she considered man's power disturbing and degrading to women, she would not make it grounds for permanent intergender enmity, at least partly because she feared an impairment of the female artist's rise to literary greatness once she succumbed to an obsessive rage against the male.

Reproving hostility, Woolf counseled sexual harmony between men and women as the formula that would most improve *belles lettres.* Her desire for sexual and intellectual amity and cooperation between the genders is exemplified by her metonym of the man and woman getting into a taxicab, symbol of both material progress and sexuality. "It is natural for the sexes to co-operate," Woolf stated. "One has a profound, if irrational instinct in favour of the theory that the union of man and woman makes for the greatest satisfaction, the most complete happiness."

Woolf considered it natural—"instinctual"— for men and women to feel attracted to one another, both physically and intellectually, as each complemented the other and fulfilled the other's identity. She conceived that androgyny—the harmonious union of male and female personality traits—was most fruitful for

literary creativity and productivity. Like Plato and Carl Jung—thinkers she failed to mention— Woolf argued that each sex had stored within it part of the other's mental and emotional apparatus. "Perhaps a mind that is purely masculine cannot create, any more than a mind that is purely feminine," she surmised. She deplored one paradoxically negative effect of the woman's movement upon male literature, whose reactive tone had become too self-consciously "male," making it less creative and meaningful to women, less reflective of objective "reality."

Woolf considered Shakespeare the greatest of all writers because his plays illuminated his androgyny: a condition partaking of both male and female temperaments, speaking to both genders. Woolf stressed that no one, man or woman, could be a powerful writer if they thought about their gender while writing:

> It is fatal for any one who writes to think of their sex. It is fatal to be a man or woman pure and simple; one must be woman-manly or man-womanly. It is fatal for a woman to lay the least stress on any grievance; to plead even with justice any cause; in any way to speak consciously as a woman. And fatal is no figure of speech; for anything written with that conscious bias is doomed to death.

Although Woolf acknowledged that women had been treated unjustly over the centuries and denounced their exploitation by an egoistic, male-dominated society, she advised that the creative woman writer shun vindictiveness. Like a feminist Gandhi or Martin Luther King, she envisioned women peacefully overcoming the obstacles before them, assisted by new inheritance, property, and divorce laws. In the sphere of literature, women must try to understand their male opponents, incorporate their perspectives, and in that manner surpass male as well as female points of view in the interest of a new objectivity. "Some marriage of opposites" had to be consummated before creativity took place. As Woolf poetically explained, angry writing "ceases to be fertilised. Brilliant and effective, powerful and masterly, as it may appear for a day or two, it must wither at nightfall; it cannot grow in the minds of others."

Woolf's desire that the female novelist pursue objective, universal themes led her to urge her predominantly middle-class women litterateurs to examine the lives of their disgraced, disinherited sisters: lower-class women and prostitutes. Deploring a dominant centuries-long trend in English writing, she advocated realistic, "naturalistic" novels depicting the everyday lives of average women, not merely the rich and middle classes. Though herself a member of the upper class, Woolf deplored the snobbery of many women writers. She worried that "Mary Carmichael," her mythical feminist novelist, fearful of real-life intimacy with the lower classes, would depict their lifestyle without first experiencing it. Seemingly even more disgruntled by female squeamishness and prudery than by male abuse, Woolf said: "It will be a curious sight, when it comes, to see these [poor] women as they are, but we must wait a little, for Mary Carmichael will still be encumbered with that self-consciousness in the presence of 'sin' which is the legacy of our sexual barbarity. She will still wear the shoddy old fetters of class on her feet." Only by respectfully attending to members of all socioeconomic classes would the female novelist succeed in expounding universal, objective themes.

Regarding autonomy as the writer's most important attribute, guarantor of his/her objectivity, Woolf spoke bluntly yet encouragingly to budding women authors: "So long as you write what you wish to write, that is all that matters; and whether it matters for ages or only for hours, nobody can say." "It is much more important to be oneself than anything else," she reiterates. "Do not dream of influencing other people, I would say, if I knew how to make it sound exalted. *Think of things in themselves.*" By exhibiting their true feelings, great novelists would, willy-nilly, externalize universal, objective truths.

Source: Arthur Scherr, "Friedrich Nietzsche, Virginia Woolf, and the creative artist: The Birth of Tragedy and *A Room of One's Own*," in *The Midwest Quarterly*, Vol. 43, No. 3, Spring 2002, pp. 257–273.

SOURCES

"100 Best Nonfiction," *The Modern Library*, www.random house.com/modernlibrary/100bestnonfiction.html (December 2, 2005).

Curry, Renee R., "Virginia Woolf: Overview," in *Gay & Lesbian Biography*, edited by Michael J. Tyrkus, St. James Press, 1997.

Fryer, Philip, "Virginia Woolf: *A Room of One's Own*," in *Library Journal*, Vol. 122, No. 11, June 15, 1997, pp. 110–11.

Hogan, Jane, "A Room of One's Own," in *Back Stage*, Vol. 40, No. 19, May 7, 1999, p. 30.

"The Literary Debate between Virginia Woolf and Arnold Bennett," *Case Western Reserve University* home.cwru.edu/~qxh4/debatetimeline.htm (January 30, 2006).

Rosenberg, Beth Carole, "Virginia Woolf: Overview," in *Feminist Writers*, edited by Pamela Kester-Shelton, St. James Press, 1996.

Sommers, Michael, "A Room of One's Own," in *Back Stage*, Vol. 32, No. 12, March 22, 1991, p. 32.

Werth, Andrew, "Virginia Woolf's Shakespeare: Why Woolf Made Room for the Stratford Lad in *A Room of One's Own*," in *Shakespeare Oxford Newsletter*, Vol. 36, No. 1, Spring 2000, p. 26.

Woolf, Virginia, *A Room of One's Own*, Harcourt Brace, 1989, originally published in 1929.

The Souls of Black Folk

W. E. B. DU BOIS

1903

W. E. B. Du Bois is among the most influential African American leaders in U.S. history, ranked with Frederick Douglass, Booker T. Washington, and Martin Luther King Jr. Du Bois believed in immediate and uncompromising equality between the races. His accomplishments include becoming the first African American to receive a Ph.D. from Harvard; co-founding the NAACP (National Association for the Advancement of Colored People); editing the NAACP magazine, *Crisis*; and teaching at several major American universities. His groundbreaking work on the status of African Americans at the turn of the twentieth century, *The Souls of Black Folk*, was published in 1903 and remains a seminal text in African American history and literature. While many of Du Bois's other writings followed a strict format of sociology, politics, or fiction, *The Souls of Black Folk* combines scientific studies with essay, personal narrative, poem, and song. Widely available in print by various publishers, *The Souls of Black Folk* famously declares, "The problem of the twentieth century is the problem of the color-line."

In his writing, Du Bois introduces the concept of "the Veil," a metaphor for the separation and misunderstanding between the black and white races in America. The Veil describes how African Americans must constantly consider both how they present themselves and how the surrounding white culture views them. Needing

"THE HISTORY OF THE AMERICAN NEGRO IS THE HISTORY OF THIS STRIFE,—THIS LONGING TO ATTAIN SELF-CONSCIOUS MANHOOD, TO MERGE HIS DOUBLE SELF INTO A BETTER AND TRUER SELF.... HE SIMPLY WISHES TO MAKE IT POSSIBLE FOR A MAN TO BE BOTH A NEGRO AND AN AMERICAN, WITHOUT BEING CURSED AND SPIT UPON BY HIS FELLOWS, WITHOUT HAVING THE DOORS OF OPPORTUNITY CLOSED ROUGHLY IN HIS FACE."

white approval to gain any power in early twentieth century America, Du Bois explains, African Americans struggle with a "double consciousness" as they attempt to fulfill their own dreams while at the same time placating white people. The idea of double consciousness continues to resonate in African American philosophy and literature a century later.

Du Bois uses his unique and bountiful years of academic training to develop some of the first comprehensive sociological studies of the African American community. Prior to his work, considerations of African American society were vague and unscientific, leading to African Americans being blamed for the majority of the country's racial strife. Applying sociological frameworks to his examinations, Du Bois produced primary research by visiting many communities and conducting countless interviews. He delivered the first collections of quantitative research focused on African American culture, providing an accurate picture of African American life in the twentieth century. Du Bois assigns responsibility for racial advancement to both the black and white communities, calling upon both groups to actively work on racial progress.

Du Bois records the events of his life and expresses his evolving theories of race and politics in two different autobiographies, *Dusk of Dawn: An Essay Toward an Autobiography of a Race Concept* (1940), and *The Autobiography of W. E. B. Du Bois: A Soliloquy on Viewing My*

Life From the Last Decade of Its First Century (1968).

PLOT SUMMARY

The Forethought

Addressing both white and black readers, Du Bois explains that all people should be interested in understanding the culture of African Americans; if America is ever to achieve racial harmony, he argues, it must understand "the strange meaning of being black." He goes on to outline the main topics of the book, addressing Emancipation, Negro leadership, life within and without the racial divide, the black lower classes, and the legacy of slavery. He closes by setting out to lift the cover, or "the Veil," so all people can see what life is really like for African Americans. He also indicates that each chapter will begin with an excerpt from a Sorrow Song, the songs created by the slaves.

Chapter I: Of Our Spiritual Strivings

Du Bois relates that people are often uncomfortable around him because he is black and that he knows they wonder what it must be like to be part of the group that has endured so much. Less charitably, Du Bois also guesses that people wonder, "How does it feel to be a problem?" He then relates story of the first time he recognized that his race made him different from the majority population and the anger and drive that followed that realization. That moment inaugurates life behind the Veil for Du Bois, because he becomes aware of the barrier between himself and the white world. He explains that this barrier develops in African Americans a double consciousness with which they must view themselves, not only through their own eyes but also through the eyes of the dominant white culture.

The goal of the African American is to live with equal opportunity. Du Bois argues that the difficulties African Americans face are caused by self-doubt and unclear goals, which result from prejudice and the legacy of slavery. Education for the mind and the body, as well as more significant representation through voting, will allow African Americans to achieve progress. Despite the burdens of slavery and racism, black people have made significant contributions to the larger culture through the only

BIOGRAPHY

W. E. B. DU BOIS

Born on February 23, 1868, in a black community in Massachusetts, William Edward Burghardt Du Bois was raised primarily by his mother. Spared by geography from the devastating racism in the South of his youth, Du Bois met any denial he did face with academic ambition. Excelling in school, Du Bois earned a scholarship to the prominent historically black college, Fisk University. He completed another bachelor's degree at Harvard University after graduating from Fisk. Continuing his studies at Harvard, he completed a doctorate in African American history, studying briefly in Berlin, Germany.

Du Bois used his education to fight for African American civil rights. Teaching sociology, economics, and history at the University of Pennsylvania and Atlanta University, Du Bois became a respected national and international figure. He believed he could change racial stereotypes by presenting facts about African Americans before and after slavery, as well as about the social circumstances of the American South. These topics were the subject of many of Du Bois's novels, essays, poems, and plays.

When racial progress proved slow, Du Bois's beliefs became radical, and he eventually turned his back on the United States. He joined the Communist Party, renounced his U.S. citizenship, and moved to Ghana. He died in Africa on August 27, 1963, the day before the historic civil rights March on Washington.

---

original American music—the Sorrow Songs and unique folklore through oral narrative.

Chapter II: Of the Dawn of Freedom

This chapter opens and closes with the phrase, "The problem of the twentieth century is the problem of the color-line." Du Bois illustrates how that problem developed during the nineteenth century and flows into the next century by examining the aftermath of Emancipation. After numerous organizations grew up to help the freed slaves, the government worked to establish its own central Freedmen's Bureau to distribute food, land, and other aid. Du Bois chronicles the many forms this Bureau took, and shows how, due to competing political interests, former slaves did not receive adequate attention. Despite some successes, mostly in establishing a school system throughout the South, the Bureau promised much but delivered little. Land distribution, for instance, would have provided ex-slaves plots to farm for their own profit. Because the Bureau never thoroughly organized, most African Americans either moved into towns or became tenant farmers and suffered extreme poverty. Land ownership was a long-held dream of many slaves, and the U.S. government's bungling of the project caused lasting disappointment and hardship.

Du Bois again cites the Bureau's biggest success as the implementation of a free school system and declares that this organization was better for helping freed slaves than none at all. If the government had enacted a permanent Bureau to study and aid in African American affairs, Du Bois believes, many of the community's problems may have been solved. He concludes then that the legacy of the Freedmen's Bureau is that "the Negro is not free."

Chapter III: Of Mr. Booker T. Washington and Others

Du Bois analyzes the popularity held by the most prominent African American leader of the late nineteenth century, Booker T. Washington. Citing Washington's famous 1895 speech at the Atlanta Exposition in which he declared that black people may be unified in purpose but separate in practice from white people, Du Bois develops a contrary argument. Known especially for his theory of African American

W. E. B. DuBois *The Library of Congress*

industrial training, or training in manual labor, Washington took an accommodating stance toward white culture. He asked for the freedom to work for a living but did not demand equal rights in all areas of life. Du Bois claims that, despite Washington's great popularity, his theories perpetuate ideas of black inferiority. Instead, Du Bois proposes that black people should demand full political participation, share complete civil rights, and pursue enlightenment through higher education.

Du Bois does not roundly condemn Washington, recognizing his vast achievements despite disagreeing with him. In order to resolve many of the race problems in the United States, Du Bois believes, both the black and white communities must turn away from some of Washington's more destructive ideas. Both communities bear the burden for the problems of the African American, and both must work to alleviate them.

Chapter IV: Of the Meaning of Progress
Du Bois describes his teaching experiences in rural Tennessee, where he observed the thirst for knowledge amid desperate poverty. For several summers during his undergraduate education, the young Du Bois served as the sole schoolteacher in a black community without any consistent education system. The children who attended his classes were of all ages and abilities, and their attendance was sporadic because of their unpredictable family fortunes. When most seats in his classroom remained empty, Du Bois traveled to each family home to promote his school. Many of the families distrusted an academic education, believing that their children should devote their energy to helping out at home. Readers learn of several individual students to whom Du Bois feels a special attachment.

Du Bois revisited the area ten years later, after graduating from college. He researched the fortunes of his previous students, only to find further desperation. Most of the children grew up and had children, causing only more financial burden. Some of Du Bois's favorite students unfortunately died young after facing a series of personal tragedies. Du Bois concludes, "How hard a thing is life to the lowly, and yet how human and real!"

Chapter V: Of the Wings of Atalanta
Du Bois invokes the myth of Atalanta, a woman who is seduced with the help of some golden apples, to explain the problems of Atlanta, and the U.S. South in general, after the Civil War. He believes materialism looms as a large problem of the developing region. Money and material gain have their place, he explains, because the region needs to rebuild its industry and vitality after the devastation of the war. Further, the removal of slavery undermined a steady economy in the South; farmers need to reinvent their business if the South is to regenerate. However, Du Bois observes that Southerners seek financial gain above all else and reject the higher ideals of life. He regrets this transformation in the black community as well, where the higher ideals of virtue and truth are replaced by a crass desire for wealth. As evidence of this change, Du Bois cites the decline in respect for ministers and teachers among blacks; merchants and businesspeople, those who generate higher incomes, enjoy prominence in this new black community.

The solution to growing materialism, Du Bois asserts, lies in valuing higher education. Universities teach individuals the higher goals of life and emphasize ideas that transcend money. Here, Du Bois implicitly addresses

Booker T. Washington's endorsement of industrial education; he claims that a true education teaches students what life is about rather than merely how to sustain that life. Du Bois believes that there is a place for the thinking black man, and that man, if properly educated, can help uplift the entire community.

Chapter VI: Of the Training of Black Men

Again, Du Bois addresses the differences between strictly industrial education and a better, more academic one. He illustrates how the history of education in the South leaves large gaps in the training of African Americans, and proposes that industrial education is only a means to maintaining one's life. Higher ideals are as necessary to the progress of the black community as labor skills. Because of the confused educational goals in the South, many people question whether higher education will benefit black people. Du Bois answers with a resounding "yes," referring to the "Talented Tenth" of the black population who gain education and lead their people.

Du Bois calls for the reform of sub-par black colleges. Higher education can help the larger black population avoid succumbing to the bitterness and rage of their desperate situations. While industrial education helps African Americans maintain their physical existence, higher education helps them become full, enlightened human beings. Higher education is the path to life beyond the Veil.

Chapter VII: Of the Black Belt

Du Bois travels through Georgia and uses this trip as an opportunity to analyze the circumstances of the state's black populations, and those of the South as a whole. He describes the remnants of plantation life during slavery, showing how dilapidated the formerly booming economy has become. During slavery, the cotton crops brought extravagant success to the South due to both high market prices of the cotton and forced labor of the slaves. Without the slave labor and with fluctuating cotton prices, the region suffers decline. Du Bois speaks to many black people in southern Georgia, only to find most of them in serious debt. He explains how the tenant system cheats black farmers out of a fair living: landowners rent the black farmers land at exorbitant prices and then also loan them their feed and equipment at high interest

rates. There are no government safeguards in place to protect the black farmers, and therefore their lives revolve around paying off high-interest, never-ending debt. The circumstances in the Black Belt, Du Bois concludes, appear desperate.

Chapter VII: Of the Quest of the Golden Fleece

Examining more thoroughly the situation of black Southern farmers, Du Bois describes their meager housing, working, and general living conditions. Many cotton farmers, he explains, live in crowded, one-room houses, inadequately maintained by the property owners. Their situation will not improve because the workers do not complain and the owners do not realize they can use better quarters as incentive for better work. The effect is circular because the workers, constantly living in poverty, have no reason to work more efficiently.

Defending the black farmers' integrity, Du Bois explains how farming families work hard and try to maintain a decent living. He defends their work ethic and their morality despite their living under conditions little better than slavery. The landowners believe the only way to encourage the tenants to work is to keep them in debt, and so the tenant farmers have no hope of getting ahead. Why should the tenants work excessively when their efforts provide little reward, Du Bois asks. The problem is not black workers' laziness, but instead lack of honest opportunity.

Chapter IX: Of the Sons of Master and Man

This chapter aims to describe the relationship between whites and blacks at the turn of the twentieth century. To do so, Du Bois discusses the key elements of sociological interaction, including home location, economics, politics, and religion. These many areas of life remain highly separate between the races and thus cause misunderstanding and inequality. Southerners, for instance, live in strictly segregated neighborhoods, creating little interaction between whites and blacks. Further, law and custom allow continued exploitation of black workers. Blacks face similar challenges in exercising their right to vote, making their political participation difficult. These many levels of social separation breed distrust between the races that can only be repaired with cooperation, argues Du Bois. Life cannot remain separate and allow equal opportunity; the races must interact to begin building a just society.

Chapter X: Of the Faith of the Fathers

Du Bois describes Southern black religion and its influence on the black community. The black church provides a central location for black people to gather, and it coordinates many more activities than strictly religious events. The black community depends upon its church to provide leadership, aid, education, and entertainment; most people remain associated with the church even if they are not official members.

Du Bois chronicles the history of the church, citing how slave masters strictly forbade any exercise of African religion among their newly arrived slaves. The banning of African spirituality, combined with the rupture of the family through slave trade, helped establish the Christian church as an important unifying element in the African American community. During slavery, Du Bois continues, freedom became akin to salvation. After Emancipation, African Americans were forced to reevaluate their view of freedom, and thus of religion, because of the enormous difficulties they faced. Du Bois asserts that freedom without proper training or social support is not freedom at all.

Chapter XI: Of the Passing of the First-Born

Du Bois shares the story of how his only son died as a young child. First relating his detachment from the newborn child, Du Bois then poetically relates how he grew to love the boy deeply. He describes his physical appearance, noting how the child's golden hair made him realize that the races intermingle in his own bloodlines. His son becomes his greatest joy in life until the young boy becomes ill. Despite the doctor's care, the boy's health declines and he eventually dies. Du Bois's grief is compounded by his contemplation of race relations in America. Is it better, he wonders, for the boy to have died than to have faced life behind the Veil, and all the pain the Veil brings? He concludes not. The child might have been more resilient than the past generation, Du Bois believes.

Chapter XII: Of Alexander Crummell

Du Bois eulogizes the Episcopalian priest Alexander Crummell, who fought for equal rights for African Americans within the church. He chronicles Crummell's religious education, as he is first refused admittance to seminary because of his race. Once ordained, Crummell moves from church to church, meeting variously congregational indifference or community racism. In Philadelphia, Crummell faces rejection by his Episcopal leadership. Crummell follows his religious calling to England and Africa, fighting to strengthen the Christian church at the same time as bolstering the black community. Despite his tireless efforts, Crummell dies without much earthly success. Du Bois respects Crummell's constant work, and not only mourns his loss but also mourns his lack of recognition. Du Bois hopes his tribute will bring respect to a strong black leader.

Chapter XIII: Of the Coming of John

Telling a story of two different men named John, Du Bois shows how racism causes devastation in the South. Black John and white John meet as young children, and both eventually leave their same small town for university training in the North. Black John has an affable, careless nature that eventually leads to his dismissal from school. Desperately wanting to continue his education, black John redoubles his efforts and works to get readmitted to classes. He works tirelessly and graduates from college. White John also works hard and graduates from college. Throughout their college years, each family at home awaits the return of their beloved son.

Black John moves north and encounters white John at a symphony; white John watches as black John is removed from the theater because of his race. Black John decides to return home and help educate his community by becoming a schoolteacher. The community does not understand the newly educated black John, but works hard to accept him back into the fold. Black John promises his white supervisor that he will not use his position as teacher to inflame the black community with ideas about equality, which is a lie. When Black John ultimately catches white John assaulting his sister Jennie, black John kills white John. The chapter closes with black John awaiting the lynch mob that comes to kill him; he dies with symphony music playing in his head.

Chapter XIV: The Sorrow Songs

Du Bois argues that the Negro spirituals are the only original American music because they blend the feelings of the African with the culture of the American. Du Bois explains how the songs gain popularity in mainstream America as the Fisk Jubilee Singers travel around the nation singing and raising money for Fisk University. The slaves used Sorrow Songs to communicate with each other and to soothe themselves; their message remains alive in the songs themselves. Listeners hear poetic lyrics about nature and work, and understand emotional melodies about loneliness and hope. The ultimate desire conveyed by the Sorrow Songs is that of final justice for the wrongs of slavery.

The Sorrow Songs are one contribution of the slaves to American culture. Du Bois also argues that the slaves built much of the American frontier as well as established the economy on cotton sales. Du Bois asks, "Would America have been America without her Negro people?"

The Afterthought

Du Bois hopes that readers will be inspired by his writing to work for equality, and to right the wrongs of the past. He hopes his efforts will spawn greater understanding between the races and not fall on deaf ears.

THEMES

Education

Du Bois uses several chapters in *The Souls of Black Folk* to present an extended argument against Booker T. Washington's theory of industrial education. Beyond the chapter specifically addressing Washington's ideas, Du Bois establishes his own theories of how higher education can help lift up the troubled African American community. Whereas Washington believes that the black community needs to learn the value of hard work, Du Bois claims they already work hard. Whereas Washington maintains the white community's innocence in the problems of blacks, Du Bois holds whites equally responsible for the problems faced by blacks in America. Finally, whereas Washington's theories encourage blacks to use menial labor to better their condition, Du Bois encourages the black community to pursue higher education to achieve progress.

Chief among Du Bois's theories is his idea of the "Talented Tenth," the name he gives to the portion of the black community gifted with academic aptitude. This group, he argues, must become educated at well-equipped colleges so that they may then become leaders for the black community. The Talented Tenth have the ability both to bring self-respect and dignity to individual blacks and to push for equal rights in the larger American society. Higher education will teach African Americans about the values of civilization and the mysteries of life itself. "The true college will ever have one goal," Du Bois writes, "not to earn meat, but to know the end and aim of that life which meat nourishes." This education allows human beings to find enlightenment; he asserts that college, "finally, beyond all this ... must develop men." Du Bois believes that educated African Americans present the only hope to living beyond the present racial divide. Du Bois dreams of the day when he can say, "wed with Truth, I dwell above the Veil."

Historical Causes of the Racial Divide

Du Bois pursued extensive education in African American history, studying all aspects of black culture. His training led him to believe that sociological facts might aid in relieving the complex web of racism that gripped America at the beginning of the twentieth century. He thought that, since the society did not understand the historical and social causes of the race problem, the problem was largely one of ignorance. Writing to educate the larger society about the roots of white and black discord in America, Du Bois truly believed that an informed population would let go of racism. *The Souls of Black Folk* is a treatise whose goals include gaining civil rights through factual observation of the African American's experience in the United States.

Du Bois focuses on the lasting legacy of slavery and the role of that legacy in perpetuating the assumption of the inherent inferiority of African Americans. He explains how, under slavery, black people were given little incentive to work most efficiently because they drew no reward from such effort. After Emancipation, this situation only worsened. As tenant farmers were unable to gain any profit from their farming, they farmed only as much as was needed to survive. Du Bois explains how the high rent and interest rates caused Southern black farmers to stay in debt. Lack of land ownership and constant indebtedness would deaden the ambitions of any human, and this combination

Slaves picking cotton The Library of Congress

caused the majority of black Southerners to lose hope.

He also blames the U.S. government for conspiring to place ex-slaves in their current predicament. Rather than dedicating serious national resources toward the training of freed slaves, the government left the slaves to fend for themselves in a hostile environment. Not only did slaves know little about life outside of forced labor, but they also faced angry and violent white Southerners who believed their freedom to be criminal. Ex-slaves had little chance of success in these circumstances, and they continued to battle hostility throughout the early twentieth century. Du Bois emphasizes how the mishandling of Emancipation and Reconstruction greatly contributed to the African American's desperate situation throughout much of the South. Du Bois concludes that legislation at the turn of the twentieth century continues this legacy of governmental abandonment, and needs to be rectified in order to give the African American a fighting chance for progress.

HISTORICAL OVERVIEW

Slavery and the Civil War

The Souls of Black Folk was published forty years after the Emancipation of the slaves, and in it Du Bois aims to explain how post–Civil War policies affected the African American population over the years. He asserts that the U.S. government's inattention to the training and well-being of the newly freed population caused many of the problems African Americans faced in the twentieth century.

Slavery in the American colonies began with the abduction and importation of African peoples in the seventeenth century, although slavery existed in other colonies much earlier. The North outlawed slavery gradually after the Revolutionary War; the South embraced slavery as it helped build an agricultural economy. The movement for abolition of slavery developed strength in the nineteenth century. The Civil War lasted from 1860 to 1865 under the leadership of president Abraham Lincoln.

While slaves were emancipated in 1863, their freedom was constantly challenged in the southern states. Many white Southerners believed that African Americans should not be free, and actively blocked their progress in various ways. Although some black people made strides under early Reconstruction, gaining economic advancement and public leadership positions, political opponents quickly dismantled this progress. By the end of the nineteenth century, African Americans faced a constant struggle to make a living. Increased immigration from Europe caused fierce competition, and even more fierce racism, in the growing industrial marketplace. Turmoil erupted around the swelling working class at the turn of the twentieth century, and African Americans suffered further abuse because of lack of structured workers' rights. Unions and labor laws developed in the early decades of the twentieth century, but they protected primarily white workers, leaving African Americans, women, and many immigrant groups in relative limbo. Rural African Americans continued to be subject to the whims of corrupt landowners because the government refused to provide substantial protection from exploitation. Du Bois details many of these injustices in *The Souls of Black Folk*, blaming them for the extreme poverty plaguing much of the African American community.

Booker T. Washington and W. E. B. Du Bois

History has cast Du Bois and Washington as oppositional African American leaders. Washington made famous his views on African American progress in his well-known 1895 speech at the Atlanta Cotton Exposition. This speech, included in chapter 14 of Washington's autobiography *Up From Slavery,* expresses an accommodating view to his white audience. Promoting manual labor as the source of African American progress, he entreats black people to "Cast down your bucket where you are" and utilize the thirst-quenching "water" all around them—to take up agricultural and other menial jobs. "It is at the bottom of life we must begin," he writes, "and not at the top." Washington further endorsed separate social circumstances, asking only for the chance to work for a living: "In all things that are purely social we can be as separate as the fingers, yet as one as the hand in all things essential to mutual progress." Not surprisingly, white audiences praised

Washington's views because he did not blame them for the dismal circumstances African Americans found themselves in at the turn of the twentieth century; he asked little of white Americans, thus becoming a widely popular figure in the mainstream culture. Washington used that popularity to raise money and fund a school to teach his theories: the Tuskegee Normal and Industrial Institute in Alabama.

Du Bois strongly disagreed with Washington's accommodationist perspective, instead defending the rights of African Americans. First, Du Bois demanded that white Americans share responsibility for the desperate poverty of many black people. Second, he refused to believe that black people were incapable of intellectual enlightenment. Because they are indeed capable, he encouraged those with academic facility to pursue higher education, as university training would provide a foundation for future strong black leaders. Finally, he demanded equal civil rights as the birthright of every American, black and white. He did not compromise on these views, inspiring later, uncompromising African American leaders such as Malcolm X. Du Bois believed so strongly in immediate civil rights for black Americans that when they were not granted over his lifetime, he disavowed his U.S. citizenship and moved to Ghana.

Negro Spirituals

What Du Bois calls "Sorrow Songs" are also commonly known as Negro Spirituals. The songs slaves developed to pass time in the fields, soothe their hurts, and communicate with each other have been recorded in various forms. Surviving through oral tradition, many have been transcribed and anthologized. After Emancipation, groups of ex-slaves traveled the country singing slave songs to raise money for Southern schools; Du Bois describes the most famous of these groups, the Fisk Jubilee Singers. *The Jubilee Singers and Their Songs* by J. B. T Marsh (2003) details the Fisk Singers' fundraising tour (including texts of the songs) that not only earned enough money to sustain the university but also brought the group to the White House and all over the world. Many other groups attempted the same type of tour, but never reached the fame of the Fisk Singers. The Carolina Singers were one such group; Paula Bernat Bennett's anthology, *Nineteenth-Century American Women Poets,* tells their story and includes texts of several of their songs. Bennett explains that slaves "passed their songs along from one community and generation to the next, creating and enhancing a slave culture which they shared in common with each other across time and location." The secret of the slave songs lies in their multiple meanings. While the slave song may sound like a simple lament of a hard day's work, it might also signal to a slave's plan to escape. Bennett continues:

> The spirituals became . . . a way for the slaves in the fields or in their cabins to communicate in public yet privately to each other. . . . Wholly indigenous to American experience, yet indelibly shaped by their creators' African origins, they are part of the cultural glue that holds this country in its very diversity together.

The Sorrow Songs that Du Bois highlights in his writing represent some of the earliest African American poetry and embody a great contribution to American poetry in general.

CRITICAL OVERVIEW

The Souls of Black Folk established Du Bois as a formidable sociologist and a controversial African American leader. His collection of essays, some of which had been published previously, found immediate popularity, but the collection also positioned him in opposition to the already-famous Booker T. Washington. Because of that opposition, many white reviewers only cautiously recommended the book, whereas black reviewers championed it. For much of his career, and certainly since, Du Bois was treated as oppositional to Washington in studies of African American politics and literature. Early reviews of *The Souls of Black Folk* are available in a study by Erica Griffin.

Du Bois's book maintained popularity throughout his lifetime and beyond. Du Bois himself wondered whether the many different genres of writing found in the collection created an uneven effect; on the contrary, the variety of essays attracts various readers and commentaries. Despite his prolific publication history and several changes in philosophy (he embraced socialism late in life), Du Bois remains most well received for the combination of theory and literature presented in *The Souls of Black Folk*. In the "W. E. B. Du Bois" entry in *African American Writers*, George P. Cunningham argues that *The Souls of Black Folk* "has an unshakable place in the African American

MEDIA ADAPTATIONS

The Souls of Black Folk was released in an unabridged version on six cassettes by Blackstone Audiobooks in August 1994. It is narrated by Walter Covell.

The Souls of Black Folk was released in an unabridged version on six audio CDs by Phoenix Publishing Corporation in 2001. It is narrated by Theodore Eagans.

literary canon." Some groups during the Civil Rights movement used Du Bois's ideas as their foundation, and academics in the African American literary studies movement of the 1970s and 1980s named Du Bois as a central figure. Critical scholarship is plentiful, as evidenced by a full-length autobiography by prominent scholar David Levering Lewis.

Near the one-hundredth anniversary of the publication of *The Souls of Black Folk*, interest in the work increased. A 1999 review in *Contemporary Review* notes that the book "has long been seen as a watershed in the history of American race relations." In "A Timeless Legacy: Celebrating 100 Years of W. E. B. Du Bois' *The Souls of Black Folk*," Kendra Hamilton acknowledges the courage it must have taken Du Bois to write this book, and states that the book itself "has lost none of its intellectual or emotional power since the day of its publication." Some members of academia suggest using *The Souls of Black Folk* in both English and American history courses. In a review of the book in *Teaching History: A Journal of Methods*, former professor Raymond J. Jirran writes that the book "has a classic quality appropriate for every survey history course." Further, a collection of essays edited by Dolan Hubbard, *The Souls of Black Folk One Hundred Years Later*, includes works by numerous important academics representing a wide array of critical perspectives. A review for *Publishers Weekly* of the book *Reconsidering the Souls of Black Folk:*

Thoughts of the Classic Work of W. E. B. Du Bois, by Stanley Crouch and Playthell Benjamin, notes Du Bois's "nuanced and pathbreaking explorations of black culture and psychology." These collections underline how important Du Bois's writing remains, even a century after its initial publication.

CRITICISM

Scott Herring

In the following excerpt, Herring argues that DuBois's reflection and simultaneous rejection of the minstrel image in Souls of Black Folk *establishes the cultural validity of African American music specifically and art more generally.*

W. E. B. Du Bois's *The Souls of Black Folk* is not a book that can be read in ignorance of its historic milieu; to focus exclusively on the text would be to cripple it. First published in 1903, it was written in an America in which the white majority only grudgingly accepted the idea that black folk even had souls. The images most white Americans had of blacks were stereotypical; blacks were a demonized group which had to be controlled by terror or an idealized group of self-sacrificing Uncle Toms and Mammys; they were seen as embodying a sexual potency and promiscuity secretly envied by whites, or they were represented as primitive, laughable clowns. All these stereotypes were given form and (for many Northerners) largely brought into being by the century-old tradition of minstrelsy, in which white comics blackened their faces with burnt cork and performed an imitation of black life for a (usually delighted) white audience. It is this tradition and its effects that Du Bois seeks to subvert in *The Souls of Black Folk*; he removes what Houston Baker calls the "minstrel mask" from his entire race, taking back from the blackface theater the characteristic art form of his race, its music, which the minstrels had appropriated for their own purposes.

I read *The Souls of Black Folk* as a political text, embedded in its historical environment and at odds with the dominant culture—a reading shaped by some of the insights of new historicism. New historicists, such as Stephen Greenblatt, have posited "transactions" or "negotiations" between components of a society (Greenblatt's term is "exchanges" in his essay on Shakespeare and the exorcists, to which my title pays an oblique homage). This essay will use the term "appropriation" for the process of cultural exchange, because the exchange that motivates *The Souls of Black Folk* is less a transaction than a theft. The blackface theater appropriated black music and transformed it to suit its own ends, the fairly straightforward ones of getting laughs and making money. Not all but a significant number of whites adopted the images of the minstrel fiction and applied them to the African American reality, seeing in the streets characters from the stage; blacks very quickly learned, in their dealings with whites, to put on the mask. For Du Bois, the mask is a Veil to be rent. In *Souls*, he addresses two audiences: for white readers, he wishes to demonstrate the worth—even the humanity—of the race many have imagined the minstrel comedian to adequately represent; and to blacks, especially young black artists, he communicates the richness of their heritage. The latter project is accomplished largely by the re-appropriation and rehabilitation of the music that minstrelsy had deformed, music being a vital form of expression for a people only recently literate (and, in 1903, still only partly so). After considering some of the implications of minstrelsy's variegated appropriation and distortion of black culture, and popular response to it, this essay will examine Du Bois's project of retaking black American music.

Du Bois's dominant metaphor for the communicative impasse which exists between the races is the Veil. It is an image that has received considerable critical attention. . . . Into this single image, then, the color line and all the evils that flow from it are compressed.

Like the color line, the veil is insubstantial; it is much more a construct of perception and attitude than of any tangible difference. It is a creation of, among other influences, the minstrel fantasy. The fantasy itself is destructive (for instance, what banker would risk a loan to a black when he believes this person to be a happy, childlike clown?), and by showing black folk to be as human as white folk, Du Bois seeks to deconstruct both the fantasy and the color line. Although he does not often mention minstrelsy by name, he challenges the minstrel tradition quite clearly in his commitment to re-appropriating the Sorrow Songs.

Du Bois reveals that he is very much aware that an appropriation has taken place, and he specifically identifies the minstrel theater as a culprit. "Away back in the thirties the melody of these slave songs stirred the nation, but the songs were soon half forgotten. Some, like 'Near the lake where drooped the willow,' passed into current airs and their source was forgotten; others were caricatured on the 'minstrel' stage and their memory died away." He understates the popularity and staying power of the many hit songs minstrelsy produced, all based ultimately on slave music: "Turkey in the Straw," "Dixie," "Camptown Races," "Old Folks at Home," "My Old Kentucky Home," "Old Black Joe," "Beautiful Dreamer," all were minstrel songs. They also all exhibit key elements of the minstrel fantasy; when sung by the blackface performer, they expressed the sentiments of a simple, playful people, homesick for massa and the plantation. Along with other "debasements and imitations," Du Bois in *The Souls of Black Folk* refers to the minstrel tradition as "a mass of music in which the novice may easily lose himself and never find the real Negro music . . . " In subverting the minstrel renditions by returning to the forgotten roots from which these songs sprang, his work of re-appropriation is partly a means to an end; showing black folk to possess a creative art form uniquely their own further rends the Veil.

"They tell us in these eager days that life was joyous to the black slave, careless and happy. I can easily believe this of some, of many. But not all the past South, though it rose from the dead, can gainsay the heart-touching witness of these songs."

But Du Bois's re-appropriation is also an end in itself; his recovery of the Sorrow Songs is a project which underlies the entire book. We see this in those odd, enigmatic bars of music which stand as silent epigraphs at the head of each chapter. To the reader who cannot decipher music notation—which is to say, most readers today—they are as meaningful as the lines of poetry which accompany them would be to an illiterate slave. It is not until the final chapter that we learn the names of the songs to which these bars of music belong, and their lyrics. It is so by design. By the end of the book, the white reader has been introduced to life behind the Veil. If Du Bois's aim has been fulfilled, he or she will know that black folk possess souls as intricate as his or her own. If not thus prepared, the white reader might dismiss these slave songs as minstrel foolishness. *The Souls of Black Folk* is at least partly structured to enable such a reader to accept these songs as works of art.

It would be difficult to overemphasize the marginal status of the Sorrow Songs, from the time of their composition until Du Bois came to their aid.

Most are religious in nature, but they were rarely permitted to be sung in church, especially before Emancipation. In the North, even black ministers disapproved of them as vulgar. Daniel Alexander Payne, for instance, at different times a minister, historian, and bishop of the African Methodist Episcopal Church, condemned the Sorrow Songs, calling them "cornfield ditties." In the South, religious gatherings of slaves, like all gatherings, were suppressed; but even in their secret gatherings, or in those permitted by lenient masters, "the slaves generally adhered to conventional forms of worship," singing only psalms and hymns approved by the Methodist or Baptist churches. "Judging from the evidence, the singing of religious folksongs was not encouraged in formal services. Plantation owner and memoirist R. Q. J. Mallard seemed to be proud of the fact that sometimes, when in a generous mood, he would let the slaves sing 'their own improvised spiritual' at church services." And while the success of the Fisk Jubilee Singers, among other touring black college groups, certainly lifted the status of the Sorrow Songs, such performances were no longer what they had been, by Du Bois's day.

Independent of the liberties minstrelsy had taken with slave music, it enjoyed no great prestige when Du Bois took up its cause.

Du Bois communicates his sense of the cultural importance the Sorrow Songs possess in the first chapter: "there is no true American music but the wild sweet melodies of the Negro slave." This statement is reinforced by, again, Du Bois's dual chapter epigraphs. In this case, he plays a subtle and little noticed joke on the white reader. All fourteen of the slave song epigraphs are examples of "true American music," works of art belonging to a genre which is distinctly ours. But what of the poets whose works stand above those of the anonymous slaves? Byron, Elizabeth Barrett Browning (twice), Swinburne, Tennyson, Arthur Symons—the list is rather British.

"The music of Negro religion...[,]despite caricature and defilement, still remains the most original and beautiful expression of human life and longing yet born on American soil."

But the importance of the Sorrow Songs does not lie merely in their ability to satisfy the literary nationalist; its potential role is too vital for that. As noted, Du Bois is confident that black folk have much to offer whites, and one of their latent gifts is their music. "Will America be poorer if she replace...her vulgar music with the soul of the Sorrow Songs?" Robert Stepto refers to this as Du Bois's "call for a truly plural American culture," involving "nothing less than his envisioning fresh spaces in which black and white Americans discover bonds beyond those generated by social-structured race rituals." The Veil is not merely to be lifted; positive cultural bonds are to replace it.

Du Bois's re-appropriation of the Sorrow Songs is not, however, a project aimed at rehabilitating them in the eyes of white Americans alone. Even more important is their rehabilitation in the eyes of the Talented Tenth of his fellow blacks.

> The innate love of harmony and beauty that set the ruder souls of his people a-dancing and a-singing raised but confusion and doubt in the soul of the black artist; for the beauty revealed to him was the soul-beauty of a race which his larger audience despised, and he could not articulate the message of another people.

According to James Weldon Johnson, Du Bois succeeded. In *Along This Way*, Johnson refers to *The Souls of Black Folk* as "a work which, I think, has had a greater effect upon and within the Negro race in America than any other single book published in this country since Uncle Tom's Cabin."

Du Bois was not the first to treat the slave songs as something more than the raw material for minstrel buffoonery. As noted, the Fisk Jubilee Singers had already brought the Sorrow Songs before the white public, and with considerable success, earning the astonishing sum of $150,000 toward the support of Fisk University. Du Bois, however, may be the first to argue that the Sorrow Songs are works of art

as important—and really no different—than the high poetry with which they share his chapter headings.

In this way, Du Bois's project of re-appropriation anticipates in a surprising way—and by about eight decades—one of the central arguments of new historicism—that the border between the literary and non-literary, between high art and low pastime, is an artificial construct of the ideology that prevails at any given time, and that such borders are permeable. His violation of the boundaries between high and low art is a radical one; beneath each of his chapter titles, the very highest and very lowest mix as equals. It is not so surprising when one reflects that all cultures possess a literature.

In an analphabetic culture, the literature will be an oral one. The legendary Homer, the anonymous Beowulf poet, the "Turoldus" who recites the *Song of Roland* (and who is to us, like Jim Crow, no more than a name)—all three, whoever they were, produced works regarded as great literature by Du Bois's America, and our own. Though the forms are different ("primary" epic versus folk song), they were engaged in the same cultural pursuit as the slaves who created the Sorrow Songs. Still, for Du Bois to equate the Sorrow Songs with the work of Byron, Tennyson, Shiller, and all the others is a subversive act indeed.

In so doing, he lays the foundations of the Harlem Renaissance, during which Alain Locke would declare black spirituals to be

> thematically rich, in idiom of rhythm and harmony richer still, in potentialities of new musical forms and new technical traditions so deep as to be accessible only to genus, they have the respect of the connoisseur even while still under the sentimental and condescending patronage of the amateur.

The Renaissance would have happened without Du Bois, of course. However, his confident assertion of equality between native black forms of aesthetic expression and those of the white majority—remarkably confident, at that early date—is an important precursor to Locke's very similar assertion.

By re-appropriating the music which minstrelsy had debased, Du Bois provides the Harlem Renaissance with an example of an art form which is distinctively African American. His was the pioneering voice. As Johnson's *Ex-Colored Man* puts it, the future black novelist or poet will have an opportunity "to give the country something new and unknown, in depicting the life, the ambitions, the struggles, and the passions of those of their race who are striving to break the narrow limits of traditions. A beginning has already been made in that remarkable book by Dr. Du Bois, *The Souls of Black Folk*."

Source: Scott Herring, "DuBois and the Minstrels," in *Melus*, Vol. 22, No. 2, Summer 1997, pp. 3–17.

SOURCES

Bennett, Paula Bernat, *Nineteenth-Century American Women Poets: An Anthology*, edited by Paula Bernat Bennett, Blackwell Publishers, 1998, pp. 262–75.

Cunningham, George P., "W. E. B. Du Bois," in *African American Writers*, Charles Scribner's Sons, 1991, pp. 7186.

Du Bois, W. E. B., *The Autobiography of W. E. B. Du Bois: A Soliloquy on Viewing my Life From the Last Decade of Its First Century*, International Publishers, 1968.

———, *Dusk of Dawn: An Essay Toward an Autobiography of a Race Concept*, Transaction Publishers, 1983, originally published in 1940.

———, *The Souls of Black Folk,* Barnes & Noble Classics, 2003, originally published in 1903.

Griffin, Erica L., "Reviews of The Souls of Black Folk," in *The Souls of Black Folk One Hundred Years Later*, University of Missouri Press, 2003, pp. 18–33.

Hamilton, Kendra, "A Timeless Legacy: Celebrating 100 Years of W. E. B. Du Bois' *The Souls of Black Folk*," in *Black Issues in Higher Education*, Vol. 19, No. 26, February 13, 2003, pp. 24–30.

Hubbard, Dolan, ed., *The Souls of Black Folk One Hundred Years Later*, University of Missouri Press, 2003.

Jirran, Raymond J., Review of *The Souls of Black Folk*, in *Teaching History: A Journal of Methods*, Vol. 25, No. 2, Fall 2000, pp. 106–107.

Lewis, David Levering, *W. E. B. Du Bois: Biography of a Race, 1868–1919*, Holt, 1993.

Review of *Reconsidering the Souls of Black Folk: Thoughts of the Classic Work of W. E. B. Du Bois*, *Publishers Weekly*, www.publishersweekly.com (March 10, 2003).

Review of *The Souls of Black Folk* in *Contemporary Review*, Vol. 275, No. 1607, December 1999, p. 334.

Washington, Booker T., *Up From Slavery*, Project Gutenberg, www.gutenberg.org/dirs/etext00/slvry10.txt (October 2000), originally published in 1901.

To Kill a Mockingbird

HARPER LEE

1960

To Kill a Mockingbird is the Pulitzer Prize–winning exploration of prejudice in a small Alabama town. The novel was published in 1960 as the civil rights movement was gathering momentum and is set in the early 1930s during the years of the author's childhood. The story deals with the coming of age of Scout and her brother Jem as they try to understand the ugly aspects of life in Maycomb, their quiet, close-knit community. Lee herself described it as a love story. Most people assume that the love she is referring to is a daughter's love for her father, Atticus Finch, who is the voice of wisdom and moral clarity in the novel. When a black man is falsely accused of raping a white woman, Atticus defends the man, even though he and his children suffer abuse for it at the hands of their fellow townspeople. Despite the ugliness they endure and despite the fact that Tom, the defendant, is wrongfully convicted and ultimately killed, Atticus tries to help his children view the residents of Maycomb with compassion and understanding, rather than bitterness and anger. His message is that people must learn to see things from other people's points of view, and that despite their flaws, most humans are basically decent.

Lee's novel could also be seen as the story of the love between a lonely recluse, Boo Radley, and the children he helps. Both the kind black man Tom and the painfully shy Boo are figurative mockingbirds, people who are put at risk by society's destructiveness despite their own

BIOGRAPHY

MOCKINGBIRDS DON'T DO ONE THING BUT MAKE MUSIC FOR US TO ENJOY. THEY DON'T EAT UP PEOPLE'S GARDENS, DON'T NEST IN CORNCRIBS, THEY DON'T DO ONE THING BUT SING THEIR HEARTS OUT FOR US. THAT'S WHY IT'S A SIN TO KILL A MOCKINGBIRD."

fundamental goodness. Atticus tells his children not to shoot mockingbirds because they cause no harm and make beautiful music. The children easily empathize with Tom and mourn his downfall. They spend most of the novel learning to understand Boo and to separate the gossip they have heard from their own experiences of the man. In the end, Boo saves them from the murderous Bob Ewell, helping to restore the children's faith in human nature following the disastrous outcome of Tom's ordeal. Scout both sees the world from Boo's eyes and recognizes the sinfulness of subjecting him to public scrutiny, which she compares to killing a mockingbird. This realization constitutes a moral victory and exemplifies Atticus's message.

To Kill a Mockingbird is widely taught in high schools throughout America today, and its compassionate message continues to affect readers, even as its politics have become somewhat outmoded. Like *The Adventures of Huckleberry Finn*, it has a problematic quality that complicates its reception: it addresses racism, while at the same time seeming to prop up racist stereotypes, particular through its frequent use of the word "nigger."

The novel continues to resonate with many Americans: in "The Strange Career of Atticus Finch," Joseph Crespino noted that in 1991 the Book of the Month Club surveyed its members, who selected *To Kill a Mockingbird* as the book that, after the Bible, had made the biggest difference in their lives. In 1962, it was made into a movie starring Gregory Peck, which earned ten Academy Award nominations and three Academy Awards. It was recently adapted into a play by Christopher Sergel, and its popularity suggests how relevant many readers and audience members continue to find Lee's work.

HARPER LEE

Nelle Harper Lee was born in 1926 in Monroeville, Alabama. *To Kill a Mockingbird* draws on her experiences growing up as the daughter of a progressive lawyer in a small southern town. Writer Truman Capote was a close friend from childhood and served as the model for the character Dill in her novel. Lee attended the University of Alabama and studied law after graduating, intending to follow in her father's footsteps. However, she withdrew one semester before completing her law degree to pursue a writing career. *To Kill a Mockingbird* is her first and only novel and was an immediate popular and critical success, winning a Pulitzer Prize in 1961. Although she was reported to be working on another novel in the mid-1960s, Lee has not published any major work since *To Kill a Mockingbird*; her retreat from writing is a source of much speculation to her readers. As of 2006, Lee divides her time between New York and Monroeville.

PLOT SUMMARY

Part 1
Chapter 1

To Kill a Mockingbird is narrated by the adult Scout Finch, who is recalling her childhood. Scout tells that she and her brother Jem had recently bickered amiably over the events that led to his breaking his arm when he was nearly thirteen. Although Jem's injury was not severe, she says it was part of a chain of events involving the very history of the state of Alabama. She describes their widowed father Atticus, a lawyer, their cook Calpurnia, and their small hometown of Maycomb. She begins the narrative when she and Jem are six and nine years old, respectively, the summer they first meet Dill, an eccentric and imaginative boy from Mississippi visiting his

Harper Lee AP Images

aunt, Miss Rachel, who lives next door to the Finches.

The three children discuss their neighbor, Boo Radley, whose mysterious life fascinates Dill. The Radleys are a reclusive family. When their son Boo was a teenager, he had fallen in with a crowd of low-level delinquents. Boo's father promised the judge Boo would never trouble Maycomb again if he were released into his father's custody. Boo disappeared into his family's house and was not seen again for the next fifteen years. Then one afternoon, he stabbed his father in the leg with a pair of scissors. This time, the authorities wanted to send him to an asylum, but his father refused out of pride, and Boo was again ensconced in the family home. By the summer of Dill's arrival in Maycomb, Boo has developed a reputation as the neighborhood bogeyman, and the children view him with a combination of apprehension and curiosity.

Chapters 2–3

That autumn, Scout attends school for the first time. At the age of six, Scout is a fluent newspaper reader, a fact that scandalizes her teacher,

Miss Caroline. The teacher is even more put off by Scout's interpretation of social class; Scout tries to explain to her why Walter Cunningham will not accept the loan of a quarter for lunch—because Cunninghams never accept anything that they cannot pay back. Bewildered by Miss Caroline's indignant response to her explanation, Scout decides that it must all be Walter's fault and attacks him during the lunch break. Jem, more sensitive and experienced than his sister, drags Scout off the boy and invites him home for lunch.

The intersection of school and social class continues to present Scout with difficulties. Miss Caroline is horrified to see lice crawling through the hair of Burris Ewell. Burris becomes hostile and leaves. The Ewells, a classmate explains, only come to school on the first day of class anyway. Scout, who has developed a hearty loathing for school, asks her father why she has to go if the Ewells do not. Atticus explains that sometimes communities make exceptions to laws in special cases, and that the Ewells, with their generations of extreme poverty, petty criminality, and ignorance, constitute a special case. Trying to drag them out of their degradation would, he suggests, cause the Ewells more harm than leaving them in their uneducated and lawless state.

Chapters 4–8

As the school year comes to a close, Scout begins to discover things hidden in the hollow of an oak tree on the edge of the Radley property: first some gum, then some Indianhead pennies. After some debate, she and Jem keep the things they find. Their fascination with Boo continues, and when Dill arrives for the summer, the three play a game in which they enact their melodramatic interpretation of Boo's life story, complete with a stabbing scene. Next, they decide to try to communicate with Boo. Dill and Jem compose a note and put it on the end of a fishing pole so they can try to drop it in a window of the Radley house. Atticus catches them and tells them to leave the Radleys alone, but Jem and Dill remain enthralled and decide to try again. This time, the three children creep onto the Radley property at night to peek into one of the windows. As Jem peers inside, a man comes around the house. The three flee across the yard as a shotgun is fired over their heads. They wriggle under a fence to escape, but Jem's pants get caught and he has to leave them behind. He tells Scout that when he returned for his pants that night, he found them folded and clumsily mended. One morning, they discover that Nathan Radley, Boo's elder brother, had filled the hole in the tree with cement. He claims the tree was sick, but it looked perfectly healthy. That night, Scout is surprised to catch Jem crying silently. Atticus rouses the children and rushes them outside during a house fire in the neighborhood one night; afterward, Scout is bewildered to find herself with an unfamiliar blanket. Atticus explains that Boo slipped out of his house and placed it around her shoulders while she was preoccupied with the fire.

Chapter 9

Scout runs into a new kind of trouble at school. The other children start taunting Scout because her father "defends niggers." Not really comprehending what they mean, she understands that it is a slur and gets into a fight to defend Atticus's honor. He later explains that he has been appointed to defend a black man, Tom Robinson. Atticus tells Scout that she must not fight anymore, and she tries to grasp why he has to do something that their friends and fellow townspeople think is wrong. Trusting that her father is right even if she does not understand it, for a few weeks she successfully walks away from fights, even when the other children call her a coward. Then, at the family gathering for Christmas, a cousin taunts Scout saying that Atticus is disgracing the family and calling him a "nigger-lover" over and over until she attacks him. Later, she overhears her father explaining that he took the case in hopes of preventing his children from "catching Maycomb's usual disease" of racism.

Chapter 10

At this difficult time, the children begin to wish their father was more like other fathers, who are younger and able to play football. Jem in particular wishes that his bespectacled father—who dislikes guns and tells them not to shoot mockingbirds because they make beautiful music— were more traditionally manly. However, when a rabid dog appears on their street, the county sheriff, Heck Tate, asks Atticus to shoot it for him. Reluctantly, he picks up the gun, drops his glasses, and shoots the dog in the head from halfway down the street. The children are impressed to discover that Atticus was once

known as "One-Shot Finch" and was the best shot in the county.

Chapter 11

An elderly neighbor, Mrs. Henry Lafayette Dubose, habitually hurls abuse at the children and Atticus from her front porch, yet Atticus is unfailingly polite to her because he knows she is ill. When she becomes especially vituperative during the buildup to the court case, Jem loses his temper and attacks her flower garden. In reparation, Jem has to read to her every day for a month. The symptoms of the woman's illness are very disturbing, and she insults the children freely, but they endure it. Shortly after the end of the month, Mrs. Dubose dies, and Atticus reveals that Mrs. Dubose's symptoms were due to morphine withdrawal. Mrs. Dubose had become addicted during her illness, but had determined to free herself from her addiction before her death. Atticus had wanted Jem to recognize that even though she was elderly, a woman, and a rather nasty personality, she was capable of great moral courage.

Part 2
Chapters 12–15

While Atticus is out of town, Calpurnia takes Jem and Scout to her church in the black community. One congregation member, Lula, objects to the white children's attendance at the black church, but the pastor and other members welcome them. Jem and Scout learn a little about the conditions of the black community in Maycomb (most of the congregation is illiterate, for example) and about how the church functions as a community, raising money to help one another and supporting members who need it, like Tom and his wife Helen. The children are surprised to learn that Helen cannot get work since her husband is accused of raping a white woman, Mayella Ewell. They are also perplexed by the different way Calpurnia speaks in the black community than when she is home with them. She explains that the best way to deal with a diverse and divided community is not to try to argue people into a shared system of values, but to adapt yourself to different people's abilities to understand you. This is why she uses a black dialect at her church, but a white dialect at the Finch house, she tells Scout.

Atticus's sister, the children's Aunt Alexandra, comes to stay for a while and starts trying to mold Scout and Jem into a proper lady and gentleman. The children resist and Atticus seems uncomfortable with his sister's instruction, but he tells the children that it is for their own good. Before going to bed one night, Scout steps on something by her bed that startles her. She asks Jem to check under her bed for snakes, and they discover their friend Dill hiding here. He explains that he has run away from home in Mississippi and traveled alone to Maycomb. They tell Atticus about Dill, who gets permission for the boy to stay with his aunt in Alabama.

One night, Atticus arouses the children's curiosity by driving into town rather than walking, as is his custom. Tom Robinson has been moved back to the Maycomb jail for the trial, and the children take a walk to find out what Atticus is up to. They see him sitting in front of the jail, reading a book. Four cars drive up, and a group of men emerge. They tell Atticus to step aside and let them in, which he refuses to do. The children emerge from hiding to the surprise of all the adults there, and when Scout recognizes Walter Cunnigham's father in the group, she tries to strike up a polite conversation with him. She asks about an inheritance case Atticus had helped him with and sends her greeting to his son. The mob stares at her silently while she chatters innocently, until finally the stunned Mr. Cunningham says, "I'll tell him you said hey, little lady" and tells his friends to clear out. After the tense situation relaxes, Atticus and the children learn that another downtown businessman had been silently at the ready with a shotgun, in case the mob had been more aggressive.

Chapters 16–23

The next day, the children try to grasp how people they know could be willing to hurt Atticus. He says that people can be good yet have what he calls "blind spots." He believes one of the most important traits people can develop is empathy for others. Atticus tells Scout, "You children last night made Walter Cunningham stand in my shoes for a minute. That was enough [to stop him]."

The trial begins. The children attend, and since there are no seats on the ground floor when they arrive, Reverend Sykes from Calpurnia's church offers them a seat in the black gallery upstairs. Sheriff Tate testifies first, saying that Bob Ewell summoned him to his house because his daughter Mayella had been raped. When he arrived, he saw that Mayella had been severely beaten. Under Atticus's examination, Mr. Tate specified that Mayella's right eye had been blackened and that the bruises went all around her throat. Mr. Ewell takes the stand and reminds Scout of a bantam rooster—boastful, puffed up, and vulgar. The unemployed, alcoholic Mr. Ewell and his teeming motherless family live behind the dump in a flimsy shack with a yard full of refuse. The only relief to the ugliness and disorder is six pots of red geraniums that Mayella maintains. He tells the court that he looked in the window and saw "that black nigger yonder a-ruttin' on my Mayella!" During questioning Atticus demonstrates that no medical proof of the rape had been established and that Mr. Ewell is left-handed.

Next, Mayella takes the stand. She tells the prosecutor that she had needed a chiffarobe (a piece of furniture) chopped for firewood and asked Tom to do it for a nickel. She claims that Tom had followed her into the house, throttled her, hit her, and raped her. Atticus has her describe her life, which is isolated and forlorn, suggesting how desperately she has craved companionship and kindness. He highlights the inconsistencies in her statement—she could not remember whether or not Tom hit her, and she could not explain why she was unable to run away or why no one heard her screams.

Finally, Tom Robinson testifies. He says that Mayella embraced him and he tried to disengage himself. At the same time, Bob Ewell saw them through the window and yelled. Tom says that he fled the house, scared. Atticus shows the court Tom's left arm, the muscles withered as the result of an accident, indicating that it would have been difficult for him to blacken Mayella's left eye or throttle her. The prosecutor cross-examines Tom about why he used to help Mayella around the house. Tom says that he felt sorry for her, and the whites in the courtroom are shocked by the idea that he could pity them. Dill starts crying in response to Mr. Gilmer's aggressive prosecutorial tactics, so the children go outside.

While the three are discussing Mr. Gilmer's treatment of Tom, they meet Mr. Dolphus Raymond, a well-to-do white man with a plantation who lives with a black woman and their biracial children, and who prefers the company of blacks. It turns out that the paper bag that Mr. Dolphus publicly drinks from contains a bottle of Coca-Cola, not liquor, as they thought. He explains that he fosters the appearance of being a drunk because it helps people understand why he chooses to live the way he does. He says, "You see they could never, never understand that I live like I do because that's the way I want to live." Rather than confronting the townspeople's prejudices, he works within parameters they understand.

They return to the courtroom in the midst of Atticus's closing argument. He tells the jury, perhaps with intentional irony, "This case is as simple as black and white." He says that Mayella accused Tom to cover up her own sense of guilt at having broken Maycomb's implicit racial code by tempting a black man. He also points out that there was no medical evidence that the crime had in fact been committed and that the witnesses for the prosecution contradicted themselves. Moreover, evidence suggested that a left-handed man, such as Bob Ewell, had beaten Mayella.

Despite the flimsiness of the evidence, the jury finds Tom guilty. Despite the loss, the black citizens in the courtroom stand as Atticus exits and leave tokens of appreciation on the Finches' porch. Jem struggles to understand how people can seem to be good, yet do bad things, and how the community could have let this obvious perversion of justice happen. Miss Maudie tells him that some people in Maycomb did try to help Tom. Tom's black friends did and the Judge did by appointing a principled and experienced lawyer like Atticus. Jem remains depressed, and he and Scout argue over whether all people are fundamentally the same, or whether there are different kinds of people. Scout says, "I think there's just one kind of folks. Folks." Jem thinks that she must be wrong; he does not know how else to account for the bigotry he has witnessed, telling her,

> That's what I thought, too, ... when I was your age. If there's just one kind of folks, why can't they get along with each other? If they're all alike, why do they go out of their way to despise each other? Scout, I think I'm beginning to understand something. I think I'm beginning to understand why Boo Radley's stayed shut up in the house all this time ... it's because he *wants* to stay inside."

Chapters 24–25
After the trial, Scout is increasingly exposed to the society of grown women. Aunt Alexandra hosts missionary circle meetings at the Finches' house. Scout attends one and watches as the women subtly insult her and her father. She hears them pity the uncivilized Mrunas, for whom they are sponsoring a mission, yet speak cruelly and stupidly about the black women working in their own homes. In the middle of the gathering, Atticus comes home with the news that Tom was shot while trying to escape from prison. After Atticus and Calpurnia go to tell Tom's widow the news, Scout gets a glimpse behind her aunt's veneer of propriety and discovers a compassionate woman proud of her brother's bravery. A newspaper editorial "likened Tom's death to the senseless slaughter of songbirds by hunters and children."

Chapters 26–27
As school starts in the fall, Scout realizes she has outgrown her fear of Boo Radley. After a classmate gives a current events report on Hitler's early persecution of the Jews in Germany, Scout's teacher gives a lesson about what it means to be a democracy: "Equal rights for all, special privileges for none." Meanwhile, Bob Ewell, Mayella's father, begins to threaten the people associated with the trial. He spits on Atticus, harasses Tom's widow, Helen, and tries to break into the judge's house. Nonetheless, Atticus believes that Ewell is all talk.

Chapters 28–31
In autumn, the school holds an agricultural pageant, in which Scout is to represent a cured ham. On the way home, she and Jem are attacked, and Scout, still in her restrictive costume, cannot escape. Jem is grabbed and then someone tries to strangle Scout in her costume. Then her assailant is pulled away, and Scout hears scuffling, wheezing, and sobbing. When she is able to crawl out of her costume, she sees a man carrying Jem toward their house and she runs after them. The doctor arrives and says that Jem's arm is broken but that both children will be fine. Sheriff Tate joins them in Jem's room and tells them that he found Bob Ewell dead with a kitchen knife between his ribs. From the state of Scout's costume, Mr. Tate tells Atticus that the attacker "meant business." Scout tells the sheriff her story, but is unclear on the details about what went on in the scuffle. Atticus points out the man who had carried Jem home, who had been standing silently in the

corner of the room the whole time. Even though she has never seen his face Scout realizes that this is Boo Radley and greets him with friendly familiarity.

Mr. Tate recognizes that it is Boo who killed Ewell, but he decides to let the official story be that Bob Ewell fell on his own knife. Mr. Tate says that Boo prevented a crime and killed the man who was responsible for Tom's death. In addition, Mr. Tate says that with Boo's "shy ways," he would hate being thrust into the public eye, even if it only brought appreciation. Exposing him would be, Scout concludes, like killing a mockingbird.

Scout walks Boo home and looks down the street from his front porch. She realizes how her games with Jem and Dill must have looked to him and understands how he became attached to them and why he helped them. When she gets home, she tells Atticus that Boo was "real nice," and Atticus tells her that most people are, when you get to know them.

THEMES

Racism

To Kill a Mockingbird deals with two related aspects of racism: white refusal to recognize black equality before the law and white treatment of blacks as less than human. The main action of the story—the trial of a black man accused of raping a white woman—is racially motivated. The woman is beaten by her racist father who is enraged at the thought that she could have wanted a black man's attention and that he could have dared to provide it. The Finch children must endure the taunts of classmates and whispers of adults in Maycomb because of their father's stand in defense of the black man, and in opposition to the white accuser. Atticus repeatedly stands for fairness and equality before the law, but Maycomb's white residents cannot comprehend how "right" and "white" are not the same thing. His closing argument to the jury stresses the ideal that in the eyes of the court, all men are created equal.

The novel also hints at the broader implications of racism in society. At Aunt Alexandra's missionary circle meeting, the women's callous discussions of the black community reveal their refusal to recognize the humanity of their black employees. The distinct perspective that the novel provides on the subject is articulated by the eccentric Mr. Dolphus Raymond, who befriends Dill because the boy is able to "cry about the simple hell people give other people—without even thinking. Cry for the hell white people give colored folks without even stopping to think that they're people, too." After Tom Robinson's death, Scout struggles to understand how it could have possibly been an injustice, after the man had a legal jury trial. She starts to see that a racist system is inherently unjust.

Gradualism

All of the adults that Scout trusts and respects favor slow, gradual changes in Southern attitudes toward race. Atticus, Miss Maudie, Mr. Dolphus Raymond, and even Calpurnia are reluctant to rupture the delicate fabric of the community with aggressive calls for change. The only politically radical character in the novel—Lula—is disliked even in the African American community. However, the novel itself illustrates the problem with this gradualist approach, which is that innocent people suffer and die while waiting for the South to slowly change its mind about racial equality.

Class

The theme of class prejudice also pervades *To Kill a Mockingbird*. When Scout attends school, she learns about different social classes even among the poor: the one to which Walter Cunningham belongs—agricultural and rigidly honest—and the class to which the Ewells belong—unemployed, illiterate, and dishonorable. She learns to perceive people's worth based on their attitudes and behavior, not their financial situation. During the trial, the Ewells' dishonesty is signaled to the reader by class markers such as their dirtiness, the vulgarity of Mr. Ewell's language, and their hostility. The figure who serves as the strongest indicator of class division in the novel is Aunt Alexandra, whom Claudia Johnson, in her article "The Secret Courts of Men's Hearts," says, "brings with her a code that delineates very narrowly ladies and gentlemen, black and white, 'good' families and trash. She files them in their proper, neat, separate boxes."

The novel's perspective on this complicated interweaving of social groups is ambivalent. For example, when Alexandra prohibits Scout from inviting young Walter Cunningham to dinner,

Gregory Peck, as Atticus Finch, delivers a speech to the jury in a scene from the 1962 film To Kill a Mockingbird *The Kobal Collection. Reproduced by permission*

Atticus allows Alexandra's ruling to stand. And while Scout and Atticus clearly recognize the good qualities in people like Walter Cunningham and the Little Chuck Little ("another member of the population who didn't know where his next meal was coming from, but he was a born gentleman"), both of them view the Ewells as "trash"—disposable and interchangeable people whose home, full of bits of refuse, merges with the garbage dump they live behind. At the same time, both characters recognize that Maycomb itself bears some responsibility for the Ewells' poverty and near-feral status; Scout notes, "Maycomb gave them Christmas baskets, welfare money, and the back of its hand."

Facing these mixed signals from Atticus and Alexandra, Jem and Scout try to understand what the fuss about class and family means.

Jem concludes that different kinds of people are determined by whose family has been reading the longest. Scout argues that there are not different kinds of people: "I think there's just one kind of folks. Folks." Jem replies, "That's what I thought, too, . . . when I was your age. If there's just one kind of folks, why can't they get along with each other?"

Gender

Scout, the motherless protagonist in the novel, is unfettered by gender roles in the egalitarian home she shares with her father and brother. She sees femininity as a weakness. Early in the novel, Jem taunts Scout when they have a disagreement by telling her that she is acting "like a girl." A single father, Atticus focuses on raising his children according to his high moral ideals—intellect, reason, tolerance, honor—and does not emphasize superficial trappings of appearances. When challenged by Alexandra about Scout's clothes, he defends himself weakly, saying, "I do the best I can with them!" Aunt Alexandra is a different matter. Unlike Calpurnia, Atticus, or Jem, Alexandra loathes Scout's overalls—the symbol of her freedom from gender constraints—and tries to make her wear a dress as often as possible. When Scout overhears Alexandra arguing with Atticus over her behavior, she feels "the starched walls of a pink cotton penitentiary closing in" on her.

The key scene in Scout's battle over her identity as a female is the missionary circle luncheon, at which Scout is offended by the women's malicious gossip and self-righteousness. Even the levelheaded Miss Maudie participates in this vapid and vicious world of missionary luncheons and Southern ladyhood. At the end of the missionary circle chapter, she resolves to imitate her Aunt's composure under pressure, saying, "After all, if Aunty could be a lady at a time like this, so could I." Like the sad realization that racism is part of her world, it shows Scout's maturation that she sees the value of learning to operate within society's expectations, even though it will be harder than just acting on her childlike impulses.

Empathy

To Kill a Mockingbird maintains that empathy is the instrument with which people can traverse the complicated issues of race, class, and gender differences. Atticus tells his daughter, "You never really understand a person until you consider things from his point of view," a recurring idea throughout the novel. He is shown teaching these lessons early in the novel, such as when he pours syrup over his dinner to make young Walter Cunningham feel at ease and when he sends Jem to read to an elderly neighbor. As Scout learns the power of compassion, she makes the lynch mob back down when they come for Tom at the jail by innocently reminding them of their humanity. Atticus's rule that the children must not kill mockingbirds, with its symbolic connection to the innocents Boo and Tom, is another face of this same idea. After Boo saves the Finch children from Bob Ewell, the sheriff decides on an alternate explanation of Ewell's death to protect the reclusive Boo from the damages of publicity and scrutiny.

HISTORICAL OVERVIEW

The American Civil Rights Movement

To Kill a Mockingbird is influenced both by racial issues of the 1930s, when the novel is set, and of the 1950s, when it was being written. There had been increasing violence against African Americans since the 1890s, accompanied by formal measures to deny them the ability to vote and access to economic and educational opportunities. An upsurge in racially motivated violence and lynchings came amid the economic uncertainty of the 1930s. With so many people out of work and facing hard times, tensions ran high as people looked for a target and outlet for their fears. The 1950s saw the beginning of a movement to address these injustices. In the early 1950s, civil rights activists focused their energies on bringing about change through legislation and court cases. After the brutal and unpunished 1955 murder of a teenage African American named Emmett Till, activists turned their attention to direct action, including civil disobedience and demonstrations.

Some of the most effective approaches were boycotts, such as the Montgomery Bus Boycott of 1955–1956; sit-ins at segregated businesses and restaurants, such as the influential Greensboro sit-in of 1960; freedom rides; marches; and voter-registration drives. The National Association for the Advancement of Colored People was responsible for most early civil rights action. This organization was later joined by Martin Luther King's Southern Christian Leadership Conference, the Student Nonviolent Coordinating Committee (which organized the freedom rides), and a variety of grassroots, often church-based groups. These organizations shared the goals of ending segregation, ensuring equal access to voting, and an end to discrimination in employment, fair housing, and legislation to protect civil rights, among other reforms. At the time *To Kill a Mockingbird* was written, the *Brown v. Topeka Board of Education* case ending legalized racial segregation in 1954 and was a major recent civil rights victory. The crowning achievements of the next decade were the Civil Rights Acts of 1964 and 1968, which prohibited discrimination in the workplace and in housing, and the Voting Rights Act of 1965, which protected citizens' access to vote.

The Scottsboro Boys

Several civil rights court cases strongly influenced this novel. The first are the Scottsboro cases, a series of trials of nine black teenagers, aged twelve to eighteen, for allegedly raping two white women on a train in Tennessee in 1931. The boys had been involved in an altercation with some white men and forced them off the train. These men complained at the next train station, and the black teens were arrested at the train's next stop in Scottsboro, Alabama. Two women were also found on the train, and in the course of the arrests, one of them claimed to have been raped. After trials that featured only dubious evidence and an apathetic defense lawyer, eight of the nine were sentenced to death. The obvious inequities of the trials and the sensational nature of the charges garnered national attention in the 1930s. It took twenty years, two Supreme Court cases, and numerous appeals, retrials, and pardons before all nine were free men. The "Scottsboro Boys" case parallels Tom Robinson's trial in its chronology, the rape charge, the race of supposed victims, and the obvious innocence of the defendants. In addition, both cases featured a committed, liberal white defense lawyer working strenuously to free his clients.

Emmett Till

The Emmett Till case was at least as influential as the case of the Scottsboro Boys in shaping *To Kill a Mockingbird* and in the public's response to the novel. While visiting family in Mississippi in the summer of 1955, Emmett Till, an African American from Chicago, supposedly spoke with, whistled at, and/or touched a white woman in a store. The woman's husband and a friend kidnapped, tortured, and killed the fourteen-year-old boy. A liberal white judge and prosecutor tried to achieve justice for the murdered boy, but the white jury chose to acquit the defendants despite the evidence of their guilt. The case aroused outrage throughout the United States and abroad, helping to fuel the civil rights movement and alerting the public to the gravity of the problem of racism in the South. The trial was additionally relevant to the novel because of Lee's interest in the role of law in prejudice. According to critic Patrick Chura in his article "Prolepsis and Anachronism: Emmett Till and the Historicity of *To Kill a Mockingbird*," due to "a decline of 'faith in legalism' at the unconscionable verdict of the Till trial, blacks in the South were moved to attempt more concrete forms of protest."

Brown v. Topeka Board of Education

Brown v. Topeka Board of Education (1954), which challenged segregation in public schools, was a major triumph for the civil rights movement. The decision explicitly struck down *Plessy v. Ferguson,* which in 1896 had established the constitutionality of "separate but equal" public facilities for blacks and whites. The unanimous decision stated explicitly that "separate educational facilities are inherently unequal," striking a major blow against the South's Jim Crow laws. Unfortunately, the immediate response to the case was a stiffening of resolve among the segregationists and racists to resist integration for more than another decade, resistance that would feature famous showdown between state and federal forces in Alabama, Mississippi, and Arkansas. *To Kill a Mockingbird,* with its defense of the personhood and value of all humans, can be seen as an attempt to assuage white race fears in the wake of *Brown.* In "The Strange Career of Atticus Finch," Crespino cites Scout's behavior during the lynch mob scene as reinforcing the importance of children in racial progress, and thus supporting the need for school desegregation.

CRITICAL OVERVIEW

Bearing a message of compassion and humanism at a point in time when moderate white Americans were beginning to recognize the magnitude of the injustices suffered by blacks in America, *To Kill a Mockingbird* was immediately viewed as a major artistic achievement and an important analysis of the problem of racism. It won the Pulitzer Prize in 1961 and garnered attention at home and abroad. The *Times Literary Supplement* (London) said in 1960 that the novel came "laden with well-deserved praise" and carrying a message that "can stand repetition." In a review titled "A Keen Scalpel on Racial Ills" (1964), Edwin Bruell compares it to Alan Paton's anti-racist novel *Cry, the Beloved Country,* citing the novels' "twin powers of compassion and understanding." It has remained popular and admired: *To Kill a Mockingbird* went through ninety-four reprints by 1975, which put it among the top five best-selling novels of the twentieth century, according to Christopher Metress in "*To Kill a Mockingbird*: Threatening Boundaries." White conservatives and segregationists, on the other hand, objected to the novel, and although it was widely assigned in high schools by the mid-1960s, it was also one of the most attacked works in the high school curriculum, according to the National Education Association.

By the end of the 1960s, *To Kill a Mockingbird* came to be criticized more by black radicals than by white conservatives. Its approach to social change came to seem increasingly hesitant and inadequate; moreover, it created the impression that social change was to be brought about exclusively through the kindness of elite white liberals. As Isaac Saney puts it in "The Case Against *To Kill a Mockingbird*" (2003), "perhaps the most egregious characteristic of the novel is the denial of historical agency of Black people. They are robbed of their role as subjects of history, reduced to mere objects who are passive hapless victims; mere spectators and bystanders in the struggle against their own oppression and exploitation."

Many academics share this perception of the novel's shortcomings. In "*To Kill a Mockingbird*: Threatening Boundaries," Christopher Metress notes that despite the novel's popularity in high schools, *To Kill a Mockingbird* had not been the focus of a dissertation before 1995, and few critical articles had been published on the novel. Ironically, it is social conservatives who now most strongly endorse Lee's massage. According to Crespino in "The Strange Career of Atticus Finch" (2000), the novel suggests that racism is a problem of individuals and should be dealt with on an individual (rather than a legislative) basis. He notes, "this is the strangeness of Atticus Finch's career: once a tool of liberal radical politics, Atticus has now become the pawn of racial conservatism." Other critics have voiced similar reservations; Eric Sundquist observes in "Blues for Atticus Finch: Scottsboro, Brown, and Harper Lee" that "*To Kill a Mockingbird* is a masterpiece of indirection that allows young readers to face racism through the deflecting screen of a frightening adventure story, just as it allows Americans to face racism through a tale that deflects the problem to the South."

While the novel's racial politics are clearly dated, its basic message of compassion and understanding is perennially relevant. This is

MEDIA ADAPTATIONS

To Kill a Mockingbird was adapted as a film in 1962 by Horton Foote, starring Gregory Peck, Robert Duvall, and Mary Badham. It is available from MCA/Universal Home Video.

To Kill a Mockingbird has been adapted as a play by Christopher Sergel. It was published in 1995 and is available from Heinemann Educational Books.

Sissy Spacek recorded an audiobooks version of *To Kill a Mockingbird* available on CD as of September 2006 from Caedmon.

To Kill a Mockingbird was released in an unabridged version on audiocassette by Audio Partners in 1997. It is narrated by Roses Prichard. This audiocassette is out of print and has limited availability.

particularly true if we remember that the focus of *To Kill a Mockingbird* includes a wider spectrum of social problems than race. It reminds us that, in Jem's words, people "go out of their way to despise each other," and that the first step to social progress is the ability to recognize the humanity of all kinds of people. Crespino, reflecting on the complicated legacy of the novel in his article "The Strange Career of Atticus Finch," suggests that we should view early liberals like Atticus Finch within their historical context, "celebrating their courage and success, lamenting the limits of their vision."

CRITICISM

Joseph Crespino
In the following excerpt, Crespino discusses how Lee's depiction of Atticus Finch was meant to be an example of how southern liberalism could alleviate racism, and how modern critics, academics, and the general public continue to respond to Atticus.

In the twentieth century, *To Kill a Mockingbird* is probably the most widely read book dealing with race in America, and its protagonist, Atticus Finch, the most enduring fictional image of racial heroism. Published in the fall of 1960, the novel had already sold five hundred thousand copies and been translated into ten languages by the time it received the Pulitzer Prize in 1961. The story was almost immediately snatched up by Hollywood, and the Alan Pakula–directed film had the double distinction of landing Gregory Peck an Oscar for his portrayal of Finch and giving Robert Duvall, with a brief role as the mysterious Boo Radley, the first of his seemingly countless screen appearances. It is estimated that by 1982 *To Kill a Mockingbird* had sold over fifteen million copies, and a 1991 American "Survey of Lifetime Reading Habits" by the Book-of-the-Month Club and the Library of Congress revealed that next to the Bible the book was "most often cited in making a difference" in people's lives.

Evidence of the novel's continuing influence on rising generations can be found on the internet, where dozens of high school and college chat groups discuss the adventures of the Finch children or debate the meaning of the Radley neighbors. Atticus Finch himself remains a touchstone figure of decency and respect. Given this legacy, the dearth of critical commentary on the novel is surprising. Literary critic Eric Sundquist writes, "It is something of a mystery that the book has failed to arouse the antagonism now often prompted by another great novelistic depiction of the South ... *Adventures of Huckleberry Finn*, which arguably uses the word nigger with more conscious irony than does *To Kill a Mockingbird* and whose antebellum framework and moral complexity ought to be a far greater bulwark against revisionist denunciation."

The enduring career of *To Kill a Mockingbird* as a story of racial justice, and of Atticus Finch as a racial hero, reveals much about American racial politics in the second half of the twentieth century. From 1960s liberalism to 1990s multiculturalism, from the inchoate conservatism of Goldwater through that of the Reagan-Bush era, Atticus Finch has been both admired and scorned by liberals and conservatives alike. Tracing Atticus's place within the American imagination reveals some of the major fault lines in the struggle for racial equality over the past forty years and allows us to look again at how competing groups have framed racial issues in America.

The early success of *To Kill a Mockingbird* and Atticus Finch's warm reception can be explained in part by the way Finch embodies what historians have called the "liberal consensus" of mid-twentieth-century America. With the defeat of the Depression at home and fascism abroad, postwar Americans were confident that democracy and western capitalism could answer basic questions of material need and class inequality that plagued the nation in prior decades.

Lee's characters and choice of narrative strategies in *To Kill a Mockingbird* reflect the moral tensions that all liberals faced in the Jim Crow South. They combine the passion and ambivalence characteristic of southerners drawn to the South's agrarian tradition and heritage but frustrated by the South's ugly racial history. Lee's political consciousness was formed during a period when the Georgia novelist Lillian Smith emerged as the most acerbic and outspoken liberal southerner. Smith's nonfiction work *Killers of the Dream* (1949) explored the deleterious effects of segregation on children and, like antilynching reformer Jesse Daniel Ames, exposed the links between racial and gender inequality.

Lee and Smith imagined a form of racial change that would occur through the leadership of people like Atticus Finch—in other words, through elite southern white liberals.

Lee's vision of liberal racial change remained distinctly regional; Atticus Finch is not a wild-eyed reformer who rejects his southern heritage. Lee believed that racial change would come through liberalism refined by a certain understanding of how the world works—particularly how white southerners work when it comes to the explosive issue of race. Atticus understands that America's historic claim to justice and equality could not be realized without racial justice in the South, but he recognizes as well the extreme difficulties involved, given the prejudices of his region.

Part of Atticus Finch's heroic power lies in his ability to embrace the need and the moral imperative for racial change without rejecting his native South. He reminds Scout that though this time they were not fighting against "the Yankees, we're fighting our friends," she should hold no grudges because "no matter how bitter things get, they're still our friends and this is still our home." But in this scene Lee comforts white southerners fearful of the change that was imminent in the South. As Eric Sundquist writes, "Just as the South closed ranks against the nation at the outset of desegregation … so *To Kill a Mockingbird* carefully narrows the terms on which changed race relations are going to be brought about in the South." Through Atticus Finch, Lee reassured anxious white southerners that civil rights change could come to the South peacefully, without bitterness, and without dividing the white southern community. After all, the southern liberals leading the change were longtime friends and neighbors; they were, first and foremost, southerners.

Atticus is a modern hero who, while embodying the most noble aspects of the southern tradition, also transcended the limits of that tradition and attained a liberal, morally rational racial viewpoint that was seen as quintessentially American.

Atticus's elite class position within the small southern town of Maycomb is an essential part of his heroism. Atticus is a paternal figure not only for blacks but poor whites as well. In a telling passage, Jem explains to his sister Maycomb's four different classes: "There's four kinds of folks in the world. There's the ordinary kind like us and the neighbors, there's the kind like the Cunninghams out in the woods, the kind like the Ewells down at the dump, and the Negroes." While Scout denies these distinctions, she lives in a world clearly divided along class lines. Atticus explains to Jem, "You and Jean Louise … are not from run-of-the-mill people … you are the product of several generations' gentle breeding … and you should try to live up to your name." Though they are both members of the white working class, the novel distinguishes between the Cunninghams and the Ewells based on the degree to which they aspire to bourgeois values—the degree to which they accommodate themselves to the hegemony of the dominant class. The young Walter Cunningham goes hungry rather than borrow money from the teacher that he knows he cannot pay back. Mr. Cunningham diligently pays back his legal debt to Atticus Finch through subsistence crops from his farm. Although Mr. Cunningham is a member of Tom Robinson's potential lynch mob, he politely retreats when faced by Scout's authentic moral presence. In contrast, the Ewells place no value on education, showing up the first

day and never coming to school again. Mr. Ewell breaks the law by hunting out of season, and Mayella Ewell breaks the fundamental code of middle-class southern womanhood by desiring the black body of Tom Robinson.

In the context of Black Power politics, one of the book's peripheral characters—Lula, the black-separatist member of Calpurnia's church—becomes one of its most interesting. Lula challenges Calpurnia for bringing the Finch children to worship at the black church: "You ain't got no business bringin' white chillun here—they got their church, we got our'n. It is our church, ain't it, Miss Cal?" Lula reminds Cal that she is a servant to the Finches, not an equal: "Yeah, an' I reckon you's company at the Finch house durin' the week." Calpurnia verbally spars with Lula in front of the church, reverting to an African American dialect that the children had never heard from her before. Lula mysteriously disappears from the scene, and the rest of the church comforts the children, telling them they should ignore Lula: "She's a troublemaker from way back, got fancy ideas an' haughty ways— we're mighty glad to have you all." Lee uses this scene to reveal her expectations for what the proper African American response to the white presence should be Lula objects to both the white children's freedom to enter the black world and the inordinate respect they receive once they are there. Lula's position in relation to Calpurnia reproduces Black Power's position toward African American liberals during the civil rights era. Lee removes all doubt as to which model white America prefers; as one critic observes, "Lee makes it clear that people like Lula are not what is expected in the Blacks who hope to be protected by the white law."

Although *To Kill a Mockingbird* has maintained its popularity as a modern-day race tale, in the aftermath of Black Power and with conservative ascendancy, both liberals and conservatives have become markedly more ambivalent in their views of Atticus Finch as an American racial hero. Certain school districts across the country have censored the novel for its sexual content, and more recently some have banned it because of its depiction of societal racism. *To Kill a Mockingbird* has increasingly become a battleground where cultural critics from the left and right debate their respective views of contemporary racial politics. For example, a

1992 debate among legal scholars amounted to a public trial of Atticus Finch. Monroe Freedman, a law professor at Hofstra University, wrote an article in *Legal Times* titled "Atticus Finch, Esq., R.I.P." that questioned Finch's role as a model of humanity and morality for the legal profession. Freedman argued that as a state legislator and community leader in a segregated society, Finch was the "passive participant in that pervasive injustice." Freedman would extend his comments later in a symposium at the University of Alabama: "Throughout his relatively comfortable and pleasant life in Maycomb, Atticus Finch knows about the grinding, ever-present humiliation and degradation of the black people of Maycomb; he tolerates it; and sometimes he even trivializes and condones it." Freedman de-emphasizes the personal heroism of Finch to focus on the larger structural racism of which he was a part and which, in Freedman's estimation, he did little to combat.

Freedman's critique appalled many of his colleagues. One legal commentator attacked Freedman personally, pointing out the violence, abuse, and crime of Freedman's own hometown of New York and asking why he wasn't "putting [his] butt on the line for these people instead of criticizing Atticus Finch, who did put his butt on the line for an innocent black man." In his eagerness to challenge notions of legal ethics, Freedman does ignore Finch's more commendable character traits, but the public outcry against his article suggests that something more was involved.

As Freedman pointed out, Atticus Finch acted heroically in 1930s segregated Alabama, but to a modern reader the limits of his heroism should be fairly evident. Racism today does not always rear its head in such blatant and perverse forms as it did in Depression-era Alabama. Even unreconstructed liberals, however, would admit that the discrimination of the Jim Crow South that American liberalism defeated in the 1950s and early 1960s did not end racism in America. Carmichael and Hamilton warned of liberal blindness to institutional racism, which "is less overt, far more subtle, less identifiable in terms of specific individuals committing the acts. But it is no less destructive of human life." At its core, the debate is over the nature of the racism at work in the post-civil rights era. If institutional racism survived the civil rights struggles of the

mid-1960s, as the Black Power movement maintained, to what degree does holding up the model of Atticus Finch as racial hero obscure structural forms of racial discrimination?

This is the strangeness of Atticus Finch's career: once a tool of liberal racial politics, Atticus has now become the pawn of racial conservatism. The right, in its insistence on focusing on racial bias on the personal level, glorifies Atticus Finch–style racial heroism. If racism exists only on an individual basis, then racial reform can occur only through individual moral reform—not through social or structural change that might challenge the legal, economic, or political status quo. As conservatives beatify the racial heroism of Atticus Finch, they fight the symptoms of the disease and fail to look for a cure that might get at the issue of white privilege.

Source: Joseph Crespino, "The Strange Career of Atticus Finch," in *Southern Cultures*, Vol. 6, No. 2, Summer 2000, pp. 9–29.

SOURCES

Bruell, Edwin, "Keen Scalpel on Racial Ills," in *English Journal*, Vol. 53, December 1964, pp. 656–61.

Chura, Patrick, "Prolepsis and Anachronism: Emmett Till and the Historicity of *To Kill a Mockingbird*," in *Southern Literary Journal*, Vol. 32, No. 2, Spring 2000, pp. 1–26.

Crespino, Joseph, "The Strange Career of Atticus Finch," in *Southern Culture*, Vol. 6, No. 2, Summer 2000, pp. 9–29.

Johnson, Claudia, "The Secret Courts of Men's Hearts: Code and Law in Harper Lee's *To Kill a Mockingbird*," in *Studies in American Fiction* Vol. 19, No. 2, Autumn 1991, pp. 129–39.

Lee, Harper, *To Kill a Mockingbird*, Warner Books, 1960.

Metress, Christopher, "*To Kill a Mockingbird*: Threatening Boundaries," in the *Mississippi Quarterly*, Vol. 48, No. 2, Spring 1995, pp. 397–402.

Review of *To Kill a Mockingbird*, in the *Times Literary Supplement* (London), October 28, 1960, p. 697.

Saney, Isaac, "The Case Against *To Kill a Mockingbird*," in *Race & Class*, Vol. 45, No. 1, July–September 2003, pp. 99–110.

Sundquist, Eric, "Blues for Atticus Finch: Scottsboro, Brown, and Harper Lee," in *The South as an American Problem*, edited by Larry J. Griffin and Don Doyle, University of Georgia Press, 1995, pp. 181–209.

Uncle Tom's Cabin

HARRIET BEECHERSTOWE

1852

Legend holds that upon meeting Harriet Beecher Stowe, President Abraham Lincoln greeted her as "the little lady who started the big war." Although the story remains unsubstantiated—and the American Civil War was the result of many complex factors—Stowe's novel brought the slavery question to the forefront in an already divided nation. When first published in 1851 as part of a magazine series, Stowe had little idea of the international phenomenon that would result. In writing the fictional account of slavery in various circumstances in the South, Stowe focuses on the inhumane and un-Christian spirit of considering human beings property under the law. When the novel was published as a full book in 1852, it set all-time sales records: ten thousand copies in the first week and three-hundred thousand in the first year. At the time, the only book to sell more copies than *Uncle Tom's Cabin* was the Bible. But the story's popularity did not end there; innumerable plays, songs, and merchandise based on Stowe's characters flooded the marketplace for decades. Stowe became an international celebrity by dramatizing the troubling question of American slavery nearly ten years before the Civil War. She drew crowds of admiring fans from America to Great Britain, but the effects of her famous novel have been questioned ever since.

Stowe described two sources of inspiration for *Uncle Tom's Cabin*: a piece of American

IF IT WERE *YOUR* HARRY, MOTHER, OR YOUR WILLIE, THAT WERE GOING TO BE TORN FROM YOU BY A BRUTAL TRADER, TO-MORROW MORNING,—IF YOU HAD SEEN THE MAN, AND HEARD THAT THE PAPERS WERE SIGNED AND DELIVERED, AND YOU HAD ONLY FROM TWELVE O'CLOCK TILL MORNING TO MAKE GOOD YOUR ESCAPE,—HOW FAST COULD *YOU* WALK?"

BIOGRAPHY

HARRIET BEECHER STOWE

Born Harriet Beecher on June 14, 1811, in Connecticut, Stowe was raised mostly by her father and sisters after her mother's early death. Her father and six brothers were successful ministers, making a strong Christian and Calvinist impression on the young Stowe. Raised with an extensive classical education uncommon for women of her time, Stowe wrote on many topics, from household economy and women's rights to slavery in the American South. Most famous for her bestseller *Uncle Tom's Cabin*, Stowe learned her politics at home, from her religious and abolitionist parents and siblings. She married a professor from her father's seminary in 1836, and together they helped runaway slaves through the Underground Railroad. Stowe observed many of the details she included in *Uncle Tom's Cabin* while living in Ohio in the 1830s. Later, when the Fugitive Slave Law prohibited citizens from aiding runaway slaves, Stowe's sister-in-law encouraged her to write something that would move the nation to action. Stowe maintained her international fame and continued to be a prolific writer throughout her life, publishing on numerous domestic and political topics until her death in 1896.

legislation and a personal vision. Raised in a family of activists and reformers, Stowe always harbored abolitionist sentiments, questioning slavery's presence in a supposedly democratic and Christian nation. But it was not until the Compromise of 1850, including the Fugitive Slave Law that required Northern non-slave states to aid in the apprehension and return of escaped slaves, that Stowe became incensed enough to write an extended story on the subject. Until then, she had published several short stories and essays, but nothing that captured the public's interest the way *Uncle Tom's Cabin* did. Stowe's main character of Uncle Tom appeared to her in a vision, she says, as she sat in church. She imagined a strong black slave being beaten to death, yet withstanding the pain and forgiving his tormentors through the strength of his Christian faith. This scene provides both the climax and the foundation for this book about slavery's horrors and the necessity of a Christian response to them.

While Stowe's writing helped invigorate the abolitionist movement in America, its reception was not entirely positive, neither at the time of its publication nor since. The novel itself, while attempting to humanize slaves who were thought to be property, also reinforces several problematic stereotypes of African Americans. Attributing submissiveness, leisure, and affability to the race as a whole, Stowe's depiction of African Americans is offensive by modern standards. The book also spawned countless loose versions of her story, often called "Tom shows," in which white actors in blackface (makeup used to create the appearance of color) portray slave characters as buffoons. Although Stowe never endorsed these coarse and racist portrayals, their existence exemplifies much of how society since has viewed *Uncle Tom's Cabin*. These offensive stereotypes, combined with twentieth century readers' increased appreciation of more complex literary portrayals of race and prejudice, caused this popular but highly emotional novel's reputation to flag considerably. It was not until the 1980s that Stowe's bestseller appeared on college reading lists, once again enjoying wide publication. The racial and literary legacy of *Uncle Tom's Cabin* continues to be debated, but its profound influence on the culture and politics of its time remains indisputable.

PLOT SUMMARY

Chapters 1–6

Uncle Tom's Cabin opens in an opulent house on a Kentucky plantation. Two men—the owner of the plantation, Mr. Shelby, and a slave trader named Haley—sit in the parlor and discuss the buying and selling of Shelby family slaves. Mr. Shelby, apparently a kind master, regrets having to sell his best farm manager, Tom, but sees no other solution to the problem of his increasing debts. A house slave, Eliza, enters with her young son Harry, and Haley asks to buy the boy as well. Eliza overhears parts of the conversation and becomes fearful that her son will be sold away from her. She asks Mrs. Shelby about these plans and is reassured that none exist.

George Harris, Eliza's husband and the slave of a neighboring master, encounters difficulty. George performs admirably at his factory job, even inventing a time-saving machine for which his owner receives a patent. But the slave's success irritates and threatens his master, so he removes George from his job and forces him to perform unskilled labor. Also, his master announces that George's marriage to Eliza is no longer valid, and that George will marry a woman on his own estate. Unable to endure the drudgery and humiliation any longer, George plans his escape to Canada; he visits Eliza and his son Harry and says his goodbyes. In a tearful exchange, Eliza implores George to have faith in God and to be as careful as possible.

The scene changes to Uncle Tom's cabin, where the reader sees a slave family's domestic life. Aunt Chloe makes dinner and tends to the children while Tom prepares for the evening's Christian meeting. The slaves come to sing and hear the Bible read to them, led by both Tom and the young Master George Shelby.

Haley and Mr. Shelby sign the papers for the sale of both Tom and young Harry. Haley describes his own idea of "humane" treatment of his purchases, encouraging Mr. Shelby to take Eliza's son away when she is not around in order to contain any emotional outbursts. Mrs. Shelby confronts Mr. Shelby about his plans and learns that Eliza was, in fact, correct about the sale of her son. She implores her husband to change his mind but he refuses. Eliza hides in a closet during this exchange, and learns of her son's fate. Intent on escaping rather than seeing her son sold, she visits Tom's cabin in the night to share the news

Harriet Beecher Stowe Public Domain

of the impending sales. She encourages him to join her in flight, but Tom refuses. He chooses to be sold rather than endanger the rest of the slaves on the plantation—Mr. Shelby would be required to sell several of them if Tom runs away.

The next morning, Haley finds that Eliza has escaped; Mrs. Shelby secretly delays Haley's attempts to capture her. The other slaves contribute to this delay through a series of forced mishaps and mistakes.

Chapters 7–13

Eliza escapes from the Shelbys at night, desperate to save her son from being sold away. She and Harry arrive at the Ohio River, able to travel undetected because their skin is light enough that they can both pass as white people without suspicion. Once at the river, Eliza is disappointed because it is too icy for boats to cross. She rests in a nearby house just as Haley arrives in town. Frantic, Eliza grabs her son and sets out on foot across the tumultuous, icy river. Upon reaching the other side, an acquaintance of

Mr. Shelby recognizes Eliza but still aids her because of her impressive feat of bravery and strength. Sorely disappointed, Haley enlists the help of two slave catchers to apprehend Eliza with whatever methods they see fit.

The Ohio senator and his wife, Mrs. Bird, discuss the Fugitive Slave Law inside their cozy home. The senator emphasizes that the national interest of state harmony is more important than individual sympathies in the matter of slavery. Mrs. Bird maintains that, although she normally stays out of public issues in favor of domestic ones, she would never forgo her Christian duty to aid a runaway slave. Senator Bird disagrees, but then goes back on his word when an exhausted and faint Eliza shows up at his door. The senator invites her into his home, and makes preparations to take her and Harry to a nearby safe haven. Mrs. Bird maintains her wifely silence, allowing her husband to contradict himself without a word of reproach.

Haley returns to the Shelby plantation, frustrated by his inability to catch Eliza and Harry. Tom says an emotional goodbye to his wife and children and receives a sad send-off from the rest of the plantation family. Haley shackles Tom around the ankles and drives away with him. Young George Shelby, away during Tom's departure, chases Haley down so that he may say goodbye. Tom's heart is warmed by George's effort.

At a nearby bar, several rough-looking men discuss the difficulties of managing intelligent slaves. Mr. Wilson, George Harris's former factory employer, enters but does not agree with the harsh commentary. A Spanish-looking man enters, calling himself Henry Butler, and makes eye contact with Wilson. Butler—who is actually the fugitive George Harris in disguise—realizes that Wilson recognizes him and invites him into his private room. Although at first determined to send him back to his master, Wilson listens to George's impassioned speech about freedom, and changes his mind. At their parting, Wilson gives George money and promises to keep his whereabouts secret.

Haley travels with Tom to a slave auction in order to buy more slaves to add to his gang. Tom must stay in jail while Haley shops for slaves, and feels humiliated by the harsh environment. At the slave auction, men examine slaves as if they were horses, opening their mouths and looking at their teeth; mothers are sold separately from their children, causing anguish for both. Haley takes his slave gang to a Mississippi riverboat that will carry them south for resale. At one stop, a woman and her young son board the boat after being sold without their knowledge to Haley. Haley sells the son to a passenger, and takes him away without telling the mother. Overwhelmed with despair, the slave mother jumps overboard.

Eliza travels to a Quaker settlement in order to continue her escape. The Hallidays house and care for Eliza, citing the Bible's teachings as their reason for helping runaway slaves. Amid the domestic bliss of the family's life, Eliza finds some rest for herself and her son. All are pleased to find Eliza's husband George nearby, and the fugitive family celebrates their reunion.

Chapters 14–20

On the riverboat, Tom encounters wealthy New Orleans slave owner Augustine St. Clare; his lovely young daughter, Evangeline, or Eva; and his Northern cousin, Ophelia. Tom befriends Eva during their journey by giving her small trinkets and playing games with her. When Eva falls overboard, Tom jumps in the water and saves her. Eva feels sorry that Tom is separated from his family, and persuades her father to buy him and bring him to their New Orleans home. Augustine has a tragic romantic history that renders him detached, though affable and kind. When his beloved married another, Augustine, in his despair, married a rich, selfish Southern woman named Marie. After the marriage, Augustine learned that his beloved remained unmarried, and his heart is forever broken. His only true devotion is to his angelic daughter, Eva.

Augustine's cousin Ophelia has agreed to move to New Orleans to care for Eva, since Marie is too self-involved to properly watch over her. Ophelia follows a strict code of Protestant morality, and keeps her life and her surroundings in unflinching order. She provides a contrast to the loose, leisurely mores of the St. Clare family. Once they have arrived at the St. Clare home, Tom meets all the slaves, who are treated fairly well and allowed many personal freedoms. Marie St. Clare feigns illness to gain attention, forcing her slaves to wait on her day and night. Believing that slaves should be treated harshly in order to teach them their place, Marie's selfishness pervades all of her actions. She feels justified after attending a church service where the sermon supports Southern racial hierarchy using the Bible as proof. Augustine seems to perceive the injustice of slavery but cannot see a practical solution.

At the Quaker settlement, the newly reunited family learns that the slave catchers know of their plans to escape to the North. Accompanied by one of the Quakers, George, Eliza, and Harry set out in their carriage but are quickly overtaken by Haley's hired men. The slaves hide in nearby rocks, and draw the slave catchers out to pursue them. George warns that he will fire at anyone who comes too close, and Tom Loker, one of the slave catchers, disregards the threat. George shoots him and then the Quaker pushes him off the rocks. Seriously wounded, Loker is abandoned by his companions. The slaves, now safe, decide to save Loker's life, bring him to a Quaker home, and nurse him back to health.

At the St. Clare home, Tom shows true concern for his master and encourages Augustine to give up drinking and have faith in God. Ophelia struggles with running the leisurely and often chaotic house efficiently; she especially clashes with cook, Dinah, whose kitchen is unorganized but whose cooking is highly successful. Augustine again explains the practical difficulties of the established slave system in America, where both owners and slaves become debased. Evidence of the horrors of slavery appears in the character of Prue, a neighboring slave whom Tom befriends. Prue tells Tom how she has suffered greatly under slavery as, among other injustices, she is forced to stand by as her newborn starves to death. Later, Prue's owners whip her for drinking away her sorrows, and leave her in the cellar to die. Ophelia expresses her outrage to Augustine, who explains that although slavery is essentially evil, he is powerless to help individual slaves. He tells how his family history influences his opinion and how slavery has become ingrained in Southern culture. Throughout these events, Tom quietly becomes accustomed to life with the St. Clares but is homesick. Augustine helps him send a letter to the Shelby plantation.

In order to test Ophelia's self-righteous attitude toward slavery, Augustine purchases a young slave girl named Topsy and places her in Ophelia's charge. Ophelia's personal prejudices arise as she does not want to become personally involved with a black person. St. Clare convinces her to educate the spirited, manipulative, and unloved young girl. Topsy challenges Ophelia's patience, but Eva befriends her and provides a contrast to the mischievous girl.

Chapters 21–28

Back at the Shelby plantation, Aunt Chloe misses Tom deeply. She approaches Mrs. Shelby with a plan to hire herself out as a confectioner in order to earn money and help buy Tom back. Mrs. Shelby not only assents to the plan but says she will also contribute to Tom's purchase. The family sends Tom a letter informing him of the plans for his repurchase, and Tom is so overjoyed that he wants to frame the note.

Eva and Tom begin reading the Bible together. One afternoon, Eva tells Tom that she will be going to heaven soon and that she feels peaceful about her own death. Tom then notices that Eva appears to be getting ill, although Augustine denies it. Soon afterward, Eva's cousin Henrique visits and beats a slave in front of Eva. The compassionate Eva, who befriends all slaves, condemns Henrique for his actions. After various discussions of slavery among the family, Henrique promises to be more kind to his slaves for Eva's sake.

As Eva's health declines, Marie seems not to notice, instead focusing on her own manufactured illnesses. Once it is clear that Eva will die, Marie assumes the role of long-suffering mother, again attempting to gain the spotlight. Eva, by contrast, exhibits selflessness and peace as she faces certain death, positively influencing those around her. She entreats her father promise to free Tom and work for abolition after she dies. Topsy promises Eva she will try to be good, for Eva's sake. Ophelia also admits her own prejudices, and vows to be more devoted and kind to Topsy. On her deathbed, Eva addresses all of the household's slaves. She asks them to have Christian faith, and gives them a lock of her golden hair as a token by which to remember her. Ophelia tends to all of Eva's needs while her mother feigns exhaustion and grief. Tom will not venture far from Eva, providing a spiritual companion to the young girl soon to die. When Eva finally dies, she has a vision and exclaims, "O! love,—joy,—peace!"

After Eva's death, many characters vow to improve morally because of Eva's example. Ophelia, for instance, pledges to love Topsy and instruct her well. Tom implores Augustine to become a Christian, and the two pray together. Augustine enjoys Tom's company because it makes him feel closer to his lost daughter, and he begins the process to free Tom according to his promise. Further, Augustine gives ownership of Topsy over to Ophelia in case of his own death. Ophelia encourages him to make similar allowances for all of his slaves, and he responds that he will in due time. The cousins earnestly discuss the complexities of slavery, with Augustine posing whether, if the South frees its slaves, the North will provide the necessary education to help them become productive members of society. Out for a drink, Augustine becomes involved in a fight and is stabbed. At home, with his plans to free his own slaves incomplete, Augustine has a spiritual awakening and dies while holding Tom's hand.

Chapters 29–34

Marie becomes a harsh mistress, planning to sell all the slaves, including Tom, despite Augustine and Eva's wishes. Ophelia appeals to Marie on behalf of the slaves and is rebuffed. Marie starts her reign with the whipping of one slave, then sends all the slaves to be auctioned off. The slaves are dispersed, and Tom and an attractive young girl named Emmeline, recently separated from her mother, become the property of a callous slave holder, Simon Legree.

Legree treats his slaves cruelly, declaring "*I'm* your church now!" He demands that his slaves not only obey but also act happy, forcing them to sing and dance on command. As Legree takes his slaves down the Red River, Stowe alludes to the Middle Passage, in which Africans were brought as slaves to the Americas.

Legree's plantation bears the marks of inattention and disrepair. Legree cares only for his farm's production, and thus spends little time maintaining his property, neglecting house and slaves alike. Following Legree's lead, his slaves treat each other brutally. This dissension among the slaves keeps them from any collective action and thus serves Legree well. Despite the harsh circumstances, Tom makes friends through his kindness and Christianity. The moral question arises, however, of how a loving God could allow such brutality to exist unchecked. Eva comes to Tom in a dream, however, encouraging him in his faith.

Legree feels disdain for Tom's kindnesses and watches him closely, looking for opportunities to punish him. Tom contributes cotton to the baskets of weaker slaves in the fields, which is strictly forbidden. Legree's longtime, unwitting mistress, Cassy, warns Tom not to help other slaves or he will risk a beating. When caught helping a slave whose basket comes up short, Tom is ordered to whip the slave for punishment. He refuses on the grounds that his faith forbids him to hurt another human being, and Legree orders a severe beating for Tom. Cassy sneaks to Tom's side in order to nurse his wounds, and encourages him to give up his resistance. Tom cites God's strength and shares his faith with Cassy. Cassy tells her history full of family separation, rape, and murder, giving insight into her hard heart. When Tom again entreats her to believe in God, Cassy says that God is not there.

Chapters 35–41

Legree's history reveals his lifelong cruelty. When a slave brings Legree the locket of Eva's hair that Tom treasures, Legree reacts violently. The locket of hair reminds him of his mother's hair, whom he continues to see as a specter in the house. His mother died attempting to reform Legree, to no avail. The slave owner's superstitions cause him to become even more paranoid. Emmeline and Cassy discuss their terrible predicament of being Legree's slaves, in both body and soul. Legree continues to think about his mother, leading to a disturbing nightmare. He is determined to force Tom to apologize for his disobedience, but Cassy warns him to leave Tom alone. Legree begins to fear the strange strength Tom exhibits.

At the Quaker home with Eliza and George, the slave-catcher Loker is nursed back to health. Because of the Quakers' kindness, Loker abandons slave catching in favor of hunting animals in the North. He gives Eliza and George tips for reaching Canada safely and avoiding any other slave catchers. On Loker's recommendation, George, Eliza, and Harry disguise themselves to travel by boat to Canada. Despite encountering Loker's former partner, Marks, the family arrives in Canada undetected. The slaves enjoy their first taste of freedom and hope to make the most of their newfound liberty.

At Legree's plantation, Tom grows weary from daily drudgery. He even doubts God's presence, wondering if all he believed in has abandoned him. At his lowest moment, however, Tom has a vision of Jesus dying on the cross and his faith is renewed. Tom feels kinship to Jesus' suffering, and begins to constantly make sacrifices for those around him, offering physical assistance as well as words of kindness to his brutal fellow slaves. As Tom steers the slaves toward Christianity, Legree feels threatened and enraged. Cassy tries to convince Tom to murder Legree for the good of the slaves, but Tom again refuses to hurt another human being, no matter the reason. Seeing Cassy and Emmeline's despair at being Legree's sexual victims, Tom encourages them to escape. When they agree, Tom refuses to accompany them in favor of completing his Christian mission among Legree's slaves.

Setting her plan to escape in motion, Cassy plays upon Legree's superstitions by arranging for ghostly sounds in the house's garret; Legree begins to fear the garret more than any other place, and thus Cassy can use the upper room to stockpile supplies for her and Emmeline's escape. After putting all the pieces in place, Cassy and Emmeline escape to a nearby swamp, careful to do so in plain view of other slaves. When the slaves alert Legree of their escape, the master and slaves return to the plantation and put together a search party. Heading back to the swamp, the search party blindly passes by Cassy and Emmeline, who have doubled back to the plantation and are hiding up in the garret. The women set up house and plan to stay in the garret until an opportunity to escape arises. Emmeline becomes like a daughter to Cassy, and helps soften her heart.

Legree projects his anger at losing the runaway slaves onto Tom. Tom admits to knowing where the women are hiding, but refuses to disclose their location. When Legree orders his fatal whipping, Tom commends his spirit to God and forgives Legree for murdering him. Although Legree is moved by Tom's actions, he continues with his beating. The two slaves who beat Tom throughout the night on Legree's behalf are impressed by the dying man's faith; they repent for their participation in his death and sincerely but futilely attempt to nurse him back to health. Tom forgives the two slaves, and they both become Christians. Many of Legree's other slaves, including Cassy, find inspiration from Tom's sacrifice and become Christians as well.

Before dying, Tom only feels sad that the Shelby family failed in their promise to bring him back to his home. In the time since Tom left, however, Mr. Shelby has died and the family affairs remain confused. Once Mrs. Shelby establishes control over the plantation's business, she sets out to locate Tom, which proves difficult. George Shelby, now a grown man, rushes to purchase Tom once he finds him. George arrives after Tom's beating, only in time to hear his dying words. Tom rejoices at George's arrival, and sends farewell messages to his family. After Tom's death, George knocks Legree down in anger and takes Tom's body for a proper burial. George vows to work toward slavery's end, although he refuses to buy two of Legree's pleading slaves.

Chapters 42–45

After Tom's death, Legree becomes obsessed with ghostly apparitions to the point of illness, allowing Cassy and Emmeline to escape easily. The runaway slaves encounter George Shelby on the boat heading North, and confide their story to him. In a series of coincidences, George realizes that Eliza must be Cassy's daughter, sold away from her many years ago. He also becomes acquainted with a sophisticated woman aboard the boat who turns out to be George Harris's long-lost sister. George Shelby helps the three women travel to Canada and reunite with George, Eliza, Harry, and their new daughter, Eliza. George and Eliza live comfortably in Canada, having established a moderate livelihood on free soil. George's sister, now a wealthy widow, offers to finance George's education in France. The happily reunited extended family travels overseas. Once George's education is complete, the family decides that America only offers bitter memories for them and instead chooses to move to Liberia. The land established specifically for former slaves offers the Harrises their best hope for a homeland, and they set their sights on Africa.

Updating readers on the fates of the novel's other characters, the narrator informs readers that Topsy grows up successfully in New England to eventually become a missionary in Africa. Further, Cassy eventually locates her lost son, Henry, who will presently follow his family to Liberia.

George Shelby returns to the plantation and informs Aunt Chloe of Tom's death. All on the plantation mourn their friend's loss and admire his Christian witness while George follows through on his promise to free the slaves. Unwilling to leave the Shelby plantation, however, the slaves instead maintain their residences and become wage workers for the family.

Concluding the fictional account of Tom and the slaves, Stowe closes her novel by describing the various real-life inspirations for many characters in her story. She maintains that all the events, though not specifically biographical, parallel the experiences of many slaves in America. Stowe also attributes the Fugitive Slave Law with inspiring her to write the story. Appealing to mothers especially, Stowe entreats her readers to consider the sin inherent in separating families and treating human beings like property. She encourages her readers to *"feel right"* about slavery, and condemn it in their hearts. Her argument continues, stating that slaves deserve reparations and should be freed and offered an education. They should then be allowed to move to Liberia, where they can establish a future as a race. As evidence that her plan could succeed, she offers examples of freed slaves who were able to support themselves by the work of their own hands. The final words of the novel warn of God's wrath toward those who ignore the evils of slavery.

THEMES

Slavery

From the start, *Uncle Tom's Cabin* rejects the premise that slavery only hurts the slave. Instead, Stowe argues throughout the novel that both the white Southern citizens and their enslaved servants suffer serious moral degradation as a result of the institution. For instance, when Mrs. Shelby cannot convince her husband against selling both Tom and little Harry, she exclaims, "This is God's curse on slavery!—a bitter, bitter, most accursed thing!—a curse to the master and a curse to the slave!" As one of the most sympathetic, intelligent, and compassionate characters in the novel, Mrs. Shelby is assumed to voice Stowe's own beliefs. She emphasizes that even as kind slaveholders, the act of denying a human being freedom is evil itself. Stowe here counters the popular defense of slavery that says slaves, under just masters, actually enjoy slavery and benefit from its

sheltering influence. This view often sets forth a model of benevolent patriarchy, where the plantation master cares for his slaves as if they were his children. Mrs. Shelby contradicts this argument early in the novel, however, when she declares,

> I was a fool to think I could make anything good out of such a deadly evil. It is a sin to hold a slave under laws like ours.... I thought, by kindness, and care, and instruction, I could make the condition of mine better than freedom—fool that I was!

Further illustrating the destructive effects of slavery, Stowe uses Legree's plantation to dramatize the level of brutality to which both master and slave are reduced. Legree, certainly the villain of the novel, enjoys his harsh treatment of slaves and takes pleasure in their humiliation. Initiating new slaves into his policies, Legree warns, "You's every one on ye got to toe the mark, I tell ye; quick,—straight,—the moment I speak.... So, now, mind yerselves; for I don't show no mercy!" His love of power over others keeps him from repenting, despite being given numerous chances. As a result of their master's treatment, Legree's slaves exhibit animal-like brutality. "Legree had trained them in savageness and brutality as systematically as he had his bulldogs; and, by long practice in hardness and cruelty, brought their whole nature to about the same range of capacities." Stowe is quick to attribute the base brutality not to an innate inferiority of the Africans but instead to the slave owner himself. By relating human beings, both master and slave, as brutes, Stowe presents a moral argument about the unnatural and inhumane spirit at the core of slavery.

Because everyone involved in the institution suffers, Stowe's story pleads for the end of slavery. Through a discussion between Augustine St. Clare and Ophelia, however, she acknowledges the difficulties of freeing the slaves outright. Augustine agrees that slavery should be abolished, but he wonders how the population of slaves, raised to be subservient and dependent, will survive as free people. Augustine wonders what skills they have to help them survive. "In many cases," he explains, "it is a gradual hardening process on both sides,—the owner growing more and more cruel, as the servant more and more callous." A slave's experience may not serve him well if free, Augustine believes. He asks Ophelia, "suppose we should rise up tomorrow and emancipate, who would educate these millions, and teach them how to use their freedom?" Stowe illustrates that although slavery debases everyone involved, simply freeing the slaves would not solve the problem of race in America.

Racism

Although Stowe's novel does much to portray the humanity of African Americans, at the same time it develops an argument for racial essentialism. According to Amanda Claybaugh in her introduction to *Uncle Tom's Cabin*, the nineteenth century popularized a concept called racialism, assigning essential and separate characteristics to each race of human. At times in her story, Stowe argues that all races are the same, and appeals to white mothers to sympathize with slave mothers whose children may be sold away from them at any moment. In other sections, though, Stowe develops the contradictory argument that the African race exhibits different characteristics from the Anglo-Saxon race. Because the races differ in essence, Stowe declares, their fates are separate. In the end, Stowe even supports sending all freed slaves to the African country of Liberia in order for their race to fulfill its distinct destiny.

In many instances throughout the novel, Stowe describes traits of black people, some of which support offensive racial stereotypes. For example, in describing both the Shelby and the St. Clare cooks—Aunt Chloe and Dinah, respectively—Stowe writes that cooking is "an indigenous talent of the African race." She extends her labeling further, saying that "common among the negroes" are "wild, grotesque songs." These descriptions reinforce stereotypes of the African American alternately as servant or entertainer. Describing the assumed emotional nature of Africans, Stowe's opinion becomes even more problematic according to twenty-first-century standards:

> it must be remembered that all the instinctive affections of that race are peculiarly strong. Their local attachments are very abiding. They are not naturally daring and enterprising but home-loving and affectionate.... patient, timid and unenterprising.

According to Stowe, the Anglo-Saxon or white race differs from the African in that it is enterprising and adventurous, "hot and hasty." She argues, "To the Anglo-Saxon race has been intrusted the destinies of the world." Attributing such distinct characteristics to different races reinforces a hierarchy among them, specifically attributing more positive and powerful characteristics to whites and more negative and passive characteristics to blacks. Stowe's message about racial harmony and the destiny of white and black people in America is unclear; does she espouse racial equality and freedom, or does she promote racial separatism and, ultimately, prejudice? Certainly the legacy of *Uncle Tom's Cabin*, and of race relations in America in general, shows signs of both.

HISTORICAL OVERVIEW

The Compromise of 1850

As Stowe recounts, the Compromise of 1850 inspired her to write a story dramatizing the horrors of slavery. The Compromise combined several pieces of legislation in order to pacify both Northern and Southern interests regarding slavery. For the North, trading slaves in Washington, D.C., became illegal, and the new California territory would enter the Union as a free state. The territories of New Mexico, Utah, Nevada, and Arizona were organized with the slavery issue to be decided later, by state vote. For the South, the Compromise enacted a new Fugitive Slave Law, requiring Northern citizens to return runaway slaves to the South. Stowe's character of Senator Bird dramatizes one opinion about the law, declaring that the public interest of Union harmony surpasses the private sympathy one might feel for a runaway slave. Mrs. Bird, by contrast, states that the only Christian priority is the private duty to help one in need. Stowe obviously agrees with Mrs. Bird's analysis, but both perspectives were common in mid-nineteenth-century culture.

Slavery in the United States

Uncle Tom's Cabin was published nine years before the Civil War began, and over a decade before President Lincoln issued the Emancipation Proclamation in 1863. The book did not directly cause either of these significant historical events; it did, however, fan the flames of the conflict between Northerners and Southerners over the matter of slavery. Should new territories enter the Union as slave or free states? How should free states respond to freed men and women and runaway slaves? These questions prompted much heated debate in the mid-nineteenth century, and Stowe's novel gave shape and language to that debate.

The transatlantic slave trade had been bringing Africans to America for almost two hundred years when Congress prohibited the practice on January 1, 1808. By this time, however, there were enough slaves, principally in the southern states, to sustain the slave population through reproduction. Slaves were considered the property of their owners, and could be bought and sold at will. Slave auctions were held in towns and cities across the South, where slaves were examined and bid upon by would-be owners. Owning slaves became a symbol of wealth and power, and many poor farmers and sharecroppers aspired to someday own slaves as a sign of their financial success. Only one-quarter of landowners in the South owned slaves, and it was rare to find more than fifty slaves on any one plantation or farm.

Slaves were used for all kinds of physical labor, from working in cotton and tobacco fields to cooking and keeping house for their white masters. They were forced to live in cramped and unsanitary quarters, with limited amounts of nutrition and long work days. They were often punished if their owners deemed them to not work hard enough, or if they were suspected of stealing or running away. Slaves that did not run away were often punished in place of those who did, and they were encouraged to alert their owners to runaways, as happens at Legree's farm in the book.

The Underground Railroad

Those slaves who did escape often found help from the Underground Railroad, a system of safe houses that provided cover and assistance for slaves making their way to the North and Canada. Underground Railroad "conductors" were individuals and religious groups, former slaves, free blacks, and whites. Bounty hunters and slave catchers were constantly after runaways, but the Underground Railroad was largely successful in keeping its routes and safe houses ("stations") secret. It is estimated that between thirty thousand and one hundred thousand slaves were aided by the Underground Railroad in the first half of the nineteenth century.

Gender Roles

The mid-nineteenth century saw the rise of what has been termed by scholars as "the cult of domesticity." According to this philosophy, gender roles followed strict divisions, attributing all public concerns to men and relegating all private and domestic concerns to women. Men concerned themselves with employment and politics while women ruled over domestic and spiritual matters. In fact, women who held jobs out of financial necessity were regarded as less feminine. Stowe reflects this division in her narrative as she consistently and directly addresses female readers, appealing to their views of home and family. "And you, mothers of America," Stowe implores, "I beseech you, pity those mothers that are constantly made childless by the American slave-trade! And say, mothers of America, is this a thing to be defended, sympathized with, passed over in silence?"

Stowe reinforces the cultural division between the sexes in her novel, maintaining that women should restrict their activities to the home. But instead of then deeming slavery a political and thus masculine concern, as many people did at the time, Stowe instead illustrates why slavery fully pervades the domestic sphere. One of Stowe's characters states, amid the cruel selling of children away from their unsuspecting mothers, "The most dreadful part of slavery, to my mind, is its outrages on the feelings and affections,—the separating of families, for example." The home and family represent the basis for all of society according to nineteenth-century standards, and together they become the sacred territory and the moral pride of upper-class women. As Stowe appeals to the common ground of motherhood, she is making a connection among all women, slave and free, that upper-class white women would not readily make on their own. Stowe pleads for her readers to put themselves in the slave woman's place, a place the reader probably never considered a personal possibility. Stowe's novel at once maintains the conservative gender roles of her time while simultaneously and radically redefining what constitutes the woman's domain.

CRITICAL OVERVIEW

Uncle Tom's Cabin was a spectacular seller as soon as it was published. Americans flocked not only to bookstores but to theaters to watch dramatic versions of the story and to gift shops to purchase trinkets related to Stowe's plot and characters. Stowe drew celebrity attention in America and abroad, and famous writers from Charles Dickens to George Sand wrote glowing reviews of her novel. The review in *The National Era*, the journal that originally published *Uncle Tom's Cabin* in serial form, calls the novel "a wonderful work" of "rare dramatic genius." The journal editors' esteem for Harriet Beecher Stowe is so great that they "cannot refrain from applying to her sacred words, and exclaiming, 'Blessed art thou among women!'" *Putnam's Monthly Review* calls the success of the book "a miracle.... the first real success in book-making." In a review for *Liberator Review*, William Lloyd Garrison praises Stowe's "rare descriptive powers," and argues that "the effect of such a work upon all intelligent and humane minds coming in contact with it ... cannot be estimated."

Although enjoying thriving sales in the North, *Uncle Tom's Cabin* received a frigid reception in the South. Not even carried in many locations, the book and its author faced severe criticism. The *Southern Literary Messenger* called the entire story, its characters, and its premise a complete fiction. In an unsigned review in the *Southern Press Review*, the critic calls the book "a caricature of slavery" that selects only "the most odious features." However, it was not just southern publications that panned Stowe's depiction of slavery. While the *Boston Morning Post Review* concedes that *Uncle Tom's Cabin* "is the finest picture yet painted of the abominable horrors of slavery," it also states that the novel:

> produces a picture which we are happy to believe does not do justice to practical slavery in our Southern States. In a word, the effect of *Uncle Tom's Cabin*, as a whole, is grossly to exaggerate the actual evils of negro slavery in this country.

The *New York Daily Times* ran an extensive four-part review and rebuttal to *Uncle Tom's Cabin* in the summer of 1853. The reviews are written by a "Southern gentleman, a lawyer of distinction, an accomplished scholar, and who has filled very high and responsible public stations with honor." The reviewer remains unnamed, and the articles are given the byline of "A Southerner." In the four subsequent reviews, the Southerner rebuts what he calls the

exaggerated and extravagant descriptions of slavery in Stowe's novel, which he believes unfairly damages the South's reputation. He argues that Stowe is writing for political reasons, not literary ones, and in the third review, that "her book is intended to turn the indignation of the whole world against the social system of the Southern States." As he extols the "comforts" of Southern slaves as compared to working-class people in England, he argues that the book "seeks to expose the *abuses* of Slavery; it does not discuss the question of Slavery as an institution." That institution, he writes, is for the most part kind, paternal, and civilized, and adds, "Slavery is consistent with the highest, the noblest, the freest, and the happiest civilization which the world has so far exhibited," referring to ancient Greece.

As Claybaugh explains in her introduction, many Southern writers even wrote revisions of Stowe's text, dramatizing pastoral and idyllic harmony among masters and slaves. Stowe attempted to validate her picture of slavery in 1853 by attributing each event in the novel to a particular experience in *A Key to Uncle Tom's Cabin*, but many Southerners continued to deny any abuses of slavery despite overwhelming physical evidence.

From its racist stereotypes to its overly emotional prose, *Uncle Tom's Cabin* has faced serious criticism that, despite its contemporary popularity, caused its reputation to flag throughout most of the twentieth century. For modern readers, Stowe's writing style may be described as sentimental and ornate. She employs melodramatic dialogue and over-the-top characters, though in her time these were common literary techniques. Directly addressing the reader, as Stowe consistently does throughout her narrative, was also popular.

The novel's mass appeal further doomed *Uncle Tom's Cabin* to obscurity for a time. Critics found popular literature to be low, instead valuing texts that were unappreciated in their time. Henry David Thoreau's cerebral tome *Walden* is an example of a highly praised literary work that sold poorly during Thoreau's lifetime. Labeling Stowe's work more propaganda than literature, scholars overlooked and devalued *Uncle Tom's Cabin* for most of the twentieth century.

MEDIA ADAPTATIONS

The first film adaptation of *Uncle Tom's Cabin* was a silent film directed by Harry A. Pollard in 1927. It stars black actor James B. Lowe as Tom, though many of the other black character parts are played by white actors in blackface makeup. The DVD by Republic Pictures includes production background by film historian David Pierce.

Uncle Tom's Cabin was adapted to film again in 1969, this time directed by Géza von Radványi. It is available in VHS format from Xenon.

Another film adaptation of *Uncle Tom's Cabin* was produced in 1987. It is directed by Stan Lathan, and stars Samuel L. Jackson and Phylicia Rashad. It is available on VHS from Republic Pictures.

Uncle Tom's Cabin was released in an unabridged version on audio CD by Brilliance Audio in 2005. It is narrated by Buck Schirner.

An abridged version of *Uncle Tom's Cabin* was released on audio CD by Naxos Audiobooks in 1999.

Literary critics Jane Tompkins and Philip Fisher initiated the academic rejuvenation of *Uncle Tom's Cabin* in 1985. Both writers published analyses of Stowe's work that re-legitimized her masterpiece. In their writings, they argue that if readers consider Stowe's project within its own cultural context, the novel must be considered crucial to the history of American literature. Since the publication of Fisher's and Tompkins's scholarship, many prominent critics, including Lawrence Buell and Eric Sundquist, have given Stowe a place in the literary canon. *Uncle Tom's Cabin* now regularly appears on university reading lists, and critics once again appreciate the enormous impact of Stowe's writing on American letters.

CRITICISM

Jane Tompkins

In the following excerpt, Tompkins argues for a serious academic, political, and social interpretation of Uncle Tom's Cabin, *which is more typically overlooked as lightweight, feminine writing*

Despite the influence of the women's movement, despite the explosion of work in nineteenth-century American social history, and despite the new historicism that is infiltrating literary studies, the women, like Stowe, whose names were household words in the nineteenth century—women such as Susan Warner, Sarah J. Hale, Augusta Evans, Elizabeth Stuart Phelps, her daughter Mary, who took the same name, and Frances Hodgson Burnett—these women remain excluded from the literary canon. And while it has recently become fashionable to study their works as examples of cultural deformation, even critics who have invested their professional careers in that study and who declare themselves feminists still refer to their novels as trash.

In reaction against their world view, and perhaps even more against their success, twentieth-century critics have taught generations of students to equate popularity with debasement, emotionality with ineffectiveness, religiosity with fakery, domesticity with triviality, and all of these, implicitly, with womanly inferiority.

Uncle Tom's Cabin was, in almost any terms one can think of, the most important book of the century. It was the first American novel ever to sell over a million copies and its impact is generally thought to have been incalculable. Expressive of and responsible for the values of its time, it also belongs to a genre, the sentimental novel, whose chief characteristic is that it is written by, for, and about women. In this respect, *Uncle Tom's Cabin* is not exceptional but representative. It is the *summa theologica* of nineteenth-century America's religion of domesticity, a brilliant redaction of the culture's favorite story about itself—the story of salvation through motherly love. Out of the ideological materials at their disposal, the sentimental novelists elaborated a myth that gave women the central position of power and authority in the culture; and of these efforts *Uncle Tom's Cabin* is the most dazzling exemplar.

I have used words like "monumental" and "dazzling" to describe Stowe's novel and the tradition of which it is a part because they have for too long been the casualties of a set of critical attitudes that equate intellectual merit with a certain kink of argumentative discourse and certain kinds of subject matter. A long tradition of academic parochialism has enforced this sort of discourse through a series of cultural contrasts: light "feminine" novels vs. tough-minded intellectual treatises; domestic "chattiness" vs. serious thinking; and summarily, the "damned mob of scribbling women" vs. a few giant intellects, unappreciated and misunderstood in their time, struggling manfully against a flood of sentimental rubbish.

Let us consider the episode in *Uncle Tom's Cabin* most often cited as the epitome of Victorian sentimentalism—the death of little Eva—because it is the kind of incident most offensive to the sensibilities of twentieth-century academic critics. It is on the belief that this incident is nothing more than a sob story that the whole case against sentimentalism rests. Little Eva's death, so the argument goes, like every other sentimental tale, is awash with emotion but does nothing to remedy the evils it deplores. Essentially, it leaves the slave system and the other characters unchanged. This trivializing view of the episode is grounded in assumptions about power and reality so common that we are not even aware they are in force. Thus generations of critics have commented with condescending irony on little Eva's death. But in the system of belief that undergirds Stowe's enterprise, dying is the supreme form of heroism. In *Uncle Tom's Cabin*, death is the equivalent not of defeat but of victory; it brings an access of power, not a loss of it; it is not only the crowning achievement of life, it *is* life and Stowe's entire presentation of little Eva is designed to dramatize this fact.

Stories like the death of little Eva are compelling for the same reason that the story of Christ's death is compelling; they enact a a philosophy, as must political as religious, in which the pure and powerless die to save the powerful and corrupt, and thereby show themselves more powerful than those they save. They enact, in short, a *theory* of power in which the ordinary or "common sense" view of what is efficacious and what is not (a view to which most modern critics are committed) is simply reversed, as the very possibility of social action is made dependent on the action taking place in individual hearts. Little Eva's death enacts the drama of

which all the major episodes of the novel are transformations, the idea, central to Christian soteriology, that the highest human calling is to give one's life for another. It presents one version of the ethic of sacrifice on which the entire novel is based and contains in some form all of the motifs that, by their frequent recurrence, constitute the novel's ideological framework.

Of course, it could be argued by critics of sentimentalism that the prominence of stories about the deaths of children is precisely what is wrong with the literature of the period; rather than being cited as a source of strength, the presence of such stories in *Uncle Tom's Cabin* could be regarded as an unfortunate concession to the age's fondness for lachrymose scenes. But to dismiss such scenes as "all tears and flapdoodle" is to leave unexplained the popularity of the novels and sermons that are filled with them, unless we choose to believe that a generation of readers was unaccountably moved to tears by matters that are intrinsically silly and trivial. That popularity is better explained, I believe, by the relationship of these scenes to a pervasive cultural myth which invests the suffering and death of an innocent victim with just the kind of power that critics deny to Stowe's novel: the power to work in, and change, the world.

The eschatological vision, by putting all individual events in relation to an order that is unchanging, collapses the distinctions among them so that they become interchangeable representations of a single timeless reality. Groups of characters blend into the same character, while the plot abounds with incidents that mirror one another. These features are the features, not of classical nineteenth-century fiction, but of typological narrative. It is this tradition rather than that of the English novel that *Uncle Tom's Cabin* reproduces and extends; for this novel does not simply quote the Bible, it rewrites the Bible as the story of a Negro slave. Formally and philosophically, it stands opposed to works like *Middlemarch* and *The Portrait of a Lady* in which everything depends on human action and decision unfolding in a temporal sequence that withholds revelation until the final moment. The truths that Stowe's narrative conveys can only be reembodied, never discovered, because they are already revealed from the beginning. Therefore, what seem from a modernist point of view to be gross stereotypes in characterization and a needless proliferation of incident, are essential properties of a narrative aimed at demonstrating that human history is a continual reenactment of the sacred drama of redemption. It is the novel's reenactment of this drama that made it irresistible in its day.

Uncle Tom's Cabin retells the culture's central religious myth—the story of the crucifixion—in terms of the nation's greatest political conflict—slavery—and of its most cherished social beliefs—the sanctity of motherhood and the family. It is because Stowe is able to combine so many of the culture's central concerns in a narrative that is immediately accessible to the general population that she is able to move so many people so deeply. The novel's typological organization allows her to present political and social situations both as themselves and as transformations of a religious paradigm which interprets them in a way that readers can both understand and respond to emotionally. For the novel functions both as a means of describing the social world and as a means of changing it. It not only offers an interpretive framework for understanding the culture, and, through the reinforcement of a particular code of values, recommends a strategy for dealing with cultural conflict, but it is itself an agent of that strategy, putting into practice the measures it prescribes. As the religious stereotypes of "Sunday-school fiction" define and organize the elements of social and political life, so the "melodrama" and "pathos" associated with the underlying myth of crucifixion put the reader's heart in the right place with respect to the problems the narrative defines. Hence, rather than making the enduring success of *Uncle Tom's Cabin* inexplicable, these popular elements which puzzled Whicher and have puzzled so many modern scholars—melodrama, pathos, Sunday-school fiction—are the *only* terms in which the book's success can be explained.

Uncle Tom's Cabin, however, unlike its counterparts in the sentimental tradition, was spectacularly persuasive in conventional political terms: it helped convince a nation to go to war and to free its slaves. But in terms of its own conception of power, a conception it shares with other sentimental fiction, the novel was a political failure. Stowe conceived her book as an instrument for bringing about the day when the world would be ruled not by force, but by Christian love. The novel's deepest political aspirations are expressed only secondarily in its

devastating attack on the slave system; the true goal of Stowe's rhetorical undertaking is nothing less than the institution of the kingdom of heaven on earth. Embedded in the world of *Uncle Tom's Cabin*, which is the fallen world of slavery, there appears an idyllic picture, both utopian and Arcadian, of the form human life would assume if Stowe's readers were to heed her moral lesson. In this vision, described in the chapter entitled "The Quaker Settlement," Christian love fulfills itself not in war, but in daily living, and the principle of sacrifice is revealed not in crucifixion, but in motherhood. The form that Stowe's utopian society takes bears no resemblance to the current social order. Man-made institutions—the church, the courts of law, the legislatures, the economic system—are nowhere in sight. The home is the center of all meaningful activity; women perform the most important tasks; work is carried on in a spirit of mutual cooperation; and the whole is guided by a Christian woman who, through the influence of her "loving words," "gentle moralities," and "motherly loving kindness," rules the world from her rocking-chair.

Source: Jane Tompkins, "Sentimental Power: Uncle Tom's Cabin and the Politics of Literary History," in *Sensational Designs: The Cultural Work of American Fiction 1790–1860*, Oxford University Press, 1985.

SOURCES

Claybaugh, Amanda, Introduction, in *Uncle Tom's Cabin*, Barnes & Noble Classics, 2003, pp. xvi, xxvii.

Garrison, William Lloyd, Review of *Uncle Tom's Cabin*, *The Institute for Advanced Technology in Humanities at the University of Virginia*, www.iath.virginia.edu/utc/reviews/rehp.html (1998), originally published in the *Liberator Review*, March 26, 1852.

Review of *Uncle Tom's Cabin*, *The Institute for Advanced Technology in Humanities at the University of Virginia*, www.iath.virginia.edu/utc/reviews/rehp.html (1998), originally published in the *Boston Morning Post Review*, 1852.

Review of *Uncle Tom's Cabin*, *The Institute for Advanced Technology in Humanities at the University of Virginia*, www.iath.virginia.edu/utc/reviews/rehp.html (1998), originally published in *The National Era*, April 22, 1852.

Review of *UncleTom's Cabin*, *The Institute for Advanced Technology in Humanities at the University of Virginia*, www.iath.virginia.edu/utc/reviews/rehp.html (1998), originally published in four parts in *New York Daily Times*, June 22–July 15, 1853.

Review of *Uncle Tom's Cabin*, The Institute for Advanced Technology in Humanities at the University of Virginia, www.iath.virginia.edu/utc/reviews/rehp.html (1998), originally published in *Putnam's Monthly Review*, January 1853.

Review of *Uncle Tom's Cabin*, The Institute for Advanced Technology in Humanities at the University of Virginia, www.iath.virginia.edu/utc/reviews/rehp.html (1998), originally published in the *Southern Press Review*, 1852.

Review of *Uncle Tom's Cabin*, The Institute for Advanced Technology in Humanities at the University of Virginia, www.iath.virginia.edu/utc/reviews/rehp.html (1998), originally published in *The Southern Literary Messenger*, October 1852.

Stowe, Harriet Beecher, *Uncle Tom's Cabin*, Barnes & Noble Classics, 2003; originally published in 1852.

A Vindication of the Rights of Woman

A Vindication of the Rights of Woman (1792), by
Mary Wollstonecraft, was published in London
during the third year of the French Revolution
and the fifth year of George Washington's pre-
sidency of the new United States of America.
Responding to other writers who praised or
attacked these antimonarchical uprisings, the
tone of the book is by turn confrontational,
instructive, harshly critical, sarcastically funny,
idealistic, and visionary. Rooting her argument
that women deserve an education equal to men's
on the human duty to use God's gift of reason,
Wollstonecraft set traditional gender roles on
their ear. Though she states that she loves man
as her "fellow," she is clear that "his scepter, real,
or usurped, extends not to me, unless the reason
of an individual demands my homage; and even
then the submission is to reason, and not to
man."

Long cited as the fundamental text of
Western feminism, the book continues to contribute to modern social thought in many ways.
Wollstonecraft repeatedly makes the connection
between slaves and Western women—even those
in the middle class. She delves into the psychology of the materially dependent to examine why
women generally play along with the prejudices
held against them. She links race-based chattel
slavery to gendered bondage, exposing how
"masters" of women benefit from creating a sub-
human female to fulfill their designs. Referring
to gendered oppression as slavery, she brings the

MARY WOLLSTONECRAFT
1792

"MAKE [WOMEN] FREE, AND THEY WILL QUICKLY BECOME WISE AND VIRTUOUS, AS MEN BECOME MORE SO; FOR THE IMPROVEMENT MUST BE MUTUAL, OR THE INJUSTICE WHICH ONE HALF OF THE HUMAN RACE ARE OBLIGED TO SUBMIT TO ... THE VIRTUE OF MAN WILL BE WORM-EATEN BY THE INSECT WHOM HE KEEPS UNDER HIS FEET."

nebulous "woman question" into the spotlight of civil and human rights and lifts to public awareness the relationship between public political systems (the divine right of kings) and private personal systems (the divine right of husbands).

Wollstonecraft sought to improve philosopher Jean-Jacques Rousseau's (1712–1788) educational philosophy (the goal of education is to learn how to live) by leaps and bounds. Insisting that females had been created not merely to complement males, but with duties to carry out in public and spiritual realms, she urges that children of both sexes be taught to "begin to think." Rather than viewing knowledge as something to acquire and own, she suggests a process fueled by life experiences, which would allow thinkers to reason though events and ideally arrive at the practice of moral virtue. This is a process of lifelong learning. She applied her own method throughout her life, hence her philosophy (consisting of seven published volumes) kept changing. For example, in 1792, *A Vindication of the Rights of Woman* emphasized the view that human sexuality that was meant to be short-lived and supplanted by other duties. But after her love affair with Gilbert Imlay, her own work challenged this naive opinion, pondering the relationship of society to female desire. This method of applying reason and book-learning to life experience, and shining the lamp of the latter on the former, is known today as feminist pedagogy.

A Vindication of the Rights of Woman touches on many other strands in the mesh of

social injustice. Readers will notice the repetition of certain topics and key words. These point to the history behind Wollstonecraft's concerns and highlight concerns of the day. Some of these concepts include "tyrant," "mob," "despotism," "liberty," "natural" (versus "artful"), "moral," "virtue," "vice," "revolution," and "reason." The source of these words can be traced to the Western philosophical movement known as the Enlightenment, and to uprisings that were overthrowing old forms of government based on monarchies. Her structure is also designed to appeal to her contemporaries. Wollstonecraft's writing is elliptical: rather than attack certain issues head-on, she returns to them over and over again, establishing their importance by examining them from many different angles. This method was intended to better appeal to the day's literate British audience, which she said suffered from a "fear of innovation." Therefore *A Vindication of the Rights of Woman* is written with a layered effect, mimicking the way prejudices affect layer after layer of human experience.

Far from offering dead debates, *A Vindication of the Rights of Woman* continues to address today's concerns. For instance, Wollstonecraft argues that neither the soul nor the mind has a sex. At the same time, she acknowledges that men are, in general, physically stronger, while women are naturally inclined to please and relate. Some bio-determinists direct their research to debating and supporting the same gender claims. In "The New Science of Sex" (2003), Iain Murray, for example, cites Andrew Sullivan's research claiming that because of high rates of testosterone, men think more, "especially about concrete problems in the immediate present," and they are more "frustrated" when action is thwarted. Murray also notes that some bio-determinists believe humans may be similar to mice when it comes to "a gene that determines 'good' motherhood." Murray also cites Cambridge University psychologist Simon Baron-Cohen, whose research indicates that men are "much more likely" to have a systematizing-type brain, while women exhibit a brain type known as empathizing. Two hundred years after her death, many issues that Wollstonecraft raised in her essay have shifted shape, but are still just as pressing and relevant.

BIOGRAPHY

MARY WOLLSTONECRAFT

Mary Wollstonecraft, the eldest daughter of a violent, impoverished "gentleman," was born in 1759 in Hoxton, England. In her twenties, she founded a school for the children of the Dissenters, a group that lived by the twin codes of reason and piety while working for an egalitarian British society. After the school closed in 1785, she was offered work as an editorial assistant, writer, and reviewer for the radical London publisher Joseph Johnson. In this capacity, her intellectual circle expanded to include famous political thinkers such as Thomas Paine and William Blake.

After the publication of *A Vindication of the Rights of Woman* in 1792, she traveled to France to write about the ongoing Revolution, where she fell in love with an American, Gilbert Imlay.

They had a daughter, Francis. Imlay sent Wollstonecraft to Scandinavia on business, then abandoned her. The ill-fated love affair left her musing about the brutal consequences that conventional societies impose on female sexual desire.

Returning to London, Wollstonecraft began a relationship with William Godwin. When she found herself pregnant, she convinced Godwin to wed. While pregnant, she worked on *The Wrongs of Woman,* a kind of sequel to *A Vindication of the Rights of Woman.* The book was never finished, as Wollstonecraft died on September 10, 1797, of complications from childbirth. She had delivered a daughter who would become Mary Shelley, author of the Gothic masterpiece *Frankenstein.*

PLOT SUMMARY

Introduction and Chapter I: The Rights and Involved Duties of Mankind Considered

In 1792, all eyes in the Western world were on the French Revolution. Wollstonecraft writes her introduction in response to Talleyrand, who has reviewed a new version of the French Constitution and agrees that girls should be educated with boys, but only until the age of eight. *A Vindication of the Rights of Woman* vehemently defends females as full human beings, who for several reasons deserve the same education that men receive. Wollstonecraft intends to persuade readers that serious social harm can come from limiting women's mental and moral abilities.

In Chapter I, Wollstonecraft asserts that only reason lifts humans above the animal kingdom, and invites readers to get back to basics. She poses three questions, giving clear, concise answers in the style of a catechism. First, what entitles humans to dominate animals and the earth? The answer is reason. Second, what does

a human gain throughout life that can improve his goodness or value? The answer is virtue. Third, why does God allow humans to feel various passions, when these have the power to lead them astray? The answer is that they might have experiences. Experiences lead people, through reason, to attain knowledge. Wollstonecraft sees these three activities as the dynamic links through which humans can perfect their natures, move closer to God, and create earthly happiness. All human beings—male and female—have the right to take part in the process by which they can refine their understanding. For only by this route can they learn to make moral choices and put their virtues into action. Enlightenment-seeking societies must be careful that men do not stop this process, which leads to goodness, by creating professions that rest first on privilege and later on tyranny.

Chapter II: The Prevailing Opinion of a Sexual Character Discussed

Wollstonecraft states that the "tyranny of man" is preserved through a number of clever arguments that promote irreconcilable gendered differences. Her argument, on the other hand, bases itself in the similarities between males and females, for both were created human by God. Hence, both share the same task of seeking perfection through living full, virtuous lives. Wollstonecraft promotes a concept of virtue (a commendable quality or behavior) that is not attainable by conforming to rules, but must be discovered and chosen when people face challenges in their lives.

Touching on Milton's portrayal of Eve in *Paradise Lost* (1667), Wollstonecraft recalls the old argument that women lack souls. She insists that females are soulful, and therefore fully human. They are insulted by "those who advise us only to render ourselves gentle, domestic brutes.... [with a] winning softness ... that governs by obeying." Gentleness and softness, childishness and innocence, in any adult's behavior, equate with weakness. Wollstonecraft compares career officers and courtiers to affluent women, for all are "taught to please, and they only live to please." Thus women (and other servile dependents) "acquire manners before morals." Their virtues are sham, superficial, and used to manipulate, and they become prey to the prejudices of the authority figures to whom they submit.

In this chapter, Wollstonecraft first touches on what constitutes a good marriage. She finds love to be a "common passion"—a device to avoid the practices of choice, reason, and long-lasting friendship between women and men. She insists that the main purposes of marriage are to raise a family and to perfect oneself in the virtues in preparation for the ecstasies of the afterlife.

Chapter III: The Same Subject Continued

Wollstonecraft continues to discuss ways in which women are defined as "fair defects" of nature. She introduces the relationship between a strong body and a strong mind. Women of the higher classes have been trained to cultivate physical fragility as a sign of refined femininity. Wollstonecraft argues that actual physical strength is essential to all who would undertake intellectual passions. She asks why women should not undertake them. The one superior trait inherent in men appears to be brawn—not brains, and not virtue. She urges women not to seek short-term favor with authority by conforming to a model of constitutional weakness,

and appeals to mothers to pass human dignity on to their daughters, rather than teaching them constraint and making them ill. Young girls, like young boys, she declares, would much rather "frolic in the open air" than be half-starved and sedentary. Likewise, though girls are said to have an innate fondness for pretty things, especially dressing up, this is because such narrow pleasures are all that are offered them.

In Chapter III, Wollstonecraft begins to critique the gender theory of Jean-Jacques Rousseau, still revered as the most-quoted, most-admired educator of the Enlightenment. She imagines a middle-class woman whose qualities conform to Rousseau's description of the ideal female. If such a woman is widowed, with no ready skills or the reasoning power to learn them, she must find a way to raise her children. Even if she is plucky rather than vain and vacuous, she may soon prove the adage that "the blind may as easily be led into a ditch as along the beaten road." In contrast, Wollstonecraft imagines a woman trained to reason independently. In the same situation, this widow is able to take good care of her family, find love in her children, and pin her happiness on the afterlife.

Chapter IV: Observations on the State of Degradation to Which Woman is Reduced by Various Causes

Wollstonecraft returns to the issue of the relationship between the soul and education, again emphasizing that females have immortal souls. Therefore, since experience leads to the soul's cultivation, women should cease to be valued according to physical beauty and submissive manners, and be trained toward reaching perfection. Wollstonecraft points out many factors that combine to degrade the female sex—in actual behavior, as well as by stereotype. Here the author first delves into how prejudice morphs into self-fulfilling prophecy. The ways in which females have been degraded have produced a history in which they have "always been either a slave or a despot" and either role "equally retards the progress of reason."

Some methods through which women become susceptible to accepting gendered difference, says Wollstonecraft, include social rewards for giving men beauty and pleasure. These play upon a female tendency to gratify emotions above loving reason: thus women vie to win a man's love. Women have also been trained to delight in sensation more than in performing their duties well. Encouraged to pamper their fleeting passions and ever seeking a state of physiological charge, women are not drawn toward delayed satisfactions that rise from the more demanding process of reason. Their training of "amiable weakness" authorizes them to seek the protection of men.

Women are taught to believe that they are the sensitive, emotional half of a heterosexual unit—the natural complement to the logical male. In childhood they are trained to appear docile, patient, and good humored, masking their true feelings and denying their intellects. Their training is seldom ordered toward expertise in a subject, but geared toward domestic life. Referring always to women "of quality," the author cites examples of how women become parodies of themselves. Rousseau's model is mentioned again, because he details desirable feminine qualities for the partner of Emilius (usually known as Émile), the ideal (male) product of an enlightened education. Wollstonecraft reexamines these reason-denying female qualities, pointing out how they are socially produced.

Chapter V: Animadversions on Some of the Writers Who Have Rendered Women Objects of Pity, Bordering on Contempt
Now the author strikes out in great detail at Rousseau's ideal gender model, and sometimes at the man himself. She quotes from Rousseau's *Émile, or On Education* (1762) extensively to attack his model. Rousseau's Sophia, the ideal wife, is as famous as Emilius himself. But while Rousseau holds that Emilius must be educated according to his reasonable, assertive, and independent nature, Sophia—and all good women, should learn:

> To please us, to be useful to us, to make us love and esteem them, to educate us when young, ... to advise, to console us, to render our lives easy and agreeable: these are the duties of women at all times, and what they should be taught in their infancy.

In addition to learning restraint from the cradle, Sophia-women should be taught to tolerate a moody husband, while also appealing to their "master" sexually, so that an educated man will desire to stay with his family, despite his natural fondness for liberty. Wollstonecraft takes issue with Rousseau's daydream. She declares, "The being who patiently endures injustice, and silently bears insults, will soon become unjust, or unable to discern right from wrong." She questions whether a "beautiful, innocent and silly" wife can entice a reasoning man to remain faithful. In any case, this is too high a price for a woman to pay—sacrificing her ability to reason in order to maintain her temporary position as seductive, compliant "mistress" of her husband's desire.

The author addresses the words of several advisors to female readers. Dr. Fordyce explains that a woman is loveliest when in "pious recollection ... she assumes, without knowing it ... the beauties of holiness," which brings her into kinship with angels. Wollstonecraft scoffs at the intentions behind such "idle, empty words" that aim to create slaves, not full human beings. Fordyce goes on to blame the young wives of abusive or neglectful husbands for their own plight: why have they not coaxed out his better qualities, overlooked his mistakes, and submitted to his authority? Wollstonecraft retorts, "Such a woman ought to be an angel—or she is an ass," but she lacks human character. Another would-be consultant is Dr. Gregory, who writes to his daughters to warn them of the common deceptions of men. Wollstonecraft agrees that men can be deceitful, but doubts that "decorum" can protect girls from villains, as Dr. Gregory suggests. An education that "make[s] the heart clean, and give[s] the head employment" would be better protection.

A Vindication of the Rights of Woman discusses some female writers of the time who attempt to preserve the gendered status quo, as well as activist female voices. The author salutes Catharine Macaulay, and then closes by noting her dislike of the dogmatic pedagogy promoted by Lord Chesterfield. By requiring students to accept "moss-covered opinions" rather than experience life and develop moral reasoning skills, he wants to short-circuit the practical-spiritual process of true education.

Chapter VI: The Effect Which an Early Association of Ideas Has Upon the Character
In this chapter, the author examines effects of poor education and negative trends on small children. Education is meant to provide the young with a basic mental content to draw on during associative thinking. Glitches occur when they are taught to habitually associate certain

ideas and impressions (mechanical thinking), or to associate impressions with emotions rather than with reason. Such faulty mental processes encourage a form of mental slavery.

Yet Wollstonecraft defends women for generally being rote learners: after all, they have been taught to obey, not to question, and not to focus on rigorous topics. Rather, they have been instructed to produce manners—not morals—and to concentrate on love, which the author terms an arbitrary passion with no basis in reason (unlike esteem). A practical example of her focus on passion rather than reason shows up in how women look for a mate. Many women prefer the dashing but unstable qualities of a "rake," because such men are thrilling. A virtuous husband's stability and disrespect for weakness, on the other hand, may be viewed as unappealing. But the rake's character is lacking in sense, as well as principles: he will introduce his wife to misery, bad habits, and the dangerous morals of a life based on titillation.

Chapter VII: Modesty—Comprehensively Considered and Not as a Sexual Virtue

Modesty is a virtue, the author claims, to be sought by both men and women. It is not a performance piece enacted by women to prove they are sweet, innocent, and feminine. Nor does modesty sprout from sexual avoidance. It is, rather, the "child of reason," and is a behavior steeped in "respect for man, as man, is the foundation of every noble sentiment."

Wollstonecraft begins this chapter by spoofing the flowery graces attributed to female modesty, but her assessment of the attribute is serious. She defends it as the most enhancing virtue because it "teaches a man not to think of himself more highly than he ought to think," while yet not humbling or debasing himself. Personal reserve, not blushes, gives rise to modesty. In relationships, modesty thrives not on sensibility but on affection. And if women truly wish to learn it, they must pursue knowledge of the world, for modesty lives "in close union with humanity."

Chapter VIII: Mortality Undermined by Sexual Notions of the Importance of a Good Reputation

Wollstonecraft once again compares courtiers and women in general as both having to appear appealing to those they depend on. Not concerned with truly moral behavior,

it is the eye of man that they have been taught to dread—and if they can lull their Argus to sleep, they seldom think of heaven or themselves, because their reputation is safe; and it is reputation, not chastity and all its fair train, that they are employed to keep free from spot, not as a virtue, but to preserve their station in the world.

The author tells tales of women of high reputation who have carried out clandestine intrigues. She laments the social system that creates "female depravity" and deception in sexual matters. This occurs due to the double standard that says women who are unchaste can never again be "respectable," while men are admired for having affairs. She also critiques those "like the Pharisees" who seek to fool others with their high reputations, but whose laudable actions are only for show. In reality, God reads all human hearts, so people are wise not to judge one another. All humans harbor vice and mistakes, but from these they can learn to reason, improve, and sympathize. She urges married women to avoid carnal "intemperance" because men and women marry, primarily, to parent the young and produce virtue. Virtue should be respected for its own sake, not as a sign of a clean reputation.

Chapter IX: Of the Pernicious Effects Which Arise from the Unnatural Distinctions Established in Society

As a pearl grows within an oyster, virtue cannot develop without the friction that people encounter daily while carrying out private and public duties. One of the basic duties that assists the growth of virtue is earning a living. While those who inherit wealth may be cushioned from need, and thus free to indulge in vanities and titillations, they lack a vital element that would allow them to perfect their characters. Wollstonecraft asserts that women who inherit wealth are even more handicapped in character than men; for male heirs can still enter public life as soldiers or statesmen, while rich women are still restricted to a domestic existence. These problems would be lessened if there were more equality of wealth and of rank in society, but women, Wollstonecraft asserts, will never develop their highest potentials until they take up a career.

Why should they assist, Wollstonecraft asks, becoming nurses rather than doctors? Why not prepare to become businesswomen, or for a post in politics? Why think small? Dedicated motherhood and full responsibility for the household should also be the task of women, wealthy or not. Instead, they are encouraged to be "the wanton solace of men" fit only for "frothy pleasure." In an abrupt rhetorical move, Wollstonecraft asks enlightened males to help women—now vain and slavishly obedient—to "snap [their] chains" and become motivated to seek "respectable" duties. She laments how few women of economic privilege are willing to, on their own initiative, seek the path of enlightenment: "Proud of their weakness . . . they must always be protected, guarded from care, and all the rough toils that dignify the mind." They are not willing to "resign the privileges of rank and sex for the privileges of humanity."

Chapter X: Parental Affection

In this chapter, Wollstonecraft identifies parental affection as the appropriate foundation for parental power. She notes that parents can use their position to impose the duty of obedience on their offspring, extending a "despotic stretch of power." She warns that women must be strong, enlightened parents if they hope to raise intelligent and dutiful children, and that "meek wives are, in general, foolish mothers." Mothers who shirk their motherly responsibilities by sending their children to a wetnurse and then to a boarding school have no right to expect loyalty from their adult children, she contends: "they who do their duty by proxy should not murmur if they miss the reward of duty—parental affection produces filial duty."

Chapter XI: Duty to Parents

Parents should raise their children to be rational, independent people, because such children will have the most devotion to their own parents, just as they become superior parents of superior children themselves. Daughters trained to be obedient to their parents are ready to become obedient wives, but not good mothers, she explains. Girls taught to be so obedient that they "never think of consulting their inclination ... become adulteresses, and neglect the education of their children." The author believes that parents' attitudes toward their children should be as follows:

> It is your interest to obey me till you can judge for yourself; ... but when your mind arrives at maturity, you must only obey me, or rather respect my opinions, so far as they coincide with the light that is breaking in your own mind.

Chapter XII: On National Education

From Plato's time, Western philosophers have speculated about the sort of education that might create citizens who would build the ideal nation-state. In this pivotal chapter, Wollstonecraft outlines her own National Education program for Britain, recommending that children of both sexes should learn together. The author is strongly opposed to boarding schools, which she feels teach vice, folly, arbitrary direction, insincerity, debauchery, and "the system of tyranny and abject slavery which is established among the [students], to say nothing of the slavery of forms, which makes religion less than a farce." She admires day schooling because it can foster affection within the family—an affection that can expand into warmth for all humankind. Day schools allow students to live at home and develop through family relations, but also to mix with their peers of both sexes, to learn to "begin to think." Although she is personally against the inequities of marriage, Wollstonecraft, considering her less-radical audience ("the fear of innovation, in this country, extends to every thing"), urges a shared male-female curriculum and coeducation, because:

> If marriage be the cement of society, mankind should all be educated after the same model, or the intercourse of the sexes will never deserve the name of fellowship, nor will women ever fulfil [*sic*] the peculiar duties of their sex, till they become enlightened citizens ... [and] are prepared to be [men's] companions rather than their mistresses.

Wollstonecraft declares that a state of war exists between the sexes. Both employ cunning and wiles to get what they want from the other. Women, in the political sense, are slaves, for women must gain their power indirectly and "are debased by their exertions to obtain illicit sway." In order to rectify this, women must be educated. A day school coed environment, "free and open to all classes" and run by the government to avoid the caprices of patrons, would raise girls to become competent mothers, wise citizens, and participants in public governance. Until the age of nine both genders' physical development would be prioritized. A wide range of subjects would be studied, but "these pursuits should never encroach on gymnastic plays in the open air."

Past the age of nine, students would be separated according to earning expectations. Boys and girls from the lower classes would study together in the morning, but in the afternoon girls would attend classes in such fields as sewing and weaving while boys might study mechanics, or something similar. The children of the upper classes would study subject matter appropriate to professional careers and intellectual interests. The author addresses the fears of her audience that boys and girls might become romantically involved. Early marriage is actually a good thing, says Wollstonecraft, but she concedes that arranged marriage will still remain custom, whether or not students take likings to each other. Day schools will be more "moral" than boarding schools are, at any rate.

Wollstonecraft's proposal specifies youth should be educated until the age of majority (eighteen years old) and that courses for non-vocational students should develop the reflective abilities needed to form sound judgments. Physical development must grow apace; hence dancing, music, and drawing will be offered. Ethics also receive attention: kindness to animals and sensitivity to social underlings are considered essential. From various angles, throughout the discussion of her educational proposal, Wollstonecraft returns to the dishonest wiles and devious ways through which uneducated women have had to try to fill needs and desires. She compares such nonvirtuous paths to the options that reasoning women can choose. Morally educated women will no longer be "vile and foolish"; at school they will learn to be friends to both women and men. They will become more interesting conversationalists and more appealing to men, by acquiring the virtue and sense that can "give a human appearance to an animal appetite." These secondary enticements are meant to appeal for support for national co-educational schools, so that women will be allowed "to participate [in] the inherent rights of mankind."

Not for the first time, the author confronts the general societal fear that an educated woman will no longer be fit for mothering—considered her natural obligation. Wollstonecraft tries to allay this fear with anecdotes from her own observation and experience. She herself has engaged with the world, tested what she found against her education, and arrived at new, moral, solutions.

Chapter XIII: Some Instances of the Folly Which the Ignorance of Women Generates; with Concluding Reflections on the Moral Improvement That a Revolution in Female Manners Might Naturally Be Expected to Produce

In this final chapter, the author examines the generally low state of character that women of quality now exhibit, repeating that a wise education would revolutionize their ways of seeing and being. The tone of her opening is harsh and direct: she accuses women of sin, weakness, and folly. But these flaws exist because men have worked to impel and maintain them. The first "folly" she addresses relates to the "fashionable deception" of paying fortune-tellers to read the future. If they knew how to reason, she explains, women would understand that it is not a human's place to try to comprehend the incomprehensible, nor second-guess divine will.

The second "feminine weakness of character" discussed is a "sentimental" twist of mind, which is constantly reignited by reading romantic novels. The fondness for novels should be corrected, because they caricature the human race. A preference for histories, essays, and moral discussions should slowly be introduced. Wollstonecraft looks once more at the manipulation of women's general desire to please. This is deformed into making females eager to obey. Next, the author states mildly that people worldwide, of both genders, enjoy dress as a form of self-expression. The problem with Western women who can afford it, she says, is that dressing well becomes a form of rivalry, in the great competition for superlative physical beauty.

Wollstonecraft asks then if women, not educated to be morally aware, are fit to raise their own young: for they are unstable and whimsical, and often model vanity, volatility, and servant abuse. She concludes this chapter, and *A Vindication of the Rights of Woman*, by projecting the middle- and upper-class woman, through an education that promotes her interests in gaining genuine virtue and wisdom beyond the domestic sphere, into the public sector—where both her liberty and her responsibilities lie. "Private duties," the author concludes, "are never properly fulfilled unless . . . understanding enlarges the heart; and . . . public virtue is only an aggregate of private." All the faults of women, so comprehensively discussed up till now in the book, are "the natural consequence of their

Children in a wagon in a parade of suffragettes The Library of Congress. George Grantham Bain Collection.

education and station in society." Therefore, if their education and station are improved, women will rise from their vices and folly to virtue and wisdom. Conversely, if enlightened men refuse to allow women to become their partners in reason, they must bear responsibility for being slave masters.

THEMES

Gender

A Vindication of the Rights of Woman dismisses the Eve of the Bible and of Milton's *Paradise Lost* as the kind of woman patriarchy longs for. (In a patriarchy, society is organized around male supremacy, the dependence of wives and children on fathers, and legal descent/inheritance through the male line. In such a setup, males control most social power.) According

to Wollstonecraft, the myths and behaviors of males in Western societies (especially the rich) produce power relationships that squeeze women into a desired mold, preventing them from developing their full human potential. Men are able to establish patriarchies even in relatively liberal Western societies through laws and customs, lack of access for women to public spheres like politics and education, and female economic dependence.

Gender is the set of behavioral, cultural, and psychological qualities typically associated with a sex (sex being determined by biological evidence). For example, as Wollstonecraft points out, females were encouraged to behave with childlike obedience, docility, gentleness, and patience, and to exhibit sexual innocence through modesty (or as Wollstonecraft charges, ignorance). Of course, poor and working-class women had to toil beside men of their class to survive, so they had little time to spend on such elegant behaviors. The author writes that, culturally, females were expected to demonstrate vanity, interests in clothes and adornments, and a "spaniel-like affection" for the men in their world. Physically, they were to cultivate bodily weakness (a sign of delicacy) and carry the burden of extreme emotion—which caused their judgments to be based on prejudice, and made them both unstable mothers and easy victims.

Wollstonecraft acknowledges that the women of her social class have been taught to fulfill the twisted gender expectations, which serve the patriarchy well. These women have become adept at manipulating their way through a society that would not let them live as equals. In addition to displaying subservient qualities, they are competitive, selfish, flirtatious, and insincere as they struggle to win male attention. They hide behind appearances in order to survive, and take their shallow pleasures as they can. Such is the design of patriarchy:

> Strengthen the female mind by enlarging it, and there will be an end to blind obedience; but, as blind obedience is ever sought for by power, tyrants and sensualists are in the right when they endeavor to keep women in the dark, because the former only want slaves, and the latter a play-thing.

If women are given a full, equal education, claims the author, they will not only be able to support themselves through a career in times of need, but will occupy their minds with important matters. They will become more interesting partners in marriage (for the best marriage is a life-long friendship—the sensual aspect of love inevitably fades) and be able to perfect their souls.

It is hard to assess the vision and courage of a woman who, in 1792, wrote, "Is one half of the human species, like the poor African, to be subject to prejudices that brutalize them?" Repeatedly in *A Vindication of the Rights of Woman*, Wollstonecraft alludes to the pampered slave position of British women, underscoring the assertion that the affluent men who oppress the slaves are as degraded by the oppression as the slaves themselves. Equating women to slaves in an era that was becoming increasingly abolitionist may have, in fact, aided in Wollstonecraft's argument.

Sexuality

Gender is naturalized (made to seem part of what creation intended) by rooting it partly in sexuality. Wollstonecraft tries to tackle aspects of gendered sexuality by touching on the double standard that condemns seduced women, while rewarding male seducers. In an age when few career options existed for well-bred women, she asks readers to reconsider financial and ethical pressures that forced women into the "refuge" of prostitution in order to survive. She offers the solution of education to expand female career options. An entire chapter is dedicated to reconsidering modesty, which Wollstonecraft observes is not about a lowered gaze, or blushing to indicate one's worldly "innocence." Rather, it is a proper self-perspective in relation to one's gifts and one's social duties.

She addresses in various ways the rationale that females are hypersensual, easily tempted, overemotional beings; therefore men must control women's sexuality for their own good. Yet while Wollstonecraft chastises the male with no interest in his own chastity and calls him a "lustful prowler," she attests that good wives have the right to their husbands' caresses and urges parents not to teach daughters that the "common appetites" of human nature that women feel are immodest.

Wollstonecraft is writing to a heterosexual audience in the conservative eighteenth century. Many of her ideas about gender and sexuality are radical and liberal for the time, though she strives to reassure readers that a woman's best place is as wife and mother. It is in these roles (rooted in parental friendship and equality) that she hopes women will best develop virtue, knowledge, and purpose.

Social Stigma

Wollstonecraft warns her readers that the perks of rank and privilege that the coddled "fair defect" enjoys will have to be given up in favor of the deep pleasures of reason. She addresses the general fear (promoted for another century) that "a sensible woman" who engages in such pursuits for reason and knowledge may be stigmatized as "an unnatural mother." She freely admits that rationality in women will often induce the "severest censure." But in the end, if women are to rise above a slave mentality, they—and the good men who support them—must press toward competence and freedom.

HISTORICAL OVERVIEW

Historical Philosophies on Women

Aristotle predated the Christian West, but was the most esteemed of its philosophers from the Middle Ages to the Enlightenment. He contended that God created males with more life force and heat than females. In procreation, therefore, males were the agents of life, while females merely furnished growth materials. Male energy always intended to reproduce itself, but sometimes something went wrong. Then, because of a defect or weakness, a female was conceived (hence Wollstonecraft's reference to women as not being merely "fair defects").

Aristotle announced *Femina est mas occasionatus*—the female is an accident. He took the implications of the "defect" in female nature further, to examine its social implications. He claimed that whenever humans engaged in politics, the soul's qualities were called into play, and women's souls were not equipped for the public sphere. Aristotle repeatedly likened women to slaves, in that both groups were found to be lacking and needed control by men. Therefore, he deduced, a woman could not make sound judgments. She could neither direct nor lead people, and she lacked virtue, too. Aristotle insisted the courage in a man's soul was best seen when he commanded, while the courage in the inferior soul of a woman was best seen when she obeyed.

The early Christian philosophers who developed their own interpretations of what God intended drew heavily on Aristotle. With subtle refinements and changes, thinkers like Augustine, Tertullian, and Thomas Aquinas also concluded that women had not been created equal to men. These beliefs were commonplace in Wollstonecraft's day, enforced by both religion and the state. They even continue to find adherents in some areas of the modern world.

The Enlightenment

The Enlightenment was an eighteenth-century intellectual movement in Western Europe and North America. Many events, such as the rise of a large middle class, exposure to various civilizations as a result of colonialism, and the increasing gap between rich (nobles) and poor (peasants), helped it develop. In the words of humanist scholar Paul Brians in "The Enlightenment":

> [Enlightenment philosophers] believed that human reason could be used to combat ignorance, superstition, and tyranny and to build a better world. Their principal targets were religion ... and the domination of society by a hereditary aristocracy.

Enlightenment thinkers believed that people, through hard work and personal merit, could use their scientific reason to improve their lot in life, rather than obeying church or state laws. Brians writes that "individualism, freedom and change replaced community, authority, and tradition as core European values." In fact, human beings' essential rights of liberty, and an ongoing quest to keep on bettering their lives, became the international hot topic. The main seats of Enlightenment thought were Paris and London, although the American colonies contributed actively, too. In Europe, perhaps the two most revered and influential thinkers for enlightened social change were Voltaire and Jean-Jacques Rousseau. Voltaire hoped that educated aristocrats could leave behind despotism and dogma. Rousseau, however, distrusted the upper classes. He pinned his hopes on an educated middle class, stating that the moment of birth is when one becomes a citizen, and as such, one should exercise that duty immediately. In his still-studied book *Émile* (1762), Rousseau outlines the sort of education that could create a free man. He writes that nature and experience are part of the education that makes man whole.

Revolutionary Rights

More than a century before Wollstonecraft's birth, there was the British revolution of 1688. By 1690, King James II had been ousted from power along with his leading nobles. William of Orange, his Dutch son-in-law, was invited to ascend the throne after he accepted the English Bill of Rights (1689). These rights guaranteed free, fair elections; the right to free speech through debates in Parliament; and the need to obtain Parliament's consent before the king could levy a tax or maintain a standing army. This revolution was relatively bloodless, and although it fostered the growth of English democracy, it also left the rural and urban poor without recourse while allowing most aristocrats to retain their wealth.

Nearly a century later, the American Revolution (1775–1783), which rejected unfair taxation and with it the control of the British monarchy, served as a huge inspiration to Europeans discontented with their own hereditary governments. The American Declaration of Independence led off with a list of "inalienable rights" of men. A vibrant exchange of visits and ideas flowed between American and European philosophers from the 1770s onward. The successful revolution and establishment of self-rule in the New World inspired Europeans. Wollstonecraft refers to the American Revolution several times in *A Vindication of the Rights of Woman*.

The French Revolution (1789–1799) was in its fourth year when *A Vindication of the Rights of Woman* was published. This was to be the last year of its moderate phase. The values of the Enlightenment had chipped away at church authority and toppled the concept of the divine right of kings. No longer were people too intimidated to defy the lavish abuses of their hereditary rulers. Both the poor and the middle class (the bourgeoisie) objected to overwhelming taxes, high food prices, and enormous public debt. As a result, King Louis XVI convened the Estates-General for the first time in almost two centuries, but a faction of this emergency law-making body, drawn from commoners, low-ranking clergy, and a few nobles, rebelled and declared themselves a new National Assembly and vowed not to disband until a new French constitution had been written. The Assembly drafted a constitution in 1791 that created a limited (rather than absolute, divine-right) monarchy, with a legislature to be voted in by property-owning men. The Constitution started with the *Declaration of the Rights of Man and Citizen*.

Wollstonecraft wrote *A Vindication of the Rights of Woman* partly in response to what social activists on all sides of the question had said about the French Revolution. She critiques the remarks British conservative Edmund Burke made in *Reflections on the Revolution in France* (1790) and refers to Thomas Paine, the radical author of *The Rights of Man* (1791). She was also inspired by the French revolutionary Olympe de Gouges, who wrote *Declaration of the Rights of Women* in 1791. De Gouges, a Parisian playwright, objected to the status of women as passive citizens with restricted rights, no matter their class background. As historian Jenifer D. Clark notes in "Women in the French Revolution: the Failure of the Parisian Women's Movement in Relation to the Theories of Feminism of

Rousseau and Condorcet," de Gouges argued the need to fully endorse the "'natural, inalienable rights' of women"—including "wide job opportunities ... [and] schooling for girls." De Gouges also demanded free speech for women, and like Wollstonecraft, insisted "if the grounds for universal human rights are to be meaningful ... they must apply to all sentient beings without exception" (quoted in Clark).

CRITICAL OVERVIEW

A Vindication of the Rights of Woman was first printed in 1792 by Joseph Johnson in London. Later that same year, it was reprinted in England and published in the United States and France. Heather E. Wallace, in "Sophie: Women's Education According to Rousseau and Wollstonecraft," reports, "Contemporary reactions ranged from shock to amusement to enthusiasm." The treatise was indeed shocking and revolutionary, and while some forward thinkers embraced and even tried to adopt its principles, the most famous conservatives of the day, such as Horace Walpole and Hannah More, considered it dangerous to social order. On the other hand, though, several famous humanists applauded the book, and the American advocates of "Republican Motherhood" echoed Wollstonecraft's argument that mothers of able citizens needed to be educated in order to parent well.

A Vindication of the Rights of Woman was printed in 1796 for the last time for almost fifty years. William Godwin, Wollstonecraft's widower, produced the infamous *Memoirs of the Author of the Vindication of the Rights of Woman* in 1798. Godwin revealed intimate details of his wife's emotional and sexual behavior. Soon the world knew that she had lovers, bore an illegitimate child, and attempted suicide. This information clouded the public's opinion of Wollstonecraft, and according to Janet Todd in "Mary Wollstonecraft: A 'Speculative and Dissenting Spirit,'" she became "hugely reviled as a 'prostitute' and 'unsex'd female.'" In a subtle yet also damaging way, Godwin reinforced the gender roles his wife had railed against, claiming the voice of reason for himself, while attributing a highly passionate sensibility to Wollstonecraft.

MEDIA
ADAPTATIONS

In 1986, Knowledge Products of Boston released a two-cassette set of Wollstonecraft's *A Vindication of the Rights of Woman* along with *On Liberty* by John Stuart Mills. Scripted by Wendy McElroy and narrated by Craig Deitschman, with voice characterizations by several guest readers. It was re-released in 2006.

Selections from *A Vindication of the Rights of Woman* read by Shirley Williams appear on the cassette entitled *Classic Politics*, produced by Politico's Media in 2000.

British media outlet ITV produced twelve-part miniseries, including a segment on *A Vindication of the Rights of Woman*, in 2006. The program, authored and presented by Melvyn Bragg, examines twelve English-language books Bragg believes have changed the world.

Public outcry was intense. Wollstonecraft was denounced as a monster, a prostitute, and as philosopher Karen Green writes in "For Wollstonecraft (Obituary)," a "hyena in petticoats." Writing on the 1997 publication of her collected works, Green notes, "Like other women thinkers, her works have languished in relative obscurity for want of ... institutional support." Victorian feminists tried to distance themselves from Wollstonecraft because of her scandalous personal life. Dr. Barbara Caine, in "Victorian Feminism and the Ghost of Mary Wollstonecraft," tells readers that while Wollstonecraft's work went unacknowledged, her life "served as a constant and sometimes unwelcome reminder of the ways in which personal rebellion and feminist commitment were connected" in the conservative mind. Because Victorian feminists, desperately seeking the vote, were rarely wealthy or high wage earners, they could not afford to alienate male mentors. It was crucial to their struggle to uphold the image of a female voter who would be sober, chaste, nurturing, and unthreatening.

The few Victorian feminists who mentioned Wollstonecraft were dismissive (her interests were too narrow; her personal life denied her philosophy, etc.). But Caine reports that George Eliot did write an essay for *The Leader* in 1855 that supported *A Vindication of the Rights of Woman*. Caine relays Eliot's feelings about the book:

> In some quarters a vague prejudice against the *Rights of Woman* as in some way or other a reprehensible book, but readers who go to it with this impression will be surprised to find it eminently serious [and] severely moral.... [with its author exhibiting] the brave bearing of a strong and truthful nature, the beating of a loving woman's heart.

However, until the 1890s, when Wollstonecraft's embrace of social "duty" was rediscovered, *A Vindication of the Rights of Woman* was abandoned by feminists, despite its courageous ideas. Not until the 1920s, with women's suffrage and concerns about female economic and cultural oppression once again in the foreground, was Wollstonecraft's unraveling of the double moral standard, with its attendant evils, taken to heart. Since then, several waves of modern feminists have identified with a variety of her concerns, finding her work ahead of its time and immense in its applications. Scholars in a number of fields are currently plumbing *A Vindication of the Rights of Woman* to extract connections Wollstonecraft made between gender and racial oppression; gender and class inequities; critiques of the traditional nuclear family; links between state and domestic tyranny; and other pertinent topics. As Green notes, in addition to holding its own as the fundamental Western feminist text, *A Vindication of the Rights of Woman* deserves to be "seriously studied as one of the foundational political texts of modern democratic thought."

CRITICISM

Barbara Taylor

In the following excerpt, Taylor writes about why feminists, from Wollstonecraft's time to today, have feared romantic love. While noting some startling dangers that have not changed much over time, she repeats Wollstonecraft's words:

"Suppressing the demands of the heart … is no liberation."

Loving men, feminists have argued, women become bound to the oppressor by the ties of their own hearts; refusing that love, heterosexual feminists have often disavowed desire tout court—a repudiation whose costs are felt in both their lives and politics. The conundrum is as old as feminism itself.

In 1792 Mary Wollstonecraft published *A Vindication of the Rights of Woman*, the founding text of modern western feminism.

If one reads Wollstonecraft's *Rights of Woman* on its own, the impression is of a dour puritanism reminiscent of today's moral conservatives. Sexual feelings, she argues, are "bestial" and "degraded", and those who indulge in them are "debauched." Men are particularly condemned for their "animal lust", while women are chastised for romantic sentimentalism. Outside marriage, she claims, erotic passion is particularly invidious in its effects on women, who become the mere sexual "playthings" of men. But even inside marriage sexual lust erodes domestic morality and encourages adultery. "In order to fulfil the duties of life … which form the moral character, a master and mistress of a family ought not to continue to love each other with passion. I mean to say that they ought not to indulge those emotions which distrub the order of society …"

This highly censorious view of heterosexual love was to cast a long shadow over Wollstonecraft's feminist successors.

But to see Wollstonecraft and the feminist tradition that succeeded her as eternally locked into an anti-male, anti-sexual stance is much too simple. The anxiety about erotic love is certainly there, but so also—as voiced in Wollstonecraft's letters and fiction—is the passionate desire for what feminists have seen as an authentic form of female loving, one based on mutual affection and respect and, above all, on genuine equality. "Perfect love and perfect trust have never yet existed except between equals," as Wollstonecraft's great admirer, the suffragist Elizabeth Wolstenholme Elmy, quoted at her readers in 1897, while a century earlier Wollstonecraft herself provided a model for such a "perfect" union. Once she had recovered from Imlay, she became the lover of England's best-known radical philosopher, William Godwin. She and Godwin argued about politics

and religion, maintained separate homes (even after they finally wed), and had great sex: "When the heart and reason accord there is no flying from voluptuous sensations, I find, do what a woman can—Can a philosopher do more?" (13 September 1796).

These tensions in the relationship between "heart and reason" are at the centre of the feminist project as Wollstonecraft helped to define it. For Wollstonecraft herself, their resolution was short-lived: she died only a year after she and Godwin became lovers. Nonetheless, for nearly two centuries her reputation as a theorist was overshadowed by her sexual history, which was construed as (in the words of the suffragist Millicent Garrett Fawcett) "irregular relations" which "sickened" the feminist mind. The overtly anti-erotic message of the *Rights of Woman* was largely forgotten, as its author came to symbolise uncontrolled female libidinism. Feminist interpretations of her life became a barometer of their attitudes toward sexual love.

In 200 years, a lot has changed; a lot hasn't. For women of Wollstonecraft's day, and for more than 150 years afterwards, it was impossible to think about heterosexual love apart from sexual reproduction. Women's vulnerability—to men who might impregnate them, desert them, infect them with venereal disease—was enormous, as were the dangers of childbirth (Wollstonecraft, like so many women, died of complications following childbirth). The celebration of celibate unions found in much feminist writing, "marriages of true minds" involving only minimal sexual contact, needs to be seen in this context, as well as in terms of the dehumanising attitudes toward women prevalent among 18th- and 19th-century male sexual libertarians.

Two centuries later, both the practicalities and attitudes have changed: or have they? Fear of pregnancy, fear of Aids, fear of establishing families in an economic depression—the price for uninhibited passion can be very high. Even in the swinging sixties the feminist voice was a cautionary one, reminding women of these potential costs. Here is one latter-day Mary Wollstonecraft, Germaine Greer, in *The Female Eunuch*: "Women must recognise in the cheap ideology of being in love the essential persuasion to take an irrational and self-destructive step … Sexual religion is the opiate of the supermenial." Libertarian radicals such as Greer might display a sexual flamboyance unimaginable in previous phases of feminism, but always with an anxious eye out for potential pain, humiliation, degradation. Poised between the recognition of women's own erotic desires and the culture that still demeans and exploits them, feminists tread carefully on love's wilder shores.

Suppressing the demands of the heart, as Wollstonecraft herself had discovered, is no liberation. Expecting those demands to be met easily, without pain or conflict, is empty utopianism. As another generation of Wollstonecraft's daughters, that's one difficult lesson we've begun to learn.

Source: Barbara Taylor, "Love and Trouble (Feminists Who Love Men)," in *New Statesman & Society*, Vol. 6, No. 239, February 12, 1993, pp. 35–36.

Iain Murray

In the following excerpt, Murray refutes Wollstonecraft's claim that "the mind has no sex." Building his case on biological determinism, he asserts that males think more, especially about concrete problems; while females exhibit a more "empathetic" brain type.

Two centuries ago, protofeminist Mary Wollstonecraft wrote a treatise entitled "*A Vindication of the Rights of Woman*" in which she theorized that men and women are essentially the same. The roles they play, she suggested, are merely social constructs. The buzz phrase since then has been that "the mind has no sex."

But there is growing scientific evidence that the mind does have a sex, and that other unexpected components of the body have a sex as well. There are significant differences between men and women in their brains and genes as well.

There are two strands to this data: animal research and human research. Among animals, it seems to be testosterone that is associated with "male" behavior.

Much the same is true in humans. One study Sullivan cited showed that men (and women) with high testosterone levels "experienced more arousal and tension than those low in testosterone... They spent more time thinking, especially about concrete problems in the immediate present. They wanted to get things done and felt frustrated when they could not." Human studies show that our testosterone levels rise in response to confrontation and sexual situations. Athletes' testosterone rises in competition, and it remains high in the event of victory, but lowers in defeat. The same is true, interestingly, of the fans following the sport.

All this holds true for both men and women. The crucial difference is that men have 250 to 1,000 nanograms of testosterone per deciliter of blood plasma, while women have 15 to 70. Testosterone is crucial in making men men— literally. It is an infusion of testosterone around six weeks after conception that makes an embryo male (the default sex for humanity is female), and it is a further rush at puberty that lowers male voices, produces body hair and builds muscles. Testosterone is clearly associated with aggression and risk-taking.

We know, however, that testosterone levels can be influenced by the social environment. An Emory University study found that an alpha-male monkey had, as expected, high testosterone levels, but that placing him in an environment with hostile females lowered his testosterone levels to those of submissive males. His initially high testosterone levels did not protect him or maintain his dominance. So while testosterone is important, it does not seem to be the final determining factor in what makes men and women different.

What about genetics, then? Males possess a Y chromosome, which women do not. The role of genetics in sex is much deeper than that, though. It is now generally accepted, for instance, that it is the father's genes that build the placenta. This is one aspect of a mysterious process known as "imprinting," whereby the genes of placental mammals seem to remember from which parent they come. This is why, so far, it has proved very difficult to create a functioning embryo from the genes of "parents" of the same sex (and why it proved so difficult to create a viable mammalian clone).

One of the most interesting aspects of imprinting is that, in mice, there is a gene that determines "good" motherhood. A female mouse who fails to have the gene imprinted is perfectly normal except that she will build a poor nest, allow her pups to wander off, and fail to keep them clean. Her pups, not surprisingly, usually die. The responsible gene is inherited from the father. The mother's gene never imprints.

Something similar may apply to humans. A study by researchers from the Institute of Child

Health in London looked at "Turner's Syndrome" girls, who are missing the paternal X chromosome. These girls scored lower on recognizing other people's feelings, realizing the effect of their behavior on others, obeying commands, and interacting socially. They acted like geeky men.

Simon Baron-Cohen, a psychiatrist at Cambridge University, is one of the world's leading experts on autism, which affects boys more than girls by a factor of eight to one. Autistic children can be extremely withdrawn, but they are not stupid. Many are exception ally good at certain tasks, generally involving systematizing. They are, however, exceptionally bad—to the point of being unable to function in society—at tasks that involve empathizing with others (just like the Turner's Syndrome girls).

Baron-Cohen has concluded that most people have a mixture of brain types: S for systematizing and E for empathizing. Men, however, are much more likely to lean toward the S-type brain, and women toward the E-type. In his new book *The Essential Difference: The Truth about the Male and Female Brain*, Baron-Cohen concludes that autism is an example of the "extreme male brain." He provides evidence that sex differences in brain types show up again and again in tests, even in babies as young as one day old.

It should be stressed that not all men have male brains, and not all women have female brains. We are talking about general patterns here. In the case of hormones, genes, and brain architecture there is clear evidence that nature tends in different directions for men and women, but obviously individuals vary. And the way a person is raised—the nurture in addition to nature—plays a role in his or her sexual identity as well.

But most often, nature will win out.

And then there are the genetic revelations. Scientists have found that the Y chromosome is not as small and stunted as previously believed. Humans and chimpanzees famously share 98.5 percent of the same DNA. Judging by the new scientific discoveries, it appears that men and women differ genetically by up to 2 percent. So, genetically speaking, a man is as much like a woman as he is like a chimpanzee.

Source: Iain Murray, "The New Science of Sex," in *The American Enterprise*, Vol. 14, No. 6, September 2003, pp. 34–35.

SOURCES

Brians, Paul, "The Enlightenment," *Washington State University*, www.wsu.edu (May 18, 2000).

Caine, Barbara, "Victorian Feminism and the Ghost of Mary Wollstonecraft," in *Women's Writings*, Vol. 4, No. 2, 1997, pp. 261–75.

Clark, Jenifer D., "Women in the French Revolution: The Failure of the Parisian Women's Movement in Relation to the Theories of Feminism of Rousseau and Condorcet," in the *Concord Review*, Vol. 7, 1992, pp. 115–27.

Green, Karen, "For Wollstonecraft (Obituary)," in *Hypatia*, Vol. 12, No. 4, Fall 1997, pp. ix–x.

Murray, Iain, "The New Science of Sex," in *The American Enterprise* Vol. 14, No. 6, September 2003, pp. 34–35.

Todd, Janet, "Mary Wollstonecraft: A 'Speculative and Dissenting Spirit,'" *British Broadcasting Association*, www.bbc.co.uk/history/society_culture/protest_reform/wollstonecraft_01.shtml (April 19, 2002).

Wallace, Heather E., "Sophie: Woman's Education According to Rousseau and Wollstonecraft," *Georgetown University*, www.georgetown.edu/faculty/irvinem/english016/franken/sophie.txt (January 20, 2000).

Wollstonecraft, Mary, *A Vindication of the Rights of Woman*, in *A Vindication of the Rights of Men, A Vindication of the Rights of Woman, An Historical and Moral View of the French Revolution*, Oxford University Press, 1999, originally published in 1792.

"What You Pawn I Will Redeem"

SHERMAN ALEXIE

2003

"What You Pawn I Will Redeem," first published in the April 2003 issue of *The New Yorker* magazine, is Sherman Alexie's contemporary take on the classic quest tale. The main character, Jackson Jackson, embarks on a journey to reclaim his grandmother's stolen powwow regalia, a quest that becomes a journey toward fulfillment and personal identity. Along the way, Jackson's interactions with friends and strangers help fill in the details of his life and his character. As a homeless Spokane Indian far from home and without family, Jackson's mission to reclaim his family heirloom becomes a link to his past, his future, and his cultural identity.

Alexie creates a world in which Jackson, who describes himself as "a Spokane Indian boy, an Interior Salish," must come to terms with his literal and figurative homelessness, despite the fact that his "people have lived within a one-hundred-mile radius of Spokane, Washington, for at least ten thousand years." The reader cannot ignore Jackson's candid references to the history of violence, oppression, and displacement that have long since characterized the indigenous experience in America. Yet Jackson's lighthearted wit and sharp sense of humor make him less like an object of pity, and more reminiscent of the Shakespearean fool—one whose keen observations, although often dismissed as the mere ramblings of an incompetent, somehow capture the essence of truth as it is experienced within the narrative.

> I AM LIVING PROOF OF THE HORRIBLE DAMAGE
> THAT COLONIALISM HAS DONE TO US SKINS. BUT
> I'M NOT GOING TO LET YOU KNOW HOW SCARED I
> SOMETIMES GET OF HISTORY AND ITS WAYS."

Jackson is a generous character, embodying his own assertion that "Indians are great story-tellers." He constantly struggles to assert his own identity in terms of his "Indian-ness" without falling into the pitfalls of stereotyping. He is comfortable making declarations like "it's an Indian thing," while also being capable of explaining the subtleties and cultural differences between Indian tribes. The story has a simple structure and a somewhat predictable outcome, but Alexie relies on the strength of Jackson's character to pull the reader along on his adventure. As Ann Patchett, a 2005 O. Henry Prize Juror, remarks in her essay explaining why she picked "What You Pawn I Will Redeem" to be distinguished as a *Juror Favorite*, "Sherman Alexie is in love with his homeless Spokane Indian narrator and so he simply steps aside to let his character have every inch of the stage."

Thematically, "What You Pawn I Will Redeem" is Alexie's attempt to play with and subvert the common motifs of the "lone Indian" and the "noble savage" that pervade much of American literature. Alexie goes beyond the stock images of Native Americans in his portrayal of Jackson and allows the character to develop a voice beyond his cultural caricature into that of an individual. Although Jackson's interactions with white men during the course of the story are pivotal, they echo with unfulfilled treaties, broken promises, and the resultant landlessness of the Native American. "What You Pawn I Will Redeem" appears as part of a collection of nine short stories, *Ten Little Indians* (2003).

PLOT SUMMARY

"What You Pawn I Will Redeem" is the story of a financially strapped Spokane Indian man faced with the task of coming up with nearly

BIOGRAPHY

SHERMAN ALEXIE

Sherman Joseph Alexie Jr. was born in Spokane, Washington, on October 7, 1966, to Sherman Joseph, a Coeur d'Alene Indian, and Lillian Agnes Cox, a Spokane Indian. He grew up on the Spokane Indian Reservation. As an infant, he was diagnosed with hydrocephalus, an abnormal swelling of the brain due to excess fluid, and was not expected to survive to adulthood. At six months, he had surgery to correct the problem, but his head remained enlarged. This caused him to isolate himself from others as a child. Alexie turned to books to escape the poverty and alcoholism of the reservation, and by age twelve he had read all of the books at the Wellpinit School Library. When Alexie finished Washington State University, he was one of the first members of his tribe to graduate from college.

Much of Alexie's writing focuses on reshaping the idea of the Native American within the context of the mainstream American imagination, and he draws inspiration from his youth spent on the reservation. Alexie's unromantic depictions of reservation life and the highly politicized nature of his writing have made him a controversial figure in contemporary American literature. Other works by Alexie include the short story collection *The Lone Ranger and Tonto Fistfight in Heaven* (1993), the novel *Indian Killer* (1996), and the screenplay for *Smoke Signals* (1999).

one thousand dollars in twenty-four hours in order to reclaim his grandmother's stolen pow-wow attire from a pawnshop. The story takes place in Seattle over the course of one day, and is narrated by the central character, Jackson Jackson.

Jackson introduces himself to the reader by telling of his move twenty-three years ago from

Spokane to Seattle to go to college, where he "flunked out within two semesters, worked various blue- and bluer-collar jobs for many years, married two or three times, fathered two or three kids, and then went crazy." Jackson then introduces the people he hangs out with on the street, his "teammates" Rose of Sharon and Junior, both also Indians. The three spend the morning panhandling in front of Pike Place Market and earn five dollars, which they promptly decide to spend on a bottle of liquor. On their way to 7-Eleven, the group passes a pawnshop, and Jackson immediately recognizes his grandmother's powwow regalia hanging in the display window. He had only seen the regalia in photos because it was stolen fifty years ago, but he knows it is hers. The group goes into the shop to speak to the owner about getting the stolen regalia back.

In order to convince the pawnshop owner the regalia is his grandmother's, Jackson tells the pawnbroker to search for a yellow bead hidden somewhere on the costume. He explains that "Indian people sew flaws into their powwow regalia" because "they don't want to be perfect." After some searching, they come upon the single yellow bead hidden beneath the armpit. The pawnbroker feels bad about the situation, but he does not want to give the regalia away because he just paid one thousand dollars for it. Jackson considers the white pawnbroker's reaction to the situation, saying, "He sounded sad about that. Like he was sorry for taking advantage of our disadvantages." Rose of Sharon and Junior suggest going to the police, but Jackson wants to be fair to the pawnbroker. The pawnbroker offers to sell the stolen regalia to Jackson for nine hundred and ninety-nine dollars, but only if Jackson can return with the money by noon the following day. The shop owner even gives Jackson twenty dollars to start him on his quest.

At 1:00 P.M., the friends stop at 7-Eleven and spend all of the cash on "three bottles of imagination" to help them think of how to raise the rest of the money. Jackson and Junior fall asleep in an alley, and then they awake, Rose of Sharon is gone. Jackson says he hears later she has gone back to live with her sister on the reservation. Junior is still passed out, so Jackson decides to set off by himself. His mission leads him to the wharf, where he meets three Aleut cousins who are staring out at the bay,

crying. Jackson explains that many of the homeless Indians in Seattle come from Alaska. They work their way down the coast on fishing and transport boats, and end up "broke and broker . . . trying to find [their] way back to the boat and the frozen north." The men smell like salmon even though they have been away from their boat for eleven years. He asks to borrow some money, but they do not have any.

At three in the afternoon, Jackson checks in on Junior, who is still unconscious. He thinks about his grandmother, Agnes, who died of breast cancer when he was fourteen years old. He wonders if her cancer had in fact started to develop when someone stole her powwow regalia, and not when she was run over by a motorcycle, as his mother always suspected, or because of the uranium mine on the reservation, as his father had thought.

Inspired once again to restore a sense of order to his world, Jackson sets off. This time, he ends up at the Real Change newspaper office. Jackson knows Real Change's mission statement by heart—"Real Change is a multifaceted organization that publishes a newspaper, supports cultural products that empower the poor and homeless, and mobilizes the public around poverty issues"—because he sometimes sells their newspapers on the streets for money. To sell the newspapers, he must stay sober and Jackson confesses, "I'm not always good at staying sober." He must pay thirty cents per newspaper, but he can sell them for a dollar each. He asks the "Big Boss" at Real Change for 1,430 copies of the paper, the number he would have to sell to make a thousand dollars. Like the pawnbroker before, the Big Boss sympathizes with Jackson's situation but tells him it would be impossible to sell that many papers in one day. Plus, Jackson would need over four hundred dollars to buy the papers in the first place. After hearing Jackson's story about his grandmother's regalia, the Big Boss gives Jackson fifty free papers to sell.

Back at the wharf at 5:00 P.M., Jackson manages to sell five papers before giving up. He heads straight to McDonald's and spends the money he has just made on four cheeseburgers. Soon after eating them, he vomits on the sidewalk, noting, "As an alcoholic Indian with a busted stomach, I always hope I can keep enough food in my stomach to stay alive." Returning to check on Junior, he thinks again about his grandmother. He recalls a story she told him about her time as a nurse during World War II. He claims she told him this story when he was sixteen, yet he previously told the reader his grandmother died when he was fourteen. Finding Junior still passed out, he takes two dollars and fifty cents from him and heads toward the Korean grocery store in Pioneer Square.

At the store, Jackson talks to Kay, the owners' daughter. He spends the money he took from Junior on a fifty-cent cigar and two scratch-off lottery tickets that cost a dollar each, hoping to win the maximum prize of five hundred dollars per ticket, but his lottery tickets yield no cash prize. Luckily, though, one of them does win him another ticket, which turns out to be a hundred-dollar winner. He gives Kay twenty dollars of his winnings, saying "it's tribal. It's an Indian thing. When you win, you're supposed to share with your family." Kay protests that she is not his family, but he tells her that she is and she keeps the money. Upon returning to share the good news of his windfall, he discovers Junior is gone. He later hears that Junior "had hitchhiked down to Portland, Oregon, and died of exposure in an alley behind the Hilton Hotel."

"Lonely for Indians," Jackson takes his remaining eighty dollars to an Indian bar called Big Heart's, located in South Downtown. There he divides his money equally among the bar patrons, buying five whiskey shots for each of his Indian "cousins" in the bar. He explains, "I didn't know any of them, but Indians like to belong, so we all pretend to be cousins." He meets and drinks with Irene Muse, a Duwamish Indian, and Honey Boy, a bisexual Crow Indian. As the evening winds down, a very drunk Jackson is beaten up and kicked out of the bar. At four in the morning, he falls asleep on the train tracks, wrapped in a plastic tarp he has taken off a truck. Two hours later, he is awoken by Officer Williams, the "second-best cop" Jackson has ever known. Williams listens to the story of Jackson's grandmother's stolen regalia and the pawnbroker's deal. Williams chides Jackson for sleeping on the train tracks and takes him toward the detox facility so he can sober up. Jackson protests, playfully pointing out "that place is awful.... It's full of drunk Indians." In the police car on the way, the two men discuss Jackson's grandmother's death in 1972, his grandfather's murder, and the ironic

sense of humor Williams sees in Native Americans. To this, Jackson explains: "The two funniest tribes I've ever been around are Indians and Jews, so I guess that says something about the inherent humor of genocide."

Jackson tells Williams he reminds him of his grandfather, a tribal cop who "never arrested people. He took care of them." He explains the situation that led to his grandfather getting killed in the line of duty, saying, "We aren't like those crazy Sioux or Apache or any of those other warrior tribes.... we Spokane, we're passive, you know? We're mean with words." Having convinced Williams that the success of his quest is more important than detox, Williams offers Jackson thirty dollars toward the cost of the regalia, telling him, "I believe in what you believe.... I hope you can turn thirty bucks into a thousand somehow."

Eight o'clock finds Jackson back at the wharf with "those three Aleut men still wait[ing] on the wooden bench." Jackson convinces them to sing some ceremonial songs for him and they do. He says, "They sang about my grandmother and their grandmothers. They were lonely for the cold and the snow. I was lonely for everybody." Two hours later, the Aleuts finish their singing and Jackson thanks them. He offers to treat them all to breakfast at a diner called Mother's Kitchen and the Aleuts accept. At the restaurant, the men eat in silence and Jackson spends all but five dollars on the meal and the tip for the waitress.

At noon, Jackson and the Aleuts part company. He explains that later on he hears that "the Aleuts had waded into the saltwater near Dock 47 and disappeared. Some Indians said the Aleuts walked on the water and headed north. Other Indians saw the Aleuts drown." At his noon deadline, Jackson returns to the pawnshop. He initially has trouble finding it, circling block after block until he sees it "located in a space I swore it hadn't been filling up a few minutes before." He offers the owner his remaining five-dollar bill. The owner wants to know if Jackson worked hard for the money and when Jackson tells him yes, the owner closes his eyes and thinks. Then he steps into his back room and returns with the regalia. He holds it out to Jackson, but Jackson protests that he does not have the money, and that he wanted to "win it." The owner responds, "You did win it. Now, take it before I change my mind."

"Do you know how many good men live in this world? Too many to count!" Jackson remarks to himself as he walks outside and dons the regalia. He steps into the intersection, where he begins to dance. Cars and pedestrians stop to watch: "They all watched me dance with my grandmother. I was my grandmother, dancing."

THEMES

Cultural Homelessness

"What You Pawn I Will Redeem" begins with the line, "One day you have a home and the next you don't." It is a deceptively simple, almost glib statement, referring both to Jackson's literal homelessness, living on the streets of Seattle, as well as his cultural homelessness as a Spokane Indian. Jackson, like all Native Americans, is culturally connected to a history of dispossession, forced removal, and lost lands. In this way, Jackson's homelessness resonates throughout the story. It represents not only his material state, but his psychological and cultural states as well.

In some ways, Jackson's quest to reclaim his grandmother's stolen powwow regalia can be paralleled with the history of the Spokane tribe. Just as Jackson's grandmother's regalia was stolen and has become an item for purchase, the Spokane suffered centuries of exploitation at the hands of white settlers and the U.S. government. Before he regains the regalia, Jackson is relatively invisible as part of the homeless population in Seattle: "Homeless Indians are everywhere in Seattle. We're common and boring, and you walk right on by us, with maybe a look of anger or disgust or even sadness." But when Jackson dons his grandmother's regalia at the end of the story, his triumph is both personally and culturally significant. Reunited with his history and his heritage, he becomes instantly visible. Whereas before he had gone unnoticed, when dressed in the regalia he literally stops traffic: "Pedestrians stopped. Cars stopped. The city stopped. They all watched me dance with my grandmother." This moment signifies a shift in Jackson's status from an invisible, ignored homeless man to a spectacle of triumph, however brief. He has found a home—a place of belonging and comfort—in his grandmother's regalia.

Stereotyping and Individual Identity

One of the major themes in "What You Pawn I Will Redeem" is the notion of identity. Jackson introduces himself as a middle-aged, homeless, alcoholic Spokane Indian man. When he describes his life before becoming homeless, he does not romanticize his past. His life was not unlike other working-class American males, except that he went crazy, and has been homeless for six years. Before he tells the story of how he found and reclaimed his dead grandmother's powwow regalia, Jackson clarifies the elements of his life that seem to beg the most explanations.

Of his mental illness, Jackson informs the reader that he has been diagnosed with asocial disorder, which sounds a bit as though he could be violent or dangerous. He goes on to clarify that he has "never hurt another human being ... physically," and is only a "boring heartbreaker," rather than a malicious "serial killer or something." Also, Jackson is noticeably unperturbed by his homelessness. He describes his homelessness as "probably the only thing [he's] ever been good at." Being homeless, therefore, is an important part of his identity. He proudly explains the special treatment he receives from restaurant and store managers who allow him to use their employee bathrooms. It makes him feel "truthworthy" and distinguished from other homeless Indians in Seattle.

As Jackson emphasizes his individuality, he also introduces the notion of a collective Indian identity. Throughout the story, Jackson identifies himself as American Indian. His concept of what it means to be part of an indigenous culture is shaped largely by his own experiences and memories, as well as by popular stereotypes. He sees himself as separate from the stereotypes often used to describe Native Americans, yet he underscores these designations with statements such as "we Indians are great storytellers," and "we Indians have built-in pawn-shop radar."

Jackson says, "I'm not going to tell you my particular reasons for being homeless, because it's my secret story, and Indians have to work hard to keep secrets from hungry white folks." This statement reveals Jackson's assumptions about both groups of people. By setting himself apart from mainstream white society (as both a homeless person and a Native American), Jackson risks being seen as a stereotypical Indian. As a countermeasure, Jackson suggests his own, more flattering stereotype—that of the cautious or secretive Indian who refuses to be exploited by whites. This tactic allows Jackson to define himself in his own terms, while nodding toward the historical basis for that decision.

When speaking of homeless Indians in Seattle, Jackson says that passersby largely ignore them, except to perhaps bear "a look of anger or disgust or even sadness at the terrible fate of the noble savage." However, he also notes that "we have dreams and families" like anyone else. Here, Jackson acknowledges the common stereotype of the noble savage that has been used for centuries to stigmatize the American Indian, and he dismisses it. He has replaced the idea of the noble savage with the idea of dreams and families, in an attempt to allow for more compassion and humanity. It is important to Jackson to distance himself from negative images of Native Americans like the noble savage, yet a few lines later he declares, "we Indians are great storytellers and liars and mythmakers"—a statement that reinforces the idea that Native Americans can be discussed in terms of generalizations.

Stereotypes focus on identifying particular behaviors or traits often associated with a given race or culture. Jackson is a product of this sort of stereotyping. But Alexie has created a character that is able to see himself both as an individual man with unique experiences, and as a member of a larger group. Jackson allows himself to associate and belong within a wider framework of people who can identify themselves similarly, thereby finding validation for his own personal experiences. At the same time, he takes pains to assert his own individuality. Throughout the story, the reader sees Jackson's attempt to render his identity both in terms of his individual nature as well as in terms of his shared Native American experience without being reduced to a stereotype.

Ethnic Heritage

In the story, Jackson launches his quest after he sees his grandmother's traditional powwow costume in a pawnshop window. He must then find a way to buy back his family's stolen heirloom before the pawnshop owner sells it to someone else. His journey, both literally and symbolically, is a journey to reclaim his ethnic heritage.

At the beginning of the story, Jackson has in many ways turned his back on his Spokane heritage. Most dramatically, he has moved away from the Spokane region to Seattle, even though his ancestors "have lived within a one-hundred-mile radius of Spokane, Washington, for at least ten thousand years." In Seattle, he pursued an average American life by attending college (where he flunked out within two semesters), working various low-level jobs, getting married "two or three times," and having children. His attempts to achieve this idealized lifestyle have met with utter failure.

Over the course of the story, Jackson meets other Indians who have also strayed from their heritage and homelands in one way or another. Like Jackson, his friends Rose of Sharon and Junior have been drawn to Seattle from their ancestral homelands. As the story progresses, both Rose of Sharon and Junior leave Seattle to different fates. Rose of Sharon returns to the reservation and lives with her sister, while Junior, who travels even farther from his Colville homeland to Portland, dies in an alley from exposure. One returns to her roots and survives; the other turns his back on his roots and dies. Jackson also meets three Aleut fishermen who want nothing more than to go back home to Alaska; he later hears that they "waded into the saltwater near Dock 47 and disappeared. Some Indians said the Aleuts walked on the water and headed north. Other Indians saw the Aleuts drown."

At the end of the story, Jackson manages to reclaim part of his ethnic heritage by obtaining his grandmother's powwow regalia from the pawnshop. He puts on the outfit and dances, feeling his grandmother's spirit within him. In this way, he once again embraces the history of his family and his tribe.

HISTORICAL OVERVIEW

Native American Displacement

"[M]y people have lived within a one-hundred-mile radius of Spokane, Washington, for at least ten thousand years," Jackson notes in "What You Pawn I Will Redeem." This estimation is corroborated by David Wynecoop in his book *Children of the Sun*, which offers a detailed history of the Spokane Indian tribe from precolonial times. Shortly after white settlers entered the Spokane country in 1807, Wynecoop notes that initially "little else changed" beyond profitable fur trading and intermarriage between whites and Indians. However, he notes, the arrival of the Christian missionaries "had a more lasting influence than even the white man's guns," as the Native Americans were forced to convert and were made subject to church laws and governance. With the acceptance of the white man's religion, Native Americans largely abandoned their traditional beliefs, which permanently altered their communities, traditions, and unique identities.

In 1850, Congress passed the Donation Act, which released "non-settled" (or Indian-occupied) lands for white settlement. The law allowed any citizen to claim up to three hundred and twenty acres in the Oregon Territory, which included present-day Oregon, Washington, Idaho, and parts of Wyoming and Montana. In order for Indians to retain claim of their land, they would have to sever any tribal affiliation and become American citizens. Most Native Americans refused this offer. Thousands of whites came to settle in the Oregon Territory, and many Indians were displaced from their homes.

Establishing the Spokane Reservation

Tensions increased between the white settlers and the indigenous population in the Oregon Territory. On January 18, 1881, President Rutherford B. Hayes issued an executive order establishing the Spokane Indian Reservation. The area set aside for the reservation reduced what had once been Indian land by 80 percent, from over three million acres to just over 150,000 acres. The document states that a "tract of land, situated in Washington Territory, be, and the same is hereby, set aside and reserved for the use and occupancy of the Spokane Indians." Wynecoop notes in *Children of the Sun* that the Lower Spokanes moved onto the reservation shortly after it was established, while "the Upper and Middle bands refused to relocate on the Reservation land" because they wanted compensation before ceding land title to the government. They argued that the reservation land was not ideal for hunting and fishing purposes, and there was concern about the religious differences between the various cultures of Spokane. The Upper and Middle bands came to an agreement with the U.S. government in 1887, in which they

ceded title to all lands they claimed and moved onto one of the established reservations. Even after conceding to the demands of the government, the Spokane still had to deal with further encroachments by white settlers on their allotted territory. Wynecoop quotes a newspaper article that appeared in the *Spokesman Review* on November 10, 1907:

> The first of the new year will witness a general house cleaning of the Colville and Spokane Reservations. All person [sic] who have no claim to allotment on these reservations will be required to leave the reservation and seek homes elsewhere. This will greatly facilitate the work of allotment. A strain of Indian blood is a valuable asset at present, and it is wonderful how many white skins have turned red lately.

As the article indicates, it was not uncommon at this time for whites to claim Native American ancestry for the sole purpose of acquiring land that had been allotted to the Spokane tribe. These and similar acts have long since contributed to the erosion of the Spokane reservation lands, and reveal the historical basis for Jackson's comment in "What You Pawn I Will Redeem": "One day you have a home and the next you don't.... Indians have to work hard to keep secrets from hungry white folks."

The Grand Coulee Dam

The Grand Coulee Dam was built on the Columbia River in Washington between 1933 and 1943, and is one of the largest generators of hydroelectric power in the world. The reservoir behind the dam covers reservation land once considered essential by the Colville and Spokane tribes. Additionally, the dam prevents the natural migration of many spawning fish species such as salmon, an important food source for many reservation Indians. In 1940, the federal government paid the Colville tribe $63,000 and the Spokane tribe $4,700 for use of their land. Since then, both tribes have actively pursued similar claims for "water power values," lost fisheries, financial losses, and additional compensation for general land usage. In 1994, the Colville tribe received a lump sum of over fifty million dollars, as well as an agreement for millions of dollars in annual payments; nearly ten years later, when Alexie wrote "What You Pawn I Will Redeem," members of the Spokane tribe had yet to receive any additional compensation.

one of the premiere Native American authors writing today.

CRITICAL OVERVIEW

"What You Pawn I Will Redeem" appeared in *The New Yorker* magazine in April 2003. It is also part of Sherman Alexie's collection of short stories *Ten Little Indians*, published later that year. The bestselling book was distinguished as a *Los Angeles Times* Best of the Best Selection, a *San Francisco Chronicle* Best Book, and a *Publishers Weekly* Book of the Year. The story was included in the 2004 collection *The Best American Short Stories* and was a 2005 O. Henry Prize Juror's Favorite. In her essay on why she selected "What You Pawn I Will Redeem" as her favorite story of 2005, novelist and O. Henry juror Ann Patchett remarks, "As I read [this story,] I was moved by sorrow, compassion, and joy."

In "Way Off the Reservation: The Indians in Alexie's Fiction are Out for Redemption," *San Francisco Chronicle* writer David Kipen writes that *Ten Little Indians* is "a bookful of keepers ... [that] belong to the rich tradition of assimilation fiction." Though he notes that the time element of "What You Pawn I Will Redeem" makes it a "gimmick story," it is also a "funny, sad, sentimental but villainless fable." In "Where the Men are Manly and the Indians Bemused," a review for the *New York Times*, Janet Maslin calls Alexie's writing in the collection "his winsome best," noting "What You Pawn I Will Redeem" as "especially stirring." William J. Cobb's review for the *Houston Chronicle*, "Stories Blend Comic, Tragic Situations," labels "What You Pawn I Will Redeem" as "Perhaps the finest story in the collection." A review in *Publishers Weekly* calls Alexie's writing "Fluent, exuberant and supremely confident," and writes that *Ten Little Indians* is a "slam dunk collection sure to score with readers everywhere." In "Stateless in Seattle," Maya Jaggi of *The Guardian* (London) applauds how the "stories irreverently explore the yearning for the sacred. In some of the best, Alexie lends the bleak minutiae of the street an epic resonance ... but with more laughs." Alexie has become popular among academics and non-academics alike as

CRITICISM

Natasha Marin

Marin is a literature scholar, freelance writer, and poet. In the following excerpt, she examines the nature of Indian identity by exploring how duality is inscribed within the role of the "native informant" in Sherman Alexie's short story "What You Pawn I Will Redeem."

Like many other writers of color, Sherman Alexie has shouldered the burden of speaking on behalf of his people, whose voices are seldom heard in the predominantly white world of contemporary American literature. He does so with an unflinching sense of humor. His stories navigate the often treacherous terrain of love, politics, human weakness, and failure. Yet, in his literary work he is most concerned with redefining the Native American experience, or as he prefers, the *Indian* experience, by establishing a new collective identity based on the individual lives and voices of the personae he creates. As in the real world, Alexie's characters encounter their own "Indian-ness" both publicly and privately. Consequently, his characters must employ this "double consciousness" while constructing their identities. These characters are endowed with Alexie's own awareness of the negative stereotypes associated with indigenous peoples, and they therefore respond, interrogate, and interact with the images most often used to describe them. The effect is a text peopled with characters who understand that they are indeed performing and fulfilling the role of "Indian" within the larger narrative beyond the page into our natural world.

This is certainly the case in Alexie's "What You Pawn I Will Redeem," the story of Jackson Jackson's quest to retrieve his grandmother's powwow regalia found in a pawnshop fifty years after it was stolen. Jackson's desire to reconnect with what he feels is rightfully his is complicated by his financial instability. Jackson is homeless and broke, making the task of finding $999 to buy the regalia that much more challenging. The complications that arise and what eventually follows allow the reader to witness Jackson's experiences while maintaining some cultural distance from him. This distance

> THE COMPLICATIONS THAT ARISE AND
> RESOLUTION THAT FOLLOWS ALLOW THE READER TO
> WITNESS JACKSON'S EXPERIENCES WHILE
> MAINTAINING SOME CULTURAL DISTANCE FROM HIM.
> THIS DISTANCE EPITOMIZES THE OVERALL CONCEPT OF
> THE NATIVE INFORMANT, WHICH ALEXIE EMPLOYS IN
> "WHAT YOU PAWN I WILL REDEEM" TO REEDUCATE HIS
> AUDIENCE."

epitomizes the overall concept of the native informant, which Alexie employs in "What You Pawn I Will Redeem" to reeducate his audience.

Jackson, the protagonist and narrator in "What You Pawn I Will Redeem," begins his story with the following lines:

> One day you have a home and the next you don't, but I'm not going to tell you my particular reasons for being homeless, because it's my secret story, and Indians have to work hard to keep secrets from hungry white folks.

This opening immediately draws attention to the distance between Jackson's and the reader's societal positions. He is revealing an experience that is outside of the reader's own cultural context. This is established when the narrator references "you," the reader. He equates this exchange between himself and the reader to those that occur between the Indian and the "hungry white folks," who presumably want to obtain his "secret story." Jackson first establishes that a story is being told, then he reiterates that the story is being told to someone who is markedly different from himself; namely, a white person. Jackson intends to tell his own story and is aware that by doing so, he prevents his own exploitation.

Jackson goes on to explain that he is "a Spokane Indian boy, an Interior Salish," who "grew up in Spokane, moved to Seattle," and led a relatively normal life before going "crazy." He refers to his mental illness with self-effacing wit, noting that having an "asocial disorder" does not make him "a serial killer or

something." Moments like this one, where relevant information is divulged to the audience, characterize Jackson's extratextual interactions with the reader. These details are important to understanding Jackson and his story, but they are not necessarily part of the plot. They allow communication between the characters within the story and the reader. Speaking directly to the reader throughout the story, Jackson educates or reeducates the reader by providing additional details that simultaneously reveal his own (possibly erroneous) cultural presumptions.

After clarifying the relative harmlessness of his condition, it is important for Jackson to establish his identity—to define both himself and the parameters of his story. The importance of this background is made clear by its position in the text—Alexie dedicates the first few pages of this short story to these details from Jackson's past. Rather than accepting the terms others have used to define him, Jackson names himself a "crazy" "Spokane Indian," who after a life of "various blue- and bluer-collar jobs" finds himself homeless. He establishes himself as both an indigent and a Spokane Indian because he feels that these two factors most succinctly summarize his experience while setting up the action of his story. Jackson insists that, "Being homeless is probably the only thing I've been good at" and that "homeless Indians are everywhere in Seattle," before he goes on to describe the peripheral nature of his existence by saying, "We're common and boring, and you walk right on by us, with maybe a look of anger or disgust or even sadness at the terrible fate of the noble savage."

Jackson's introduction defines his relationship to the reader. Jackson represents himself as Indian while he performs the role of storyteller. This storytelling role is often associated with the popular stereotype of Indian-ness, which motivates his comment that "we Indians are great storytellers and liars and mythmakers."

In her essay, "Reconfiguring the Native Informant: Positionality and the Global Age," Shahnaz Khan notes that "Anthropologists identify the native informant as the person who translates [his or] her culture for the researcher, the outsider." She goes on to say that personally, having herself been "recruited into this role":

> I do not make any claims about producing authentic knowledge about [my] culture. Instead, I complicate the process of knowledge production and claim that you, the reader, can

only know about my research ... via an analysis of my own location [outside that culture].

Perhaps this is what Alexie is doing by creating a character who sees himself not only as a complex individual, but also as one who is performing a racial and cultural service for the reader.

If the term "native informant" is applied to Jackson, then the readers must consider themselves to be "the researchers" or "the outsiders" that Khan refers to in her essay. As outsiders, readers interact with the native informant as they might a tour guide. In this way, Jackson takes the reader on a tour of what it means to be an Indian—specifically, a homeless Spokane Indian in Seattle. Therefore, the native informant in this story is a go-between for two cultures. He exists for the purpose of facilitating interaction between the "I" and the "Other" in pursuit of a mutual understanding. This dynamic—this exchange of information—is key to understanding the concept of the native informant.

Joseph Jeyaraj adds to this definition of the native informant in his essay "Native Informants, Ethos, and Unsituated Rhetoric: Some Rhetorical Issues in Postcolonial Discourses." He calls attention to the status of the native informant as one who occupies the space between his or her own society, and the society of the outsider or colonizer. The distance this distinction creates makes the native informant separate, and therefore more valid than the native, who is consequently defined as such by a marked lack of utility. The native informant is then perceived by the outsiders, as well as himself, as a valuable commodity. This objectification confers relevance, that is, a position of importance, within the new, postcolonial society. Jeyaraj speculates to this effect saying, "It may be that there is an eliteness associated with the personal lives of postcolonial native informants."

While introducing himself, Jackson makes a point of distinguishing himself from the others by including distinguishing details:

> I've made friends with restaurant and convenience-store managers who let me use their bathrooms. I don't mean the public bathrooms either. I mean the employees' bathrooms, the clean ones hidden in the back of the kitchen or the pantry or the cooler. I know it sounds strange to be proud of, but it means a lot to me, being truthworthy [sic] enough to piss in

somebody else's clean bathroom. Maybe you don't understand the value of a clean bathroom, but I do.

These details and others set Jackson apart from those who are not capable of interacting to this extent with outsiders. His ability to communicate a culturally sensitive story without fear of exploitation indicates that Jackson has been cast by Alexie in the role of native informant. Jackson and other native informants, as Jeyaraj describes it, "have a strong tendency to occupy these [roles] partly because these [roles] offer many perks and partly because there is [outside] pressure ... to make them occupy these [roles]."

At many times during the story, Jackson delivers information to the reader for the purpose of contributing to a multicultural understanding of "Indian-ness." For example, shortly after introducing two of his companions, Jackson says, "I am living proof of the horrible damage that colonialism has done to us Skins." He goes on to say, "I'm a strong man, and I know that silence is the best way of dealing with white folks." These statements establish certain complex cultural "truths" within the framework created by Jackson's Indian authority. The reader is in no position to disagree with Jackson, who has already established his narrative authority simply by distinguishing himself as separate from and speaking for the other Indians. These attempts to distinguish himself from or align himself with other Indians function as a means to divulge crucial information to the reader, who has now become the outsider Kahn mentions. For instance, the term "skins" calls to mind the systematic exploitation, assimilation, and elimination of indigenous cultures in the Western Hemisphere as a direct result of European colonialism. By using this racial slur himself, Jackson alludes to its history without neutering or excusing the word itself.

As the story develops, Jackson allows his native authority to underscore comments like, "we Indians have built-in pawnshop radar" and "because they don't want to be perfect, because only God is perfect, Indian people sew flaws into their powwow regalia." These statements read a lot like stereotypes, but they recast the role of "Indian" on Jackson's terms, thereby reeducating and informing the reader of specific cultural cues. The reader must then decide whether or not to accept Jackson's authority as the native informant based on his performance as "Indian," or to deny his representation of "Indian-ness" on the basis of unreliability.

Jackson's narrative authority may indeed be questioned in terms of his propensity to deliver edicts on subjects like "pawnshop radar," but it is reconfirmed by his singularity as the Indian voice within the text. Throughout the story, Jackson interacts with members of other indigenous tribes—Aleut, Plains, and Crow, all of whom are distinguished from Spokane Indians with descriptors like, "these Aleuts smelled like salmon." Each of these characters vanishes suddenly from the narrative, leaving only Jackson's voice behind. Near the end of the story, after leaving his Aleut companions, Jackson remarks, "I later heard the Aleuts had waded into the saltwater near Dock 47 and disappeared." These disappearing acts, which are not uncommon in the story, reinforce Jackson's status as *the* Indian spokesperson, and thereby reinforce his status as the native informant. In this way, the dominance of Jackson's voice is furthered by his singularity. Even though Jackson says, "Indians are everywhere," the reader only encounters Jackson's point of view. However problematic his conceptualization of the "Indian" is, Jackson is the only character who informs the reader of what it means to be Indian.

In "What You Pawn I Will Redeem," Alexie has demonstrated his capacity to display and fulfill the role of native informant by allowing Jackson's Indian perspective to supersede all others. As the native informant, Jackson is able to interact with the reader in a manner that both deconstructs and sustains the cultural space between "us" and "them" by capitalizing on the storyteller/listener dynamic. This process of conveying knowledge, be it fact or legend, is fundamental to the role of the native informant. In this way, Alexie's "What You Pawn I Will Redeem" contributes to the already fascinating discourse surrounding the definition or redefinition of the

Native American (or *Indian*) experience as it is viewed in a contemporary and culturally sensitive context.

SOURCES

Alexie, Sherman, "What You Pawn I Will Redeem," in *Ten Little Indians*, Grove Press, 2003, pp. 169–194.

Cobb, William J., "Stories Blend Comic, Tragic Situations," *Houston Chronicle*, www.chron.com/disp/story.mp/ae/books/reviews/2021476.html (August 1, 2003).

Hayes, Rutherford B., "Executive Order of President R. B. Hayes Establishing the Spokane Reservation, 18 January 1881," *Center for Columbia River History*, www.ccrh.org/comm/river/treaties/spokane.htm (December 20, 2005), originally issued January 18, 1881.

Jaggi, Maya, "Stateless in Seattle," in *The Guardian* (London), January 31, 2004.

Jeyaraj, Joseph, "Native Informants, Ethos, and Unsituated Rhetoric: Some Rhetorical Issues in Postcolonial Discourses," in *Pretexts: Literal and Cultural Studies*, Vol. 12, No. 1, 2003, pp. 80–81.

Khan, Shahnaz, "Reconfiguring the Native Informant: Positionality in the Global Age," in *Signs: Journal of Women and Culture and Society*, Vol. 30, No. 4, 2005, pp. 2022–23.

Kipen, David, "Way Off the Reservation: The Indians in Alexie's Fiction are Out for Redemption," *San Francisco Chronicle*, www.sfgate.com (June 29, 2003).

Maslin, Janet, "Where the Men are Manly and the Indians Bemused," *New York Times*, www.nytimes.com (May 26, 2003).

Patchett, Ann, "The O. Henry Prize Stories: Juror's Favorite," *Random House,*, www.randomhouse.com/anchor/ohenry/jury.html (December 19, 2005).

Review of *Ten Little Indians*, *Publishers Weekly*, www.publishersweekly.com (May 5, 2003).

Wynecoop, David, *Children of the Sun*, Wellpinit *(Washington) School District Website*, www.wellpinit.wednet.edu/sal-cos, (December 19, 2005), originally published in 1969.

Subthemes

Class and Caste

Introduction

In literature dealing with race and prejudice, class is often intertwined with race and ethnicity; those who are discriminated against due to race are more likely to be trapped in a lower level of society. Conversely, those who exist in the lower classes are more likely to be discriminated against by those in the upper classes. This creates a vicious undertow that can trap victims of racial or ethnic prejudice, making it extremely difficult for them to attain a higher social status. However, literature dealing with social class prejudice and conflict shows that such treatment frequently exists without regard for race or ethnicity.

Born Unlucky

One of the most observant chroniclers of Victorian England's class struggles is novelist Charles Dickens. In *Oliver Twist* (1838), one of the great author's most famous works, a young boy named Oliver is born into England's harsh workhouse system. Dickens spends much time satirizing the "benefits" of this system and its treatment of the poor; for example, he notes that lawmakers granted poor people substantial freedom, allowing them to choose between "being starved by a gradual process in the [work]house, or by a quick one out of it." He also illustrates how an essentially good person like Oliver can be tempted to perform criminal acts by those willing to take advantage of his

People sit in front of shacks in the slum village of Cross Roads, South Africa, 1978 P. Mugabane / The United Nations

desperation. Although Oliver ultimately receives a substantial inheritance and a life that will continue happily-ever-after, Dickens's searing portrait of working-class existence in nineteenth-century England is just as heartrending today as when it first made the Victorian public aware of the desolation in their midst.

Dorothy Allison's *Bastard Out of Carolina* (1992), also portrays class issues not rooted in race or ethnicity. The story focuses on the relationship between Ruth Anne Boatwright, nicknamed "Bone," and her too-young mother Anney in 1950s South Carolina. The Boatwrights are a close-knit lower-class family known for fighting and drinking. Anney gives birth to Bone at only fifteen; the birth certificate is marked with undeniable evidence of her lower-class roots: the word "Illegitimate" stamped across it.

Anney eventually marries an abusive man Bone calls Daddy Glen, who is from a middle-class family. His father owns a dairy, one brother practices medicine, and the other practices law. Allison suggests that it is Glen's failure to meet his family's middle-class expectations that result

in the rage and violence that he focuses on Bone throughout the novel. Ultimately, Anney chooses the cruel and abusive Glen over her own daughter. Before she leaves, however, she gives her daughter an opportunity to escape the social stigma she was born into by obtaining a new copy of Bone's birth certificate—one without the cruel "Illegitimate" stamp.

Haves and Have-nots

In Katherine Mansfield's short story "The Garden-Party" (1921), class distinctions are revealed in layers as the story progresses. At the start, the Sheridan family estate is described in an almost idyllic manner. The estate is being prepared for a lavish lawn party the Sheridans are hosting for all their wealthy acquaintances. It soon becomes clear, however, that the people doing all the actual work—and shouldering the blame for any missteps that occur—are the working-class servants and tradespeople who cater to the Sheridans' whims. The Sheridans themselves appear comfortable with this distinction, though one of the daughters, Laura, seems to have a dawning awareness of the differences between her family and the workers who serve them.

When she hears that a working-class neighbor has died, Laura wonders if the party should take place at all. Her family does not understand why she would even consider canceling it after all the trouble they have gone to; Laura relents, and the party goes on. Afterward, Laura's mother makes her take the leftover food from the party to the grieving family. Laura feels such a gesture is inappropriate, but does as her mother insists. Once there, she is so affected by the sight of the dead man and his family that she seems fundamentally changed. It is left to the reader to decide if Laura has truly overcome her family's condescending view of the lower classes.

The Grapes of Wrath, by John Steinbeck, (1939) tells the tale of the Joads, an Oklahoma farm family who lose their land during the Great Depression. Like countless other Midwestern families, the loss of their home is the loss of their livelihood. To the farmers, the villain is the upper-class banker, he who extends credit, then calls their debts and forecloses when they cannot pay. Steinbeck even describes the banks themselves as hungry beasts: "They breathe profits; they eat the interest on money. If they don't get it, they die the way you die without air, without side-meat."

When they hear of farming opportunities out west in California, the Joads sell their possessions and make the grueling journey across the parched, dusty landscape. When they arrive in California, they discover that the only opportunities available are for migrant laborers—a thankless, low-paying, and temporary occupation. Other Californians contemptuously call these displaced Midwesterners "Okies." Singled out as "others," they are treated as second-class citizens, and rarely find basic shelter or even enough food to survive. When some of the workers attempt to organize for a better wage, they are harassed and arrested. Steinbeck makes a clear distinction between the classes: the dispossessed Okies are the downtrodden lower-class heroes, while the bankers and landowners are upper-class villains intent on squeezing every last penny of profit from a desperate labor force. It is this dichotomy—between the haves and the have-nots—that fuels the narrative. As one character comments:

> The whole United States ain't that big. It ain't that big. It ain't big enough. There ain't room

A migrant worker mother with her children, photographed by Dorothea Lange, Nipomo, California, 1936 (c) Dorothea Lange / The Library of Congress

enough for you an' me, for your kind an' my kind, for rich and poor together all in one country, for thieves and honest men. For hunger and fat.

Thankless Jobs

Upton Sinclair's *The Jungle* (1906) and Barbara Ehrenreich's *Nickel and Dimed* (2001) both offer accounts of the hazards and tribulations of lower-class occupations. In the novel *The Jungle*, the Rudkus family leaves Lithuania for the promise of prosperity in America. After arriving in Chicago, however, they realize that such hopes are false empty. They encounter greed and discrimination and are forced to take dangerous jobs that pay little. Young newlywed Jurgis finds work in a slaughterhouse, the filthy conditions of which—based on the author's real-life investigations—appalled readers upon its publication. Unfortunately, Sinclair's attempt to shed light on the class inequalities of capitalism instead focused world attention on the failures of the U.S. meatpacking industry. As Sinclair noted afterward, "I aimed for the public's heart but by accident I hit it in the stomach."

> **THINGS THAT WERE QUITE UNSPEAKABLE WENT ON THERE IN THE PACKING HOUSES ALL THE TIME, AND WERE TAKEN FOR GRANTED BY EVERYBODY; ONLY THEY DID NOT SHOW, AS IN THE OLD SLAVERY TIMES, BECAUSE THERE WAS NO DIFFERENCE IN COLOR BETWEEN MASTER AND SLAVE."**

> *Upton Sinclair,* The Jungle

Ehrenreich's *Nickel and Dimed* is a nonfiction account of one woman's attempt to live off minimum-wage earnings at the turn of the twenty-first century. Though the author's methods are unscientific, and her perspective is as biased as Sinclair's, she nonetheless draws an alarming picture of the state of America's lowest-class citizens: the work they perform is backbreaking, the pay is low, and job security is nonexistent. As one of the author's coworkers says about corporations, "They don't cut you no slack. You give and you give, and they take." Like Sinclair, Ehrenreich hoped to call attention to class distinctions and inequities. Unfortunately, like Sinclair, her main message was nearly overshadowed by what many readers viewed as an exposé of franchise housecleaning services.

Indian Caste

Of all modern world literature, the literature of India is especially focused on the theme of social class. Traditional Indian society is divided into rigid social classes known as castes; a person born into a certain caste is unlikely to ever become a member of a higher-level caste, which means that individuals retain the social status of their ancestors. As India has become a more modern and independent nation, these class issues have become a fertile subject for Indian literature.

"Untouchables" are a group so low that it is not even considered a caste. Members of this lowest class are tasked with jobs such as disposal of waste and the dead and are consequently considered impure or dirty by members of the higher castes. Mulk Raj Anand's

Untouchable (1935) is the first novel to feature a member of India's lowest social class as a hero. Bakha, the main character, is an eighteen-year-old who spends his days cleaning latrines. Although Bakha evokes sympathy for the injustices he must endure, Anand does not offer any sort of ultimate vindication or resolution for his main character. His message, perhaps, is that as long as India retains its caste system, there will be no happy ending for the untouchables.

Although Salim, the hero of V. S. Naipul's *A Bend in the River* (1979), is far from an untouchable—he is Indian only in ancestry and runs a business in a troubled region of Africa—he also witnesses firsthand the devastation visited upon the lowest classes of society. As the region undergoes a revolution led by a violent anticolonialist dictator, many of the very people who work for the region's poor are murdered because they represent a colonial past. This chaos affects the lowest classes most directly, though by the end of the novel, Salim realizes that no one who stays in the region is safe.

Nectar in a Sieve (1950), by Kamala Markandaya, and *The God of Small Things* (1997), by Arundhati Roy, offer two more views of India's social structure, one from the perspective of a farmer's wife and another from the perspective of a wealthy family. *Nectar in a Sieve* tells the story of Rukmani, a woman whose husband in an arranged marriage, Nathan, is a tenant farmer in a rural village. The Hindu villagers in the tale are largely depicted as illiterate yet sympathetic, while the landowner is shown as wealthy and uncaring. Likewise, the Muslims who run the newly built tannery in the village consistently display their lack of respect for the lower-class farmers. Over several decades, Rukmani's family is torn apart as her children turn their backs on rural life and industry forces the aging couple off their farmland.

In *The God of Small Things*, the Kochamma family owns a successful pickle and preserves business. Although the family suffers its fair share of hardships, the primary class conflict occurs when young wife and mother Ammu Kochamma begins a love affair with Velutha, an untouchable who works in the family's factory. This scandalous act is at the core of the family's subsequent disintegration. The worst

The interior of a room in the Williamsburg Housing Project, Brooklyn, New York, 1935 National Archives and Records Administration

fate, however, is reserved for the untouchable who dares to behave as if he belongs to a higher class: he is arrested and beaten for a crime he did not commit, and dies in jail before the truth becomes known. His treatment by the police indicates their view of untouchables:

> If they hurt Velutha more than they intended to, it was only because any kinship, any connection between themselves and him, any implication that if nothing else, at least biologically he was a fellow creature—had been severed long ago.

Knowledge is Power

In the modern world, people can rise to a higher class than the one they are born into, and education is one of the surest ways to achieve such a change. Those denied adequate education are the ones that suffer today. Martin Espada's poem "Public School 190, Brooklyn 1963" addresses the inferior opportunities for members of marginalized classes. Espada's poem takes place on the day John F. Kennedy is assassinated; he describes the abysmal conditions of a public school that serves working-class Brooklyn children. "The

inkwells had no ink," he writes, noting the utter lack of necessities in the school. The descriptions make it clear that many of the students are members of minorities, and imply that such conditions would not be considered acceptable for wealthier, white children. The day's national tragedy is far removed from the reality of the students at Public School 190, who do not fully understand the event; these students, after all, live their own tragedy every day, regardless of Kennedy's death.

In contrast, E. R. Braithwaite's *To Sir, With Love* (1959) takes the reader's expectations about class and race and turns them upside down. In the novel, which is based on the author's own experiences, a black man from Guyana accepts a teaching position in London's impoverished East End. The white students are the troubled products of working-class families, and at first resist any effort to better themselves through education. By overcoming barriers of race and class, the students and teacher together learn important life lessons. This "racial reversal" of the classes illustrates that the struggles of the individual are often more universal than they might appear.

Conclusion

Literature dealing with social class issues is nearly always a reflection of the society in which its author lives. Themes of social class conflict usually result from the author's own experiences or observations and most often reflect the author's dissatisfaction with the way a certain class is treated. In that way, themes of class struggle parallel themes of race and prejudice in literature. While race and class do not always go hand-in-hand, mistreatment on the basis of either arises from fear, ignorance, and prejudice. Literature about both serves to assure the afraid, enlighten the ignorant, and inspire the victims as well as the victimizers to reject the prejudice that burdens them both.

SOURCES

Dickens, Charles, *Oliver Twist*, Signet Classics, 3d Reissue Edition, 1961, pp. 34–35, originally published in 1838.

Ehrenreich, Barbara, *Nickel and Dimed: On (Not) Getting By in America*, Metropolitan Books, 2001, p. 22.

Espada, Martin, "Public School 190, Brooklyn 1963," from *Imagine the Angels of Bread*, W. W. Norton, 1996, p. 25.

Roy, Arundhati, *The God of Small Things*, Random House, 1997, p. 293.

Sinclair, Upton, Introduction, *The Brass Check: A Study of American Journalism*, University of Illinois Press, 2003, p. x, quote originally published in *Cosmopolitan*, October 1906.

———, *The Jungle: The Uncensored Original Edition*, See Sharp Press, 2003, p. 97, originally published in 1906.

Steinbeck, John, *The Grapes of Wrath*, Penguin Books, 1997, pp. 35, 121, originally published in 1939.

Disabilities, Illness, and Social Stigma

Introduction

The appearance of differentness often creates a frame of stigma within which those who are "different" must learn to live. Many individuals throughout the world approach illness and disability with great trepidation. The social stigma associated with disability and illness means that the afflicted must struggle for acceptance. Wanting to belong and fearing the position of the "other"—a social space in which one is misunderstood, devalued, and subjugated—many powerful writers have pushed for acceptance and understanding with personal tales and affecting fiction.

Disabilities

Memoirs of those who have triumphed despite physical challenges are among the most remarkable in literature. Their stories would be astounding for able-bodied people, and their further drive to physically create the text is as awesome as the rarest athletic performance. Both Helen Keller's *The Story of My Life* (1903) and Christy Brown's *My Left Foot* (1954) represent the fortitude of the human spirit when physically challenged individuals find the strength to lead exceptional lives despite phenomenal obstacles. Helen Keller's *The Story of My Life* is the most well known of the famous deaf and blind activist's numerous books and articles. After losing her sight and hearing as a toddler, Helen's inability to communicate left

her isolated. Anne Sullivan, a young visually impaired teacher, taught Helen as a child to make hand signs for letters and to spell words: "somehow the mystery of language was revealed to me." After entering the public awareness with her autobiography, Helen Keller spent the next six decades of her life as an activist and advocate for the blind and was one of the most inspiring people of the twentieth century. The autobiography is the basis for the well-known play *The Miracle Worker* and a movie of the same name.

Irish writer and artist Christy Brown's autobiography *My Left Foot* (1954) demonstrates a similar triumph over physical disability. Stricken with cerebral palsy, Brown could neither speak nor move any part of his body other than his left foot. Brown's descriptions in the early section of his book provide access to the person inside the disfigured body, leaving the reader eager to know more about his difficult birth, the doctors' dismissiveness, and Brown's family's persistent hope. When, at age five, Brown grabs chalk from his sister's hand with his left foot and traces the letter A, he proves that his intellect is intact and he can communicate with his family and the world.

In addition to memoirs, conventional fiction also helps readers recognize and confront their own prejudices. Virginia Fleming's *Be Good to Eddie Lee* (1993) is a children's book that helps youngsters understand those who are different and see diversity as a positive aspect of human relations. "God didn't make mistakes, and Eddie Lee was a mistake if there ever was one," muses Christy, a young girl trying to justify her reluctance to be kind to Eddie Lee, the neighborhood boy with Down Syndrome. Setting out with her friend Jim Bud hoping to find frogs' eggs, Christy eventually begins to see the beauty of the woods through Eddie Lee's eyes as he insists on tagging along, ultimately showing a superior knowledge of and sensitivity to nature. *Be Good to Eddie Lee* helps readers of all ages realize how children like Eddie Lee, though different, can enrich the lives of others, both despite and because of their talents and weaknesses.

Illness

No disease in modern memory has caused the hysterical reaction—the fear, the blame, and the mistreatment—that HIV/AIDS has. The play *Angels in America* (1992), by Tony Kushner, dramatically explores the racial, sexual,

Jean Driscoll, two-time Olympic silver medalist, celebrates after wining the Boston Marathon Elise Amendola / AP Images

political, religious, and social issues confronting the United States during the Reagan years, the time during which the AIDS epidemic was emerging. *Angels in America* won the 1993 Pulitzer Prize for Drama for its attention to a wide range of reactions to illness, both by its main characters who have AIDS and by those around them. The play opens with a rabbi saying that in the American "melting pot," nothing melts. The audience quickly meets Prior, an individual with AIDS who questions his own sanity as he is visited by ghosts of his ancestors and selected by angels to be a prophet. While every situation in the play is viewed from at least two sometimes conflicting perspectives, the audience learns that much of the nation's reaction to AIDS and healthcare is highly politicized and prejudiced. Characters struggle to find meaning and while some fail, others break free of the various problems that have been their prisons or find meaning in compassion and commitment to others.

❝ YOU THINK THIS IS TOO HORRIBLE TO HAVE REALLY HAPPENED, THIS IS TOO AWFUL TO BE THE TRUTH! BUT, PLEASE. IT'S STILL HARD FOR ME TO HAVE A CLEAR MIND THINKING ON IT. BUT IT'S THE TRUTH EVEN IF IT DIDN'T HAPPEN.❞

Ken Kesey, One Flew Over the Cuckoo's Nest

The collection of poems in Tory Dent's *HIV, Mon Amour* (1999) explores the AIDS epidemic and popular culture from a highly personal perspective. Echoing Marguerite Duras's famous book *Hiroshima, Mon Amour,* Dent's collection takes the reader on a journey into an honest, angry, and gripping view of living with HIV through an assortment of cultural allusions. Chosen for the 1999 Academy of American Poets James Laughlin Award, *HIV, Mon Amour* demonstrates one woman's resilience and determination to cling to love and life in the face of devastating illness.

The mentally ill often face the same cruel, irrational, and judgmental reactions as those with any misunderstood disease. Literature about mental illness often provides a firsthand look into a world that most cannot imagine. Anne Sexton's poetry was not only technically excellent, but also meaningful to readers who empathized with her fear and angst. Readers readily believed that her poems echoed her life, reflecting her intermittent institutionalization due to several attempts at suicide in the late 1950s. "Noon Walk On The Asylum Lawn," (1960) anthologized in *To Bedlam and Part Way Back,* juxtaposes reassuring words of protection from Psalm 23 against her own terrifying observations:

> The grass speaks.
> I hear green chanting all day.
> *I will fear no evil, fear no evil*
> The blades extend
> and reach my way.

One Flew Over the Cuckoo's Nest (1962), by Ken Kesey, is set among the patients and workers in a mental institution and is narrated by Chief Broom, a catatonic half-Indian everyone

believes is deaf and dumb. McMurphy, a con man and patient who has sought institutionalization in order to escape the rigors of a prison work farm, challenges policy and procedure at the institution. Through his constant skirmishes with Miss Ratched, the dictatorial nurse who controls the inmates' daily routines, McMurphy alters the destiny of all the men in the ward. After his final, violent encounter with Ratched, McMurphy disappears and eventually returns, after being lobotomized. Chief Broom, more aware than his peers realize, smothers McMurphy with a pillow to end his misery. Kesey's part-time work in a mental ward as an orderly shaped his belief that mental patients were not necessarily crazy, just more individualized than society was willing to accept.

Susanna Kayson's *Girl, Interrupted* (1993) addresses the stigma of mental illness. She recounts her two-year stay in a Boston psychiatric hospital and her frustrating experience in the "parallel universe" of madness, one of many places that "exist alongside this world and resemble it, but are not in it." Kayson's memoir, written from a cool, rational, and controlled perspective, asks readers to consider the thin line that separates madness from sanity. Kayson suggests that some forms of mental disturbance are not actually illnesses, but instead labels our society has applied to states of confusion and unhappiness, and that "deviance" and "normalcy" might be considered reflections of socially constructed ideas rather than social truth.

Stigma

William Faulkner's *The Sound and the Fury* (1929) is an American classic. It depicts the decline of the once-aristocratic Compson family from different points of view. Each perspective relates a different piece of the four-part novel, thus providing the reader with vastly different but connected glimpses into the Compson family's dysfunction and the effect that daughter Caddy's scandalous behavior has on the other family members. The first and most difficult section recounts the novel's earliest events via flashback from the point of view of Benjy Compson, a thirty-three-year-old "idiot." Benjy's brother Quentin narrates the second part of the novel, and while his perceptive understanding of the events of the Compson's family downfall differ from Benjy's, he believes deeply that triumph over the human condition is impossible.

Helen Keller, who was both blind and deaf, sits with her teacher, Anne Sullivan AP Images

Quentin ultimately commits suicide to release himself from the pain of his past. Both brothers are undone by their sister's shame.

John Steinbeck's *Of Mice and Men* (1937) traces the story of Lennie and George, two displaced migrant farm workers in California during the period of the Great Depression. George, a tough and shrewd farmhand, takes care of Lennie, who is mentally retarded but a strong worker. Although George often bemoans this attachment to Lennie—"I could get along so easy and so nice if I didn't have you on my tail"—readers eventually see a symbiotic relationship between the two men. When Lennie's urge to touch soft things results in a false rape accusation, George and Lennie are forced to leave town and find work at a ranch near Soledad, California. Hoping to save enough money to buy a small farm of their own, Lennie chooses to care for rabbits. The dream collapses when Lennie accidentally kills the wife of Curley, the ranch boss's son. Lennie flees to the river, the safe place where George directed him to go if he ever got into trouble, where George shoots him in an attempt to spare him

Curley's vengeance. Lennie continually tries to protect George and finally does so by killing him. Stigma keeps George and Lennie in the shadows, unable to find the understanding that may have protected both George and those he accidentally hurts.

Staying Fat for Sarah Byrnes (1993), by Chris Crutcher, addresses the theme of body image, an ever-present concept in modern society. Eric Calhoune and Sarah Byrnes struggle with themselves in vastly different ways— Eric has been humiliated by his weight his entire life and Sarah suffers through the stigma of horrible facial scars she has had since her father pushed her into a hot stove at the age of three. Unlikely best friends their whole lives, Eric finds Sarah in the hospital in a catatonic state. Eric, now slim from his work on the swim team, visits every day trying to get a response. When Sarah finally answers him, she lets him know she has been aware all along and intends to leave her unbalanced father. With the help of a sympathetic teacher, Eric searches for Sarah's mother and also struggles with overeating, his old pattern, as a response to his successful weight loss that appears to threaten his and Sarah's long-standing friendship. Though both are victims of shame, narrow-mindedness, and abuse, Eric ultimately helps Sarah find her way back into the world.

Another powerful memoir is poet Lucy Grealy's *Autobiography of a Face* (1994). Diagnosed as a child with cancer of the jawbone, Grealy illuminates the pain, suffering, and confusion she felt at age nine as she endured several surgeries and more than two years of intensive chemotherapy and radiation treatments. Although hospital stays are anxious and painful, being at home is worse. An insider in the hospital corridors, Grealy feels both guilt and shame at home, blaming herself for the arguments over money, family tension, and her mother's depression, although the family dynamic had existed prior to her illness. Once well enough to return to school, Grealy's disfigured face draws attention and taunts, helping ultimately convince her that, perceived as ugly, she will never be loved.

During years of reconstructive surgery, Grealy makes complex rationalizations to give meaning to her suffering, and relies on two passions to keep her grounded and sane: a love of horses and poetry. "The journey back to my face was a long one," she writes. More than just an illness narrative, Grealy's account of disfigurement and catastrophic childhood illness provides moving insights into the nature of suffering, demonstrating the incongruities in how others see us and how we see ourselves.

Conclusion

Mental and physical illness and the stigmas that accompany any kind of social difference have always plagued our social consciousness. While intolerance begets intolerance, the choices of a understanding society can reduce the unnecessary fear and prejudice toward those otherwise marginalized and shunned. Stories by and about those who are stigmatized show us the destructive power of careless, thoughtless prejudices.

SOURCES

Dent, Tory, *HIV, Mon Amour*, Sheep Meadow Press, 1999, p. 81.

Faulkner, William, *The Sound and the Fury*, The Modern Library, 1992, originally published in 1929, p. 76.

Fleming, Virginia, *Be Good to Eddie Lee*, Philomel Books, 1993, p. 2.

Grealy, Lucy, *Autobiography Of A Face*, Houghton Mifflin Company, 1994, p. 220.

Kayson, Susanna, *Girl, Interrupted*, Vintage Books, 1993, p. 5.

Keller, Helen, *The Story of My Life*, Bantam Books, 1990, p. 16.

Kesey, Ken, *One Flew Over the Cuckoo's Nest*, Signet, 1993, originally published in 1963, p. 13.

Sexton, Anne, "Noon Walk on the Asylum Lawn" in *To Bedlam and Part Way Back*, Houghton Mifflin Company, 1960, p. 39.

Steinbeck, John, *Of Mice and Men*, Penguin Books, 2002, originally published in 1937, pp. 6–7.

Ethnic Cleansing, Genocide, and Exile

Introduction

In her book *"The Problem from Hell": America and the Age of Genocide*, Samantha Power recounts the story of Raphael Lemkin, a Polish Jew, who was determined to find a word that would capture the barbarity of the Nazi agenda and also carry the moral implications of targeting a specific ethnic group. Lemkin finally settled on the term we commonly associate with the horrors of the Holocaust: genocide. It is a combination of the Greek *geno*, which means "race" or "tribe," and the Latin derivative *cide*, which means "to kill."

Many people consider the term "ethnic cleansing" to be synonymous with genocide. In *The Specter of Genocide: Mass Murder in Historical Perspective*, for example, Robert Gellately and Ben Kiernan explain that "'ethnic cleansing' involves the 'purification' of a territory, not necessarily of a population. This means the deportation, usually threatening but not necessarily violent, of an ethnic group from the territory." The less violent result of ethnic cleansing can be exile; the most extreme is genocide. The literature of these horrors serves to bring the world's attention to events the perpetrators want to go unnoticed, to remember the humanity and individuality of the victims, and to improve the outlook for the future by bearing witness to the past.

NEVER SHALL I FORGET THAT NIGHT, THE FIRST NIGHT IN CAMP, WHICH HAS TURNED MY LIFE INTO ONE LONG NIGHT, SEVEN TIMES CURSED AND SEVEN TIMES SEALED. NEVER SHALL I FORGET THAT SMOKE. NEVER SHALL I FORGET THE LITTLE FACES OF THE CHILDREN, WHOSE BODIES I SAW TURNED INTO WREATHS OF SMOKE BENEATH A SILENT BLUE SKY.**

Elie Wiesel, Night

Race and Religion

Anne Frank's *The Diary of a Young Girl* (1947) is not just a book about a young girl coming of age, though that is a key motif, but also a vivid illustration of the wretched conditions among a the Jewish population in Nazi Germay—a population deemed undesirable by those in power. Readers who identify with Anne, and even become emotionally involved with her struggles in the cramped quarters that she inhabits, are also mindful that beyond the inconvenience of the situation lies real danger. The truth of this is driven home by the fact that this young girl dies in a concentration camp less than a year after the diary ends. Elie Wiesel's memoir *Night* (1960) presents a different view of life in Nazi Germany. Wiesel—himself a survivor of the concentration camps—focuses his attention on the specific horrors that he experienced. Readers will find it difficult to remain unaffected by the inhuman treatment that Wiesel describes, whether it is the general mistreatment of the captives or the brutal, indiscriminant killings of men, women, and children. The fact that both of these works are autobiographical enhances their power.

In brutalizing the innocent, persecutors so cheapen human life as to lose their own humanity. Such seems to be the case with the SS medical officer Fritz Jemand von Niemand who, feeling his work is religiously justifiable, forces the title character of William Styron's *Sophie's Choice* (1976) to choose which of her two children will live—even though Sophie's incarceration has nothing to do with her religion. The memory haunts Sophie, and even though years have passed and she has since rediscovered freedom, friendship, and love, she opts to quiet her guilt with cyanide. Such is the aftermath of so terrible a trauma; Sophie seems unable to regain a sense of the humanity that was lost in this violent psychological oppression.

While the Holocaust is the most well-known case of genocide, sadly, the twentieth century saw numerous other instances of such atrocities. Just after the turn of the century, for example, the Turkish government experienced a growing nationalism. Predominantly Islamic Turkey had a checkered relationship with its Christian Armenian population, and the desire of the Turks to assert their cultural roots, including Islam, prompted acts of genocide. Turkey began deporting Armenians during Word War I, claiming they were an internal threat to their war effort. Deportations, however, often escalated into mass killings. In the end, around a million of the over two million Armenian Turks died. In *A Summer Without Dawn: An Armenian Epic* (2000), Agop J. Hacikyan follows the lives of Vartan Balian and his wife and son who, after being separated, experience different fates. What is significant about Hacikyan's book is that he portrays the humanity of members of both sides. Julia Pascal in the *Independent* (London) explains, "Hacikyan clearly blames the Ottoman Empire for the mass murder of the Armenians, but he avoids blanket condemnation of the Turks."

In his novel for young adults, *Under the Sun* (2004), Arthur Dorros portrays the events in Sarajevo in the early 1990s, where the dissolution of Yugoslavia has left a political void, and a power struggle along both ethnic and religious lines ensues. Christian Serbs, wanting an independent and culturally pure country of their own, begin the methodic expulsion of Croats and Bosnian Muslims. Dorros's book follows the thirteen-year-old Ehmet, whose father is a Muslim and whose mother is a Catholic Croat. Faced with the realities of war, he must flee his home. The book traces his progress to safety, which is found in an old village peacefully inhabited by the full ethnic and religious spectrum of the war's orphans, Dorros's final comment on the war.

Politics

An old tactic in politics is to win over the population by blaming a distinct group for some national hardship. The Nazis blamed Jews for Germany's financial ruin, while in Bosnia the violence stemmed from fears that the Muslims minority would hinder the Serbs' efforts to achieve independence. Gaining and keeping power serve as the driving forces behind such political maneuvering.

In 1937, the Dominican Republic dictator Generalissimo Rafael Trujillo tried to "whiten" the mixed-race country, partly by ridding his country of its darker-skinned Haitian immigrants. Near the border between the two countries, along the river that divided them, Trujillo had his soldiers kill tens of thousands of Haitians. This massacre forms the background for Haitian American Edwidge Danticat's 1998 novel *The Farming of Bones*. Danticat continued exploring the crimes against her forbears in her 2004 novel *The Dew Breaker*. The novel focuses on exiles from the tyrannical regime that ruled Haiti from the early 1970s to the mid-1980s, that of Jean-Claude "Baby Doc" Duvalier. The personal stories center around a Haitian immigrant to New York who, it turns out, was not a victim, but a perpetrator of the crimes. As he explains to his daughter, "You see, Ka, your father was the hunter, he was not the prey."

Racial distinctions are arbitrary. They may be assigned by outsiders, such as colonizers who assert control by creating these artificial distinctions among the indigenous peoples. The conflict between the Hutus and Tutsis in Rwanda, for example, can be traced back to distinctions made by the colonizing Belgians who singled out the taller, lighter-skinned natives (considered Tutsis) for office jobs while the stockier, darker people (considered Hutus) were relegated to manual labor. When Rwanda gained its independence in 1962, the Hutu majority gained power and retaliated by discriminating against the Tutsi. Hutu extremists, fearing a power shift, went on a hundred-day killing spree in 1994, murdering one million Tutsis and moderate Hutus. *Shake Hands with the Devil: The Failure of Humanity in Rwanda* (2003) explores the tragedy caused by governmental inaction. In this book, Lieutenant-General Romeo Dallaire recounts his experience in the midst of the genocide. Dallaire focuses his frustrations on the larger political failures of the United Nations and other world powers, whom he believes could have stopped the massacre, but instead merely stood by as the killings continued.

Sometimes groups have been targeted for being of a particular socioeconomic class, rather than a religion or ethnicity. While most instances of crimes against humanity are tied to race and ethnicity, Eric Weitz explains in *A Century of Genocide* (2003) that, under Stalin, the Soviet Union worked hard to define the various levels of society based on economics. When it determined that a particular class became a threat, it strove to eliminate the entire social group, in most cases by sending them into exile to live in work camps where many of them died of cold and hunger. Alexander Solzhenitsyn describes a typical day in one of these camps, based on his own experience, in *One Day in the Life of Ivan Denisovich* (1962). Though it is only one of the 3,653 days of his sentence, it is "almost a happy day" that starts and ends with extra food:

> [S]till clutching the hunk of bread, he drew his feet out of his valenki, deftly leaving inside them his foot rags and spoon, crawled barefoot up to his bunk, widened a little hole in the mattress, and there, amidst the sawdust, concealed his half-ration.

The United States is not without its own sordid past, and ethnic cleansing is among the crimes accrued during the drive to expand the borders of the nation "from sea to shining sea." The victims were the Native Americans who, because of westward expansion, were displaced to reservations and often became victims of violence. In *Bury my Heart at Wounded Knee* (1971), Dee Brown gives a historical account of the final years of the "Indian Wars." Brown describes a score of major incidents between different Native American tribes and the U.S. government between 1860 and 1890. In 1868, a Comanche chief named Tosawi surrendered to U.S. General Sheridan with the reassurance that he was a "good Indian." Sheridan's reply summed up the United States' attitude at the time: "The only good Indians I ever saw were dead."

Many authors who treat the subject of genocide focus on frustrations caused by governmental interference, particularly by a government attempting to cover up its involvement in ethnic killings. In his novel *Anil's Ghost* (2000), Michael Ondaatje dramatizes recent struggles in Sri Lanka, where Buddhist Sinhala and Hindu Tamils have been engaged in civil war since 1983. Here, the Sinhalese use their political power to cover up violence against the insurgent Tamils. While the protagonist's return to her native Sri Lanka is in part a personal quest, Rachel Cusk suggests in the *New Statesman* that "she quickly finds herself among people who live and die for their work, who labour in an atmosphere of political terror, bloodshed, and mortal danger." The climax of the novel occurs when the protagonist, a forensic anthropologist, discovers that a recently uncovered body was a person killed by the government. In her attempts to expose the results, she finds she is confounded by all sides.

Conclusion

Most instances of ethnic cleansing result in the displacement of many people who find themselves in new cultures. Some attempt to assimilate so not to draw attention to themselves, while others work to salvage their cultural identities. In either case, the descendants of the displaced will often wonder about their heritage. In *Everything is Illuminated* (2002), Jonathan Safran Foer makes his narrator his namesake, though one must remember that the account is fiction. He does, though, draw on his own search into his family's past to learn about a woman who may have saved his grandfather's life during World War II:

> "We will search for Augustine, who you think saved your grandfather from the Nazis."
> "Yes. . . . And then," I said, "if we find her?" The hero was a pensive person. "I don't know what then. I suppose I'd thank her."

To understand himself, the fictional Foer must face his past.

In the same way, each account of genocide is an attempt to preserve such a remembrance, an attempt to piece back together what was torn asunder. The act of genocide is more than mass murder; it is an attempt to rid the world of a particular racial, ethnic, or religious group. Genocide kills cultures and traditions and, by extension, it destroys the heritage of many individuals. Each account of genocide, each recollection by the survivors of genocide, serves as an attempt to reconstruct what was lost. More importantly, though, each account insists that its readers open their eyes to the horrors of the past so that some day we can all truly say, "never again."

SOURCES

Brown, Dee, *Bury My Heart at Wounded Knee: An Indian History of the American West*, Owl Books, 2001, originally published in 1971, p. 170.

Cusk, Rachel, "Sri Lankan Skeletons," in *New Statesman*, May 8, 2000, p. 55.

Danticat, Edwidge, *The Dew Breaker*, Random House, 2004.

Foer, Jonathan Safran, *Everything is Illuminated* Harper Perennial, 2003, p. 60.

Gellately, Robert, and Ben Kiernan, "The Study of Mass Murder and Genocide," in *The Specter of Genocide: Mass Murder in Historical Perspective*, edited by Robert Gellately and Ben Kiernan, Cambridge University Press, 2003, p. 20.

Pascal, Julia, "Friday Book: Tales from the Heart of a Forgotten Holocaust," in the *Independent*, August 11, 2000, enjoyment.independent.co.uk/books/reviews/article155254.ece (March 23, 2006).

Power, Samantha, *"A Problem from Hell": America and the Age of Genocide*, Perennial, 2002.

Solzhenitsyn, Alexander, *One Day in the Life of Ivan Denisovich*, translated by Ralph Parker, Signet Classics, 1993, p. 21.

Weitz, Eric D., *A Century of Genocide: Utopias of Race and Nation*, Princeton University Press, 2003.

Wiesel, Elie, *Night*, Bantam Books, 1960, p. 32.

Ethnicity

Introduction

Ethnicity is a powerful glue for many groups in society. It typically includes several factors, such as race, religion, culture, and language. The idea of ethnic identity can be found in every culture in the world, and it is often what groups use to separate themselves from other groups in a multicultural society. Ethnic groups can be either a minority or a majority in a society. The dominant group sets its own standards for what is considered "normal" in their society. Stories that deal with ethnicity often tell of minority groups, or of those that are oppressed, discriminated against, ostracized, or even simply misunderstood. Distinct ethnic groups inside a society are frequently from minority groups and also often immigrants. Immigrants from other cultures are most likely to stand out from the overall culture.

Desire to Fit In

Sometimes an individual within an ethnic group is ostracized for exhibiting the very traits the group most wants to reject in themselves. For example, Pecola Breedlove, the young African American girl in Toni Morrison's first novel *The Bluest Eye* (1970), rejects herself and experiences the rejection of her peers because she is "black and ugly." She wants nothing more than to be the very opposite of what she is. The other African Americans in Pecola's town shun and

The Lafayette Theater in Harlem at the time of the Harlem Renaissance (c) *Corbis*

abuse her because they have designated her family the lowest in town, the one that makes the others feel better because they are higher than the Breedloves: "All of us—all who knew her—felt so wholesome after we cleaned ourselves on her." When her father rapes and impregnates her, Pecola escapes into madness. The children laugh at her and the adults blame her for her misfortune: "when the land kills of its own volition, we acquiesce and say the victim had no right to live. We are wrong, of course, but it doesn't matter. It's too late."

Those who shun Pecola and laugh at her impossible dream do so precisely because they, too, secretly long to be blonde, blue-eyed, and white. Pecola's blackness makes them so ashamed of their own that they reject her. They hate her because they hate themselves. Their ethnic identity is based on what they can never be—someone else.

Similarly, Archie and Samad in Zadie Smith's uproarious novel *White Teeth* (2000)

both discover that life in multicultural London of the 1970s is tough. Samad accepts an arranged marriage to a woman from his own culture and ends up with two alienated sons. Archie marries a Jamaican woman. They first meet when Samad saves Archie from a suicide attempt. The characters in the novel are basically unhappy with themselves, regardless of their ethnic group. Archie's daughter, Irie, thinks, "Sometimes you want to be different. And sometimes you'd give the hair on your head to be the same as everybody else." At the hairdresser, Irie has tamed her Afro in favor of short, straight hair, hating her non-English appearance. But Irie's friends and family do not approve, and her attempts to pass as white like her father go in vain. About this self-hatred among immigrants and their children in England, the author muses, a "churchgoing lady was determined to go to her grave with long fake nails and a weave-on. Strange as it sounds, there are plenty of people who refuse to meet the Lord with an Afro."

Mixed-Race Identity

Irie comes from two different ethnic groups, Jamaican and English, belonging entirely to neither and rejected by one or both. This lack of a specific ethnic identity also occurs in James McBride's memoir about his white mother, *The Color of Water* (1997), and in the young half-Vietnamese girl, Loi, in Sherry Garland's young adult novel *Song of the Buffalo Boy* (1994). McBride's Jewish mother left her immigrant Polish family, who rejected her, married McBride's African American father, and converted to Christianity. Her children found themselves caught between two worlds. But their mother's love turned this mix of cultures into a strength, not a weakness. In contrast, Loi, the child of her Vietnamese mother's liason with an American soldier, is an outcast. The bitter villagers reject her because to them, she represents the American invaders who destroyed their homes and killed their relatives, and their shame at not being able to stop this invasion. But they also reject her out of their own rigidity and racism against outsiders. Refusing to accept this injustice, Loi flees to Saigon to find her father and to escape an arranged marriage. Her search ends unhappily, but it does lead to find a place in Vietnamese society with the one she loves, Khai the "Buffalo Boy."

Oppression

Stories about ethnicity often explore uncomfortable and taboo subjects. *The Bluest Eye*, for example, explores incest, child rape, and self-hatred. *Song of the Buffalo Boy* explores the Vietnam War and the plight of the despised mixed-race children in its aftermath. Conflict between and within ethnic groups can result in shameful acts on both sides, as well as oppression and even genocide.

Gwendolyn Brooks's 1981 poem, "To the Diaspora," for example, evokes the shameful legacy of the trans-Atlantic slave trade, in which millions of Africans were kidnapped and sold to the Americas as slaves. She asks the people of the diaspora (people of African ancestry living outside Africa) what they might find when they come home to Africa. David Guterson's novel *Snow Falling on Cedars* (1994) explores lives changed by the internment of Japanese Americans during World War II. In the novel, Kabuo Miyamoto, a Japanese

fisherman living in the Pacific Northwest during the 1950s, is arrested for murdering another fisherman. His arrest is a result of his Japanese ethnicity, as suspicion and discrimination remained issues for Japanese Americans on the West Coast for at least a decade after World War II. A local white journalist, Ishmael Chambers, tries to defend him. But Ishmael has an ulterior motive—he is in love with Kabuo's wife Hatsue, with whom he grew up. Kabuo is finally released when the death is ruled an accident. Ishmael's story ends less happily when Hatsue stays with her husband. He sees Hatsue and Kabuo as essentially inscrutable:

> [T]he palpitations of Kabuo Miyamoto's heart were unknowable finally. And Hatsue's heart wasn't knowable, either, nor was Carl Heine's [the dead fisherman]. The heart of *any* other, because it had a will, would remain forever mysterious.

For Ishmael, everyone is an "other," an alien person of incomprehensible thoughts, feelings, and cultural attitudes.

Similarly, the young hero of Larry Watson's novel *Montana, 1948* (1995) at first sees the behavior of his family's Sioux housekeeper as a mystery. In both novels, white male protagonists tell the stories of female, nonwhite women who are deprived of their voices in society. When the housekeeper falls ill, she refuses to be treated by the protagonist's uncle, the town doctor. When she is later found dead, she appears to have caused her own death by refusing medical treatment. Then, accusations against the uncle begin to surface, and there are rumors that he sexually abused Sioux women under his care. The protagonist tells his story from the distance of adulthood, piecing together a story of prejudice and buried secrets from his own memories and the memories of those who still live and will speak to him. Even dominant groups in society cannot escape the poison that results from oppressing others.

Conflict can even result in the ostracism or attempted destruction of a group or individual, as in Rumer Goddon's young adult novel *Gypsy Girl* (1972). In it, Kizzy Lovell lives on the edge of a village after her grandmother dies and her wagon burns. The villagers hate and fear gypsies as thieves and tramps and try to drive her out. Only after great struggle is Kizzy able to make them accept her.

Class

People in minority ethnic groups often live in poverty, as they are denied equal education, housing, and professional opportunities. In Sandra Cisneros's *The House on Mango Street* (1984), young Esperanza Cordero finds her impoverished life on Mango Street oppressive. Even though her family owns their house, she dreams of growing up to have better house of her own. For her, poverty means her family's small house and the humiliations they must endure because they cannot afford anything better. At the beginning of the novel, Esperanza explains the situation:

> The house on Mango Street is ours, and we don't have to pay rent to anybody, or share the yard with the people downstairs, or be careful not to make too much noise, and there isn't a landlord banging on the ceiling with a broom. But even so, it's not the house we'd thought we'd get.

Poverty means adjusting one's dreams downward, something that Esperanza longs to escape.

Stories about ethnicity also frequently illustrate the social and economic shocks that immigrant groups suffer when moving to another, often larger, society. The Garcia de la Torre girls, of Julia Alvarez's *How the Garcia Girls Lost Their Accents* (1991), for example, come from the very top of a rich, but oppressive society in the Dominican Republic. When they move to America, their father struggles for work and their mother struggles with a much lower place in her new society. In assimilating into American society, the four daughters are not just attracted by the wider opportunities of America, but also repelled by the closed and oppressive nature of their old society. The young Dominican men are similarly confused. They like the freedoms of America, but they do not want to share them with the women of their families:

> Mundín's eyes do a double blink. For all his liberal education in the States, and all his sleeping around there and here, and all his eager laughter when his Americanized cousins recount their misadventures, his own sister has to be pure.

Even those who want to assimilate the most do not want to change the old system if it means that others in their group will get ahead of them.

WHEN I SIT IN THE DRAFTY BASEMENT THAT IS THE NEW WORLD CABARET WITH A WHITE PERSON, MY COLOR COMES. WE ENTER CHATTING ABOUT ANY LITTLE NOTHING THAT WE HAVE IN COMMON AND ARE SEATED BY THE JAZZ WAITERS. IN THE ABRUPT WAY THAT JAZZ ORCHESTRAS HAVE, THIS ONE PLUNGES INTO A NUMBER. . . . I FOLLOW THOSE HEATHEN— FOLLOW THEM EXULTINGLY. . . . THE MEN OF THE ORCHESTRA WIPE THEIR LIPS AND REST THEIR FINGERS. I CREEP BACK SLOWLY TO THE VENEER WE CALL CIVILIZATION WITH THE LAST TONE AND FIND THE WHITE FRIEND SITTING MOTIONLESS IN HIS SEAT SMOKING CALMLY."

Zora Neale Hurston, "How It Feels to Be Colored Me"

Social Change

Some people find strength in embracing not only the successes among their ethnic group, but also the tragic failures in their midst. In Ernest Gaines's novel *A Lesson before Dying* (1993), an African American teacher, Grant Wiggins, is asked by his aunt to help Jefferson, a condemned man from his community, face death with dignity. Jefferson, a mentally challenged man who witnessed a liquor store shoot-out that killed two black men and the white store owner, is tried as an accomplice to murder. His defense attorney tells the all-white jury, "Why, I would just as soon put a hog in the electric chair as this."

Jefferson is condemned to death, despite clearly being unable to comprehend the charges against him or the crime he was supposed to have committed. Grant does not want to help Jefferson at first. Jefferson symbolizes everything about his town that Wiggins tried to leave behind by going to college. But eventually, he realizes that Jefferson is teaching him something far more important about dying that Grant is teaching him. A witness to the execution later

Japanese Americans boarding trains for the Manzanar Relocation Center Crown Publishers

tells Grant, "He was the strongest man in that crowded room."

People who embrace their ethnic identity may also find great strength in the specialness it confers. Zora Neale Hurston's essay "How It Feels to Be Colored Me" (1928) celebrates her African American heritage instead of dwelling on the pain of slavery, segregation, or forced assimilation. "I am not tragically colored," she insists. She describes going to a nightclub with a white friend. She is caught up, willingly and joy-fully, in the wild mood of the jazz music. At the end of the piece, she turns to her white friend, who has been completely unmoved by the music, and she feels sorry for his ignorance. His tonal deafness seems, to her, a function of his drab, colorless ethnic background and she wants no part in it, dominant or not.

Language

In Yoshiko Ushida's novel *Picture Bride* (1997), Hana Omiya, a young Japanese woman, comes to America at the turn of the century for an arranged marriage with a young, rich business-man. When her husband turns out to be both poor and middle-aged, she is disappointed, but remains true to him. She does so by trying to maintain a Japanese home in the United States. Her English remains limited and broken as she proudly clings to her Japanese language and customs. Language becomes a link to her identity.

Language also marks those who assimilate into a new society. In *How the Garcia Girls Lost Their Accents,* Yolanda resists maintaining her Spanish roots, fearing it will affect her English:

> The more she practices, the sooner she'll be back into her native tongue, the aunts insist. Yes, and when she returns to the States, she'll find herself suddenly going blank over some word in English or, like her mother, mixing up some common phrase.

To Yolanda, assimilation is easier than a daily compromise between different cultures,

Young girls in a Cinco de Mayo parade, New York, 1997 (c) *Catherine Karnow | Corbis*

because it is less confusing. But it also leads to losing a part of one's self. By refusing to keep her Spanish, Yolanda loses that childhood part of her that speaks and thinks in her native tongue.

Keeping one's culture can go even further than holding onto language and daily customs. Antonio, the young hero of Rudolpho A. Anaya's novel *Bless Me Ultima* (1994), learns Native American shamanic traditions in 1940s New Mexico. These magical traditions give a surreal quality to the boy's memories when he grows up, but they also enable him to preserve his Native ethnic identity. Not only does his the old healer Ultima speak a different language from English and freely live an impoverished lifestyle that most immigrants would avoid and try to escape, but she has mysterious traditions

that defy Western rational thought. The protagonist strives to retain these traditions, even to the point of rejecting the dominant American culture. They give him an especially strong ethnic identity.

Conclusion

When ethnic identity makes the person feel stronger rather than weaker, superior rather than inferior, that person will struggle to retain that identity. When a person holds a weaker position in the old culture than in the new one, his or her attachment to the old ethnic identity likewise becomes weaker. Thus, the Garcia girls lose their accents and Esperanza flees Mango Street. In traditional, non-Western cultures, women are usually required to suppress their own identities as individuals in favor of bolstering their ethnic culture and the identities of their husbands, brothers, fathers, and sons. They are expected to bear the burden of carrying on the culture by maintaining their households and raising their children in traditional ways, like Hana Omiya in *Picture Bride*. Stories about ethnic identity often show women fighting and rejecting traditional ethnic ties as too hostile and confining.

However, people like Hurston and characters like Antonio and Ultima can surmount these weaknesses and turn them into strengths. Hurston freely adopts the traditionally male persona of a hunter when listening to jazz music. She converts traditional roles to her own use, making something new and vibrant out of something that is neither purely African nor purely American. Antonio juggles Spanish and Native American culture and comes up with something of both that works for him. Fiction about ethnicity rarely shows such a happy blend of traditions, but the protagonists of such stories often hope for such a solution to

their confusion. A healthy culture can mix new traditions with old ones and maintain continuity.

SOURCES

Alvarez, Julia, *How the Garcia Girls Lost Their Accents*, Algonquin Books of Chapel Hill, 1991, pp. 7, 125.

Cisneros, Sandra, *The House on Mango Street*, Alfred A. Knopf, 2005, pp. 3–4.

Gaines, Ernest J., *A Lesson Before Dying*, Alfred A. Knopf, 1993, pp. 8, 253.

Guterson, David, *Snow Falling on Cedars*, Harcourt Brace, 1994, p. 345.

Hurston, Zora Neale, *How It Feels to Be Colored Me*, *Barnard Electronic Archive and Teaching Library*, beatl. barnard.columbia.edu/wsharpe/citylit/colored_me.htm (February 4, 2006).

Morrison, Toni, *The Bluest Eye*, Alfred A. Knopf, 2005, pp. 203–204.

Smith, Zadie, *White Teeth*, Random House, 2000, pp. 227, 237.

Gender

Introduction

Imagine you lived in a world in which you could not vote, hold elected office, or own property no matter how old you are. Consider how limited your life would be if you were not encouraged to go to school or pursue a career. Think about how frustrating it would be to marry a spouse who maintained final authority over every aspect of your life, a spouse who in some places could administer corporal punishment to you with the full consent and encouragement of the law. Until comparatively recent times, most women lived in such a world, for discrimination based on gender was the rule in almost every culture. Yet even in the most repressive times and places, writers of both sexes have protested the discrimination against women that was so thoroughly woven into the fabric of society that many people simply could not recognize the inequities.

Women and Literature

Many people associate feminism with political activism and believe the feminist movement to be only a few decades old. In reality, the issues and ideals of feminism have been sources of debate and discussion for thousands of years. One of the earliest and most important feminist works of Western literature is *Antigone* (approx. 440 B.C.), by Sophocles.

The play concerns the conflict between Antigone and her uncle, Creon, who is the king

of Thebes. Creon has come to power because his nephews—Antigone's brothers—have killed each other during a war for control of Thebes. Because Creon considers one brother, Polynices, a traitor, he orders the body to be left unburied, which is a terrible insult. Antigone believes it is her responsibility to bury her brother, and when she attempts to do so, her own uncle condemns her to die. His decision ultimately leads to the demise of Creon's wife and son, as well as his niece.

The earliest audiences of Sophocles' play realized that the author was illustrating the consequences awaiting any man so full of *hubris,* or enormous self-pride. Yet, it is also likely that they picked up on the conflict between the sexes that seems foremost to modern readers. After all, as the daughter of King Oedipus, Antigone should herself be in line for the throne, but Antigone is never given an opportunity to prove herself as a leader. Furthermore, the fact that Creon wields absolute authority and Antigone is rendered essentially powerless because of her gender is a ready symbol of the imbalance of power between all men and women in Sophocles' time. This imbalance is further illustrated through Ismene, Antigone's sister, who meekly submits to Creon's excessive decree:

> Do but consider how most miserably
> We too shall perish, if despite of law
> We traverse the behest or power of kings.
> We must remember we are women born,
> Unapt to cope with men; and, being ruled
> By mightier than ourselves, we have to hear
> These things—and worse. For my part, I will
> . . . yield obedience
> To them that walk in power; to exceed
> Is madness, and not wisdom.

One of the most influential works to protest discrimination against women appeared in 1792. *A Vindication of the Rights of Woman,* by Mary Wollstonecraft, is often cited as the first modern feminist manifesto. Wollstonecraft did publish other material, but *A Vindication of the Rights of Woman,* with its passionate yet well-reasoned call to provide increased educational and vocational choices for women, is the only piece of hers that is still widely read. Referring to the prevailing notion that knowledge is closely associated with morality, Wollstonecraft asserts that "truth must be common to all, or it will be ineffacacious with respect to its influence on general practice." Tragically, Wollstonecraft's own pursuit of female equality was cut short when she

died a few days after giving birth to her daughter, Mary Godwin, who later achieved literary immortality as Mary Shelley, the author of *Frankenstein.*

For almost a century, the novels of Jane Austen have remained among the most popular in English literature. Austen's gift for wry social commentary gained attention with *Sense and Sensibility* (1811). Her second book, *Pride and Prejudice* (1813), remains equally beloved and was actually drafted years earlier than her first published novel. *Pride and Prejudice* examines the lengths to which the five Bennet sisters will go in order to marry happily. Austen suggests that a society that encourages marriages for social and financial gain while discouraging female independence and autonomy is destined to produce materialistic and shallow citizens. As the author ironically notes in *Pride and Prejudice,* "It is a truth universally acknowledged, that a single man in possession of a good fortune, must be in want of a wife."

European writers and philosophers had long espoused principles that promoted democracy and equality; these principles inspired the American Revolution, which ended with the establishment of a new nation that supposedly guaranteed its citizens "life, liberty, and the pursuit of happiness." Yet, even in the United States, the freedoms were initially reserved for white male property owners. As the nineteenth century progressed, a movement to abolish slavery gained momentum; many abolitionists also advocated increased rights for women. Among the highlights of this movement was Sojourner Truth's appearance at a women's rights convention in Akron, Ohio, in 1851. Born a slave, Truth was an illiterate but powerful and persuasive advocate for the rights of African Americans and women. Her brief address, "Ain't I A Woman?" electrified the conventioneers and remains one of the great American speeches, an inspirational call for civil rights for all. Truth firmly denounces the idea that women cannot be equal to men because Jesus was male. Truth asks, "Where did your Christ come from?" then provides the answer: "From God and a woman! Man had nothing to do with Him."

Henrik Ibsen's play *A Doll's House* (1879) is another influential work that continues to fascinate and challenge readers. *A Doll's House* is the story of Nora, a cheerful, somewhat immature housewife who was stifled and sheltered first by her father, then her husband. Nora has saved her banker husband's life by secretly borrowing money from an unsavory employee of the bank. When Nora's husband, Torvald, learns what she has done, he explodes in a rage and reveals that he cares more for his profession and position in society than he does for his own wife. Torvald quickly apologizes and tries to make amends, but a sadder, wiser Nora decides to leave him in order to find her own place in the world. The harshness of the slamming door at Nora's departure at the play's end underscores the likely grim fate of Ibsen's protagonist; after all, without money or education in a world that discriminates against independent women, how will Nora survive?

Thomas Hardy's *Tess of the d'Urbervilles* (1891) is the tragic story of a poor girl's gradual descent into ruin. Tess Durbeyfield seeks help for her impoverished family from the wealthy d'Urbervilles, to whom she believes she is distantly related. Rakish Alec d'Urberville takes advantage of her, and Tess returns home to give birth to a child who dies shortly thereafter. Angel, a local minister's son, falls in love with Tess, but he rejects her after they marry because of her sexual past. Eventually, Tess kills Alec and is briefly reunited with Angel, but she is ultimately arrested and executed for murder. Hardy repeatedly attacks the stringent social codes that separate Tess from both aristocratic Alec and middle-class Angel, as well as the double standard that excuses and even encourages males to indulge in premarital sex while simultaneously vilifying any female who does the same.

As feminist critics continue to study the role of women's literature throughout history, they frequently uncover ignored or forgotten texts that illuminate the condition of women in the past. An excellent example of such a "recovered text" is Charlotte Perkins Gilman's "The Yellow Wallpaper" (1892). Gilman's work was largely forgotten after her death in 1935. After "The Yellow Wallpaper" was reprinted in the early 1970s, however, the story earned a place among the most significant works in American literature. In this first-person narrative, a doctor's wife is forced to undergo the "rest cure," which requires absolute quiet and confinement in bed. As the story unfolds, the female narrator becomes obsessed with an unusual patch of wallpaper in her bedroom that seems to contain an image of an imprisoned woman trying to escape.

Ultimately, the reader realizes that the narrator identifies with the wallpaper image and now imagines herself fleeing from the confinement prescribed by her husband. The symbolism of a woman with intelligence and imagination being prevented from expressing herself can be applied to many contemporary gender issues.

Kate Chopin's short story "The Story of an Hour" (1894) enjoys a cachet similar to Gilman's "The Yellow Wallpaper." Chopin's tale chronicles the last sixty minutes in the life of Mrs. Mallard, a sickly housewife who is shocked to learn that her husband, Brently, has been killed in a railroad accident. At first devastated by the news, Mrs. Mallard gradually realizes that her husband's death has provided her with an opportunity to live her own life, on her own terms, as opposed to his:

> There would be no one to live for during those coming years; she would live for herself. There would be no powerful will bending hers in that blind persistence with which men and women believe they have a right to impose a private will upon a fellow-creature. A kind intention or a cruel intention made the act seem no less a crime as she looked upon it in that brief moment of illumination.

When her husband shows up alive and well, Mrs. Mallard suddenly dies, suffering a heart attack from what her doctors call "joy that kills." Readers, of course, realize that Mrs. Mallard expires because her heart has broken under the realization that her taste of freedom will not last.

Another work by Chopin that illustrates the restrictions placed on a woman's independence and right to live according to her own standards is *The Awakening* (1899). This short novel traces the development of Edna Pontellier, a young wife and mother who finds marriage and family stifling and repressive. While her husband is away, Edna engages in an affair with another man and sends her children away in order to enjoy time to herself. However, Edna's world forbids such shocking displays of independence for women, and Edna drowns herself rather than return to her old way of living. Chopin's title refers to Edna's sexual and intellectual rebirth, acknowledged as Edna swims out to her death feeling "like some new-born creature, opening its eyes in a familiar world that it had never known." For Edna, death itself is a kind of awakening. Chopin's novel was met with such condemnation by an outraged public that she rarely published again. After her death in 1904, Chopin's book, like Gilman's short story, fell into obscurity until revived by feminist critics decades later.

The House of Mirth (1905), Edith Wharton's first major novel, introduced Lily Bart to the world. Lily is a daughter of wealth and privilege who finds herself limited not only by the social restrictions on women, but more specifically by the expectations of the American upper class: Lily has been taught to revere the security and luxury guaranteed by a wealthy husband, so she refuses to marry her true love, Lawrence Selden, who is not rich. She eventually commits suicide after losing her fortune and the prospect of finding a rich husband. Clearly, even women of means are oppressed when they cannot imagine marrying below their station in life.

British author Virginia Woolf discusses the needs of writers, particularly female authors, in *A Room of One's Own* (1929). Woolf claims that women need five hundred pounds (in British currency) to support themselves while pursuing writing careers. Elsewhere in the book, Woolf describes the fate of William Shakespeare's hypothetical sister. If Shakespeare had a sister, Woolf points out, she would not have been allowed a formal education and would have been discouraged from expressing herself either as a writer or an actress (since women were forbidden from performing on the Elizabethan stage). Ultimately, "any woman born with a great [artistic] gift in the sixteenth century would certainly have gone crazed, shot herself, or ended her days in some lonely cottage outside the village," Woolf claims.

In the wake of the feminist movement of the 1960s, a number of authors have questioned the assumptions of gender roles and challenged discrimination based not just on sex, but on race and sexual persuasion as well. Adrienne Rich's poem "Diving into the Wreck" (1972) uses deep-sea diving imagery to recount metaphorically the quest of women to establish their own identities independent of men and hints at the validity of lesbian relationships. In *The Woman Warrior* (1976), Maxine Hong Kingston's memoir of her life as a young Chinese American, several stories recount discrimination based on race as well as gender. The most compelling of these tales, "No Name Woman," describes the sad fate of an aunt driven to suicide in China long before Kingston's birth. This aunt, whose name the

> I KNOW THAT LIBERTINES WILL ALSO EXCLAIM, THAT WOMAN WOULD BE UNSEXED BY ACQUIRING STRENGTH OF BODY AND MIND, AND THAT BEAUTY, SOFT BEWITCHING BEAUTY! WOULD NO LONGER ADORN THE DAUGHTERS OF MEN. I AM OF A VERY DIFFERENT OPINION, FOR I THINK, THAT, ON THE CONTRARY, WE SHOULD THEN SEE DIGNIFIED BEAUTY, AND TRUE GRACE; TO PRODUCE WHICH, MANY POWERFUL PHYSICAL AND MORAL CAUSES WOULD CONCUR."

> *Mary Wollstonecraft,* A Vindication of the Rights of Woman

family is forbidden to mention, killed herself after shaming her family by getting pregnant outside of wedlock. Though it is likely this relative was seduced or raped, "her betrayal so maddened them, they saw to it she would suffer forever, even after death." Alice Walker's Pulitzer Prize–winning novel, *The Color Purple* (1982) traces the development of Celie, who grows up in the rural South facing extreme poverty, racism, and abuse. Married against her will to the cruel Albert, Celie eventually finds the strength and courage to reject her husband. After experiencing real love with Albert's mistress, Celie is finally able to experience many different forms of love with her extended family.

Writers have explored gender discrimination in some highly unusual cultural contexts as well. Margaret Atwood's *The Handmaid's Tale* (1986) depicts a futuristic world in which women have been stripped of their human rights. Because most couples have been rendered infertile, young women such as the novel's protagonist, Offred, are compelled to bear children to be raised by the male-dominated ruling class. Witi Ihimaera's *The Whale Rider* (1987) introduces readers to Kahu, a young Maori girl in New Zealand. Kahu's birth disappoints her aging great-grandfather, who longs for a boy to continue his name and preserve his culture's traditions, but in time, Kahu proves herself a worthy heir to carry on her people's way of life. Jeffrey Eugenides won a Pulitzer Prize for his novel

Middlesex (2002), an epic history of a Greek American family narrated by Cal Stephanides, who is a hermaphrodite: "I was born twice: first as a baby girl, on a remarkably smogless Detroit day in January of 1960; and then again, as a teenage boy, in an emergency room near Petoskey, Michigan, in August of 1974."

Conclusion

Cal's development mirrors the evolution of America in the late twentieth century, a time when gender discrimination was overcome in many instances. Yet, the last few decades have witnessed new forms of prejudice, including intolerance of individuals whose gender identification does not align with their biological sex. As the next century and eras yet to come present new challenges to the expectations and assumptions of contemporary society, writers will undoubtedly continue to illustrate and illuminate the debate in the campaign against this, and any and all, discrimination.

SOURCES

Atwood, Margaret, *The Handmaid's Tale,* 1986, Anchor Books, 1998.

Austen, Jane, *Pride and Prejudice,* edited by Donald Gray, W. W. Norton, 1993, p. 3, originally published in 1813.

Chopin, Kate, *The Awakening,* 1899, Dover Publications, 1993, p. 115.

———, "The Story of An Hour," *East of the Web,* www.eastoftheweb.com/short-stories/UBooks/StorHour.shtml (February 6, 2006).

Eugenides, Jeffrey, *Middlesex,* Farrar, Straus and Giroux, 2002, p. 3.

Gilman, Charlotte Perkins, "The Yellow Wallpaper," edited by Dale M. Bauer, Bedford Books, 1998, originally published in 1892.

Hardy, Thomas, *Tess of the d'Urbervilles,* Penguin Books, 2003, originally published in 1891.

Ibsen, Henrik, *A Doll's House,* Dover Publications, 1992, originally published in 1879.

Ihimaera, Witi, *The Whale Rider,* Harcourt Paperbacks, 2003, originally published in 1987.

Kingston, Maxine Hong, *The Woman Warrior,* Vintage Books, 1989, p. 16, originally published in 1976.

Rich, Adrienne, "Diving Into the Wreck," in *Adrienne Rich's Poetry and Prose,* edited by Barbara Charlesworth Gelpi and Albert Gelpi, W. W. Norton, 1993, p. 53.

Sophocles, *Antigone,* Dover Publications, 1993, p. 3.

Truth, Sojourner, "Ain't I A Woman?", *Inquiry: Questioning, Reading, Writing,* 2d ed., edited by Lynn Z. Bloom and Edward M. White, Pearson / Prentice Hall, 2004, p. 369.

Walker, Alice, *The Color Purple,* Pocket Books, 1990, originally published in 1982.

Wharton, Edith, *The House of Mirth,* edited by Shari Benstock, Bedford / St. Martin's, 1994, originally published in 1905.

Wollstonecraft, Mary, *A Vindication of the Rights of Woman,* Dover Publications, 1996, p. 2, originally published in 1792.

Woolf, Virginia, *A Room of One's Own,* in *The Norton Anthology of Theory and Criticism,* edited by Vincent B. Leitch et al., W. W. Norton, 2001, p. 1023, originally published in 1929.

Religion

Introduction

In literature that explores the issues of race and prejudice, religion often emerges as the foundation of conflict and divisiveness between individuals or groups. This is not surprising, since such literature by definition centers on ideas of exclusion and intolerance. In addition, religions are often closely associated with specific ethnic or racial groups, as with Judaism; in these cases, religion can become a source of persecution for a character or group. However, religion can also appear as a positive force that unifies and sustains those who endure suffering borne of racism and prejudice.

Religion in Literature

Arthur Miller's *The Crucible* (1953) is a classic example of how religion can become a lightning rod for hysteria that divides a community and targets individuals for persecution. The play depicts the infamous witch trials in Salem, Massachusetts, in 1692. In the drama, the townspeople engage in a frenzy of accusation and confession that culminates in the hangings of several innocent people. The charges that fracture the austere Puritan community center on people suspected of interacting with the devil. Once indicted, a defendant can either confess to the sin and implicate others, or face death. These accusations are made based on personal grudges and prejudices instead of evidence, and the

A T'ang-era figure of the Buddha seated sitting cross-legged

"I LOOK FOR JOHN PROCTOR THAT TOOK ME FROM MY SLEEP AND PUT KNOWLEDGE IN MY HEART! I NEVER KNEW WHAT PRETENSE SALEM WAS, I NEVER KNEW THE LYING LESSONS I WAS TAUGHT BY ALL THESE CHRISTIAN WOMEN AND THEIR COVENANTED MEN! AND NOW YOU BID ME TEAR THE LIGHT OUT OF MY EYES? I WILL NOT, I CANNOT! YOU LOVED ME, JOHN PROCTOR, AND WHATEVER SIN IT IS, YOU LOVE ME YET!"

Arthur Miller, The Crucible

ruling bodies equate protestations with guilt: as Deputy Governor Danforth puts it, "you must understand, sir, that a person is either with this court or he must be counted against it, there be no road between." Although people's religious beliefs are apparently behind the persecution in the play, the work also parallels the entirely political movement of McCarthyism that was sweeping the nation at the time it was written.

Religion is also a divisive force in *Midnight's Children* (1980), by Salman Rushdie. The novel parallels the rise of India as a free nation with the birth and growth of two Indian boys—one Muslim, one Hindu—who are switched at birth. The book illustrates the devastating effects of religious intolerance and separatism, depicting the chaotic formation of the Muslim and Hindu nations of Pakistan and India, as well as the later independence of Bangladesh. At the same time, Rushdie demonstrates how people's religion is often simply a trait assigned by their birth.

In *The Crusades Through Arab Eyes*, Amin Maalouf offers a historical account of the medieval Euro-Christian assault on the "holy lands" from the perspective of the Muslims who fended off the Christian intruders, a point of view rarely presented. Here, religion serves two purposes that might seem contradictory: Christianity is used to unify Europeans in their desire to reclaim the holy lands, while at the same time casting those of any other religion as unfit to care for such a sacred place. Ultimately, religion acts as a unifying force, bringing together different Muslim groups in the region to repel the invading Christian hordes.

Religion also serves a dual purpose in Graham Greene's *The Power and the Glory* (1940; first published in the United States under the title *The Labyrinthine Ways*). In the book, a Catholic priest discovers he is the last of his kind in the Tabasco region of Mexico, where Communist revolutionaries have forced all other priests to either flee or renounce their faith by marrying. The goal of the revolutionaries is simple: "No more money for saying prayers, no more money for building places to say prayers in. We'll give people food instead, teach them to read, give them books. We'll see they don't suffer." The priest's insistence on continuing to serve his followers makes him a target and eventually leads to his execution. In the end, the priest tells his captor that "if there's ever been a single man in this state damned, then I'll be damned too." The priest accepts his fate. Although he has more than one opportunity to

Muslims in prayer near the Dome of the Rock Mosque, Jerusalem Khaled Zigari | AP Images

escape unharmed, his duty to his religion is more important than his own well-being. In this way, religion sustains his spirit even as it is the very reason for his persecution.

A similar situation exists for Primo Levi and his fellow Jews in "A Good Day," a chapter from Levi's memoir *Survival in Auschwitz* (1947). As they journey to the factory where they are forced to work, the prisoners see the hills that mark the gas chambers at Birkenau, where they believe they will soon meet their end. They are all resigned to this fate except "a group of Greeks, those admirable and terrible Jews of Salonica," whose faith leads them to sing songs of their upcoming freedom. All ten thousand in their camp are imprisoned simply because they are Jews; their nationalities range from Italian to Polish to Greek, but their religion means that they are all equally condemned. Here, the faith that dooms them also sustains some of them. However, Levi points out that in such dire circumstances—bitter cold, starvation,

hard labor, hopelessness—their "only purpose is to reach the spring."

The trappings of religion are used to explore race and ethnicity in Jhumpa Lahiri's "This Blessed House," found in her short story collection *Interpreter of Maladies* (1999). In the story, a newly wedded Indian American couple discovers many Christian ornaments scattered throughout the house they have just purchased. Sanjeev, the husband, wants to throw them out since he and his wife are not Christian; however, his wife—who goes by the name Twinkle—finds them beautiful. She begins to display them on the mantle above the fireplace, partly because she enjoys them and partly because she feels a need to assert some level of independence in their relationship. Sanjeev is worried only that others will see the artifacts and incorrectly assume the couple is Christian. He implies a certain prejudice toward Christian Indians. Ultimately, the objects help the couple define their expectations for each other in their new marriage.

The artifacts themselves hold power beyond their religious association.

Conclusion

Religion is often intertwined with ethnic or racial identity and is therefore a common sub-theme in literature dealing with race and prejudice. Religion is sometimes presented as the basis for discrimination, but it can provide the strength that helps the persecuted endure and the inspiration that helps the persecutors discover their humanity. As in life, religion may have as many purposes in literature, the best of which will instruct, inspire, and elevate.

SOURCES

Greene, Graham, *The Power and the Glory*, Penguin, 1991, pp. 194, 200, originally published in 1940.

Lahiri, Jhumpa, "This Blessed House," in *Interpreter of Maladies*, Mariner Books, 1999, pp. 136–57.

Levi, Primo, "A Good Day," in *Survival in Auschwitz*, translated by Stuart Woolf, Simon & Schuster, 1996, pp. 71–76, originally published in 1947.

Miller, Arthur, *The Crucible*, in Vol. 2 of *The Heath Anthology of American Literature*, 2d edition, edited by Paul Lauter, Heath, 1994, pp. 1980–2053, originally published in 1953.

Segregation

Introduction

At the heart of most literature about race and prejudice is the idea of exclusion—exclusion from opportunities, exclusion from resources, and even exclusion from physical spaces. Segregation is the physical separation of people of a certain race, ethnicity, or class from other people. Sometimes this involves wholesale relocation, as with American Indians in the nineteenth century and Japanese Americans during World War II. However, segregation can also manifest itself as exclusion from certain places or services; during the first half of the twentieth century, for example, many restaurants in the American South refused entrance or service to "coloreds." Despite these examples, segregation is not limited to the history and literature of Americans; a survey of world literature reveals that segregation is a common theme across all boundaries of culture and geography.

Jim Crow

From the end of post–Civil War Reconstruction in 1877 to the Civil Rights Act of 1964, legalized racism flourished in the southern United States with the encouragement and protection of "Jim Crow" laws—laws that kept black and white Americans segregated in many areas of life. One of the most well-known figures in the fight to end segregation in America is Dr. Martin Luther King Jr. In 1956, he helped organize a boycott of the Montgomery, Alabama, bus

system in an attempt to end segregation on public transportation. Eight years later, on the steps of the Lincoln Memorial in Washington, D.C., King gave what would become his most famous speech: "I Have A Dream." In it, he notes the promise of Lincoln's Emancipation Proclamation, which was meant to free blacks from "the long night of captivity" that was slavery. One hundred years later, King argues, blacks are still not free, but are "crippled by the manacles of segregation and the chains of discrimination." According to King, segregation has created "a lonely island of poverty" for blacks "in the midst of a vast ocean of material prosperity" for whites. The speech is a plea for all Americans to settle for nothing less than an end to segregation:

> There are those who are asking the devotees of civil rights, "When will you be satisfied?" We can never be satisfied as long as our bodies, heavy with the fatigue of travel, cannot gain lodging in the motels of the highways and the hotels of the cities.

In fact, a deeper reading reveals that King's stated goal is not just an end to segregation; the "dream" King mentions in the speech is genuine *integration*. He dreams of an America where, as he describes it, "little black boys and black girls will be able to join hands with little white boys and white girls and walk together as sisters and brothers." King did not dream just of equality, but of cooperation and brotherhood between races.

The Autobiography of Malcolm X (1965), written by Malcolm X and Alex Haley, offers a different perspective on the issue of black segregation in America. After a troubled early adulthood that leads to crimes and prison, Malcolm X becomes active in the separatist Nation of Islam movement, which seeks to end the injustice of whites against blacks by forming an entirely separate nation for blacks. The first part of the book represents his early endorsement of segregation for the benefit of those who are oppressed; in doing so, it offers the cynical viewpoint that whites and nonwhites might never be able to achieve the harmony sought by Dr. King. Instead, Malcolm X proposes that black Americans seek common ground outside their home country:

> I reflected many, many times to myself upon how the American Negro has been entirely brainwashed from ever seeing or thinking of himself, as he should, as a part of the non-white peoples of the world.

I SEE ONLY ONE HOPE FOR OUR COUNTRY, AND THAT IS WHEN WHITE MEN AND BLACK MEN, DESIRING NEITHER POWER NOR MONEY, BUT DESIRING ONLY THE GOOD OF THEIR COUNTRY, COME TOGETHER AND WORK FOR IT.

HE WAS GRAVE AND SILENT, AND THEN HE SAID SOMBRELY, I HAVE ONE GREAT FEAR IN MY HEART, THAT ONE DAY WHEN THEY ARE TURNED TO LOVING, THEY WILL FIND WE ARE TURNED TO HATING."

Alan Paton, Cry, the Beloved Country

Some statements toward the end of the book—as well as his formal break with the Nation of Islam—indicate a softening of Malcolm X's militant separatist views. His 1964 journey to Mecca in particular expands his ideas about how whites and blacks can interact. However, once he returns to America, he still routinely denies whites the opportunity to join his movement. He is assassinated the following year, before he has a chance to solidify any practical shift in his attitudes toward segregation and separatism.

Harper Lee's *To Kill a Mockingbird* (1960) is widely regarded as a classic coming-of-age story that tackles the issue of race relations in the American South. It tells the story of an innocent black man named Tom Robinson put on trial for the rape of a white woman through the eyes of the white girl whose father is defending the case. The incident reveals how quickly the small, tight-knit town of Maycomb divides almost to a person along racial lines; only the white Finch family breaks the color barrier, with father Atticus defending Robinson and the Finch children watching the trial from the "colored" balcony in the courthouse.

However, *To Kill a Mockingbird* also depicts a different kind of prejudice and segregation equally important to the novel's theme. Boo Radley, a neighbor of the Finches, is a mysterious shut-in who is feared by the neighborhood children. His appearance and harsh upbringing are obstacles that prevent him from becoming a

Federal troops escort nine black students to Little Rock High School, Arkansas, 1957, after the 1954 U. S. Supreme Court ruling ordering integration of public schools AP Images

part of normal society. Throughout the course of the novel, the children come to understand that their initial prejudices about Boo were wrong. In response, they encourage Boo to extend himself into the world outside his home, and accept him as a part of their community. This acceptance of others is a central theme of the novel, and is hinted at in Chapter Three by Atticus himself: "You never really understand a person until you consider things from his point of view . . . until you climb into his skin and walk around in it."

In *Black Like Me* (1961), a white journalist named John Howard Griffin takes Atticus Finch's suggestion a step further. With the goal of confronting white Americans with the realities of segregation and racism in the American South, Griffin undergoes skin treatments that darken his skin, then travels the South posing as a black man so he can chronicle the experience firsthand. After weeks of being denied basic rights and services by whites, Griffin decides to alternate his appearance in the same location; first he enters a town as a black man, and then later returns as a white man. The difference in treatment only confirms what he has already

come to know: even when white and black Americans are not segregated geographically, they exist in two entirely different worlds.

Apartheid

While American writers have helped to provide a deeper understanding of black segregation, especially in the South prior to and during the civil rights movement, world literature contains many works that document equally compelling experiences in other countries. In particular, the issue of segregation strikes a resonant chord with many writers from South Africa who lived with the country's history of state-sponsored racial segregation, apartheid. The word "apartheid," which comes from the Afrikaans language spoken by white Dutch settlers of South Africa, actually means "separateness."

The books *Cry, the Beloved Country*, by Alan Paton (1948), and *A Dry White Season*, by André Brink, (1984) offer two different views of apartheid in the South African city of Johannesburg—one black, and the other white. *Cry, the Beloved Country* tells of a rural black reverend's quest to recover his family from the

Child refugees push a cart filled with their belongs through Katlehong, South Africa AP Images

danger and decay that eats away their spirits in urban Johannesburg. The reverend, Stephen Kumalo, discovers that his estranged son Absalom is involved in the killing of a white man named Arthur Jarvis. Absalom is tried and sentenced to death. Kumalo meets the victim's father, James Jarvis, and the two form an unlikely friendship born from the tragedy. In *A Dry White Season*, a white teacher named Ben du Toit becomes friends with Gordon Ngubene, a black janitor at the school where Ben teaches. When Gordon's son disappears during an anti-apartheid demonstration, Gordon becomes suspicious; Ben, however, is not willing to believe that the government would be involved in malfeasance. After both Gordon and his son turn up dead, Ben is forced to confront the ugly truth behind his country's peacekeeping methods. Although the two books were published more than three decades apart, they show that apartheid was a perverse evil that often brought tragedy to both black and white South Africans.

Long Walk to Freedom: The Autobiography of Nelson Mandela (1995) tells the story of one of South Africa's most important opponents of apartheid. Mandela grows up in a rural part of South Africa still ruled by tribal custom, isolated

from the white Afrikaner areas of the country. As he gets older—and as apartheid becomes official state policy—he realizes that the separation of races is being enforced by violence and oppression, and that the government is attempting to create "homelands" for blacks separate from the "real" South Africa to keep them from being classified as citizens. Mandela notes that tribalism further divides black South Africans, making it difficult for blacks to fight for equality against the minority population of whites.

Although the young Mandela supports sabotage and destruction to achieve goals, he does not see the situation between blacks and whites as hopeless. Even at his 1964–1965 trial for sabotage, which results in a sentence of life imprisonment, he speaks clearly against separatism and segregation:

> I have fought against white domination, and I have fought against black domination. I have cherished the ideal of a democratic and free society in which all persons live together in harmony and with equal opportunities.

Mandela is eventually released from prison in 1990, as the South African government begins the process of dismantling apartheid. He becomes the first democratically elected president of South Africa four years later, and is awarded the Nobel Peace Prize along with former South African President F. W. de Klerk. However, Mandela cautions that even though apartheid has been defeated, the long walk to freedom is an ongoing journey.

Beyond Black and White

Wladyslaw Szpilman's *The Pianist: The Extraordinary True Story of One Man's Survival in Warsaw, 1939–1945* (1999; originally published in Polish in 1945) offers a glimpse at a specific, swift, and brutal example of segregation: Jewish relocation and internment by the Nazi government during World War II. In Warsaw, where Szpilman works as a classical musician, German occupying troops first force all Jews into a "ghetto," or a district designated specifically for a certain minority. Later, as the Nazis decide upon the "Final Solution" for dealing with Jews, the Warsaw ghetto is cleared and all inhabitants are forced into concentration camps, where many are systematically killed. Szpilman stays behind, hiding out in an attic and depending upon the essential goodness of others— including one sympathetic Nazi officer—to survive the unspeakable genocide that befalls so many other Polish Jews. Even amidst the terror, hatred, and methodical murder by the Nazis, it is Szpilman's ability to recognize and appreciate universal humanness that keeps him alive that makes his account so memorable and important.

In some ways, the oppressed become the oppressors in Joe Sacco's *Palestine* (1993–1995), a graphic novel that depicts the turbulence of the Middle East through the author's own experiences and through the stories of others. Sacco's work concentrates on the Palestinian population that lives under occupation by Israeli troops. Intent on securing the safety of their homeland, the Israelis insist that they must occupy this area to protect themselves. After centuries of persecution, the Israelis are so determined to keep themselves safe that they

engage in forced relocations and violent tactics against Palestinians. Though such actions are not always unprovoked, and Sacco is careful to depict the frequent ugliness of Palestinian behavior as well, the book can be seen as a warning about the dangers of oppression in any form, for even the most understandable reasons.

Conclusion

Segregation as a theme in literature underscores the all-too-real tendency toward exclusion of certain people that has existed throughout human history. This might seem disheartening at first glance, but literature's greatest accomplishment is the expression of the universality of the human experience. The fact that such works can evoke outrage, indignation, and understanding in readers across all cultural boundaries shows that literature's power lies in its ability to *include* rather than exclude. Perhaps the theme of segregation, then, appears so often because it acts as a unifying force—a call for self-examination and a challenge for all readers to be better humans.

SOURCES

King, Martin Luther, Jr., "I Have A Dream," as printed in *Martin Luther King, Jr.: The Peaceful Warrior*, by Ed Clayton, Simon Pulse, 1991, originally published in 1968, pp. 110–18.

Lee, Harper, *To Kill a Mockingbird*, HarperCollins, 1999, p. 33, originally published in 1959.

Mandela, Nelson, *Long Walk to Freedom: The Autobiography of Nelson Mandela*, Back Bay Books, 1995, p. 368.

Paton, Alan, *Cry, the Beloved Country*, Scribner, 2003, p. 71, originally published in 1948.

X, Malcolm, and Alex Haley, *The Autobiography of Malcolm X*, Ballantine Books, 1992, p. 398, originally published in 1965.

Sexual Orientation

Introduction

Since the end of the Victorian era, industrialized societies across the globe have followed a gradual but persistent path toward openness when discussing topics once considered off-limits. Although frank discussions of sexual behavior still often inhabit the realm of low humor, the general public has become increasingly tolerant of serious discussion regarding the issue of sexual orientation, especially as it relates to individual rights and attempts to forge identity.

The emergence of sexual orientation issues in mainstream society has been controversial. One only has to consider the ongoing disputes over same-sex marriages to realize the impact of issues of sexual orientation on American culture. While it is true that matters of sexual orientation have come to the forefront in modern America, explorations of the topic can be found in many of the greatest literary works produced in the past century. Works ranging from Tennessee Williams's *Cat on a Hot Tin Roof* to Annie Proulx's "Brokeback Mountain" demonstrate the influence that literature has had on the way issues of sexual orientation are viewed. These works, among others, have shone a light on the challenges faced by gay men and women in society. Usually, such literature underscores the discrimination—even violence—that gays encounter, as well as the identity issues that result from one's sexual orientation.

Burl Ives, Elizabeth Taylor, and Paul Newman in a scene from the movie Cat On A Hot Tin Roof *MGM /*
The Kobal Collection

Discrimination and Violence

Throughout the course of human history, when discrimination has occurred it has almost always been against a minority group that somehow deviates from established traditions of what is considered normal or appropriate. This is certainly the case for those who are homosexual or exhibit signs of ambivalence in terms of their sexual orientation.

Since religion prescribes standards for acceptable behavior, it is no surprise that religion often figures prominently in literature about discrimination based on sexual orientation. Jeanette Winterson's *Oranges Are Not the Only Fruit* (1985) explores the tribulations faced by a girl whose sexuality is greatly complicated by the religious tradition in which she was reared. When her affair with another woman at the church is exposed, the protagonist becomes the center of her church's lesson on "unnatural

passions and the mark of the demon." She is told that her decision to practice homosexuality is "an immoral proposition that cannot be countenanced" and will result in her eternal damnation.

While Winterson's novel sympathetically portrays the experience of being the target of discrimination, Proulx's short story "Brokeback Mountain" (1997) goes further, exploring how prejudice can escalate into violence. In Proulx's story, two young men fall in love while herding sheep on Brokeback Mountain one summer in the 1960s. Though they both settle in different parts of the country, get married, and have children as the years pass, Jack and Ennis keep returning to each other to rekindle their romance. Ennis is afraid, because as a child he had seen the body of a man tortured to death for being a homosexual. While Ennis is cautious and hesitant about his relationship with Jack, Jack is less cautious and has several affairs with local

A parade during Gay Pride week in Central Park, New York John-Marshall Mantel | Corbis

men. When Ennis is told that Jack died in a freak accident, he knows it "had been the tire iron" that killed Jack, too. It is a violence made all the more stunning because of its predictability: Ennis never doubted that in their particular time and place, openly following such feelings between two men would ultimately lead to death.

The hate, fear, and violence in *Oranges Are Not the Only Fruit* and "Brokeback Mountain" illustrate the prejudice often encountered by homosexuals. As the literature reflects, it can be an uphill battle for those whose sexual orientation is not considered "normal": they may simply be shunned by society, or they may pay the ultimate price for their choices. They must struggle to become accepted members of society, and they often find that they are not judged by their worth as individuals but rather by their sexual choices.

Identity Crisis

Fearing that they will not be accepted by their friends, families, or society at large, homosexuals often struggle to come to grips with their personal identities. Dreading the stigma associated with a sexual orientation that is considered by some to be perverse, gays often find themselves questioning who they are and perhaps even wishing that they could be something different. Literature that focuses on this identity crisis can not only map out the difficult path many face due to their sexual orientation, but also offer a potential source of inspiration and affirmation for readers grappling with those same issues.

The theme of inability to come to terms with one's own sexual identity recurs throughout the novels, dramas, and poems that deal with the issue of sexual orientation. For instance, in Proulx's "Brokeback Mountain," Ennis is unwilling to admit his homosexuality even to Jack, declaring, "I'm not no queer." Likewise, Jeanette in *Oranges Are Not the Only Fruit* struggles with her sexual identity, begging "the Lord to set [her] free." Virginia Woolf, who was quite free in her expression of sexuality, explores the sometimes bewildering nature of sexual identity in her novel *Orlando* (1928). As a novel written in biography style, *Orlando* is the story of a man

*"*LATER, THAT DOZY EMBRACE SOLIDIFIED IN HIS MEMORY AS THE SINGLE MOMENT OF ARTLESS, CHARMED HAPPINESS IN THEIR SEPARATE AND DIFFICULT LIVES. NOTHING MARRED IT, EVEN THE KNOWLEDGE THAT ENNIS WOULD NOT THEN EMBRACE HIM FACE TO FACE BECAUSE HE DID NOT WANT TO SEE NOR FEEL THAT IT WAS JACK HE HELD. AND MAYBE, HE THOUGHT, THEY'D NEVER GOT MUCH FARTHER THAN THAT. LET BE, LET BE.*"*

Annie Proulx, "Brokeback Mountain"

who spontaneously turns into a woman, further emphasizing the confusion of identity faced by those who live a life of questioned sexuality. Frank O'Hara (1926–1966) voices the familiar concern over admitting to one's sexuality in his poem "Homosexuality": "So we are taking off our masks, are we, and keeping / our mouths shut?" The need to keep "mouths shut" in the 1950s and 1960s reflects a similar atmosphere to that of "Brokeback Mountain," when mainstream America generally considered homosexuals to be deviants. That same time period is the setting for Tennessee Williams's play *Cat on a Hot Tin Roof* (1955). The main character, Brick, is influenced by commonly held views on homosexuality, referring to homosexuals as "queers," "fairies," and "dirty old men." Yet at the same time, Brick's own feelings are extremely ambiguous throughout the play, leading one to question his willingness to honestly identify his own sexuality. As a former football star living in the conservative South, Brick's public persona is at odds with the possibility of being gay, and he is unwilling or unable to reconcile the two.

In contrast to these works stands Michael Cunningham's novel *A Home at the End of the World* (1990), in which sexuality is treated as something that can be expressed freely. Indeed, the novel redefines society's typical views of the ideal family, showing how those who have non-conforming ideas of sexuality can live together and have a productive life. Cunningham's novel shows the relative erasure of social barriers that affected Winterson, Jack, Ennis, Orlando, O'Hara, and Brick. Though society has not wholly embraced homosexuality and questions of identity remain a hurdle to some in the gay community, the progress that has been made against prejudice and discrimination is evident in Cunningham's novel.

Conclusion

Literature dealing with issues of sexual orientation brings to light the difficulties of living a lifestyle outside the norm. Openness about one's sexuality, in particular homosexuality, is shown as an arduous journey during which one must confront demons—both personal and societal—in a struggle for acceptance. Just as the literature illustrates that prejudice and violence are often part of a lonely journey to establish one's identity, it also provides a map and a comfort to the individuals and the societies still in the process.

SOURCES

O'Hara, Frank, "Homosexuality," *American Poems Project*, www.americanpoems.com/poets/Frank-OHara/4846 (January 12, 2006).

Proulx, Annie, "Brokeback Mountain," in *Close Range: Wyoming Stories*, Simon & Schuster, 2000.

Winterson, Jeanette, *Oranges Are Not the Only Fruit*, Grove Press, 1985, pp. 105, 121, 151.

Slavery

Introduction

The history of slavery testifies not only to the economic benefits it provides the enslavers, but also to the credence that certain people are innately inferior to others. Whether it is chattel slavery—absolute ownership of a person—or indentured servitude with the promise of eventual freedom, slavery has occurred in some form in every part of the inhabited world. Literature about slavery reveals the physical, emotional, and spiritual legacy left by this institution on both individuals and societies.

Conditions under Slavery

The conditions a slave must endure are typically harsh and oppressive, resulting from the belief that the slave belongs to a group of people that are inferior by birth or circumstance. Many novels about slavery expose its inhumane nature and the squalid conditions in which slaves are forced to suffer. Harriet Beecher Stowe wrote *Uncle Tom's Cabin* (1852) to draw attention to such conditions in the American South. Alarmed by what she considered the un-Christian nature of owning another human as property, Stowe wrote the novel as an appeal to women and mothers to stand up against slavery and prevent families from being separated. As Tom, the main character, is bought and sold several times, he encounters both compassionate and harsh masters. He faces the loss of his family, routine beatings, and the indignity of being treated like an

An engraving of a slave auction, Charleston, South Carolina, 1861 Archive Photos / Getty Images

animal at auction. Despite Tom's kind and patient nature, his owner Legree treats him with hate and contempt and decides to beat Tom to death simply because he can: "I *hate* him! And isn't he MINE? Can't I do what I like with him?" Stowe's novel is considered one spark that ignited the national debate over slavery, a factor that led to the Civil War.

Gone with the Wind (1936), by Margaret Mitchell, presents a radically different perspective than *Uncle Tom's Cabin*. Written by a Southerner during a time when the antebellum era was highly romanticized, *Gone with the Wind* presents an idealized image of slavery. Though the novel is largely set on a Georgia plantation during and after the Civil War, the institution of slavery is at most a background issue. Main slave characters such as Mammy, Pork, and Prissy appear devoted to the O'Hara family and never utter a complaint or indicate a desire to be free. They are depicted as if, given the choice, they would choose slavery. Though the protagonist Scarlett loves Mammy like a second mother, she also expects her to obey and follow orders. They

are never equals. In *Gone with the Wind*, slave masters are depicted as kind and benevolent and slaves' conditions as comfortable and fair. In fact, after the war, Scarlett even thinks "the Yankees have poisoned [former slaves] against us," suggesting that Northerners have brainwashed freed slaves into thinking slavery was evil and wrong. Mitchell and Stowe write from distinctly different backgrounds and time periods, which results in contrasting views on slavery and its effects.

Occasionally, a slave arrangement may exist that is not inherently oppressive. Anthropologist Amitav Ghosh examines one such relationship in *In an Antique Land: History in the Guise of a Traveler's Tale* (1992). In this book, which is part fiction, part historical fact, and part anthropological study, Ghosh presents an unexpected master/slave relationship. In the era before colonialism, the area between Spain, North Africa, and India was a harmonious world without borders where Arabs, Jews, and Indians could move freely. In *In an Antique Land*, Ghosh presents a twelfth-century Tunisian Jew who travels to

India and obtains a slave. Unlike the hard work that slaves must perform in *Uncle Tom's Cabin* and *Gone with the Wind*, the Tunisian has his slave make business arrangements and even travel overseas on his behalf. Unlike Mammy and Scarlett, the Tunisian and his slave appear to have genuine respect for one another. Slavery as depicted in *In an Antique Land* is an apprenticeship, a gateway to opportunities and a higher social class. Ghosh's story about this unconventional relationship contributes a largely unknown perspective on the institution of slavery and the dynamics between master and slave.

Rebellion

Though the main slave characters in Mitchell, Stowe, and Ghosh's work do not seek freedom from their bondage, literature is filled with stories of escape, rebellion, and liberty ultimately achieved.

Mark Twain's landmark novel *Adventures of Huckleberry Finn* (1885) is the story of an unlikely friendship between a young boy and a runaway slave on the Mississippi River in the 1840s. When Jim learns that his master is going to sell him down to New Orleans, he escapes and sets up camp on an island in the river, where he eventually meets Huck. Jim considers that he is rich now that he has escaped, because as a slave he was valued at eight hundred dollars: "I's rich now, come to look at it. I own myself, en I's wuth eight hund'd dollars." When Jim and Huck encounter people along their journey who want to turn Jim in for a forty-dollar bounty, Huck must decide whether to turn Jim in or to follow his instincts and help Jim escape. Huck feels guilty about his compassion for Jim, but he thinks the flaw is in himself, rather than in his society. He agonizes over the stigma he would have if anyone found out that "Huck Finn helped a nigger to get to his freedom," yet he cannot bring himself to return his friend to a life of slavery. Twain's novel explores the bravery required to stand up for a moral right over a legal one. It also illustrates the freedom that both a slave and a free man can feel by refusing to abide by an oppressive institution.

Adventures of Huckleberry Finn illustrates the obstacles that a single escaped slave faces in his journey toward freedom. *Testimony of an Irish Slave Girl* (2002), by Kate McCafferty,

> I WAS BROKEN IN BODY, SOUL, AND SPIRIT. MY NATURAL ELASTICITY WAS CRUSHED, MY INTELLECT LANGUISHED, THE DISPOSITION TO READ DEPARTED, THE CHEERFUL SPARK THAT LINGERED ABOUT MY EYE DIED; THE DARK NIGHT OF SLAVERY CLOSED IN UPON ME; AND BEHOLD A MAN TRANSFORMED INTO A BRUTE!"
>
> *Frederick Douglass,* Narrative of the Life of Frederick Douglass

shows the power of the masses when slaves revolt against their bondage. In the seventeenth century, the British government forced thousands of English and Irish citizens into indentured servitude on plantations in the Caribbean. Most were never able to buy their freedom and essentially became slaves for the rest of their lives. *Testimony of an Irish Slave Girl* is the story of Cot, a ten-year-old girl kidnapped from Ireland and forced to work on a sugar plantation in Barbados. After participating in a mixed-race slave revolt, Cot is imprisoned. There, she gives her testimony to a government official evaluating how various races of slaves perform in the fields. The truth that McCafferty's novel underscores is that anyone can be exploited as a slave; there is no "better" skin color or ethnicity in a system that treats people as property.

Though the rebellion in *Testimony of an Irish Slave Girl* does not bring freedom, the rebellion that Madison Smartt Bell fictionalizes in *All Souls' Rising* (1995) resulted in an entirely free nation. *All Souls' Rising* is set in the late eighteenth century, in the wake of the French Revolution and its "Declaration of the Rights of Man" in 1789. The principles set forth in the declaration had a strong effect on the French colony of Haiti in the Caribbean, and the slaves were determined to assert their human rights. The rebellion, which engulfed the entire island for over a decade, was led by Toussaint L'Ouverture, a former slave and one of the main characters of Bell's novel. The rebellion effectively ended white rule in Haiti, as all slaves

Slaves working in a cotton field W. A. Walker / Corbis

were liberated. The novel is a reminder that freedom from slavery carries a high cost.

Personal Narratives

Slave narratives allow readers to glimpse into the lives of individuals who endured horrific conditions and lived to share the tale. The aim of a slave narrative is not only to tell the individual's own story, but also to speak on behalf of those who cannot speak for themselves.

During the seventeenth century, North African slave traders routinely captured Europeans at sea and in the coastal villages of France, Italy, England, and Spain for slave markets in North Africa. Eleven-year-old Englishman Thomas Pellow was captured on a boat in the Mediterranean and became the Sultan of Morocco's personal servant. He was held as the Sultan's slave for twenty-three years before escaping and making his way back to London. Upon his return, he published stories about his experience in the English newspapers. The stories were immensely popular, though they were likely embellished in order to make them more dramatic. Giles Milton writes about Pellow, his

narratives, and the European slave trade in *White Gold: The Extraordinary Story of Thomas Pellow and Islam's One Million White Slaves* (2005).

Narrative of the Life of Frederick Douglass, by Frederick Douglass (1845), may be the most well-known of slave narratives. In it, Douglass recounts his story as an American slave born to a slave woman and a white man. Introduced to reading, writing, and the abolitionist movement while working in Baltimore shipyards, he recalls his thoughts as he began planning his escape in 1836: "Why am I a slave? I will run away. I will not stand it. Get caught, or get clear, I'll try it." He was jailed when his plan was discovered but eventually escaped to the North in 1838. Douglass was drawn to the anti-slavery movement in hopes of helping other slaves still in bonds. As he reflects on his calling as a reformer, which began with speaking at an anti-slavery meeting in Massachusetts in 1841, "I have been engaged in pleading the cause of my brethren— with what success, and with what devotion, I leave those acquainted with my labors to decide." His devotion and success is unquestionable. In the

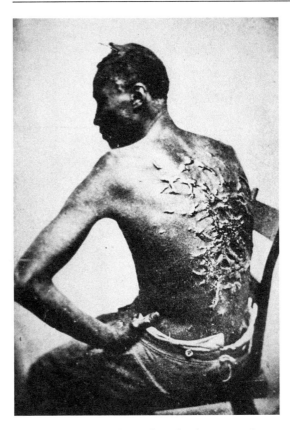

A slave or former slave whose back is severely scarred from whip lashes National Archives and Records Administration

raiders in 1994. She was sent to the capital, Khartoum, and became a maid for a wealthy, cruel family. As their unpaid servant, she was physically and sexually abused, worked harshly, and made to sleep in the shed. After several years she was sent to London to work—again, unpaid—for a Sudanese diplomat. With the help of several Sudanese families in London, she was able to escape in 2000. Just as Douglass's narrative helped raise awareness about pre–Civil War slavery, Nazer's narrative is helping raise awareness about modern slavery in Africa, which occurs not only in Sudan, but also in Mauritania, Mali, Nigeria, and the Ivory Coast.

Conclusion

Literature about slavery ranges from books that oppose the institution to those that defend it and contains many narrative accounts from those who have lived through it themselves. It is full of unforgettable characters, heartbreaking situations, and stark examples of racism, hatred, and oppression. But there is also the hope that future generations will not know the pain and oppression of slavery and the hope that slavery will someday exist only in books.

years leading up to the Civil War, Douglass's slave narrative gave a personal face to the institution of slavery and helped to humanize slaves in the minds of free citizens.

Slavery is by no means a relic of less-enlightened times. Slavery continues to exist in many parts of the world, often undetected or unreported. For this reason, slave narratives such as Mende Nazer's *Slave: A Modern Account of Slavery* (2002) take on even greater significance, as they inform the public of brutal slave practices that might otherwise go unnoticed.

Twelve-year-old Nazer was kidnapped from her Sudanese tribal home by Arab

SOURCES

Douglass, Frederick, *Narrative of the Life of Frederick Douglass, An American Slave, Written by Himself*, Pocket Books Enriched Classics, 2004, pp. 90, 91, 141, originally published in 1845.

Mitchell, Margaret, *Gone with the Wind*, Warner Books, 1936, p. 641.

Stowe, Harriet Beecher, *Uncle Tom's Cabin*, Pocket Books Enriched Classics, 2004, p. 499, originally published in 1852.

Twain, Mark, *Adventures of Huckleberry Finn*, in *A Case Study in Critical Controversy: Adventures of Huckleberry Finn by Mark Twain*, edited by Gerald Graff and James Phelan, Bedford Books of St. Martin's Press, 1995, pp. 201, 202, originally published in 1885.

What Do I Read Next?

What Do I Read Next?

Ethnicity

Though it has long been assumed that Native Americans before European colonization lived in primitive societies, Charles C. Mann's *1491: New Revelations of the Americas Before Columbus* (2005) posits a different possibility. Mann's book speculates that Native American societies throughout the Americas were far more technologically, socially, and culturally advanced than previously thought.

Harriet Wilson, one of the first African American novelists, published *Our Nig: or, Sketches from the Life of a Free Black* in 1859. It is the story of Frado, a young black girl forced into a life of servitude in antebellum New England, determined to surmount the obstacles that she faces, defend her meager rights, and improve herself and her place in the world. The book points out the mistreatment free blacks endured in the North, which was not talked about much in the antebellum United States.

Iola Leroy, or Shadows Uplifted (1892), by Frances E. W. Harper, focuses on the intangible and arbitrary distinctions of race. Written after the Civil War but set in the slave era, its protagonist is a white daughter of privilege who is enslaved after her father's death, only then learning that her mother was, in fact, her father's fair-skinned slave. She soon wins her freedom, but must grapple with issues of "passing" as white

and social restrictions for women and African Americans in the nineteenth century.

Mark Twain's *Pudd'nhead Wilson* (1894) tells the tale of the son of a white plantation owner and a light-skinned slave who are switched at birth. The novel centers on issues of identity and self-determination, the arbitrariness of race, and people's ability to recreate themselves. The novel is full of people assuming the identities of others, and being taken at face value. Twain comically shows the absurdity of judging people for anything other than their character.

The first novel by a black author to win the National Book Award, Ralph Ellison's *Invisible Man* (1952) is a groundbreaking story of the African American experience in the twentieth century. The narrator is a nameless southern man who moves to New York in the 1930s and struggles with his personal identity and his larger, racial identity. He claims to be invisible because people choose not to see him.

James Baldwin's short story "Sonny's Blues" (1957) presents opposite views of the African American experience in pre–Civil Rights America. One man tries to fit into white society and faces limited opportunities because he is black, while his brother, who does not try to assimilate, faces different struggles outside of mainstream society.

The play *Joe Turner's Come and Gone* (1986), by Pulitzer Prize–winner August Wilson, is set in 1911 in a boardinghouse in Pittsburgh, where many Southern blacks had come to find opportunities and better lives than they could hope for in the South. The title refers to a Tennessee figure who illegally kept slaves into the twentieth century. Herald Loomis, one of the characters in the play, is trying to piece his life back together after being freed from Turner. The play focuses on the challenges faced by African Americans trying to establish new communities and identities as free citizens.

The first Southern courtroom drama from popular writer John Grisham, *A Time to Kill* (1989) looks at racism and justice in modern-day Mississippi. A black man stands trial for murdering the white men who raped his young daughter, and racial tension explodes as the case progresses. It is a modern story with the basic structure of *To Kill a Mockingbird*, with a black man defended by a white native son. But instead

of being innocent, the accused is guilty—and justified.

Louise Erdrich examines life on a modern Indian reservation with her collection of short stories, *Love Medicine* (1993). The many Native American characters in these short stories interact with the world outside the reservation with varying degrees of success: some die, some lose their identity, and some become iconic representations of Indian-ness for the white world. Regardless of their experiences, however, the characters each retain a connection to their home on the reservation, and with their family's cultural identity.

Randall Kenan's *Walking on Water: Black American Lives at the Turn of the Twenty-First Century* (2000) presents a sweeping view of African American lives across the country. From Vermont to Alaska, Mississippi to Montana, Kenan travels throughout the country and investigates how black Americans live. The results are as diverse as the environments he visits.

In *The Human Stain* (2000), Philip Roth explores the irony of an African American man who has passed as white his whole adult life being accused of racism against blacks in his career as a college professor. The novel looks at the lies that scaffold his identity, both inwardly and externally.

Chitra Banerjee Divakaruni delves into the experiences of Indian immigrants to the United States in her short story collection *The Unknown Errors of Our Lives* (2001). Nine stories of alienation and assimilation focusing on female protagonists in the United States and India comprise the collection.

A nonfiction account of one Mexican family's quest for a better life in the North, *Crossing Over: A Mexican Family on the Migrant Trail* (2001), by journalist Ruben Martinez, reveals the motives and tragedies that underlie the U.S. migrant culture. It is a first-person account of the months the author spent on the immigrant trail from Mexico to different parts of the United States, following the often-tragic stories of different members of the Chavez family.

Sandra Cisneros's *Caramelo* (2002) chronicles a Mexican American family as their bicultural evolution becomes clear to the daughter, Lala, through visits from her home in Chicago to her extended family in Mexico City. Through touching, heartbreaking, and funny episodes, Lala learns of Mexico's past and her family's connections to it. She comes to appreciate the family matriarch, whom she once thought of as "Awful Grandmother." As she matures, she struggles to find her own place in American society.

Cynthia Kadohata's young adult novel *Kira-Kira* (2004) tells the story of a young Japanese American girl growing up in Georgia in the 1950s, highlighting the experiences of Japanese Americans in the pre–Civil Rights era. The narrator documents the racism, poverty, illness, and hardship that her family faces, but she emphasizes the hope and love that allow them to go on.

Inspired by *Howards End*, Zadie Smith's *On Beauty* (2005) is an interracial satire set in New England academia. The relaxed Belsey family and the conservative Kippses intertwine as the mothers bond and the fathers clash. Conflicts about class, culture, and family between the white English protagonist and his rival, wife, and children (all black or biracial) drive the story.

Gender

Sophocles' classical drama *Antigone* (approx. 440 B.C.) concerns the conflict between Antigone and her uncle, King Creon. Antigone dooms herself by defying an unjust decree, as well as her place in the patriarchal society of ancient Greece. In this classic example of *hubris*—arrogance that provokes the gods—Creon holds himself above natural law, and is punished for it.

Often cited as the first English-language novel, Daniel Defoe's *Moll Flanders* (1722) is the fictional "biography" of a woman with no security or social standing, forced to turn to immoral behavior to survive. Defoe presents his heroine with great sympathy and humor, and spares her from the dire consequences that the moral climate of eighteenth-century England would have expected for such a "fallen" woman.

Hope Leslie: or, Early Times in the Massachusetts (1827), by Catharine Maria Sedgwick, features a plucky, free-thinking heroine in repressive colonial times. It is the story of a cross-cultural friendship between two independent-minded girls—a Puritan and a Pequot—who embody the mores of the author's progressive nineteenth-century attitudes.

In *Ruth Hall: A Domestic Tale of the Present Time* (1855), Sarah Willis, under the pseudonym Fanny Fern, fictionalizes her true experience as a young widow rising above social and gender discrimination to become one of the most successful writers of the pre–Civil War United States.

Set in 1870s New York, Edith Wharton's *The Age of Innocence* (1920) explores the constraints of social mores on women. May, the proper, meek, dutiful woman wins marriage and family with Newland, but her husband remains fascinated by Ellen, a disgraced woman who flouts convention. Ellen cares more for the value of social standing than Newland, and ultimately helps him preserve his position by leaving him.

Featuring one of the most renowned female protagonists of the twentieth century, Margaret Mitchell's *Gone with the Wind* (1936) is the story of Scarlett O'Hara's struggle amid the adversities of the Civil War–torn South. Determined and resourceful, Scarlett makes her own destiny throughout most of the book. She employs her feminine wiles to get her way in most things, using marriage as a means to an end.

Their Eyes Were Watching God (1937), by Harlem Renaissance writer Zora Neale Hurston, follows Janie, a woman raised by her grandmother who is a former slave. As Janie finds her path in life, she comes to grips with conflicting generational ideas about gender and race.

Renowned memoirist, poet, and activist Maya Angelou has inspired generations with her writings of struggle and triumph since her first autobiography was published in 1970. *Phenomenal Woman: Four Poems Celebrating Women* (1994) is a slim, stirring volume that includes "Phenomenal Woman, " "Still I Rise," "Weekend Glory," and "Our Grandmothers." The collection commemorates the strength of women of generations past and rejoices in the power of modern African American women.

Yentl the Yeshiva Boy (1983), by Isaac Singer, is the tale of a Jewish woman who opts to live as a man to follow her dreams. Set in Poland in the early 1900s, the title character disguises herself as her brother to study the Torah, a practice forbidden to women.

Naomi Wolf's 1991 nonfiction blockbuster *The Beauty Myth* is a pillar of the modern feminism debate. In it, she posits that Western culture keeps women preoccupied and insecure about their appearance, and that women must recognize and reject the "Beauty Myth" to neutralize it as a societal force.

Alice Walker, the Pulitzer Prize–winning author of *The Color Purple*, tells the story of one African woman's trauma and madness as the result of female circumcision in *Possessing the Secret of Joy* (1992). Tashi, Celie's daughter-in-law in *The Color Purple*, is the protagonist. She voluntarily has the traditional procedure, then must fight for her very sanity as she is forced to come to grips with the mutilation carried out against members of her gender and her race.

A female perspective of life in the time of the Old Testament is given in Anita Diamant's *The Red Tent* (1997). The "Red Tent" is where women stay during their menstrual periods and childbirth, and where, away from the men that control their lives, the women's world emerges.

Memoirs of a Geisha (1997), by Walter Golden, presents a woman's life in World War II–era Japan. Born poor, the protagonist experiences life as an ornamental figure, but also must shed those superficialities to survive the war. It is a beautiful portrait of the modern world's encroachment on traditional customs, and a woman's struggle to survive as her world evolves.

Religion

In *Wise Blood* (1952), by Flannery O'Connor, Hazel Motes returns home to Tennessee after serving in World War II. He begins street preaching, and decides to start his own sect, "Church Without Christ," bent on rejecting the pursuit of redemption. After a rival group takes over his message and attracts his followers, Motes begins to embrace suffering as the path to atonement.

Rudolfo Anaya tells of a Hispanic American boy's spiritual awakening in *Bless Me, Ultima* (1972). In post–World War II New Mexico, the boy is conflicted trying to balance his Catholic upbringing with the traditional faith healing of an elderly family friend.

The familiar Arthurian legends are the foundation for *The Mists of Avalon* (1982), by Marion Zimmer Bradley. Told from the women's point of view, the novel recasts the stories of chivalry and quests as a battle between the emerging

Christianity and the pagan religion of the ancient Britons. Arthur holds Christianity's advance at bay for a generation, long enough for the symbols and deities of the old religion to become incorporated into the new one.

The Merchant of Venice has inspired many novels and plays. One example is popular novelist Erica Jong's fantasy *Serenissima: A Novel of Venice* (1987), which takes an American actress back to sixteenth-century Venice where she is transformed into Jessica, the daughter of a local Jew, and meets the young William Shakespeare, who is visiting the city.

The Satanic Verses (1988) is a comedy that earned its author, Salman Rushdie, an order of death in Iran for blasphemy. The novel centers on two Indian celebrities in England who, after surviving an airplane bombing, are transformed into the literal embodiments of good and evil. The battle plays out along religious, cultural, and philosophical lines, revealing the complexities and interdependence in all dichotomies.

The national drama of predominantly Muslim Pakistan's 1947 emergence from mainly Hindu India is played out on a personal level in *Cracking India* (1991) by Bapsi Sidhwa. Narrated by a young Parsee (Zoroastrian) girl, the novel presents the chaos and violence that takes place among Hindus, Muslims, and Sikhs from a neutral but highly relevant point of view.

The child of secular Indian zookeepers, the protagonist of Yann Martel's *Life of Pi* (2001) embraces the three major world religions—Islam, Hinduism, and Christianity—equally. After a shipwreck, the boy uses all his intellect and all his faith to survive in the company of a Bengal tiger on a lifeboat adrift on the ocean for many months. Introduced as "a story that will make you believe in God," the novel leaves the reader with a clear choice about how to understand Pi's miraculous experience.

Nick Hornby explores how religion can alter a marriage in his novel *How to be Good* (2001). Katie's husband David undergoes a radical religious conversion, which inspires him to give away their possessions, take in homeless people, and try to change the world. Katie must decide whether to stay with David or follow through on her plan to leave him. His recent conversion has changed him so much that she is not sure which is the "real" David.

Sexual Orientation

In Lillian Hellman's play *The Children's Hour* (1934), two teachers at a girls' boarding school are accused of being involved in a lesbian affair. Lies, rumor, and homophobia ruin the women's lives. Like *The Crucible*, in which Arthur Miller would later dramatize mass hysteria, *The Children's Hour* explores people's willingness to manipulate the fear of others for personal gain.

Ferdinand García Lorca's *Poet in New York* (1940) includes "Ode to Walt Whitman," in which he condemns the tawdry, effeminate, urban gay underground and pays tribute to the artistic, sensitive, solitary gay men. Himself a closeted homosexual, García Lorca addresses the "virile," "beautiful," "macho" Walt Whitman in this poem while he expresses his sympathy for others in his lonely situation.

The complicated relationships in James Baldwin's *Another Country* (1962) are affected by each character's race, class, and sexuality. Trying to understand what caused the suicide of a friend, the novel's characters are drawn together seeking answers. The struggle for acceptance of themselves and each other—on many levels—drives the plot.

Quentin Crisp's memoir *The Naked Civil Servant* (1968) made him a gay icon. His witty, unapologetic account of his life as a young gay man in prewar London recounts prejudice and acceptance, and made its author a celebrity for simply being himself.

David Carter chronicles the 1969 New York City riots that launched the American gay rights movement in *Stonewall: The Riots that Sparked the Gay Revolution* (2004). Carter starts by sketching the environment in the late 1960s that led to the riots, gives a detailed account of the days of crisis, and follows with a description of the progress made in the organized gay rights movement in the years after Stonewall.

Originally a newspaper serial starting in 1976, Armistead Maupin's *Tales of the City* (1978) captures San Francisco life in the pre-AIDS heyday of sexual freedom. Focusing on residents in the same apartment house, the stories deal comically and sympathetically with a diverse cast of characters drawn together by circumstance.

In Rita Mae Brown's comic novel *Venus Envy* (1993), the protagonist, a former Southern debutante who believes she is dying, writes letters to her family and friends to reveal her true identity as a lesbian. When she does not die as expected, she must deal with the fallout in her relationships.

While England Sleeps (1993), by David Leavitt, is a historical romance between an upper-class English writer and his working-class Communist lover. The writer believes that his homosexuality is merely a temporary phase, and is surprised by his feelings as he tries to save his lover, who has gone to fight in the Spanish Civil War.

The memoir of Cuban dissident writer Reinaldo Arenas, *Before Night Falls* (1993), was published three years after the author's suicide. Openly gay and jailed in Cuba in the 1970s for his political ideology, Arenas sought asylum in the United States in 1980. The autobiography chronicles his disillusionment with communism, his imprisonment, and his battle with AIDS while living in New York in the 1980s.

Juani, a twenty-four-year-old Cuban-born American lesbian, is the narrator of *Memory Mambo* (1996), by Achy Obejas. Juani strives to uncover the truth in her memories, her relationships with her family, and her family's relationship with its Cuban past and American present.

Winner of the 2004 Man Booker Prize, Alan Hollinghurst's *The Line of Beauty: A Novel* (2004) follows a young university graduate trying to balance his bourgeoning awareness of his homosexuality and his attraction to the excesses and privileges of power in Thatcher-era England.

Social Class and Caste

Charles Dickens's classic *Great Expectations* (1861) focuses on Pip, a poor orphan who is exposed to wealth as a child and mysteriously inherits a fortune. Pip has flaws, and he matures from an idealistic boy to an ambitious, proud, and superficial man. In the time of the Industrial Revolution, when social class began to have more to do with wealth than birth, Pip becomes a gentleman, but learns that social class and character are not the same.

A collection of short stories, Sherwood Anderson's *Winesburg, Ohio* (1919) explores the ordinary, flawed, "grotesque" inhabitants of a small Midwestern town after World War I, isolated in the modern world, dissatisfied and longing for more, lamenting their missed connections to each other.

Considered by many to be the quintessential American novel, F. Scott Fitzgerald's *The Great Gatsby* (1925) explodes the notion that money and class can buy happiness. After Daisy rejects the young Gatsby, he transforms himself into a wealthy, mysterious man of culture for the sole purpose of winning her back. Although he acquires the trappings of Daisy's world, Gatsby cannot penetrate the psyche of that realm.

The Grapes of Wrath (1939), which won the Pulitzer Prize for fiction in 1940, is John Steinbeck's masterpiece about the plight of the American farmer during the Great Depression. It follows an Oklahoma family, the Joads, as they migrate west in search of work and food. The novel contrasts the decency of poor people with the harsh inhumanity of government and industry.

"Greenleaf" (1965) is an O. Henry Award–winning short story by Flannery O'Connor that illustrates how tentative class distinctions can be. Mrs. May prides herself on her breeding and etiquette, and continually asserts her superiority over her farm manager, Greenleaf. Like in most of O'Connor's short stories, characters who insist on clinging to their class pretensions are in for a rude awakening.

Pulitzer Prize–winning journalist Rick Bragg parlayed his intellectual gifts into opportunity, using both to escape the brutal poverty of his childhood in rural Alabama. His memoir, *All Over But the Shoutin'* (1997), pays tribute to his mother, who bravely left an abusive, alcoholic husband to protect herself and her children, even though it meant a life of struggle and sacrifice.

In *The Impressionist* (2002), Hari Kunzru takes the reader through numerous social strata of India, England, and Africa during the early twentieth century, as the hero assumes and discards identities as they best help him survive over two decades prior to World War II.

Random Family: Love, Drugs, Trouble, and Coming of Age in the Bronx (2003), by Adrian Nicole LeBlanc, follows several members of a Bronx neighborhood over a decade, and chronicles their life decisions, their struggles, the obstacles they face, and their disappointments. LeBlanc shows the humanity in these individuals who struggle to survive in working-class America.

Another Bullsh—t Night in Suck City (2004) is Nick Flynn's memoir of his encounter with his long-lost father in a Boston homeless shelter. As a volunteer at the shelter, Flynn sees firsthand the way that the homeless are treated by society, yet when he encounters the father that had run out on his family so many years before, he finds his threshold for compassion and sympathy sorely tested.

Disability, Illness, and Social Stigma

F. Scott Fitzgerald's novel *Tender Is the Night* (1934) chronicles the relationship between Dick and Nicole Diver as they travel around Europe seeking a cure for Nicole's mental condition. Dick is Nicole's psychoanalyst, and the strain of treating Nicole and keeping up appearances becomes a heavy burden on their relationship, eventually ruining Dick. Fitzgerald's own wife, Zelda, was treated for mental illness throughout their marriage.

Carson McCullers's *The Heart Is a Lonely Hunter* (1940) features several misfits, including John Singer, an intelligent, sensitive deaf-mute man. When his best friend, also deaf, is institutionalized, Singer is isolated and lonely. He moves in with the Kelly family and gets to know Mick Kelly, a teenaged girl who is as lonely as he is. Although he meets many other people who come to believe he understands them, Singer suffers from the feeling that no one actually understands him.

In *The Best Little Girl in the World* (1978), eating disorder expert Steven Levenkron begins the introduction of anorexia nervosa into the mainstream consciousness. Fifteen-year-old Kessa first begins to lose weight after a comment from her ballet teacher. As she gets thinner and thinner, Francesca becomes obsessed with achieving "perfection" as her image of herself becomes critically distorted. When her parents finally notice that she is wasting away, they turn to a psychotherapist for help.

A blind man teaches a sighted man to sense things beyond his sight in Raymond Carver's short story "Cathedral" (1983). The narrator exhibits disdain for his wife's blind friend early in the story, but in the end learns that there is a world beyond what he can see with his eyes. The blind man leads the narrator to a moment of illumination, helping him discover and share things he did not know he knew.

The Snapper (1990), by Roddy Doyle, is a comical look at the crisis of an out-of-wedlock pregnancy in a working-class Irish family. Twenty-year-old Sharon shocks her family and community with the news of her pregnancy and compounds the gossip and speculation when she refuses to name the father. The family's comic but caring response to the approaching birth of Sharon's baby (or "snapper") creates a sensitive, genuine story of the courage to reject society's stigmas.

Peter Carey fictionalizes the tale of Australia's true-life outlaw hero in *True History of the Kelly Gang* (2000), which won the Man Booker Prize in 2001. Facing execution, Kelly writes to explain himself to his yet-unborn child. He describes how his Irish family came to Australia, his failed attempts at making an honest living, and the harassment of his family by British colonial authorities. Kelly, his brother, and two friends turned to a fabled and flamboyant life as outlaws, all the while maintaining that they had been unfairly targeted.

In 1992, free-spirited Christopher McCandless rid himself of all of his possessions and turned his back on society. He hitchhiked across the country, heading into Alaska to live off the land. In *Into the Wild* (1996), Jon Krakauer traces McCandless's journey, in hopes of discovering what motivated the young man's decision to live a life outside the norm.

The Dive from Clausen's Pier (2002), by Ann Packer, rests on an intriguing premise: what obligations does a person have toward another after a debilitating accident? When Carrie's fiancé, with whom she is about to break up, is paralyzed after diving into shallow water, Carrie is unsure what to do. Afraid that leaving Michael will make her a social pariah, she also knows she cannot commit to caring for him for the rest of her life. Carrie must discover a path for herself that allows her to come to a decision in peace.

The literary headline grabber of 2005, James Frey's fictionalized "memoir" *A Million Little Pieces* (2003) is a gripping tale of addiction and recovery. As brash as it is harsh, the story is not self-pitying, self-congratulatory, or instructive. It challenges conventional wisdom about recovery as the protagonist finds his own path.

T. C. Boyle's *Drop City* (2003) takes place in the 1960s among a community of hippies and nonconformists. After being kicked out of their house in California, the group heads to Alaska in order to create their own utopian society. Locals in Alaska frown on the group's decision to relocate in their area, and the harsh winter landscape soon takes its toll on everyone.

Ethnic Cleansing, Genocide, and Exile

Nobel Peace laureate Elie Wiesel's memoir *Night* (1960) reveals the horror of life and the reality of death inside Nazi concentration camps. The slim book is a sort of historical sequel to Anne Frank's diary, which had been known to readers for more than a decade when Wiesel revealed the nightmare that followed capture. Wiesel was one of the first survivors to expose his nightmarish experiences, sharing his wrenching anguish with readers who, through his account, understand and feel humanity's loss.

National Book Award–winner *Mr. Sammler's Planet* (1970), by Saul Bellow, views 1960s America through the eyes of a seventy-year-old Jewish holocaust survivor. Though he narrowly escaped death more than once during World War II, it is life in the liberal United States that makes the old man fear the downfall of civilization. The novel tells of one survivor's journey back to humanity.

Alexander Solzhenitsyn was a Soviet Army commander when he was arrested for criticizing Stalin in a letter and sentenced to eight years in a prison camp. *The Gulag Archipelago* (1973) is his three-volume memoir of that imprisonment and history of the Soviet prison camp system in general. Solzhenitsyn relays his own experience and that of hundreds of other prisoners, shocking the world with his account of systematic brutality in the Soviet Union.

The young adult novel *And the Violins Stopped Playing* (1986), by Alexander Ramati, was inspired by the true story of Roman Mirga, a teenager who experiences firsthand the Nazi campaign to exterminate European Roma (Gypsies). The story follows the family from their home, through escape and capture to the death camp at Auschwitz, where Roman and his father are forced to abet the horror as they try to survive.

I, Rigoberta Menchú: An Indian Woman in Guatemala (1987) is the memoir of the devastation inflicted on indigenous people in Central America by those of European descent. In the 1970s, Guatemala's human rights violations garnered the world's attention as the military government struggled to hold power from the guerilla resistance. Although its author is a Nobel Peace Prize–winning activist, the memoir is controversial and many of its facts are disputed.

The shame, responsibility, and reconciliation in post–World War II Germany serves as the backdrop of Bernhard Schlink's *The Reader* (1997). Forced to confront the war crimes of a mysterious loved one, a young man is profoundly changed by the revelation.

Adam Hochschild tells of the era of Conrad's *Heart of Darkness* in *King Leopold's Ghost: A Story of Greed, Terror, and Heroism in Colonial Africa* (1998). In the late 1800s, Belgium's King Leopold II claimed much of central Africa as his own personal property, plundered its natural resources, and devastated its population. Leopold took control of what he called the Congo Free State in 1885, and governed it ruthlessly until 1908 when he passed control to the government of Belgium.

In about one hundred days in 1994, between five hundred thousand and one million Rwandans died in an attempt by some of the country's Hutu population to wipe out their Tutsi neighbors . In *We Wish to Inform You That Tomorrow We Will Be Killed with Our Families* (1998), journalist Philip Gourevitch documents the atrocity through interviews with witnesses and victims of this genocide.

Philip Roth reimagines American history in *The Plot Against America* (2004). In Roth's novel, celebrated airman and noted anti-Semite Charles Lindbergh wins the 1940 presidential election, defeating Franklin D. Roosevelt and allying with Hitler. The Roths, a Jewish family in New Jersey, soon begin to see changes in the country that suggest Lindbergh is planning to enact the same racist policies as Nazi Germany.

Art Spiegelman's graphic novels *Maus: A Survivor's Tale: My Father Bleeds History* (1986) and *Maus II: A Survivor's Tale: And Here My Troubles Began* (1992) are autobiographical comics describing the impact of the Holocaust on the child of two Auschwitz survivors. The author casts his stories as an animal fable, portraying the Jews as mice and the Germans as cats.

Slavery

The History of Mary Prince, a West Indian Slave, Related by Herself (1831) galvanized the British antislavery movement when it was published in London. Prince's slave narrative, one of the first by a woman, shocked readers with its humanity in the face of brutality and prompted Great Britain to abolish slavery in 1834.

Escaped slave and abolitionist William Wells Brown explores the rumor that Thomas Jefferson fathered children by his slave in *Clotel: Or, the President's Daughter* (1853). The novel follows three generations of Jefferson's fictional slave descendants through a culture where the notion of race is as important as it is fluid.

Up from Slavery (1901) is the autobiography of Booker T. Washington, the influential African American educator and political leader. Born into slavery, Washington went on to earn a Ph.D. from Harvard and open the Tuskegee Institute, an institute of higher education for black men in Alabama. *Up from Slavery* outlines Washington's philosophy that all Americans are tainted by the effects of slavery and that education is the path to equality.

Pearl Buck's Pulitzer Prize–winning novel *The Good Earth* (1931) depicts the life of a former slave in China around the turn of the twentieth century. She and her husband work to overcome their poverty and find their fortunes tied to the land. Her life is still one of servitude even after she gains her freedom; it consists of endless toil and abuse, and she is not appreciated until it is too late to make a difference.

Alex Haley's Queen: The Story of an American Family (1993) is another compelling family history from Alex Haley, the author of *Roots*. It tells the fact-based story of his grandmother, Queen Haley, the daughter of a slave and her owner. The saga follows Queen as she lives alternately as white and black and has relationships with a former slave master as well as a former slave. Haley died before finishing the book, which was completed by David Stevens.

Segregation

A masterpiece of the Harlem Renaissance, *Cane* (1923) is a collection of stories and poems by Jean Toomer. The sketches portray African American life in the South after Reconstruction but before the Civil Rights movement. It was lauded for its rejection of stereotypes and rich picture of the black experience in the early 1900s.

A collection of lectures about desegregation by Yale historian C. Vann Woodward, *The Strange Career of Jim Crow* (1955) was published nearly a decade before the Civil Rights

Act of 1964 finally banned legal segregation. Woodward traces the history of segregation in the South and the flawed logic that was keeping the institution alive. Dr. Martin Luther King Jr. called it "the historical Bible of the civil rights movement."

Thirty years before he became the first Poet Laureate of the United States, Robert Penn Warren published *Segregation: The Inner Conflict in the South* (1956). The book gives the account of interviews the Pulitzer Prize–winner conducted with Southerners in the wake of the 1954 *Brown v. Board of Education* ruling, which outlawed segregation in public education. Warren argues that white southerners must abandon their "romanticized segregationist" views.

Towards the Mountain (1980) is the first of Alan Paton's autobiographies. The book focuses on the influences and events that led him, a white South African, to become politically active in the antiapartheid movement and to write *Cry, The Beloved Country* (1948), which alerted the world to the growing oppression of blacks in South Africa.

Kaffir Boy in America (1989) is Mark Mathabane's second autobiographical book, picking up where *Kaffir Boy: The True Story of a Black Youth's Coming of Age in Apartheid South Africa* (1986) ends, as Mathabane leaves his homeland for a tennis scholarship in the United States. He tells the story of his life on several American college campuses, his encounters with American racism, and his attempts to help his family in South Africa.

In 1994, after the fall of apartheid and the enfranchisement of black South Africans, the country granted amnesty to those who committed politically motivated crimes under apartheid, on the condition that they made full confessions to the Truth and Reconciliation Commission. In *No Future Without Forgiveness* (1999), Nobel Peace laureate Archbishop Desmond Tutu recounts his years as the chairman of the commission.

The Journal of Biddy Owens: The Negro Leagues, Birmingham, Alabama, 1948 (2001) is a novel for young adults by Walter Dean Myers. It is the fictional first-person account of the teenage equipment manager for a black baseball team in the segregated South. As the narrator struggles with racism in his daily life, his interests turn from sports to education.

Achmat Dangor delves into the aftermath of apartheid in *Bitter Fruit* (2004). In the novel, a black South African couple must confront atrocities in their past. Their world is thrown into disarray when a white former police officer who raped the wife years earlier seeks forgiveness from the Truth and Reconciliation Commission, publicly confessing the crime the victim has tried to erase from her reality.

Media
Adaptations

Media Adaptations

Ethnicity

D. W. Griffith's *The Birth of a Nation* (1915), starring Lillian Gish, was one of film's earliest blockbusters. It is lauded for its technical innovations, but decried for its overtly racist message. It portrays newly freed slaves as dangerous criminals, and glorifies the Ku Klux Klan as the saviors of white people. It inspired the twentieth-century revival of the KKK, a group that was outlawed during Reconstruction. The U.S. Library of Congress selected this film for preservation in the National Film Registry in 1992 for its "cultural relevance." It is available on DVD from Image Entertainment and Delta.

Amos & Andy was originally an immensely popular radio show produced first by WMAQ in 1928, then by NBC, with the white writer and comedian team of Freeman Gosden and Charles Correll playing a circle of working-class African American friends living in Chicago and then Harlem. The radio show was adapted for television by CBS in the 1950s, with black actors playing the leads. While the series is, by modern standards, offensive and racist, considering the time in which it was made and in comparison with other works from that era, its characters were actually portrayed sympathetically and with more than the usual degree of complexity. Radio broadcasts are available on CD and cassette from Radio Spirits; several DVD editions of the television episodes are available, including

a complete edition by Restoration Filmworks and a smaller collection from Education 2000.

Porgy and Bess (1935) is an opera by George Gershwin about African American life in coastal South Carolina. The story, told through such famous songs as "Summertime," "It Ain't Necessarily So," and "A Woman Is a Sometime Thing," records the internal and external pressures that bring tragedy to the community of Catfish Row. Although the opera has always been controversial in its depictions of African Americans, it has helped to launch the careers of many black singers and has become a standard in the operatic repertoire. Angel Records has released a DVD of the Trevor Nunn and Simon Rattle production of *Porgy and Bess*; the opera is also available on CD in a number of versions, including Miles Davis's jazz rendition on the Sony label and Leontyne Price and William Warfield's traditional operatic version by RCA.

"Strange Fruit," most often associated with singer Billie Holiday, is a haunting and disturbing song inspired by the lynching of two black men in Indiana. It was written by a Jewish man, Abel Meeropol, after seeing the photograph of the lynched and tortured bodies of Thomas Shipp and Abraham Smith. It includes the lines, "Southern trees bear a strange fruit, / blood on the leaves and blood at the root, / black body swinging in the Southern breeze, / strange fruit hanging from the poplar trees." Holiday's version of "Strange Fruit" is available on a CD of the same name on the Import label.

In 1948, sculptor Korczak Ziolkowski began work on a memorial to Oglala Sioux Chief Crazy Horse, who fought to preserve his people and their way of life. The monument is on the side of a South Dakota mountain, and is being made on a much larger scale than Mount Rushmore. The project is entirely funded by the general public. Work on the memorial continues today. The official website is www.crazyhorse.org.

The musical stage play *Show Boat* (1927), by Jerome Kern and Oscar Hammerstein II, highlights racism against biracial people in the generations after Emancipation. At a stop along the Mississippi River, a local sheriff stops the performance on the showboat because the star is a mulatto woman married to a white man. She disappears, and the boat captain's daughter takes over. The play features the songs "Ol' Man River" and "Can't Help Lovin' Dat Man." It was innovative because it was the first musical in which black and white performers appeared onstage together, but it was criticized for inaccurately portraying the vernacular of black Americans. The 1936 film adaptation, starring Irene Dunne and Paul Robeson, is available on VHS and DVD from MGM. The 1951 film adaptation, starring Ava Gardner and Howard Keel, is available on VHS and DVD from MGM. A revival production of the stage musical was staged in Toronto in 1993, moving to Broadway in 1994. A 1994 cast recording is available on CD from Quality Video.

Guess Who's Coming to Dinner (1967), directed by Stanley Kramer, is a classic comedy about the discrepancies between people's politics and how they actually behave. Katharine Hepburn and Spencer Tracy play progressive, modern parents who have difficulty coming to terms with their daughter's choice of a black fiancé (Sydney Poitier). The movie won two Academy Awards and was nominated for ten; it is available on VHS and DVD from Sony Pictures.

Jacob Lawrence (1917–2000) was an African American painter who came to fame during the Harlem Renaissance. He painted important figures and events in African American history, among them depictions of the abolitionist John Brown, Haitian revolutionary Toussaint l'Ouverture, and "Underground Railroad Conductor" Harriet Tubman. He was awarded the U.S. National Medal of the Arts in 1990. Many of his works are displayed in New York at the Queens Museum of Art (www.queensmuseum.org) and The Museum of Modern Art (www.moma.org).

Mississippi Burning (1988) was inspired by the true story of the 1964 disappearance of three civil rights workers. The action centers on two FBI agents, played by Gene Hackman and Willem Dafoe, as they try to solve the case and deal with escalating racial violence. It is available from MGM on VHS and DVD.

Writer-director Spike Lee's breakout film was *Do the Right Thing* (1989). Lee also acted in this controversial film, which portrays the events in a New York neighborhood on a sweltering summer day. Tempers flare and tensions rise between the African American and Italian American residents of Bedford-Stuyvesant until a riot erupts. Some journalists and theater owners feared violence would start among audiences watching the film, but none occurred. In 1999, the film was deemed "culturally significant" by the U.S. Library of Congress and selected for preservation in the National Film Registry. It is available from Universal Studios on DVD.

Driving Miss Daisy (1989) focuses on the friendship between a Jewish woman and a black man in the Civil Rights–era South. Based on Alfred Uhry's Pulitzer Prize–winning play, the movie stars Jessica Tandy as Miss Daisy and Morgan Freeman as Hoke, and it won four Academy Awards. Forced to accept Hoke when her son hires him to be her chauffeur, Miss Daisy initially resists, but comes to understand how much a rich white woman and a poor black man can have in common. It is available on DVD from Warner Home Video.

Miss Saigon (1989), by Claude-Michel Schonberg and Alan Boublil, is a retelling of Giacomo Puccini's opera *Madame Butterfly*, which is about an inexperienced Asian woman who has a child by an American soldier and is abandoned by him. The original story is set in Japan, while *Miss Saigon* takes place during and after the Vietnam War. The musical's racial focus is more explicit than the original opera's, involving not just the challenges faced by the heroine, but also the fate of the thousands of children born to Vietnamese mothers from American fathers in the 1960s and 1970s. The original London cast recording is available on CD from Decca.

The Civil Rights Memorial, created by Maya Lin and dedicated in 1989, is in front of the Southern Poverty Law Center in Montgomery, Alabama. The memorial uses black granite and water to embody the demands of civil rights activists. In the words of Dr. Martin Luther King Jr., "we will not be satisfied until justice rolls down like waters and righteousness like a mighty stream." Echoing the artist's Vietnam Veterans Memorial, the Civil Rights Memorial is carved with the date and description of more than fifty key events in the civil rights movement, from the 1954 *Brown v. Board of Education* decision to the 1968 assassination of Martin Luther King Jr. The official website for the memorial is www.splcenter.org/crm/memorial.jsp

In *Romper Stomper* (1992), Russell Crowe plays Hando, the leader of a violent gang of white supremacist skinheads targeting Vietnamese immigrants in Melbourne, Australia. Available from Twentieth Century Fox on DVD.

Based on a novel by Amy Tan, *The Joy Luck Club* (1993) tells the stories of four women who immigrated to the United States from China, and of their four first-generation American daughters. All struggle to accept and honor the past while moving forward with their American lives. Available on DVD from Buena Vista Home Entertainment.

The Boondocks is a daily comic strip by Aaron McGruder. First published in 1997 in the student newspaper at the University of Maryland, College Park, it was nationally syndicated in 1999. *The Boondocks* explores American culture through the eyes of a pessimistic ten-year-old black radical named Huey Freeman, who lives with his brother and grandfather in a white neighborhood. In the fall of 2005, The Boondocks debuted as an animated television series for Cartoon Network. The daily comic is available at www.ucomics.com/boondocks and is widely syndicated in newspapers. Four collections have been published as books, in 2000, 2001, 2002, and 2005.

Smoke Signals (1998) is a road trip movie about two teen-aged American Indians who travel from Idaho to Arizona to retrieve the body of one boy's father. The movie depicts the intersection of mainstream popular culture and life on the reservation. Available on VHS and DVD from Miramax.

In the comedy *A Day without a Mexican* (2004), residents of California wake up one day to find that all the state's Latino residents have disappeared. Californians are left to deal with their lives without the help of many of the blue-collar, white-collar, retail, and domestic workers they rely on. Available from Xenon on VHS and DVD.

Crash (2004) is a movie about the complexities of racism and prejudice is modern America. The movie brings together characters from a range of social classes and racial backgrounds whose interactions show that racism affects all Americans in one way or another. *Crash* was directed by Paul Haggis and stars an ensemble cast that includes Sandra Bullock, Don Cheadle, and Matt Dillon. The movie won the Academy Award for Best Picture. It is available on VHS and DVD from Lion's Gate.

Gender

Mary Cassatt (1844–1926) was an American-born painter who worked in France. She painted scenes of domesticity and maternity, and was among the first artists to explore the mundane details of women's daily lives. Many of her paintings are in the collection held at the National Gallery of Art, in Washington, D.C. (www.nga.gov).

Iron Jawed Angels (2004) depicts the U.S. women's suffrage movement in the 1910s. Led by Alice Paul (Hilary Swank) and Lucy Burns (Frances O'Connor), suffragists demonstrate, protest, and eventually go on hunger strikes to draw attention to their cause. It is available on DVD from HBO Home Video.

Gertrude "Ma" Rainey (1886–1939) was a pioneering American blues singer. She began performing while a young teenager, and had been a professional entertainer for more than twenty years before she made her first recordings in 1923. Fully at ease with her sexuality, she sang of the joys of both men and women, as well as of infidelity, domestic violence, and women's dissatisfaction in traditional roles. Several CDs of her music are currently available. She inspired *Ma Rainey's Black Bottom* (1982), a play by Pulitzer Prize–winning writer August Wilson.

The Mary Tyler Moore Show (1970–1977) was a pioneering character-driven situation comedy starring Mary Tyler Moore as Mary Richards, a single career woman making it "on her own," without the help of a husband. The show focuses on Mary's workplace, a Minneapolis newsroom, and her relationships with friends and coworkers, portrayed by Ed Asner, Ted Knight, Cloris Leachman, and Betty White, among others. The first four seasons are available on DVD from Twentieth Century Fox.

Vagina Monologues (1996) is a play written by Eve Ensler. It is a series of monologues, based on interviews with hundreds of different women, about a broad range of experiences related to their vaginas. It premiered in New York in 1996. At first, Ensler performed all the monologues herself, but late the play was modified to feature three or more actresses. A DVD featuring Ensler performing the monologues is available from HBO Home Video.

In *Whale Rider* (2002), a modern-day Maori girl (the only hereditary descendant of the chief) must prove that she can be the first woman to lead her tribe. Available on DVD from Sony Home Video.

Transamerica (2005) is a road picture following pre-operative transsexual Bree (Felicity Huffman) and the son she is surprised to learn of, fathered years before. She does not immediately make her role in the boy's life known, and the two travel cross-country together. Slowly, both of them reveal their secrets and seek understanding from each other.

Religion

Fifteenth-century Spanish artist Pedro Berruguete captures a seminal event of his time in the painting *St. Dominic Presiding at an Auto-da-fe* (Burning of the Heretics). Berruguete lived in the time of the Spanish Inquisition and Reconquista, or Catholicism's "reconquest" of the Iberian Peninsula from Islamic forces. The painting shows a public gathering to watch men being burned at the stake. The painting was created around the turn of the sixteenth century and is part of the collection at Museo del Prado in Madrid.

In the early twentieth century, Russian-born artist Marc Chagall portrayed the looming disaster for European Jews in *The White Crucifixion* (1938). Although Jewish himself, Chagall often used the New Testament figure of Christ to symbolize all humanity and the crucifixion to symbolize all human suffering. The painting has a large crucifixion at the center with many smaller images of an army advancing, people fleeing, and buildings burning all around it. The work is on display at the Art Institute of Chicago.

The play *Inherit the Wind* (1955) by Jerome Lawrence and Robert Edwin Lee is a fictionalized account of the famous Scopes "Monkey" Trial that took place in Tennessee thirty years earlier. In the play, as in the actual court case, a public school science teacher is prosecuted for teaching Darwin's theory of evolution. The trial became a battle of religious faith and scientific reason. The play was adapted as a film Starring Spencer Tracy and Fredric March in 1960. It is available on VHS and DVD from MGM.

Witness (1985) gives a look inside an Amish community. When a young boy witnesses a murder outside the community, an inner-city police detective (played by Harrison Ford) goes to protect him and his mother (Kelly McGillis) by hiding inside their plain, simple, nontechnological community. It is available on DVD from Paramount.

Based on a novel by Peter Mathiessen, *At Play in the Fields of the Lord* (1991), directed by Hector Babenco, is the story of two threats to the indigenous Brazilians by two different forces: native missionaries and industrial interests, the former represented by John Lithgow, and the latter by Tom Berenger. Released on VHS by Twentieth Century Fox.

In *Nowhere in Africa* (2001), a German Jewish family flees to Kenya shortly before World War II, where they struggle to adapt to their new life in an alien world. The German-language film won the 1992 Academy Award for Best Foreign Film. It is available on DVD from Sony Pictures, in German with English subtitles.

Saved! (2003) is a sardonic comedy about religious hypocrisy. When the religious teen Mary (Jena Malone) becomes pregnant as a result of her endeavors to convert her closeted boyfriend (Chad Faust) to heterosexuality, she discovers surprising kindness and acceptance from the misfits at her Baptist high school. Directed by Brian Dannelly, *Saved!* is available on VHS and DVD from MGM.

Steven Spielberg's *Munich* (2005) is based on true events surrounding the murder of eleven Israeli athletes by Arab extremists at the 1972 Olympics in Munich, Germany. The screenplay was written by George Jones and Tony Kushner. Eric Bana stars as the Israeli chosen to lead the mission to locate and assassinate the terrorists. In the aftermath, his team members become targets, too.

Sexual Orientation

Paul Cadmus generated controversy and notoriety when his 1934 painting *The Fleet's In!* was included in the Public Works of Art Project exhibit at the Corcoran Gallery in Washington, D.C. This painting features a handful of sailors on shore leave flirting with women. There is one civilian man in the painting, and he is wearing a red tie, which many viewers took to indicate his homosexuality. The painting launched Cadmus's long career and is now usually on display at the Navy Art Gallery in Washington, D.C. (www.history.navy.mil/ac/cadmus/cadmus.htm).

Director Ang Lee's 1993 film *The Wedding Banquet* features a Taiwanese man in a gay relationship who asks his female friend to pose as his fiancée when his parents visit. With the encouragement of his traditional parents, the Taiwanese man, his white American lover, and his Chinese female friend form an unconventional domestic arrangement. It is available on VHS and DVD from MGM.

Two gay Australian drag queens and a transsexual named Bernadette travel by bus across the Outback in *The Adventures of Priscilla, Queen of the Desert* (1994). Along the way, they encounter white locals and Aborigines with both closed and open minds, and learn about each other's heartaches. Terrence Stamp, Hugo Weaving, and Guy Pearce star. It is available on VHS and DVD from MGM.

Boys Don't Cry (1999) is the true story of Brandon Teena, transgender female-to-male living as a teenage boy in a small Nebraska town, hanging out with boys and dating girls. Tragedy follows when Brandon's friends discover his secret. Hillary Swank won the Academy Award for Best Actress for her portrayal of Brandon. The movie is available on DVD from Twentieth Century Fox.

Following the different lives that have inhabited the same house over different generations, *If These Walls Could Talk 2* (2000) looks at the challenges faced by lesbians in the late twentieth century. It stars Vanessa Redgrave, Michelle Williams, Chloë Sevigny, Ellen Degeneres, and Sharon Stone in three vignettes set in three decades. It is available on DVD from HBO Home Video.

The debonair ghost of Cary Grant (Kyle MacLachlan) haunts the film *Touch of Pink* (2004). In this comedy, Grant is the lifelong imaginary friend of Alim, a Muslim Pakistani Canadian who lives in London with his boyfriend. He gives the sort of advice that made sense in 1950s romantic comedies, but does not serve Alim well as he tries to hide the truth about his identity from his family. The movie is available on DVD from Sony Pictures.

The cinematic sensation of 2005, Ang Lee's groundbreaking *Brokeback Mountain* depicts the decades-long closeted homosexual romance between two sheepherders—Jack Twist and Ennis Del Mar (Jake Gyllenhaal and Heath Ledger)—that begins when both are in their twenties working in Wyoming. They both go on to marry and have families, but cannot leave each other behind. Based on a short story by Annie Proulx, the film is available on DVD from Universal.

Social Class and Caste

Jane Austen's 1811 novel *Sense and Sensibility* (1995) was adapted for film with a screenplay by actress Emma Thompson, who also stars. It follows the Dashwood sisters as they try to navigate the strict moral codes of nineteenth-century England to find love, marriage, and happiness. In addition to Thompson, who won an Academy Award for her screenplay, the film stars Kate Winslet (who won an Academy Award for her acting), Hugh Grant, and Alan Rickman. It is available on DVD from Sony Pictures.

Dorothea Lange (1895–1965) was a documentary photographer who captured images of human misery during the Great Depression. She was hired by the Farm Security Administration (FSA) to document the struggles of displaced migrant farm families. Her best-known work is probably *Migrant Mother*, which shows a young mother with an expression of great worry surrounded by her many listless children. The complete catalog of Lange's FSA photographs is online at the Library of Congress website at memory.loc.gov/ammem/fsahtml/fahome.html.

Michael Moore's first documentary, *Roger and Me* (1989), records his persistent attempts to meet with the CEO of General Motors to discuss the layoffs that devastated his hometown of Flint, Michigan. Moore also investigates several other faulty attitudes and institutions in the town he believes to be partly responsible for the town's economic collapse. The satirical documentary is available on DVD from Warner Home Video.

The documentary *Born into Brothels* (2004) exposes the reality of children born to prostitutes in Calcutta's red light district. Filmmakers Zana Briski and Ross Kauffman gave the children cameras and taught them photography, hoping to improve their outlooks and prospects in life. The film won the Academy Award for best documentary feature and is available on VHS and DVD from Thinkfilm.

Disability, Illness, and Social Stigma

William Gibson's play *The Miracle Worker* (1959) is based upon Helen Keller's *The Story of My Life*. It tells the story of the beginning of the relationship between the deaf, mute, and blind girl and her teacher Annie Sullivan, who helped Helen communicate, against all odds. Adapted as a film in 1962, it won Academy Awards for both lead actresses: Patty Duke (as Helen) and Anne Bancroft (as Annie Sullivan). It is available on VHS and DVD from MGM

Children of a Lesser God (1986) dramatizes the romantic relationship between a teacher for the deaf with a deaf woman, who resists his attempts to draw her into the hearing world. William Hurt plays the teacher, and Marlee Matlin, a deaf actress, plays the passionate, mercurial object of his affection. Matlin, in her debut performance, won the Academy Award for Best Actress. It is available on DVD from Paramount.

Artist and AIDS activist Keith Haring (1958–1990) captured the mood of the late-1980s struggle against the stigma of the disease with his 1989 painting *Silence = Death*. The activist organization AIDS Coalition to Unleash Power (ACT UP) adopted the pink triangle, the Nazi symbol to identify homosexuals, and the motto "Silence = Death" in 1987. Haring's interpretation of the logo imposed his distinctive cartoon of human figures covering their eyes, ears, and mouths in the familiar "hear no evil, see no evil, speak no evil" poses. The painting is online at www.haring.com/cgi-bin/art.cgi?date = 1989&genre = Painting.

Life Goes On (1989–1993) was an hour-long drama on ABC television focused on the life of the Thatcher family and their two adolescent children, one of whom is disabled. It broke ground in television by featuring a major character with Down syndrome (Corky), played by an actor (Chris Burke) with Down syndrome. Much of the series depicts the struggles as Corky tries to function in mainstream society, but plotlines also center on the other main characters and their lives. The first season is available on DVD from Warner Home Video.

In *Proof* (1991), Hugo Weaving plays Martin, an aloof, independent blind man who tentatively seeks connections with others despite his basic distrust. He takes photographs, which he labels with one person's description, and asks others to verify that what is in the picture is as it was originally described. The story follows the interplay between Martin, the woman who helps around his house, and his friend Andy, played by Russell Crowe. It is available on DVD from New Line Home Video.

The groundbreaking movie *Philadelphia* (1993) was the first mainstream film to address AIDS. In it, an attorney played by Tom Hanks is fired after his partners at his firm learn that he is gay and has AIDS. He sues for wrongful termination with the only lawyer he could find to help, a homophobe played by Denzel Washington. Hanks won the Academy Award for Best Actor for his performance in the movie, which is available from Sony Home Video on DVD.

The true story of quadriplegic Ramón Sampedro's three-decade battle for the right to end his life is dramatized in *The Sea Inside* (2004). Spanish actor Javier Bardem plays Sampedro. It won the Academy Award for Best Foreign Language Film, and is available from New Line Home Video on DVD

British artist Alison Lapper was born with no arms and very short legs due to a congenital disorder. In 2005, a nude marble sculpture of her eight-months pregnant by Marc Quinn, *Alison Lapper Pregnant* was unveiled in London's Trafalgar Square. The statue is controversial, with advocates hailing it as a modern tribute to femininity, disability, and motherhood. It can be seen at www.alisonlapper.com/statue.

Ethnic Cleansing, Genocide, and Exile

In the late 1970s, the Khmer Rouge communist regime in Cambodia set about exterminating every person with sympathy for the former government. Between one and three million people were murdered in four years. *The Killing Fields* (1984) tells the true story of Pulitzer Prize–winning New York Times journalist Sydney Schanberg (Sam Waterston), who reported from Cambodia at the time. Haing S. Ngor won an Academy Award for his supporting role as Schanberg's assistant. This film is available on DVD from Warner Home Video.

Roberto Benigni co-wrote, directed, and starred in *Life is Beautiful* (1997), a movie about life in a Nazi concentration camp. His character, Guido, tries to protect his son from the horror of their reality by pretending the whole experience is an elaborate game, in which they are vying for a prize. Available in Italian with English subtitles on DVD from Miramax.

The Oscar-winning documentary *Into the Arms of Strangers: Stories of the Kindertransport* (2000) tells the stories of the children who were sent by their parents from Germany to seek asylum in England in the late 1930s. Over ten thousand children's lives were saved as a result of the kindertransport. Narrated by Dame Judi Dench

and directed by Mark Jonathan Harris, this film is available on DVD from Warner Home Video.

An unusual view of World War II is presented in *Conspiracy* (2001). Portraying the historical 1942 Wannsee Conference, Nazi and SS leaders gather around a conference table and negotiate the "Final Solution to the Jewish Question." Kenneth Branagh plays SS-General Reinhard Heydrich, the main proponent of extermination. It is available on DVD from HBO Home Video.

Ararat (2002) is a film within a film, about the making of a historical movie about the Armenian Holocaust, in which over one million Armenian Christians were killed by Islamic Turkish forces between 1915 and 1918. The movie follows characters involved in producing the film in several plotlines. It is available on DVD from Miramax.

Hotel Rwanda (2004) depicts the beginning of the 1994 genocide in Rwanda, telling the true story of Hutu hotelier Paul Rusesabagina and the many lives—Hutu and Tutsi—he saves while waiting for foreign assistance. It is available on VHS and DVD from MGM.

Slavery

Thomas Nast (1840–1902), considered the father of American political cartooning, used his talent to focus the country's attention on the tragedy of slavery. His illustrations in *Harper's Weekly* rallied public support to President Lincoln and the cause of the Union during the Civil War. Some of his antislavery illustrations can be seen at www.sonofthesouth.net/Emancipated_Slaves.htm.

Aida (1871) is an opera by Giuseppe Verdi, about an Ethiopian princess enslaved in ancient Egypt. One commander is torn between his love for the slave and his loyalty to the Pharaoh. Many versions are available on CD. A musical drama was adapted for the stage in 2000, with music by Elton John and lyrics by Tim Rice. The Broadway production ran until 2004. The 2000 Broadway cast recording is available on CD from Disney.

Released by Warner Brothers and directed by Roland Joffé, *The Mission* (1986) depicts the colonial era of eighteenth-century South America. In 1750, Spain gave part of their South American territory to Portugal, touching off the conflict between profiteering slave traders and Jesuit missionaries intent on protecting the native peoples of the region. *The Mission* stars Robert DeNiro as a redeemed slaver and Jeremy Irons as the head of a Jesuit mission. It is available on DVD from Warner Home Video.

The story of the 1839 slave revolt at sea and the ensuing court battle about the status of the captives is told in *Amistad* (1997), directed by Steven Spielberg. Anthony Hopkins portrays ex-president John Quincy Adams, who argues on the Africans' behalf. It is available on DVD from Dreamworks Video.

Africans in America: America's Journey Through Slavery (1998) recounts the history of slavery in the United States. It resonates using dramatic and first-person accounts read by actors and other famous Americans, including General Colin Powell. The six-hour documentary is available on DVD from WGBH Boston.

Oprah Winfrey produced and stars in the movie adaptation of Toni Morrison's Pulitzer Prize–winning *Beloved* (1998). Also starring Danny Glover and Thandie Newton, *Beloved* examines a newly freed slave family as they try to come to terms with their past. It is available on DVD from Walt Disney Video.

Segregation

Cry Freedom (1987) dramatizes the actual events that brought Steven Biko to the world's attention as an antiapartheid martyr. Black nationalist Steven Biko (Denzel Washington) and white newspaper editor Donald Woods (Kevin Kline) get to know each other in South Africa in the 1960s, where Biko is an early organizer to end apartheid. After Biko dies in police custody in 1977, Woods campaigns to expose the crime. It is based on Woods's books *Biko* and *Asking for Trouble*, and is available on DVD from Universal Studios.

A Dry White Season (1989) stars Donald Sutherland and Marlon Brando in this courtroom drama about a white man seeking justice after the murder of a black boy in apartheid-era South Africa. It is available on VHS and DVD from MGM.

The Montgomery Bus Boycott of 1955–1956 is the driving force of *The Long Walk Home* (1990). Sissy Spacek stars as a white housewife who gets involved in the protest when she begins driving her black maid around town, rather than have her spend her time and energy walking. Whoopi Goldberg, stars as Odessa, the maid. It is available on DVD from Live/Artisan.

Glossary

abstract: as an adjective applied to writing or literary works, abstract refers to words or phrases that name things not knowable through the five senses. Examples of abstracts include the *Cliffs Notes* summaries of major literary works. Examples of abstract terms or concepts include "idea," "guilt," "honesty," and "loyalty."

aestheticism: a literary and artistic movement of the nineteenth century. Followers of the movement believed that art should not be mixed with social, political, or moral teaching. The statement "art for art's sake" is a good summary of aestheticism. The movement had its roots in France, but it gained widespread importance in England in the last half of the nineteenth century, where it helped change the Victorian practice of including moral lessons in literature.

Age of Johnson: the period in English literature between 1750 and 1798, named after the most prominent literary figure of the age, Samuel Johnson. Works written during this time are noted for their emphasis on "sensibility," or emotional quality. These works formed a transition between the rational works of the Age of Reason, or Neoclassical period, and the emphasis on individual feelings and responses of the Romantic period. Significant writers during the Age of Johnson included the novelists Ann Radcliffe and Henry Mackenzie, dramatists Richard Sheridan and Oliver Goldsmith, and poets William Collins and Thomas Gray.

Age of Reason: see *neoclassicism*

Age of Sensibility: see *Age of Johnson*

agrarians: a group of Southern American writers of the 1930s and 1940s who fostered an economic and cultural program for the South based on agriculture, in opposition to the industrial society of the North. The term can refer to any group that promotes the value of farm life and agricultural society. Members of the original Agrarians included John Crowe Ransom, Allen Tate, and Robert Penn Warren.

allegory: a narrative technique in which characters representing things or abstract ideas are used to convey a message or teach a lesson. Allegory is typically used to teach moral, ethical, or religious lessons but is sometimes used for satiric or political purposes. Examples of allegorical works include Edmund Spenser's *The Faerie Queene* and John Bunyan's *The Pilgrim's Progress*.

allusion: a reference to a familiar literary or historical person or event, used to make an idea more easily understood. For example, describing someone as a "Romeo" makes an allusion to William Shakespeare's famous young lover in *Romeo and Juliet*.

amerind literature: the writing and oral traditions of Native Americans. Native American literature was originally passed on by word of mouth, so it consisted largely of stories and events that were easily memorized. Amerind prose is often rhythmic like poetry because it was recited to the beat of a ceremonial drum. Examples of Amerind literature include the autobiographical *Black Elk Speaks*, the works of N. Scott Momaday, James Welch, and Craig Lee Strete, and the poetry of Luci Tapahonso.

analogy: a comparison of two things made to explain something unfamiliar through its similarities to something familiar, or to prove one point based on the acceptedness of another. Similes and metaphors are types of analogies. Analogies often take the form of an extended simile, as in William Blake's aphorism: "As the caterpillar chooses the fairest leaves to lay her eggs on, so the priest lays his curse on the fairest joys."

angry young men: a group of British writers of the 1950s whose work expressed bitterness and disillusionment with society. Common to their work is an anti-hero who rebels against a corrupt social order and strives for personal integrity. The term has been used to describe Kingsley Amis, John Osborne, Colin Wilson, John Wain, and others.

antagonist: the major character in a narrative or drama who works against the hero or protagonist. An example of an evil antagonist is Richard Lovelace in Samuel Richardson's *Clarissa*, while a virtuous antagonist is Macduff in William Shakespeare's *Macbeth*.

anthropomorphism: the presentation of animals or objects in human shape or with human characteristics. The term is derived from the Greek word for "human form." The fables of Aesop, the animated films of Walt Disney, and Richard Adams's *Watership Down* feature anthropomorphic characters.

anti-hero: a central character in a work of literature who lacks traditional heroic qualities such as courage, physical prowess, and fortitude. Anti-heros typically distrust conventional values and are unable to commit themselves to any ideals. They generally feel helpless in a world over which they have no control. Anti-heroes usually accept, and often celebrate, their positions as social outcasts. A well-known anti-hero is Yossarian in Joseph Heller's novel *Catch-22*.

anti-novel: a term coined by French critic Jean-Paul Sartre. It refers to any experimental work of fiction that avoids the familiar conventions of the novel. The anti-novel usually fragments and distorts the experience of its characters, forcing the reader to construct the reality of the story from a disordered narrative. The best-known anti-novelist is Alain Robbe-Grillet, author of *Le voyeur*.

antithesis: the antithesis of something is its direct opposite. In literature, the use of antithesis as a figure of speech results in two statements that show a contrast through the balancing of two opposite ideas. Technically, it is the second portion of the statement that is defined as the "antithesis"; the first portion is the "thesis." An example of antithesis is found in the following portion of Abraham Lincoln's "Gettysburg Address"; notice the opposition between the verbs "remember" and "forget" and the phrases "what we say" and "what they did": "The world will little note nor long remember what we say here, but it can never forget what they did here."

apocrypha: writings tentatively attributed to an author but not proven or universally accepted to be their works. The term was originally applied to certain books of the Bible that were not considered inspired and so were not included in the "sacred canon." Geoffrey Chaucer, William Shakespeare, Thomas Kyd, Thomas Middleton, and John Marston all have apocrypha. Apocryphal books of the Bible include the Old Testament's Book of Enoch and New Testament's Gospel of Peter.

apprenticeship novel: see *bildungsroman*

archetype: the word archetype is commonly used to describe an original pattern or model from which all other things of the same kind are made. This term was introduced to literary criticism from the psychology of Carl Jung. It expresses Jung's theory that behind every person's "unconscious," or repressed memories of the past, lies the "collective unconscious" of the human race: memories of the countless typical experiences of our ancestors. These memories are said to prompt illogical associations that trigger powerful emotions in the reader. Often, the emotional process is primitive, even primordial. Archetypes are the literary images that grow out of the "collective unconscious." They appear in literature as incidents and plots that repeat basic patterns of life. They may also appear as stereotyped characters. Examples of literary archetypes include themes such as birth and death and characters such as the Earth Mother.

argument: the argument of a work is the author's subject matter or principal idea. Examples of defined "argument" portions of works include John Milton's *Arguments* to each of the books of *Paradise Lost* and the "Argument" to Robert Herrick's *Hesperides.*

art for art's sake: see *aestheticism*

audience: the people for whom a piece of literature is written. Authors usually write with a certain audience in mind, for example, children, members of a religious or ethnic group, or colleagues in a professional field. The term "audience" also applies to the people who gather to see or hear any performance, including plays, poetry readings, speeches, and concerts. Jane Austen's parody of the gothic novel, *Northanger Abbey,* was originally intended for (and also pokes fun at) an audience of young and avid female gothic novel readers.

autobiography: a connected narrative in which an individual tells his or her life story. Examples include Benjamin Franklin's *Autobiography* and Henry Adams's *The Education of Henry Adams.*

automatic writing: writing carried out without a preconceived plan in an effort to capture every random thought. Authors who engage in automatic writing typically do not revise their work, preferring instead to preserve the revealed truth and beauty of spontaneous expression. Automatic writing was employed by many of the Surrealist writers, notably the French poet Robert Desnos.

avant-garde: French term meaning "vanguard." It is used in literary criticism to describe new writing that rejects traditional approaches to literature in favor of innovations in style or content. Twentieth-century examples of the literary *avant-garde* include the Black Mountain School of poets, the Bloomsbury Group, and the Beat Movement.

B

baroque: a term used in literary criticism to describe literature that is complex or ornate in style or diction. Baroque works typically express tension, anxiety, and violent emotion. The term "Baroque Age" designates a period in Western European literature beginning in the late sixteenth century and ending about one hundred years later. Works of this period often mirror the qualities of works more generally associated with the label "baroque" and sometimes feature elaborate conceits. Examples of Baroque works include John Lyly's *Euphues: The Anatomy of Wit,* Luis de Gongora's *Soledads,* and William Shakespeare's *As You Like It.*

baroque age: see *baroque*

baroque period: see *baroque*

beat generation: see *beat movement*

beat movement: a period featuring a group of American poets and novelists of the 1950s and 1960s—including Jack Kerouac, Allen Ginsberg, Gregory Corso, William S. Burroughs, and Lawrence Ferlinghetti—who rejected established social and literary values. Using such techniques as stream of consciousness writing and jazz-influenced free verse and focusing on unusual or abnormal states of mind—generated by religious ecstasy or the use of drugs—the Beat writers aimed to create works that were unconventional in both form and subject matter. Kerouac's *On the Road* is perhaps the best-known example of a Beat Generation novel, and Ginsberg's *Howl* is a famous collection of Beat poetry.

beats, the: see *beat movement*

belles- lettres: a French term meaning "fine letters" or "beautiful writing." It is often used as a synonym for literature, typically referring to imaginative and artistic rather than scientific or expository writing. Current usage sometimes restricts the meaning to light or humorous writing and appreciative essays about literature. Lewis Carroll's *Alice in Wonderland* epitomizes the realm of *belles-lettres*.

bildungsroman: a German word meaning "novel of development." The *bildungsroman* is a study of the maturation of a youthful character, typically brought about through a series of social or sexual encounters that lead to self-awareness. *Bildungsroman* is used interchangeably with *erziehungsroman*, a novel of initiation and education. When a *bildungsroman* is concerned with the development of an artist (as in James Joyce's *A Portrait of the Artist as a Young Man*), it is often termed a *kunstlerroman*. Well-known *bildungsroman* include J. D. Salinger's *The Catcher in the Rye*, Robert Newton Peck's *A Day No Pigs Would Die*, and S. E. Hinton's *The Outsiders*.

biography: a connected narrative that tells a person's life story. Biographies typically aim to be objective and closely detailed. James Boswell's *The Life of Samuel Johnson*, is a famous example of the form.

black aesthetic movement: a period of artistic and literary development among African Americans in the 1960s and early 1970s. This was the first major African-American artistic movement since the Harlem Renaissance and was closely paralleled by the civil rights and black power movements. The black aesthetic writers attempted to produce works of art that would be meaningful to the black masses. Key figures in black aesthetics included one of its founders, poet and playwright Amiri Baraka, formerly known as LeRoi Jones; poet and essayist Haki R. Madhubuti, formerly Don L. Lee; poet and playwright Sonia Sanchez; and dramatist Ed Bullins. Works representative of the Black Aesthetic Movement include Amiri Baraka's play *Dutchman*, a 1964 Obie award-winner; *Black Fire: An Anthology of Afro-American Writing*, edited by Baraka and playwright Larry Neal and published in 1968; and Sonia Sanchez's poetry collection *We a BaddDDD People*, published in 1970.

black arts movement: see *black aesthetic movement*

black comedy: see *black humor*

black humor: writing that places grotesque elements side by side with humorous ones in an attempt to shock the reader, forcing him or her to laugh at the horrifying reality of a disordered world. Joseph Heller's novel *Catch-22* is considered a superb example of the use of black humor. Other well-known authors who use black humor include Kurt Vonnegut, Edward Albee, Eugene Ionesco, and Harold Pinter.

bloomsbury group: a group of English writers, artists, and intellectuals who held informal artistic and philosophical discussions in Bloomsbury, a district of London, from around 1907 to the early 1930s. The Bloomsbury Group held no uniform-philosophical beliefs but did commonly express an aversion to moral prudery and a desire for greater social tolerance. At various times the circle included Virginia Woolf, E. M. Forster, Clive Bell, Lytton Strachey, and John Maynard Keynes.

bon mot: a French term meaning "good word." A *bon mot* is a witty remark or clever observation. Charles Lamb and Oscar Wilde are celebrated for their witty *bon mots*. Two examples by Oscar Wilde stand out: (1) "All women become their mothers. That is their tragedy. No man does. That's his." (2) "A man cannot be too careful in the choice of his enemies."

burlesque: any literary work that uses exaggeration to make its subject appear ridiculous, either by treating a trivial subject with profound seriousness or by treating a dignified subject frivolously. The word "burlesque" may also be used as an adjective, as in "burlesque show," to mean "striptease act." Examples of literary burlesque include the comedies of Aristophanes, Miguel de Cervantes's *Don Quixote*, Samuel Butler's poem "Hudibras," and John Gay's play *The Beggar's Opera*.

C

Celtic renaissance: a period of Irish literary and cultural history at the end of the nineteenth century. Followers of the movement aimed to create a romantic vision of Celtic myth and legend. The most significant works of the Celtic Renaissance typically present a dreamy, unreal world, usually in reaction against the reality of contemporary problems. William Butler Yeats's *The Wanderings of*

Oisin is among the most significant works of the Celtic Renaissance.

Celtic twilight: see *Celtic Renaissance*

character: broadly speaking, a person in a literary work. The actions of characters are what constitute the plot of a story, novel, or poem. There are numerous types of characters, ranging from simple, stereotypical figures to intricate, multifaceted ones. In the techniques of anthropomorphism and personification, animals—and even places or things—can assume aspects of character. "Characterization" is the process by which an author creates vivid, believable characters in a work of art. This may be done in a variety of ways, including (1) direct description of the character by the narrator; (2) the direct presentation of the speech, thoughts, or actions of the character; and (3) the responses of other characters to the character. The term "character" also refers to a form originated by the ancient Greek writer Theophrastus that later became popular in the seventeenth and eighteenth centuries. It is a short essay or sketch of a person who prominently displays a specific attribute or quality, such as miserliness or ambition. Notable characters in literature include Oedipus Rex, Don Quixote de la Mancha, Macbeth, Candide, Hester Prynne, Ebenezer Scrooge, Huckleberry Finn, Jay Gatsby, Scarlett O'Hara, James Bond, and Kunta Kinte.

characterization: see *character*

chronicle: a record of events presented inchronological order. Although the scope and level of detail provided varies greatly among the chronicles surviving from ancient times, some, such as the *Anglo-Saxon Chronicle,* feature vivid descriptions and a lively recounting of events. During the Elizabethan Age, many dramas—appropriately called "chronicle plays"—were based on material from chronicles. Many of William Shakespeare's dramas of English history as well as Christopher Marlowe's *Edward II* are based in part on Raphael Holinshead's *Chronicles of England, Scotland, and Ireland.*

classical: in its strictest definition in literary criticism, classicism refers to works of ancient Greek or Roman literature. The term may also be used to describe a literary work of recognized importance (a "classic") from any time period or literature that exhibits the traits of classicism. Classical authors from ancient Greek and Roman times include Juvenal and Homer. Examples of later works and authors now described as classical include French literature of the seventeenth century, Western novels of the nineteenth century, and American fiction of the mid-nineteenth century such as that written by James Fenimore Cooper and Mark Twain.

classicism: a term used in literary criticism to describe critical doctrines that have their roots in ancient Greek and Roman literature, philosophy, and art. Works associated with classicism typically exhibit restraint on the part of the author, unity of design and purpose, clarity, simplicity, logical organization, and respect for tradition. Examples of literary classicism include Cicero's prose, the dramas of Pierre Corneille and Jean Racine, the poetry of John Dryden and Alexander Pope, and the writings of J. W. von Goethe, G. E. Lessing, and T. S. Eliot.

climax: the turning point in a narrative, the moment when the conflict is at its most intense. Typically, the structure of stories, novels, and plays is one of rising action, in which tension builds to the climax, followed by falling action, in which tension lessens as the story moves to its conclusion. The climax in James Fenimore Cooper's *The Last of the Mohicans* occurs when Magua and his captive Cora are pursued to the edge of a cliff by Uncas. Magua kills Uncas but is subsequently killed by Hawkeye.

colloquialism: a word, phrase, or form of pronunciation that is acceptable in casual conversation but not in formal, written communication. It is considered more acceptable than slang. An example of colloquialism can be found in Rudyard Kipling's *Barrack-room Ballads:* "When 'Omer smote 'is bloomin' lyre He'd 'eard men sing by land and sea; An' what he thought 'e might require 'E went an' took—the same as me!"

coming of age novel: see *bildungsroman*

concrete: concrete is the opposite of abstract, and refers to a thing that actually exists or a description that allows the reader to experience an object or concept with the senses. Henry David Thoreau's *Walden* contains much concrete description of nature and wildlife.

connotation: the impression that a word gives beyond its defined meaning. Connotations may be universally understood or may be significant only to a certain group. Both "horse" and "steed" denote the same animal, but "steed" has a different connotation, deriving from the chivalrous or romantic narratives in which the word was once often used.

convention: any widely accepted literary device, style, or form. A soliloquy, in which a character reveals to the audience his or her private thoughts, is an example of a dramatic convention.

crime literature: a genre of fiction that focuses on the environment, behavior, and psychology of criminals. Prominent writers of crime novels include John Wainwright, Colin Watson, Nicolas Freeling, Ruth Rendell, Jessica Mann, Mickey Spillane, and Patricia Highsmith.

D

dadaism: a protest movement in art and literature founded by Tristan Tzara in 1916. Followers of the movement expressed their outrage at the destruction brought about by World War I by revolting against numerous forms of social convention. The Dadaists presented works marked by calculated madness and flamboyant nonsense. They stressed total freedom of expression, commonly through primitive displays of emotion and illogical, often senseless, poetry. The movement ended shortly after the war, when it was replaced by surrealism. Proponents of Dadaism include Andre Breton, Louis Aragon, Philippe Soupault, and Paul Eluard.

decadent: see *decadents*

decadents: the followers of a nineteenth-century literary movement that had its beginnings in French aestheticism. Decadent literature displays a fascination with perverse and morbid states; a search for novelty and sensation—the "new thrill"; a preoccupation with mysticism; and a belief in the senselessness of human existence. The movement is closely associated with the doctrine Art for Art's Sake. The term "decadence" is sometimes used to denote a decline in the quality of art or literature following a period of greatness. Major French decadents are Charles Baudelaire and Arthur Rimbaud. English decadents include Oscar Wilde, Ernest Dowson, and Frank Harris.

deduction: the process of reaching a conclusion through reasoning from general premises to a specific premise. An example of deduction is present in the following syllogism: Premise: All mammals are animals. Premise: All whales are mammals. Conclusion: Therefore, all whales are animals.

denotation: the definition of a word, apart from the impressions or feelings it creates in the reader. The word "apartheid" denotes a political and economic policy of segregation by race, but its connotations—oppression, slavery, inequality—are numerous.

denouement: a French word meaning "the unknotting." In literary criticism, it denotes the resolution of conflict in fiction or drama. The *denouement* follows the climax and provides an outcome to the primary plot situation as well as an explanation of secondary plot complications. The *denouement* often involves a character's recognition of his or her state of mind or moral condition. A well-known example of *denouement* is the last scene of the play *As You Like It* by William Shakespeare, in which couples are married, an evildoer repents, the identities of two disguised characters are revealed, and a ruler is restored to power.

description: descriptive writing is intended to allow a reader to picture the scene or setting in which the action of a story takes place. The form this description takes often evokes an intended emotional response—a dark, spooky graveyard will evoke fear, and a peaceful, sunny meadow will evoke calmness. An example of a descriptive story is Edgar Allan Poe's *Landor's Cottage*, which offers a detailed depiction of a New York country estate.

detective story: a narrative about the solution of a mystery or the identification of a criminal. The conventions of the detective story include the detective's scrupulous use of logic in solving the mystery; incompetent or ineffectual police; a suspect who appears guilty at first but is later proved innocent;

and the detective's friend or confidant—often the narrator—whose slowness in interpreting clues emphasizes by contrast the detective's brilliance. Edgar Allan Poe's "Murders in the Rue Morgue" is commonly regarded as the earliest example of this type of story. With this work, Poe established many of the conventions of the detective story genre, which are still in practice. Other practitioners of this vast and extremely popular genre include Arthur Conan Doyle, Dashiell Hammett, and Agatha Christie.

dialogue: in its widest sense, dialogue is simply conversation between people in a literary work; in its most restricted sense, it refers specifically to the speech of characters in a drama. As a specific literary genre, a "dialogue" is a composition in which characters debate an issue or idea. The Greek philosopher Plato frequently expounded his theories in the form of dialogues.

diary: a personal written record of daily events and thoughts. As private documents, diaries are supposedly not intended for an audience, but some, such as those of Samuel Pepys and Anais Nin, are known for their high literary quality. *The Diary of Anne Frank* is an example of a well-known diary discovered and published after the author's death. Many writers have used the diary form as a deliberate literary device, as in Nikolai Gogol's story "Diary of a Madman."

diction: the selection and arrangement of words in a literary work. Either or both may vary depending on the desired effect. There are four general types of diction: "formal," used in scholarly or lofty writing; "informal," used in relaxed but educated conversation; "colloquial," used in everyday speech; and "slang," containing newly coined words and other terms not accepted in formal usage.

didactic: a term used to describe works of literature that aim to teach some moral, religious, political, or practical lesson. Although didactic elements are often found in artistically pleasing works, the term "didactic" usually refers to literature in which the message is more important than the form. The term may also be used to criticize a work that the critic finds "overly didactic," that is, heavy-handed in its delivery of a lesson.

Examples of didactic literature include John Bunyan's *Pilgrim's Progress,* Alexander Pope's *Essay on Criticism,* Jean-Jacques Rousseau's *Emile,* and Elizabeth Inchbald's *Simple Story.*

doppelganger: a literary technique by which a character is duplicated (usually in the form of an alter ego, though sometimes as a ghostly counterpart) or divided into two distinct, usually opposite personalities. The use of this character device is widespread in nineteenth- and twentieth- century literature, and indicates a growing awareness among authors that the "self" is really a composite of many "selves." A well-known story containing a *doppelganger* character is Robert Louis Stevenson's *Dr. Jekyll and Mr. Hyde,* which dramatizes an internal struggle between good and evil.

double entendre: a corruption of a French phrase meaning "double meaning." The term is used to indicate a word or phrase that is deliberately ambiguous, especially when one of the meanings is risque or improper. An example of a *double entendre* is the Elizabethan usage of the verb "die," which refers both to death and to orgasm.

double, the: see *doppelganger*

draft: any preliminary version of a written work. An author may write dozens of drafts which are revised to form the final work, or he or she may write only one, with few or no revisions. Dorothy Parker's observation that "I can't write five words but that I change seven" humorously indicates the purpose of the draft.

dramatic irony: occurs when the audience of a play or the reader of a work of literature knows something that a character in the work itself does not know. The irony is in the contrast between the intended meaning of the statements or actions of a character and the additional information understood by the audience. A celebrated example of dramatic irony is in Act V of William Shakespeare's *Romeo and Juliet,* where two young lovers meet their end as a result of a tragic misunderstanding. Here, the audience has full knowledge that Juliet's apparent "death" is merely temporary; she will regain her senses when the mysterious "sleeping potion" she has taken wears off. But Romeo, mistaking Juliet's drug-induced trance for true death, kills himself in grief. Upon awakening, Juliet discovers Romeo's corpse and, in despair, slays herself.

dramatis personae: the characters in a work of literature, particularly a drama. The list of characters printed before the main text of a play or in the program is the *dramatis personae*.

dream allegory: see *dream vision*

dream vision: a literary convention, chiefly of the Middle Ages. In a dream vision a story is presented as a literal dream of the narrator. This device was commonly used to teach moral and religious lessons. Important works of this type are *The Divine Comedy* by Dante Alighieri, *Piers Plowman* by William Langland, and *The Pilgrim's Progress* by John Bunyan.

dystopia: an imaginary place in a work of fiction where the characters lead dehumanized, fearful lives. Jack London's *The Iron Heel*, Yevgeny Zamyatin's *My*, Aldous Huxley's *Brave New World*, George Orwell's *Nineteen Eighty-four*, and Margaret Atwood's *Handmaid's Tale* portray versions of dystopia.

E

Edwardian: describes cultural conventions identified with the period of the reign of Edward VII of England (1901–1910). Writers of the Edwardian Age typically displayed a strong reaction against the propriety and conservatism of the Victorian Age. Their work often exhibits distrust of authority in religion, politics, and art and expresses strong doubts about the soundness of conventional values. Writers of this era include George Bernard Shaw, H. G. Wells, and Joseph Conrad.

Edwardian age: see *Edwardian*

electra complex: a daughter's amorous obsession with her father. The term Electra complex comes from the plays of Euripides and Sophocles entitled *Electra,* in which the character Electra drives her brother Orestes to kill their mother and her lover in revenge for the murder of their father.

Elizabethan age: a period of great economic growth, religious controversy, and nationalism closely associated with the reign of Elizabeth I of England (1558–1603). The Elizabethan Age is considered a part of the general renaissance—that is, the flowering of arts and literature—that took place in Europe during the fourteenth through sixteenth centuries. The era is considered the golden age of English literature. The most important dramas in English and a great deal of lyric poetry were produced during this period, and modern English criticism began around this time. The notable authors of the period—Philip Sidney, Edmund Spenser, Christopher Marlowe, William Shakespeare, Ben Jonson, Francis Bacon, and John Donne—are among the best in all of English literature.

empathy: a sense of shared experience, including emotional and physical feelings, with someone or something other than oneself. Empathy is often used to describe the response of a reader to a literary character. An example of an empathic passage is William Shakespeare's description in his narrative poem *Venus and Adonis* of "the snail, whose tender horns being hit, Shrinks backward in his shelly cave with pain." Readers of Gerard Manley Hopkins's *The Windhover* may experience some of the physical sensations evoked in the description of the movement of the falcon.

enlightenment, the: an eighteenth-century philosophical movement. It began in France but had a wide impact throughout Europe and America. Thinkers of the Enlightenment valued reason and believed that both the individual and society could achieve a state of perfection. Corresponding to this essentially humanist vision was a resistance to religious authority. Important figures of the Enlightenment were Denis Diderot and Voltaire in France, Edward Gibbon and David Hume in England, and Thomas Paine and Thomas Jefferson in the United States.

epigram: a saying that makes the speaker's point quickly and concisely. Samuel Taylor Coleridge wrote an epigram that neatly sums up the form: "What is an Epigram? A Dwarfish whole, Its body brevity, and wit its soul."

epilogue: a concluding statement or section of a literary work. In dramas, particularly those of the seventeenth and eighteenth centuries, the epilogue is a closing speech, often in verse, delivered by an actor at the end of a play and spoken directly to the audience. A famous epilogue is Puck's speech at the end of William Shakespeare's *A Midsummer Night's Dream*.

epiphany: a sudden revelation of truth inspired by a seemingly trivial incident. The term was widely used by James Joyce in his critical writings, and the stories in Joyce's *Dubliners* are commonly called "epiphanies."

episode: an incident that forms part of a story and is significantly related to it. Episodes may be either self- contained narratives or events that depend on a larger context for their sense and importance. Examples of episodes include the founding of Wilmington, Delaware in Charles Reade's *The Disinherited Heir* and the individual events comprising the picaresque novels and medieval romances.

episodic plot: see *plot*

epistolary novel: a novel in the form of letters. The form was particularly popular in the eighteenth century. Samuel Richardson's *Pamela* is considered the first fully developed English epistolary novel.

epitaph: an inscription on a tomb or tombstone, or a verse written on the occasion of a person's death. Epitaphs may be serious or humorous. Dorothy Parker's epitaph reads, "I told you I was sick."

epithet: a word or phrase, often disparaging or abusive, that expresses a character trait of someone or something. "The Napoleon of crime" is an epithet applied to Professor Moriarty, arch-rival of Sherlock Holmes in Arthur Conan Doyle's series of detective stories.

erziehungsroman: see *bildungsroman*

essay: a prose composition with a focused subject of discussion. The term was coined by Michel de Montaigne to describe his 1580 collection of brief, informal reflections on himself and on various topics relating to human nature. An essay can also be a long, systematic discourse. An example of a longer essay is John Locke's An Essay Concerning Human Understanding.

exempla: see *exemplum*

exemplum: a tale with a moral message. This form of literary sermonizing flourished during the Middle Ages, when *exempla* appeared in collections known as "example-books." The works of Geoffrey Chaucer are full of *exempla*.

existentialism: a predominantly twentieth-century philosophy concerned with the nature and perception of human existence. There are two major strains of existentialist thought: atheistic and Christian. Followers of atheistic existentialism believe that the individual is alone in a godless universe and that the basic human condition is one of suffering and loneliness. Nevertheless, because there are no fixed values, individuals can create their own characters—indeed, they can shape themselves—through the exercise of free will. The atheistic strain culminates in and is popularly associated with the works of Jean-Paul Sartre. The Christian existentialists, on the other hand, believe that only in God may people find freedom from life's anguish. The two strains hold certain beliefs in common: that existence cannot be fully understood or described through empirical effort; that anguish is a universal element of life; that individuals must bear responsibility for their actions; and that there is no common standard of behavior or perception for religious and ethical matters. Existentialist thought figures prominently in the works of such authors as Eugene Ionesco, Franz Kafka, Fyodor Dostoyevsky, Simone de Beauvoir, Samuel Beckett, and Albert Camus.

expatriates: see *expatriatism*

expatriatism: the practice of leaving one's country to live for an extended period in another country. Literary expatriates include English poets Percy Bysshe Shelley and John Keats in Italy, Polish novelist Joseph Conrad in England, American writers Richard Wright, James Baldwin, Gertrude Stein, and Ernest Hemingway in France, and Trinidadian author Neil Bissondath in Canada.

exposition: writing intended to explain the nature of an idea, thing, or theme. Expository writing is often combined with description, narration, or argument. In dramatic writing, the exposition is the introductory material which presents the characters, setting, and tone of the play. An example of dramatic exposition occurs in many nineteenth-century drawing-room comedies in which the butler and the maid open the play with relevant talk about their master and mistress; in composition, exposition relays factual information, as in encyclopedia entries.

expressionism: an indistinct literary term, originally used to describe an early twentieth-century school of German painting. The term applies to almost any mode of unconventional, highly subjective writing that distorts reality in some way. Advocates of expressionism include dramatists George Kaiser, Ernst Toller, Luigi Pirandello, Federico Garcia Lorca, Eugene O'Neill, and Elmer Rice; poets George Heym, Ernst Stadler, August Stramm, Gottfried Benn, and Georg Trakl; and novelists Franz Kafka and James Joyce.

F

Fable: a prose or verse narrative intended to convey a moral. Animals or inanimate objects with human characteristics often serve as characters in fables. A famous fable is Aesop's "The Tortoise and the Hare."

fairy tales: short narratives featuring mythical beings such as fairies, elves, and sprites. These tales originally belonged to the folklore of a particular nation or region, such as those collected in Germany by Jacob and Wilhelm Grimm. Two other celebrated writers of fairy tales are Hans Christian Andersen and Rudyard Kipling.

falling action: see *denouement*

fantasy: a literary form related to mythology and folklore. Fantasy literature is typically set in non-existent realms and features supernatural beings. Notable examples of fantasy literature are *The Lord of the Rings* by J. R. R. Tolkien and the Gormenghast trilogy by Mervyn Peake.

farce: a type of comedy characterized by broad humor, outlandish incidents, and often vulgar subject matter. Much of the "comedy" in film and television could more accurately be described as farce.

femme fatale: a French phrase with the literal translation "fatal woman." A *femme fatale* is a sensuous, alluring woman who often leads men into danger or trouble. A classic example of the *femme fatale* is the nameless character in Billy Wilder's *The Seven Year Itch,* portrayed by Marilyn Monroe in the film adaptation.

festschrift: a collection of essays written in honor of a distinguished scholar and presented to him or her to mark some special occasion. Examples of *festschriften* are *Worlds of Jewish Prayer: A Festschrift in Honour of Rabbi Zalman M. Schachter-Shalomi* and *The Organist as Scholar: Essays in Memory of Russell Saunders.*

fiction: any story that is the product of imagination rather than a documentation of fact. Characters and events in such narratives may be based in real life but their ultimate form and configuration is a creation of the author. Geoffrey Chaucer's *The Canterbury Tales,* Laurence Sterne's *Tristram Shandy,* and Margaret Mitchell's *Gone with the Wind* are examples of fiction.

figurative language: a technique in writing in which the author temporarily interrupts the order, construction, or meaning of the writing for a particular effect. This interruption takes the form of one or more figures of speech such as hyperbole, irony, or simile. Figurative language is the opposite of literal language, in which every word is truthful, accurate, and free of exaggeration or embellishment. Examples of figurative language are tropes such as metaphor and rhetorical figures such as apostrophe.

figures of speech: writing that differs from customary conventions for construction, meaning, order, or significance for the purpose of a special meaning or effect. There are two major types of figures of speech: rhetorical figures, which do not make changes in the meaning of the words, and tropes, which do. Types of figures of speech include simile, hyperbole, alliteration, and pun, among many others.

fin de siecle: a French term meaning "end of the century." The term is used to denote the last decade of the nineteenth century, a transition period when writers and other artists abandoned old conventions and looked for new techniques and objectives. Two writers commonly associated with the *fin de siecle* mindset are Oscar Wilde and George Bernard Shaw.

first person: see *point of view*

flashback: a device used in literature to present action that occurred before the beginning of the story. Flashbacks are often introduced as the dreams or recollections of one or more characters. Flashback techniques are often used in films, where they are typically set off by a gradual changing of one picture to another.

foil: a character in a work of literature whose physical or psychological qualities contrast strongly with, and therefore highlight, the corresponding qualities of another character. In his Sherlock Holmes stories, Arthur Conan Doyle portrayed Dr. Watson as a man of normal habits and intelligence, making him a foil for the eccentric and wonderfully perceptive Sherlock Holmes.

folklore: traditions and myths preserved in a culture or group of people. Typically, these are passed on by word of mouth in various forms—such as legends, songs, and proverbs—or preserved in customs and ceremonies. This term was first used by W. J. Thoms in 1846. Sir James Frazer's *The Golden Bough* is the record of English folklore; myths about the frontier and the Old South exemplify American folklore.

folktale: a story originating in oral tradition. Folktales fall into a variety of categories, including legends, ghost stories, fairy tales, fables, and anecdotes based on historical figures and events. Examples of folktales include Giambattista Basile's *The Pentamerone,* which contains the tales of Puss in Boots, Rapunzel, Cinderella, and Beauty and the Beast, and Joel Chandler Harris's Uncle Remus stories, which represent transplanted African folktales and American tales about the characters Mike Fink, Johnny Appleseed, Paul Bunyan, and Pecos Bill.

foreshadowing: a device used in literature to create expectation or to set up an explanation of later developments. In Charles Dickens's *Great Expectations,* the graveyard encounter at the beginning of the novel between Pip and the escaped convict Magwitch foreshadows the baleful atmosphere and events that comprise much of the narrative.

form: the pattern or construction of a work that identifies its genre and distinguishes it from other genres. Examples of forms include the different genres, such as the lyric form or the short story form, and various patterns for poetry, such as the verse form or the stanza form.

futurism: a flamboyant literary and artistic movement that developed in France, Italy, and Russia from 1908 through the 1920s. Futurist theater and poetry abandoned traditional literary forms. In their place, followers of the movement attemp-ted to achieve total freedom of expression through bizarre imagery and deformed or newly invented words. The Futurists were self-consciously modern artists who attempted to incorporate the appearances and sounds of modern life into their work. Futurist writers include Filippo Tommaso Marinetti, Wyndham Lewis, Guillaume Apollinaire, Velimir Khlebnikov, and Vladimir Mayakovsky.

G

genre: a category of literary work. In critical theory, genre may refer to both the content of a given work—tragedy, comedy, pastoral—and to its form, such as poetry, novel, or drama. This term also refers to types of popular literature, as in the genres of science fiction or the detective story.

genteel tradition: a term coined by critic George Santayana to describe the literary practice of certain late nineteenth- century American writers, especially New Englanders. Followers of the Genteel Tradition emphasized conventionality in social, religious, moral, and literary standards. Some of the best-known writers of the Genteel Tradition are R. H. Stoddard and Bayard Taylor.

gilded age: a period in American history during the 1870s characterized by political corruption and materialism. A number of important novels of social and political criticism were written during this time. Examples of Gilded Age literature include Henry Adams's *Democracy* and F. Marion Crawford's *An American Politician.*

gothic: see *gothicism*

gothicism: in literary criticism, works characterized by a taste for the medieval or morbidly attractive. A gothic novel prominently features elements of horror, the supernatural, gloom, and violence: clanking chains, terror, charnel houses, ghosts, medieval castles, and mysteriously slamming doors. The term "gothic novel" is also applied to novels that lack elements of the traditional Gothic setting but that create a similar atmosphere of terror or dread. Mary Shelley's *Frankenstein* is perhaps the best-known English work of this kind.

gothic novel: see *gothicism*

great chain of being: the belief that all things and creatures in nature are organized in a hierarchy from inanimate objects at the bottom to God at the top. This system of belief was popular in the seventeenth and eighteenth centuries. A summary of the concept of the great chain of being can be found in the first epistle of Alexander Pope's *An Essay on Man,* and more recently in Arthur O. Lovejoy's *The Great Chain of Being: A Study of the History of an Idea.*

grotesque: in literary criticism, the subject matter of a work or a style of expression characterized by exaggeration, deformity, freakishness, and disorder. The grotesque often includes an element of comic absurdity. Early examples of literary grotesque include Francois Rabelais's *Pantagruel* and *Gargantua* and Thomas Nashe's *The Unfortunate Traveller,* while more recent examples can be found in the works of Edgar Allan Poe, Evelyn Waugh, Eudora Welty, Flannery O'Connor, Eugene Ionesco, Gunter Grass, Thomas Mann, Mervyn Peake, and Joseph Heller, among many others.

H

hamartia: in tragedy, the event or act that leads to the hero's or heroine's downfall. This term is often incorrectly used as a synonym for tragic flaw. In Richard Wright's *Native Son,* the act that seals Bigger Thomas's fate is his first impulsive murder.

Harlem renaissance: the Harlem Renaissance of the 1920s is generally considered the first significant movement of black writers and artists in the United States. During this period, new and established black writers published more fiction and poetry than ever before, the first influential black literary journals were established, and black authors and artists received their first widespread recognition and serious critical appraisal.

Among the major writers associated with this period are Claude McKay, Jean Toomer, Countee Cullen, Langston Hughes, Arna Bontemps, Nella Larsen, and Zora Neale Hurston. Works representative of the Harlem Renaissance include Arna Bontemps's poems "The Return" and "Golgotha Is a Mountain," Claude McKay's novel *Home to Harlem,* Nella Larsen's novel *Passing,* Langston Hughes's poem "The Negro Speaks of Rivers," and the journals *Crisis* and *Opportunity,* both founded during this period.

Hellenism: imitation of ancient Greek thought or styles. Also, an approach to life that focuses on the growth and development of the intellect. "Hellenism" is sometimes used to refer to the belief that reason can be applied to examine all human experience. A cogent discussion of Hellenism can be found in Matthew Arnold's *Culture and Anarchy.*

hero/heroine: the principal sympathetic character (male or female) in a literary work. Heroes and heroines typically exhibit admirable traits: idealism, courage, and integrity, for example. Famous heroes and heroines include Pip in Charles Dickens's *Great Expectations,* the anonymous narrator in Ralph Ellison's *Invisible Man,* and Sethe in Toni Morrison's *Beloved.*

heroine: see *hero/heroine*

historical criticism: the study of a work based on its impact on the world of the time period in which it was written. Examples of postmodern historical criticism can be found in the work of Michel Foucault, Hayden White, Stephen Greenblatt, and Jonathan Goldberg.

holocaust: see *holocaust literature*

holocaust literature: literature influenced by or written about the Holocaust of World War II. Such literature includes true stories of survival in concentration camps, escape, and life after the war, as well as fictional works and poetry. Representative works of Holocaust literature include Saul Bellow's *Mr. Sammler's Planet,* Anne Frank's *The Diary of a Young Girl,* Jerzy Kosinski's *The Painted Bird,* Arthur Miller's *Incident at Vichy,* Czeslaw Milosz's *Collected Poems,* William Styron's *Sophie's Choice,* and Art Spiegelman's *Maus.*

horatian satire: see *satire*

humanism: a philosophy that places faith in the dignity of humankind and rejects the medieval perception of the individual as a weak, fallen creature. "Humanists" typically believe in the perfectibility of human nature and view reason and education as the means to that end. Humanist thought is represented in the works of Marsilio Ficino, Ludovico Castelvetro, Edmund Spenser, John Milton, Dean John Colet, Desiderius Erasmus, John Dryden, Alexander Pope, Matthew Arnold, and Irving Babbitt.

humors: mentions of the humors refer to the ancient Greek theory that a person's health and personality were determined by the balance of four basic fluids in the body: blood, phlegm, yellow bile, and black bile. A dominance of any fluid would cause extremes in behavior. An excess of blood created a sanguine person who was joyful, aggressive, and passionate; a phlegmatic person was shy, fearful, and sluggish; too much yellow bile led to a choleric temperament characterized by impatience, anger, bitterness, and stubbornness; and excessive black bile created melancholy, a state of laziness, gluttony, and lack of motivation. Literary treatment of the humors is exemplified by several characters in Ben Jonson's plays *Every Man in His Humour* and *Every Man out of His Humour*.

humours: see *humors*

hyperbole: in literary criticism, deliberate exaggeration used to achieve an effect. In William Shakespeare's *Macbeth,* Lady Macbeth hyperbolizes when she says, "All the perfumes of Arabia could not sweeten this little hand."

I

idiom: a word construction or verbal expression closely associated with a given language. For example, in colloquial English the construction "how come" can be used instead of "why" to introduce a question. Similarly, "a piece of cake" is sometimes used to describe a task that is easily done.

image: a concrete representation of an object or sensory experience. Typically, such a representation helps evoke the feelings associated with the object or experience itself.

Images are either "literal" or "figurative." Literal images are especially concrete and involve little or no extension of the obvious meaning of the words used to express them. Figurative images do not follow the literal meaning of the words exactly. Images in literature are usually visual, but the term "image" can also refer to the representation of any sensory experience. In his poem "The Shepherd's Hour," Paul Verlaine presents the following image: "The Moon is red through horizon's fog;/ In a dancing mist the hazy meadow sleeps." The first line is broadly literal, while the second line involves turns of meaning associated with dancing and sleeping.

imagery: the array of images in a literary work. Also, figurative language. William Butler Yeats's "The Second Coming" offers a powerful image of encroaching anarchy: "Turning and turning in the widening gyre The falcon cannot hear the falconer; Things fall apart...."

in medias res: a Latin term meaning "in the middle of things." It refers to the technique of beginning a story at its midpoint and then using various flashback devices to reveal previous action. This technique originated in such epics as Virgil's *Aeneid.*

induction: the process of reaching a conclusion by reasoning from specific premises to form a general premise. Also, an introductory portion of a work of literature, especially a play. Geoffrey Chaucer's "Prologue" to the *Canterbury Tales,* Thomas Sackville's "Induction" to *The Mirror of Magistrates,* and the opening scene in William Shakespeare's *The Taming of the Shrew* are examples of inductions to literary works.

intentional fallacy: the belief that judgments of a literary work based solely on an author's stated or implied intentions are false and misleading. Critics who believe in the concept of the intentional fallacy typically argue that the work itself is sufficient matter for interpretation, even though they may concede that an author's statement of purpose can be useful. Analysis of William Wordsworth's *Lyrical Ballads* based on the observations about poetry he makes in his "Preface" to the second edition of that work is an example of the intentional fallacy.

interior monologue: a narrative technique in which characters' thoughts are revealed in a way that appears to be uncontrolled by the author. The interior monologue typically aims to reveal the inner self of a character. It portrays emotional experiences as they occur at both a conscious and unconscious level. Images are often used to represent sensations or emotions. One of the best-known interior monologues in English is the Molly Bloom section at the close of James Joyce's *Ulysses*. The interior monologue is also common in the works of Virginia Woolf.

Irish literary renaissance: a late nineteenth- and early twentieth-century movement in Irish literature. Members of the movement aimed to reduce the influence of British culture in Ireland and create an Irish national literature. William Butler Yeats, George Moore, and Sean O'Casey are three of the best-known figures of the movement.

irony: in literary criticism, the effect of language in which the intended meaning is the opposite of what is stated. The title of Jonathan Swift's "A Modest Proposal" is ironic because what Swift proposes in this essay is cannibalism—hardly "modest."

J

Jacobean age: the period of the reign of James I of England (1603-1625). The early literature of this period reflected the worldview of the Elizabethan Age, but a darker, more cynical attitude steadily grew in the art and literature of the Jacobean Age. This was an important time for English drama and poetry. Milestones include William Shakespeare's tragedies, tragi-comedies, and sonnets; Ben Jonson's various dramas; and John Donne's metaphysical poetry.

jargon: language that is used or understood only by a select group of people. Jargon may refer to terminology used in a certain profession, such as computer jargon, or it may refer to any nonsensical language that is not understood by most people. Literary examples of jargon are Francois Villon's *Ballades en jargon*, which is composed in the secret language of the *coquillards,* and Anthony Burgess's *A Clockwork Orange,* narrated in the fictional characters' language of "Nadsat."

journalism: writing intended for publication in a newspaper or magazine, or for broadcast on a radio or television program featuring news, sports, entertainment, or other timely material. The essays and reviews written by H. L. Mencken for the *Baltimore Morning Herald* and collected in his *Prejudices* are an example of journalism.

juvenalian satire: see *satire*

K

knickerbocker group: a somewhat indistinct group of New York writers of the first half of the nineteenth century. Members of the group were linked only by location and a common theme: New York life. Two famous members of the Knickerbocker Group were Washington Irving and William Cullen Bryant. The group's name derives from Irving's *Knickerbocker's History of New York.*

kunstlerroman: see *bildungsroman*

L

leitmotiv: see *motif*

literal language: an author uses literal language when he or she writes without exaggerating or embellishing the subject matter and without any tools of figurative language. To say "He ran very quickly down the street" is to use literal language, whereas to say "He ran like a hare down the street" would be using figurative language.

literature: literature is broadly defined as any written or spoken material, but the term most often refers to creative works. Literature includes poetry, drama, fiction, and many kinds of nonfiction writing, as well as oral, dramatic, and broadcast compositions not necessarily preserved in a written format, such as films and television programs.

lost generation: a term first used by Gertrude Stein to describe the post-World War I generation of American writers: men and women haunted by a sense of betrayal and emptiness brought about by the destructiveness of the war. The term is commonly applied to Hart Crane, Ernest Hemingway, F. Scott Fitzgerald, and others.

M

mannerism: exaggerated, artificial adherence to a literary manner or style. Also, a popular style of the visual arts of late sixteenth-century Europe that was marked by elongation of the human form and by intentional spatial distortion. Literary works that are self-consciously high-toned and artistic are often said to be "mannered." Authors of such works include Henry James and Gertrude Stein.

memoirs: an autobiographical form of writing in which the author gives his or her personal impressions of significant figures or events. This form is different from the autobiography because it does not center around the author's own life and experiences. Early examples of memoirs include the Viscount de Chateaubriand's *The Memoirs of Chateaubriand* and Giacomo Casanova's *History of My Life,* while modern memoirs include reminiscences of World War II by Dwight Eisenhower, Viscount Montgomery, and Charles de Gaulle.

metaphor: a figure of speech that expresses an idea through the image of another object. Metaphors suggest the essence of the first object by identifying it with certain qualities of the second object. An example is "But soft, what light through yonder window breaks? / It is the east, and Juliet is the sun" in William Shakespeare's *Romeo and Juliet*. Here, Juliet, the first object, is identified with qualities of the second object, the sun.

modernism: modern literary practices. Also, the principles of a literary school that lasted from roughly the beginning of the twentieth century until the end of World War II. Modernism is defined by its rejection of the literary conventions of the nineteenth century and by its opposition to conventional morality, taste, traditions, and economic values. Many writers are associated with the concepts of Modernism, including Albert Camus, Marcel Proust, D. H. Lawrence, W. H. Auden, Ernest Hemingway, William Faulkner, William Butler Yeats, Thomas Mann, Tennessee Williams, Eugene O'Neill, and James Joyce.

mood: the prevailing emotions of a work or of the author in his or her creation of the work. The mood of a work is not always what might be expected based on its subject matter. The poem "Dover Beach" by Matthew Arnold offers examples of two different moods originating from the same experience: watching the ocean at night. The mood of the first three lines—"The sea is calm tonight The tide is full, the moon lies fair Upon the straights...." is in sharp contrast to the mood of the last three lines— "And we are here as on a darkling plain Swept with confused alarms of struggle and flight, Where ignorant armies clash by night."

motif: a theme, character type, image, metaphor, or other verbal element that recurs throughout a single work of literature or occurs in a number of different works over a period of time. For example, the various manifestations of the color white in Herman Melville's *Moby Dick* is a "specific" *motif,* while the trials of star-crossed lovers is a "conventional" *motif* from the literature of all periods.

motiv: see *motif*

muckrakers: an early twentieth-century group of American writers. Typically, their works exposed the wrongdoings of big business and government in the United States. Upton Sinclair's *The Jungle* exemplifies the muckraking novel.

muses: nine Greek mythological goddesses, the daughters of Zeus and Mnemosyne (Memory). Each muse patronized a specific area of the liberal arts and sciences. Calliope presided over epic poetry, Clio over history, Erato over love poetry, Euterpe over music or lyric poetry, Melpomene over tragedy, Polyhymnia over hymns to the gods, Terpsichore over dance, Thalia over comedy, and Urania over astronomy. Poets and writers traditionally made appeals to the Muses for inspiration in their work. John Milton invokes the aid of a muse at the beginning of the first book of his *Paradise Lost:* "Of Man's First disobedience, and the Fruit of the Forbidden Tree, whose mortal taste Brought Death into the World, and all our woe, With loss of Eden, till one greater Man Restore us, and regain the blissful Seat, Sing Heav'nly Muse, that on the secret top of Oreb, or of Sinai, didst inspire That Shepherd, who first taught the chosen Seed, In the

Beginning how the Heav'ns and Earth Rose out of Chaos...."

mystery: see *suspense*

myth: an anonymous tale emerging from the traditional beliefs of a culture or social unit. Myths use supernatural explanations for natural phenomena. They may also explain cosmic issues like creation and death. Collections of myths, known as mythologies, are common to all cultures and nations, but the best-known myths belong to the Norse, Roman, and Greek mythologies. A famous myth is the story of Arachne, an arrogant young girl who challenged a goddess, Athena, to a weaving contest; when the girl won, Athena was enraged and turned Arachne into a spider, thus explaining the existence of spiders.

N

narration: the telling of a series of events, real or invented. A narration may be either a simple narrative, in which the events are recounted chronologically, or a narrative with a plot, in which the account is given in a style reflecting the author's artistic concept of the story. Narration is sometimes used as a synonym for "storyline." The recounting of scary stories around a campfire is a form of narration.

narrative: a verse or prose accounting of an event or sequence of events, real or invented. The term is also used as an adjective in the sense "method of narration." For example, in literary criticism, the expression "narrative technique" usually refers to the way the author structures and presents his or her story. Narratives range from the shortest accounts of events, as in Julius Caesar's remark, "I came, I saw, I conquered," to the longest historical or biographical works, as in Edward Gibbon's *The Decline and Fall of the Roman Empire,* as well as diaries, travelogues, novels, ballads, epics, short stories, and other fictional forms.

narrator: the teller of a story. The narrator may be the author or a character in the story through whom the author speaks. Huckleberry Finn is the narrator of Mark Twain's *The Adventures of Huckleberry Finn.*

naturalism: a literary movement of the late nineteenth and early twentieth centuries. The movement's major theorist, French novelist Emile Zola, envisioned a type of fiction that would examine human life with the objectivity of scientific inquiry. The Naturalists typically viewed human beings as either the products of "biological determinism," ruled by hereditary instincts and engaged in an endless struggle for survival, or as the products of "socioeconomic determinism," ruled by social and economic forces beyond their control. In their works, the Naturalists generally ignored the highest levels of society and focused on degradation: poverty, alcoholism, prostitution, insanity, and disease. Naturalism influenced authors throughout the world, including Henrik Ibsen and Thomas Hardy. In the United States, in particular, Naturalism had a profound impact. Among the authors who embraced its principles are Theodore Dreiser, Eugene O'Neill, Stephen Crane, Jack London, and Frank Norris.

negritude: a literary movement based on the concept of a shared cultural bond on the part of black Africans, wherever they may be in the world. It traces its origins to the former French colonies of Africa and the Caribbean. Negritude poets, novelists, and essayists generally stress four points in their writings: One, black alienation from traditional African culture can lead to feelings of inferiority. Two, European colonialism and Western education should be resisted. Three, black Africans should seek to affirm and define their own identity. Four, African culture can and should be reclaimed. Many Negritude writers also claim that blacks can make unique contributions to the world, based on a heightened appreciation of nature, rhythm, and human emotions—aspects of life they say are not so highly valued in the materialistic and rationalistic West. Examples of Negritude literature include the poetry of both Senegalese Leopold Senghor in *Hosties noires* and Martiniquais Aime-Fernand Cesaire in *Return to My Native Land.*

negro renaissance: see *Harlem renaissance*

neoclassical period: see *neoclassicism*

neoclassicism: in literary criticism, this term refers to the revival of the attitudes and styles of expression of classical literature. It is generally used to describe a period in European history beginning in the late seventeenth century and lasting until about 1800. In its purest form, Neoclassicism marked a return to order, proportion, restraint, logic, accuracy, and decorum. In England, where Neoclassicism perhaps was most popular, it reflected the influence of seventeenth- century French writers, especially dramatists. Neoclassical writers typically reacted against the intensity and enthusiasm of the Renaissance period. They wrote works that appealed to the intellect, using elevated language and classical literary forms such as satire and the ode. Neoclassical works were often governed by the classical goal of instruction. English neoclassicists included Alexander Pope, Jonathan Swift, Joseph Addison, Sir Richard Steele, John Gay, and Matthew Prior; French neoclassicists included Pierre Corneille and Jean-Baptiste Moliere.

neoclassicists: see *Neoclassicism*

new criticism: a movement in literary criticism, dating from the late 1920s, that stressed close textual analysis in the interpretation of works of literature. The New Critics saw little merit in historical and biographical analysis. Rather, they aimed to examine the text alone, free from the question of how external events—biographical or otherwise—may have helped shape it. This predominantly American school was named "New Criticism" by one of its practitioners, John Crowe Ransom. Other important New Critics included Allen Tate, R. P. Blackmur, Robert Penn Warren, and Cleanth Brooks.

new journalism: a type of writing in which the journalist presents factual information in a form usually used in fiction. New journalism emphasizes description, narration, and character development to bring readers closer to the human element of the story, and is often used in personality profiles and in-depth feature articles. It is not compatible with "straight" or "hard" newswriting, which is generally composed in a brief, fact-based style. Hunter S. Thompson, Gay Talese, Thomas Wolfe, Joan Didion, and John McPhee are well-known New Journalists.

new journalists: see *new journalism*

new negro movement: see *Harlem renaissance*

noble savage: the idea that primitive man is noble and good but becomes evil and corrupted as he becomes civilized. The concept of the noble savage originated in the Renaissance period but is more closely identified with such later writers as Jean-Jacques Rousseau and Aphra Behn. First described in John Dryden's play *The Conquest of Granada,* the noble savage is portrayed by the various Native Americans in James Fenimore Cooper's "Leatherstocking Tales," by Queequeg, Daggoo, and Tashtego in Herman Melville's *Moby Dick,* and by John the Savage in Aldous Huxley's *Brave New World.*

novel: a long fictional narrative written in prose, which developed from the novella and other early forms of narrative. A novel is usually organized under a plot or theme with a focus on character development and action. The novel emerged as a fully evolved literary form in the mid-eighteenth century in Samuel Richardson's *Pamela; or, Virtue Rewarded.*

novella: an Italian term meaning "story." This term has been especially used to describe fourteenth-century Italian tales, but it also refers to modern short novels. The tales comprising Giovanni Boccaccio's *Decameron* are examples of the novella. Modern novellas include Leo Tolstoy's *The Death of Ivan Ilich,* Fyodor Dostoyevsky's *Notes from the Underground,* Joseph Conrad's *Heart of Darkness,* and Henry James's "The Aspern Papers."

novel of ideas: a novel in which the examination of intellectual issues and concepts takes precedence over characterization or a traditional storyline. Examples of novels of ideas include Aldous Huxley's *Crome Yellow, Point Counter Point,* and *After Many a Summer.*

novel of manners: a novel that examines the customs and mores of a cultural group. The novels of Jane Austen and Edith Wharton are widely considered novels of manners.

O

objective correlative: an outward set of objects, a situation, or a chain of events corresponding to an inward experience and evoking this experience in the reader. The term frequently appears in modern criticism in discussions of authors' intended effects on the emotional responses of readers. This term was originally used by T. S. Eliot in his 1919 essay "Hamlet."

objectivity: a quality in writing characterized by the absence of the author's opinion or feeling about the subject matter. Objectivity is an important factor in criticism. The novels of Henry James and, to a certain extent, the poems of John Larkin demonstrate objectivity, and it is central to John Keats's concept of "negative capability." Critical and journalistic writing usually are or attempt to be objective.

Oedipus complex: a son's amorous obsession with his mother. The phrase is derived from the story of the ancient Theban hero Oedipus, who unknowingly killed his father and married his mother. Literary occurrences of the Oedipus complex include Andre Gide's *Oedipe* and Jean Cocteau's *La Machine infernale,* as well as the most famous, Sophocles' *Oedipus Rex.*

omniscience: see *point of view*

onomatopoeia: the use of words whose sounds express or suggest their meaning. In its simplest sense, onomatopoeia may be represented by words that mimic the sounds they denote such as "hiss" or "meow." At a more subtle level, the pattern and rhythm of sounds and rhymes of a line or poem may be onomatopoeic. A celebrated example of onomatopoeia is the repetition of the word "bells" in Edgar Allan Poe's poem "The Bells."

oxymoron: a phrase combining two contradictory terms. Oxymorons may be intentional or unintentional. The following speech from William Shakespeare's *Romeo and Juliet* uses several oxymorons: "Why, then, O brawling love! O loving hate! O anything, of nothing first create! O heavy lightness! serious vanity! Mis-shapen chaos of well-seeming forms! Feather of lead, bright smoke, cold fire, sick health! This love feel I, that feel no love in this."

P

pantheism: the idea that all things are both a manifestation or revelation of God and a part of God at the same time. Pantheism was a common attitude in the early societies of Egypt, India, and Greece—the term derives from the Greek *pan* meaning "all" and *theos* meaning "deity." It later became a significant part of the Christian faith. William Wordsworth and Ralph Waldo Emerson are among the many writers who have expressed the pantheistic attitude in their works.

parable: a story intended to teach a moral lesson or answer an ethical question. In the West, the best examples of parables are those of Jesus Christ in the New Testament, notably "The Prodigal Son," but parables also are used in Sufism, rabbinic literature, Hasidism, and Zen Buddhism.

paradox: a statement that appears illogical or contradictory at first, but may actually point to an underlying truth. "Less is more" is an example of a paradox. Literary examples include Francis Bacon's statement, "The most corrected copies are commonly the least correct," and "All animals are equal, but some animals are more equal than others" from George Orwell's *Animal Farm.*

parallelism: a method of comparison of two ideas in which each is developed in the same grammatical structure. Ralph Waldo Emerson's "Civilization" contains this example of parallelism: "Raphael paints wisdom; Handel sings it, Phidias carves it, Shakespeare writes it, Wren builds it, Columbus sails it, Luther preaches it, Washington arms it, Watt mechanizes it."

parnassianism: a mid nineteenth-century movement in French literature. Followers of the movement stressed adherence to well-defined artistic forms as a reaction against the often chaotic expression of the artist's ego that dominated the work of the Romantics. The Parnassians also rejected the moral, ethical, and social themes exhibited in the works of French Romantics such as Victor Hugo. The aesthetic doctrines of the Parnassians strongly influenced the later symbolist and decadent movements. Members of the Parnassian school include Leconte de Lisle, Sully Prudhomme, Albert Glatigny, Francois Coppee, and Theodore de Banville.

parody: in literary criticism, this term refers to an imitation of a serious literary work or the signature style of a particular author in a ridiculous manner. A typical parody adopts the style of the original and applies it to an inappropriate subject for humorous effect. Parody is a form of satire and could be considered the literary equivalent of a caricature or cartoon. Henry Fielding's *Shamela* is a parody of Samuel Richardson's *Pamela.*

pastoral: a term derived from the Latin word "pastor," meaning shepherd. A pastoral is a literary composition on a rural theme. The conventions of the pastoral were originated by the third-century Greek poet Theocritus, who wrote about the experiences, love affairs, and pastimes of Sicilian shepherds. In a pastoral, characters and language of a courtly nature are often placed in a simple setting. The term pastoral is also used to classify dramas, elegies, and lyrics that exhibit the use of country settings and shepherd characters. Percy Bysshe Shelley's "Adonais" and John Milton's "Lycidas" are two famous examples of pastorals.

pelado: literally the "skinned one" or shirtless one, he was the stock underdog, sharp-witted picaresque character of Mexican vaudeville and tent shows. The *pelado* is found in such works as Don Catarino's *Los effectos de la crisis* and *Regreso a mi tierra.*

pen name: see *pseudonym*

persona: a Latin term meaning "mask." *Personae* are the characters in a fictional work of literature. The *persona* generally functions as a mask through which the author tells a story in a voice other than his or her own. A *persona* is usually either a character in a story who acts as a narrator or an "implied author," a voice created by the author to act as the narrator for himself or herself. *Personae* include the narrator of Geoffrey Chaucer's *Canterbury Tales* and Marlow in Joseph Conrad's *Heart of Darkness.*

personae: see *persona*

personal point of view: see *point of view*

personification: a figure of speech that gives human qualities to abstract ideas, animals, and inanimate objects. William Shakespeare used personification in *Romeo and Juliet* in the lines "Arise, fair sun, and kill the envious moon, / Who is already sick and pale with grief." Here, the moon is portrayed as being envious, sick, and pale with grief—all markedly human qualities.

phenomenology: a method of literary criticism based on the belief that things have no existence outside of human consciousness or awareness. Proponents of this theory believe that art is a process that takes place in the mind of the observer as he or she contemplates an object rather than a quality of the object itself. Among phenomenological critics are Edmund Husserl, George Poulet, Marcel Raymond, and Roman Ingarden.

picaresque novel: episodic fiction depicting the adventures of a roguish central character ("picaro" is Spanish for "rogue"). The picaresque hero is commonly a low-born but clever individual who wanders into and out of various affairs of love, danger, and farcical intrigue. These involvements may take place at all social levels and typically present a humorous and wide-ranging satire of a given society. Prominent examples of the picaresque novel are *Don Quixote* by Miguel de Cervantes, *Tom Jones* by Henry Fielding, and *Moll Flanders* by Daniel Defoe.

plagiarism: claiming another person's written material as one's own. Plagiarism can take the form of direct, word-for- word copying or the theft of the substance or idea of the work. A student who copies an encyclopedia entry and turns it in as a report for school is guilty of plagiarism.

Platonic criticism: a form of criticism that stresses an artistic work's usefulness as an agent of social engineering rather than any quality or value of the work itself. Platonic criticism takes as its starting point the ancient Greek philosopher Plato's comments on art in his *Republic.*

Platonism: the embracing of the doctrines of the philosopher Plato, popular among the poets of the Renaissance and the Romantic period. Platonism is more flexible than Aristotelian Criticism and places more emphasis on the supernatural and unknown aspects of life. Platonism is expressed in the love poetry of the Renaissance, the fourth book of Baldassare Castiglione's *The Book of the Courtier,* and the poetry of William Blake, William Wordsworth, Percy Bysshe Shelley, Friedrich Holderlin, William Butler Yeats, and Wallace Stevens.

plot: in literary criticism, this term refers to the pattern of events in a narrative or drama. In its simplest sense, the plot guides the author in composing the work and helps the reader follow the work. Typically, plots exhibit causality and unity and have a beginning, a middle, and an end. Sometimes, however, a plot may consist of a series of disconnected events, in which case it is known as an "episodic plot." In his *Aspects of the Novel,* E. M. Forster distinguishes between a story, defined as a "narrative of events arranged in their time- sequence," and plot, which organizes the events to a "sense of causality." This definition closely mirrors Aristotle's discussion of plot in his *Poetics.*

poetic justice: an outcome in a literary work, not necessarily a poem, in which the good are rewarded and the evil are punished, especially in ways that particularly fit their virtues or crimes. For example, a murderer may himself be murdered, or a thief will find himself penniless.

poetic license: distortions of fact and literary convention made by a writer—not always a poet—for the sake of the effect gained. Poetic license is closely related to the concept of "artistic freedom." An author exercises poetic license by saying that a pile of money "reaches as high as a mountain" when the pile is actually only a foot or two high.

poetics: this term has two closely related meanings. It denotes (1) an aesthetic theory in literary criticism about the essence of poetry or (2) rules prescribing the proper methods, content, style, or diction of poetry. The term poetics may also refer to theories about literature in general, not just poetry.

point of view: the narrative perspective from which a literary work is presented to the reader. There are four traditional points of view. The "third person omniscient" gives the reader a "godlike" perspective, unrestricted by time or place, from which to see actions and look into the minds of characters. This allows the author to comment openly on characters and events in the work. The "third person" point of view presents the events of the story from outside of any single character's perception, much like the omniscient point of view, but the reader must understand the action as it takes place and without any special insight into characters' minds or motivations. The "first person" or "personal" point of view relates events as they are perceived by a single character. The main character "tells" the story and may offer opinions about the action and characters which differ from those of the author. Much less common than omniscient, third person, and first person is the "second person" point of view, wherein the author tells the story as if it is happening to the reader. James Thurber employs the omniscient point of view in his short story "The Secret Life of Walter Mitty." Ernest Hemingway's "A Clean, Well-Lighted Place" is a short story told from the third person point of view. Mark Twain's novel *Huck Finn* is presented from the first person viewpoint. Jay McInerney's *Bright Lights, Big City* is an example of a novel which uses the second person point of view.

polemic: a work in which the author takes a stand on a controversial subject, such as abortion or religion. Such works are often extremely argumentative or provocative. Classic examples of polemics include John Milton's *Aeropagitica* and Thomas Paine's *The American Crisis.*

pornography: writing intended to provoke feelings of lust in the reader. Such works are often condemned by critics and teachers, but those which can be shown to have literary value are viewed less harshly. Literary works that have been described as pornographic include Ovid's *The Art of Love,* Margaret of Angouleme's *Heptameron,* John Cleland's *Memoirs of a Woman of Pleasure; or, the Life of Fanny Hill,* the anonymous *My Secret Life,* D. H. Lawrence's *Lady Chatterley's Lover,* and Vladimir Nabokov's *Lolita.*

post-aesthetic movement: an artistic response made by African Americans to the black aesthetic movement of the 1960s and early 1970s. Writers since that time have adopted a somewhat different tone in their work, with less emphasis placed on the disparity between black and white in the United States. In the words of post-aesthetic authors such as Toni Morrison, John Edgar Wideman, and Kristin Hunter, African Americans are portrayed as looking inward for answers to their own questions, rather than always looking to the outside world. Two well-known examples of works produced as part of the post-aesthetic movement are the Pulitzer Prize-winning novels *The Color Purple* by Alice Walker and *Beloved* by Toni Morrison.

postmodernism: writing from the 1960s forward characterized by experimentation and continuing to apply some of the fundamentals of modernism, which included existentialism and alienation. Postmodernists have gone a step further in the rejection of tradition begun with the modernists by also rejecting traditional forms, preferring the anti-novel over the novel and the anti-hero over the hero. Postmodern writers include Alain Robbe-Grillet, Thomas Pynchon, Margaret Drabble, John Fowles, Adolfo Bioy-Casares, and Gabriel Garcia Marquez.

pre-Raphaelites: a circle of writers and artists in mid nineteenth-century England. Valuing the pre-Renaissance artistic qualities of religious symbolism, lavish pictorialism, and natural sensuousness, the Pre-Raphaelites cultivated a sense of mystery and melancholy that influenced later writers associated with the Symbolist and Decadent movements. The major members of the group include Dante Gabriel Rossetti, Christina Rossetti, Algernon Swinburne, and Walter Pater.

primitivism: the belief that primitive peoples were nobler and less flawed than civilized peoples because they had not been subjected to the tainting influence of society. Examples of literature espousing primitivism include Aphra Behn's *Oroonoko: Or, The History of the Royal Slave,* Jean-Jacques Rousseau's *Julie ou la Nouvelle Heloise,* Oliver Goldsmith's *The Deserted Village,* the poems of Robert Burns, Herman Melville's stories *Typee, Omoo,* and *Mardi,* many poems of William Butler Yeats and Robert Frost, and William Golding's novel *Lord of the Flies.*

prologue: an introductory section of a literary work. It often contains information establishing the situation of the characters or presents information about the setting, time period, or action. In drama, the prologue is spoken by a chorus or by one of the principal characters. In the "General Prologue" of *The Canterbury Tales,* Geoffrey Chaucer describes the main characters and establishes the setting and purpose of the work.

prose: a literary medium that attempts to mirror the language of everyday speech. It is distinguished from poetry by its use of unmetered, unrhymed language consisting of logically related sentences. Prose is usually grouped into paragraphs that form a cohesive whole such as an essay or a novel. Recognized masters of English prose writing include Sir Thomas Malory, William Caxton, Raphael Holinshed, Joseph Addison, Mark Twain, and Ernest Hemingway.

prosopopoeia: see *personification*

protagonist: the central character of a story who serves as a focus for its themes and incidents and as the principal rationale for its development. The protagonist is sometimes referred to in discussions of modern literature as the hero or anti-hero. Well-known protagonists are Hamlet in William Shakespeare's *Hamlet* and Jay Gatsby in F. Scott Fitzgerald's *The Great Gatsby.*

protest fiction: protest fiction has as its primary purpose the protesting of some social injustice, such as racism or discrimination. One example of protest fiction is a series of five novels by Chester Himes, beginning in 1945 with *If He Hollers Let Him Go* and ending in 1955 with *The Primitive.* These works depict the destructive effects of race and gender stereotyping in the context of interracial relationships. Another African American author whose works often revolve around themes of social protest is John Oliver Killens. James Baldwin's essay "Everybody's Protest Novel" generated controversy by attacking the authors of protest fiction.

proverb: a brief, sage saying that expresses a truth about life in a striking manner. "They are not all cooks who carry long knives" is an example of a proverb.

pseudonym: a name assumed by a writer, most often intended to prevent his or her identification as the author of a work. Two or more authors may work together under one pseudonym, or an author may use a different name for each genre he or she publishes in. Some publishing companies maintain "house pseudonyms," under which any number of authors may write installations in a series. Some authors also choose a pseudonym over their real names the way an actor may use a stage name. Examples of pseudonyms (with the author's real name in parentheses) include Voltaire (Francois-Marie Arouet), Novalis (Friedrich von Hardenberg), Currer Bell (Charlotte Bronte), Ellis Bell (Emily Bronte), George Eliot (Maryann Evans), Honorio Bustos Donmecq (Adolfo Bioy-Casares and Jorge Luis Borges), and Richard Bachman (Stephen King).

pun: a play on words that have similar sounds but different meanings. A serious example of the pun is from John Donne's "A Hymne to God the Father": "Sweare by thyself, that at my death thy sonne Shall shine as he shines now, and hereto fore; And, having done that, Thou haste done; I fear no more."

R

realism: a nineteenth-century European literary movement that sought to portray familiar characters, situations, and settings in a realistic manner. This was done primarily by using an objective narrative point of view and through the buildup of accurate detail. The standard for success of any realistic work depends on how faithfully it transfers common experience into fictional forms. The realistic method may be altered or extended, as in stream of consciousness writing, to record highly subjective experience. Seminal authors in the tradition of Realism include Honore de Balzac, Gustave Flaubert, and Henry James.

renaissance: the period in European history that marked the end of the Middle Ages. It began in Italy in the late fourteenth century. In broad terms, it is usually seen as spanning the fourteenth, fifteenth, and sixteenth-centuries, although it did not reach Great Britain, for example, until the 1480s or so. The Renaissance saw an awakening in almost every sphere of human activity, especially science, philosophy, and the arts. The period is best defined by the emergence of a general philosophy that emphasized the importance of the intellect, the individual, and world affairs. It contrasts strongly with the medieval worldview, characterized by the dominant concerns of faith, the social collective, and spiritual salvation. Prominent writers during the Renaissance include Niccolo Machiavelli and Baldassare Castiglione in Italy, Miguel de Cervantes and Lope de Vega in Spain, Jean Froissart and Francois Rabelais in France, Sir Thomas

More and Sir Philip Sidney in England, and Desiderius Erasmus in Holland.

repartee: conversation featuring snappy retorts and witticisms. Masters of *repartee* include Sydney Smith, Charles Lamb, and Oscar Wilde. An example is recorded in the meeting of "Beau" Nash and John Wesley: Nash said, "I never make way for a fool," to which Wesley responded, "Don't you? I always do," and stepped aside.

resolution: the portion of a story following the climax, in which the conflict is resolved. The resolution of Jane Austen's *Northanger Abbey* is neatly summed up in the following sentence: "Henry and Catherine were married, the bells rang and every body smiled."

restoration: see *restoration age*

restoration age: a period in English literature beginning with the crowning of Charles II in 1660 and running to about 1700. The era, which was characterized by a reaction against Puritanism, was the first great age of the comedy of manners. The finest literature of the era is typically witty and urbane, and often lewd. Prominent Restoration Age writers include William Congreve, Samuel Pepys, John Dryden, and John Milton.

rhetoric: in literary criticism, this term denotes the art of ethical persuasion. In its strictest sense, rhetoric adheres to various principles developed since classical times for arranging facts and ideas in a clear, persuasive, appealing manner. The term is also used to refer to effective prose in general and theories of or methods for composing effective prose. Classical examples of rhetorics include *The Rhetoric of Aristotle,* Quintillian's *Institutio Oratoria,* and Cicero's *Ad Herennium.*

rhetorical question: a question intended to provoke thought, but not an expressed answer, in the reader. It is most commonly used in oratory and other persuasive genres. The following lines from Thomas Gray's "Elegy Written in a Country Churchyard" ask rhetorical questions: "Can storied urn or animated bust Back to its mansion call the fleeting breath? Can Honour's voice provoke the silent dust, Or Flattery soothe the dull cold ear of Death?"

rising action: the part of a drama where the plot becomes increasingly complicated. Rising action leads up to the climax, or turning point, of a drama. The final "chase scene" of an action film is generally the rising action which culminates in the film's climax.

rococo: a style of European architecture that flourished in the eighteenth century, especially in France. The most notable features of *rococo* are its extensive use of ornamentation and its themes of lightness, gaiety, and intimacy. In literary criticism, the term is often used disparagingly to refer to a decadent or over-ornamental style. Alexander Pope's "The Rape of the Lock" is an example of literary *rococo*.

Roman a clef: a French phrase meaning "novel with a key." It refers to a narrative in which real persons are portrayed under fictitious names. Jack Kerouac, for example, portrayed various real-life beat generation figures under fictitious names in his *On the Road*.

romance: a broad term, usually denoting a narrative with exotic, exaggerated, often idealized characters, scenes, and themes. Nathaniel Hawthorne called his *The House of the Seven Gables* and *The Marble Faun* romances in order to distinguish them from clearly realistic works.

romantic age: see *romanticism*

romanticism: this term has two widely accepted meanings. In historical criticism, it refers to a European intellectual and artistic movement of the late eighteenth and early nineteenth centuries that sought greater freedom of personal expression than that allowed by the strict rules of literary form and logic of the eighteenth-century neoclassicists. The Romantics preferred emotional and imaginative expression to rational analysis. They considered the individual to be at the center of all experience and so placed him or her at the center of their art. The Romantics believed that the creative imagination reveals nobler truths—unique feelings and attitudes—than those that could be discovered by logic or by scientific examination. Both the natural world and the state of childhood were important sources for revelations of "eternal truths." "Romanticism" is also used as a general term to refer to a type of sensibility found in all periods of literary history and usually considered to be in opposition to the principles of classicism. In this sense, Romanticism signifies any work or philosophy in which the exotic or dreamlike figure strongly, or that is devoted to individualistic expression, self-analysis, or a pursuit of a higher realm of knowledge than can be discovered by human reason. Prominent Romantics include Jean-Jacques Rousseau, William Wordsworth, John Keats, Lord Byron, and Johann Wolfgang von Goethe.

romantics: see *romanticism*

Russian symbolism: a Russian poetic movement, derived from French symbolism, that flourished between 1894 and 1910. While some Russian Symbolists continued in the French tradition, stressing aestheticism and the importance of suggestion above didactic intent, others saw their craft as a form of mystical worship, and themselves as mediators between the supernatural and the mundane. Russian symbolists include Aleksandr Blok, Vyacheslav Ivanovich Ivanov, Fyodor Sologub, Andrey Bely, Nikolay Gumilyov, and Vladimir Sergeyevich Solovyov.

S

satire: a work that uses ridicule, humor, and wit to criticize and provoke change in human nature and institutions. There are two major types of satire: "formal" or "direct" satire speaks directly to the reader or to a character in the work; "indirect" satire relies upon the ridiculous behavior of its characters to make its point. Formal satire is further divided into two manners: the "Horatian," which ridicules gently, and the "Juvenalian," which derides its subjects harshly and bitterly. Voltaire's novella *Candide* is an indirect satire. Jonathan Swift's essay "A Modest Proposal" is a Juvenalian satire.

science fiction: a type of narrative about or based upon real or imagined scientific theories and technology. Science fiction is often peopled with alien creatures and set on other planets or in different dimensions. Karel Capek's *R.U.R.* is a major work of science fiction.

second person: see *point of view*

semiotics: the study of how literary forms and conventions affect the meaning of language. Semioticians include Ferdinand de Saussure, Charles Sanders Pierce, Claude Levi-Strauss,

Jacques Lacan, Michel Foucault, Jacques Derrida, Roland Barthes, and Julia Kristeva.

setting: the time, place, and culture in which the action of a narrative takes place. The elements of setting may include geographic location, characters' physical and mental environments, prevailing cultural attitudes, or the historical time in which the action takes place. Examples of settings include the romanticized Scotland in Sir Walter Scott's "Waverley" novels, the French provincial setting in Gustave Flaubert's *Madame Bovary,* the fictional Wessex country of Thomas Hardy's novels, and the small towns of southern Ontario in Alice Munro's short stories.

short story: a fictional prose narrative shorter and more focused than a novella. The short story usually deals with a single episode and often a single character. The "tone," the author's attitude toward his or her subject and audience, is uniform throughout. The short story frequently also lacks *denouement*, ending instead at its climax. Well-known short stories include Ernest Hemingway's "Hills Like White Elephants," Katherine Mansfield's "The Fly," Jorge Luis Borge's "Tlon, Uqbar, Orbis Tertius," Eudora Welty's "Death of a Travelling Salesman," Yukio Mishima's "Three Million Men," and Milan Kundera's "The Hitchhiking Game."

signifying monkey: a popular trickster figure in black folklore, with hundreds of tales about this character documented since the 19th century. Henry Louis Gates Jr. examines the history of the signifying monkey in *The Signifying Monkey: Towards a Theory of Afro-American Literary Criticism,* published in 1988.

simile: a comparison, usually using "like" or "as", of two essentially dissimilar things, as in "coffee as cold as ice" or "He sounded like a broken record." The title of Ernest Hemingway's "Hills Like White Elephants" contains a simile.

slang: a type of informal verbal communication that is generally unacceptable for formal writing. Slang words and phrases are often colorful exaggerations used to emphasize the speaker's point; they may also be shortened versions of an often-used word or phrase. Examples of American slang from the 1990s include "yuppie" (an acronym for Young Urban Professional), "awesome" (for "excellent"), wired (for "nervous" or "excited"), and "chill out" (for relax).

slave narrative: autobiographical accounts of American slave life as told by escaped slaves. These works first appeared during the abolition movement of the 1830s through the 1850s. Olaudah Equiano's *The Interesting Narrative of Olaudah Equiano, or Gustavus Vassa, The African* and Harriet Ann Jacobs's *Incidents in the Life of a Slave Girl* are examples of the slave narrative.

social realism: see *socialist realism*

socialist realism: the Socialist Realism school of literary theory was proposed by Maxim Gorky and established as a dogma by the first Soviet Congress of Writers. It demanded adherence to a communist worldview in works of literature. Its doctrines required an objective viewpoint comprehensible to the working classes and themes of social struggle featuring strong proletarian heroes. A successful work of socialist realism is Nikolay Ostrovsky's *Kak zakalyalas stal* (*How the Steel Was Tempered*).

stereotype: a stereotype was originally the name for a duplication made during the printing process; this led to its modern definition as a person or thing that is (or is assumed to be) the same as all others of its type. Common stereotypical characters include the absent-minded professor, the nagging wife, the troublemaking teenager, and the kind-hearted grandmother.

stream of consciousness: a narrative technique for rendering the inward experience of a character. This technique is designed to give the impression of an ever-changing series of thoughts, emotions, images, and memories in the spontaneous and seemingly illogical order that they occur in life. The textbook example of stream of consciousness is the last section of James Joyce's *Ulysses*.

structuralism: a twentieth-century movement in literary criticism that examines how literary texts arrive at their meanings, rather than the meanings themselves. There are two major types of structuralist analysis: one examines the way patterns of linguistic structures unify a specific text and emphasize certain elements of that text, and the other interprets the way literary forms and conventions affect the meaning of language itself. Prominent structuralists include Michel Foucault, Roman Jakobson, and Roland Barthes.

structure: the form taken by a piece of literature. The structure may be made obvious for ease of understanding, as in nonfiction works, or may be obscured for artistic purposes, as in some poetry or seemingly "unstructured" prose. Examples of common literary structures include the plot of a narrative, the acts and scenes of a drama, and such poetic forms as the Shakespearean sonnet and the Pindaric ode.

sturm und drang: a German term meaning "storm and stress." It refers to a German literary movement of the 1770s and 1780s that reacted against the order and rationalism of the enlightenment, focusing instead on the intense experience of extraordinary individuals. Highly romantic, works of this movement, such as Johann Wolfgang von Goethe's *Gotz von Berlichingen*, are typified by realism, rebelliousness, and intense emotionalism.

style: a writer's distinctive manner of arranging words to suit his or her ideas and purpose in writing. The unique imprint of the author's personality upon his or her writing, style is the product of an author's way of arranging ideas and his or her use of diction, different sentence structures, rhythm, figures of speech, rhetorical principles, and other elements of composition. Styles may be classified according to period (Metaphysical, Augustan, Georgian), individual authors (Chaucerian, Miltonic, Jamesian), level (grand, middle, low, plain), or language (scientific, expository, poetic, journalistic).

subject: the person, event, or theme at the center of a work of literature. A work may have one or more subjects of each type, with shorter works tending to have fewer and longer works tending to have more. The subjects of James Baldwin's novel *Go Tell It on the Mountain* include the themes of father-son relationships, religious conversion, black life, and sexuality. The subjects of Anne Frank's *Diary of a Young Girl* include Anne and her family members as well as World War II, the Holocaust, and the themes of war, isolation, injustice, and racism.

subjectivity: writing that expresses the author's personal feelings about his subject, and which may or may not include factual information about the subject. Subjectivity is demonstrated in James Joyce's *Portrait of the Artist as a Young Man*, Samuel Butler's *The Way of All Flesh*, and Thomas Wolfe's *Look Homeward, Angel*.

subplot: a secondary story in a narrative. A subplot may serve as a motivating or complicating force for the main plot of the work, or it may provide emphasis for, or relief from, the main plot. The conflict between the Capulets and the Montagues in William Shakespeare's *Romeo and Juliet* is an example of a subplot.

surrealism: a term introduced to criticism by Guillaume Apollinaire and later adopted by Andre Breton. It refers to a French literary and artistic movement founded in the 1920s. The Surrealists sought to express unconscious thoughts and feelings in their works. The best-known technique used for achieving this aim was automatic writing—transcriptions of spontaneous outpourings from the unconscious. The Surrealists proposed to unify the contrary levels of conscious and unconscious, dream and reality, objectivity and subjectivity into a new level of "super-realism." Surrealism can be found in the poetry of Paul Eluard, Pierre Reverdy, and Louis Aragon, among others.

suspense: a literary device in which the author maintains the audience's attention through the buildup of events, the outcome of which will soon be revealed. Suspense in William Shakespeare's *Hamlet* is sustained throughout by the question of whether or not the Prince will achieve what he has been instructed to do and of what he intends to do.

syllogism: a method of presenting a logical argument. In its most basic form, the syllogism consists of a major premise, a minor premise, and a conclusion. An example of a syllogism is: Major premise: When it snows, the streets get wet. Minor premise: It is snowing. Conclusion: The streets are wet.

symbol: something that suggests or stands for something else without losing its original identity. In literature, symbols combine their literal meaning with the suggestion of an abstract concept. Literary symbols are of two types: those that carry complex associations of meaning no matter what their contexts, and those that derive their suggestive meaning from their functions in specific literary works. Examples of symbols are sunshine suggesting happiness, rain suggesting sorrow, and storm clouds suggesting despair.

symbolism: this term has two widely accepted meanings. In historical criticism, it denotes an early modernist literary movement initiated in France during the nineteenth century that reacted against the prevailing standards of realism. Writers in this movement aimed to evoke, indirectly and symbolically, an order of being beyond the material world of the five senses. Poetic expression of personal emotion figured strongly in the movement, typically by means of a private set of symbols uniquely identifiable with the individual poet. The principal aim of the Symbolists was to express in words the highly complex feelings that grew out of everyday contact with the world. In a broader sense, the term "symbolism" refers to the use of one object to represent another. Early members of the Symbolist movement included the French authors Charles Baudelaire and Arthur Rimbaud; William Butler Yeats, James Joyce, and T. S. Eliot were influenced as the movement moved to Ireland, England, and the United States. Examples of the concept of symbolism include a flag that stands for a nation or movement, or an empty cupboard used to suggest hopelessness, poverty, and despair.

symbolist: see *symbolism*

symbolist movement: see *symbolism*

T

tale: a story told by a narrator with a simple plot and little character development. Tales are usually relatively short and often carry a simple message. Examples of tales can be found in the work of Rudyard Kipling, Somerset Maugham,

Saki, Anton Chekhov, Guy de Maupassant, and Armistead Maupin.

tall tale: a humorous tale told in a straightforward, credible tone but relating absolutely impossible events or feats of the characters. Such tales were commonly told of frontier adventures during the settlement of the west in the United States. Tall tales have been spun around such legendary heroes as Mike Fink, Paul Bunyan, Davy Crockett, Johnny Appleseed, and Captain Stormalong as well as the real-life William F. Cody and Annie Oakley. Literary use of tall tales can be found in Washington Irving's *History of New York,* Mark Twain's *Life on the Mississippi,* and in the German R. F. Raspe's *Baron Munchausen's Narratives of His Marvellous Travels and Campaigns in Russia.*

textual criticism: a branch of literary criticism that seeks to establish the authoritative text of a literary work. Textual critics typically compare all known manuscripts or printings of a single work in order to assess the meanings of differences and revisions. This procedure allows them to arrive at a definitive version that (supposedly) corresponds to the author's original intention. Textual criticism was applied during the Renaissance to salvage the classical texts of Greece and Rome, and modern works have been studied, for instance, to undo deliberate correction or censorship, as in the case of novels by Stephen Crane and Theodore Dreiser.

theme: the main point of a work of literature. The term is used interchangeably with thesis. The theme of William Shakespeare's *Othello*—jealousy—is a common one.

thesis: a thesis is both an essay and the point argued in the essay. Thesis novels and thesis plays share the quality of containing a thesis which is supported through the action of the story. A master's thesis and a doctoral dissertation are two theses required of graduate students.

thesis novel: see *thesis*

third person: see *point of view*

tone: the author's attitude toward his or her audience may be deduced from the tone of the work. A formal tone may create distance or convey politeness, while an informal tone may encourage a friendly, intimate, or intrusive feeling in the reader. The author's attitude toward his or her subject matter may also be deduced from the tone of the words he or she uses in discussing it. The tone of John F. Kennedy's speech which included the appeal to "ask not what your country can do for you" was intended to instill feelings of camaraderie and national pride in listeners.

transcendentalism: an American philosophical and religious movement, based in New England from around 1835 until the Civil War. Transcendentalism was a form of American romanticism that had its roots abroad in the works of Thomas Carlyle, Samuel Coleridge, and Johann Wolfgang von Goethe. The Transcendentalists stressed the importance of intuition and subjective experience in communication with God. They rejected religious dogma and texts in favor of mysticism and scientific naturalism. They pursued truths that lie beyond the "colorless" realms perceived by reason and the senses and were active social reformers in public education, women's rights, and the abolition of slavery. Prominent members of the group include Ralph Waldo Emerson and Henry David Thoreau.

trickster: a character or figure common in Native American and African literature who uses his ingenuity to defeat enemies and escape difficult situations. Tricksters are most often animals, such as the spider, hare, or coyote, although they may take the form of humans as well. Examples of trickster tales include Thomas King's *A Coyote Columbus Story,* Ashley F. Bryan's *The Dancing Granny* and Ishmael Reed's *The Last Days of Louisiana Red.*

U

understatement: see *irony*

urban realism: a branch of realist writing that attempts to accurately reflect the often harsh facts of modern urban existence. Some works by Stephen Crane, Theodore Dreiser, Charles Dickens, Fyodor Dostoyevsky, Emile Zola, Abraham Cahan, and Henry Fuller feature urban realism. Modern examples include Claude Brown's *Manchild in the Promised Land* and Ron Milner's *What the Wine Sellers Buy.*

utopia: a fictional perfect place, such as "paradise" or "heaven." Early literary utopias were included in Plato's *Republic* and Sir Thomas More's *Utopia,* while more modern utopias can be found in Samuel Butler's *Erewhon,* Theodor Herzka's *A Visit to Freeland,* and H. G. Wells' *A Modern Utopia.*

utopian: see *utopia*

utopianism: see *utopia*

V

verisimilitude: literally, the appearance of truth. In literary criticism, the term refers to aspects of a work of literature that seem true to the reader. Verisimilitude is achieved in the work of Honore de Balzac, Gustave Flaubert, and Henry James, among other late nineteenth-century realist writers.

Victorian: refers broadly to the reign of Queen Victoria of England (1837-1901) and to anything with qualities typical of that era. For example, the qualities of smug narrowmindedness, bourgeois materialism, faith in social progress, and priggish morality are often considered Victorian. This stereotype is contradicted by such dramatic intellectual developments as the theories of Charles Darwin, Karl Marx, and Sigmund Freud (which stirred strong debates in England) and the critical attitudes of serious Victorian writers like Charles Dickens and George Eliot. In literature, the Victorian Period was the great age of the English novel, and the latter part of the era saw the rise of movements such as decadence and symbolism. Works of Victorian literature include the poetry of Robert Browning and Alfred, Lord Tennyson, the criticism of Matthew Arnold and John Ruskin, and the novels of Emily Bronte, William Makepeace Thackeray, and Thomas Hardy.

Victorian age: see *Victorian*

Victorian period: see *Victorian*

W

weltanschauung: a German term referring to a person's worldview or philosophy. Examples of *weltanschauung* include Thomas Hardy's view of the human being as the victim of fate, destiny, or impersonal forces and circumstances, and the disillusioned and laconic cynicism expressed by such poets of the 1930s as W. H. Auden, Sir Stephen Spender, and Sir William Empson.

weltschmerz: a German term meaning "world pain." It describes a sense of anguish about the nature of existence, usually associated with a melancholy, pessimistic attitude. *Weltschmerz* was expressed in England by George Gordon, Lord Byron in his *Manfred* and *Childe Harold's Pilgrimage,* in France by Viscount de Chateaubriand, Alfred de Vigny, and Alfred de Musset, in Russia by Aleksandr Pushkin and Mikhail Lermontov, in Poland by Juliusz Slowacki, and in America by Nathaniel Hawthorne.

Z

zeitgeist: a German term meaning "spirit of the time." It refers to the moral and intellectual trends of a given era. Examples of *zeitgeist* include the preoccupation with the more morbid aspects of dying and death in some Jacobean literature, especially in the works of dramatists Cyril Tourneur and John Webster, and the decadence of the French Symbolists.

Author/Title Index

Nationality/Ethnicity Index

African American

Angelou, Maya
I Know Why the Caged Bird Sings,
2: 307–319
Brooks, Gwendolyn
Blacks, 1: 128–139
Du Bois, W.E.B.
The Souls of Black Folk,
2: 456–469
Ellison, Ralph
King of the Bingo Game, 2: 333–344
Haley, Alex
The Autobiography of Malcolm X,
1: 101–113
Hansberry, Lorraine
A Raisin in the Sun, 2: 412–425
Hughes, Langston
The Negro Speaks of Rivers,
2: 374–384
King, Martin Luther Jr.
I Have a Dream, 1: 294–306
Malcolm X
The Autobiography of Malcolm X,
1: 101–113
Taylor, Mildred D.
Roll of Thunder, Hear My Cry,
2: 426–440
Walker, Alice
The Color Purple, 1: 172–185
Wright, Richard
Native Son, 2: 360–373

American

Alexie, Sherman
What You Pawn I Will Redeem,
2: 515–525

Angelou, Maya
*I Know Why the Caged Bird
Sings*, 2: 307–319
Brooks, Gwendolyn
Blacks, 1: 128–139
Brown, Dee
*Bury My Heart at Wounded
Knee*, 1: 140–155
Chopin, Kate
The Awakening, 1: 114–127
Cisneros, Sandra
The House on Mango Street,
1: 279–293
Du Bois, W.E.B.
The Souls of Black Folk,
2: 456–469
Ellison, Ralph
King of the Bingo Game,
2: 333–344
Gaines, Ernest J.
*The Autobiography of Miss Jane
Pittman*, 1: 72–85
Haley, Alex
The Autobiography of Malcolm X,
1: 101–113
Hansberry, Lorraine
A Raisin in the Sun, 2: 412–425
Houston, James D.
*Farewell to Manzanar: A True
Story of Japanese American
Experience During and After the
World War II Internment*,
1: 227–240
Houston, Jeanne Wakatsuki
*Farewell to Manzanar: A True
Story of Japanese American

*Experience During and After the
World War II Internment*,
1: 227–240
Hughes, Langston
The Negro Speaks of Rivers,
2: 374–384
Keyes, Daniel
Flowers for Algernon, 1: 241–255
King, Martin Luther Jr.
I Have a Dream, 1: 294–306
Kushner, Tony
Angels in America, 1: 72–85
Lee, Harper
To Kill a Mockingbird,
2: 470–483
Malcolm X
The Autobiography of Malcolm X,
1: 101–113
Marmon Silko, Leslie
Ceremony, 1: 156–171
O'Connor, Flannery
*Everything that Rises Must
Converge*, 1: 214–226
Sone, Monica
Nisei Daughter, 2: 385–397
Stowe, Harriet Beecher
Uncle Tom's Cabin, 2: 484–498
Taylor, Mildred D.
Roll of Thunder, Hear My Cry,
2: 426–440
Twain, Mark
*The Adventures of Huckleberry
Finn*, 1: 55–71
Walker, Alice
The Color Purple, 1: 172–185
Wright, Richard
Native Son, 2: 360–2373

English

Conrad, Joseph
Heart of Darkness, 1: 267–278
Forster, E.M.
A Passage to India, 2: 398–411
Shakespeare, William
The Merchant of Venice, 2: 345–359
Wollstonecraft, Mary
A Vindication of the Rights of Woman, 2: 499–514
Woolf, Virginia
A Room of One's Own, 2: 441–455

German

Frank, Anne
The Diary of a Young Girl, 1: 199–213

Italian

Levi, Primo
A Good Day, 1: 256–266

Japanese American

Houston, Jeanne Wakatsuki
Farewell to Manzanar: A True Story of Japanese American Experience During and After the World War II Internment, 1: 227–240
Sone, Monica
Nisei Daughter, 2: 385–397

Jewish

Frank, Anne
The Diary of a Young Girl, 1: 199–213
Kushner, Tony
Angels in America, 1: 72–85

Mexican American

Cisneros, Sandra
The House on Mango Street, 1: 279–293

Native American

Marmon Silko, Leslie
Ceremony, 1: 156–171

South African

Mathabane, Mark
Kaffir Boy: The True Story of a Black Youth's Coming of Age in Apatheid South Africa, 2: 320–332
Paton, Alan
Cry, the Beloved Country, 1: 186–198

Ukrainian

Conrad, Joseph
Heart of Darkness, 1: 267–278